Defect
Detect

DUmps Binaries Logs INternals
School of Security

Windows
Memory Dump Analysis
Advanced

with Data Structures

Version 5

Dmitry Vostokov
Software Diagnostics Services

Published by OpenTask, Republic of Ireland

Product and company names mentioned in this book may be trademarks of their owners.

OpenTask books and magazines are available through booksellers and distributors worldwide. For further information or comments, send requests to press@opentask.com.

A CIP catalog record for this book is available from the British Library.

ISBN-l3: 978-1-912636-95-2 (Paperback)

Revision 5.01 (March 2024)

Contents

About the Author

Dmitry Vostokov is an internationally recognized expert, speaker, educator, scientist, inventor, and author. He founded the pattern-oriented software diagnostics, forensics, and prognostics discipline (Systematic Software Diagnostics) and Software Diagnostics Institute (DA+TA: DumpAnalysis.org + TraceAnalysis.org). Vostokov has also authored over 50 books on software diagnostics, anomaly detection and analysis, software and memory forensics, root cause analysis and problem solving, memory dump analysis, debugging, software trace and log analysis, reverse engineering, and malware analysis. He has over 25 years of experience in software architecture, design, development, and maintenance in various industries, including leadership, technical, and people management roles. Dmitry also founded Syndromatix, Anolog.io, BriteTrace, DiaThings, Logtellect, OpenTask Iterative and Incremental Publishing (OpenTask.com), Software Diagnostics Technology and Services (former Memory Dump Analysis Services) PatternDiagnostics.com, and Software Prognostics. In his spare time, he presents various topics on Debugging.TV and explores Software Narratology, its further development as Narratology of Things and Diagnostics of Things (DoT), Software Pathology, and Quantum Software Diagnostics. His current interest areas are theoretical software diagnostics and its mathematical and computer science foundations, application of formal logic, artificial intelligence, machine learning and data mining to diagnostics and anomaly detection, software diagnostics engineering and diagnostics-driven development, diagnostics workflow and interaction. Recent interest areas also include cloud native computing, security, automation, functional programming, applications of category theory to software development and big data, and diagnostics of artificial intelligence.

Presentation Slides and Transcript

Windows
Memory Dump Analysis
Advanced

with Data Structures

Version 5

Dmitry Vostokov
Software Diagnostics Services

Hello everyone, my name is Dmitry Vostokov, and I teach this course.

Prerequisites

Basic and intermediate level
Windows memory dump analysis

These prerequisites are hard to define. Software development experience is a definite help for some exercises. Familiarity with software design and Unified Modeling Language would be beneficial when I show some diagrams, but if you have never seen or used UML, I added a relevant crash course to this edition. The ability to read assembly language has some advantages but is not necessary for this training. If you attended Accelerated training[1], then it may also help because this training extends the former one and presupposes familiarity with its topics.

---

[1] https://www.patterndiagnostics.com/accelerated-windows-memory-dump-analysis-book

Training Goals

- Use UML for communication

- Learn fundamentals of device drivers

- Learn specialized analysis techniques and commands in the context of x64 complete memory dumps

- Learn how to navigate data structures such as linked lists and arrays

Our primary goal is to learn various analysis techniques and debugging commands beyond listing modules, processes, threads, and their stack traces. When discussing modules, memory structures, and kernel objects, it is necessary to use some graphical notation to communicate concepts, so my choice was to use UML (Unified Modeling Language[2]). If you are unfamiliar with it, please don't worry as I explain notation along the way. We use only the necessary minimum of it.

---

[2] https://en.wikipedia.org/wiki/Unified_Modeling_Language

Training Principles

◉ Talk only about what I can show

◉ Lots of pictures

◉ Lots of examples

◉ Original content and examples

There were many training formats to consider, and I decided that the best way is to concentrate on hands-on exercises. Specifically, for this training, I developed 16 of them. Slides are kept to a minimum.

Practice Exercises

Practice Exercises

Now, we come to practice immediately.

Links

⊙ Memory Dumps:

Included in Exercise 0

⊙ Exercise Transcripts:

Included in this book

Exercise 0

- **Goal:** Install WinDbg or Debugging Tools for Windows, or pull Docker image, and check that symbols are set up correctly

- **Patterns:** Stack Trace; Incorrect Stack Trace

- \AdvWMDA-Dumps\Exercise-0-Download-Setup-WinDbg.pdf

Exercise 0: Download, set up, and verify your WinDbg or Debugging Tools for Windows installation, or Docker Debugging Tools for Windows image

Goal: Install WinDbg or Debugging Tools for Windows, or pull Docker image, and check that symbols are set up correctly.

Patterns: Stack Trace; Incorrect Stack Trace.

1.   Download memory dump files if you haven't done that already and unpack the archive:

https://www.patterndiagnostics.com/Training/AdvWMDA/AdvWMDA-V4-Dumps-Part1.zip
https://www.patterndiagnostics.com/Training/AdvWMDA/AdvWMDA-V4-Dumps-Part2.zip

Note: Part2 dump is only needed for Exercise C11.

2.   Install WinDbg (or upgrade existing WinDbg Preview) from https://learn.microsoft.com/en-gb/windows-hardware/drivers/debugger. Run WinDbg.

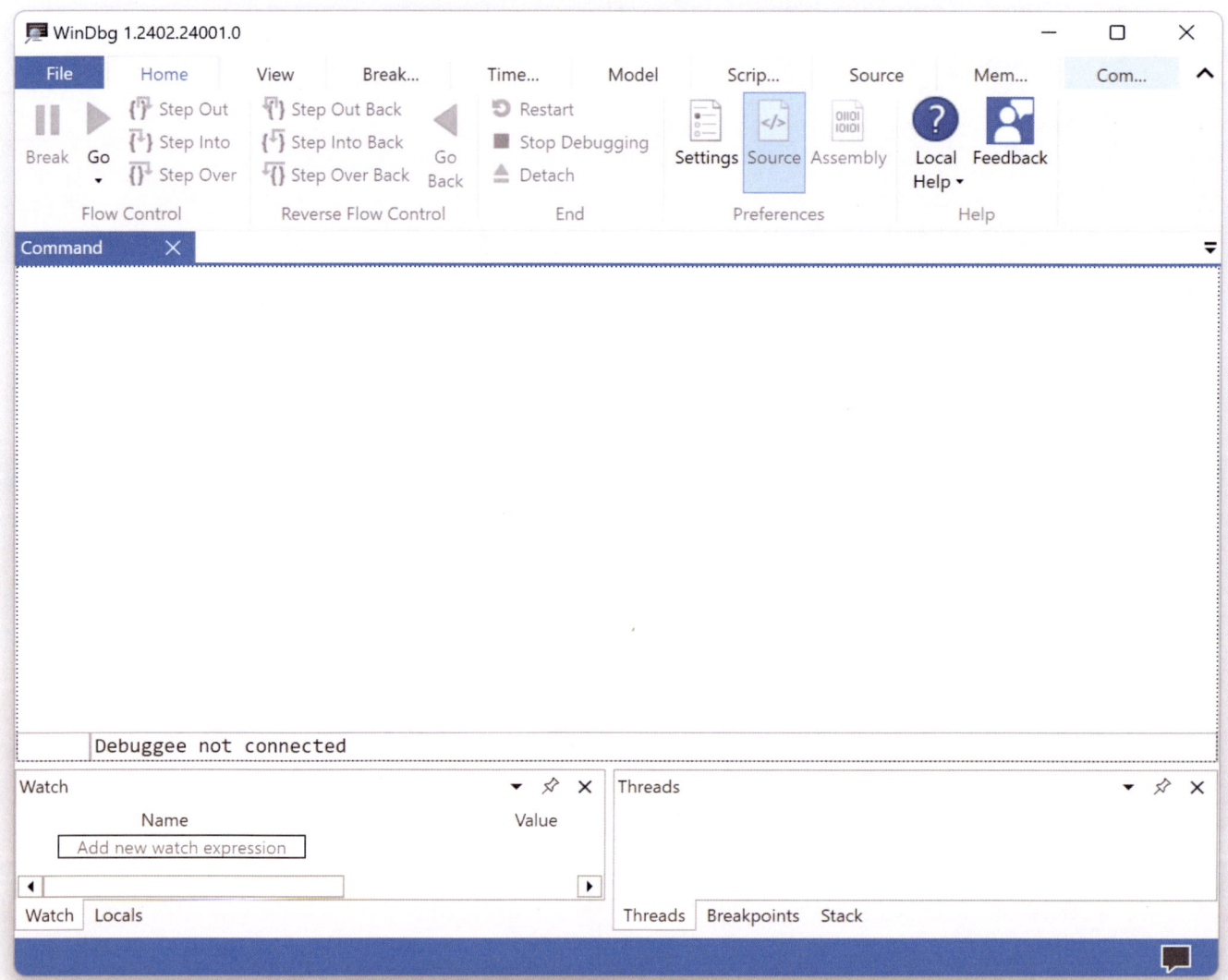

3.   Open \AdvWMDA-Dumps\x64\wordpad.DMP:

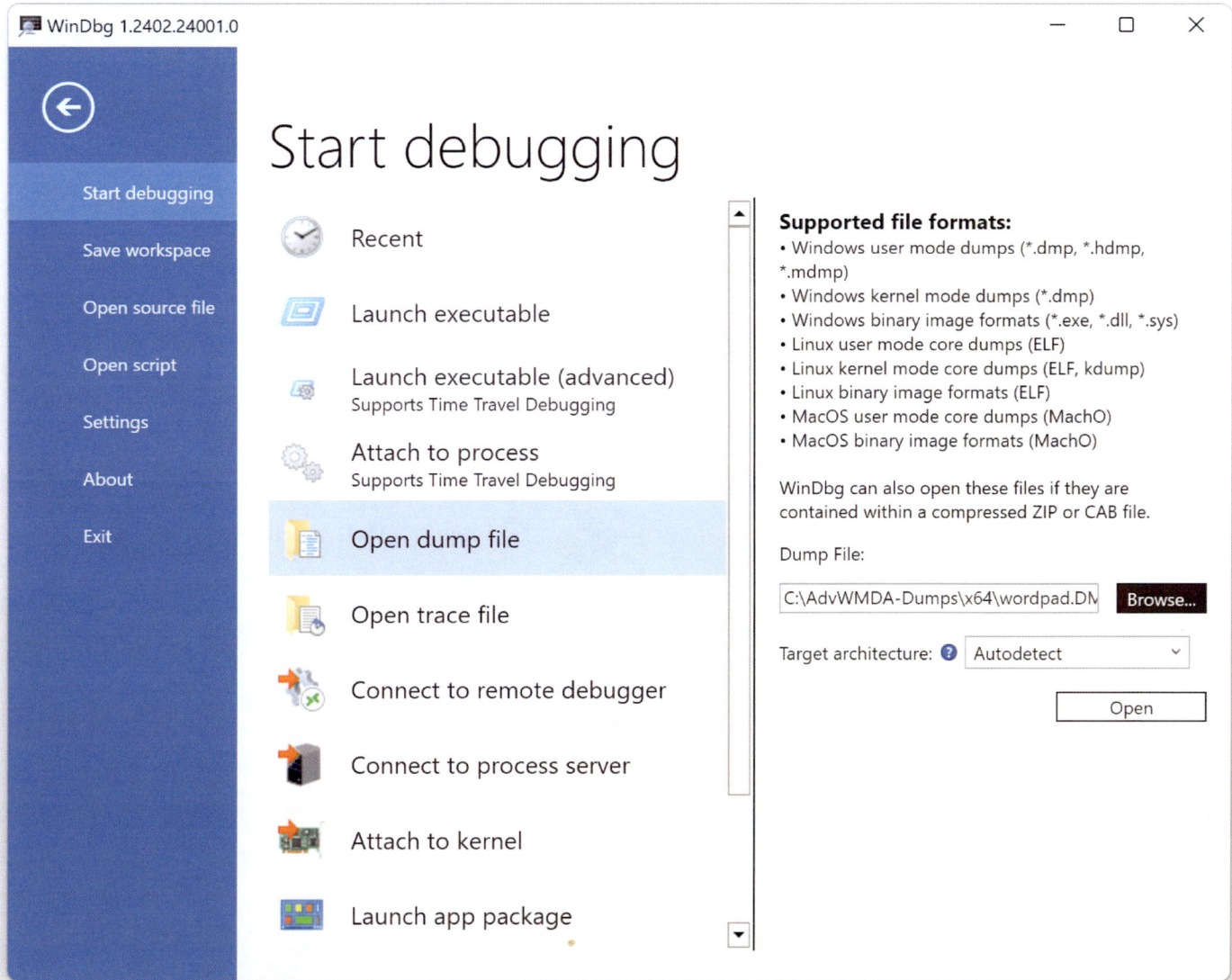

4.   We get the dump file loaded:

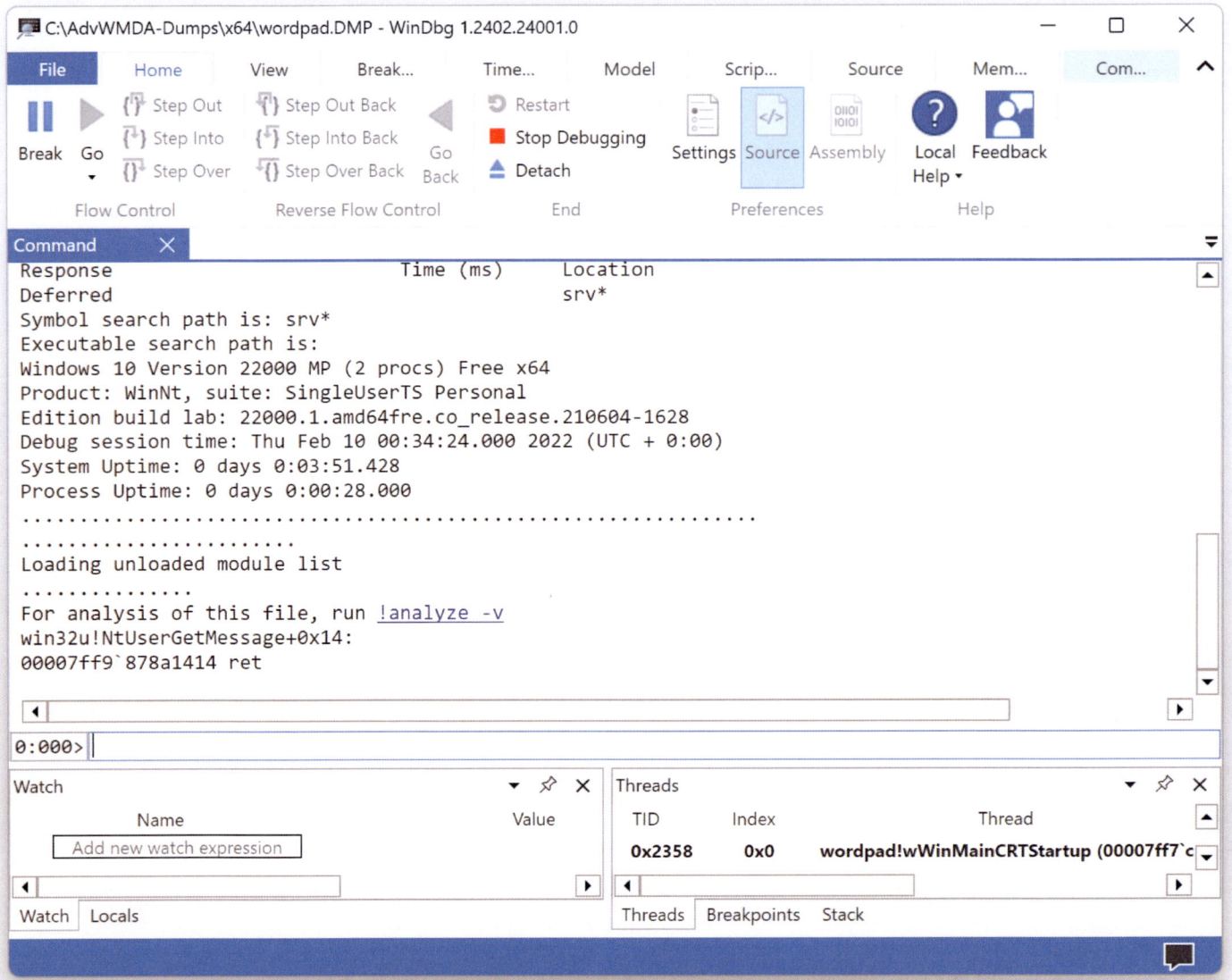

```
C:\AdvWMDA-Dumps\x64\wordpad.DMP - WinDbg 1.2402.24001.0                              —   □   ✕
```

File Home View Break... Time... Model Scrip... Source Mem... Com...

Break Go Step Out Step Out Back Restart Settings Source Assembly Local Feedback
          Step Into Step Into Back Stop Debugging   Help
          Step Over Step Over Back Detach
                     Go Back

Flow Control   Reverse Flow Control   End   Preferences   Help

Command   ✕

```
Response                        Time (ms)       Location
Deferred                                        srv*
Symbol search path is: srv*
Executable search path is:
Windows 10 Version 22000 MP (2 procs) Free x64
Product: WinNt, suite: SingleUserTS Personal
Edition build lab: 22000.1.amd64fre.co_release.210604-1628
Debug session time: Thu Feb 10 00:34:24.000 2022 (UTC + 0:00)
System Uptime: 0 days 0:03:51.428
Process Uptime: 0 days 0:00:28.000
.......................................................
........................
Loading unloaded module list
...............
For analysis of this file, run !analyze -v
win32u!NtUserGetMessage+0x14:
00007ff9`878a1414 ret
```

```
0:000> |
```

Watch   ▼ 📌 ✕   Threads   ▼ 📌 ✕

Name	Value
Add new watch expression	

TID	Index	Thread
0x2358	0x0	wordpad!wWinMainCRTStartup (00007ff7`c

Watch Locals   Threads Breakpoints Stack

5.   We can execute the **k** command to get the stack trace:

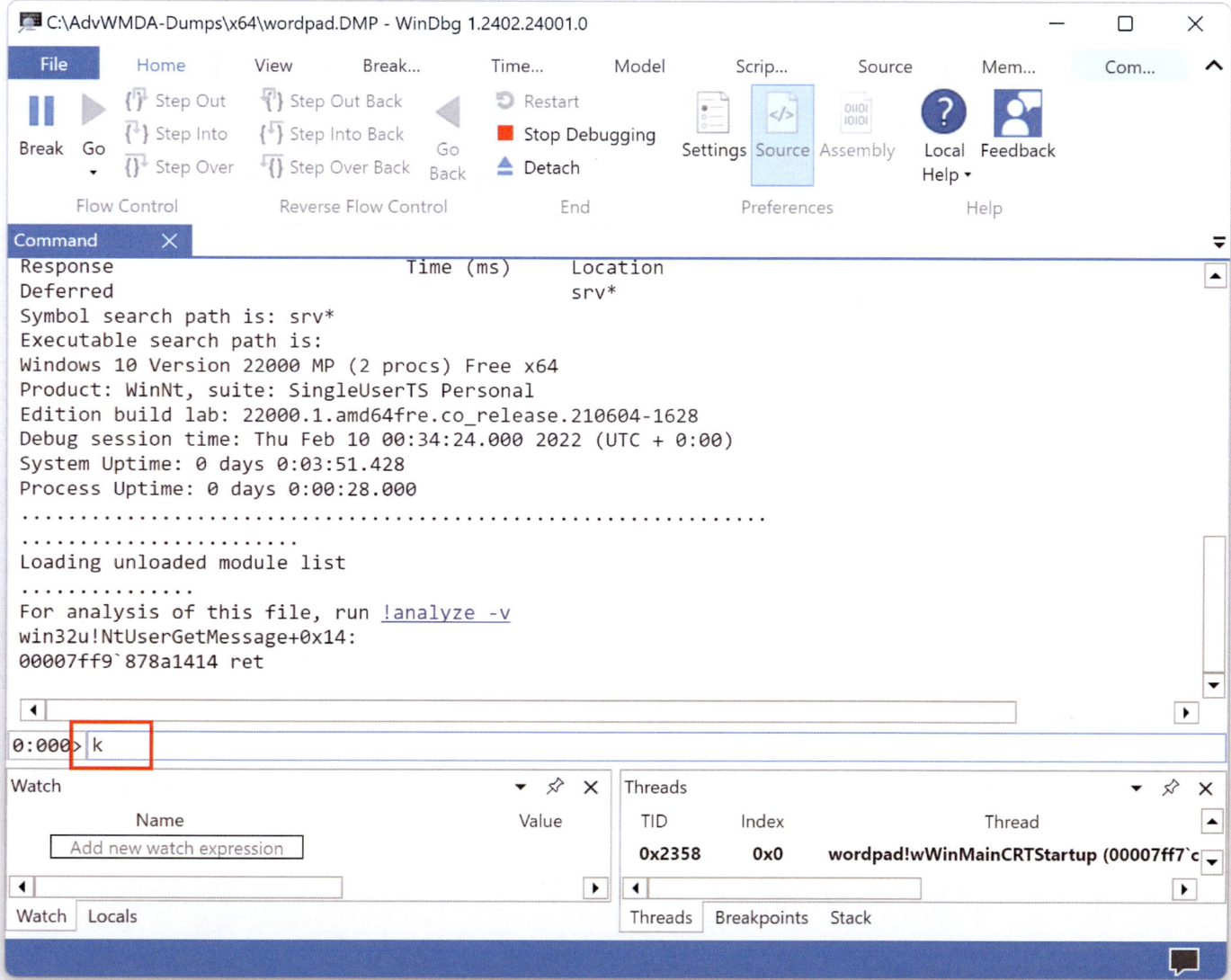

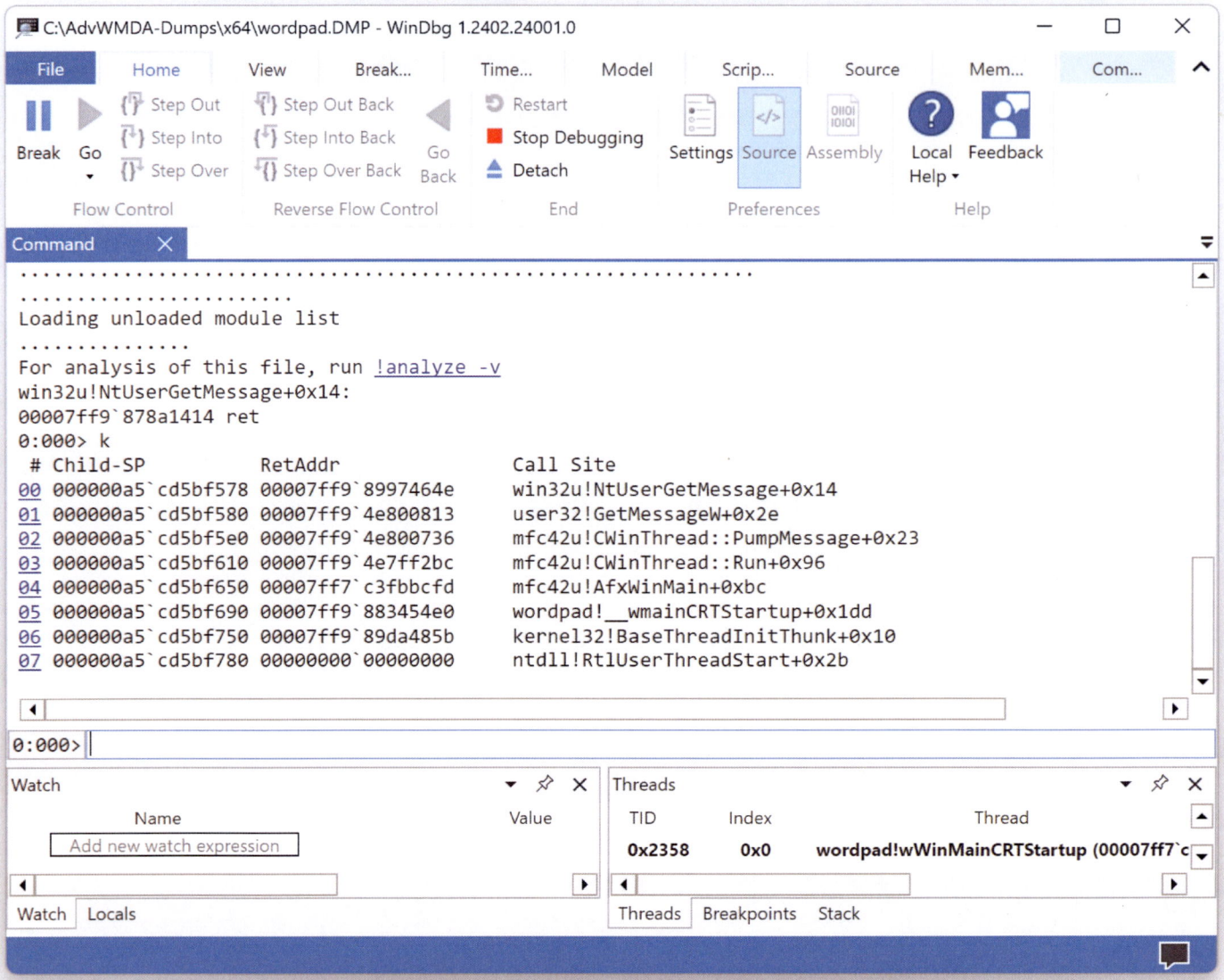

```
C:\AdvWMDA-Dumps\x64\wordpad.DMP - WinDbg 1.2402.24001.0
```

Home / View / Break... / Time... / Model / Scrip... / Source / Mem... / Com...

Break Go Step Out Step Out Back Restart Settings Source Assembly Local Help Feedback
        Step Into Step Into Back Go Back Stop Debugging
        Step Over Step Over Back Detach

Flow Control | Reverse Flow Control | End | Preferences | Help

```
Command                X

........................................................
........................
Loading unloaded module list
...............
For analysis of this file, run !analyze -v
win32u!NtUserGetMessage+0x14:
00007ff9`878a1414 ret
0:000> k
 # Child-SP          RetAddr               Call Site
00 000000a5`cd5bf578 00007ff9`8997464e     win32u!NtUserGetMessage+0x14
01 000000a5`cd5bf580 00007ff9`4e800813     user32!GetMessageW+0x2e
02 000000a5`cd5bf5e0 00007ff9`4e800736     mfc42u!CWinThread::PumpMessage+0x23
03 000000a5`cd5bf610 00007ff9`4e7ff2bc     mfc42u!CWinThread::Run+0x96
04 000000a5`cd5bf650 00007ff7`c3fbbcfd     mfc42u!AfxWinMain+0xbc
05 000000a5`cd5bf690 00007ff9`883454e0     wordpad!__wmainCRTStartup+0x1dd
06 000000a5`cd5bf750 00007ff9`89da485b     kernel32!BaseThreadInitThunk+0x10
07 000000a5`cd5bf780 00000000`00000000     ntdll!RtlUserThreadStart+0x2b

0:000>
```

Watch

Name	Value
Add new watch expression	

Watch | Locals

Threads

TID	Index	Thread
0x2358	0x0	wordpad!wWinMainCRTStartup (00007ff7`c

Threads | Breakpoints | Stack

6.   The output of the **k** command should be this:

```
0:000> k
 # Child-SP          RetAddr               Call Site
00 000000a5`cd5bf578 00007ff9`8997464e     win32u!NtUserGetMessage+0x14
01 000000a5`cd5bf580 00007ff9`4e800813     user32!GetMessageW+0x2e
02 000000a5`cd5bf5e0 00007ff9`4e800736     mfc42u!CWinThread::PumpMessage+0x23
03 000000a5`cd5bf610 00007ff9`4e7ff2bc     mfc42u!CWinThread::Run+0x96
04 000000a5`cd5bf650 00007ff7`c3fbbcfd     mfc42u!AfxWinMain+0xbc
05 000000a5`cd5bf690 00007ff9`883454e0     wordpad!__wmainCRTStartup+0x1dd
06 000000a5`cd5bf750 00007ff9`89da485b     kernel32!BaseThreadInitThunk+0x10
07 000000a5`cd5bf780 00000000`00000000     ntdll!RtlUserThreadStart+0x2b
```

22

If it has this form below with a large offset, then your symbol files were not set up correctly – **Incorrect Stack Trace** pattern:

```
0:000> k
 # Child-SP          RetAddr           Call Site
00 000000a5`cd5bf578 00007ff9`8997464e win32u!NtUserGetMessage+0x14
01 000000a5`cd5bf580 00007ff9`4e800813 user32!GetMessageW+0x2e
02 000000a5`cd5bf5e0 00007ff9`4e800736 mfc42u!Ordinal5730+0x23
03 000000a5`cd5bf610 00007ff9`4e7ff2bc mfc42u!Ordinal6054+0x96
04 000000a5`cd5bf650 00007ff7`c3fbbcfd mfc42u!Ordinal1584+0xbc
05 000000a5`cd5bf690 00007ff9`883454e0 wordpad+0xbcfd
06 000000a5`cd5bf750 00007ff9`89da485b kernel32!BaseThreadInitThunk+0x10
07 000000a5`cd5bf780 00000000`00000000 ntdll!RtlUserThreadStart+0x2b
```

7.   [Optional] Download and install Debugging Tools for Windows (See windbg.org for quick links, WinDbg Quick Links \ Download Debugging Tools for Windows) as a standalone toolset. For this training, we use WinDbg 10.0.22621.3233 from Windows SDK 10.0.22621 for Windows 11, version 23H2.

8.   Launch WinDbg from Windows Kits \ WinDbg (X64).

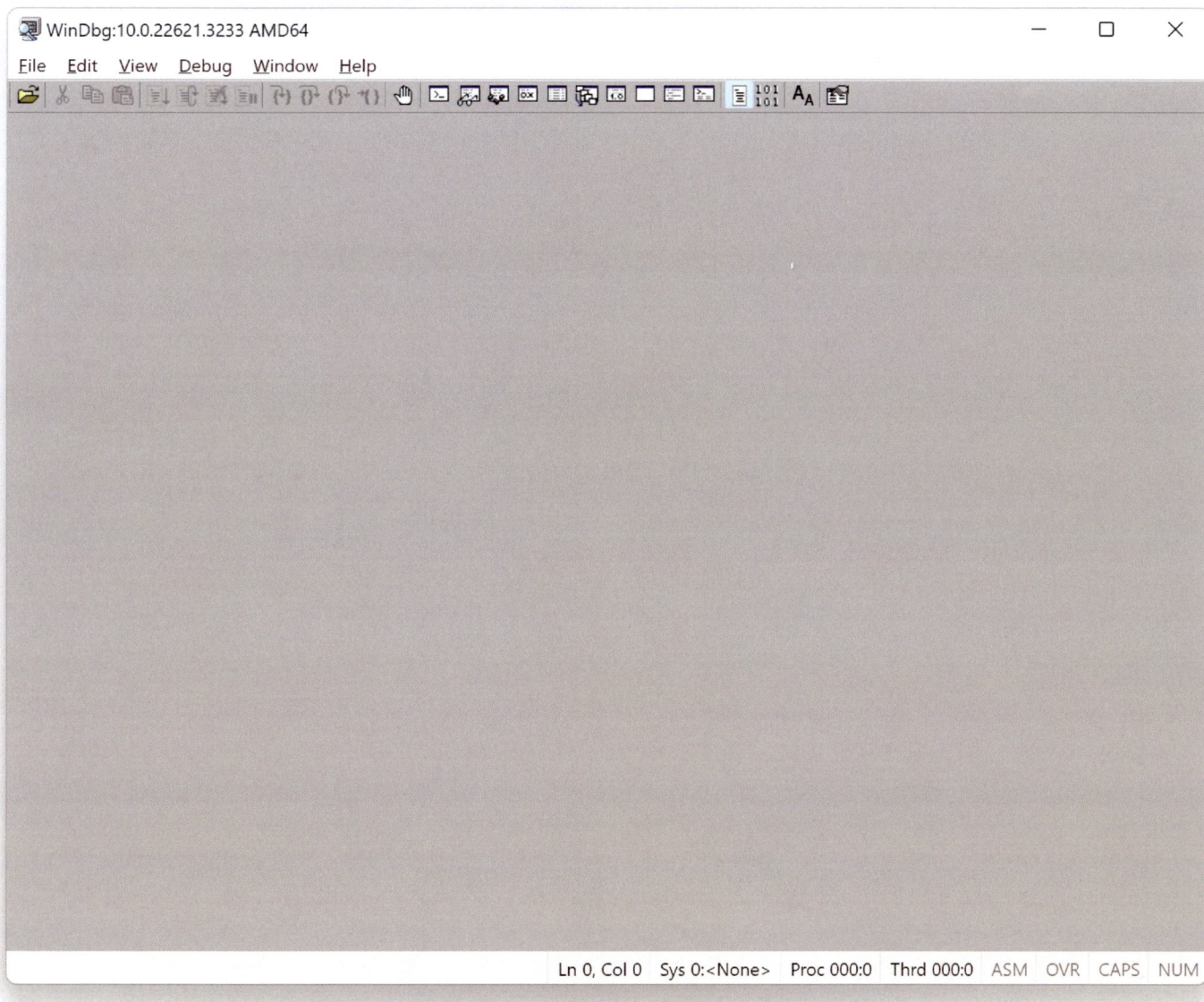

9.   Open \AdvWMDA-Dumps\x64\wordpad.DMP:

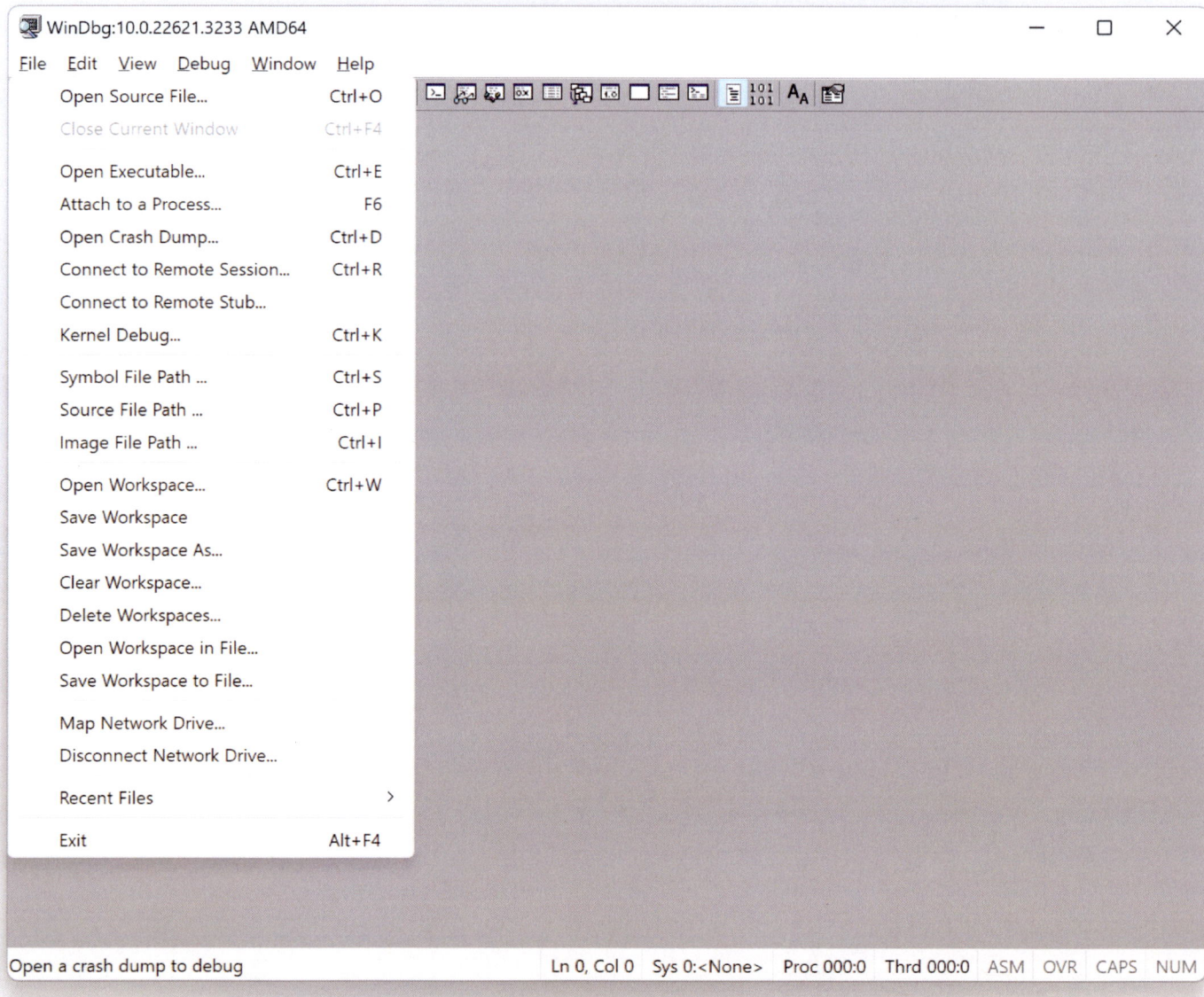

WinDbg:10.0.22621.3233 AMD64

File   Edit   View   Debug   Window   Help

Open Source File...	Ctrl+O
Close Current Window	Ctrl+F4
Open Executable...	Ctrl+E
Attach to a Process...	F6
Open Crash Dump...	Ctrl+D
Connect to Remote Session...	Ctrl+R
Connect to Remote Stub...	
Kernel Debug...	Ctrl+K
Symbol File Path ...	Ctrl+S
Source File Path ...	Ctrl+P
Image File Path ...	Ctrl+I
Open Workspace...	Ctrl+W
Save Workspace	
Save Workspace As...	
Clear Workspace...	
Delete Workspaces...	
Open Workspace in File...	
Save Workspace to File...	
Map Network Drive...	
Disconnect Network Drive...	
Recent Files	>
Exit	Alt+F4

Open a crash dump to debug   Ln 0, Col 0   Sys 0:<None>   Proc 000:0   Thrd 000:0   ASM   OVR   CAPS   NUM

10.   We get the dump file loaded:

```
Dump C:\AdvWMDA-Dumps\x64\wordpad.DMP - WinDbg:10.0.22621.3233 AMD64

File   Edit   View   Debug   Window   Help

Command - Dump C:\AdvWMDA-Dumps\x64\wordpad.DMP - WinDbg:10.0.22621.3233...

Microsoft (R) Windows Debugger Version 10.0.22621.3233 AMD64
Copyright (c) Microsoft Corporation. All rights reserved.


Loading Dump File [C:\AdvWMDA-Dumps\x64\wordpad.DMP]
User Mini Dump File with Full Memory: Only application data is available

Symbol search path is: srv*
Executable search path is:
Windows 10 Version 22000 MP (2 procs) Free x64
Product: WinNt, suite: SingleUserTS Personal
Edition build lab: 22000.1.amd64fre.co_release.210604-1628
Machine Name:
Debug session time: Thu Feb 10 00:34:24.000 2022 (UTC + 0:00)
System Uptime: 0 days 0:03:51.428
Process Uptime: 0 days 0:00:28.000
............................................................
.....................
Loading unloaded module list
..............
For analysis of this file, run !analyze -v
win32u!NtUserGetMessage+0x14:
00007ff9`878a1414 c3              ret

0:000> |
```

Ln 0, Col 0   Sys 0:C:\AdvW   Proc 000:2350   Thrd 000:2358   ASM   OVR   CAPS   NUM

11. Type the **k** command to verify the correctness of the stack trace:

```
Command - Dump C:\AdvWMDA-Dumps\x64\wordpad.DMP - WinDbg:10.0.22621.3233 AMD64          □    ✕

Microsoft (R) Windows Debugger Version 10.0.22621.3233 AMD64
Copyright (c) Microsoft Corporation. All rights reserved.


Loading Dump File [C:\AdvWMDA-Dumps\x64\wordpad.DMP]
User Mini Dump File with Full Memory: Only application data is available

Symbol search path is: srv*
Executable search path is:
Windows 10 Version 22000 MP (2 procs) Free x64
Product: WinNt, suite: SingleUserTS Personal
Edition build lab: 22000.1.amd64fre.co_release.210604-1628
Machine Name:
Debug session time: Thu Feb 10 00:34:24.000 2022 (UTC + 0:00)
System Uptime: 0 days 0:03:51.428
Process Uptime: 0 days 0:00:28.000
...........................................................
.......................
Loading unloaded module list
..............
For analysis of this file, run !analyze -v
win32u!NtUserGetMessage+0x14:
00007ff9`878a1414 c3              ret

0:000> k
```

```
Command - Dump C:\AdvWMDA-Dumps\x64\wordpad.DMP - WinDbg:10.0.22621.3233 AMD64          □    ✕

Executable search path is:
Windows 10 Version 22000 MP (2 procs) Free x64
Product: WinNt, suite: SingleUserTS Personal
Edition build lab: 22000.1.amd64fre.co_release.210604-1628
Machine Name:
Debug session time: Thu Feb 10 00:34:24.000 2022 (UTC + 0:00)
System Uptime: 0 days 0:03:51.428
Process Uptime: 0 days 0:00:28.000
...........................................................
.......................
Loading unloaded module list
..............
For analysis of this file, run !analyze -v
win32u!NtUserGetMessage+0x14:
00007ff9`878a1414 c3              ret
0:000> k
 # Child-SP          RetAddr               Call Site
00 000000a5`cd5bf578 00007ff9`8997464e     win32u!NtUserGetMessage+0x14
01 000000a5`cd5bf580 00007ff9`4e800813     user32!GetMessageW+0x2e
02 000000a5`cd5bf5e0 00007ff9`4e800736     mfc42u!CWinThread::PumpMessage+0x23
03 000000a5`cd5bf610 00007ff9`4e7ff2bc     mfc42u!CWinThread::Run+0x96
04 000000a5`cd5bf650 00007ff7`c3fbbcfd     mfc42u!AfxWinMain+0xbc
05 000000a5`cd5bf690 00007ff9`883454e0     wordpad!__wmainCRTStartup+0x1dd
06 000000a5`cd5bf750 00007ff9`89da485b     kernel32!BaseThreadInitThunk+0x10
07 000000a5`cd5bf780 00000000`00000000     ntdll!RtlUserThreadStart+0x2b
0:000>
```

12.   [Optional] Another approach is to use a Docker container image that contains preinstalled WinDbg x64 and WinDbg x86 with the required symbol files for this course's memory dump files:

```
C:\AdvWMDA-Dumps>docker pull patterndiagnostics/windbg:10.0.22621.3233-advwmda
```

```
C:\AdvWMDA-Dumps>docker run -it -v C:\AdvWMDA-Dumps:C:\AdvWMDA-Dumps
patterndiagnostics/windbg:10.0.22621.3233-advwmda

Microsoft Windows [Version 10.0.20348.2322]
(c) Microsoft Corporation. All rights reserved.

C:\WinDbg>windbg C:\AdvWMDA-Dumps\x64\wordpad.DMP

Microsoft (R) Windows Debugger Version 10.0.22621.3233 AMD64
Copyright (c) Microsoft Corporation. All rights reserved.


Loading Dump File [C:\AdvWMDA-Dumps\x64\wordpad.DMP]
User Mini Dump File with Full Memory: Only application data is available


************* Path validation summary **************
Response                        Time (ms)       Location
OK                                              C:\WinDbg\mss
Symbol search path is: C:\WinDbg\mss
Executable search path is:
Windows 10 Version 22000 MP (2 procs) Free x64
Product: WinNt, suite: SingleUserTS Personal
Edition build lab: 22000.1.amd64fre.co_release.210604-1628
Machine Name:
Debug session time: Thu Feb 10 00:34:24.000 2022 (UTC + 0:00)
System Uptime: 0 days 0:03:51.428
Process Uptime: 0 days 0:00:28.000
................................................................
.........................
Loading unloaded module list
...............
For analysis of this file, run !analyze -v
win32u!NtUserGetMessage+0x14:
00007ff9`878a1414 c3              ret
```

```
0:000> k
Child-SP          RetAddr               Call Site
000000a5`cd5bf578 00007ff9`8997464e     win32u!NtUserGetMessage+0x14
000000a5`cd5bf580 00007ff9`4e800813     user32!GetMessageW+0x2e
000000a5`cd5bf5e0 00007ff9`4e800736     mfc42u!CWinThread::PumpMessage+0x23
000000a5`cd5bf610 00007ff9`4e7ff2bc     mfc42u!CWinThread::Run+0x96
000000a5`cd5bf650 00007ff7`c3fbbcfd     mfc42u!AfxWinMain+0xbc
000000a5`cd5bf690 00007ff9`883454e0     wordpad!__wmainCRTStartup+0x1dd
000000a5`cd5bf750 00007ff9`89da485b     kernel32!BaseThreadInitThunk+0x10
000000a5`cd5bf780 00000000`00000000     ntdll!RtlUserThreadStart+0x2b
```

```
0:000> .load mex
Mex External 3.0.0.7172 Loaded!
```

```
0:000> q
quit:
NatVis script unloaded from 'C:\Program Files\Windows
Kits\10\Debuggers\x64\Visualizers\atlmfc.natvis'
NatVis script unloaded from 'C:\Program Files\Windows
Kits\10\Debuggers\x64\Visualizers\ObjectiveC.natvis'
NatVis script unloaded from 'C:\Program Files\Windows
Kits\10\Debuggers\x64\Visualizers\concurrency.natvis'
```

```
NatVis script unloaded from 'C:\Program Files\Windows
Kits\10\Debuggers\x64\Visualizers\cpp_rest.natvis'
NatVis script unloaded from 'C:\Program Files\Windows
Kits\10\Debuggers\x64\Visualizers\stl.natvis'
NatVis script unloaded from 'C:\Program Files\Windows
Kits\10\Debuggers\x64\Visualizers\Windows.Data.Json.natvis'
NatVis script unloaded from 'C:\Program Files\Windows
Kits\10\Debuggers\x64\Visualizers\Windows.Devices.Geolocation.natvis'
NatVis script unloaded from 'C:\Program Files\Windows
Kits\10\Debuggers\x64\Visualizers\Windows.Devices.Sensors.natvis'
NatVis script unloaded from 'C:\Program Files\Windows
Kits\10\Debuggers\x64\Visualizers\Windows.Media.natvis'
NatVis script unloaded from 'C:\Program Files\Windows
Kits\10\Debuggers\x64\Visualizers\windows.natvis'
NatVis script unloaded from 'C:\Program Files\Windows
Kits\10\Debuggers\x64\Visualizers\winrt.natvis'
```

`C:\WinDbg>`**`exit`**

`C:\AdvWMDA-Dumps>`

If you find any symbol problems, please use the Contact form on www.patterndiagnostics.com to report them.

We recommend exiting WinDbg after each exercise.

Complete Memory Dumps

Exercises C1 – C13

Complete memory dumps were saved from the Windows 11 system under VMware Workstation Pro. We learn more than 40 memory analysis patterns.

Exercise C1A

- **Goal:** Learn how to get stack traces related to sessions, processes and threads; diagnose different process relationships and thread types

- **Patterns:** Stack Trace Collection (Unmanaged Space); Active Thread; Passive Thread; Coupled Processes (Weak); Coupled Processes (Strong); Wait Chain (ALPC); Zombie Processes; Stack Trace Collection (Predicate); Stack Trace Collection (CPUs); Input Thread; Truncated Stack Trace; Memory Data Model

- \AdvWMDA-Dumps\Exercise-C1A-Stack-Trace-Collection.pdf

Exercise C1A: Stack Trace Collection

Goal: Learn how to get stack traces related to sessions, processes, and threads; diagnose different process relationships and thread types.

Patterns: Stack Trace Collection (unmanaged space); Active Thread; Passive Thread; Coupled Processes (weak); Coupled Processes (strong); Wait Chain (ALPC); Zombie Processes; Stack Trace Collection (Predicate); Stack Trace Collection (CPUs); Input Thread; Truncated Stack Trace; Memory Data Model.

1.   Launch WinDbg.

2.   Open \AdvWMDA-Dumps\x64\MEMORY-Normal.DMP

3.   We get the dump file loaded:

```
Microsoft (R) Windows Debugger Version 10.0.27553.1004 AMD64
Copyright (c) Microsoft Corporation. All rights reserved.


Loading Dump File [C:\AdvWMDA-Dumps\x64\MEMORY-Normal.DMP]
Kernel Bitmap Dump File: Full address space is available


************* Path validation summary **************
Response                      Time (ms)      Location
Deferred                                     srv*
Symbol search path is: srv*
Executable search path is:
Windows 10 Kernel Version 22000 MP (2 procs) Free x64
Product: WinNt, suite: TerminalServer SingleUserTS Personal
Edition build lab: 22000.1.amd64fre.co_release.210604-1628
Kernel base = 0xfffff807`62000000 PsLoadedModuleList = 0xfffff807`62c29bc0
Debug session time: Thu Feb 10 01:11:26.439 2022 (UTC + 0:00)
System Uptime: 0 days 0:07:45.422
Loading Kernel Symbols
...............................................................
...............................................................
...............................................................
..
Loading User Symbols
..............................................
Loading unloaded module list
........
For analysis of this file, run !analyze -v
nt!KeBugCheckEx:
fffff807`62416220 mov     qword ptr [rsp+8],rcx ss:0018:ffffa28c`9d8d8690=000000000000000a
```

4.   We open a log file:

```
1: kd> .logopen C:\AdvWMDA-Dumps\x64\C1A.log
Opened log file 'C:\AdvWMDA-Dumps\x64\C1A.log'
```

5.   We list running sessions:

```
1: kd> !session
unable to get nt!PspSessionIdBitmap
Sessions on machine: 2
Valid Sessions: 0 1
Current Session 1
```

Note: The error in gray color wasn't available in the previous versions of WinDbg and can be ignored.

6.   We check the current process:

```
1: kd> !process
PROCESS ffffbe0c8c2cd0c0
    SessionId: 1  Cid: 243c    Peb: 34f5f83000  ParentCid: 1070
    DirBase: 12ea72002  ObjectTable: ffff800edff979c0  HandleCount: 176.
    Image: notmyfault64.exe
    VadRoot ffffbe0c8c233dc0 Vads 83 Clone 0 Private 428. Modified 15. Locked 0.
    DeviceMap ffff800eda519d60
    Token                             ffff800ee01df060
    ElapsedTime                       00:00:19.477
    UserTime                          00:00:00.000
    KernelTime                        00:00:00.000
    QuotaPoolUsage[PagedPool]         194192
    QuotaPoolUsage[NonPagedPool]      11616
    Working Set Sizes (now,min,max)   (3317, 50, 345) (13268KB, 200KB, 1380KB)
    PeakWorkingSetSize                3240
    VirtualSize                       4234 Mb
    PeakVirtualSize                   4250 Mb
    PageFaultCount                    3390
    MemoryPriority                    FOREGROUND
    BasePriority                      8
    CommitCharge                      475
    Job                               ffffbe0c8a7a36b0

        THREAD ffffbe0c8974f080  Cid 243c.1938  Teb: 00000034f5f84000 Win32Thread: ffffbe0c8cccb2a0 RUNNING on processor 1
        THREAD ffffbe0c8b5e0080  Cid 243c.24a8  Teb: 00000034f5f86000 Win32Thread: 0000000000000000 WAIT: (WrQueue) UserMode Alertable
            ffffbe0c8b617400  QueueObject

        THREAD ffffbe0c8be7c080  Cid 243c.2484  Teb: 00000034f5f88000 Win32Thread: 0000000000000000 WAIT: (WrQueue) UserMode Alertable
            ffffbe0c8b617400  QueueObject
```

Note: We used the *NotMyFault* tool to force a complete memory dump:

https://docs.microsoft.com/en-us/sysinternals/downloads/notmyfault

7.   We set the current session to 0 and examine its implicit process:

```
1: kd> !session -s 0
Sessions on machine: 2
Implicit process is now ffffbe0c`87f2b080
Using session 01
```

```
1: kd> !process ffffbe0c`87f2b080 3f
PROCESS ffffbe0c87f2b080
    SessionId: 0  Cid: 01fc    Peb: 3901e58000  ParentCid: 01f0
    DirBase: 01932002  ObjectTable: ffff800ed7355c00  HandleCount: 537.
    Image: csrss.exe
    VadRoot ffffbe0c897bf550 Vads 164 Clone 0 Private 277. Modified 258. Locked 0.
    DeviceMap ffff800ed4822520
    Token                             ffff800ed73f8060
    ElapsedTime                       00:07:13.525
    UserTime                          00:00:00.000
    KernelTime                        00:00:00.468
    QuotaPoolUsage[PagedPool]         239472
    QuotaPoolUsage[NonPagedPool]      23032
    Working Set Sizes (now,min,max)   (1369, 50, 345) (5476KB, 200KB, 1380KB)
    PeakWorkingSetSize                1469
    VirtualSize                       2101339 Mb
    PeakVirtualSize                   2101340 Mb
    PageFaultCount                    2742
```

```
MemoryPriority                     BACKGROUND
BasePriority                       13
CommitCharge                       485

PEB at 0000003901e58000
InheritedAddressSpace:    No
ReadImageFileExecOptions:  No
BeingDebugged:            No
ImageBaseAddress:         00007ff6d7380000
NtGlobalFlag:             400
NtGlobalFlag2:            0
Ldr                       00007ffe5b0fa120
Ldr.Initialized:          Yes
Ldr.InInitializationOrderModuleList: 0000015013a03e70 . 0000015013a2b560
Ldr.InLoadOrderModuleList:          0000015013a04000 . 0000015013a2b540
Ldr.InMemoryOrderModuleList:        0000015013a04010 . 0000015013a2b550
         Base TimeStamp                     Module
    7ff6d7380000 064903e5 May 05 12:13:41 1973 C:\WINDOWS\system32\csrss.exe
    7ffe5af80000 931cda92 Mar 18 10:55:14 2048 C:\WINDOWS\SYSTEM32\ntdll.dll
    7ffe58450000 51a03181 May 25 04:35:29 2013 C:\WINDOWS\SYSTEM32\CSRSRV.dll
    7ffe58430000 d987e1f9 Aug 25 07:58:01 2085 C:\WINDOWS\system32\basesrv.DLL
    7ffe58410000 ec122896 Jul 04 11:16:54 2095 C:\WINDOWS\system32\winsrv.DLL
    7ffe58a00000 72a6f702 Dec 15 06:00:34 2030 C:\WINDOWS\System32\kernelbase.dll
    7ffe5a2c0000 7b65e245 Aug 09 13:17:09 2035 C:\WINDOWS\System32\kernel32.dll
    7ffe583e0000 864193e6 May 18 00:04:06 2041 C:\WINDOWS\SYSTEM32\winsrvext.dll
    7ffe58d80000 2eab7211 Oct 24 09:36:33 1994 C:\WINDOWS\System32\win32u.dll
    7ffe58e20000 0b2998f3 Dec 08 12:58:27 1975 C:\WINDOWS\System32\GDI32.dll
    7ffe588e0000 f03395da Sep 13 13:08:58 2097 C:\WINDOWS\System32\gdi32full.dll
    7ffe58610000 1fb7fd57 Nov 12 03:53:59 1986 C:\WINDOWS\System32\msvcp_win.dll
    7ffe584f0000 00e78ce9 Jun 25 16:14:49 1970 C:\WINDOWS\System32\ucrtbase.dll
    7ffe59000000 95c2e8f0 Aug 14 19:33:20 2049 C:\WINDOWS\System32\USER32.dll
    7ffe583d0000 203620ec Feb 15 20:11:24 1987 C:\WINDOWS\system32\sxssrv.DLL
    7ffe582e0000 a2eb73f0 Aug 12 22:00:32 2056 C:\WINDOWS\system32\sxs.dll
    7ffe5a210000 ce622c7b Sep 21 17:46:51 2079 C:\WINDOWS\System32\ADVAPI32.dll
    7ffe5a160000 90483ed2 Sep 15 20:49:38 2046 C:\WINDOWS\System32\msvcrt.dll
    7ffe5ad10000 31ec7be5 Jul 17 06:36:37 1996 C:\WINDOWS\System32\sechost.dll
    7ffe596c0000 7ff0ec4a Jan 07 16:46:02 2038 C:\WINDOWS\System32\RPCRT4.dll
    7ffe581f0000 7ac2022e Apr 07 06:01:34 2035 C:\WINDOWS\system32\ServicingCommon.dll
    7ffe58470000 a34302f0 Oct 18 07:57:52 2056 C:\WINDOWS\System32\bcryptPrimitives.dll
SubSystemData:     0000000000000000
ProcessHeap:       0000015013890000
ProcessParameters: 0000015013a034f0
CurrentDirectory:  'C:\WINDOWS\system32\'
WindowTitle:  '< Name not readable >'
ImageFile:    'C:\WINDOWS\system32\csrss.exe'
CommandLine:  '%SystemRoot%\system32\csrss.exe ObjectDirectory=\Windows SharedSection=1024,20480,768 Windows=On SubSystemType=Windows
ServerDll=basesrv,1 ServerDll=winsrv:UserServerDllInitialization,3 ServerDll=sxssrv,4 ProfileControl=Off MaxRequestThreads=16'
DllPath:      '< Name not readable >'
Environment:  0000015013a02a00
    ComSpec=C:\WINDOWS\system32\cmd.exe
    DriverData=C:\Windows\System32\Drivers\DriverData
    NUMBER_OF_PROCESSORS=2
    OS=Windows_NT

Path=C:\WINDOWS\system32;C:\WINDOWS;C:\WINDOWS\System32\Wbem;C:\WINDOWS\System32\WindowsPowerShell\v1.0\;C:\WINDOWS\System32\OpenSSH\;C:\Program
Files\dotnet\;C:\Program Files (x86)\dotnet\
    PATHEXT=.COM;.EXE;.BAT;.CMD;.VBS;.VBE;.JS;.JSE;.WSF;.WSH;.MSC
    PROCESSOR_ARCHITECTURE=AMD64
    PROCESSOR_IDENTIFIER=Intel64 Family 6 Model 142 Stepping 10, GenuineIntel
    PROCESSOR_LEVEL=6
    PROCESSOR_REVISION=8e0a
    PSModulePath=%ProgramFiles%\WindowsPowerShell\Modules;C:\WINDOWS\system32\WindowsPowerShell\v1.0\Modules
    SystemDrive=C:
    SystemRoot=C:\WINDOWS
    TEMP=C:\WINDOWS\TEMP
    TMP=C:\WINDOWS\TEMP
    USERNAME=SYSTEM
    windir=C:\WINDOWS


    THREAD ffffbe0c87d1a580  Cid 01fc.020c  Teb: 0000003901e5f000 Win32Thread: ffffbe0c87ff3c50 WAIT: (WrLpcReceive) UserMode Non-Alertable
        ffffbe0c87d1aa58  Semaphore Limit 0x1
    Not impersonating
    DeviceMap                 ffff800ed4822520
    Owning Process            ffffbe0c87f2b080      Image:         csrss.exe
    Attached Process          N/A            Image:        N/A
    Wait Start TickCount      29729          Ticks: 58 (0:00:00.906)
    Context Switch Count      817            IdealProcessor: 0
    UserTime                  00:00:00.000
    KernelTime                00:00:00.156
    Win32 Start Address CSRSRV!CsrApiRequestThread (0x00007ffe58451820)
    Stack Init ffffa28c9cfa1c70 Current ffffa28c9cfa13d0
    Base ffffa28c9cfa2000 Limit ffffa28c9cf9c000 Call 0000000000000000
    Priority 14 BasePriority 13 PriorityDecrement 0 IoPriority 2 PagePriority 5
Unable to load image \??\C:\WINDOWS\system32\drivers\myfault.sys, Win32 error 0n2
    Child-SP          RetAddr           Call Site
    ffffa28c`9cfa1410 fffff807`623327f7 nt!KiSwapContext+0x76
    ffffa28c`9cfa1550 fffff807`623346a9 nt!KiSwapThread+0x3a7
    ffffa28c`9cfa1630 fffff807`6232e5c4 nt!KiCommitThreadWait+0x159
    ffffa28c`9cfa16d0 fffff807`6222fdc6 nt!KeWaitForSingleObject+0x234
    ffffa28c`9cfa17c0 fffff807`6268caf0 nt!AlpcpWaitForSingleObject+0x3e
```

```
ffffa28c`9cfa1800 fffff807`6274caad     nt!AlpcpCompleteDeferSignalRequestAndWait+0x3c
ffffa28c`9cfa1840 fffff807`6274d4d3     nt!AlpcpReceiveMessagePort+0x3ad
ffffa28c`9cfa18d0 fffff807`6274d01e     nt!AlpcpReceiveMessage+0x333
ffffa28c`9cfa19b0 fffff807`62428775     nt!NtAlpcSendWaitReceivePort+0xfe
ffffa28c`9cfa1a70 00007ffe`5b0248c4     nt!KiSystemServiceCopyEnd+0x25 (TrapFrame @ ffffa28c`9cfa1ae0)
00000039`01d7f7f8 00007ffe`58451926     ntdll!NtAlpcSendWaitReceivePort+0x14
00000039`01d7f800 00007ffe`5af84873     CSRSRV!CsrApiRequestThread+0x106
00000039`01d7fea0 00000000`00000000     ntdll!RtlUserThreadStart+0x43
```

    THREAD ffffbe0c887d60c0 Cid 01fc.0228 Teb: 0000003901e63000 Win32Thread: ffffbe0c8a6f1b20 WAIT: (WrLpcReply) UserMode Non-Alertable
        ffffbe0c887d6598 Semaphore Limit 0x1
    Waiting for reply to ALPC Message ffff800ed83f7a50 : queued at port ffffbe0c89022b20 : owned by process ffffbe0c891020c0
    Not impersonating
    DeviceMap   ffff800ed4822520
    Owning Process   ffffbe0c87f2b080   Image: csrss.exe
    Attached Process   N/A   Image: N/A
    Wait Start TickCount   4008   Ticks: 25779 (0:00:06:42.796)
    Context Switch Count   8   IdealProcessor: 0
    UserTime   00:00:00.000
    KernelTime   00:00:00.015
    Win32 Start Address winsrvext!TerminalServerRequestThread (0x00007ffe583ee680)
    Stack Init ffffa28c9cfeec70 Current ffffa28c9cfee3b0
    Base ffffa28c9cfef000 Limit ffffa28c9cfe9000 Call 0000000000000000
    Priority 15 BasePriority 15 PriorityDecrement 0 IoPriority 2 PagePriority 5
    Child-SP   RetAddr   Call Site
    ffffa28c`9cfee3f0 fffff807`623327f7   nt!KiSwapContext+0x76
    ffffa28c`9cfee530 fffff807`623346a9   nt!KiSwapThread+0x3a7
    ffffa28c`9cfee610 fffff807`6232e5c4   nt!KiCommitThreadWait+0x159
    ffffa28c`9cfee6b0 fffff807`622c45ed   nt!KeWaitForSingleObject+0x234
    ffffa28c`9cfee7a0 fffff807`6274e0c6   nt!AlpcpSignalAndWait+0x13d
    ffffa28c`9cfee830 fffff807`6274dc1f   nt!AlpcpReceiveSynchronousReply+0x56
    ffffa28c`9cfee890 fffff807`6274d0f6   nt!AlpcpProcessSynchronousRequest+0x36f
    ffffa28c`9cfee9b0 fffff807`62428775   nt!NtAlpcSendWaitReceivePort+0x1d6
    ffffa28c`9cfeea70 00007ffe`5b0248c4   nt!KiSystemServiceCopyEnd+0x25 (TrapFrame @ ffffa28c`9cfeeae0)
    00000039`01dff958 00007ffe`583ee984   ntdll!NtAlpcSendWaitReceivePort+0x14
    00000039`01dff960 00007ffe`5af84873   winsrvext!TerminalServerRequestThread+0x304
    00000039`01dffac0 00000000`00000000   ntdll!RtlUserThreadStart+0x43

    THREAD ffffbe0c888020c0 Cid 01fc.0230 Teb: 0000003901e67000 Win32Thread: 0000000000000000 WAIT: (UserRequest) UserMode Alertable
        ffffbe0c87c87be0 SynchronizationEvent
        ffffbe0c87c87ae0 SynchronizationEvent
        ffffbe0c84db6ee0 SynchronizationEvent
    Not impersonating
    DeviceMap   ffff800ed4822520
    Owning Process   ffffbe0c87f2b080   Image: csrss.exe
    Attached Process   N/A   Image: N/A
    Wait Start TickCount   2076   Ticks: 27711 (0:00:07:12.984)
    Context Switch Count   4   IdealProcessor: 0
    UserTime   00:00:00.000
    KernelTime   00:00:00.000
    Win32 Start Address winsrvext!NotificationThread (0x00007ffe583e3430)
    Stack Init ffffa28c9cffcc70 Current ffffa28c9cffbee0
    Base ffffa28c9cffd000 Limit ffffa28c9cff7000 Call 0000000000000000
    Priority 3 BasePriority 13 PriorityDecrement 0 IoPriority 2 PagePriority 5
    Kernel stack not resident.

    THREAD ffffbe0c888130c0 Cid 01fc.0234 Teb: 0000003901e69000 Win32Thread: 0000000000000000 WAIT: (UserRequest) UserMode Alertable
        ffffbe0c87c879e0 SynchronizationEvent
    Not impersonating
    DeviceMap   ffff800ed4822520
    Owning Process   ffffbe0c87f2b080   Image: csrss.exe
    Attached Process   N/A   Image: N/A
    Wait Start TickCount   2076   Ticks: 27711 (0:00:07:12.984)
    Context Switch Count   2   IdealProcessor: 1
    UserTime   00:00:00.000
    KernelTime   00:00:00.000
    Win32 Start Address winsrvext!PowerNotificationThread (0x00007ffe583e3950)
    Stack Init ffffa28c9ca97c70 Current ffffa28c9ca97650
    Base ffffa28c9ca98000 Limit ffffa28c9ca92000 Call 0000000000000000
    Priority 15 BasePriority 13 PriorityDecrement 0 IoPriority 2 PagePriority 5
    Kernel stack not resident.

    THREAD ffffbe0c87efb080 Cid 01fc.0238 Teb: 0000003901e6b000 Win32Thread: 0000000000000000 WAIT: (WrLpcReceive) UserMode Non-Alertable
        ffffbe0c87efb558 Semaphore Limit 0x1
    Not impersonating
    DeviceMap   ffff800ed4822520
    Owning Process   ffffbe0c87f2b080   Image: csrss.exe
    Attached Process   N/A   Image: N/A
    Wait Start TickCount   2077   Ticks: 27710 (0:00:07:12.968)
    Context Switch Count   3   IdealProcessor: 0
    UserTime   00:00:00.000
    KernelTime   00:00:00.000
    Win32 Start Address CSRSRV!CsrSbApiRequestThread (0x00007ffe584574b0)
    Stack Init ffffa28c9cdf7c70 Current ffffa28c9cdf7410
    Base ffffa28c9cdf8000 Limit ffffa28c9cdf2000 Call 0000000000000000
    Priority 14 BasePriority 13 PriorityDecrement 0 IoPriority 2 PagePriority 5
    Kernel stack not resident.

    THREAD ffffbe0c88893080 Cid 01fc.0268 Teb: 0000003901e6d000 Win32Thread: ffffbe0c87ff5eb0 WAIT: (WrLpcReceive) UserMode Non-Alertable
        ffffbe0c88893558 Semaphore Limit 0x1
    Not impersonating

```
DeviceMap              ffff800ed4822520
Owning Process         ffffbe0c87f2b080       Image:          csrss.exe
Attached Process       N/A         Image:         N/A
Wait Start TickCount   29374       Ticks: 413 (0:00:00:06.453)
Context Switch Count   952         IdealProcessor: 1
UserTime               00:00:00.031
KernelTime             00:00:00.062
Win32 Start Address CSRSRV!CsrApiRequestThread (0x00007ffe58451820)
Stack Init ffffa28c9ce3ec70 Current ffffa28c9ce3e3d0
Base ffffa28c9ce3f000 Limit ffffa28c9ce39000 Call 0000000000000000
Priority 14 BasePriority 13 PriorityDecrement 0 IoPriority 2 PagePriority 5
Child-SP          RetAddr           Call Site
ffffa28c`9ce3e410 fffff807`623327f7 nt!KiSwapContext+0x76
ffffa28c`9ce3e550 fffff807`623346a9 nt!KiSwapThread+0x3a7
ffffa28c`9ce3e630 fffff807`6232e5c4 nt!KiCommitThreadWait+0x159
ffffa28c`9ce3e6d0 fffff807`6222fdc6 nt!KeWaitForSingleObject+0x234
ffffa28c`9ce3e7c0 fffff807`6268caf0 nt!AlpcpWaitForSingleObject+0x3e
ffffa28c`9ce3e800 fffff807`6274caad nt!AlpcpCompleteDeferSignalRequestAndWait+0x3c
ffffa28c`9ce3e840 fffff807`6274d4d3 nt!AlpcpReceiveMessagePort+0x3ad
ffffa28c`9ce3e8d0 fffff807`6274d01e nt!AlpcpReceiveMessage+0x333
ffffa28c`9ce3e9b0 fffff807`62428775 nt!NtAlpcSendWaitReceivePort+0xfe
ffffa28c`9ce3ea70 00007ffe`5b0248c4 nt!KiSystemServiceCopyEnd+0x25 (TrapFrame @ ffffa28c`9ce3eae0)
00000039`01cbf518 00007ffe`58451926 ntdll!NtAlpcSendWaitReceivePort+0x14
00000039`01cbf520 00007ffe`5af84873 CSRSRV!CsrApiRequestThread+0x106
00000039`01cbfbc0 00000000`00000000 ntdll!RtlUserThreadStart+0x43


THREAD ffffbe0c888b4080 Cid 01fc.0278 Teb: 0000003901e6f000 Win32Thread: ffffbe0c87ff5140 WAIT: (WrUserRequest) KernelMode Non-Alertable
    ffffbe0c87447b40 QueueObject
    ffffbe0c87ff54b0 NotificationTimer
    ffffbe0c87ff5820 SynchronizationTimer
    ffffbe0c87ca65c0 SynchronizationEvent
    fffff80762c23960 NotificationEvent
    ffffbe0c886fd7e0 SynchronizationEvent
    ffffbe0c886fd8e0 Semaphore Limit 0x7fffffff
    ffffbe0c886fd0e0 SynchronizationEvent
    ffffbe0c887fd340 SynchronizationTimer
    ffffbe0c886fdce0 SynchronizationEvent
    ffffbe0c886fd960 SynchronizationEvent
    ffffbe0c886fde60 SynchronizationEvent
    ffffbe0c886fdee0 SynchronizationEvent
    ffffbe0c886fd5e0 Semaphore Limit 0x7fffffff
    ffffbe0c886fd260 SynchronizationEvent
    ffffbe0c887fe270 SynchronizationTimer
    ffffbe0c887ff350 SynchronizationTimer
    ffffbe0c887fc0b0 SynchronizationTimer
    ffffbe0c887fc260 SynchronizationTimer
    ffffbe0c887fda00 SynchronizationTimer
    ffffbe0c886fdc60 SynchronizationEvent
    ffffbe0c886fda60 SynchronizationEvent
    ffffbe0c886fd160 SynchronizationEvent
    ffffbe0c886fdfe0 SynchronizationEvent
    ffffbe0c886fd860 SynchronizationEvent
    ffffbe0c886fe060 SynchronizationEvent
Not impersonating
DeviceMap              ffff800ed4822520
Owning Process         ffffbe0c87f2b080       Image:          csrss.exe
Attached Process       N/A         Image:         N/A
Wait Start TickCount   29701       Ticks: 86 (0:00:00:01.343)
Context Switch Count   126         IdealProcessor: 0
UserTime               00:00:00.000
KernelTime             00:00:00.000
Win32 Start Address winsrvext!StartCreateSystemThreads (0x00007ffe583e3fc0)
Stack Init ffffa28c9ce5ac70 Current ffffa28c9ce5a250
Base ffffa28c9ce5b000 Limit ffffa28c9ce55000 Call 0000000000000000
Priority 16 BasePriority 16 PriorityDecrement 0 IoPriority 2 PagePriority 5
Child-SP          RetAddr           Call Site
ffffa28c`9ce5a290 fffff807`623327f7 nt!KiSwapContext+0x76
ffffa28c`9ce5a3d0 fffff807`623346a9 nt!KiSwapThread+0x3a7
ffffa28c`9ce5a4b0 fffff807`6228ed51 nt!KiCommitThreadWait+0x159
ffffa28c`9ce5a550 fffbc92`8e121ec5 nt!KeWaitForMultipleObjects+0x2b1
ffffa28c`9ce5a650 fffbc92`8e7a4576 win32kbase!LegacyInputDispatcher::WaitAndDispatch+0x95
ffffa28c`9ce5a720 fffbc92`8e192904 win32kfull!RawInputThread+0x796
ffffa28c`9ce5a890 fffbc92`8e192684 win32kbase!xxxCreateSystemThreads+0x214
ffffa28c`9ce5a9b0 fffbc92`8dc4a612 win32kbase!NtUserCreateSystemThreads+0x144
ffffa28c`9ce5aab0 fffff807`62428775 win32k!NtUserCreateSystemThreads+0x16
ffffa28c`9ce5aae0 00007ffe`58d88cd4 nt!KiSystemServiceCopyEnd+0x25 (TrapFrame @ ffffa28c`9ce5aae0)
00000039`0213fdf8 00007ffe`583e3fdc win32u!NtUserCreateSystemThreads+0x14
00000039`0213fe00 00007ffe`5af84873 winsrvext!StartCreateSystemThreads+0x1c
00000039`0213fe30 00000000`00000000 ntdll!RtlUserThreadStart+0x43


THREAD ffffbe0c888b6080 Cid 01fc.027c Teb: 0000003901e71000 Win32Thread: ffffbe0c87ff5320 WAIT: (WrUserRequest) UserMode Non-Alertable
    ffffbe0c87ca68c0 SynchronizationEvent
    ffffbe0c87ca79d0 SynchronizationEvent
    ffffbe0c87447700 QueueObject
Not impersonating
DeviceMap              ffff800ed4822520
Owning Process         ffffbe0c87f2b080       Image:          csrss.exe
Attached Process       N/A         Image:         N/A
Wait Start TickCount   3863        Ticks: 25924 (0:00:06:45.062)
Context Switch Count   83          IdealProcessor: 1
UserTime               00:00:00.000
```

```
KernelTime                     00:00:00.015
Win32 Start Address winsrvext!StartCreateSystemThreads (0x00007ffe583e3fc0)
Stack Init ffffa28c9ce61c70 Current ffffa28c9ce61260
Base ffffa28c9ce62000 Limit ffffa28c9ce5c000 Call 0000000000000000
Priority 16 BasePriority 16 PriorityDecrement 0 IoPriority 2 PagePriority 5
Child-SP          RetAddr           Call Site
ffffa28c`9ce612a0 fffff807`623327f7 nt!KiSwapContext+0x76
ffffa28c`9ce613e0 fffff807`623346a9 nt!KiSwapThread+0x3a7
ffffa28c`9ce614c0 fffff807`6228ed51 nt!KiCommitThreadWait+0x159
ffffa28c`9ce61560 ffffbc92`8e121ec5 nt!KeWaitForMultipleObjects+0x2b1
ffffa28c`9ce61660 ffffbc92`8e6f15b4 win32kbase!LegacyInputDispatcher::WaitAndDispatch+0x95
ffffa28c`9ce61730 ffffbc92`8e6f1349 win32kfull!xxxDesktopThreadWaiter+0xe0
ffffa28c`9ce617a0 ffffbc92`8e192904 win32kfull!xxxDesktopThread+0x359
ffffa28c`9ce61890 ffffbc92`8e192684 win32kbase!xxxCreateSystemThreads+0x214
ffffa28c`9ce619b0 ffffbc92`8dc4a612 win32kbase!NtUserCreateSystemThreads+0x144
ffffa28c`9ce61ab0 fffff807`62428775 win32k!NtUserCreateSystemThreads+0x16
ffffa28c`9ce61ae0 00007ffe`58d88cd4 nt!KiSystemServiceCopyEnd+0x25 (TrapFrame @ ffffa28c`9ce61ae0)
00000039`0217fe48 00007ffe`583e3fdc win32u!NtUserCreateSystemThreads+0x14
00000039`0217fe50 00007ffe`5af84873 winsrvext!StartCreateSystemThreads+0x1c
00000039`0217fe80 00000000`00000000 ntdll!RtlUserThreadStart+0x43

THREAD ffffbe0c889c8040  Cid 01fc.03a0  Teb: 0000003901e73000 Win32Thread: ffffbe0c888fce20 WAIT: (WrQueue) UserMode Alertable
    ffffbe0c87e707c0  QueueObject
Not impersonating
DeviceMap                      ffff800ed4822520
Owning Process                 ffffbe0c87f2b080       Image:          csrss.exe
Attached Process               N/A             Image:          N/A
Wait Start TickCount           2843            Ticks: 26944 (0:00:07:01.000)
Context Switch Count           16              IdealProcessor: 0
UserTime                       00:00:00.015
KernelTime                     00:00:00.000
Win32 Start Address ntdll!TppWorkerThread (0x00007ffe5af96950)
Stack Init ffffa28c9d110c70 Current ffffa28c9d110360
Base ffffa28c9d111000 Limit ffffa28c9d10b000 Call 0000000000000000
Priority 14 BasePriority 13 PriorityDecrement 0 IoPriority 2 PagePriority 5
Kernel stack not resident.


THREAD ffffbe0c890b6080  Cid 01fc.0008  Teb: 0000003901e75000 Win32Thread: ffffbe0c89097980 WAIT: (WrUserRequest) UserMode Non-Alertable
    ffffbe0c890b0c40  QueueObject
Not impersonating
DeviceMap                      ffff800ed4822520
Owning Process                 ffffbe0c87f2b080       Image:          csrss.exe
Attached Process               N/A             Image:          N/A
Wait Start TickCount           2578            Ticks: 27209 (0:00:07:05.140)
Context Switch Count           5               IdealProcessor: 1
UserTime                       00:00:00.000
KernelTime                     00:00:00.000
Win32 Start Address winsrvext!StartCreateSystemThreads (0x00007ffe583e3fc0)
Stack Init ffffa28c9d1cdc70 Current ffffa28c9d1cd170
Base ffffa28c9d1ce000 Limit ffffa28c9d1c8000 Call 0000000000000000
Priority 14 BasePriority 12 PriorityDecrement 0 IoPriority 2 PagePriority 5
Kernel stack not resident.


THREAD ffffbe0c89a9a080  Cid 01fc.0cd0  Teb: 0000003901e77000 Win32Thread: ffffbe0c898d7b60 WAIT: (WrLpcReceive) UserMode Non-Alertable
    ffffbe0c89a9a558  Semaphore Limit 0x1
Not impersonating
DeviceMap                      ffff800ed4822520
Owning Process                 ffffbe0c87f2b080       Image:          csrss.exe
Attached Process               N/A             Image:          N/A
Wait Start TickCount           29353           Ticks: 434 (0:00:00:06.781)
Context Switch Count           670             IdealProcessor: 0
UserTime                       00:00:00.031
KernelTime                     00:00:00.015
Win32 Start Address CSRSRV!CsrApiRequestThread (0x00007ffe58451820)
Stack Init ffffa28c9e030c70 Current ffffa28c9e0303d0
Base ffffa28c9e031000 Limit ffffa28c9e02b000 Call 0000000000000000
Priority 14 BasePriority 13 PriorityDecrement 0 IoPriority 2 PagePriority 5
Child-SP          RetAddr           Call Site
ffffa28c`9e030410 fffff807`623327f7 nt!KiSwapContext+0x76
ffffa28c`9e030550 fffff807`623346a9 nt!KiSwapThread+0x3a7
ffffa28c`9e030630 fffff807`6232e5c4 nt!KiCommitThreadWait+0x159
ffffa28c`9e0306d0 fffff807`6222fdc6 nt!KeWaitForSingleObject+0x234
ffffa28c`9e0307c0 fffff807`6268caf0 nt!AlpcpWaitForSingleObject+0x3e
ffffa28c`9e030800 fffff807`6274caad nt!AlpcpCompleteDeferSignalRequestAndWait+0x3c
ffffa28c`9e030840 fffff807`6274d4d3 nt!AlpcpReceiveMessagePort+0x3ad
ffffa28c`9e0308d0 fffff807`6274d01e nt!AlpcpReceiveMessage+0x333
ffffa28c`9e0309b0 fffff807`62428775 nt!NtAlpcSendWaitReceivePort+0xfe
ffffa28c`9e030a70 00007ffe`5b0248c4 nt!KiSystemServiceCopyEnd+0x25 (TrapFrame @ ffffa28c`9e030ae0)
00000039`0203f288 00007ffe`58451926 ntdll!NtAlpcSendWaitReceivePort+0x14
00000039`0203f290 00007ffe`5af84873 CSRSRV!CsrApiRequestThread+0x106
00000039`0203f930 00000000`00000000 ntdll!RtlUserThreadStart+0x43


THREAD ffffbe0c89fb6040  Cid 01fc.10ac  Teb: 0000003901e79000 Win32Thread: ffffbe0c8a6fa400 WAIT: (WrQueue) UserMode Alertable
    ffffbe0c87e707c0  QueueObject
Not impersonating
DeviceMap                      ffff800ed4822520
Owning Process                 ffffbe0c87f2b080       Image:          csrss.exe
Attached Process               N/A             Image:          N/A
Wait Start TickCount           4270            Ticks: 25517 (0:00:06:38.703)
Context Switch Count           17              IdealProcessor: 1
UserTime                       00:00:00.000
```

```
KernelTime                      00:00:00.000
Win32 Start Address ntdll!TppWorkerThread (0x00007ffe5af96950)
Stack Init ffffa28c9e60dc70 Current ffffa28c9e60d360
Base ffffa28c9e60e000 Limit ffffa28c9e608000 Call 0000000000000000
Priority 15 BasePriority 13 PriorityDecrement 0 IoPriority 2 PagePriority 5
Child-SP          RetAddr           Call Site
ffffa28c`9e60d3a0 fffff807`623327f7 nt!KiSwapContext+0x76
ffffa28c`9e60d4e0 fffff807`623346a9 nt!KiSwapThread+0x3a7
ffffa28c`9e60d5c0 fffff807`62337106 nt!KiCommitThreadWait+0x159
ffffa28c`9e60d660 fffff807`62336b18 nt!KeRemoveQueueEx+0x2b6
ffffa28c`9e60d710 fffff807`6233937c nt!IoRemoveIoCompletion+0x98
ffffa28c`9e60d830 fffff807`62428775 nt!NtWaitForWorkViaWorkerFactory+0x39c
ffffa28c`9e60da70 00007ffe`5b027304 nt!KiSystemServiceCopyEnd+0x25 (TrapFrame @ ffffa28c`9e60dae0)
00000039`0223f848 00007ffe`5af96c2f ntdll!NtWaitForWorkViaWorkerFactory+0x14
00000039`0223f850 00007ffe`5af84873 ntdll!TppWorkerThread+0x2df
00000039`0223fb40 00000000`00000000 ntdll!RtlUserThreadStart+0x43


THREAD ffffbe0c8bfbc040  Cid 01fc.26d8  Teb: 0000003901e7d000 Win32Thread: 0000000000000000 WAIT: (WrQueue) UserMode Alertable
    ffffbe0c87e71780  QueueObject
Not impersonating
DeviceMap                       ffff800ed4822520
Owning Process                  ffffbe0c87f2b080       Image:         csrss.exe
Attached Process                N/A            Image:         N/A
Wait Start TickCount            28424          Ticks: 1363 (0:00:00:21.296)
Context Switch Count            4              IdealProcessor: 1
UserTime                        00:00:00.000
KernelTime                      00:00:00.000
Win32 Start Address ntdll!TppWorkerThread (0x00007ffe5af96950)
Stack Init ffffa28ca0317c70 Current ffffa28ca0317360
Base ffffa28ca0318000 Limit ffffa28ca0312000 Call 0000000000000000
Priority 13 BasePriority 13 PriorityDecrement 0 IoPriority 2 PagePriority 5
Child-SP          RetAddr           Call Site
ffffa28c`a03173a0 fffff807`623327f7 nt!KiSwapContext+0x76
ffffa28c`a03174e0 fffff807`623346a9 nt!KiSwapThread+0x3a7
ffffa28c`a03175c0 fffff807`62337106 nt!KiCommitThreadWait+0x159
ffffa28c`a0317660 fffff807`62336b18 nt!KeRemoveQueueEx+0x2b6
ffffa28c`a0317710 fffff807`6233937c nt!IoRemoveIoCompletion+0x98
ffffa28c`a0317830 fffff807`62428775 nt!NtWaitForWorkViaWorkerFactory+0x39c
ffffa28c`a0317a70 00007ffe`5b027304 nt!KiSystemServiceCopyEnd+0x25 (TrapFrame @ ffffa28c`a0317ae0)
00000039`01cffc58 00007ffe`5af96c2f ntdll!NtWaitForWorkViaWorkerFactory+0x14
00000039`01cffc60 00007ffe`5af84873 ntdll!TppWorkerThread+0x2df
00000039`01cfff50 00000000`00000000 ntdll!RtlUserThreadStart+0x43
```

Note: We see that the current process has changed. We specified **3f** flags to have the process context changed to that of *csrss.exe* during the execution of the **!process** command. We also notice passive threads waiting for ALPC notification, for example, **ffffbe0c87d1a580** (weakly coupled processes) and **ffffbe0c887d60c0** thread waiting for ALPC request reply from *svchost.exe* process (strongly coupled processes):

```
1: kd> !alpc /m ffff800ed83f7a50
Invalid reserved message id 0xffff800ed83f7a50
```

Note: The previous versions of WinDbg showed this (you can also use classic WinDbg), and we could check the thread:

```
1: kd> !alpc /m ffff800ed83f7a50

Message ffff800ed83f7a50
  MessageID             : 0x0008 (8)
  CallbackID            : 0x0339 (825)
  SequenceNumber        : 0x00000003 (3)
  Type                  : LPC_REQUEST
  DataLength            : 0x4048 (16456)
  TotalLength           : 0x4070 (16496)
  Canceled              : No
  Release               : No
  ReplyWaitReply        : No
  Continuation          : Yes
  OwnerPort             : ffffbe0c89115d60 [ALPC_CLIENT_COMMUNICATION_PORT]
  WaitingThread         : ffffbe0c887d60c0
  QueueType             : ALPC_MSGQUEUE_PENDING
```

```
QueuePort               : ffffbe0c89022b20 [ALPC_CONNECTION_PORT]
QueuePortOwnerProcess   : ffffbe0c891020c0 (svchost.exe)
ServerThread            : ffffbe0c89111080
QuotaCharged            : Yes
CancelQueuePort         : 0000000000000000
CancelSequencePort      : 0000000000000000
CancelSequenceNumber    : 0x00000000 (0)
ClientContext           : 0000000000000000
ServerContext           : 0000000000000000
PortContext             : 0000029537e331f0
CancelPortContext       : 0000000000000000
SecurityData            : 0000000000000000
View                    : 0000000000000000
HandleData              : 0000000000000000
```

```
1: kd> !thread ffffbe0c89111080 3f
```

```
THREAD ffffbe0c89111080  Cid 01b4.0240  Teb: 000000e56c471000 Win32Thread: 0000000000000000 WAIT:
(WrQueue) UserMode Alertable
    ffffbe0c890b3c40  QueueObject
Not impersonating
DeviceMap               ffff800ed4822520
Owning Process          ffffbe0c891020c0       Image:          svchost.exe
Attached Process        N/A            Image:          N/A
Wait Start TickCount    26624          Ticks: 3163 (0:00:00:49.421)
Context Switch Count    1227           IdealProcessor: 0
UserTime                00:00:00.062
KernelTime              00:00:00.062
Win32 Start Address ntdll!TppWorkerThread (0x00007ffe5af96950)
Stack Init ffffa28c9d230c70 Current ffffa28c9d230360
Base ffffa28c9d231000 Limit ffffa28c9d22b000 Call 0000000000000000
Priority 11 BasePriority 8 PriorityDecrement 48 IoPriority 2 PagePriority 5
Child-SP          RetAddr               Call Site
ffffa28c`9d2303a0 fffff807`623327f7     nt!KiSwapContext+0x76
ffffa28c`9d2304e0 fffff807`623346a9     nt!KiSwapThread+0x3a7
ffffa28c`9d2305c0 fffff807`62337106     nt!KiCommitThreadWait+0x159
ffffa28c`9d230660 fffff807`62336b18     nt!KeRemoveQueueEx+0x2b6
ffffa28c`9d230710 fffff807`6233937c     nt!IoRemoveIoCompletion+0x98
ffffa28c`9d230830 fffff807`62428775     nt!NtWaitForWorkViaWorkerFactory+0x39c
ffffa28c`9d230a70 00007ffe`5b027304     nt!KiSystemServiceCopyEnd+0x25 (TrapFrame @ ffffa28c`9d230ae0)
000000e5`6c8ff9a8 00007ffe`5af96c2f     ntdll!NtWaitForWorkViaWorkerFactory+0x14
000000e5`6c8ff9b0 00007ffe`5a2d54e0     ntdll!TppWorkerThread+0x2df
000000e5`6c8ffca0 00007ffe`5af8485b     KERNEL32!BaseThreadInitThunk+0x10
000000e5`6c8ffcd0 00000000`00000000     ntdll!RtlUserThreadStart+0x2b
```

Note: You can also use the port option instead of the message:

```
1: kd> !alpc /p ffffbe0c89022b20
```

```
Port ffffbe0c89022b20
  Type                      : ALPC_CONNECTION_PORT
  CommunicationInfo         : ffff800ed8a33420
    ConnectionPort          : ffffbe0c89022b20 (SmSsWinStationApiPort), Connections
    ClientCommunicationPort : 0000000000000000
    ServerCommunicationPort : 0000000000000000
  OwnerProcess              : ffffbe0c891020c0 (svchost.exe), Connections
  SequenceNo                : 0x00000002 (2)
  CompletionPort            : ffffbe0c890b3c40
  CompletionList            : 0000000000000000
  ConnectionPending         : No
  ConnectionRefused         : No
  Disconnected              : No
  Closed                    : No
  FlushOnClose              : Yes
  ReturnExtendedInfo        : No
  Waitable                  : No
```

```
Security              : Static
Wow64CompletionList   : No

8 thread(s) are registered with port IO completion object:

   THREAD ffffbe0c89110040  Cid 01b4.01f0  Teb: 000000e56c46f000 Win32Thread: 0000000000000000 WAIT
   THREAD ffffbe0c89111080  Cid 01b4.0240  Teb: 000000e56c471000 Win32Thread: 0000000000000000 WAIT
   THREAD ffffbe0c8911c040  Cid 01b4.02d0  Teb: 000000e56c473000 Win32Thread: 0000000000000000 WAIT
   THREAD ffffbe0c8927e080  Cid 01b4.054c  Teb: 000000e56c475000 Win32Thread: 0000000000000000 WAIT
   THREAD ffffbe0c89def040  Cid 01b4.1b68  Teb: 000000e56c477000 Win32Thread: 0000000000000000 WAIT
   THREAD ffffbe0c8b4d9040  Cid 01b4.04cc  Teb: 000000e56c479000 Win32Thread: 0000000000000000 WAIT
   THREAD ffffbe0c8b5da040  Cid 01b4.22c8  Teb: 000000e56c47b000 Win32Thread: 0000000000000000 WAIT
   THREAD ffffbe0c8b53f040  Cid 01b4.26d4  Teb: 000000e56c47f000 Win32Thread: 0000000000000000 WAIT

 Main queue is empty.


 Direct message queue is empty.


 Large message queue is empty.


 Pending queue has 2 message(s)

   ffff800ed890a8d0 00000084 0000000000000250:000000000000029c ffffbe0c888ca080 ffffbe0c8927e080 LPC_REQUEST
   ffff800ed83f7a50 00000008 00000000000001fc:0000000000000228 ffffbe0c887d60c0 ffffbe0c89111080 LPC_REQUEST

 Canceled queue is empty.
```

Note: ALPC wait chains in *csrss.exe* are normal and expected. We can get the list of all ALPC receiver threads and threads waiting for a reply using Microsoft MEX Debugging Extension:

https://www.microsoft.com/en-us/download/details.aspx?id=53304

After downloading, extracting, and unzipping, we copy \x64*mex.dll* to our dump files folder, for example, C:\AdvWMDA-Dumps\x64. If you use the classic WinDbg from Debugging Tools for Windows, you can copy it to the WinDbg installation folder (for example, *C:\Program Files (x86)\Windows Kits\10\Debuggers\x64*). If you use the Docker environment, then it is already installed.

```
1: kd> .load C:\AdvWMDA-Dumps\x64\mex
Mex External 3.0.0.7172 Loaded!
```

```
1: kd> !mex.help
Mex currently has 255 extensions available.  Please specify a keyword to search.
Or browse by category:

All PowerShell[6] SystemCenter[3] Networking[12] Process[5] Mex[2] Kernel[27] DotNet[32] Decompile[15] Utility[40] Thread[27] Binaries[6] General[22]
```

```
1: kd> !mex.help -all
[...]
```

```
1: kd> !mex.wrlpcreceive
Process               PID  Thread           Id  CSwitches User  Kernel State        Time Reason    Wait Function
==================== ==== ================ ==== ========= ===== ====== ======= ========= ========= ================================
System                  4 ffffbe0c87808040  164       60     0      0 Waiting 5m:03.562 WrLpcReceive nt!AlpcpSignalAndWait+0x13d
csrss.exe             1fc ffffbe0c87d1a580  20c      817     0  156ms Waiting     906ms WrLpcReceive CSRSRV!CsrApiRequestThread+0x106
csrss.exe             1fc ffffbe0c87efb080  238        3     0      0 Waiting 7m:12.968 WrLpcReceive Kernel stack not resident
csrss.exe             1fc ffffbe0c88893080  268      952  31ms   63ms Waiting    6s.453 WrLpcReceive CSRSRV!CsrApiRequestThread+0x106
csrss.exe             1fc ffffbe0c89a9a080  cd0      670  31ms   16ms Waiting    6s.781 WrLpcReceive CSRSRV!CsrApiRequestThread+0x106
csrss.exe             250 ffffbe0c887e5080  264      942  63ms  156ms Waiting     796ms WrLpcReceive CSRSRV!CsrApiRequestThread+0x106
csrss.exe             250 ffffbe0c888d9080  2ac        3     0      0 Waiting 7m:12.593 WrLpcReceive Kernel stack not resident
csrss.exe             250 ffffbe0c888eb080  2ec      912  78ms  125ms Waiting     796ms WrLpcReceive CSRSRV!CsrApiRequestThread+0x106
csrss.exe             250 ffffbe0c89116080  254        5     0      0 Waiting 7m:08.765 WrLpcReceive Kernel stack not resident
csrss.exe             250 ffffbe0c89122080  300      885  94ms   47ms Waiting    1s.437 WrLpcReceive CSRSRV!CsrApiRequestThread+0x106
lsass.exe             294 ffffbe0c8881b5c0  2c4        3     0      0 Waiting 7m:12.562 WrLpcReceive Kernel stack not resident
dwm.exe               310 ffffbe0c89368080  66c      147     0      0 Waiting 7m:10.046 WrLpcReceive Kernel stack not resident
svchost.exe (Themes)  884 ffffbe0c841c9080  8d4      389     0      0 Waiting    6s.171 WrLpcReceive themeservice!CAPIConnection::Listen+0x81
svchost.exe (FontCache) 8b8 ffffbe0c895a1080 92c     814  78ms   31ms Waiting    8s.875 WrLpcReceive fntcache!AlpcServer::ProcessMessage+0xe1
```

```
ctfmon.exe        11ec ffffbe0c8978e080 878      568    0      0 Waiting    5s.453 WrLpcReceive MSCTF!CCtfServerPort::ServerLoop+0x18f
splwow64.exe      13b4 ffffbe0c8764b080 11e0      27    0      0 Waiting 1m:42.109 WrLpcReceive splwow64!LPCConnMsgsServingThread+0x5d
Count: 16
```

Note: The command takes some time to execute since it has to scan all threads. MEX command also changed the current CPU from 1 to 0.

```
0: kd> !mex.wrlpcreply
Process                PID  Thread            Id   CSwitches User Kernel State     Time Reason    Waiting On                                                  Wait Function
====================== ==== ================= ==== ========= ==== ====== ======= ========= ========= =========================================================== =====================================================================
csrss.exe              1fc  ffffbe0c887d60c0  228       8   0      16ms Waiting 6m:42.796 WrLpcReply Thread: ffffbe0c8911080 in svchost.exe (LSM) (0n436)        winsrvext!TerminalServerRequestThread+0x304
csrss.exe              250  ffffbe0c888ca080  29c      38   0         0 Waiting 6m:42.812 WrLpcReply Thread: ffffbe0c8927e080 in svchost.exe (LSM) (0n436)        winsrvext!TerminalServerRequestThread+0x304
svchost.exe (netprofm) 694  ffffbe0c8a860080 1458       1   0         0 Waiting 6m:39.171 WrLpcReply Thread: ffffbe0c8a861080 in svchost.exe (SSDPSRV) (0n6052)  ssdpapi!GetNotificationLoop+0x84
svchost.exe (SensrSvc)  720  ffffbe0c8a411080  818       1   0         0 Waiting 7m:09.359 WrLpcReply Thread: ffffbe0c89116080 in csrss.exe (0n592)            Kernel stack not resident
svchost.exe (TokenBroker) 130c ffffbe0c8a92a040 18c0   665 94ms         0 Waiting 5m:01.718 WrLpcReply Message queued to SystemSettings.exe (0n9128)             combase!CMessageCall::RpcSendRequestReceiveResponse+0xb9
svchost.exe (BITS)     1758 ffffbe0c8978f080  fa0       1   0         0 Waiting 6m:29.468 WrLpcReply Thread: ffffbe0c8a8e8040 in svchost.exe (SSDPSRV) (0n6052)  SSDPAPI!GetNotificationLoop+0x84
SearchHost.exe          49c ffffbe0c8ad6f080 1b20       9   0         0 Waiting 6m:32.750 WrLpcReply Thread: ffffbe0c8acc5040 in dllhost.exe (0n6644)
SearchHost.exe          49c ffffbe0c8a3f6080 1c54      10   0         0 Waiting 6m:26.718 WrLpcReply Thread: ffffbe0c8acbe040 in dllhost.exe (0n6644)
RuntimeBroker.exe      184c ffffbe0c84ca3040 11b4     631 31ms         0 Waiting   36s.015 WrLpcReply Message queued to SearchHost.exe (0n1180)                 combase!CMessageCall::RpcSendRequestReceiveResponse+0xb9
RuntimeBroker.exe      1d80 ffffbe0c8ac020c0 1d9c      60   0      16ms Waiting 6m:06.140 WrLpcReply Message queued to YourPhone.exe (0n6248)                  combase!CMessageCall::RpcSendRequestReceiveResponse+0xb9
msedge.exe             1200 ffffbe0c8760a080 25dc       1   0         0 Waiting    859ms WrLpcReply Thread: ffffbe0c89591040 in svchost.exe (-p) (0n2100)     DNSAPI!SyncResolverQueryRpc+0x1d7
SearchHost.exe         2434 ffffbe0c8b41e500  e40      10   0         0 Waiting   12s.140 WrLpcReply Thread: ffffbe0c8acb7080 in dllhost.exe (0n6644)          edgehtml!WebPlatStorageEventsManager::BackgroundThreadProc+0x15c
SearchHost.exe         2434 ffffbe0c8b419080  bf4       9   0         0 Waiting   11s.125 WrLpcReply Thread: ffffbe0c8acc0040 in dllhost.exe (0n6644)          edgehtml!WebPlatStorageEventsManager::BackgroundThreadProc+0x15c
Count: 13
```

8.   Now we try to list processes and threads from session 1:

```
0: kd> !sprocess 1 3f
Dumping Session 1
```

Note: The WinDbg extension command fails in this debugger version (you may also get **Cannot read session list message** or **Cannot find nt!_MM_SESSION_SPACE type** instead), so we address this bug in Exercise C3B after learning how to navigate linked lists. However, we can still see the list of session 1 processes and also their bitness by using the MEX extension **tasklist** command:

```
0: kd> !mex.tasklist -s 1
PID              Address            Name                              Ses
==============   ================   ================================  ===
0x250  0n592     ffffbe0c888840c0   csrss.exe                          1
0x2b4  0n692     ffffbe0c888dc080   winlogon.exe                       1
0x340  0n832     ffffbe0c889b11c0   fontdrvhost.exe                    1
0x310  0n784     ffffbe0c89120080   dwm.exe                            1
0x1160 0n4448    ffffbe0c8a2320c0   sihost.exe                         1
0x11f8 0n4600    ffffbe0c898c10c0   svchost.exe(CDPUserSvc)            1
0x1204 0n4612    ffffbe0c8a3340c0   svchost.exe(WpnUserService)        1
0x12d0 0n4816    ffffbe0c8a337080   taskhostw.exe                      1
0x1070 0n4208    ffffbe0c8a455080   explorer.exe                       1
0x1518 0n5400    ffffbe0c8a4f7080   svchost.exe(cbdhsvc)               1
0x49c  0n1180    ffffbe0c8a982080   SearchHost.exe                     1
0x6d8  0n1752    ffffbe0c8aa020c0   StartMenuExperienceHost.exe        1
0x184c 0n6220    ffffbe0c8aaa00c0   RuntimeBroker.exe                  1
0x18d4 0n6356    ffffbe0c8ab52080   svchost.exe(UdkUserSvc)            1
0x18fc 0n6396    ffffbe0c8aa37080   RuntimeBroker.exe                  1
0x19f4 0n6644    ffffbe0c8acd6080   dllhost.exe                        1
0x1868 0n6248    ffffbe0c8ae6f080   YourPhone.exe                      1
0x11ec 0n4588    ffffbe0c8ae72080   ctfmon.exe                         1
0x1b70 0n7024    ffffbe0c8aeeb0c0   TabTip.exe                         1
0x1d80 0n7552    ffffbe0c8af240c0   RuntimeBroker.exe                  1
0x1df8 0n7672    ffffbe0c8ac98080   smartscreen.exe                    1
0x1e28 0n7720    ffffbe0c84120080   SecurityHealthSystray.exe          1
0x1e7c 0n7804    ffffbe0c8aedd080   vmtoolsd.exe                       1
0x1ef8 0n7928    ffffbe0c8b2080c0   ApplicationFrameHost.exe           1
0x1f04 0n7940    ffffbe0c8ad84080   TextInputHost.exe                  1
0x1fd8 0n8152    ffffbe0c8af55080   vm3dservice.exe                    1
0x1188 0n4488    ffffbe0c8b49a080   OneDrive.exe                       1
0x484  0n1156    ffffbe0c8b4020c0   Cortana.exe                        1
0x1fd4 0n8148    ffffbe0c8b417080   RuntimeBroker.exe                  1
```

```
0x1390 0n5008 ffffbe0c8b4b2080 svchost.exe(NPSMSvc)                  1
0x2040 0n8256 ffffbe0c8b092080 svchost.exe(AarSvc)                   1
0x23a8 0n9128 ffffbe0c8b5e60c0 SystemSettings.exe                    1
0x1414 0n5140 ffffbe0c8b4b60c0 UserOOBEBroker.exe                    1
0x2068 0n8296 ffffbe0c8b3d5080 svchost.exe(UnistackSvcGroup)         1
0xf0c  0n3852 ffffbe0c8b4d80c0 msedge.exe                            1
0x1e8c 0n7820 ffffbe0c8ad810c0 msedge.exe                            1
0x83c  0n2108 ffffbe0c8b0d60c0 msedge.exe                            1
0x1200 0n4608 ffffbe0c8cce90c0 msedge.exe                            1
0x20d8 0n8408 ffffbe0c8b224080 msedge.exe                            1
0x23a4 0n9124 ffffbe0c8b6960c0 msedge.exe                            1
0x7cc  0n1996 ffffbe0c8b5b30c0 msedge.exe                            1
0x12bc 0n4796 ffffbe0c8af460c0 msedge.exe                            1
0x2288 0n8840 ffffbe0c8b0e20c0 MiniSearchHost.exe                    1
0x1b24 0n6948 ffffbe0c870210c0 Notepad.exe                           1
0x22a8 0n8872 ffffbe0c876480c0 dllhost.exe                           1
0x236c 0n9068 ffffbe0c84caf080 CalculatorApp.exe                     1
0xce8  0n3304 ffffbe0c8b538080 RuntimeBroker.exe                     1
0x1d98 0n7576 ffffbe0c8be620c0 wordpad.exe*32                        1
0x13b4 0n5044 ffffbe0c8bed8080 splwow64.exe                          1
0x2384 0n9092 ffffbe0c84c990c0 svchost.exe(PrintWorkflowUserSvc)     1
0x1260 0n4704 ffffbe0c8a7a6080 LINQPad7.exe                          1
0x2478 0n9336 ffffbe0c8b318080 LINQPad7.Query.exe                    1
0x2560 0n9568 ffffbe0c8c9d3080 cmd.exe                               1
0x2568 0n9576 ffffbe0c8b317080 conhost.exe                           1
0x2678 0n9848 ffffbe0c877ec080 Taskmgr.exe                           1
0x243c 0n9276 ffffbe0c8c2cd0c0 notmyfault64.exe                      1
0x2434 0n9268 ffffbe0c8bfb10c0 SearchHost.exe                        1
============= ================ ================================== ===
PID          Address          Name                                Ses
```

Warning! Zombie process(es) detected (not displayed). Count: 7 [zombie report]

Note: For the complete list or **tasklist** command options, please use **-?** parameter. We explore *wordpad.exe* stack traces in the next Exercise C1B.

We can list zombie processes or get a shorter report about them using these commands:

```
0: kd> !mex.tasklist -z
PID          Address          Name                    Ses Thd Obj Handles Obj Pointers
============= ================ ====================== === === =========== ============
0x1234 0n4660 ffffbe0c8a0c4080 taskhostw.exe            1   0           0            1
0xbb0  0n2992 ffffbe0c8a454080 userinit.exe             1   0           1            1
0x1b78 0n7032 ffffbe0c8ae760c0 svchost.exe              0   0           0            1
0x12c8 0n4808 ffffbe0c8b4e90c0 msedge.exe               1   0           0            1
0x2328 0n9000 ffffbe0c89a020c0 Win32Bridge.Server.exe   1   0           1        32767
0x22f8 0n8952 ffffbe0c8b3960c0 identity_helper.exe      1   0           1        32768
0x25ac 0n9644 ffffbe0c8c5760c0 TabTip.exe               1   0           1        32763
============= ================ ====================== === === =========== ============
PID          Address          Name                    Ses Thd Obj Handles Obj Pointers
```

```
0: kd> !mex.tasklist -z -r
Count Name                    Ses Thd Obj Handles Obj Pointers
===== ====================== === === =========== ============
    1 identity_helper.exe      1   0           1        32768
    1 msedge.exe               1   0           0            1
    1 svchost.exe              0   0           0            1
```

```
      1 TabTip.exe              1   0            1         32763
      1 taskhostw.exe           1   0            0             1
      1 userinit.exe            1   0            1             1
      1 Win32Bridge.Server.exe  1   0            1         32767
===== ====================== === === =========== =============
Count Name                     Ses Thd Obj Handles Obj Pointers
    7
```

Sometimes, we are interested in *svchost.exe* to service name translation:

```
0: kd> !mex.tasklist -svc
PID            Address          Name
============== ================ =======================================
0x0    0n0     fffff80762d32b00 Idle
0x4    0n4     ffffbe0c840eb040 System
0x64   0n100   ffffbe0c84136080 Registry
0x168  0n360   ffffbe0c8780f040 smss.exe
0x1fc  0n508   ffffbe0c87f2b080 csrss.exe
0x244  0n580   ffffbe0c887d4080 wininit.exe
0x250  0n592   ffffbe0c888840c0 csrss.exe
0x28c  0n652   ffffbe0c888c9100 services.exe
0x294  0n660   ffffbe0c888cb0c0 lsass.exe
0x2b4  0n692   ffffbe0c888dc080 winlogon.exe
0x340  0n832   ffffbe0c889b11c0 fontdrvhost.exe
0x348  0n840   ffffbe0c889af1c0 fontdrvhost.exe
0x354  0n852   ffffbe0c889ae080 svchost.exe(-p)
0x3a8  0n936   ffffbe0c890130c0 WUDFHost.exe
0x3f0  0n1008  ffffbe0c889c7080 svchost.exe(-p)
0x1b4  0n436   ffffbe0c891020c0 svchost.exe(LSM)
0x310  0n784   ffffbe0c89120080 dwm.exe
0x44c  0n1100  ffffbe0c891a0080 svchost.exe(gpsvc)
0x454  0n1108  ffffbe0c8919e080 svchost.exe(-p)
0x460  0n1120  ffffbe0c891a80c0 svchost.exe(lmhosts)
0x474  0n1140  ffffbe0c891b90c0 svchost.exe(BTAGService)
0x494  0n1172  ffffbe0c891c6080 svchost.exe(BthAvctpSvc)
0x4b0  0n1200  ffffbe0c89209080 svchost.exe(bthserv)
0x4f0  0n1264  ffffbe0c89241080 svchost.exe(NcbService)
0x508  0n1288  ffffbe0c892550c0 svchost.exe(TimeBrokerSvc)
0x554  0n1364  ffffbe0c892b6080 svchost.exe(Schedule)
0x5bc  0n1468  ffffbe0c89348080 svchost.exe(DispBrokerDesktopSvc)
0x5d4  0n1492  ffffbe0c8934d080 svchost.exe(ProfSvc)
0x600  0n1536  ffffbe0c89362080 svchost.exe(DisplayEnhancementService)
0x63c  0n1596  ffffbe0c893bc080 svchost.exe(nsi)
0x644  0n1604  ffffbe0c893bf080 svchost.exe(UserManager)
0x664  0n1636  ffffbe0c89363080 svchost.exe(DeviceAssociationService)
0x694  0n1684  ffffbe0c89407080 svchost.exe(netprofm)
0x6a8  0n1704  ffffbe0c8940a080 svchost.exe(SensorService)
0x720  0n1824  ffffbe0c841ba080 svchost.exe(SensrSvc)
0x748  0n1864  ffffbe0c841b0080 svchost.exe(TabletInputService)
0x760  0n1888  ffffbe0c84185080 svchost.exe(camsvc)
0x82c  0n2092  ffffbe0c841ed080 svchost.exe(EventLog)
0x834  0n2100  ffffbe0c84135080 svchost.exe(-p)
0x864  0n2148  ffffbe0c89496080 svchost.exe(EventSystem)
0x870  0n2160  ffffbe0c895340c0 svchost.exe(SysMain)
0x884  0n2180  ffffbe0c89538080 svchost.exe(Themes)
0x8b8  0n2232  ffffbe0c89596080 svchost.exe(FontCache)
0x8f0  0n2288  ffffbe0c895b3040 MemCompression
0x910  0n2320  ffffbe0c895cc080 svchost.exe(SENS)
```

```
0x93c    0n2364   ffffbe0c895df080   svchost.exe(AudioEndpointBuilder)
0x97c    0n2428   ffffbe0c8963c080   svchost.exe(Dhcp)
0x9e8    0n2536   ffffbe0c896b1080   svchost.exe(WinHttpAutoProxySvc)
0xa0c    0n2572   ffffbe0c896d20c0   svchost.exe(-p)
0xa60    0n2656   ffffbe0c89730080   svchost.exe(-p)
0xa68    0n2664   ffffbe0c897450c0   svchost.exe(-p)
0xab4    0n2740   ffffbe0c89728080   svchost.exe(ShellHWDetection)
0xacc    0n2764   ffffbe0c897da080   svchost.exe(StateRepository)
0xb24    0n2852   ffffbe0c897ed0c0   spoolsv.exe
0xb48    0n2888   ffffbe0c897dc0c0   svchost.exe(-p)
0xb68    0n2920   ffffbe0c89895080   svchost.exe(LanmanWorkstation)
0xa24    0n2596   ffffbe0c89a07080   svchost.exe(-p)
0xb98    0n2968   ffffbe0c89a06080   svchost.exe(-p)
0xc04    0n3076   ffffbe0c89042080   svchost.exe(DPS)
0xc14    0n3092   ffffbe0c89a0a080   svchost.exe(iphlpsvc)
0xc54    0n3156   ffffbe0c89a8e0c0   svchost.exe(LanmanServer)
0xc6c    0n3180   ffffbe0c89a96080   svchost.exe(SstpSvc)
0xc7c    0n3196   ffffbe0c89aa6080   svchost.exe(TrkWks)
0xc84    0n3204   ffffbe0c89aa9080   VGAuthService.exe
0xc8c    0n3212   ffffbe0c89aaa080   vmtoolsd.exe
0xca0    0n3232   ffffbe0c89a42080   MsMpEng.exe
0xcac    0n3244   ffffbe0c89ac10c0   svchost.exe(Winmgmt)
0xcb8    0n3256   ffffbe0c89aae080   svchost.exe(WpnService)
0xdd8    0n3544   ffffbe0c899e80c0   svchost.exe(netsvcs)
0xf00    0n3840   ffffbe0c89c30080   dllhost.exe
0xfa8    0n4008   ffffbe0c89cf8080   AggregatorHost.exe
0x438    0n1080   ffffbe0c89e840c0   svchost.exe(RmSvc)
0xaf0    0n2800   ffffbe0c89f5e080   msdtc.exe
0x10e8   0n4328   ffffbe0c8a0540c0   svchost.exe(AppXSvc)
0x1278   0n4728   ffffbe0c8a0cb080   WmiPrvSE.exe
0x1160   0n4448   ffffbe0c8a2320c0   sihost.exe
0x11f8   0n4600   ffffbe0c898c10c0   svchost.exe(CDPUserSvc)
0x1204   0n4612   ffffbe0c8a3340c0   svchost.exe(WpnUserService)
0x12d0   0n4816   ffffbe0c8a337080   taskhostw.exe
0x130c   0n4876   ffffbe0c8a071080   svchost.exe(TokenBroker)
0x13a0   0n5024   ffffbe0c8a4020c0   MsMpEngCP.exe
0x13b8   0n5048   ffffbe0c8a43b080   svchost.exe(CDPSvc)
0x1070   0n4208   ffffbe0c8a455080   explorer.exe
0x1448   0n5192   ffffbe0c8a4f8080   svchost.exe(ClipSVC)
0x1518   0n5400   ffffbe0c8a4f7080   svchost.exe(cbdhsvc)
0x1564   0n5476   ffffbe0c8a4ef0c0   svchost.exe(Appinfo)
0x1590   0n5520   ffffbe0c8a4e9080   WmiPrvSE.exe
0x15c4   0n5572   ffffbe0c8a6c1080   NisSrv.exe
0x1650   0n5712   ffffbe0c8a729080   svchost.exe(lfsvc)
0x1744   0n5956   ffffbe0c8a8540c0   SearchIndexer.exe
0x1758   0n5976   ffffbe0c8a859080   svchost.exe(BITS)
0x17a4   0n6052   ffffbe0c8a9240c0   svchost.exe(SSDPSRV)
0x49c    0n1180   ffffbe0c8a982080   SearchHost.exe
0x6d8    0n1752   ffffbe0c8aa020c0   StartMenuExperienceHost.exe
0x181c   0n6172   ffffbe0c8a55b0c0   svchost.exe(WdiSystemHost)
0x184c   0n6220   ffffbe0c8aaa00c0   RuntimeBroker.exe
0x18d4   0n6356   ffffbe0c8ab52080   svchost.exe(UdkUserSvc)
0x18fc   0n6396   ffffbe0c8aa37080   RuntimeBroker.exe
0x196c   0n6508   ffffbe0c8ac07080   svchost.exe(PcaSvc)
0x19f4   0n6644   ffffbe0c8acd6080   dllhost.exe
0x1afc   0n6908   ffffbe0c8ad94080   svchost.exe(LicenseManager)
0x1868   0n6248   ffffbe0c8ae6f080   YourPhone.exe
0x11ec   0n4588   ffffbe0c8ae72080   ctfmon.exe
0x1b70   0n7024   ffffbe0c8aeeb0c0   TabTip.exe
```

```
0x1d38 0n7480 fffffbe0c8ac8e080 WmiApSrv.exe
0x1d80 0n7552 fffffbe0c8af240c0 RuntimeBroker.exe
0x1df8 0n7672 fffffbe0c8ac98080 smartscreen.exe
0x1e28 0n7720 fffffbe0c84120080 SecurityHealthSystray.exe
0x1e3c 0n7740 fffffbe0c8aee1080 SecurityHealthService.exe
0x1e7c 0n7804 fffffbe0c8aedd080 vmtoolsd.exe
0x1ef8 0n7928 fffffbe0c8b2080c0 ApplicationFrameHost.exe
0x1f04 0n7940 fffffbe0c8ad84080 TextInputHost.exe
0x1fd8 0n8152 fffffbe0c8af55080 vm3dservice.exe
0x1188 0n4488 fffffbe0c8b49a080 OneDrive.exe
0x484  0n1156 fffffbe0c8b4020c0 Cortana.exe
0x1fd4 0n8148 fffffbe0c8b417080 RuntimeBroker.exe
0x130  0n304  fffffbe0c8b37b080 svchost.exe(wuauserv)
0x1390 0n5008 fffffbe0c8b4b2080 svchost.exe(NPSMSvc)
0x2040 0n8256 fffffbe0c8b092080 svchost.exe(AarSvc)
0x20cc 0n8396 fffffbe0c876f2080 svchost.exe(DoSvc)
0x2124 0n8484 fffffbe0c8b4d6080 svchost.exe(StorSvc)
0x23a8 0n9128 fffffbe0c8b5e60c0 SystemSettings.exe
0x1ac0 0n6848 fffffbe0c8b8870c0 svchost.exe(UsoSvc)
0x1414 0n5140 fffffbe0c8b4b60c0 UserOOBEBroker.exe
0x1a3c 0n6716 fffffbe0c876f8080 SgrmBroker.exe
0x4e8  0n1256 fffffbe0c892bc080 svchost.exe(W32Time)
0x8d8  0n2264 fffffbe0c89a9b080 svchost.exe(wscsvc)
0x2068 0n8296 fffffbe0c8b3d5080 svchost.exe(UnistackSvcGroup)
0xf0c  0n3852 fffffbe0c8b4d80c0 msedge.exe
0x1e8c 0n7820 fffffbe0c8ad810c0 msedge.exe
0x83c  0n2108 fffffbe0c8b0d60c0 msedge.exe
0x1200 0n4608 fffffbe0c8cce90c0 msedge.exe
0x20d8 0n8408 fffffbe0c8b224080 msedge.exe
0x23a4 0n9124 fffffbe0c8b6960c0 msedge.exe
0x7cc  0n1996 fffffbe0c8b5b30c0 msedge.exe
0x12bc 0n4796 fffffbe0c8af460c0 msedge.exe
0x2288 0n8840 fffffbe0c8b0e20c0 MiniSearchHost.exe
0x1b24 0n6948 fffffbe0c870210c0 Notepad.exe
0x22a8 0n8872 fffffbe0c876480c0 dllhost.exe
0x236c 0n9068 fffffbe0c84caf080 CalculatorApp.exe
0xce8  0n3304 fffffbe0c8b538080 RuntimeBroker.exe
0x1d98 0n7576 fffffbe0c8be620c0 wordpad.exe*32
0x13b4 0n5044 fffffbe0c8bed8080 splwow64.exe
0x2384 0n9092 fffffbe0c84c990c0 svchost.exe(PrintWorkflowUserSvc)
0x328  0n808  fffffbe0c8be760c0 svchost.exe(wlidsvc)
0x1260 0n4704 fffffbe0c8a7a6080 LINQPad7.exe
0x2478 0n9336 fffffbe0c8b318080 LINQPad7.Query.exe
0x2560 0n9568 fffffbe0c8c9d3080 cmd.exe
0x2568 0n9576 fffffbe0c8b317080 conhost.exe
0x2678 0n9848 fffffbe0c877ec080 Taskmgr.exe
0x246c 0n9324 fffffbe0c8c2de0c0 audiodg.exe
0x243c 0n9276 fffffbe0c8c2cd0c0 notmyfault64.exe
0x2434 0n9268 fffffbe0c8bfb10c0 SearchHost.exe
============= ================ =====================================
PID          Address          Name
```

Warning! Zombie process(es) detected (not displayed). Count: 7 [zombie report]

Note: If you want to see command lines, use the **-cl** parameter. Nicely summarized additional information, such as whether *gflags.exe* was used, whether blocked, running, suspended, or waiting-for-ALPC threads exist (including overall thread count), can be seen with the **-a** parameter (pay attention to **!! Rn Ry Bk Lc IO Er** columns). It also shows PIDs in both hex and decimal formats. Consider this as a column-based **!process 0 3f**. Some columns may not show information for recent Windows versions.

9.   Another way to list all stack traces is to use the **!for_each_thread** command, where we can customize stack trace output:

```
0: kd> !for_each_thread ".thread /r /p @#Thread; kc"
.thread /r /p @#Thread; kc
Implicit thread is now ffffbe0c`841cd080
Implicit process is now ffffbe0c`840eb040
Loading User Symbols


************* Symbol Loading Error Summary **************
Module name             Error
myfault                 The system cannot find the file specified

You can troubleshoot most symbol related issues by turning on symbol loading diagnostics (!sym
noisy) and repeating the command that caused symbols to be loaded.
You should also verify that your symbol search path (.sympath) is correct.
  *** Stack trace for last set context - .thread/.cxr resets it
 # Call Site
00 nt!KiSwapContext
01 nt!KiSwapThread
02 nt!KiCommitThreadWait
03 nt!KeWaitForSingleObject
04 nt!PopIrpWorkerControl
05 nt!PspSystemThreadStartup
06 nt!KiStartSystemThread
.thread /r /p @#Thread; kc
Implicit thread is now ffffbe0c`84145080
Implicit process is now ffffbe0c`840eb040
Loading User Symbols

[...]

Implicit thread is now ffffbe0c`8c116080
Implicit process is now ffffbe0c`8bfb10c0
Loading User Symbols
..............................................................
..............................................................
...................................

************* Symbol Loading Error Summary **************
Module name             Error
vsock                   The system cannot find the file specified
vmci                    The system cannot find the file specified
WdFilter                The system cannot find the file specified
vm3dmp                  The system cannot find the file specified
vmmemctl                The system cannot find the file specified
vmhgfs                  The system cannot find the file specified
myfault                 The system cannot find the file specified

You can troubleshoot most symbol related issues by turning on symbol loading diagnostics (!sym
noisy) and repeating the command that caused symbols to be loaded.
You should also verify that your symbol search path (.sympath) is correct.
  *** Stack trace for last set context - .thread/.cxr resets it
```

```
 # Call Site
00 nt!KiSwapContext
01 nt!KiSwapThread
02 nt!KiCommitThreadWait
03 nt!KeWaitForMultipleObjects
04 nt!ObWaitForMultipleObjects
05 win32kfull!xxxMsgWaitForMultipleObjectsEx
06 win32kfull!NtUserMsgWaitForMultipleObjectsEx
07 win32k!NtUserMsgWaitForMultipleObjectsEx
08 nt!KiSystemServiceCopyEnd
09 win32u!NtUserMsgWaitForMultipleObjectsEx
0a user32!RealMsgWaitForMultipleObjectsEx
0b combase!CCliModalLoop::BlockFn
0c combase!ClassicSTAThreadWaitForHandles
0d combase!CoWaitForMultipleHandles
0e edgehtml!CDwnTaskExec::ThreadExec
0f edgehtml!CExecFT::ThreadProc
10 edgehtml!CExecFT::StaticThreadProc
11 KERNEL32!BaseThreadInitThunk
12 ntdll!RtlUserThreadStart
```

Note: We can use this script to list all processes and threads, including 32-bit stack traces, when it is possible:

!for_each_thread "!thread @#Thread 3f;.thread /w @#Thread; .reload; kb 256; .effmach AMD64"

Note: Mex **!ForEachThread** (**!fet**) can also be used. Use the **-?** option to see the syntax. The advantage of it is the ability to apply commands to a particular process (we don't need to exclude other processes in the body of the **!for_each_thread** command) and also include terminated threads (we choose *wordpad.exe*32* process address from the previous output):

```
0: kd> !mex.fet -t -p ffffbe0c8be620c0 "!thread @#Thread 3f; .thread /w @#Thread; .reload; kL
256; .effmach AMD64"
Changing to thread: ffffbe0c8beda080
THREAD ffffbe0c8beda080  Cid 1d98.1bb0  Teb: 00000000008b5000 Win32Thread: ffffbe0c8ccd5ed0
WAIT: (WrUserRequest) UserMode Non-Alertable
    ffffbe0c8bd0e580  QueueObject
Not impersonating
DeviceMap                 ffff800eda518d20
Owning Process            ffffbe0c8be620c0       Image:        wordpad.exe
Attached Process          N/A            Image:        N/A
Wait Start TickCount      29755          Ticks: 32 (0:00:00.500)
Context Switch Count      3348           IdealProcessor: 1
UserTime                  00:00:00.187
KernelTime                00:00:00.578
Win32 Start Address wordpad!wWinMainCRTStartup (0x0000000001036e40)
Stack Init ffffa28ca02c3c70 Current ffffa28ca02c3050
Base ffffa28ca02c4000 Limit ffffa28ca02be000 Call 0000000000000000
Priority 10 BasePriority 8 PriorityDecrement 0 IoPriority 2 PagePriority 5
Child-SP          RetAddr               Call Site
ffffa28c`a02c3090 fffff807`623327f7     nt!KiSwapContext+0x76
ffffa28c`a02c31d0 fffff807`623346a9     nt!KiSwapThread+0x3a7
ffffa28c`a02c32b0 fffff807`6232e5c4     nt!KiCommitThreadWait+0x159
ffffa28c`a02c3350 fffff807`6228efe0     nt!KeWaitForSingleObject+0x234
ffffa28c`a02c3440 ffffbc92`8e76afd6     nt!KeWaitForMultipleObjects+0x540
ffffa28c`a02c3540 ffffbc92`8e76ac3f     win32kfull!xxxRealSleepThread+0x2c6
ffffa28c`a02c3660 ffffbc92`8e76e08a     win32kfull!xxxSleepThread2+0xb3
```

```
ffffa28c`a02c36b0 ffffbc92`8e7b26ec    win32kfull!xxxRealInternalGetMessage+0xc5a
ffffa28c`a02c3a10 ffffbc92`8dc4645a    win32kfull!NtUserGetMessage+0x8c
ffffa28c`a02c3aa0 fffff807`62428775    win32k!NtUserGetMessage+0x16
ffffa28c`a02c3ae0 00007ffe`5ac81424    nt!KiSystemServiceCopyEnd+0x25 (TrapFrame @
ffffa28c`a02c3ae0)
00000000`00a5e1d8 00007ffe`5ac7510e    wow64win!NtUserGetMessage+0x14
00000000`00a5e1e0 00007ffe`5a0f77ca    wow64win!whNtUserGetMessage+0x2e
00000000`00a5e240 00000000`775517ba    wow64!Wow64SystemServiceEx+0x15a
00000000`00a5eb00 00000000`77551d75    wow64cpu!ServiceNoTurbo+0xb
00000000`00a5ebb0 00007ffe`5a0fe06d    wow64cpu!BTCpuSimulate+0xbb5
00000000`00a5ebf0 00007ffe`5a0fd8ad    wow64!RunCpuSimulation+0xd
00000000`00a5ec20 00007ffe`5b05f87d    wow64!Wow64LdrpInitialize+0x12d
00000000`00a5eed0 00007ffe`5b04d78c    ntdll!LdrpInitializeProcess+0x16d1
00000000`00a5f290 00007ffe`5affa993    ntdll!_LdrpInitialize+0x52dc0
00000000`00a5f310 00007ffe`5affa8be    ntdll!LdrpInitializeInternal+0x6b
00000000`00a5f590 00000000`00000000    ntdll!LdrInitializeThunk+0xe

Implicit thread is now ffffbe0c`8beda080
WARNING: WOW context retrieval requires
switching to the thread's process context.
Use .process /p ffffbe0c`89120080 to switch back.
Implicit process is now ffffbe0c`8be620c0
The context is partially valid. Only x86 user-mode context is available.
x86 context set
Loading Kernel Symbols
...........................................................
...........................................................
...........................................................
..
Loading User Symbols
.......
Loading unloaded module list
........
Loading Wow64 Symbols
...........................................................
....
 # ChildEBP          RetAddr
00 00a9fd70 758e0200     win32u!NtUserGetMessage+0xc
01 00a9fdac 75238f35     USER32!GetMessageW+0x30
02 00a9fdc8 75238fe3     MFC42u!CWinThread::PumpMessage+0x15
03 00a9fde4 7520a242     MFC42u!CWinThread::Run+0x63
04 00a9fdfc 01036d0c     MFC42u!AfxWinMain+0xa2
05 00a9fe8c 75eb6739     wordpad!__wmainCRTStartup+0x153
06 00a9fe9c 775c8e7f     KERNEL32!BaseThreadInitThunk+0x19
07 00a9fef4 775c8e4d     ntdll_77560000!__RtlUserThreadStart+0x2b
08 00a9ff04 00000000     ntdll_77560000!_RtlUserThreadStart+0x1b
Effective machine: x64 (AMD64)
[...]
```

10.   Yet another way is to use **!stacks** command (the default version omits paged out stacks):

```
0: kd> !stacks
Proc.Thread  .Thread   Ticks   ThreadState Blocker
                         [fffff80762d32b00 Idle]
    0.000000  fffff80762d35bc0 000230f  RUNNING    nt!KiIdleLoop+0x176
    0.000000  ffffce00fb70c0c0 000745b  RUNNING    nt!KiIdleLoop+0x176
    0.00002c  ffffbe0c841ab080 0003ae3  RUNNING    nt!KiSwapContext+0x76
    0.000034  ffffbe0c84178080 000745b  RUNNING    nt!KiSwapContext+0x76
                         [ffffbe0c840eb040 System]
```

```
4.000018   ffffbe0c84189080  000049a  Blocked    nt!PopFxProcessWorkPool+0xf5
4.00001c   ffffbe0c84097480  00003ba  Blocked    nt!ExpWorkQueueManagerThread+0x149
4.000020   ffffbe0c840af080  000007e  Blocked    nt!KeRemovePriQueue+0x259
4.000024   ffffbe0c8420c140  000000a  Blocked    nt!ExpWorkerFactoryManagerThread+0x3b
4.000040   ffffbe0c841ef080  00010ee  Blocked    nt!MiRebuildLargePagesThread+0x5c
4.000044   ffffbe0c84202080  0006ec8  Blocked    nt!MiZeroPageThread+0x2b
4.00004c   ffffbe0c8412d080  0000001  READY      nt!MiReadyToZeroNextLargePage+0x179
4.000050   ffffbe0c8412f080  00003d2  Blocked    nt!MiReadyToZeroNextLargePage+0x179
4.000054   ffffbe0c84113080  0000029  Blocked    nt!CcQueueLazyWriteScanThread+0xdf
4.000058   ffffbe0c84076080  0000251  Blocked    nt!CcAsyncReadWorker+0x139
4.00005c   ffffbe0c840e5080  0007437  Blocked    nt!CcAsyncReadWorker+0x139
4.000060   ffffbe0c84131080  0007437  Blocked    nt!CcAsyncReadWorker+0x139
4.00006c   ffffbe0c8413a080  0000026  Blocked    nt!KeRemovePriQueue+0x259
4.000070   ffffbe0c8413c080  0000219  Blocked    nt!KeRemovePriQueue+0x259
4.00007c   ffffbe0c84119080  0000027  Blocked    nt!KeRemovePriQueue+0x259
4.000080   ffffbe0c84153080  00068b3  Blocked    nt!KeRemovePriQueue+0x259
4.000084   ffffbe0c8411f080  000014c  Blocked    nt!EtwpLogger+0xc2
4.000088   ffffbe0c8415c080  00015df  Blocked    nt!EtwpLogger+0xc2
4.00008c   ffffbe0c8415e080  0000420  Blocked    nt!EtwpLogger+0xc2
4.000090   ffffbe0c84162080  00002f3  Blocked    nt!EtwpLogger+0xc2
4.000094   ffffbe0c84164080  00002f3  Blocked    nt!EtwpLogger+0xc2
4.000098   ffffbe0c8416b080  00015df  Blocked    nt!EtwpLogger+0xc2
4.00009c   ffffbe0c8416d080  0000419  Blocked    nt!EtwpLogger+0xc2
4.0000a0   ffffbe0c84171080  0002553  Blocked    nt!EtwpLogger+0xc2
4.0000a4   ffffbe0c84173080  0006c9e  Blocked    nt!EtwpLogger+0xc2
4.0000a8   ffffbe0c84129080  00001fc  Blocked    nt!EtwpLogger+0xc2
4.0000ac   ffffbe0c84127080  0006c9e  Blocked    nt!EtwpLogger+0xc2
4.0000b0   ffffbe0c8417c080  0006c9e  Blocked    nt!EtwpLogger+0xc2
4.0000b8   ffffbe0c84182080  0006c9e  Blocked    nt!EtwpLogger+0xc2
4.0000bc   ffffbe0c84186080  0001621  Blocked    nt!EtwpLogger+0xc2
4.0000c0   ffffbe0c8418b080  0004f52  Blocked    nt!EtwpLogger+0xc2
4.0000c4   ffffbe0c8418d080  0006c9e  Blocked    nt!EtwpLogger+0xc2
4.0000c8   ffffbe0c84191080  000742a  Blocked    nt!IopPassiveInterruptRealtimeWorker+0x16
4.0000cc   ffffbe0c84193080  000742a  Blocked    nt!IopPassiveInterruptRealtimeWorker+0x16
4.0000d0   ffffbe0c84195080  000742a  Blocked    nt!IopPassiveInterruptRealtimeWorker+0x16
4.0000d4   ffffbe0c84197080  000742a  Blocked    nt!IopPassiveInterruptRealtimeWorker+0x16
4.0000dc   ffffbe0c841a6080  0006fa5  Blocked    ACPI!ACPIWorkerThread+0x9a
4.0000e0   ffffbe0c8477e080  000594e  Blocked    nt!KeRemovePriQueue+0x259
4.0000e4   ffffbe0c84b44040  000683b  Blocked    nt!KeRemovePriQueue+0x259
4.0000e8   ffffbe0c84b46080  0000019  Blocked    nt!KeRemovePriQueue+0x259
4.0000ec   ffffbe0c84b47040  000685f  Blocked    nt!KeRemovePriQueue+0x259
4.0000f0   ffffbe0c8419e080  00073e1  Blocked    pci!RootPmeEventDispatcher+0x9b
4.0000f4   ffffbe0c84b3f100  00073e1  Blocked    ACPI!PciRootBusBiosMethodDispatcherOnResume+0x57
4.0000f8   ffffbe0c84a26100  00073d2  Blocked    Wdf01000!FxSystemThread::Thread+0x134
4.0000fc   ffffbe0c84bd0480  00015f9  Blocked    tpm!Tpm20Scheduler::SchedulerThreadFunction+0x77
4.00010c   ffffbe0c84a95040  0007383  Blocked    spaceport!SpLimiterDispatcherThreadRoutine+0x3c
4.000110   ffffbe0c84a9c080  0007382  Blocked    vsock+0x4334
4.000114   ffffbe0c84a9d040  0007382  Blocked    vmci+0x859f
4.000118   ffffbe0c849cd040  000001d  Blocked    WdFilter+0x1c629
4.00011c   ffffbe0c849ce040  00001b7  Blocked    WdFilter+0x1da07
4.000120   ffffbe0c849cf040  00000b2  Blocked    WdFilter+0x1da07
4.000124   ffffbe0c84983040  0004830  Blocked    ndis!ndisWaitForKernelObject+0x21
4.000128   ffffbe0c849db040  0006a3d  Blocked    ndis!ndisWaitForKernelObject+0x21
4.000134   ffffbe0c84c91040  000051d  Blocked    nt!KeRemovePriQueue+0x259
4.000144   ffffbe0c84eb4040  0000186  Blocked    nt!KeRemovePriQueue+0x259
4.00014c   ffffbe0c84c97040  0000f26  Blocked    nt!KeRemovePriQueue+0x259
4.000150   ffffbe0c849c8080  0001048  Blocked    nt!KeRemovePriQueue+0x259
4.000154   ffffbe0c84df8040  00070d2  Blocked    watchdog!SMgrGdiCalloutThread+0x50
4.000158   ffffbe0c84f440c0  00070c8  Blocked    rdbss!RxpIdleWorkerThread+0x25
4.00015c   ffffbe0c87aec080  0000019  Blocked    bam!BampThrottlingWorker+0xc3
4.000160   ffffbe0c87804040  00064b2  Blocked    nt!PopDirectedDripsWorkerRoutine+0x4d
4.000164   ffffbe0c87808040  0004be4  Blocked    nt!AlpcpSignalAndWait+0x13d
4.000170   ffffbe0c8780c540  0000000  READY      vm3dmp+0x16775
4.000174   ffffbe0c87824040  00070ba  Blocked    dxgkrnl!DpiPowerArbiterThread+0x67
4.000180   ffffbe0c87c68040  0000564  Blocked    nt!KeRemovePriQueue+0x259
```

```
4.00018c   ffffbe0c87d68100 00065ea Blocked    BTHport!HCI_ThreadFunction+0x172
4.000190   ffffbe0c87d4c040 0001aec Blocked    nt!KeRemovePriQueue+0x259
4.000194   ffffbe0c87daa080 0000186 Blocked    nt!KeRemovePriQueue+0x259
4.0001f8   ffffbe0c87f20080 000041f Blocked    nt!MiModifiedPageWriter+0x112
4.000214   ffffbe0c887cd5c0 0000001 Blocked    dxgmms1!VidSchiWaitForSchedulerEvents+0x211
4.000218   ffffbe0c887ef5c0 0006713 Blocked    dxgkrnl!BLTQUEUE::BltQueueWorker+0x426
4.00021c   ffffbe0c8880a5c0 0000155 Blocked    BasicRender!WARPKMADAPTER::RunGPU+0x4f8
4.000220   ffffbe0c887d1100 000011d Blocked    dxgmms2!VidSchiWaitForSchedulerEvents+0x26c
4.000224   ffffbe0c887c50c0 000015d Blocked    dxgmms2!VIDMM_WORKER_THREAD::Run+0x1bf
4.000270   ffffbe0c888aa0c0 000018b Blocked    nt!IoRemoveIoCompletion+0x98
4.0003e0   ffffbe0c89022080 0006bfd Blocked    nt!EtwpLogger+0xc2
4.000788   ffffbe0c840e0040 00001b9 Blocked    luafv!SynchronousFsControl+0x19e
4.000810   ffffbe0c84118040 0006b58 Blocked    storqosflt!SqosJobDispatcherThreadRoutine+0x63
4.000b14   ffffbe0c8980c040 0006af1 Blocked    HTTP!UlpScavengerThread+0x148
4.000b60   ffffbe0c89892040 0004bab Blocked    mpsdrv!MpsWorkerThread+0xe9
4.000bb4   ffffbe0c897fc040 00004d8 Blocked    mmcss!CiSchedulerDeepSleep+0x64
4.000be0   ffffbe0c898ca040 0001aec Blocked    nt!KeRemovePriQueue+0x259
4.000be4   ffffbe0c898c9040 0000186 Blocked    nt!KeRemovePriQueue+0x259
4.000970   ffffbe0c8974a040 0001aec Blocked    nt!KeRemovePriQueue+0x259
4.000a38   ffffbe0c898e8040 0000033 Blocked    vmmemctl+0x24ff
4.000c28   ffffbe0c89aed040 0001aed Blocked    nt!KeRemovePriQueue+0x259
4.000c2c   ffffbe0c89aec040 00000d8 Blocked    nt!KeRemovePriQueue+0x259
4.000c60   ffffbe0c89a11040 0006a96 Blocked    Ndu!NduTokenComputeTokensWorkerRoutine+0x85
4.000c64   ffffbe0c89a10040 0000037 Blocked    Ndu!NduUpdateProcessEnergyWorkerRoutine+0xb1
4.000cec   ffffbe0c89987080 0000f90 Blocked    nt!EtwpLogger+0xc2
4.000d94   ffffbe0c899c3040 0001048 Blocked    nt!KeRemovePriQueue+0x259
4.000de0   ffffbe0c89b50040 0006a45 Blocked    vmhgfs+0xdf6b
4.000de4   ffffbe0c89b4f040 0006a45 Blocked    vmhgfs+0xdf6b
4.000e58   ffffbe0c8996c040 0006a34 Blocked    srv2!RfspThreadPoolNodeManagerRun+0x81
4.000e5c   ffffbe0c89b99040 0006a34 Blocked    srv2!RfspThreadPoolNodeWorkerProcessWorkItems+0xd3
4.000e60   ffffbe0c89b98040 0006a34 Blocked    srv2!RfspThreadPoolNodeManagerRun+0x81
4.000e64   ffffbe0c89b97040 0006a34 Blocked    srv2!RfspThreadPoolNodeWorkerProcessWorkItems+0xd3
4.000e68   ffffbe0c89b96040 0006a34 Blocked    srv2!RfspThreadPoolNodeManagerRun+0x81
4.000e6c   ffffbe0c89b95040 0006a34 Blocked    srv2!RfspThreadPoolNodeWorkerProcessWorkItems+0xd3
4.000ea4   ffffbe0c89a74040 0006a28 Blocked    ndis!NdisWaitEvent+0x50
4.000ea8   ffffbe0c841fe040 0006a28 Blocked    ndis!NdisWaitEvent+0x50
4.000eac   ffffbe0c840bb040 0006a28 Blocked    ndis!NdisWaitEvent+0x50
4.000eb0   ffffbe0c896d5040 0006a28 Blocked    ndis!NdisWaitEvent+0x50
4.000eb4   ffffbe0c8952b040 0006a28 Blocked    ndis!NdisWaitEvent+0x50
4.000eb8   ffffbe0c898e4040 0006a28 Blocked    ndis!NdisWaitEvent+0x50
4.000f68   ffffbe0c89c660c0 0000c02 Blocked    nt!EtwpLogger+0xc2
4.000ff0   ffffbe0c892ad080 00010fd Blocked    nt!KeRemovePriQueue+0x259
4.000ff4   ffffbe0c89df4080 00000ac Blocked    nt!MiStoreEvictThread+0x109
4.000ba0   ffffbe0c89ec3080 0006991 Blocked    nt!EtwpLogger+0xc2
4.00105c   ffffbe0c89ce5080 0006958 Blocked    nt!EtwpLogger+0xc2
4.000ae8   ffffbe0c89caa080 0006830 Blocked    nt!EtwpLogger+0xc2
4.001d2c   ffffbe0c8a34a080 000001c Blocked    nt!EtwpLogger+0xc2
4.001dec   ffffbe0c8ac5c080 0000001 READY      nt!KxDispatchInterrupt+0x151
4.001e50   ffffbe0c8abd2080 0003ce0 Blocked    nt!EtwpLogger+0xc2
4.001e84   ffffbe0c8aef8040 0000186 Blocked    nt!KeRemovePriQueue+0x259
4.001e88   ffffbe0c8aef7040 0000233 Blocked    nt!KeRemovePriQueue+0x259
4.0012c0   ffffbe0c841a7040 0005c6b Blocked    nt!KeRemovePriQueue+0x259
4.001904   ffffbe0c8b694080 00025b6 Blocked    nt!EtwpLogger+0xc2
4.0020e0   ffffbe0c8a197080 00055ae Blocked    nt!EtwpLogger+0xc2
4.001338   ffffbe0c892c1080 0000137 Blocked    nt!EtwpLogger+0xc2
4.001f10   ffffbe0c84caa300 0000d2e Blocked    nt!KeRemovePriQueue+0x259
4.001da0   ffffbe0c8c0dd040 0001177 Blocked    nt!KeRemovePriQueue+0x259


                    [ffffbe0c84136080 Registry]
64.000068  ffffbe0c84138080 0007437 Blocked    nt!CmpDummyThreadRoutine+0x1e
64.0001e0  ffffbe0c87f2c080 00000d9 Blocked    nt!CmpLazyWriteWorker+0x47
64.0001e4  ffffbe0c87f2d080 0000644 Blocked    nt!CmpLazyWriteWorker+0x47
64.0001e8  ffffbe0c87f2e080 0001599 Blocked    nt!CmpLazyWriteWorker+0x47


                    [ffffbe0c8780f040 smss.exe]
```

49

```
                          [ffffbe0c87f2b080 csrss.exe]
   1fc.00020c  ffffbe0c87d1a580 000003a Blocked    nt!AlpcpWaitForSingleObject+0x3e
   1fc.000228  ffffbe0c887d60c0 00064b3 Blocked    nt!AlpcpSignalAndWait+0x13d
   1fc.000268  ffffbe0c88893080 000019d Blocked    nt!AlpcpWaitForSingleObject+0x3e
   1fc.000278  ffffbe0c888b4080 0000056 Blocked    win32kbase!LegacyInputDispatcher::WaitAndDispatch+0x95
   1fc.00027c  ffffbe0c888b6080 0006544 Blocked    win32kbase!LegacyInputDispatcher::WaitAndDispatch+0x95
   1fc.000cd0  ffffbe0c89a9a080 00001b2 Blocked    nt!AlpcpWaitForSingleObject+0x3e
   1fc.0010ac  ffffbe0c89fb6040 00063ad Blocked    nt!IoRemoveIoCompletion+0x98
   1fc.0026d8  ffffbe0c8bfbc040 0000553 Blocked    nt!IoRemoveIoCompletion+0x98

                          [ffffbe0c887d4080 wininit.exe]
   244.00026c  ffffbe0c888a8040 000212a Blocked    nt!IoRemoveIoCompletion+0x98
   244.000274  ffffbe0c888ab080 0005d0e Blocked    nt!IoRemoveIoCompletion+0x98

[...]

                          [ffffbe0c8c2cd0c0 notmyfault64.e]
   243c.001938 ffffbe0c8974f080 0000001 RUNNING    nt!KeBugCheckEx
   243c.0024a8 ffffbe0c8b5e0080 0000444 Blocked    nt!IoRemoveIoCompletion+0x98
   243c.002484 ffffbe0c8be7c080 0000444 Blocked    nt!IoRemoveIoCompletion+0x98

                          [ffffbe0c8bfb10c0 SearchHost.exe]
   2434.002440 ffffbe0c841d4080 0000333 Blocked    nt!ObWaitForMultipleObjects+0x2d5
   2434.002450 ffffbe0c8c2e7080 0000126 Blocked    nt!IoRemoveIoCompletion+0x98
   2434.00183c ffffbe0c8b5eb080 00002cd Blocked    nt!IoRemoveIoCompletion+0x98
   2434.00253c ffffbe0c8b5cd080 0000309 Blocked    nt!ObWaitForSingleObject+0xbb
   2434.0022b0 ffffbe0c8a2e9080 00002ff Blocked    nt!ObWaitForMultipleObjects+0x2d5
   2434.000b5c ffffbe0c8c2eb080 0000339 Blocked    nt!ObWaitForMultipleObjects+0x2d5
   2434.000814 ffffbe0c8b9d8080 00001f9 Blocked    nt!ObWaitForMultipleObjects+0x2d5
   2434.0017c8 ffffbe0c8c164080 0000325 Blocked    nt!ObWaitForMultipleObjects+0x2d5
   2434.002438 ffffbe0c8c9cb080 0000309 Blocked    nt!ObWaitForSingleObject+0xbb
   2434.000b1c ffffbe0c89ae9080 00001f9 Blocked    nt!ObWaitForMultipleObjects+0x2d5
   2434.000e88 ffffbe0c8b56d040 000023f Blocked    nt!ObWaitForMultipleObjects+0x2d5
   2434.0016cc ffffbe0c8c9a9080 0000166 Blocked    nt!ObWaitForMultipleObjects+0x2d5
   2434.000390 ffffbe0c87346080 0000333 Blocked    nt!ObWaitForMultipleObjects+0x2d5
   2434.000204 ffffbe0c8b120080 00000cf Blocked    nt!ObWaitForMultipleObjects+0x2d5
   2434.0011f4 ffffbe0c8b6a9080 00000cd Blocked    nt!ObWaitForMultipleObjects+0x2d5
   2434.000658 ffffbe0c8a346080 00001e0 Blocked    nt!KeWaitForAlertByThreadId+0xc4
   2434.00225c ffffbe0c8978a080 0000328 Blocked    nt!ObWaitForMultipleObjects+0x2d5
   2434.002350 ffffbe0c8b535080 00001e0 Blocked    nt!ObWaitForSingleObject+0xbb
   2434.001dc4 ffffbe0c8bfc9080 0000236 Blocked    nt!ObWaitForMultipleObjects+0x2d5
   2434.001f64 ffffbe0c8b3eb080 0000236 Blocked    nt!ObWaitForMultipleObjects+0x2d5
   2434.001764 ffffbe0c8a68f080 000031c Blocked    nt!IoRemoveIoCompletion+0x98
   2434.000e18 ffffbe0c8b3e0080 0000216 Blocked    nt!IoRemoveIoCompletion+0x98
   2434.0025b0 ffffbe0c8bfd7080 00002c5 Blocked    nt!ObWaitForMultipleObjects+0x2d5
   2434.001ca0 ffffbe0c8af29080 0000187 Blocked    nt!ObWaitForMultipleObjects+0x2d5
   2434.0018bc ffffbe0c8a90b080 0000046 Blocked    nt!ObWaitForMultipleObjects+0x2d5
   2434.002204 ffffbe0c8c2e8080 0000244 Blocked    nt!ObWaitForMultipleObjects+0x2d5
   2434.001308 ffffbe0c8c42b080 000001a Blocked    nt!ObWaitForMultipleObjects+0x2d5
   2434.0022ac ffffbe0c8a43a300 0000314 Blocked    nt!ObWaitForMultipleObjects+0x2d5
   2434.002260 ffffbe0c8c9680c0 0000313 Blocked    win32kfull!xxxRealSleepThread+0x2c6
   2434.000e28 ffffbe0c8c8cd0c0 000005a Blocked    nt!ObWaitForSingleObject+0xbb
   2434.0003fc ffffbe0c8c8ef0c0 00002eb Blocked    nt!ObWaitForMultipleObjects+0x2d5
   2434.0013b0 ffffbe0c8c9460c0 0000187 Blocked    nt!IoRemoveIoCompletion+0x98
   2434.0024e4 ffffbe0c8bac6080 000018d Blocked    win32kfull!xxxRealSleepThread+0x2c6
   2434.00228c ffffbe0c8c2ec080 000030c Blocked    nt!ObWaitForMultipleObjects+0x2d5
   2434.000e1c ffffbe0c8b793080 000030c Blocked    nt!ObWaitForMultipleObjects+0x2d5
   2434.00210c ffffbe0c8b69a500 000030b Blocked    win32kfull!xxxRealSleepThread+0x2c6
```

```
2434.000e8c  ffffbe0c8b763080 0000187 Blocked   win32kfull!xxxRealSleepThread+0x2c6
2434.0021e8  ffffbe0c8c0de500 000028c Blocked   nt!ObWaitForMultipleObjects+0x2d5
2434.000e40  ffffbe0c8b41e500 0000309 Blocked   nt!AlpcpSignalAndWait+0x13d
2434.0023c0  ffffbe0c8c11e080 000018c Blocked   nt!IoRemoveIoCompletion+0x98
2434.001238  ffffbe0c8bcb9540 0000187 Blocked   nt!ObWaitForMultipleObjects+0x2d5
2434.001c18  ffffbe0c8bad1080 0000306 Blocked   nt!ObWaitForMultipleObjects+0x2d5
2434.000840  ffffbe0c8baea540 0000216 Blocked   nt!IoRemoveIoCompletion+0x98
2434.001804  ffffbe0c8bee0300 000014c Blocked   nt!ObWaitForMultipleObjects+0x2d5
2434.000f24  ffffbe0c8a530540 0000216 Blocked   nt!IoRemoveIoCompletion+0x98
2434.001cd0  ffffbe0c8b511080 0000165 Blocked   nt!ObWaitForMultipleObjects+0x2d5
2434.000410  ffffbe0c894952c0 00002fd Blocked   nt!IoRemoveIoCompletion+0x98
2434.0021e0  ffffbe0c8a404580 00001e0 Blocked   nt!ObWaitForMultipleObjects+0x2d5
2434.0024d0  ffffbe0c8c1110c0 00002f2 Blocked   nt!ObWaitForMultipleObjects+0x2d5
2434.0022bc  ffffbe0c89b93040 000008a Blocked   nt!IoRemoveIoCompletion+0x98
2434.000854  ffffbe0c8a79b080 0000187 Blocked   nt!IoRemoveIoCompletion+0x98
2434.000f84  ffffbe0c8ae6e0c0 00002c8 Blocked   nt!ObWaitForSingleObject+0xbb
2434.000bf4  ffffbe0c8b419080 00002c8 Blocked   nt!AlpcpSignalAndWait+0x13d
2434.001310  ffffbe0c84ca9080 0000219 Blocked   nt!IoRemoveIoCompletion+0x98
2434.000d78  ffffbe0c89d7a080 0000235 Blocked   nt!ObWaitForMultipleObjects+0x2d5
2434.0023b0  ffffbe0c8bfd1080 0000236 Blocked   nt!ObWaitForMultipleObjects+0x2d5
2434.001c0c  ffffbe0c8c11d080 000018b Blocked   nt!IoRemoveIoCompletion+0x98
2434.001d4c  ffffbe0c8752e040 0000219 Blocked   nt!IoRemoveIoCompletion+0x98
2434.0025bc  ffffbe0c8c2b7080 000023f Blocked   nt!ObWaitForMultipleObjects+0x2d5
2434.0025c0  ffffbe0c8c2b3080 0000236 Blocked   nt!IoRemoveIoCompletion+0x98
2434.000b20  ffffbe0c8c8780c0 000021a Blocked   nt!IoRemoveIoCompletion+0x98
2434.000af4  ffffbe0c8c8130c0 000018b Blocked   nt!IoRemoveIoCompletion+0x98
2434.002240  ffffbe0c8c5ed0c0 0000217 Blocked   nt!IoRemoveIoCompletion+0x98
2434.00250c  ffffbe0c8c8de0c0 000021a Blocked   nt!IoRemoveIoCompletion+0x98
2434.002224  ffffbe0c8c89a0c0 0000218 Blocked   nt!IoRemoveIoCompletion+0x98
2434.00263c  ffffbe0c8c116080 0000216 Blocked   nt!ObWaitForMultipleObjects+0x2d5


Threads Processed: 2109
```

11.   Let's now check the processes that were waiting for user input:

```
0: kd> !stacks 2 NtUserGetMessage
Proc.Thread  .Thread  Ticks   ThreadState Blocker
                              [fffff80762d32b00 Idle]
                              [ffffbe0c840eb040 System]

                              [ffffbe0c84136080 Registry]

                              [ffffbe0c8780f040 smss.exe]

                              [ffffbe0c87f2b080 csrss.exe]

                              [ffffbe0c887d4080 wininit.exe]

                              [ffffbe0c888840c0 csrss.exe]

                              [ffffbe0c888c9100 services.exe]

                              [ffffbe0c888cb0c0 lsass.exe]

                              [ffffbe0c888dc080 winlogon.exe]

                              [ffffbe0c889b11c0 fontdrvhost.ex]

                              [ffffbe0c889af1c0 fontdrvhost.ex]

                              [ffffbe0c889ae080 svchost.exe]
```

51

```
                    [ffffbe0c890130c0 WUDFHost.exe]

                    [ffffbe0c889c7080 svchost.exe]

                    [ffffbe0c891020c0 svchost.exe]

                    [ffffbe0c89120080 dwm.exe]
310.000288  ffffbe0c89121080 0000144 Blocked    nt!KiSwapContext+0x76
                              nt!KiSwapThread+0x3a7
                              nt!KiCommitThreadWait+0x159
                              nt!KeWaitForSingleObject+0x234
                              nt!KeWaitForMultipleObjects+0x540
                              win32kfull!xxxRealSleepThread+0x2c6
                              win32kfull!xxxSleepThread2+0xb3
                              win32kfull!xxxRealInternalGetMessage+0xc5a
                              win32kfull!NtUserGetMessage+0x8c
                              win32k!NtUserGetMessage+0x16
                              nt!KiSystemServiceCopyEnd+0x25
                              win32u!NtUserGetMessage+0x14

                    [ffffbe0c891a0080 svchost.exe]

...
...
...


                    [ffffbe0c89a8e0c0 svchost.exe]

                    [ffffbe0c89a96080 svchost.exe]

                    [ffffbe0c89aa6080 svchost.exe]

                    [ffffbe0c89aa9080 VGAuthService.]

                    [ffffbe0c89aaa080 vmtoolsd.exe]

                    [ffffbe0c89a42080 MsMpEng.exe]
ca0.001aec  ffffbe0c89ca5080 0000056 Blocked    nt!KiSwapContext+0x76
                              nt!KiSwapThread+0x3a7
                              nt!KiCommitThreadWait+0x159
                              nt!KeWaitForSingleObject+0x234
                              nt!KeWaitForMultipleObjects+0x540
                              win32kfull!xxxRealSleepThread+0x2c6
                              win32kfull!xxxSleepThread2+0xb3
                              win32kfull!xxxRealInternalGetMessage+0xc5a
                              win32kfull!NtUserGetMessage+0x8c
                              win32k!NtUserGetMessage+0x16
                              nt!KiSystemServiceCopyEnd+0x25
                              win32u!NtUserGetMessage+0x14

                    [ffffbe0c89ac10c0 svchost.exe]

                    [ffffbe0c89aae080 svchost.exe]
cb8.00023c  ffffbe0c8a446080 0001b4d Blocked    nt!KiSwapContext+0x76
                              nt!KiSwapThread+0x3a7
                              nt!KiCommitThreadWait+0x159
                              nt!KeWaitForSingleObject+0x234
                              nt!KeWaitForMultipleObjects+0x540
                              win32kfull!xxxRealSleepThread+0x2c6
                              win32kfull!xxxSleepThread2+0xb3
                              win32kfull!xxxRealInternalGetMessage+0xc5a
                              win32kfull!NtUserGetMessage+0x8c
                              win32k!NtUserGetMessage+0x16
                              nt!KiSystemServiceCopyEnd+0x25
                              win32u!NtUserGetMessage+0x14

                    [ffffbe0c899e80c0 svchost.exe]

                    [ffffbe0c89c30080 dllhost.exe]
f00.000f34  ffffbe0c89c9a080 0001f06 Blocked    nt!KiSwapContext+0x76
                              nt!KiSwapThread+0x3a7
                              nt!KiCommitThreadWait+0x159
                              nt!KeWaitForSingleObject+0x234
```

```
                              nt!KeWaitForMultipleObjects+0x540
                              win32kfull!xxxRealSleepThread+0x2c6
                              win32kfull!xxxSleepThread2+0xb3
                              win32kfull!xxxRealInternalGetMessage+0xc5a
                              win32kfull!NtUserGetMessage+0x8c
                              win32k!NtUserGetMessage+0x16
                              nt!KiSystemServiceCopyEnd+0x25
                              win32u!NtUserGetMessage+0x14

                  [ffffbe0c89cf8080 AggregatorHost]

                  [ffffbe0c89e840c0 svchost.exe]

                  [ffffbe0c89f5e080 msdtc.exe]

                  [ffffbe0c8a0540c0 svchost.exe]

                  [ffffbe0c8a0cb080 WmiPrvSE.exe]
1278.00127c  ffffbe0c89be30c0 00063ad Blocked    nt!KiSwapContext+0x76
                              nt!KiSwapThread+0x3a7
                              nt!KiCommitThreadWait+0x159
                              nt!KeWaitForSingleObject+0x234
                              nt!KeWaitForMultipleObjects+0x540
                              win32kfull!xxxRealSleepThread+0x2c6
                              win32kfull!xxxSleepThread2+0xb3
                              win32kfull!xxxRealInternalGetMessage+0xc5a
                              win32kfull!NtUserGetMessage+0x8c
                              win32k!NtUserGetMessage+0x16
                              nt!KiSystemServiceCopyEnd+0x25
                              win32u!NtUserGetMessage+0x14

                  [ffffbe0c8a2320c0 sihost.exe]
1160.001330  ffffbe0c8a344080 0001bdd Blocked    nt!KiSwapContext+0x76
                              nt!KiSwapThread+0x3a7
                              nt!KiCommitThreadWait+0x159
                              nt!KeWaitForSingleObject+0x234
                              nt!KeWaitForMultipleObjects+0x540
                              win32kfull!xxxRealSleepThread+0x2c6
                              win32kfull!xxxSleepThread2+0xb3
                              win32kfull!xxxRealInternalGetMessage+0xc5a
                              win32kfull!NtUserGetMessage+0x8c
                              win32k!NtUserGetMessage+0x16
                              nt!KiSystemServiceCopyEnd+0x25
                              win32u!NtUserGetMessage+0x14

                  [ffffbe0c898c10c0 svchost.exe]

                  [ffffbe0c8a3340c0 svchost.exe]

                  [ffffbe0c8a0c4080 taskhostw.exe]

                  [ffffbe0c8a337080 taskhostw.exe]
12d0.001854  ffffbe0c8a92b080 000018b Blocked    nt!KiSwapContext+0x76
                              nt!KiSwapThread+0x3a7
                              nt!KiCommitThreadWait+0x159
                              nt!KeWaitForSingleObject+0x234
                              nt!KeWaitForMultipleObjects+0x540
                              win32kfull!xxxRealSleepThread+0x2c6
                              win32kfull!xxxSleepThread2+0xb3
                              win32kfull!xxxRealInternalGetMessage+0xc5a
                              win32kfull!NtUserGetMessage+0x8c
                              win32k!NtUserGetMessage+0x16
                              nt!KiSystemServiceCopyEnd+0x25
                              win32u!NtUserGetMessage+0x14

                  [ffffbe0c8a071080 svchost.exe]

                  [ffffbe0c8a4020c0 MsMpEngCP.exe]

                  [ffffbe0c8a43b080 svchost.exe]

                  [ffffbe0c8a454080 userinit.exe]

                  [ffffbe0c8a455080 explorer.exe]
```

```
1070.0014e0   ffffbe0c8a5e1080  0000544 Blocked    nt!KiSwapContext+0x76
                                                    nt!KiSwapThread+0x3a7
                                                    nt!KiCommitThreadWait+0x159
                                                    nt!KeWaitForSingleObject+0x234
                                                    nt!KeWaitForMultipleObjects+0x540
                                                    win32kfull!xxxRealSleepThread+0x2c6
                                                    win32kfull!xxxSleepThread2+0xb3
                                                    win32kfull!xxxRealInternalGetMessage+0xc5a
                                                    win32kfull!NtUserGetMessage+0x8c
                                                    win32k!NtUserGetMessage+0x16
                                                    nt!KiSystemServiceCopyEnd+0x25
                                                    win32u!NtUserGetMessage+0x14
1070.0014e8   ffffbe0c8a5df080  0000157 Blocked    nt!KiSwapContext+0x76
                                                    nt!KiSwapThread+0x3a7
                                                    nt!KiCommitThreadWait+0x159
                                                    nt!KeWaitForSingleObject+0x234
                                                    nt!KeWaitForMultipleObjects+0x540
                                                    win32kfull!xxxRealSleepThread+0x2c6
                                                    win32kfull!xxxSleepThread2+0xb3
                                                    win32kfull!xxxRealInternalGetMessage+0xc5a
                                                    win32kfull!NtUserGetMessage+0x8c
                                                    win32k!NtUserGetMessage+0x16
                                                    nt!KiSystemServiceCopyEnd+0x25
                                                    win32u!NtUserGetMessage+0x14
1070.001ae4   ffffbe0c8ab4c080  0000544 Blocked    nt!KiSwapContext+0x76
                                                    nt!KiSwapThread+0x3a7
                                                    nt!KiCommitThreadWait+0x159
                                                    nt!KeWaitForSingleObject+0x234
                                                    nt!KeWaitForMultipleObjects+0x540
                                                    win32kfull!xxxRealSleepThread+0x2c6
                                                    win32kfull!xxxSleepThread2+0xb3
                                                    win32kfull!xxxRealInternalGetMessage+0xc5a
                                                    win32kfull!NtUserGetMessage+0x8c
                                                    win32k!NtUserGetMessage+0x16
                                                    nt!KiSystemServiceCopyEnd+0x25
                                                    win32u!NtUserGetMessage+0x14
1070.001ae8   ffffbe0c8a74f080  00001cb Blocked    nt!KiSwapContext+0x76
                                                    nt!KiSwapThread+0x3a7
                                                    nt!KiCommitThreadWait+0x159
                                                    nt!KeWaitForSingleObject+0x234
                                                    nt!KeWaitForMultipleObjects+0x540
                                                    win32kfull!xxxRealSleepThread+0x2c6
                                                    win32kfull!xxxSleepThread2+0xb3
                                                    win32kfull!xxxRealInternalGetMessage+0xc5a
                                                    win32kfull!NtUserGetMessage+0x8c
                                                    win32k!NtUserGetMessage+0x16
                                                    nt!KiSystemServiceCopyEnd+0x25
                                                    win32u!NtUserGetMessage+0x14
1070.001f70   ffffbe0c8b218080  00001c2 Blocked    nt!KiSwapContext+0x76
                                                    nt!KiSwapThread+0x3a7
                                                    nt!KiCommitThreadWait+0x159
                                                    nt!KeWaitForSingleObject+0x234
                                                    nt!KeWaitForMultipleObjects+0x540
                                                    win32kfull!xxxRealSleepThread+0x2c6
                                                    win32kfull!xxxSleepThread2+0xb3
                                                    win32kfull!xxxRealInternalGetMessage+0xc5a
                                                    win32kfull!NtUserGetMessage+0x8c
                                                    win32k!NtUserGetMessage+0x16
                                                    nt!KiSystemServiceCopyEnd+0x25
                                                    win32u!NtUserGetMessage+0x14
1070.001f80   ffffbe0c8b21c080  0000544 Blocked    nt!KiSwapContext+0x76
                                                    nt!KiSwapThread+0x3a7
                                                    nt!KiCommitThreadWait+0x159
                                                    nt!KeWaitForMultipleObjects+0x2b1
                                                    win32kfull!xxxRealSleepThread+0x2c6
                                                    win32kfull!xxxSleepThread2+0xb3
                                                    win32kfull!xxxRealInternalGetMessage+0xc5a
                                                    win32kfull!NtUserGetMessage+0x8c
                                                    win32k!NtUserGetMessage+0x16
                                                    nt!KiSystemServiceCopyEnd+0x25
                                                    win32u!NtUserGetMessage+0x14
1070.001fec   ffffbe0c8af4a080  0000545 Blocked    nt!KiSwapContext+0x76
                                                    nt!KiSwapThread+0x3a7
                                                    nt!KiCommitThreadWait+0x159
```

```
                              nt!KeWaitForMultipleObjects+0x2b1
                              win32kfull!xxxRealSleepThread+0x2c6
                              win32kfull!xxxSleepThread2+0xb3
                              win32kfull!xxxRealInternalGetMessage+0xc5a
                              win32kfull!NtUserGetMessage+0x8c
                              win32k!NtUserGetMessage+0x16
                              nt!KiSystemServiceCopyEnd+0x25
                              win32u!NtUserGetMessage+0x14
1070.0017cc   ffffbe0c8942e080 0000545 Blocked    nt!KiSwapContext+0x76
                              nt!KiSwapThread+0x3a7
                              nt!KiCommitThreadWait+0x159
                              nt!KeWaitForMultipleObjects+0x2b1
                              win32kfull!xxxRealSleepThread+0x2c6
                              win32kfull!xxxSleepThread2+0xb3
                              win32kfull!xxxRealInternalGetMessage+0xc5a
                              win32kfull!NtUserGetMessage+0x8c
                              win32k!NtUserGetMessage+0x16
                              nt!KiSystemServiceCopyEnd+0x25
                              win32u!NtUserGetMessage+0x14
1070.0011a4   ffffbe0c8a2f1080 000050b Blocked    nt!KiSwapContext+0x76
                              nt!KiSwapThread+0x3a7
                              nt!KiCommitThreadWait+0x159
                              nt!KeWaitForMultipleObjects+0x2b1
                              win32kfull!xxxRealSleepThread+0x2c6
                              win32kfull!xxxSleepThread2+0xb3
                              win32kfull!xxxRealInternalGetMessage+0xc5a
                              win32kfull!NtUserGetMessage+0x8c
                              win32k!NtUserGetMessage+0x16
                              nt!KiSystemServiceCopyEnd+0x25
                              win32u!NtUserGetMessage+0x14
1070.0018f8   ffffbe0c8bad4080 000046f Blocked    nt!KiSwapContext+0x76
                              nt!KiSwapThread+0x3a7
                              nt!KiCommitThreadWait+0x159
                              nt!KeWaitForSingleObject+0x234
                              nt!KeWaitForMultipleObjects+0x540
                              win32kfull!xxxRealSleepThread+0x2c6
                              win32kfull!xxxSleepThread2+0xb3
                              win32kfull!xxxRealInternalGetMessage+0xc5a
                              win32kfull!NtUserGetMessage+0x8c
                              win32k!NtUserGetMessage+0x16
                              nt!KiSystemServiceCopyEnd+0x25
                              win32u!NtUserGetMessage+0x14
1070.002778   ffffbe0c8bed7080 0000446 Blocked    nt!KiSwapContext+0x76
                              nt!KiSwapThread+0x3a7
                              nt!KiCommitThreadWait+0x159
                              nt!KeWaitForSingleObject+0x234
                              nt!KeWaitForMultipleObjects+0x540
                              win32kfull!xxxRealSleepThread+0x2c6
                              win32kfull!xxxSleepThread2+0xb3
                              win32kfull!xxxRealInternalGetMessage+0xc5a
                              win32kfull!NtUserGetMessage+0x8c
                              win32k!NtUserGetMessage+0x16
                              nt!KiSystemServiceCopyEnd+0x25
                              win32u!NtUserGetMessage+0x14

                   [ffffbe0c8a4f8080 svchost.exe]

                   [ffffbe0c8a4f7080 svchost.exe]

                   [ffffbe0c8a4ef0c0 svchost.exe]

                   [ffffbe0c8a4e9080 WmiPrvSE.exe]
1590.001594   ffffbe0c8a566080 00063ad Blocked    nt!KiSwapContext+0x76
                              nt!KiSwapThread+0x3a7
                              nt!KiCommitThreadWait+0x159
                              nt!KeWaitForSingleObject+0x234
                              nt!KeWaitForMultipleObjects+0x540
                              win32kfull!xxxRealSleepThread+0x2c6
                              win32kfull!xxxSleepThread2+0xb3
                              win32kfull!xxxRealInternalGetMessage+0xc5a
                              win32kfull!NtUserGetMessage+0x8c
                              win32k!NtUserGetMessage+0x16
                              nt!KiSystemServiceCopyEnd+0x25
                              win32u!NtUserGetMessage+0x14
```

```
1590.001d30  ffffbe0c8927b080 0005f8c Blocked    nt!KiSwapContext+0x76
                                       nt!KiSwapThread+0x3a7
                                       nt!KiCommitThreadWait+0x159
                                       nt!KeWaitForSingleObject+0x234
                                       nt!KeWaitForMultipleObjects+0x540
                                       win32kfull!xxxRealSleepThread+0x2c6
                                       win32kfull!xxxSleepThread2+0xb3
                                       win32kfull!xxxRealInternalGetMessage+0xc5a
                                       win32kfull!NtUserGetMessage+0x8c
                                       win32k!NtUserGetMessage+0x16
                                       nt!KiSystemServiceCopyEnd+0x25
                                       win32u!NtUserGetMessage+0x14

                   [ffffbe0c8a6c1080 NisSrv.exe]

                   [ffffbe0c8a729080 svchost.exe]

                   [ffffbe0c8a8540c0 SearchIndexer.]

                   [ffffbe0c8a859080 svchost.exe]
1758.0017a0  ffffbe0c8a9020c0 000190b Blocked    nt!KiSwapContext+0x76
                                       nt!KiSwapThread+0x3a7
                                       nt!KiCommitThreadWait+0x159
                                       nt!KeWaitForSingleObject+0x234
                                       nt!KeWaitForMultipleObjects+0x540
                                       win32kfull!xxxRealSleepThread+0x2c6
                                       win32kfull!xxxSleepThread2+0xb3
                                       win32kfull!xxxRealInternalGetMessage+0xc5a
                                       win32kfull!NtUserGetMessage+0x8c
                                       win32k!NtUserGetMessage+0x16
                                       nt!KiSystemServiceCopyEnd+0x25
                                       win32u!NtUserGetMessage+0x14

                   [ffffbe0c8a9240c0 svchost.exe]

                   [ffffbe0c8a982080 SearchHost.exe]
49c.00193c   ffffbe0c8abfc080 00062f4 Blocked    nt!KiSwapContext+0x76
                                       nt!KiSwapThread+0x3a7
                                       nt!KiCommitThreadWait+0x159
                                       nt!KeWaitForSingleObject+0x234
                                       nt!KeWaitForMultipleObjects+0x540
                                       win32kfull!xxxRealSleepThread+0x2c6
                                       win32kfull!xxxSleepThread2+0xb3
                                       win32kfull!xxxRealInternalGetMessage+0xc5a
                                       win32kfull!NtUserGetMessage+0x8c
                                       win32k!NtUserGetMessage+0x16
                                       nt!KiSystemServiceCopyEnd+0x25
                                       win32u!NtUserGetMessage+0x14
49c.001b08   ffffbe0c8a862080 0000c9f Blocked    nt!KiSwapContext+0x76
                                       nt!KiSwapThread+0x3a7
                                       nt!KiCommitThreadWait+0x159
                                       nt!KeWaitForSingleObject+0x234
                                       nt!KeWaitForMultipleObjects+0x540
                                       win32kfull!xxxRealSleepThread+0x2c6
                                       win32kfull!xxxSleepThread2+0xb3
                                       win32kfull!xxxRealInternalGetMessage+0xc5a
                                       win32kfull!NtUserGetMessage+0x8c
                                       win32k!NtUserGetMessage+0x16
                                       nt!KiSystemServiceCopyEnd+0x25
                                       win32u!NtUserGetMessage+0x14
49c.001b14   ffffbe0c8ad72080 0000ca0 Blocked    nt!KiSwapContext+0x76
                                       nt!KiSwapThread+0x3a7
                                       nt!KiCommitThreadWait+0x159
                                       nt!KeWaitForSingleObject+0x234
                                       nt!KeWaitForMultipleObjects+0x540
                                       win32kfull!xxxRealSleepThread+0x2c6
                                       win32kfull!xxxSleepThread2+0xb3
                                       win32kfull!xxxRealInternalGetMessage+0xc5a
                                       win32kfull!NtUserGetMessage+0x8c
                                       win32k!NtUserGetMessage+0x16
                                       nt!KiSystemServiceCopyEnd+0x25
                                       win32u!NtUserGetMessage+0x14
49c.001b18   ffffbe0c8ad71080 0000c9a Blocked    nt!KiSwapContext+0x76
                                       nt!KiSwapThread+0x3a7
```

```
                                  nt!KiCommitThreadWait+0x159
                                  nt!KeWaitForSingleObject+0x234
                                  nt!KeWaitForMultipleObjects+0x540
                                  win32kfull!xxxRealSleepThread+0x2c6
                                  win32kfull!xxxSleepThread2+0xb3
                                  win32kfull!xxxRealInternalGetMessage+0xc5a
                                  win32kfull!NtUserGetMessage+0x8c
                                  win32k!NtUserGetMessage+0x16
                                  nt!KiSystemServiceCopyEnd+0x25
                                  win32u!NtUserGetMessage+0x14

                 [ffffbe0c8aa020c0 StartMenuExper]

                 [ffffbe0c8a55b0c0 svchost.exe]

                 [ffffbe0c8aaa00c0 RuntimeBroker.]
184c.001c68  ffffbe0c89eb4080 0000544 Blocked      nt!KiSwapContext+0x76
                                  nt!KiSwapThread+0x3a7
                                  nt!KiCommitThreadWait+0x159
                                  nt!KeWaitForSingleObject+0x234
                                  nt!KeWaitForMultipleObjects+0x540
                                  win32kfull!xxxRealSleepThread+0x2c6
                                  win32kfull!xxxSleepThread2+0xb3
                                  win32kfull!xxxRealInternalGetMessage+0xc5a
                                  win32kfull!NtUserGetMessage+0x8c
                                  win32k!NtUserGetMessage+0x16
                                  nt!KiSystemServiceCopyEnd+0x25
                                  win32u!NtUserGetMessage+0x14
184c.000da4  ffffbe0c8b4d4080 0000ccc Blocked      nt!KiSwapContext+0x76
                                  nt!KiSwapThread+0x3a7
                                  nt!KiCommitThreadWait+0x159
                                  nt!KeWaitForSingleObject+0x234
                                  nt!KeWaitForMultipleObjects+0x540
                                  win32kfull!xxxRealSleepThread+0x2c6
                                  win32kfull!xxxSleepThread2+0xb3
                                  win32kfull!xxxRealInternalGetMessage+0xc5a
                                  win32kfull!NtUserGetMessage+0x8c
                                  win32k!NtUserGetMessage+0x16
                                  nt!KiSystemServiceCopyEnd+0x25
                                  win32u!NtUserGetMessage+0x14

                 [ffffbe0c8ab52080 svchost.exe]

                 [ffffbe0c8aa37080 RuntimeBroker.]
18fc.001b30  ffffbe0c8a055080 0001722 Blocked      nt!KiSwapContext+0x76
                                  nt!KiSwapThread+0x3a7
                                  nt!KiCommitThreadWait+0x159
                                  nt!KeWaitForSingleObject+0x234
                                  nt!KeWaitForMultipleObjects+0x540
                                  win32kfull!xxxRealSleepThread+0x2c6
                                  win32kfull!xxxSleepThread2+0xb3
                                  win32kfull!xxxRealInternalGetMessage+0xc5a
                                  win32kfull!NtUserGetMessage+0x8c
                                  win32k!NtUserGetMessage+0x16
                                  nt!KiSystemServiceCopyEnd+0x25
                                  win32u!NtUserGetMessage+0x14

                 [ffffbe0c8ac07080 svchost.exe]

                 [ffffbe0c8acd6080 dllhost.exe]
19f4.001a44  ffffbe0c8acbd080 0001783 Blocked      nt!KiSwapContext+0x76
                                  nt!KiSwapThread+0x3a7
                                  nt!KiCommitThreadWait+0x159
                                  nt!KeWaitForSingleObject+0x234
                                  nt!KeWaitForMultipleObjects+0x540
                                  win32kfull!xxxRealSleepThread+0x2c6
                                  win32kfull!xxxSleepThread2+0xb3
                                  win32kfull!xxxRealInternalGetMessage+0xc5a
                                  win32kfull!NtUserGetMessage+0x8c
                                  win32k!NtUserGetMessage+0x16
                                  nt!KiSystemServiceCopyEnd+0x25
                                  win32u!NtUserGetMessage+0x14

                 [ffffbe0c8ad94080 svchost.exe]
```

```
                              [ffffbe0c8ae6f080 YourPhone.exe]

                              [ffffbe0c8ae72080 ctfmon.exe]

                              [ffffbe0c8ae760c0 svchost.exe]

                              [ffffbe0c8aeeb0c0 TabTip.exe]
1b70.001b7c    ffffbe0c841dc080 000612d Blocked     nt!KiSwapContext+0x76
                                       nt!KiSwapThread+0x3a7
                                       nt!KiCommitThreadWait+0x159
                                       nt!KeWaitForSingleObject+0x234
                                       nt!KeWaitForMultipleObjects+0x540
                                       win32kfull!xxxRealSleepThread+0x2c6
                                       win32kfull!xxxSleepThread2+0xb3
                                       win32kfull!xxxRealInternalGetMessage+0xc5a
                                       win32kfull!NtUserGetMessage+0x8c
                                       win32k!NtUserGetMessage+0x16
                                       nt!KiSystemServiceCopyEnd+0x25
                                       win32u!NtUserGetMessage+0x14

                              [ffffbe0c8ac8e080 WmiApSrv.exe]

                              [ffffbe0c8af240c0 RuntimeBroker.]

                              [ffffbe0c8ac98080 smartscreen.ex]

                              [ffffbe0c84120080 SecurityHealth]
1e28.001e2c    ffffbe0c8abdc080 0000543 Blocked     nt!KiSwapContext+0x76
                                       nt!KiSwapThread+0x3a7
                                       nt!KiCommitThreadWait+0x159
                                       nt!KeWaitForSingleObject+0x234
                                       nt!KeWaitForMultipleObjects+0x540
                                       win32kfull!xxxRealSleepThread+0x2c6
                                       win32kfull!xxxSleepThread2+0xb3
                                       win32kfull!xxxRealInternalGetMessage+0xc5a
                                       win32kfull!NtUserGetMessage+0x8c
                                       win32k!NtUserGetMessage+0x16
                                       nt!KiSystemServiceCopyEnd+0x25
                                       win32u!NtUserGetMessage+0x14

                              [ffffbe0c8aee1080 SecurityHealth]
1e3c.001ec4    ffffbe0c8ae91080 0000cf8 Blocked     nt!KiSwapContext+0x76
                                       nt!KiSwapThread+0x3a7
                                       nt!KiCommitThreadWait+0x159
                                       nt!KeWaitForSingleObject+0x234
                                       nt!KeWaitForMultipleObjects+0x540
                                       win32kfull!xxxRealSleepThread+0x2c6
                                       win32kfull!xxxSleepThread2+0xb3
                                       win32kfull!xxxRealInternalGetMessage+0xc5a
                                       win32kfull!NtUserGetMessage+0x8c
                                       win32k!NtUserGetMessage+0x16
                                       nt!KiSystemServiceCopyEnd+0x25
                                       win32u!NtUserGetMessage+0x14

                              [ffffbe0c8aedd080 vmtoolsd.exe]

                              [ffffbe0c8b2080c0 ApplicationFra]
1ef8.001f54    ffffbe0c8aa9d080 00004c5 Blocked     nt!KiSwapContext+0x76
                                       nt!KiSwapThread+0x3a7
                                       nt!KiCommitThreadWait+0x159
                                       nt!KeWaitForMultipleObjects+0x2b1
                                       win32kfull!xxxRealSleepThread+0x2c6
                                       win32kfull!xxxSleepThread2+0xb3
                                       win32kfull!xxxRealInternalGetMessage+0xc5a
                                       win32kfull!NtUserGetMessage+0x8c
                                       win32k!NtUserGetMessage+0x16
                                       nt!KiSystemServiceCopyEnd+0x25
                                       win32u!NtUserGetMessage+0x14
1ef8.002394    ffffbe0c8a341080 00004ba Blocked     nt!KiSwapContext+0x76
                                       nt!KiSwapThread+0x3a7
                                       nt!KiCommitThreadWait+0x159
                                       nt!KeWaitForMultipleObjects+0x2b1
                                       win32kfull!xxxRealSleepThread+0x2c6
```

```
                                  win32kfull!xxxSleepThread2+0xb3
                                  win32kfull!xxxRealInternalGetMessage+0xc5a
                                  win32kfull!NtUserGetMessage+0x8c
                                  win32k!NtUserGetMessage+0x16
                                  nt!KiSystemServiceCopyEnd+0x25
                                  win32u!NtUserGetMessage+0x14
1ef8.0011c0  ffffbe0c89dea080 0000475 Blocked    nt!KiSwapContext+0x76
                                  nt!KiSwapThread+0x3a7
                                  nt!KiCommitThreadWait+0x159
                                  nt!KeWaitForMultipleObjects+0x2b1
                                  win32kfull!xxxRealSleepThread+0x2c6
                                  win32kfull!xxxSleepThread2+0xb3
                                  win32kfull!xxxRealInternalGetMessage+0xc5a
                                  win32kfull!NtUserGetMessage+0x8c
                                  win32k!NtUserGetMessage+0x16
                                  nt!KiSystemServiceCopyEnd+0x25
                                  win32u!NtUserGetMessage+0x14

                   [ffffbe0c8ad84080 TextInputHost.]

                   [ffffbe0c8af55080 vm3dservice.ex]
1fd8.001fdc  ffffbe0c8911b080 0000544 Blocked    nt!KiSwapContext+0x76
                                  nt!KiSwapThread+0x3a7
                                  nt!KiCommitThreadWait+0x159
                                  nt!KeWaitForSingleObject+0x234
                                  nt!KeWaitForMultipleObjects+0x540
                                  win32kfull!xxxRealSleepThread+0x2c6
                                  win32kfull!xxxSleepThread2+0xb3
                                  win32kfull!xxxRealInternalGetMessage+0xc5a
                                  win32kfull!NtUserGetMessage+0x8c
                                  win32k!NtUserGetMessage+0x16
                                  nt!KiSystemServiceCopyEnd+0x25
                                  win32u!NtUserGetMessage+0x14

                   [ffffbe0c8b49a080 OneDrive.exe]
1188.001a9c  ffffbe0c8b222080 0000543 Blocked    nt!KiSwapContext+0x76
                                  nt!KiSwapThread+0x3a7
                                  nt!KiCommitThreadWait+0x159
                                  nt!KeWaitForSingleObject+0x234
                                  nt!KeWaitForMultipleObjects+0x540
                                  win32kfull!xxxRealSleepThread+0x2c6
                                  win32kfull!xxxSleepThread2+0xb3
                                  win32kfull!xxxRealInternalGetMessage+0xc5a
                                  win32kfull!NtUserGetMessage+0x8c
                                  win32k!NtUserGetMessage+0x16
                                  nt!KiSystemServiceCopyEnd+0x25
                                  win32u!NtUserGetMessage+0x14
1188.001258  ffffbe0c8b48a080 0005c1a Blocked    nt!KiSwapContext+0x76
                                  nt!KiSwapThread+0x3a7
                                  nt!KiCommitThreadWait+0x159
                                  nt!KeWaitForSingleObject+0x234
                                  nt!KeWaitForMultipleObjects+0x540
                                  win32kfull!xxxRealSleepThread+0x2c6
                                  win32kfull!xxxSleepThread2+0xb3
                                  win32kfull!xxxRealInternalGetMessage+0xc5a
                                  win32kfull!NtUserGetMessage+0x8c
                                  win32k!NtUserGetMessage+0x16
                                  nt!KiSystemServiceCopyEnd+0x25
                                  win32u!NtUserGetMessage+0x14

                   [ffffbe0c8b4e90c0 msedge.exe]

                   [ffffbe0c8b4020c0 Cortana.exe]

                   [ffffbe0c8b417080 RuntimeBroker.]

                   [ffffbe0c8b37b080 svchost.exe]

                   [ffffbe0c8b4b2080 svchost.exe]

                   [ffffbe0c8b092080 svchost.exe]

                   [ffffbe0c876f2080 svchost.exe]
```

```
                    [ffffbe0c8b4d6080 svchost.exe]

                    [ffffbe0c89a020c0 Win32Bridge.Se]

                    [ffffbe0c8b5e60c0 SystemSettings]
23a8.0023f8  ffffbe0c8b2ec080 000500c Blocked    nt!KiSwapContext+0x76
                                     nt!KiSwapThread+0x3a7
                                     nt!KiCommitThreadWait+0x159
                                     nt!KeWaitForSingleObject+0x234
                                     nt!KeWaitForMultipleObjects+0x540
                                     win32kfull!xxxRealSleepThread+0x2c6
                                     win32kfull!xxxSleepThread2+0xb3
                                     win32kfull!xxxRealInternalGetMessage+0xc5a
                                     win32kfull!NtUserGetMessage+0x8c
                                     win32k!NtUserGetMessage+0x16
                                     nt!KiSystemServiceCopyEnd+0x25
                                     win32u!NtUserGetMessage+0x14
23a8.000a98  ffffbe0c8a730080 0004ff6 Blocked    nt!KiSwapContext+0x76
                                     nt!KiSwapThread+0x3a7
                                     nt!KiCommitThreadWait+0x159
                                     nt!KeWaitForSingleObject+0x234
                                     nt!KeWaitForMultipleObjects+0x540
                                     win32kfull!xxxRealSleepThread+0x2c6
                                     win32kfull!xxxSleepThread2+0xb3
                                     win32kfull!xxxRealInternalGetMessage+0xc5a
                                     win32kfull!NtUserGetMessage+0x8c
                                     win32k!NtUserGetMessage+0x16
                                     nt!KiSystemServiceCopyEnd+0x25
                                     win32u!NtUserGetMessage+0x14

                    [ffffbe0c8b8870c0 svchost.exe]

                    [ffffbe0c8b4b60c0 UserOOBEBroker]
1414.0012cc  ffffbe0c89aea080 0004faf Blocked    nt!KiSwapContext+0x76
                                     nt!KiSwapThread+0x3a7
                                     nt!KiCommitThreadWait+0x159
                                     nt!KeWaitForSingleObject+0x234
                                     nt!KeWaitForMultipleObjects+0x540
                                     win32kfull!xxxRealSleepThread+0x2c6
                                     win32kfull!xxxSleepThread2+0xb3
                                     win32kfull!xxxRealInternalGetMessage+0xc5a
                                     win32kfull!NtUserGetMessage+0x8c
                                     win32k!NtUserGetMessage+0x16
                                     nt!KiSystemServiceCopyEnd+0x25
                                     win32u!NtUserGetMessage+0x14

                    [ffffbe0c876f8080 SgrmBroker.exe]

                    [ffffbe0c892bc080 svchost.exe]

                    [ffffbe0c89a9b080 svchost.exe]

                    [ffffbe0c8b3d5080 svchost.exe]

                    [ffffbe0c8b4d80c0 msedge.exe]
f0c.000f10  ffffbe0c87608080 0002b3f Blocked    nt!KiSwapContext+0x76
                                     nt!KiSwapThread+0x3a7
                                     nt!KiCommitThreadWait+0x159
                                     nt!KeWaitForSingleObject+0x234
                                     nt!KeWaitForMultipleObjects+0x540
                                     win32kfull!xxxRealSleepThread+0x2c6
                                     win32kfull!xxxSleepThread2+0xb3
                                     win32kfull!xxxRealInternalGetMessage+0xc5a
                                     win32kfull!NtUserGetMessage+0x8c
                                     win32k!NtUserGetMessage+0x16
                                     nt!KiSystemServiceCopyEnd+0x25
                                     win32u!NtUserGetMessage+0x14

                    [ffffbe0c8ad810c0 msedge.exe]
1e8c.000a14  ffffbe0c8a2f3080 0000544 Blocked    nt!KiSwapContext+0x76
                                     nt!KiSwapThread+0x3a7
                                     nt!KiCommitThreadWait+0x159
                                     nt!KeWaitForSingleObject+0x234
                                     nt!KeWaitForMultipleObjects+0x540
```

```
                              win32kfull!xxxRealSleepThread+0x2c6
                              win32kfull!xxxRealInternalGetMessage+0x14ff
                              win32kfull!NtUserGetMessage+0x8c
                              win32k!NtUserGetMessage+0x16
                              nt!KiSystemServiceCopyEnd+0x25
                              win32u!NtUserGetMessage+0x14

                  [ffffbe0c8b0d60c0 msedge.exe]

                  [ffffbe0c8cce90c0 msedge.exe]

                  [ffffbe0c8b224080 msedge.exe]

                  [ffffbe0c8b6960c0 msedge.exe]

                  [ffffbe0c8b3960c0 identity_helpe]

                  [ffffbe0c8b5b30c0 msedge.exe]

                  [ffffbe0c8af460c0 msedge.exe]

                  [ffffbe0c8b0e20c0 MiniSearchHost]

                  [ffffbe0c870210c0 Notepad.exe]
1b24.0010b4  ffffbe0c89789080 0000020 Blocked    nt!KiSwapContext+0x76
                              nt!KiSwapThread+0x3a7
                              nt!KiCommitThreadWait+0x159
                              nt!KeWaitForSingleObject+0x234
                              nt!KeWaitForMultipleObjects+0x540
                              win32kfull!xxxRealSleepThread+0x2c6
                              win32kfull!xxxSleepThread2+0xb3
                              win32kfull!xxxRealInternalGetMessage+0xc5a
                              win32kfull!NtUserGetMessage+0x8c
                              win32k!NtUserGetMessage+0x16
                              nt!KiSystemServiceCopyEnd+0x25
                              win32u!NtUserGetMessage+0x14

                  [ffffbe0c876480c0 dllhost.exe]
22a8.0018e8  ffffbe0c8b6af300 00001a5 Blocked    nt!KiSwapContext+0x76
                              nt!KiSwapThread+0x3a7
                              nt!KiCommitThreadWait+0x159
                              nt!KeWaitForSingleObject+0x234
                              nt!KeWaitForMultipleObjects+0x540
                              win32kfull!xxxRealSleepThread+0x2c6
                              win32kfull!xxxSleepThread2+0xb3
                              win32kfull!xxxRealInternalGetMessage+0xc5a
                              win32kfull!NtUserGetMessage+0x8c
                              win32k!NtUserGetMessage+0x16
                              nt!KiSystemServiceCopyEnd+0x25
                              win32u!NtUserGetMessage+0x14

                  [ffffbe0c84caf080 CalculatorApp.]

                  [ffffbe0c8b538080 RuntimeBroker.]
 ce8.00084c  ffffbe0c8a7b2080 0001ebb Blocked    nt!KiSwapContext+0x76
                              nt!KiSwapThread+0x3a7
                              nt!KiCommitThreadWait+0x159
                              nt!KeWaitForSingleObject+0x234
                              nt!KeWaitForMultipleObjects+0x540
                              win32kfull!xxxRealSleepThread+0x2c6
                              win32kfull!xxxSleepThread2+0xb3
                              win32kfull!xxxRealInternalGetMessage+0xc5a
                              win32kfull!NtUserGetMessage+0x8c
                              win32k!NtUserGetMessage+0x16
                              nt!KiSystemServiceCopyEnd+0x25
                              win32u!NtUserGetMessage+0x14

                  [ffffbe0c8be620c0 wordpad.exe]
1d98.001bb0  ffffbe0c8beda080 0000020 Blocked    nt!KiSwapContext+0x76
                              nt!KiSwapThread+0x3a7
                              nt!KiCommitThreadWait+0x159
                              nt!KeWaitForSingleObject+0x234
                              nt!KeWaitForMultipleObjects+0x540
                              win32kfull!xxxRealSleepThread+0x2c6
```

61

```
                                      win32kfull!xxxSleepThread2+0xb3
                                      win32kfull!xxxRealInternalGetMessage+0xc5a
                                      win32kfull!NtUserGetMessage+0x8c
                                      win32k!NtUserGetMessage+0x16
                                      nt!KiSystemServiceCopyEnd+0x25
                                      +0x7ffe5ac81424

                      [ffffbe0c8bed8080 splwow64.exe]

                      [ffffbe0c84c990c0 svchost.exe]

                      [ffffbe0c8be760c0 svchost.exe]

                      [ffffbe0c8a7a6080 LINQPad7.exe]

                      [ffffbe0c8b318080 LINQPad7.Query]

                      [ffffbe0c8c9d3080 cmd.exe]

                      [ffffbe0c8b317080 conhost.exe]
2568.002594   ffffbe0c8b537080 0000020 Blocked     nt!KiSwapContext+0x76
                                      nt!KiSwapThread+0x3a7
                                      nt!KiCommitThreadWait+0x159
                                      nt!KeWaitForSingleObject+0x234
                                      nt!KeWaitForMultipleObjects+0x540
                                      win32kfull!xxxRealSleepThread+0x2c6
                                      win32kfull!xxxSleepThread2+0xb3
                                      win32kfull!xxxRealInternalGetMessage+0xc5a
                                      win32kfull!NtUserGetMessage+0x8c
                                      win32k!NtUserGetMessage+0x16
                                      nt!KiSystemServiceCopyEnd+0x25
                                      win32u!NtUserGetMessage+0x14

                      [ffffbe0c877ec080 Taskmgr.exe]

                      [ffffbe0c8c2de0c0 audiodg.exe]

                      [ffffbe0c8c5760c0 TabTip.exe]

                      [ffffbe0c8c2cd0c0 notmyfault64.e]

                      [ffffbe0c8bfb10c0 SearchHost.exe]
2434.002260   ffffbe0c8c9680c0 0000313 Blocked     nt!KiSwapContext+0x76
                                      nt!KiSwapThread+0x3a7
                                      nt!KiCommitThreadWait+0x159
                                      nt!KeWaitForSingleObject+0x234
                                      nt!KeWaitForMultipleObjects+0x540
                                      win32kfull!xxxRealSleepThread+0x2c6
                                      win32kfull!xxxSleepThread2+0xb3
                                      win32kfull!xxxRealInternalGetMessage+0xc5a
                                      win32kfull!NtUserGetMessage+0x8c
                                      win32k!NtUserGetMessage+0x16
                                      nt!KiSystemServiceCopyEnd+0x25
                                      win32u!NtUserGetMessage+0x14
                                      user32!GetMessageW+0x2e
                                      edgehtml!CIndependentHitTestManager::IndependentHitTestThreadProc+0xa8
                                      KERNEL32!BaseThreadInitThunk+0x10
                                      ntdll!RtlUserThreadStart+0x2b
2434.0024e4   ffffbe0c8bac6080 000018d Blocked     nt!KiSwapContext+0x76
                                      nt!KiSwapThread+0x3a7
                                      nt!KiCommitThreadWait+0x159
                                      nt!KeWaitForSingleObject+0x234
                                      nt!KeWaitForMultipleObjects+0x540
                                      win32kfull!xxxRealSleepThread+0x2c6
                                      win32kfull!xxxSleepThread2+0xb3
                                      win32kfull!xxxRealInternalGetMessage+0xc5a
                                      win32kfull!NtUserGetMessage+0x8c
                                      win32k!NtUserGetMessage+0x16
                                      nt!KiSystemServiceCopyEnd+0x25
                                      win32u!NtUserGetMessage+0x14
                                      user32!GetMessageW+0x2e
                                      WebRuntimeManager!LCIEWWAServiceWorkerGlobalScopeHost::ThreadProc+0x7f
                                      edgeiso!_IsoThreadProc_WrapperToReleaseScope+0x20
                                      KERNEL32!BaseThreadInitThunk+0x10
```

```
                          ntdll!RtlUserThreadStart+0x2b
2434.00210c  ffffbe0c8b69a500 000030b Blocked    nt!KiSwapContext+0x76
                          nt!KiSwapThread+0x3a7
                          nt!KiCommitThreadWait+0x159
                          nt!KeWaitForSingleObject+0x234
                          nt!KeWaitForMultipleObjects+0x540
                          win32kfull!xxxRealSleepThread+0x2c6
                          win32kfull!xxxSleepThread2+0xb3
                          win32kfull!xxxRealInternalGetMessage+0xc5a
                          win32kfull!NtUserGetMessage+0x8c
                          win32k!NtUserGetMessage+0x16
                          nt!KiSystemServiceCopyEnd+0x25
                          win32u!NtUserGetMessage+0x14
                          user32!GetMessageW+0x2e
                          edgehtml!CRawInput::RawInputThreadProc+0x50
                          KERNEL32!BaseThreadInitThunk+0x10
                          ntdll!RtlUserThreadStart+0x2b
2434.000e8c  ffffbe0c8b763080 0000187 Blocked    nt!KiSwapContext+0x76
                          nt!KiSwapThread+0x3a7
                          nt!KiCommitThreadWait+0x159
                          nt!KeWaitForSingleObject+0x234
                          nt!KeWaitForMultipleObjects+0x540
                          win32kfull!xxxRealSleepThread+0x2c6
                          win32kfull!xxxSleepThread2+0xb3
                          win32kfull!xxxRealInternalGetMessage+0xc5a
                          win32kfull!NtUserGetMessage+0x8c
                          win32k!NtUserGetMessage+0x16
                          nt!KiSystemServiceCopyEnd+0x25
                          win32u!NtUserGetMessage+0x14
                          user32!GetMessageW+0x2e
                          edgehtml!WorkerGlobalScopeThread::RunMessageLoopForSTA+0x29
                          edgehtml!WorkerGlobalScopeThread::RunMessageLoop+0x6e
                          edgehtml!WorkerGlobalScopeThread::RunWorkerGlobalScope+0x74
                          edgehtml!WorkerGlobalScopeThread::RunThread+0x7f
                          edgehtml!WorkerGlobalScopeThread::ThreadProc+0x1f
                          KERNEL32!BaseThreadInitThunk+0x10
                          ntdll!RtlUserThreadStart+0x2b


Threads Processed: 2109
```

Note: However, if we try to search for *ReadConsole* input threads using the **!stacks** command, we would fail since the command doesn't switch to proper process context to show correct user space thread stacks, for example, having them truncated as highlighted in red for *conhost.exe* and *wordpad.exe*. In the output for *SearchHost.exe,* we accidentally have the correct stack trace because of the previous script that set the correct context for the last process in the list. To search for *ReadConsole* threads, we can use the MEX extension command:

```
0: kd> !mex.us -a ReadConsole
Unable to load image C:\Program Files\VMware\VMware Tools\glib-2.0.dll, Win32 error 0n2
Unable to load image C:\Program Files\VMware\VMware Tools\vmtoolsd.exe, Win32 error 0n2
Unable to load image C:\Program Files\VMware\VMware Tools\plugins\vmsvc\hwUpgradeHelper.dll, Win32 error 0n2
Unable to load image C:\ProgramData\Microsoft\Windows Defender\Definition Updates\{B3AF7FFC-0739-417C-99AE-
D5D78FD8A0CE}\mpengine.dll, Win32 error 0n2
Unable to load image c:\windows\system32\appxdeploymentserver.dll, Win32 error 0n2
Unable to load image C:\ProgramData\Microsoft\Windows Defender\Definition Updates\{B3AF7FFC-0739-417C-99AE-
D5D78FD8A0CE}\mpengine.dll, Win32 error 0n2
Unable to load image C:\ProgramData\Microsoft\Windows Defender\Scans\MsMpEngCP.exe, Win32 error 0n2
Unable to load image C:\Program Files\VMware\VMware Tools\plugins\vmusr\unity.dll, Win32 error 0n2
Unable to load image C:\Program Files\VMware\VMware Tools\plugins\vmusr\dndcp.dll, Win32 error 0n2
Unable to load image C:\Program Files\VMware\VMware Tools\plugins\vmusr\desktopEvents.dll, Win32 error 0n2
Unable to load image C:\Program Files\VMware\VMware Tools\glib-2.0.dll, Win32 error 0n2
Unable to load image C:\Windows\System32\vm3dservice.exe, Win32 error 0n2
Unable to load image C:\Users\dumpa\AppData\Local\Microsoft\OneDrive\22.002.0103.0004\SyncEngine.DLL, Win32 error 0n2
Unable to load image C:\Users\dumpa\AppData\Local\Microsoft\OneDrive\22.002.0103.0004\FileSyncClient.dll, Win32 error
0n2
Unable to load image C:\Users\dumpa\AppData\Local\Microsoft\OneDrive\22.002.0103.0004\OneDriveTelemetryStable.dll,
Win32 error 0n2
Unable to load image C:\Users\dumpa\AppData\Local\Microsoft\OneDrive\22.002.0103.0004\LoggingPlatform.dll, Win32 error
0n2
```

```
Unable to load image C:\Program Files (x86)\Microsoft\Edge\Application\97.0.1072.76\oneds.dll, Win32 error 0n2
Unable to load image C:\Program Files (x86)\Microsoft\Edge\Application\97.0.1072.76\msedge.dll, Win32 error 0n2
Unable to load image C:\Program Files (x86)\Microsoft\Edge\Application\msedge.exe, Win32 error 0n2
Unable to load image C:\Program Files (x86)\Microsoft\Edge\Application\msedge.exe, Win32 error 0n2
Unable to load image C:\Program Files (x86)\Microsoft\Edge\Application\msedge.exe, Win32 error 0n2
Unable to load image C:\Program Files (x86)\Microsoft\Edge\Application\msedge.exe, Win32 error 0n2
Unable to load image C:\Program Files (x86)\Microsoft\Edge\Application\msedge.exe, Win32 error 0n2
*** WARNING: Unable to verify checksum for Notepad.exe
Unable to load image C:\Program
Files\WindowsApps\Microsoft.WindowsCalculator_11.2110.4.0_x64__8wekyb3d8bbwe\CalculatorApp.dll, Win32 error 0n2
*** WARNING: Unable to verify checksum for CalculatorApp.dll
Unable to load image C:\Program Files
(x86)\Microsoft\EdgeWebView\Application\97.0.1072.76\EBWebView\x64\EmbeddedBrowserWebView.dll, Win32 error 0n2
*** WARNING: Unable to verify checksum for System.Windows.Forms.Primitives.dll
*** WARNING: Unable to verify checksum for System.Windows.Forms.dll
*** WARNING: Unable to verify checksum for Microsoft.Win32.SystemEvents.dll
Process: cmd.exe @ ffffbe0c8c9d3080
========================================================
1 thread: ffffbe0c8c9aa080
    fffff8076241dce6 nt!KiSwapContext+0x76
    fffff807623327f7 nt!KiSwapThread+0x3a7
    fffff8076233346a9 nt!KiCommitThreadWait+0x159
    fffff8076232e5c4 nt!KeWaitForSingleObject+0x234
    fffff8076276bd67 nt!IopSynchronousServiceTail+0x347
    fffff8076276b9d2 nt!IopXxxControlFile+0xc82
    fffff8076276ad36 nt!NtDeviceIoControlFile+0x56
    fffff80762428775 nt!KiSystemServiceCopyEnd+0x25
    00007ffe5b023834 ntdll!NtDeviceIoControlFile+0x14
    00007ffe58a25845 KERNELBASE!ConsoleCallServerGeneric+0xe9
    00007ffe58aad6bd KERNELBASE!ReadConsoleInternal+0x18d
    00007ffe58aad51a KERNELBASE!ReadConsoleW+0x1a
    00007ff66133ca6f cmd!ReadBufFromConsole+0x127
    00007ff661332202 cmd!FillBuf+0x11c82
    00007ff6613200fc cmd!Lex+0x4fc
    00007ff66131f2c6 cmd!GetToken+0x26
    00007ff66131f023 cmd!Parser+0x113
    00007ff66133384c cmd!main+0xf390
    00007ff6613298e1 cmd!__mainCRTStartup+0x161
    00007ffe5a2d54e0 KERNEL32!BaseThreadInitThunk+0x10
    00007ffe5af8485b ntdll!RtlUserThreadStart+0x2b

Threads matching filter: 1 out of 1

Unable to load image C:\Work\notmyfault64.exe, Win32 error 0n2
```

The command can also search for exception or bugcheck processing threads and also for non-waiting threads:

```
0: kd> !mex.us -a -crash
Unable to load image C:\Program Files\VMware\VMware Tools\glib-2.0.dll, Win32 error 0n2
Unable to load image C:\Program Files\VMware\VMware Tools\vmtoolsd.exe, Win32 error 0n2
Unable to load image C:\Program Files\VMware\VMware Tools\plugins\vmsvc\hwUpgradeHelper.dll, Win32 error 0n2
Unable to load image C:\ProgramData\Microsoft\Windows Defender\Definition Updates\{B3AF7FFC-0739-417C-99AE-D5D78FD8A0CE}\mpengine.dll, Win32 error 0n2
Unable to load image c:\windows\system32\appxdeploymentserver.dll, Win32 error 0n2
Unable to load image C:\ProgramData\Microsoft\Windows Defender\Definition Updates\{B3AF7FFC-0739-417C-99AE-D5D78FD8A0CE}\mpengine.dll, Win32 error 0n2
Unable to load image C:\ProgramData\Microsoft\Windows Defender\Scans\MsMpEngCP.exe, Win32 error 0n2
Unable to load image C:\Windows\System32\sppc.dll, Win32 error 0n2
Unable to load image C:\WINDOWS\SYSTEM32\SPPC.DLL, Win32 error 0n2
Unable to load image C:\Program Files\VMware\VMware Tools\plugins\vmusr\unity.dll, Win32 error 0n2
Unable to load image C:\Program Files\VMware\VMware Tools\plugins\vmusr\dndcp.dll, Win32 error 0n2
Unable to load image C:\Program Files\VMware\VMware Tools\plugins\vmusr\desktopEvents.dll, Win32 error 0n2
Unable to load image C:\Program Files\VMware\VMware Tools\glib-2.0.dll, Win32 error 0n2
Unable to load image C:\Windows\System32\vm3dservice.exe, Win32 error 0n2
Unable to load image C:\Users\dumpa\AppData\Local\Microsoft\OneDrive\22.002.0103.0004\SyncEngine.DLL, Win32 error 0n2
Unable to load image C:\Users\dumpa\AppData\Local\Microsoft\OneDrive\22.002.0103.0004\FileSyncClient.dll, Win32 error 0n2
Unable to load image C:\Users\dumpa\AppData\Local\Microsoft\OneDrive\22.002.0103.0004\OneDriveTelemetryStable.dll, Win32 error 0n2
Unable to load image C:\Users\dumpa\AppData\Local\Microsoft\OneDrive\22.002.0103.0004\LoggingPlatform.dll, Win32 error 0n2
Unable to load image C:\Program Files (x86)\Microsoft\Edge\Application\97.0.1072.76\oneds.dll, Win32 error 0n2
Unable to load image C:\Program Files (x86)\Microsoft\Edge\Application\97.0.1072.76\msedge.dll, Win32 error 0n2
Unable to load image C:\Program Files (x86)\Microsoft\Edge\Application\msedge.exe, Win32 error 0n2
Unable to load image C:\Program Files (x86)\Microsoft\Edge\Application\msedge.exe, Win32 error 0n2
Unable to load image C:\Program Files (x86)\Microsoft\Edge\Application\msedge.exe, Win32 error 0n2
Unable to load image C:\Program Files (x86)\Microsoft\Edge\Application\msedge.exe, Win32 error 0n2
Unable to load image C:\Program Files\WindowsApps\Microsoft.WindowsNotepad_10.2103.6.0_x64__8wekyb3d8bbwe\Notepad\Notepad.exe, Win32 error 0n2
*** WARNING: Unable to verify checksum for Notepad.exe
Unable to load image C:\Program Files\WindowsApps\Microsoft.WindowsCalculator_11.2110.4.0_x64__8wekyb3d8bbwe\CalculatorApp.dll, Win32 error 0n2
*** WARNING: Unable to verify checksum for CalculatorApp.dll
Unable to load image C:\Program Files (x86)\Microsoft\EdgeWebView\Application\97.0.1072.76\EBWebView\x64\EmbeddedBrowserWebView.dll, Win32 error 0n2
*** WARNING: Unable to verify checksum for System.Windows.Forms.Primitives.dll
*** WARNING: Unable to verify checksum for System.Windows.Forms.dll
```

```
Process: notmyfault64.exe @ ffffbe0c8c2cd0c0
================================================================
1 thread: ffffbe0c8974f080
    fffff80762416220 nt!KeBugCheckEx
    fffff80762428da9 nt!KiBugCheckDispatch+0x69
    fffff80762424f00 nt!KiPageFault+0x440
    fffff80761781530 myfault+0x1530
    fffff80761781e2d myfault+0x1e2d
    fffff80761781f88 myfault+0x1f88
    fffff80762303115 nt!IofCallDriver+0x55
    fffff8076276bbf2 nt!IopSynchronousServiceTail+0x1d2
    fffff8076276b9d2 nt!IopXxxControlFile+0xc82
    fffff8076276ad36 nt!NtDeviceIoControlFile+0x56
    fffff80762428775 nt!KiSystemServiceCopyEnd+0x25
    00007ffe5b023834 ntdll!NtDeviceIoControlFile+0x14
    00007ffe58a33ffb KERNELBASE!DeviceIoControl+0x6b
    00007ffe5a2d5f91 KERNEL32!DeviceIoControlImplementation+0x81
    00007ff72c0426ce notmyfault64+0x26ce
    00007ffe5901484b USER32!UserCallDlgProcCheckWow+0x14b
    00007ffe5901409b USER32!DefDlgProcWorker+0xcb
    00007ffe590597c9 USER32!DefDlgProcA+0x39
    00007ffe59011c4c USER32!UserCallWinProcCheckWow+0x33c
    00007ffe5901179c USER32!DispatchClientMessage+0x9c
    00007ffe59024b4d USER32!_fnDWORD+0x3d
    00007ffe5b0276a4 ntdll!KiUserCallbackDispatcherContinue
    00007ffe58d81434 win32u!NtUserMessageCall+0x14
    00007ffe590108cf USER32!SendMessageWorker+0x12f
    00007ffe59010737 USER32!SendMessageW+0x137
    00007ffe444750bf COMCTL32!Button_ReleaseCapture+0xbb
    00007ffe444a8822 COMCTL32!Button_WndProc+0x802
    00007ffe59011c4c USER32!UserCallWinProcCheckWow+0x33c
    00007ffe59010ea6 USER32!DispatchMessageWorker+0x2a6
    00007ffe59016084 USER32!IsDialogMessageW+0x104
    00007ffe44455f9f COMCTL32!Prop_IsDialogMessage+0x4b
    00007ffe44455e48 COMCTL32!_RealPropertySheet+0x2c0
    00007ffe44455abd COMCTL32!_PropertySheet+0x49
    00007ffe44520953 COMCTL32!PropertySheetA+0x53
    00007ff72c043415 notmyfault64+0x3415
    00007ff72c045c68 notmyfault64+0x5c68
    00007ffe5a2d54e0 KERNEL32!BaseThreadInitThunk+0x10
    00007ffe5af8485b ntdll!RtlUserThreadStart+0x2b

Threads matching filter: 1 out of 3

0: kd> !mex.us -a -nw
Process: Idle @ fffff80762d32b00
==============================================================
2 threads: ffffbe0c84178080 ffffbe0c841ab080
    fffff8076241dce6 nt!KiSwapContext+0x76
    fffff807623327f7 nt!KiSwapThread+0x3a7
    fffff807623be9ac nt!KiExecuteDpcDelegate+0x5c
    fffff8076241a2d4 nt!KiStartSystemThread+0x34

Threads matching filter: 2 out of 4

Process: System @ ffffbe0c840eb040
==============================================================
1 thread: ffffbe0c8ac5c080
    fffff8076241df31 nt!KxDispatchInterrupt+0x151
    fffff8076241d3b6 nt!KiDpcInterrupt+0x326
    fffff807626ccc61 nt!PfTCreateTraceDump+0x1c1
```

```
        fffff807626cca66 nt!PfTGenerateTrace+0x16
        fffff8076286b763 nt!PfTLoggingWorker+0x183
        fffff807622478f5 nt!PspSystemThreadStartup+0x55
        fffff8076241a2d4 nt!KiStartSystemThread+0x34


2 threads: ffffbe0c84167080 ffffbe0c841de080
        fffff8076241dce6 nt!KiSwapContext+0x76
        fffff807623327f7 nt!KiSwapThread+0x3a7
        fffff807623346a9 nt!KiCommitThreadWait+0x159
        fffff807622548cf nt!KeWaitForGate+0xcf
        fffff807623c7222 nt!KiExecuteDpc+0x92
        fffff807622478f5 nt!PspSystemThreadStartup+0x55
        fffff8076241a2d4 nt!KiStartSystemThread+0x34


28 threads: ffffbe0c84153080 ffffbe0c84b47040 ffffbe0c84b44040 ffffbe0c841a7040 ffffbe0c8477e080 ffffbe0c89aed040
ffffbe0c8974a040 ffffbe0c87d4c040 ffffbe0c898ca040 ffffbe0c8c0dd040 ...
        fffff8076241dce6 nt!KiSwapContext+0x76
        fffff807623327f7 nt!KiSwapThread+0x3a7
        fffff807623346a9 nt!KiCommitThreadWait+0x159
        fffff8076231d989 nt!KeRemovePriQueue+0x259
        fffff8076231d2e3 nt!ExpWorkerThread+0xd3
        fffff807622478f5 nt!PspSystemThreadStartup+0x55
        fffff8076241a2d4 nt!KiStartSystemThread+0x34


Threads matching filter: 31 out of 136


Process: dwm.exe @ ffffbe0c89120080
================================================================
1 thread: ffffbe0c89190080
        00007ffe552d2700 CoreMessaging!AlpcClientConnection::PendingPortCheck
        00007ffe552d22e4 CoreMessaging!`CFlat::DelegateImpl<System::Action,0,void
__cdecl(void),void,0>::Bind<CFlat::SmartPtr<Microsoft::CoreUI::Messaging::CrossProcessReceivePort$AlpcReceiveSource>,&
Microsoft::CoreUI::Messaging::CrossProcessReceivePort$AlpcReceiveSource::ScheduleReceiveIfNeeded>'::`2'::Thunk::Invoke
+0x24
        00007ffe552aae27 CoreMessaging!CFlat::DelegateImpl<System::Action,0,void
__cdecl(void),void,0>::MulticastInvoke+0x47
        00007ffe552ca6f6 CoreMessaging!Microsoft::CoreUI::Dispatch::EventLoop::CallYieldCheckHandler+0xa2
        00007ffe552ff321 CoreMessaging!Microsoft::CoreUI::Dispatch::Dispatcher::PeekNextItem+0x26355
        00007ffe552aa4bd CoreMessaging!Microsoft::CoreUI::Dispatch::EventLoop::Callback_RunCoreLoop+0x1ed
        00007ffe552a70ba CoreMessaging!Microsoft::CoreUI::Dispatch::Win32EventLoopBridge::Callback_Run+0x41a
        00007ffe552d280e CoreMessaging!Microsoft::CoreUI::Dispatch::EventLoop::Callback_Run+0xae
        00007ffe55290dcf CoreMessaging!Microsoft::CoreUI::IExportMessageLoopExtensions::ExportAdapter$::Run+0x19f
        00007ffe54e698c9 dwmcore!CComposition::ProcessBatches+0xb1
        00007ffe54e6999b dwmcore!CComposition::PreRender+0x77
        00007ffe54e691c2 dwmcore!CComposition::ProcessComposition+0x4a
        00007ffe54e682c7 dwmcore!CPartitionVerticalBlankScheduler::Render+0x5b
        00007ffe54e67876 dwmcore!CPartitionVerticalBlankScheduler::ProcessFrame+0x102
        00007ffe54e6684f dwmcore!CPartitionVerticalBlankScheduler::ScheduleAndProcessFrame+0x8f
        00007ffe54eed3a6 dwmcore!CConnection::MainCompositionThreadLoop+0xba
        00007ffe54eed2d6 dwmcore!CConnection::RunCompositionThread+0xfa
        00007ffe5a2d54e0 KERNEL32!BaseThreadInitThunk+0x10
        00007ffe5af8485b ntdll!RtlUserThreadStart+0x2b


Threads matching filter: 1 out of 17
3 stack(s) were not displayed because we could not switch to thread context, or stack trace was empty


Process: explorer.exe @ ffffbe0c8a455080
================================================================
1 thread: ffffbe0c8a5dd080
        fffff8076241df31 nt!KxDispatchInterrupt+0x151
        fffff8076241d5d5 nt!KiDpcInterruptBypass+0x25
        fffff80762418471 nt!KiInterruptDispatchNoLockNoEtw+0xb1
        fffff807624285d5 nt!KiSystemServiceUser+0xbb
        00007ffe5b027104 ntdll!NtTraceControl+0x14
        00007ffe5afde2e7 ntdll!EtwEventActivityIdControl+0x87
        00007ffe566a1c26 windows_storage!SHILAliasTranslate+0x1c6
        00007ffe56b5655b windows_storage!SHLogILFromFSIL+0x1b
        00007ffe3223a43a windows_storage_search!CGrepQuery::_IsNotExcludedFolder+0x8a
        00007ffe3223a7c8 windows_storage_search!CGrepQuery::_ShouldCrawlItem+0xfc
        00007ffe322390fd windows_storage_search!CGrepQuery::_CheckRecurseIntoFolder+0x15
        00007ffe321feec3 windows_storage_search!CGrepQuery::CrawlForNextItemImpl+0x321e3
        00007ffe321f882d windows_storage_search!TestHook_GrepQuery_CrawlForNextItem+0x1d
        00007ffe321f863d windows_storage_search!CGrepQuery::CrawlForNextItem+0x1d
        00007ffe321ef419 windows_storage_search!CGrepRowset::GetRowsAt+0x69
```

```
00007ffe321e30d9  windows_storage_search!CQueryResultSet::FetchResultAt+0x119
00007ffe321d6018  windows_storage_search!CRowsetEnumeration::_EnumerateRowset+0x158
00007ffe3224151e  windows_storage_search!<lambda_1ed3756976052670480a11bef8ae9396>::operator()+0x7a
00007ffe59fa4ead  shcore!WorkThreadManager::CThread::ThreadProc+0x2dd
00007ffe59fa2a7e  shcore!WorkThreadManager::CThread::s_ExecuteThreadProc+0x22
00007ffe59fc9289  shcore!<lambda_142c425290ac4fbd4d5aee2fc3f7d711>::<lambda_invoker_cdecl>+0x29
00007ffe5afa1323  ntdll!TppSimplepExecuteCallback+0xa3
00007ffe5af96fd6  ntdll!TppWorkerThread+0x686
00007ffe5a2d54e0  KERNEL32!BaseThreadInitThunk+0x10
00007ffe5af8485b  ntdll!RtlUserThreadStart+0x2b

1 thread: ffffbe0c8c9c7080
    fffff8076241df31  nt!KxDispatchInterrupt+0x151
    fffff8076241d3b6  nt!KiDpcInterrupt+0x326
    fffff8076232d060  nt!KeLeaveCriticalRegion
    ffffbc928e134a0d  win32kbase!REGION::vDeleteREGION+0x21d
    ffffbc928e14ecd5  win32kbase!DC::iCombine+0x545
    ffffbc928e14e516  win32kbase!GreIntersectClipRect+0x486
    ffffbc928e7bf933  win32kfull!NtGdiIntersectClipRect+0x13
    ffffbc928dc4d4f4  win32k!NtGdiIntersectClipRect+0x20
    fffff80762428775  nt!KiSystemServiceCopyEnd+0x25
    00007ffe58d81754  win32u!NtGdiIntersectClipRect+0x14
    00007ffe58900f02  gdi32full!IntersectClipRectImpl+0x52
    00007ffe5575562a  UxTheme!DrawThemeParentBackgroundEx+0x29a
    00007ffe3bb5ac9e  explorerframe!CBreadcrumbBar::_WndProc+0x1ae
    00007ffe3bb5aa51  explorerframe!CBreadcrumbBar::s_BreadcrumbWndProc+0x71
    00007ffe59011c4c  user32!UserCallWinProcCheckWow+0x33c
    00007ffe5901179c  user32!DispatchClientMessage+0x9c
    00007ffe59024b4d  user32!_fnDWORD+0x3d
    00007ffe5b0276a4  ntdll!KiUserCallbackDispatcherContinue
    00007ffe58d81434  win32u!NtUserMessageCall+0x14
    00007ffe590108cf  user32!SendMessageWorker+0x12f
    00007ffe59010737  user32!SendMessageW+0x137
    00007ffe5575553b  UxTheme!DrawThemeParentBackgroundEx+0x1ab
    00007ffe3bb5af2b  explorerframe!CBreadcrumbBar::_WndProc+0x43b
    00007ffe3bb5aa51  explorerframe!CBreadcrumbBar::s_BreadcrumbWndProc+0x71
    00007ffe59011c4c  user32!UserCallWinProcCheckWow+0x33c
    00007ffe5901179c  user32!DispatchClientMessage+0x9c
    00007ffe59024b4d  user32!_fnDWORD+0x3d
    00007ffe5b0276a4  ntdll!KiUserCallbackDispatcherContinue
    00007ffe58d81434  win32u!NtUserMessageCall+0x14
    00007ffe590108cf  user32!SendMessageWorker+0x12f
    00007ffe59010737  user32!SendMessageW+0x137
    00007ffe4449fa4d  comctl32!CCSendNotify+0x11d
    00007ffe444a2070  comctl32!CToolbar::TB_DrawBackground+0x48
    00007ffe444a1f2f  comctl32!CToolbar::TBPaintImpl+0x6f
    00007ffe444a22f8  comctl32!CToolbar::TBPaint+0x1c0
    00007ffe4449651e  comctl32!CToolbar::ToolbarWndProc+0x39e
    00007ffe44496094  comctl32!CToolbar::s_ToolbarWndProc+0x54
    00007ffe59011c4c  user32!UserCallWinProcCheckWow+0x33c
    00007ffe5901189e  user32!CallWindowProcW+0x8e
    00007ffe444b48a8  comctl32!CallNextSubclassProc+0xa8
    00007ffe444b47d8  comctl32!DefSubclassProc+0x88
    00007ffe3bba403f  explorerframe!CBreadcrumbBar::_TBWndProc+0x6f
    00007ffe444b48a8  comctl32!CallNextSubclassProc+0xa8
    00007ffe444b4697  comctl32!MasterSubclassProc+0xa7
    00007ffe59011c4c  user32!UserCallWinProcCheckWow+0x33c
    00007ffe5901179c  user32!DispatchClientMessage+0x9c
    00007ffe59024b4d  user32!_fnDWORD+0x3d
    00007ffe5b0276a4  ntdll!KiUserCallbackDispatcherContinue
    00007ffe58d819b4  win32u!NtUserDispatchMessage+0x14
    00007ffe59010edd  user32!DispatchMessageWorker+0x2dd
    00007ffe3bba4671  explorerframe!CExplorerFrame::FrameMessagePump+0x101
    00007ffe3bb78bac  explorerframe!BrowserThreadProc+0x90
    00007ffe3bb78c78  explorerframe!BrowserNewThreadProc+0x4c
    00007ffe3bb78ce2  explorerframe!CExplorerTask::InternalResumeRT+0x12
    00007ffe3bbb453e  explorerframe!CRunnableTask::Run+0xce
    00007ffe5678515e  windows_storage!CShellTask::TT_Run+0x46
    00007ffe56784d95  windows_storage!CShellTaskThread::ThreadProc+0xdd
    00007ffe56784a34  windows_storage!CShellTaskThread::s_ThreadProc+0x44
    00007ffe59fc4e9f  shcore!_WrapperThreadProc+0x10f
    00007ffe5a2d54e0  KERNEL32!BaseThreadInitThunk+0x10
    00007ffe5af8485b  ntdll!RtlUserThreadStart+0x2b
```

```
Threads matching filter: 2 out of 116

Process: SearchHost.exe @ ffffbe0c8a982080
===============================================================
2 threads: ffffbe0c8ab3a080 ffffbe0c89cfc080
    fffff8076241dce6 nt!KiSwapContext+0x76
    fffff807623327f7 nt!KiSwapThread+0x3a7
    fffff8076233346a9 nt!KiCommitThreadWait+0x159
    fffff80762254fa4 nt!KeWaitForAlertByThreadId+0xc4
    fffff807626c72a0 nt!NtWaitForAlertByThreadId+0x30
    fffff80762428775 nt!KiSystemServiceCopyEnd+0x25
    00007ffe5b0272a4 0x7ffe5b0272a4

Threads matching filter: 2 out of 60

Unable to load image C:\Work\notmyfault64.exe, Win32 error 0n2
Process: notmyfault64.exe @ ffffbe0c8c2cd0c0
===============================================================
1 thread: ffffbe0c8974f080
    fffff80762416220 nt!KeBugCheckEx
    fffff80762428da9 nt!KiBugCheckDispatch+0x69
    fffff80762424f00 nt!KiPageFault+0x440
    fffff80761781530 myfault+0x1530
    fffff80761781e2d myfault+0x1e2d
    fffff80761781f88 myfault+0x1f88
    fffff80762303115 nt!IofCallDriver+0x55
    fffff8076276bbf2 nt!IopSynchronousServiceTail+0x1d2
    fffff8076276b9d2 nt!IopXxxControlFile+0xc82
    fffff8076276ad36 nt!NtDeviceIoControlFile+0x56
    fffff80762428775 nt!KiSystemServiceCopyEnd+0x25
    00007ffe5b023834 ntdll!NtDeviceIoControlFile+0x14
    00007ffe58a33ffb KERNELBASE!DeviceIoControl+0x6b
    00007ffe5a2d5f91 KERNEL32!DeviceIoControlImplementation+0x81
    00007ff72c0426ce notmyfault64+0x26ce
    00007ffe5901484b USER32!UserCallDlgProcCheckWow+0x14b
    00007ffe5901409b USER32!DefDlgProcWorker+0xcb
    00007ffe590597c9 USER32!DefDlgProcA+0x39
    00007ffe59011c4c USER32!UserCallWinProcCheckWow+0x33c
    00007ffe5901179c USER32!DispatchClientMessage+0x9c
    00007ffe59024b4d USER32!_fnDWORD+0x3d
    00007ffe5b0276a4 ntdll!KiUserCallbackDispatcherContinue
    00007ffe58d81434 win32u!NtUserMessageCall+0x14
    00007ffe590108cf USER32!SendMessageWorker+0x12f
    00007ffe59010737 USER32!SendMessageW+0x137
    00007ffe444750bf COMCTL32!Button_ReleaseCapture+0xbb
    00007ffe444a8822 COMCTL32!Button_WndProc+0x802
    00007ffe59011c4c USER32!UserCallWinProcCheckWow+0x33c
    00007ffe59010ea6 USER32!DispatchMessageWorker+0x2a6
    00007ffe59016084 USER32!IsDialogMessageW+0x104
    00007ffe44455f9f COMCTL32!Prop_IsDialogMessage+0x4b
    00007ffe44455e48 COMCTL32!_RealPropertySheet+0x2c0
    00007ffe44455abd COMCTL32!_PropertySheet+0x49
    00007ffe44520953 COMCTL32!PropertySheetA+0x53
    00007ff72c043415 notmyfault64+0x3415
    00007ff72c045c68 notmyfault64+0x5c68
    00007ffe5a2d54e0 KERNEL32!BaseThreadInitThunk+0x10
    00007ffe5af8485b ntdll!RtlUserThreadStart+0x2b

Threads matching filter: 1 out of 3
```

Note: The option **-a** searches all processes. For illustration, we sometimes omit it to search the current process of interest only if it takes too long otherwise.

12.   To see stack traces from threads running on CPUs, you can use these MEX extension commands:

```
0: kd> !mex.running
Process            PID  Thread              Id  Pri Base Pri Next CPU CSwitches   User Kernel State    Time Reason
================ ==== ================ ==== === ======== ======== ========= ====== ====== ======= ==== ===========
dwm.exe            310 ffffbe0c89190080  428  15        15        0     19997 5s.266 3s.625 Running 15ms UserRequest
notmyfault64.exe 243c ffffbe0c8974f080 1938  12         8        1      1701   16ms  125ms Running 15ms WrResource

Count: 2 | Show Unique Stacks
```

```
0: kd> !mex.us -cpu
1 thread: ffffbe0c89190080
    00007ffe552d2700 CoreMessaging!AlpcClientConnection::PendingPortCheck
    00007ffe552d22e4 CoreMessaging!`CFlat::DelegateImpl<System::Action,0,void
__cdecl(void),void,0>::Bind<CFlat::SmartPtr<Microsoft::CoreUI::Messaging::CrossProcessReceivePort$AlpcReceiveSource>,&
Microsoft::CoreUI::Messaging::CrossProcessReceivePort$AlpcReceiveSource::ScheduleReceiveIfNeeded>'::`2'::Thunk::Invoke
+0x24
    00007ffe552aae27 CoreMessaging!CFlat::DelegateImpl<System::Action,0,void
__cdecl(void),void,0>::MulticastInvoke+0x47
    00007ffe552ca6f6 CoreMessaging!Microsoft::CoreUI::Dispatch::EventLoop::CallYieldCheckHandler+0xa2
    00007ffe552ff321 CoreMessaging!Microsoft::CoreUI::Dispatch::Dispatcher::PeekNextItem+0x26355
    00007ffe552aa4bd CoreMessaging!Microsoft::CoreUI::Dispatch::EventLoop::Callback_RunCoreLoop+0x1ed
    00007ffe552a70ba CoreMessaging!Microsoft::CoreUI::Dispatch::Win32EventLoopBridge::Callback_Run+0x41a
    00007ffe552d280e CoreMessaging!Microsoft::CoreUI::Dispatch::EventLoop::Callback_Run+0xae
    00007ffe55290dcf CoreMessaging!Microsoft::CoreUI::IExportMessageLoopExtensions::ExportAdapter$::Run+0x19f
    00007ffe54e698c9 dwmcore!CComposition::ProcessBatches+0xb1
    00007ffe54e6999b dwmcore!CComposition::PreRender+0x77
    00007ffe54e691c2 dwmcore!CComposition::ProcessComposition+0x4a
    00007ffe54e682c7 dwmcore!CPartitionVerticalBlankScheduler::Render+0x5b
    00007ffe54e67876 dwmcore!CPartitionVerticalBlankScheduler::ProcessFrame+0x102
    00007ffe54e6684f dwmcore!CPartitionVerticalBlankScheduler::ScheduleAndProcessFrame+0x8f
    00007ffe54eed3a6 dwmcore!CConnection::MainCompositionThreadLoop+0xba
    00007ffe54eed2d6 dwmcore!CConnection::RunCompositionThread+0xfa
    00007ffe5a2d54e0 KERNEL32!BaseThreadInitThunk+0x10
    00007ffe5af8485b ntdll!RtlUserThreadStart+0x2b


1 thread: ffffbe0c8974f080
Unable to load image C:\Work\notmyfault64.exe, Win32 error 0n2
    fffff80762416220 nt!KeBugCheckEx
    fffff80762428da9 nt!KiBugCheckDispatch+0x69
    fffff80762424f00 nt!KiPageFault+0x440
    fffff80761781530 myfault+0x1530
    fffff80761781e2d myfault+0x1e2d
    fffff80761781f88 myfault+0x1f88
    fffff80762303115 nt!IofCallDriver+0x55
    fffff8076276bbf2 nt!IopSynchronousServiceTail+0x1d2
    fffff8076276b9d2 nt!IopXxxControlFile+0xc82
    fffff80762476ad36 nt!NtDeviceIoControlFile+0x56
    fffff80762428775 nt!KiSystemServiceCopyEnd+0x25
    00007ffe5b023834 ntdll!NtDeviceIoControlFile+0x14
    00007ffe58a33ffb KERNELBASE!DeviceIoControl+0x6b
    00007ffe5a2d5f91 KERNEL32!DeviceIoControlImplementation+0x81
    00007ff72c0426ce notmyfault64+0x26ce
    00007ffe5901484b USER32!UserCallDlgProcCheckWow+0x14b
    00007ffe5901409b USER32!DefDlgProcWorker+0xcb
    00007ffe590597c9 USER32!DefDlgProcA+0x39
    00007ffe59011c4c USER32!UserCallWinProcCheckWow+0x33c
    00007ffe5901179c USER32!DispatchClientMessage+0x9c
    00007ffe59024b4d USER32!_fnDWORD+0x3d
    00007ffe5b0276a4 ntdll!KiUserCallbackDispatcherContinue
    00007ffe58d81434 win32u!NtUserMessageCall+0x14
    00007ffe590108cf USER32!SendMessageWorker+0x12f
    00007ffe59010737 USER32!SendMessageW+0x137
    00007ffe444750bf COMCTL32!Button_ReleaseCapture+0xbb
    00007ffe444a8822 COMCTL32!Button_WndProc+0x802
    00007ffe59011c4c USER32!UserCallWinProcCheckWow+0x33c
    00007ffe59010ea6 USER32!DispatchMessageWorker+0x2a6
    00007ffe59016084 USER32!IsDialogMessageW+0x104
    00007ffe44455f9f COMCTL32!Prop_IsDialogMessage+0x4b
    00007ffe44455e48 COMCTL32!_RealPropertySheet+0x2c0
    00007ffe44455abd COMCTL32!_PropertySheet+0x49
    00007ffe44520953 COMCTL32!PropertySheetA+0x53
```

```
00007ff72c043415 notmyfault64+0x3415
00007ff72c045c68 notmyfault64+0x5c68
00007ffe5a2d54e0 KERNEL32!BaseThreadInitThunk+0x10
00007ffe5af8485b ntdll!RtlUserThreadStart+0x2b
```

2 stack(s) with 2 threads displayed (2 Total threads)

Note: We use the **!mex.running** command to differentiate it from the preloaded **!kdexts.running** command:

```
0: kd> ~1s
```

```
1: kd> .thread /r /p
```

```
1: kd> !kdexts.running
```

```
System Processors:  (0000000000000003)
  Idle Processors:  (0000000000000000)


      Prcbs             Current          (pri) Next          (pri) Idle
 0    fffff807604e6180  ffffbe0c89190080 (15)                      fffff80762d35bc0  ................
 1    ffffce00fb700180  ffffbe0c8974f080 (12)                      ffffce00fb70c0c0  ................
```

Note: However, the default running command has problems loading the correct user space context for non-current processes (the **-i** option is included to list idle threads as well, if any):

```
1: kd> !kdexts.running -t -i
```

```
System Processors:  (0000000000000003)
  Idle Processors:  (0000000000000000)


      Prcbs             Current          (pri) Next          (pri) Idle
 0    fffff807604e6180  ffffbe0c89190080 (15)                      fffff80762d35bc0  ................

# Child-SP          RetAddr           Call Site
00 0000005b`47eff318 00007ffe`552d22e4 CoreMessaging!AlpcClientConnection::PendingPortCheck
01 0000005b`47eff320 00007ffe`552aae27 CoreMessaging!`CFlat::DelegateImpl<System::Action,0,void
__cdecl(void),void,0>::Bind<CFlat::SmartPtr<Microsoft::CoreUI::Messaging::CrossProcessReceivePort$AlpcReceiveSource>,&Microsoft::CoreUI
::Messaging::CrossProcessReceivePort$AlpcReceiveSource::ScheduleReceiveIfNeeded>'::`2'::Thunk::Invoke+0x24
02 0000005b`47eff350 00007ffe`552ca6f6 CoreMessaging!CFlat::DelegateImpl<System::Action,0,void
__cdecl(void),void,0>::MulticastInvoke+0x47
03 0000005b`47eff380 00007ffe`552ff321 CoreMessaging!Microsoft::CoreUI::Dispatch::EventLoop::CallYieldCheckHandler+0xa2
04 0000005b`47eff3b0 00007ffe`552aa4bd CoreMessaging!Microsoft::CoreUI::Dispatch::Dispatcher::PeekNextItem+0x26355
05 0000005b`47eff3e0 00007ffe`552a70ba CoreMessaging!Microsoft::CoreUI::Dispatch::EventLoop::Callback_RunCoreLoop+0x1ed
06 0000005b`47eff4a0 00007ffe`552d280e CoreMessaging!Microsoft::CoreUI::Dispatch::Win32EventLoopBridge::Callback_Run+0x41a
07 0000005b`47eff550 00007ffe`55290dcf CoreMessaging!Microsoft::CoreUI::Dispatch::EventLoop::Callback_Run+0xae
08 0000005b`47eff590 00007ffe`54e698c9 CoreMessaging!Microsoft::CoreUI::IExportMessageLoopExtensions::ExportAdapter$::Run+0x19f
09 0000005b`47eff600 00000000`00000001 0x00007ffe`54e698c9
0a 0000005b`47eff608 00000000`00000003 0x1
0b 0000005b`47eff610 00007ffe`54e698c9 0x3
0c 0000005b`47eff618 0000018f`4003e340 0x00007ffe`54e698c9
0d 0000005b`47eff620 0000a68b`a6149684 0x0000018f`4003e340
0e 0000005b`47eff628 0000018f`4003ea10 0x0000a68b`a6149684
0f 0000005b`47eff630 0000018f`4003ea10 0x0000018f`4003ea10
10 0000005b`47eff638 00007ffe`54e6999b 0x0000018f`4003ea10
11 0000005b`47eff640 0000018f`40038e00 0x00007ffe`54e6999b
12 0000005b`47eff648 00000000`00000040 0x0000018f`40038e00
13 0000005b`47eff650 00000000`00000000 0x40


 1    ffffce00fb700180  ffffbe0c8974f080 (12)                      ffffce00fb70c0c0  ................

# Child-SP          RetAddr           Call Site
00 ffffa28c`9d8d8688 fffff807`62428da9 nt!KeBugCheckEx
01 ffffa28c`9d8d8690 fffff807`62424f00 nt!KiBugCheckDispatch+0x69
02 ffffa28c`9d8d87d0 fffff807`61781530 nt!KiPageFault+0x440
03 ffffa28c`9d8d8960 fffff807`61781e2d myfault+0x1530
04 ffffa28c`9d8d8990 fffff807`61781f88 myfault+0x1e2d
05 ffffa28c`9d8d8ae0 fffff807`62303115 myfault+0x1f88
06 ffffa28c`9d8d8b20 fffff807`6276bbf2 nt!IofCallDriver+0x55
07 ffffa28c`9d8d8b60 fffff807`6276b9d2 nt!IopSynchronousServiceTail+0x1d2
08 ffffa28c`9d8d8c10 fffff807`6276ad36 nt!IopXxxControlFile+0xc82
09 ffffa28c`9d8d8d40 fffff807`62428775 nt!NtDeviceIoControlFile+0x56
0a ffffa28c`9d8d8db0 00007ffe`5b023834 nt!KiSystemServiceCopyEnd+0x25
0b 00000034`f5d2eb88 00007ffe`58a33ffb ntdll!NtDeviceIoControlFile+0x14
0c 00000034`f5d2eb90 00007ffe`5a2d5f91 KERNELBASE!DeviceIoControl+0x6b
```

```
0d 00000034`f5d2ec00 00007ff7`2c0426ce     KERNEL32!DeviceIoControlImplementation+0x81
0e 00000034`f5d2ec50 00007ffe`5901484b     notmyfault64+0x26ce
0f 00000034`f5d2ed50 00007ffe`5901409b     USER32!UserCallDlgProcCheckWow+0x14b
10 00000034`f5d2ee30 00007ffe`590597c9     USER32!DefDlgProcWorker+0xcb
11 00000034`f5d2eef0 00007ffe`59011c4c     USER32!DefDlgProcA+0x39
12 00000034`f5d2ef30 00007ffe`5901179c     USER32!UserCallWinProcCheckWow+0x33c
13 00000034`f5d2f0a0 00007ffe`59024b4d     USER32!DispatchClientMessage+0x9c
14 00000034`f5d2f100 00007ffe`5b0276a4     USER32!_fnDWORD+0x3d
15 00000034`f5d2f160 00007ffe`58d81434     ntdll!KiUserCallbackDispatcherContinue
16 00000034`f5d2f1e8 00007ffe`590108cf     win32u!NtUserMessageCall+0x14
17 00000034`f5d2f1f0 00007ffe`59010737     USER32!SendMessageWorker+0x12f
18 00000034`f5d2f290 00007ffe`444750bf     USER32!SendMessageW+0x137
19 00000034`f5d2f2f0 00007ffe`444a8822     COMCTL32!Button_ReleaseCapture+0xbb
1a 00000034`f5d2f320 00007ffe`59011c4c     COMCTL32!Button_WndProc+0x802
1b 00000034`f5d2f430 00007ffe`59010ea6     USER32!UserCallWinProcCheckWow+0x33c
1c 00000034`f5d2f5a0 00007ffe`59016084     USER32!DispatchMessageWorker+0x2a6
1d 00000034`f5d2f620 00007ffe`44455f9f     USER32!IsDialogMessageW+0x104
1e 00000034`f5d2f680 00007ffe`44455e48     COMCTL32!Prop_IsDialogMessage+0x4b
1f 00000034`f5d2f6c0 00007ffe`44455abd     COMCTL32!_RealPropertySheet+0x2c0
20 00000034`f5d2f790 00007ffe`44520953     COMCTL32!_PropertySheet+0x49
21 00000034`f5d2f7c0 00007ff7`2c043415     COMCTL32!PropertySheetA+0x53
22 00000034`f5d2f860 00007ff7`2c045c68     notmyfault64+0x3415
23 00000034`f5d2fa90 00007ffe`5a2d54e0     notmyfault64+0x5c68
24 00000034`f5d2fad0 00007ffe`5af8485b     KERNEL32!BaseThreadInitThunk+0x10
25 00000034`f5d2fb00 00000000`00000000     ntdll!RtlUserThreadStart+0x2b
```

```
1: kd> ~0s
```

```
0: kd> .reload /user
Loading User Symbols
..........................................................
...................

************* Symbol Loading Error Summary **************
Module name          Error
myfault              The system cannot find the file specified

You can troubleshoot most symbol related issues by turning on symbol loading diagnostics (!sym noisy) and
repeating the command that caused symbols to be loaded.
You should also verify that your symbol search path (.sympath) is correct.
```

```
0: kd> !kdexts.running -t -i

System Processors:  (0000000000000003)
  Idle Processors:  (0000000000000000)

      Prcbs            Current           (pri) Next           (pri) Idle
  0   fffff807604e6180 ffffbe0c89190080 (15)                        fffff80762d35bc0 ...............

  # Child-SP          RetAddr              Call Site
  00 0000005b`47eff318 00007ffe`552d22e4  CoreMessaging!AlpcClientConnection::PendingPortCheck
  01 0000005b`47eff320 00007ffe`552aae27  CoreMessaging!`CFlat::DelegateImpl<System::Action,0,void
  __cdecl(void),void,0>::Bind<CFlat::SmartPtr<Microsoft::CoreUI::Messaging::CrossProcessReceivePort$AlpcReceiveSource>,&Microsoft::CoreUI
  ::Messaging::CrossProcessReceivePort$AlpcReceiveSource::ScheduleReceiveIfNeeded>'::`2'::Thunk::Invoke+0x24
  02 0000005b`47eff350 00007ffe`552ca6f6  CoreMessaging!CFlat::DelegateImpl<System::Action,0,void
  __cdecl(void),void,0>::MulticastInvoke+0x47
  03 0000005b`47eff380 00007ffe`552ff321  CoreMessaging!Microsoft::CoreUI::Dispatch::EventLoop::CallYieldCheckHandler+0xa2
  04 0000005b`47eff3b0 00007ffe`552aa4bd  CoreMessaging!Microsoft::CoreUI::Dispatch::Dispatcher::PeekNextItem+0x26355
  05 0000005b`47eff3e0 00007ffe`552a70ba  CoreMessaging!Microsoft::CoreUI::Dispatch::EventLoop::Callback_RunCoreLoop+0x1ed
  06 0000005b`47eff4a0 00007ffe`552d280e  CoreMessaging!Microsoft::CoreUI::Dispatch::Win32EventLoopBridge::Callback_Run+0x41a
  07 0000005b`47eff550 00007ffe`55290dcf  CoreMessaging!Microsoft::CoreUI::Dispatch::EventLoop::Callback_Run+0xae
  08 0000005b`47eff590 00007ffe`54e698c9  CoreMessaging!Microsoft::CoreUI::IExportMessageLoopExtensions::ExportAdapter$::Run+0x19f
  09 0000005b`47eff600 00007ffe`54e6999b  dwmcore!CComposition::ProcessBatches+0xb1
  0a 0000005b`47eff640 00007ffe`54e691c2  dwmcore!CComposition::PreRender+0x77
  0b 0000005b`47eff6d0 00007ffe`54e682c7  dwmcore!CComposition::ProcessComposition+0x4a
  0c 0000005b`47eff770 00007ffe`54e67876  dwmcore!CPartitionVerticalBlankScheduler::Render+0x5b
  0d 0000005b`47eff7d0 00007ffe`54e6684f  dwmcore!CPartitionVerticalBlankScheduler::ProcessFrame+0x102
  0e 0000005b`47eff870 00007ffe`54eed3a6  dwmcore!CPartitionVerticalBlankScheduler::ScheduleAndProcessFrame+0x8f
  0f 0000005b`47eff990 00007ffe`54eed2d6  dwmcore!CConnection::MainCompositionThreadLoop+0xba
  10 0000005b`47effa00 00007ffe`5a2d54e0  dwmcore!CConnection::RunCompositionThread+0xfa
  11 0000005b`47effa30 00007ffe`5af8485b  KERNEL32!BaseThreadInitThunk+0x10
  12 0000005b`47effa60 00000000`00000000  ntdll!RtlUserThreadStart+0x2b

  1   ffffce00fb700180 ffffbe0c8974f080 (12)                        ffffce00fb70c0c0 ...............

  # Child-SP          RetAddr              Call Site
  00 ffffa28c`9d8d8688 fffff807`62428da9  nt!KeBugCheckEx
  01 ffffa28c`9d8d8690 fffff807`62424f00  nt!KiBugCheckDispatch+0x69
  02 ffffa28c`9d8d87d0 fffff807`61781530  nt!KiPageFault+0x440
```

```
03 ffffa28c`9d8d8960 fffff807`61781e2d    myfault+0x1530
04 ffffa28c`9d8d8990 fffff807`61781f88    myfault+0x1e2d
05 ffffa28c`9d8d8ae0 fffff807`62303115    myfault+0x1f88
06 ffffa28c`9d8d8b20 fffff807`6276bbf2    nt!IofCallDriver+0x55
07 ffffa28c`9d8d8b60 fffff807`6276b9d2    nt!IopSynchronousServiceTail+0x1d2
08 ffffa28c`9d8d8c10 fffff807`6276ad36    nt!IopXxxControlFile+0xc82
09 ffffa28c`9d8d8d40 fffff807`62428775    nt!NtDeviceIoControlFile+0x56
0a ffffa28c`9d8d8db0 00007ffe`5b023834    nt!KiSystemServiceCopyEnd+0x25
0b 00000034`f5d2eb88 00007ffe`58a33ffb    ntdll!NtDeviceIoControlFile+0x14
0c 00000034`f5d2eb90 00007ffe`5a2d5f91    KERNELBASE!DeviceIoControl+0x6b
0d 00000034`f5d2ec00 00007ff7`2c0426ce    KERNEL32!DeviceIoControlImplementation+0x81
0e 00000034`f5d2ec50 00000000`0004086e    0x00007ff7`2c0426ce
0f 00000034`f5d2ec58 00000034`f5d2ece9    0x4086e
10 00000034`f5d2ec60 00000034`f5d2ece9    0x00000034`f5d2ece9
11 00000034`f5d2ec68 00000000`00000000    0x00000034`f5d2ece9
```

Note: Mex **!UniqueStacks** (**!us**) and **!ForEachMatchingStack** (**!fems**) commands have many options to list and filter stack traces. Use the **-?** option to see their description.

13.   We can also use regular expressions for stack traces, treating them as a multiline string (**-m**):

```
0: kd> ~1s
```

```
1: kd> .thread /r /p
Implicit thread is now ffffbe0c`8974f080
Implicit process is now ffffbe0c`8c2cd0c0
Loading User Symbols
...............................

************* Symbol Loading Error Summary **************
Module name         Error
vsock               The system cannot find the file specified
vmci                The system cannot find the file specified
WdFilter            The system cannot find the file specified
vm3dmp              The system cannot find the file specified
vmmemctl            The system cannot find the file specified
vmhgfs              The system cannot find the file specified
myfault             The system cannot find the file specified
```

You can troubleshoot most symbol related issues by turning on symbol loading diagnostics (!sym noisy) and repeating the command that caused symbols to be loaded.
You should also verify that your symbol search path (.sympath) is correct.

```
1: kd> !mex.us -m (.*)BugCheck(.*)PageFault(.*)
Threads matching filter: 0 out of 3
```

```
0: kd> !mex.us -m (.*)BugCheck(.*)PageFault(.*)
1 thread [stats]: ffffc38c33ac3080
    fffff80662215590 nt!KeBugCheckEx
    fffff806622281a9 nt!KiBugCheckDispatch+0x69
    fffff80662224300 nt!KiPageFault+0x440
    fffff80660571981 myfault+0x1981
    fffff80660571d3d myfault+0x1d3d
    fffff80660571ea1 myfault+0x1ea1
    fffff80662102f65 nt!IofCallDriver+0x55
    fffff8066256b532 nt!IopSynchronousServiceTail+0x1d2
    fffff8066256acbf nt!IopXxxControlFile+0x5df
    fffff8066256a6c6 nt!NtDeviceIoControlFile+0x56
    fffff80662227b75 nt!KiSystemServiceCopyEnd+0x25
    00007ffc88543444 ntdll!NtDeviceIoControlFile+0x14
    00007ffc85c23edb KERNELBASE!DeviceIoControl+0x6b
    00007ffc876b5f91 KERNEL32!DeviceIoControlImplementation+0x81
```

```
00007ff7be36342f  notmyfault64+0x342f
00007ffc87fd484b  USER32!UserCallDlgProcCheckWow+0x14b
00007ffc87fd409b  USER32!DefDlgProcWorker+0xcb
00007ffc880197c9  USER32!DefDlgProcA+0x39
00007ffc87fd1c4c  USER32!UserCallWinProcCheckWow+0x33c
00007ffc87fd179c  USER32!DispatchClientMessage+0x9c
00007ffc87fe4b4d  USER32!_fnDWORD+0x3d
00007ffc885472b4  ntdll!KiUserCallbackDispatcherContinue
00007ffc85b21434  win32u!NtUserMessageCall+0x14
00007ffc87fd08cf  USER32!SendMessageWorker+0x12f
00007ffc87fd0737  USER32!SendMessageW+0x137
00007ffc73c550bf  COMCTL32!Button_ReleaseCapture+0xbb
00007ffc73c88822  COMCTL32!Button_WndProc+0x802
00007ffc87fd1c4c  USER32!UserCallWinProcCheckWow+0x33c
00007ffc87fd0ea6  USER32!DispatchMessageWorker+0x2a6
00007ffc87fd6084  USER32!IsDialogMessageW+0x104
00007ffc73c35f9f  COMCTL32!Prop_IsDialogMessage+0x4b
00007ffc73c35e48  COMCTL32!_RealPropertySheet+0x2c0
00007ffc73c35abd  COMCTL32!_PropertySheet+0x49
00007ffc73d00953  COMCTL32!PropertySheetA+0x53
00007ff7be364cd0  notmyfault64+0x4cd0
00007ff7be365292  notmyfault64+0x5292
00007ffc876b54e0  KERNEL32!BaseThreadInitThunk+0x10
00007ffc884a485b  ntdll!RtlUserThreadStart+0x2b

Threads matching filter: 1 out of 3
```

Note: As we see above, sometimes the behavior of this old extension is unpredictable: it didn't find the stack trace pattern for CPU #1 and its current thread and process context and switched to CPU #0 but didn't change current the thread and its process context there so the next command run found the pattern. If you get this output, try to change the CPU context a few times:

```
1: kd> !kdexts.running -t -i

System Processors:  (0000000000000003)
  Idle Processors:  (0000000000000000)

    Prcbs              Current        (pri) Next          (pri) Idle
  0 fffff807604e6180  ffffbe0c89190080 (15)                   fffff80762d35bc0  ...............

      ^ Current scope machine type mismatch error in '0k'

  1 ffffce00fb700180  ffffbe0c8974f080 (12)                   ffffce00fb70c0c0  ...............

      ^ Current scope machine type mismatch error in '1k'

1: kd> ~0s; ~1s
```

14. Another way to explore sessions, processes, and threads is to use the *Model* tab in WinDbg:

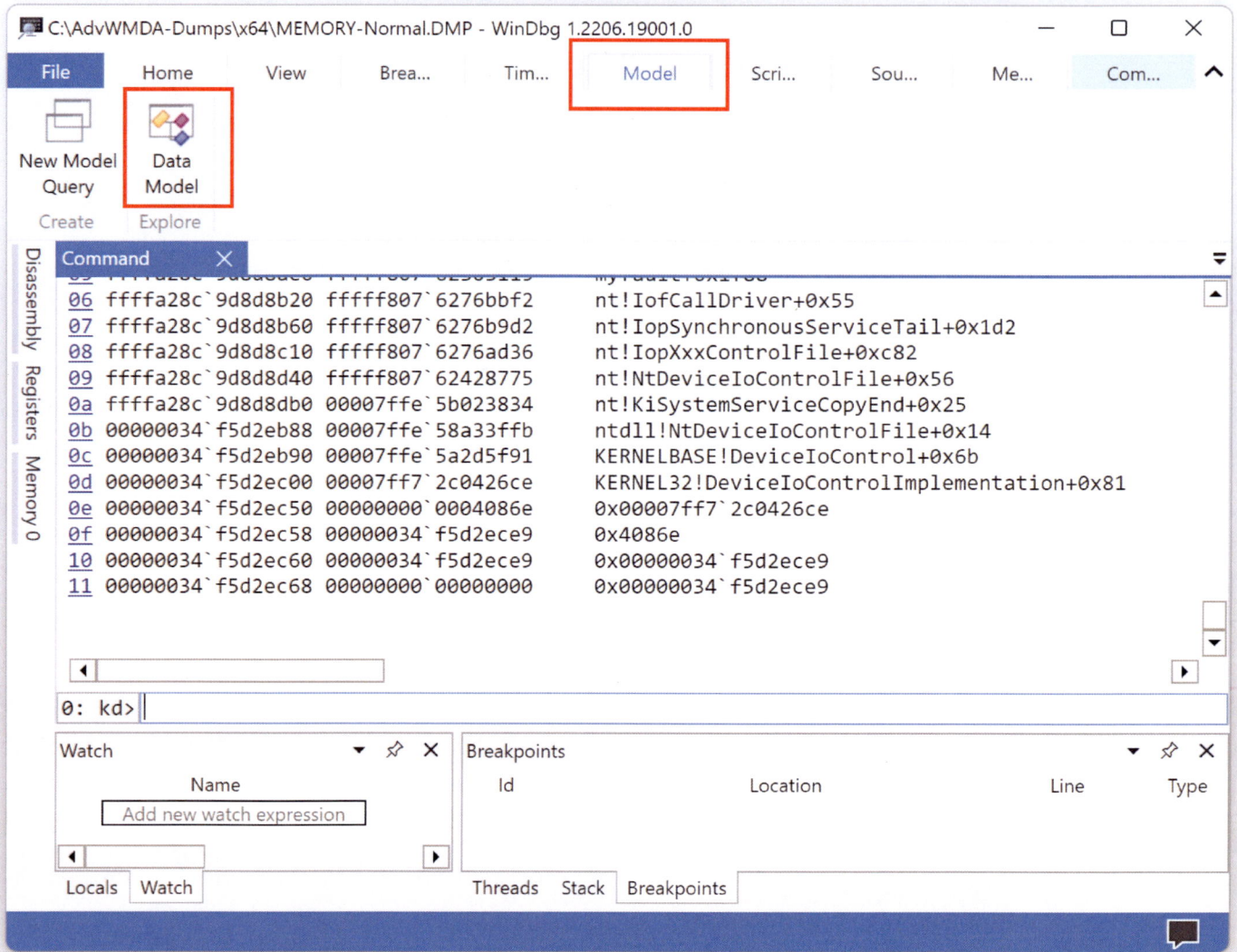

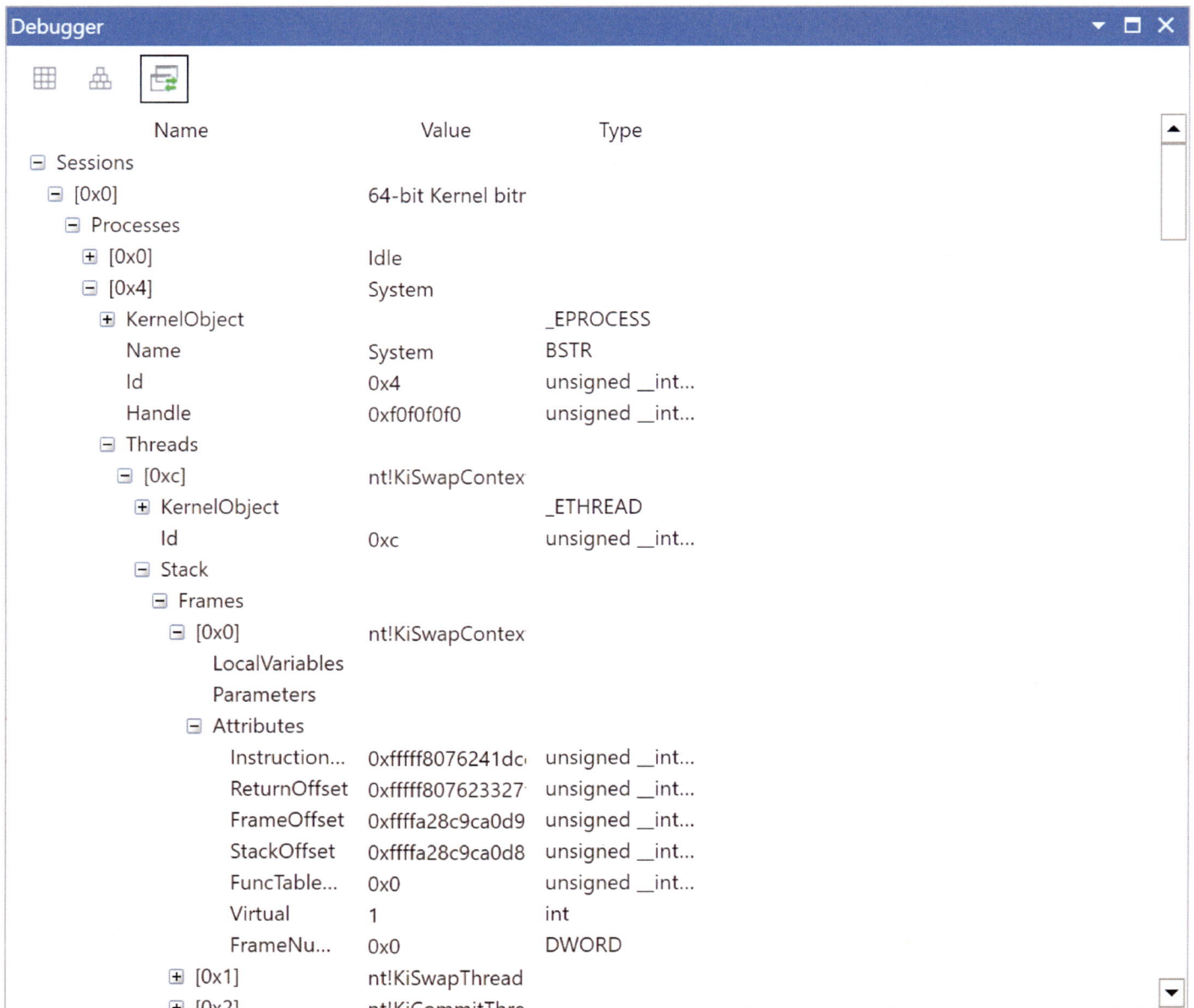

Debugger

Name	Value	Type
⊟ Sessions		
⊟ [0x0]	64-bit Kernel bitr	
⊟ Processes		
⊞ [0x0]	Idle	
⊟ [0x4]	System	
⊞ KernelObject		_EPROCESS
Name	System	BSTR
Id	0x4	unsigned __int...
Handle	0xf0f0f0f0	unsigned __int...
⊟ Threads		
⊟ [0xc]	nt!KiSwapContex	
⊞ KernelObject		_ETHREAD
Id	0xc	unsigned __int...
⊟ Stack		
⊟ Frames		
⊟ [0x0]	nt!KiSwapContex	
LocalVariables		
Parameters		
⊟ Attributes		
Instruction...	0xfffff8076241dc	unsigned __int...
ReturnOffset	0xfffff807623327	unsigned __int...
FrameOffset	0xfffffa28c9ca0d9	unsigned __int...
StackOffset	0xfffffa28c9ca0d8	unsigned __int...
FuncTable...	0x0	unsigned __int...
Virtual	1	int
FrameNu...	0x0	DWORD
⊞ [0x1]	nt!KiSwapThread	
⊞ [0x2]	nt!KiCommitThro	

15.   We close logging before exiting WinDbg:

```
0: kd> .logclose
Closing open log file C:\AdvWMDA-Dumps\x64\C1A.log
```

Note: We recommend exiting WinDbg after each exercise to avoid possible confusion and glitches.

Exercise C1B

- **Goal:** Get stack traces from WOW64 processes and reconstruct them manually.

- **Patterns:** Virtualized Process; Main Thread; Execution Residue; Past Stack Trace; Glued Stack Trace

- \AdvWMDA-Dumps\Exercise-C1B-WOW64.pdf

Exercise C1B: WOW64 Stack Trace Reconstruction

Goal: Get stack traces from WOW64 processes and reconstruct them manually.

Patterns: Virtualized Process; Main Thread; Truncated Stack Trace; Execution Residue; Past Stack Trace; Glued Stack Trace.

1.   Launch WinDbg.

2.   Open \AdvWMDA-Dumps\x64\MEMORY-Normal.DMP

3.   We get the dump file loaded (the output should be the same as in the previous exercise).

4.   We open a log file:

```
1: kd> .logopen C:\AdvWMDA-Dumps\x64\C1B.log
Opened log file 'C:\AdvWMDA-Dumps\x64\C1B.log'
```

5.   In the Excercise C1A, we noticed a 32-bit process *wordpad.exe*. Let's get its stack traces:

```
1: kd> !process 0 3f wordpad.exe
PROCESS ffffbe0c8be620c0
    SessionId: 1  Cid: 1d98    Peb: 008b3000  ParentCid: 0e3c
    DirBase: 7f5cf002  ObjectTable: ffff800edebe2180  HandleCount: 327.
    Image: wordpad.exe
    VadRoot ffffbe0c8ccd98f0 Vads 521 Clone 0 Private 3368. Modified 2454. Locked 0.
    DeviceMap ffff800eda518d20
    Token                             ffff800edee6f0a0
    ElapsedTime                       00:01:44.236
    UserTime                          00:00:00.015
    KernelTime                        00:00:00.015
    QuotaPoolUsage[PagedPool]         290304
    QuotaPoolUsage[NonPagedPool]      71096
    Working Set Sizes (now,min,max)   (13415, 50, 345) (53660KB, 200KB, 1380KB)
    PeakWorkingSetSize                15606
    VirtualSize                       197 Mb
    PeakVirtualSize                   222 Mb
    PageFaultCount                    20582
    MemoryPriority                    BACKGROUND
    BasePriority                      8
    CommitCharge                      4423


    PEB at 00000000008b3000
    InheritedAddressSpace:    No
    ReadImageFileExecOptions: No
    BeingDebugged:            No
    ImageBaseAddress:         0000000000f90000
    NtGlobalFlag:             400
    NtGlobalFlag2:            0
    Ldr                       00007ffe5b0fa120
    Ldr.Initialized:          Yes
    Ldr.InInitializationOrderModuleList: 0000000000bb5d10 . 0000000000bb67a0
    Ldr.InLoadOrderModuleList:           0000000000bb5e90 . 0000000000bb6780
    Ldr.InMemoryOrderModuleList:         0000000000bb5ea0 . 0000000000bb6790
             Base TimeStamp                      Module
           f90000 4ccb85ad Oct 30 03:40:45 2010 C:\Program Files (x86)\Windows NT\Accessories\wordpad.exe
         7ffe5af80000 931cda92 Mar 18 10:55:14 2048 C:\WINDOWS\SYSTEM32\ntdll.dll
         7ffe5a0f0000 f4699176 Dec 10 04:13:42 2099 C:\WINDOWS\System32\wow64.dll
         7ffe5a150000 05c399a6 Jan 24 06:28:54 1973 C:\WINDOWS\System32\wow64base.dll
         7ffe5ac70000 cb133f37 Dec 18 06:56:55 2077 C:\WINDOWS\System32\wow64win.dll
         7ffe596a0000 baa7118a Mar 26 08:12:58 2069 C:\WINDOWS\System32\wow64con.dll
            77550000 d7e3a9be Oct 10 14:06:06 2084 C:\WINDOWS\System32\wow64cpu.dll
    SubSystemData:      0000000000000000
    ProcessHeap:        0000000000bb0000
    ProcessParameters:  0000000000bb5510
    CurrentDirectory:   'C:\WINDOWS\'
    WindowTitle:  'C:\Program Files (x86)\Windows NT\Accessories\wordpad.exe'
    ImageFile:    'C:\Program Files (x86)\Windows NT\Accessories\wordpad.exe'
    CommandLine:  '"C:\Program Files (x86)\Windows NT\Accessories\wordpad.exe" '
    DllPath:      '< Name not readable >'
    Environment:  0000000000bb11f0
       =::=::\
```

```
ALLUSERSPROFILE=C:\ProgramData
APPDATA=C:\Users\dumpa\AppData\Roaming
CommonProgramFiles=C:\Program Files\Common Files
CommonProgramFiles(x86)=C:\Program Files (x86)\Common Files
CommonProgramW6432=C:\Program Files\Common Files
COMPUTERNAME=DESKTOP-OGPC0LO
ComSpec=C:\WINDOWS\system32\cmd.exe
DriverData=C:\Windows\System32\Drivers\DriverData
FPS_BROWSER_APP_PROFILE_STRING=Internet Explorer
FPS_BROWSER_USER_PROFILE_STRING=Default
HOMEDRIVE=C:
HOMEPATH=\Users\dumpa
LOCALAPPDATA=C:\Users\dumpa\AppData\Local
LOGONSERVER=\\DESKTOP-OGPC0LO
NUMBER_OF_PROCESSORS=2
OneDrive=C:\Users\dumpa\OneDrive
OS=Windows_NT

Path=C:\WINDOWS\system32;C:\WINDOWS;C:\WINDOWS\System32\Wbem;C:\WINDOWS\System32\WindowsPowerShell\v1.0\;C:\WINDOWS\System32\OpenSSH\;C:\Program
Files\dotnet\;C:\Program Files (x86)\dotnet\;C:\Users\dumpa\AppData\Local\Microsoft\WindowsApps;C:\Users\dumpa\.dotnet\tools;
PATHEXT=.COM;.EXE;.BAT;.CMD;.VBS;.VBE;.JS;.JSE;.WSF;.WSH;.MSC
PROCESSOR_ARCHITECTURE=AMD64
PROCESSOR_IDENTIFIER=Intel64 Family 6 Model 142 Stepping 10, GenuineIntel
PROCESSOR_LEVEL=6
PROCESSOR_REVISION=8e0a
ProgramData=C:\ProgramData
ProgramFiles=C:\Program Files
ProgramFiles(x86)=C:\Program Files (x86)
ProgramW6432=C:\Program Files
PSModulePath=C:\Program Files\WindowsPowerShell\Modules;C:\WINDOWS\system32\WindowsPowerShell\v1.0\Modules
PUBLIC=C:\Users\Public
SESSIONNAME=Console
SystemDrive=C:
SystemRoot=C:\WINDOWS
TEMP=C:\Users\dumpa\AppData\Local\Temp
TMP=C:\Users\dumpa\AppData\Local\Temp
USERDOMAIN=DESKTOP-OGPC0LO
USERDOMAIN_ROAMINGPROFILE=DESKTOP-OGPC0LO
USERNAME=Training
USERPROFILE=C:\Users\dumpa
windir=C:\WINDOWS


THREAD ffffbe0c8beda080  Cid 1d98.1bb0  Teb: 00000000008b5000 Win32Thread: ffffbe0c8ccd5ed0 WAIT: (WrUserRequest) UserMode Non-Alertable
    ffffbe0c8bd0e580  QueueObject
Not impersonating
DeviceMap                 ffff800eda518d20
Owning Process            ffffbe0c8be620c0        Image:          wordpad.exe
Attached Process          N/A              Image:         N/A
Wait Start TickCount      29755            Ticks: 32 (0:00:00.500)
Context Switch Count      3348             IdealProcessor: 1
UserTime                  00:00:00.187
KernelTime                00:00:00.578
Win32 Start Address wordpad!wWinMainCRTStartup (0x0000000001036e40)
Stack Init ffffa28ca02c3c70 Current ffffa28ca02c3050
Base ffffa28ca02c4000 Limit ffffa28ca02be000 Call 0000000000000000
Priority 10 BasePriority 8 PriorityDecrement 0 IoPriority 2 PagePriority 5
Unable to load image \??\C:\WINDOWS\system32\drivers\myfault.sys, Win32 error 0n2
Child-SP          RetAddr           Call Site
ffffa28c`a02c3090 fffff807`623327f7 nt!KiSwapContext+0x76
ffffa28c`a02c31d0 fffff807`623346a9 nt!KiSwapThread+0x3a7
ffffa28c`a02c32b0 fffff807`6232e5c4 nt!KiCommitThreadWait+0x159
ffffa28c`a02c3350 fffff807`6228efe0 nt!KeWaitForSingleObject+0x234
ffffa28c`a02c3440 ffffbc92`8e76afd6 nt!KeWaitForMultipleObjects+0x540
ffffa28c`a02c3540 ffffbc92`8e76ac3f win32kfull!xxxRealSleepThread+0x2c6
ffffa28c`a02c3660 ffffbc92`8e76e08a win32kfull!xxxSleepThread2+0xb3
ffffa28c`a02c36b0 ffffbc92`8e7b26ec win32kfull!xxxRealInternalGetMessage+0xc5a
ffffa28c`a02c3a10 ffffbc92`8dc4645a win32kfull!NtUserGetMessage+0x8c
ffffa28c`a02c3aa0 fffff807`62428775 win32k!NtUserGetMessage+0x16
ffffa28c`a02c3ae0 00007ffe`5ac81424 nt!KiSystemServiceCopyEnd+0x25 (TrapFrame @ ffffa28c`a02c3ae0)
00000000`00a5e1d8 00007ffe`5ac7510e wow64win!NtUserGetMessage+0x14
00000000`00a5e1e0 00007ffe`5a0f77ca wow64win!whNtUserGetMessage+0x2e
00000000`00a5e240 00000000`775517ba wow64!Wow64SystemServiceEx+0x15a
00000000`00a5eb00 00000000`77551d75 wow64cpu!ServiceNoTurbo+0xb
00000000`00a5ebb0 00007ffe`5a0fe06d wow64cpu!BTCpuSimulate+0xbb5
00000000`00a5ebf0 00007ffe`5a0fd8ad wow64!RunCpuSimulation+0xd
00000000`00a5ec20 00007ffe`5b05f87d wow64!Wow64LdrpInitialize+0x12d
00000000`00a5eed0 00007ffe`5b04d78c ntdll!LdrpInitializeProcess+0x16d1
00000000`00a5f290 00007ffe`5affa993 ntdll!_LdrpInitialize+0x52dc0
00000000`00a5f310 00007ffe`5affa8be ntdll!LdrpInitializeInternal+0x6b
00000000`00a5f590 00000000`00000000 ntdll!LdrInitializeThunk+0xe


THREAD ffffbe0c8b3f4080  Cid 1d98.0b94  Teb: 00000000008c5000 Win32Thread: 0000000000000000 WAIT: (UserRequest) UserMode Non-Alertable
    ffffbe0c8b7ebd70  SynchronizationTimer
Not impersonating
DeviceMap                 ffff800eda518d20
Owning Process            ffffbe0c8be620c0        Image:          wordpad.exe
Attached Process          N/A              Image:         N/A
Wait Start TickCount      27198            Ticks: 2589 (0:00:00:40.453)
Context Switch Count      5                IdealProcessor: 1
UserTime                  00:00:00.000
```

```
KernelTime                     00:00:00.000
Win32 Start Address 0x0000000075c40280
Stack Init ffffa28c9d58ec70 Current ffffa28c9d58ddf0
Base ffffa28c9d58f000 Limit ffffa28c9d589000 Call 0000000000000000
Priority 9 BasePriority 8 PriorityDecrement 0 IoPriority 2 PagePriority 5
Child-SP          RetAddr          Call Site
ffffa28c`9d58de30 fffff807`623327f7 nt!KiSwapContext+0x76
ffffa28c`9d58df70 fffff807`623346a9 nt!KiSwapThread+0x3a7
ffffa28c`9d58e050 fffff807`6232e5c4 nt!KiCommitThreadWait+0x159
ffffa28c`9d58e0f0 fffff807`6228efe0 nt!KeWaitForSingleObject+0x234
ffffa28c`9d58e1e0 fffff807`627702c5 nt!KeWaitForMultipleObjects+0x540
ffffa28c`9d58e2e0 fffff807`62686a9c nt!ObWaitForMultipleObjects+0x2d5
ffffa28c`9d58e7e0 fffff807`62428775 nt!NtWaitForMultipleObjects32+0x11c
ffffa28c`9d58ea70 00000000`77551cf3 nt!KiSystemServiceCopyEnd+0x25 (TrapFrame @ ffffa28c`9d58eae0)
00000000`04d0e9a8 00000000`7755184f wow64cpu!CpupSyscallStub+0x13
00000000`04d0e9b0 00000000`77551d75 wow64cpu!WaitForMultipleObjects32+0x1d
00000000`04d0ea60 00007ffe`5a0fe06d wow64cpu!BTCpuSimulate+0xbb5
00000000`04d0eaa0 00007ffe`5a0fd8ad wow64!RunCpuSimulation+0xd
00000000`04d0ead0 00007ffe`5affaaa8 wow64!Wow64LdrpInitialize+0x12d
00000000`04d0ed80 00007ffe`5affa993 ntdll!_LdrpInitialize+0xdc
00000000`04d0ee00 00007ffe`5affa8be ntdll!LdrpInitializeInternal+0x6b
00000000`04d0f080 00000000`00000000 ntdll!LdrInitializeThunk+0xe

THREAD ffffbe0c8a0bf040  Cid 1d98.1edc  Teb: 00000000008c9000 Win32Thread: 0000000000000000 WAIT: (WrQueue) UserMode Alertable
    ffffbe0c8bd0ce00  QueueObject
Not impersonating
DeviceMap                 ffff800eda518d20
Owning Process            ffffbe0c8be620c0       Image:         wordpad.exe
Attached Process          N/A          Image:         N/A
Wait Start TickCount      26976        Ticks: 2811 (0:00:00:43.921)
Context Switch Count      10           IdealProcessor: 0
UserTime                  00:00:00.000
KernelTime                00:00:00.000
Win32 Start Address 0x00000000775919f0
Stack Init ffffa28ca02d1c70 Current ffffa28ca02d1360
Base ffffa28ca02d2000 Limit ffffa28ca02cc000 Call 0000000000000000
Priority 8 BasePriority 8 PriorityDecrement 0 IoPriority 2 PagePriority 5
Child-SP          RetAddr          Call Site
ffffa28c`a02d13a0 fffff807`623327f7 nt!KiSwapContext+0x76
ffffa28c`a02d14e0 fffff807`623346a9 nt!KiSwapThread+0x3a7
ffffa28c`a02d15c0 fffff807`62337106 nt!KiCommitThreadWait+0x159
ffffa28c`a02d1660 fffff807`62336b18 nt!KeRemoveQueueEx+0x2b6
ffffa28c`a02d1710 fffff807`6233937c nt!IoRemoveIoCompletion+0x98
ffffa28c`a02d1830 fffff807`62428775 nt!NtWaitForWorkViaWorkerFactory+0x39c
ffffa28c`a02d1a70 00007ffe`5b027304 nt!KiSystemServiceCopyEnd+0x25 (TrapFrame @ ffffa28c`a02d1ae0)
00000000`04d9df88 00007ffe`5a0fa76a ntdll!NtWaitForWorkViaWorkerFactory+0x14
00000000`04d9df90 00007ffe`5a0f77ca wow64!whNtWaitForWorkViaWorkerFactory+0x11a
00000000`04d9e020 00000000`775517ba wow64!Wow64SystemServiceEx+0x15a
00000000`04d9e8e0 00000000`77551d75 wow64cpu!ServiceNoTurbo+0xb
00000000`04d9e990 00007ffe`5a0fe06d wow64cpu!BTCpuSimulate+0xbb5
00000000`04d9e9d0 00007ffe`5a0fd8ad wow64!RunCpuSimulation+0xd
00000000`04d9ea00 00007ffe`5affaaa8 wow64!Wow64LdrpInitialize+0x12d
00000000`04d9ecb0 00007ffe`5affa993 ntdll!_LdrpInitialize+0xdc
00000000`04d9ed30 00007ffe`5affa8be ntdll!LdrpInitializeInternal+0x6b
00000000`04d9efb0 00000000`00000000 ntdll!LdrInitializeThunk+0xe

THREAD ffffbe0c8b3f3040  Cid 1d98.1334  Teb: 00000000008cd000 Win32Thread: 0000000000000000 WAIT: (WrQueue) UserMode Alertable
    ffffbe0c8bd0ce00  QueueObject
Not impersonating
DeviceMap                 ffff800eda518d20
Owning Process            ffffbe0c8be620c0       Image:         wordpad.exe
Attached Process          N/A          Image:         N/A
Wait Start TickCount      23135        Ticks: 6652 (0:00:01:43.937)
Context Switch Count      4            IdealProcessor: 1
UserTime                  00:00:00.000
KernelTime                00:00:00.000
Win32 Start Address 0x00000000775919f0
Stack Init ffffa28c9ec21c70 Current ffffa28c9ec21360
Base ffffa28c9ec22000 Limit ffffa28c9ec1c000 Call 0000000000000000
Priority 8 BasePriority 8 PriorityDecrement 0 IoPriority 2 PagePriority 5
Child-SP          RetAddr          Call Site
ffffa28c`9ec213a0 fffff807`623327f7 nt!KiSwapContext+0x76
ffffa28c`9ec214e0 fffff807`623346a9 nt!KiSwapThread+0x3a7
ffffa28c`9ec215c0 fffff807`62337106 nt!KiCommitThreadWait+0x159
ffffa28c`9ec21660 fffff807`62336b18 nt!KeRemoveQueueEx+0x2b6
ffffa28c`9ec21710 fffff807`6233937c nt!IoRemoveIoCompletion+0x98
ffffa28c`9ec21830 fffff807`62428775 nt!NtWaitForWorkViaWorkerFactory+0x39c
ffffa28c`9ec21a70 00007ffe`5b027304 nt!KiSystemServiceCopyEnd+0x25 (TrapFrame @ ffffa28c`9ec21ae0)
00000000`0568e468 00007ffe`5a0fa76a ntdll!NtWaitForWorkViaWorkerFactory+0x14
00000000`0568e470 00007ffe`5a0f77ca wow64!whNtWaitForWorkViaWorkerFactory+0x11a
00000000`0568e500 00000000`775517ba wow64!Wow64SystemServiceEx+0x15a
00000000`0568edc0 00000000`77551d75 wow64cpu!ServiceNoTurbo+0xb
00000000`0568ee70 00007ffe`5a0fe06d wow64cpu!BTCpuSimulate+0xbb5
00000000`0568eeb0 00007ffe`5a0fd8ad wow64!RunCpuSimulation+0xd
00000000`0568eee0 00007ffe`5affaaa8 wow64!Wow64LdrpInitialize+0x12d
00000000`0568f190 00007ffe`5affa993 ntdll!_LdrpInitialize+0xdc
00000000`0568f210 00007ffe`5affa8be ntdll!LdrpInitializeInternal+0x6b
00000000`0568f490 00000000`00000000 ntdll!LdrInitializeThunk+0xe

THREAD ffffbe0c89988080  Cid 1d98.222c  Teb: 00000000008d5000 Win32Thread: 0000000000000000 WAIT: (UserRequest) UserMode Non-Alertable
    ffffbe0c8bed8080  ProcessObject
```

```
Not impersonating
DeviceMap              ffff800eda518d20
Owning Process         ffffbe0c8be620c0    Image:        wordpad.exe
Attached Process       N/A        Image:      N/A
Wait Start TickCount   23156             Ticks: 6631 (0:00:01:43.609)
Context Switch Count   4                 IdealProcessor: 1
UserTime               00:00:00.000
KernelTime             00:00:00.000
Win32 Start Address 0x000000007448ab20
Stack Init ffffa28c9dea0c70 Current ffffa28c9dea0650
Base ffffa28c9dea1000 Limit ffffa28c9de9b000 Call 0000000000000000
Priority 8 BasePriority 8 PriorityDecrement 0 IoPriority 2 PagePriority 5
Child-SP          RetAddr               Call Site
ffffa28c`9dea0690 fffff807`623327f7     nt!KiSwapContext+0x76
ffffa28c`9dea07d0 fffff807`623346a9     nt!KiSwapThread+0x3a7
ffffa28c`9dea08b0 fffff807`6232e5c4     nt!KiCommitThreadWait+0x159
ffffa28c`9dea0950 fffff807`6276ac5b     nt!KeWaitForSingleObject+0x234
ffffa28c`9dea0a40 fffff807`6276ab8a     nt!ObWaitForSingleObject+0xbb
ffffa28c`9dea0aa0 fffff807`62428775     nt!NtWaitForSingleObject+0x6a
ffffa28c`9dea0ae0 00000000`77551cf3     nt!KiSystemServiceCopyEnd+0x25 (TrapFrame @ ffffa28c`9dea0ae0)
00000000`0837eb08 00000000`77551b56     wow64cpu!CpupSyscallStub+0x13
00000000`0837eb10 00000000`77551d75     wow64cpu!Thunk0ArgReloadState+0x5
00000000`0837ebc0 00007ffe`5a0fe06d     wow64cpu!BTCpuSimulate+0xbb5
00000000`0837ec00 00007ffe`5a0fd8ad     wow64!RunCpuSimulation+0xd
00000000`0837ec30 00007ffe`5affaaa8     wow64!Wow64LdrpInitialize+0x12d
00000000`0837eee0 00007ffe`5affa993     ntdll!_LdrpInitialize+0xdc
00000000`0837ef60 00007ffe`5affa8be     ntdll!LdrpInitializeInternal+0x6b
00000000`0837f1e0 00000000`00000000     ntdll!LdrInitializeThunk+0xe
```

Note: We see it is a virtualized WOW64 process indeed, and it has the main input thread (in green).

6.   We can see its 32-bit stack trace using the standard **.thread /w** command:

```
1: kd> .thread /w ffffbe0c8beda080
Implicit thread is now ffffbe0c`8beda080
WARNING: WOW context retrieval requires
switching to the thread's process context.
Use .process /p ffffbe0c`89120080 to switch back.
Implicit process is now ffffbe0c`8be620c0
The context is partially valid. Only x86 user-mode context is available.
x86 context set
```

```
1: kd:x86> .reload
Loading Kernel Symbols
...........................................................
...........................................................
...........................................................
..
Loading User Symbols
.......
Loading unloaded module list
........
Loading Wow64 Symbols
...........................................................
....
```

```
1: kd:x86> k
  *** Stack trace for last set context - .thread/.cxr resets it
 # ChildEBP          RetAddr
00 00a9fd70 758e0200     win32u!NtUserGetMessage+0xc
01 00a9fdac 75238f35     USER32!GetMessageW+0x30
02 00a9fdc8 75238fe3     MFC42u!CWinThread::PumpMessage+0x15
03 00a9fde4 7520a242     MFC42u!CWinThread::Run+0x63
04 00a9fdfc 01036d0c     MFC42u!AfxWinMain+0xa2
05 00a9fe8c 75eb6739     wordpad!__wmainCRTStartup+0x153
06 00a9fe9c 775c8e7f     KERNEL32!BaseThreadInitThunk+0x19
07 00a9fef4 775c8e4d     ntdll_77560000!__RtlUserThreadStart+0x2b
08 00a9ff04 00000000     ntdll_77560000!_RtlUserThreadStart+0x1b
```

Note: However, in some of the WinDbg versions that we used in the previous editions of this book for the optional Docker environment, we were disappointed to see an incorrect and truncated stack trace:

```
1: kd:x86> k
  *** Stack trace for last set context - .thread/.cxr resets it
 # ChildEBP          RetAddr
WARNING: Frame IP not in any known module. Following frames may be wrong.
00 a02c3249 00000000      0x6241dce6
```

7.   To learn some additional techniques, we try to reconstruct the stack trace manually. First, we get the boundaries of a 32-bit stack region:

```
1: kd:x86> !teb
Wow64 TEB32 at 008b7000
    ExceptionList:          00a9fe7c
    StackBase:              00aa0000
    StackLimit:             00a96000
    SubSystemTib:           00000000
    FiberData:              00001e00
    ArbitraryUserPointer:   00000000
    Self:                   008b7000
    EnvironmentPointer:     00000000
    ClientId:               00001d98 . 00001bb0
    RpcHandle:              00000000
    Tls Storage:            00c8b610
    PEB Address:            008b4000
    LastErrorValue:         0
    LastStatusValue:        0
    Count Owned Locks:      0
    HardErrorMode:          0


Wow64 TEB at 008b5000
    ExceptionList:          008b7000
    StackBase:              00a5fd20
    StackLimit:             00a51000
    SubSystemTib:           00000000
    FiberData:              00001e00
    ArbitraryUserPointer:   00000000
    Self:                   008b5000
    EnvironmentPointer:     00000000
    ClientId:               00001d98 . 00001bb0
    RpcHandle:              00000000
    Tls Storage:            00000000
    PEB Address:            008b3000
    LastErrorValue:         0
    LastStatusValue:        c0000008
    Count Owned Locks:      0
    HardErrorMode:          0
```

Note: We are lucky that the **!teb** command works. But suppose it does not work. Then, we can find the address of TEB32 from a 64-bit native TEB structure (we can use either the **!sw** or **.effmach AMD64** command to switch back to the native mode):

```
1: kd:x86> .load wow64exts
```

```
1: kd:x86> !sw
Switched to Host mode


1: kd> dt nt!_TEB 008b5000
   +0x000 NtTib            : _NT_TIB
   +0x038 EnvironmentPointer : (null)
   +0x040 ClientId         : _CLIENT_ID
   +0x050 ActiveRpcHandle  : (null)
   +0x058 ThreadLocalStoragePointer : (null)
   +0x060 ProcessEnvironmentBlock : 0x00000000`008b3000 _PEB
   +0x068 LastErrorValue   : 0
   +0x06c CountOfOwnedCriticalSections : 0
   +0x070 CsrClientThread  : (null)
   +0x078 Win32ThreadInfo  : 0x00000000`00001bb0 Void
   +0x080 User32Reserved   : [26] 0
   +0x0e8 UserReserved     : [5] 0
   +0x100 WOW32Reserved    : (null)
   +0x108 CurrentLocale    : 0x1809
   +0x10c FpSoftwareStatusRegister : 0
   +0x110 ReservedForDebuggerInstrumentation : [16] (null)
   +0x190 SystemReserved1  : [30] (null)
   +0x280 PlaceholderCompatibilityMode : 0 ''
   +0x281 PlaceholderHydrationAlwaysExplicit : 0 ''
   +0x282 PlaceholderReserved : [10]  ""
   +0x28c ProxiedProcessId : 0
   +0x290 _ActivationStack : _ACTIVATION_CONTEXT_STACK
   +0x2b8 WorkingOnBehalfTicket : [8]  ""
   +0x2c0 ExceptionCode    : 0n0
   +0x2c4 Padding0         : [4]  ""
   +0x2c8 ActivationContextStackPointer : 0x00000000`008b5290 _ACTIVATION_CONTEXT_STACK
   +0x2d0 InstrumentationCallbackSp : 0
   +0x2d8 InstrumentationCallbackPreviousPc : 0
   +0x2e0 InstrumentationCallbackPreviousSp : 0
   +0x2e8 TxFsContext      : 0xfffe
   +0x2ec InstrumentationCallbackDisabled : 0 ''
   +0x2ed UnalignedLoadStoreExceptions : 0 ''
   +0x2ee Padding1         : [2]  ""
   +0x2f0 GdiTebBatch      : _GDI_TEB_BATCH
   +0x7d8 RealClientId     : _CLIENT_ID
   +0x7e8 GdiCachedProcessHandle : (null)
   +0x7f0 GdiClientPID     : 0
   +0x7f4 GdiClientTID     : 0
   +0x7f8 GdiThreadLocalInfo : (null)
   +0x800 Win32ClientInfo  : [62] 0x388
   +0x9f0 glDispatchTable  : [233] (null)
   +0x1138 glReserved1     : [29] 0
   +0x1220 glReserved2     : (null)
   +0x1228 glSectionInfo   : (null)
   +0x1230 glSection       : (null)
   +0x1238 glTable         : (null)
   +0x1240 glCurrentRC     : (null)
   +0x1248 glContext       : (null)
   +0x1250 LastStatusValue : 0xc0000008
   +0x1254 Padding2        : [4]  ""
   +0x1258 StaticUnicodeString : _UNICODE_STRING ""
   +0x1268 StaticUnicodeBuffer : [261]  ""
   +0x1472 Padding3        : [6]  ""
   +0x1478 DeallocationStack : 0x00000000`00a20000 Void
```

```
+0x1480 TlsSlots           : [64] (null)
+0x1680 TlsLinks           : _LIST_ENTRY [ 0x00000000`00000000 - 0x00000000`00000000 ]
+0x1690 Vdm                : (null)
+0x1698 ReservedForNtRpc   : (null)
+0x16a0 DbgSsReserved      : [2] (null)
+0x16b0 HardErrorMode      : 0
+0x16b4 Padding4           : [4]   ""
+0x16b8 Instrumentation    : [11] (null)
+0x1710 ActivityId         : _GUID {00000000-0000-0000-0000-000000000000}
+0x1720 SubProcessTag      : (null)
+0x1728 PerflibData        : (null)
+0x1730 EtwTraceData       : (null)
+0x1738 WinSockData        : (null)
+0x1740 GdiBatchCount      : 0
+0x1744 CurrentIdealProcessor : _PROCESSOR_NUMBER
+0x1744 IdealProcessorValue : 0x1010000
+0x1744 ReservedPad0       : 0 ''
+0x1745 ReservedPad1       : 0 ''
+0x1746 ReservedPad2       : 0x1 ''
+0x1747 IdealProcessor     : 0x1 ''
+0x1748 GuaranteedStackBytes : 0
+0x174c Padding5           : [4]   ""
+0x1750 ReservedForPerf    : (null)
+0x1758 ReservedForOle     : (null)
+0x1760 WaitingOnLoaderLock : 0
+0x1764 Padding6           : [4]   ""
+0x1768 SavedPriorityState : (null)
+0x1770 ReservedForCodeCoverage : 0
+0x1778 ThreadPoolData     : (null)
+0x1780 TlsExpansionSlots  : (null)
+0x1788 ChpeV2CpuAreaInfo  : (null)
+0x1790 Unused             : (null)
+0x1798 MuiGeneration      : 0
+0x179c IsImpersonating    : 0
+0x17a0 NlsCache           : (null)
+0x17a8 pShimData          : (null)
+0x17b0 HeapData           : 0x9daf0000
+0x17b4 Padding7           : [4]   ""
+0x17b8 CurrentTransactionHandle : (null)
+0x17c0 ActiveFrame        : (null)
+0x17c8 FlsData            : (null)
+0x17d0 PreferredLanguages : (null)
+0x17d8 UserPrefLanguages  : (null)
+0x17e0 MergedPrefLanguages : (null)
+0x17e8 MuiImpersonation   : 1
+0x17ec CrossTebFlags      : 0
+0x17ec SpareCrossTebBits  : 0y0000000000000000 (0)
+0x17ee SameTebFlags       : 0x420
+0x17ee SafeThunkCall      : 0y0
+0x17ee InDebugPrint       : 0y0
+0x17ee HasFiberData       : 0y0
+0x17ee SkipThreadAttach   : 0y0
+0x17ee WerInShipAssertCode : 0y0
+0x17ee RanProcessInit     : 0y1
+0x17ee ClonedThread       : 0y0
+0x17ee SuppressDebugMsg   : 0y0
+0x17ee DisableUserStackWalk : 0y0
+0x17ee RtlExceptionAttached : 0y0
+0x17ee InitialThread      : 0y1
```

```
+0x17ee SessionAware         : 0y0
+0x17ee LoadOwner            : 0y0
+0x17ee LoaderWorker         : 0y0
+0x17ee SkipLoaderInit       : 0y0
+0x17ee SkipFileAPIBrokering : 0y0
+0x17f0 TxnScopeEnterCallback : (null)
+0x17f8 TxnScopeExitCallback : (null)
+0x1800 TxnScopeContext      : (null)
+0x1808 LockCount            : 0
+0x180c WowTebOffset         : 0n8192
+0x1810 ResourceRetValue     : (null)
+0x1818 ReservedForWdf       : (null)
+0x1820 ReservedForCrt       : 0
+0x1828 EffectiveContainerId : _GUID {00000000-0000-0000-0000-000000000000}
+0x1838 LastSleepCounter     : 0
+0x1840 SpinCallCount        : 0
+0x1844 Padding8             : [4]  ""
+0x1848 ExtendedFeatureDisableMask : 0


1: kd> dt -r1 nt!_TEB32 008b5000 + 0n8192
+0x000 NtTib                 : _NT_TIB32
   +0x000 ExceptionList      : 0xa9fe7c
   +0x004 StackBase          : 0xaa0000
   +0x008 StackLimit         : 0xa96000
   +0x00c SubSystemTib       : 0
   +0x010 FiberData          : 0x1e00
   +0x010 Version            : 0x1e00
   +0x014 ArbitraryUserPointer : 0
   +0x018 Self               : 0x8b7000
+0x01c EnvironmentPointer : 0
+0x020 ClientId              : _CLIENT_ID32
   +0x000 UniqueProcess      : 0x1d98
   +0x004 UniqueThread       : 0x1bb0
+0x028 ActiveRpcHandle  : 0
+0x02c ThreadLocalStoragePointer : 0xc8b610
+0x030 ProcessEnvironmentBlock : 0x8b4000
+0x034 LastErrorValue   : 0
+0x038 CountOfOwnedCriticalSections : 0
+0x03c CsrClientThread  : 0
+0x040 Win32ThreadInfo  : 0
+0x044 User32Reserved   : [26] 0
+0x0ac UserReserved     : [5] 0
+0x0c0 WOW32Reserved    : 0x77556000
+0x0c4 CurrentLocale    : 0x1809
+0x0c8 FpSoftwareStatusRegister : 0
+0x0cc ReservedForDebuggerInstrumentation : [16] 0
+0x10c SystemReserved1  : [26] 0
+0x174 PlaceholderCompatibilityMode : 0 ''
+0x175 PlaceholderHydrationAlwaysExplicit : 0 ''
+0x176 PlaceholderReserved : [10]  ""
+0x180 ProxiedProcessId : 0
+0x184 _ActivationStack : _ACTIVATION_CONTEXT_STACK32
   +0x000 ActiveFrame      : 0
   +0x004 FrameListCache   : LIST_ENTRY32
   +0x00c Flags            : 2
   +0x010 NextCookieSequenceNumber : 0x1f
   +0x014 StackId          : 0x5837f
+0x19c WorkingOnBehalfTicket : [8]  ""
+0x1a4 ExceptionCode    : 0n0
```

```
+0x1a8 ActivationContextStackPointer : 0x8b7184
+0x1ac InstrumentationCallbackSp : 0
+0x1b0 InstrumentationCallbackPreviousPc : 0
+0x1b4 InstrumentationCallbackPreviousSp : 0
+0x1b8 InstrumentationCallbackDisabled : 0 ''
+0x1b9 SpareBytes         : [23]  ""
+0x1d0 TxFsContext        : 0xfffe
+0x1d4 GdiTebBatch        : _GDI_TEB_BATCH32
   +0x000 Offset          : 0y00000000000000000000000000000000 (0)
   +0x000 HasRenderingCommand : 0y0
   +0x004 HDC             : 0
   +0x008 Buffer          : [310] 0
+0x6b4 RealClientId       : _CLIENT_ID32
   +0x000 UniqueProcess   : 0x1d98
   +0x004 UniqueThread    : 0x1bb0
+0x6bc GdiCachedProcessHandle : 0
+0x6c0 GdiClientPID       : 0
+0x6c4 GdiClientTID       : 0
+0x6c8 GdiThreadLocalInfo : 0
+0x6cc Win32ClientInfo    : [62] 0
+0x7c4 glDispatchTable    : [233] 0
+0xb68 glReserved1        : [29] 0
+0xbdc glReserved2        : 0
+0xbe0 glSectionInfo      : 0
+0xbe4 glSection          : 0
+0xbe8 glTable            : 0
+0xbec glCurrentRC        : 0
+0xbf0 glContext          : 0
+0xbf4 LastStatusValue    : 0
+0xbf8 StaticUnicodeString : _STRING32
   +0x000 Length          : 0
   +0x002 MaximumLength   : 0x20a
   +0x004 Buffer          : 0x8b7c00
+0xc00 StaticUnicodeBuffer : [261]  ""
+0xe0c DeallocationStack  : 0xa60000
+0xe10 TlsSlots           : [64] 0
+0xf10 TlsLinks           : LIST_ENTRY32
   +0x000 Flink           : 0
   +0x004 Blink           : 0
+0xf18 Vdm                : 0
+0xf1c ReservedForNtRpc   : 0xab162b6b
+0xf20 DbgSsReserved      : [2] 0
+0xf28 HardErrorMode      : 0
+0xf2c Instrumentation    : [9] 0
+0xf50 ActivityId         : _GUID {00000000-0000-0000-0000-000000000000}
   +0x000 Data1           : 0
   +0x004 Data2           : 0
   +0x006 Data3           : 0
   +0x008 Data4           : [8]  ""
+0xf60 SubProcessTag      : 0
+0xf64 PerflibData        : 0
+0xf68 EtwTraceData       : 0
+0xf6c WinSockData        : 0
+0xf70 GdiBatchCount      : 0x8b5000
+0xf74 CurrentIdealProcessor : _PROCESSOR_NUMBER
   +0x000 Group           : 0
   +0x002 Number          : 0x1 ''
   +0x003 Reserved        : 0x1 ''
+0xf74 IdealProcessorValue : 0x1010000
```

```
+0xf74 ReservedPad0      : 0 ''
+0xf75 ReservedPad1      : 0 ''
+0xf76 ReservedPad2      : 0x1 ''
+0xf77 IdealProcessor    : 0x1 ''
+0xf78 GuaranteedStackBytes : 0
+0xf7c ReservedForPerf   : 0
+0xf80 ReservedForOle    : 0xbccaf8
+0xf84 WaitingOnLoaderLock : 0
+0xf88 SavedPriorityState : 0
+0xf8c ReservedForCodeCoverage : 0
+0xf90 ThreadPoolData    : 0
+0xf94 TlsExpansionSlots : 0
+0xf98 MuiGeneration     : 0
+0xf9c IsImpersonating   : 0
+0xfa0 NlsCache          : 0
+0xfa4 pShimData         : 0
+0xfa8 HeapData          : 0x86ac0000
+0xfac CurrentTransactionHandle : 0
+0xfb0 ActiveFrame       : 0
+0xfb4 FlsData           : 0xbcec00
+0xfb8 PreferredLanguages : 0
+0xfbc UserPrefLanguages : 0xbd5160
+0xfc0 MergedPrefLanguages : 0xbd5cf8
+0xfc4 MuiImpersonation  : 0
+0xfc8 CrossTebFlags     : 0
+0xfc8 SpareCrossTebBits : 0y0000000000000000 (0)
+0xfca SameTebFlags      : 0x620
+0xfca SafeThunkCall     : 0y0
+0xfca InDebugPrint      : 0y0
+0xfca HasFiberData      : 0y0
+0xfca SkipThreadAttach  : 0y0
+0xfca WerInShipAssertCode : 0y0
+0xfca RanProcessInit    : 0y1
+0xfca ClonedThread      : 0y0
+0xfca SuppressDebugMsg  : 0y0
+0xfca DisableUserStackWalk : 0y0
+0xfca RtlExceptionAttached : 0y1
+0xfca InitialThread     : 0y1
+0xfca SessionAware      : 0y0
+0xfca LoadOwner         : 0y0
+0xfca LoaderWorker      : 0y0
+0xfca SkipLoaderInit    : 0y0
+0xfca SkipFileAPIBrokering : 0y0
+0xfcc TxnScopeEnterCallback : 0
+0xfd0 TxnScopeExitCallback : 0
+0xfd4 TxnScopeContext   : 0
+0xfd8 LockCount         : 0
+0xfdc WowTebOffset      : 0n-8192
+0xfe0 ResourceRetValue  : 0xbcd3e0
+0xfe4 ReservedForWdf    : 0
+0xfe8 ReservedForCrt    : 0
+0xff0 EffectiveContainerId : _GUID {00000000-0000-0000-0000-000000000000}
   +0x000 Data1          : 0
   +0x004 Data2          : 0
   +0x006 Data3          : 0
   +0x008 Data4          : [8]  ""
+0x1000 LastSleepCounter : ??
+0x1008 SpinCallCount    : ??
+0x1010 ExtendedFeatureDisableMask : ??
```

Memory read error 00000000008b8010

8.   Next, we get symbolic execution residue, find the standard thread start function, and reconstruct the stack trace backward using 32-bit pointers (use **dds** instead of **dps** command; also, don't forget to switch to the thread context just in case you ran some other thread or process command after the **!sw** command):

```
1: kd> .thread /r /p ffffbe0c8beda080
Implicit thread is now ffffbe0c`8beda080
Implicit process is now ffffbe0c`8be620c0
Loading User Symbols
.......
Loading Wow64 Symbols
...........................................................
....

1: kd> dds 0xa96000 0xaa0000
00000000`00a96000  00000000
00000000`00a96004  00000000
00000000`00a96008  00000000
00000000`00a9600c  00000000
00000000`00a96010  00000000
00000000`00a96014  00000000
00000000`00a96018  00000000
00000000`00a9601c  00000000
00000000`00a96020  00000000
00000000`00a96024  00000000
00000000`00a96028  00000000
00000000`00a9602c  00000000
00000000`00a96030  00000000
00000000`00a96034  00000000
00000000`00a96038  00000000
00000000`00a9603c  00000000
00000000`00a96040  00000000
00000000`00a96044  00000000
00000000`00a96048  00000000
00000000`00a9604c  00000000
00000000`00a96050  00000000
00000000`00a96054  00000000
00000000`00a96058  00000000
00000000`00a9605c  00000000
00000000`00a96060  00000000
00000000`00a96064  00000000
00000000`00a96068  00000000
00000000`00a9606c  00000000
00000000`00a96070  00000000
00000000`00a96074  00000000
00000000`00a96078  00000000
00000000`00a9607c  00000000
00000000`00a96080  00000000
00000000`00a96084  00000000
00000000`00a96088  00000000
00000000`00a9608c  00000000
00000000`00a96090  00000000
00000000`00a96094  00000000
[...]
00000000`00a9f90c  0000007f
00000000`00a9f910  00030564
00000000`00a9f914  00030564
```

```
00000000`00a9f918    00000000
00000000`00a9f91c    00000000
00000000`00a9f920    00000000
00000000`00a9f924    00000000
00000000`00a9f928    00000000
00000000`00a9f92c    00000000
00000000`00a9f930    00000000
00000000`00a9f934    00a9f944
00000000`00a9f938    00bd7df8
00000000`00a9f93c    00000000
00000000`00a9f940    00000000
00000000`00a9f944    00a9f96c
00000000`00a9f948    75201eeb MFC42u!afxMapHWND+0x6b
00000000`00a9f94c    96c70f68
00000000`00a9f950    0000007f
00000000`00a9f954    00000000
00000000`00a9f958    96c70f68
00000000`00a9f95c    00a9f908
00000000`00a9f960    00a9f9bc
00000000`00a9f964    751e8232 MFC42u!CFontPropPage::`vcall'{236}'+0x9e2
00000000`00a9f968    00000000
00000000`00a9f96c    751fd78e MFC42u!AfxCallWndProc+0x13e
00000000`00a9f970    751fdef6 MFC42u!AfxWndProc+0x36
00000000`00a9f974    05302a70
00000000`00a9f978    00030564
00000000`00a9f97c    0000007f
00000000`00a9f980    00000000
00000000`00a9f984    00000000
00000000`00a9f988    751fc580 MFC42u!AfxWndProcBase
00000000`00a9f98c    00a9f9c8
00000000`00a9f990    0000007f
00000000`00a9f994    751fc580 MFC42u!AfxWndProcBase
00000000`00a9f998    7759f01c ntdll_77560000!RtlDeactivateActivationContextUnsafeFast+0x9c
00000000`00a9f99c    00000000
00000000`00a9f9a0    751fc5bd MFC42u!AfxWndProcBase+0x3d
00000000`00a9f9a4    96c70fcc
00000000`00a9f9a8    0000007f
00000000`00a9f9ac    751fc580 MFC42u!AfxWndProcBase
00000000`00a9f9b0    00030564
00000000`00a9f9b4    00000000
00000000`00a9f9b8    00bd7df8
00000000`00a9f9bc    00a9fad4
00000000`00a9f9c0    751e8069 MFC42u!CFontPropPage::`vcall'{236}'+0x819
00000000`00a9f9c4    00000000
00000000`00a9f9c8    751fc5bd MFC42u!AfxWndProcBase+0x3d
00000000`00a9f9cc    758f7dd2 USER32!_InternalCallWinProc+0x2a
00000000`00a9f9d0    00030564
00000000`00a9f9d4    0000007f
00000000`00a9f9d8    00000000
00000000`00a9f9dc    00000000
00000000`00a9f9e0    751fc580 MFC42u!AfxWndProcBase
00000000`00a9f9e4    dcbaabcd
00000000`00a9f9e8    00030564
00000000`00a9f9ec    0000007f
00000000`00a9f9f0    751fc580 MFC42u!AfxWndProcBase
00000000`00a9f9f4    00a9fae4
00000000`00a9f9f8    758d727a USER32!UserCallWinProcCheckWow+0x4aa
00000000`00a9f9fc    93a308a7
00000000`00a9fa00    00030564
```

```
00000000`00a9fa04   00a9fae4
00000000`00a9fa08   758d7459 USER32!UserCallWinProcCheckWow+0x689
00000000`00a9fa0c   758d7306 USER32!UserCallWinProcCheckWow+0x536
00000000`00a9fa10   45eebb5a
00000000`00a9fa14   751fc580 MFC42u!AfxWndProcBase
00000000`00a9fa18   00030564
00000000`00a9fa1c   036a34e0
00000000`00a9fa20   00000024
00000000`00a9fa24   00000001
00000000`00a9fa28   00000000
00000000`00a9fa2c   00000000
00000000`00a9fa30   00000070
00000000`00a9fa34   ffffffff
00000000`00a9fa38   ffffffff
00000000`00a9fa3c   758d6f53 USER32!UserCallWinProcCheckWow+0x183
00000000`00a9fa40   758d7459 USER32!UserCallWinProcCheckWow+0x689
00000000`00a9fa44   758fa7c0 USER32!_except_handler4
00000000`00a9fa48   00000000
00000000`00a9fa4c   00000000
00000000`00a9fa50   008b5800
00000000`00a9fa54   758d5fb6 USER32!HMValidateHandle+0x56
00000000`00a9fa58   00000001
00000000`00a9fa5c   45eebba2
00000000`00a9fa60   00a9fa80
00000000`00a9fa64   758d1403 USER32!RealDefWindowProcW+0x53
00000000`00a9fa68   036a00a0
00000000`00a9fa6c   00000000
00000000`00a9fa70   00000000
00000000`00a9fa74   00000000
00000000`00a9fa78   7595f038 USER32!grgbDwpLiteHookMsg
00000000`00a9fa7c   00000000
00000000`00a9fa80   00000000
00000000`00a9fa84   00000000
00000000`00a9fa88   8000c011
00000000`00a9fa8c   00000000
00000000`00a9fa90   00000000
00000000`00a9fa94   00ba1348
00000000`00a9fa98   00000000
00000000`00a9fa9c   00000001
00000000`00a9faa0   751fc580 MFC42u!AfxWndProcBase
00000000`00a9faa4   00000000
00000000`00a9faa8   00000000
00000000`00a9faac   751fc580 MFC42u!AfxWndProcBase
00000000`00a9fab0   00000000
00000000`00a9fab4   74229180 UIRibbon!COfficeSpaceUser::OnMsoWndProc
00000000`00a9fab8   00030564
00000000`00a9fabc   8000c011
00000000`00a9fac0   00ba1348
00000000`00a9fac4   00000000
00000000`00a9fac8   00000001
00000000`00a9facc   00000000
00000000`00a9fad0   00000000
00000000`00a9fad4   00a9fc88
00000000`00a9fad8   758fa7c0 USER32!_except_handler4
00000000`00a9fadc   30d26e2e
00000000`00a9fae0   fffffffe
00000000`00a9fae4   00a9fb1c
00000000`00a9fae8   758d5eaf USER32!CallWindowProcW+0x7f
00000000`00a9faec   751fc580 MFC42u!AfxWndProcBase
```

```
00000000`00a9faf0    00000000
00000000`00a9faf4    0000007f
00000000`00a9faf8    00000000
00000000`00a9fafc    00000000
00000000`00a9fb00    00000000
00000000`00a9fb04    00000000
00000000`00a9fb08    00c28b60
00000000`00a9fb0c    0000007f
00000000`00a9fb10    00000000
00000000`00a9fb14    7422a8b0 UIRibbon!COfficeSpaceUser::s_FrameListenerWndProc
00000000`00a9fb18    00000000
00000000`00a9fb1c    00a9fb5c
00000000`00a9fb20    7433bf5b UIRibbon!WndBridge::RawWndProc+0x10b
00000000`00a9fb24    751fc580 MFC42u!AfxWndProcBase
00000000`00a9fb28    00030564
00000000`00a9fb2c    0000007f
00000000`00a9fb30    00000000
00000000`00a9fb34    00000000
00000000`00a9fb38    737e8000 atlthunk!AtlThunkData
00000000`00a9fb3c    00a9fb74
00000000`00a9fb40    00030564
00000000`00a9fb44    751fc580 MFC42u!AfxWndProcBase
00000000`00a9fb48    0000007f
00000000`00a9fb4c    737e1860 atlthunk!AtlThunk_0x00
00000000`00a9fb50    7759f01c ntdll_77560000!RtlDeactivateActivationContextUnsafeFast+0x9c
00000000`00a9fb54    00000000
00000000`00a9fb58    006c8870
00000000`00a9fb5c    00a9fb7c
00000000`00a9fb60    737e189a atlthunk!AtlThunk_0x00+0x3a
00000000`00a9fb64    00c28b60
00000000`00a9fb68    0000007f
00000000`00a9fb6c    00000000
00000000`00a9fb70    00000000
00000000`00a9fb74    0000007f
00000000`00a9fb78    737e1860 atlthunk!AtlThunk_0x00
00000000`00a9fb7c    00a9fba8
00000000`00a9fb80    758f7dd2 USER32!_InternalCallWinProc+0x2a
00000000`00a9fb84    00030564
00000000`00a9fb88    0000007f
00000000`00a9fb8c    00000000
00000000`00a9fb90    00000000
00000000`00a9fb94    737e1860 atlthunk!AtlThunk_0x00
00000000`00a9fb98    dcbaabcd
00000000`00a9fb9c    00030564
00000000`00a9fba0    0000007f
00000000`00a9fba4    737e1860 atlthunk!AtlThunk_0x00
00000000`00a9fba8    00a9fc98
00000000`00a9fbac    758d727a USER32!UserCallWinProcCheckWow+0x4aa
00000000`00a9fbb0    737e1860 atlthunk!AtlThunk_0x00
00000000`00a9fbb4    93a30a6f
00000000`00a9fbb8    00a9fc98
00000000`00a9fbbc    758d7459 USER32!UserCallWinProcCheckWow+0x689
00000000`00a9fbc0    758d7306 USER32!UserCallWinProcCheckWow+0x536
00000000`00a9fbc4    45eebd26
00000000`00a9fbc8    00000000
00000000`00a9fbcc    00000388
00000000`00a9fbd0    0000007f
00000000`00a9fbd4    00000024
00000000`00a9fbd8    00000001
```

```
00000000`00a9fbdc   00000000
00000000`00a9fbe0   00000000
00000000`00a9fbe4   00000070
00000000`00a9fbe8   ffffffff
00000000`00a9fbec   ffffffff
00000000`00a9fbf0   758d6f53   USER32!UserCallWinProcCheckWow+0x183
00000000`00a9fbf4   758d7459   USER32!UserCallWinProcCheckWow+0x689
00000000`00a9fbf8   00000000
00000000`00a9fbfc   00000000
00000000`00a9fc00   fffffff0
00000000`00a9fc04   036a34e0
00000000`00a9fc08   00000000
00000000`00a9fc0c   00ba1348
00000000`00a9fc10   00000000
00000000`00a9fc14   00000001
00000000`00a9fc18   746c8870   MSFTEDIT!RichEditWndProc
00000000`00a9fc1c   775d4bc6   ntdll_77560000!NtQueryInformationProcess+0x26
00000000`00a9fc20   00a9fc48
00000000`00a9fc24   758d5001   USER32!_GetWindowLong+0xe1
00000000`00a9fc28   036a34e0
00000000`00a9fc2c   00000000
00000000`00a9fc30   00000000
00000000`00a9fc34   00000000
00000000`00a9fc38   00000000
00000000`00a9fc3c   8000c011
00000000`00a9fc40   00000000
00000000`00a9fc44   00000000
00000000`00a9fc48   00ba1348
00000000`00a9fc4c   00000000
00000000`00a9fc50   00000001
00000000`00a9fc54   737e1860   atlthunk!AtlThunk_0x00
00000000`00a9fc58   00000000
00000000`00a9fc5c   00000000
00000000`00a9fc60   737e1860   atlthunk!AtlThunk_0x00
00000000`00a9fc64   00000000
00000000`00a9fc68   00000000
00000000`00a9fc6c   00030564
00000000`00a9fc70   8000c011
00000000`00a9fc74   00ba1348
00000000`00a9fc78   00000000
00000000`00a9fc7c   00000001
00000000`00a9fc80   00a9fc9c
00000000`00a9fc84   74226609   UIRibbon!CMessageHookImpl::s_CallWndProcHookProc+0x99
00000000`00a9fc88   00a9fcec
00000000`00a9fc8c   758fa7c0   USER32!_except_handler4
00000000`00a9fc90   30d26e2e
00000000`00a9fc94   fffffffe
00000000`00a9fc98   00a9fcfc
00000000`00a9fc9c   758d6d0a   USER32!DispatchClientMessage+0xea
00000000`00a9fca0   737e1860   atlthunk!AtlThunk_0x00
00000000`00a9fca4   00000000
00000000`00a9fca8   0000007f
00000000`00a9fcac   00000000
00000000`00a9fcb0   00000000
00000000`00a9fcb4   008b5000
00000000`00a9fcb8   00000001
00000000`00a9fcbc   45eebd42
00000000`00a9fcc0   010493fc   wordpad!theApp+0x34
00000000`00a9fcc4   775f81b0   ntdll_77560000!NtdllDispatchMessage_W
```

```
00000000`00a9fcc8    010493c8  wordpad!theApp
00000000`00a9fccc    758ccbd0  USER32!fnHkINLPCWPSTRUCTW+0x60
00000000`00a9fcd0    00040000
00000000`00a9fcd4    00000001
00000000`00a9fcd8    00000000
00000000`00a9fcdc    00030564
00000000`00a9fce0    00000000
00000000`00a9fce4    00a9fcbc
00000000`00a9fce8    010493c8  wordpad!theApp
00000000`00a9fcec    00a9fd48
00000000`00a9fcf0    758fa7c0  USER32!_except_handler4
00000000`00a9fcf4    30d26ece
00000000`00a9fcf8    fffffffe
00000000`00a9fcfc    00a9fd38
00000000`00a9fd00    758dfbef  USER32!__fnDWORD+0x3f
00000000`00a9fd04    036a34e0
00000000`00a9fd08    775d4a6c  ntdll_77560000!NtCallbackReturn+0xc
00000000`00a9fd0c    758dfc07  USER32!__fnDWORD+0x57
00000000`00a9fd10    00a9fd20
00000000`00a9fd14    00000018
00000000`00a9fd18    00000000
00000000`00a9fd1c    010493fc  wordpad!theApp+0x34
00000000`00a9fd20    00000000
00000000`00a9fd24    00000000
00000000`00a9fd28    00000000
00000000`00a9fd2c    7a27552b
00000000`00a9fd30    00000000
00000000`00a9fd34    00000000
00000000`00a9fd38    00a9fdac
00000000`00a9fd3c    775d6fdc  ntdll_77560000!KiUserCallbackDispatcher+0x4c
00000000`00a9fd40    00a9fd54
00000000`00a9fd44    00000020
00000000`00a9fd48    00a9fe7c
00000000`00a9fd4c    775d6f10  ntdll_77560000!KiUserCallbackExceptionHandler
00000000`00a9fd50    00a9fd74
00000000`00a9fd54    036a34e0
00000000`00a9fd58    00000000
00000000`00a9fd5c    0000007f
00000000`00a9fd60    00000000
00000000`00a9fd64    00000000
00000000`00a9fd68    737e1860  atlthunk!AtlThunk_0x00
00000000`00a9fd6c    775f81b0  ntdll_77560000!NtdllDispatchMessage_W
00000000`00a9fd70    00007ffe
00000000`00a9fd74    758e0200  USER32!GetMessageW+0x30
00000000`00a9fd78    010493fc  wordpad!theApp+0x34
00000000`00a9fd7c    00000000
00000000`00a9fd80    00000000
00000000`00a9fd84    00000000
00000000`00a9fd88    010368d0  wordpad!CWinThread::PumpMessage
00000000`00a9fd8c    010493fc  wordpad!theApp+0x34
00000000`00a9fd90    00000001
00000000`00a9fd94    010493c8  wordpad!theApp
00000000`00a9fd98    00000001
00000000`00a9fd9c    010493c8  wordpad!theApp
00000000`00a9fda0    036a5dc0
00000000`00a9fda4    00a9fdc4
00000000`00a9fda8    75239688  MFC42u!CWinApp::OnIdle+0x88
00000000`00a9fdac    00a9fde4
00000000`00a9fdb0    75238f35  MFC42u!CWinThread::PumpMessage+0x15
```

```
00000000`00a9fdb4   010493fc  wordpad!theApp+0x34
00000000`00a9fdb8   00000000
00000000`00a9fdbc   00000000
00000000`00a9fdc0   00000000
00000000`00a9fdc4   00000000
00000000`00a9fdc8   010493c8  wordpad!theApp
00000000`00a9fdcc   75238fe3  MFC42u!CWinThread::Run+0x63
00000000`00a9fdd0   010493c8  wordpad!theApp
00000000`00a9fdd4   010368c0  wordpad!CWinApp::Run
00000000`00a9fdd8   ffffffff
00000000`00a9fddc   00f9786c  wordpad!CWordPadApp::`vftable'
00000000`00a9fde0   00000002
00000000`00a9fde4   00a9fdfc
00000000`00a9fde8   7520a242  MFC42u!AfxWinMain+0xa2
00000000`00a9fdec   00000000
00000000`00a9fdf0   00000020
00000000`00a9fdf4   00000000
00000000`00a9fdf8   010493c8  wordpad!theApp
00000000`00a9fdfc   00a9fe8c
00000000`00a9fe00   01036d0c  wordpad!__wmainCRTStartup+0x153
00000000`00a9fe04   00f90000  wordpad!type_info::`vftable' <PERF> (wordpad+0x0)
00000000`00a9fe08   00000000
00000000`00a9fe0c   00bc5804
00000000`00a9fe10   00000001
00000000`00a9fe14   e186e40a
00000000`00a9fe18   01036e40  wordpad!wWinMainCRTStartup
00000000`00a9fe1c   01036e40  wordpad!wWinMainCRTStartup
00000000`00a9fe20   008b4000
00000000`00a9fe24   00000044
00000000`00a9fe28   00bc589a
00000000`00a9fe2c   00bc587a
00000000`00a9fe30   00bc5806
00000000`00a9fe34   00000000
00000000`00a9fe38   00000000
00000000`00a9fe3c   00000000
00000000`00a9fe40   00000000
00000000`00a9fe44   00000000
00000000`00a9fe48   00000000
00000000`00a9fe4c   00000000
00000000`00a9fe50   00000001
00000000`00a9fe54   00000001
00000000`00a9fe58   00000000
00000000`00a9fe5c   00000000
00000000`00a9fe60   00000000
00000000`00a9fe64   00000000
00000000`00a9fe68   00000000
00000000`00a9fe6c   00bc5804
00000000`00a9fe70   00000000
00000000`00a9fe74   00a9fe14
00000000`00a9fe78   00000000
00000000`00a9fe7c   00a9fee4
00000000`00a9fe80   01037710  wordpad!_except_handler4
00000000`00a9fe84   e02b2c76
00000000`00a9fe88   00000000
00000000`00a9fe8c   00a9fe9c
00000000`00a9fe90   75eb6739  KERNEL32!BaseThreadInitThunk+0x19
00000000`00a9fe94   008b4000
00000000`00a9fe98   75eb6720  KERNEL32!BaseThreadInitThunk
00000000`00a9fe9c   00a9fef4
```

```
00000000`00a9fea0    775c8e7f    ntdll_77560000!__RtlUserThreadStart+0x2b
00000000`00a9fea4    008b4000
00000000`00a9fea8    93a30fcf
00000000`00a9feac    00000000
00000000`00a9feb0    00000000
00000000`00a9feb4    008b4000
00000000`00a9feb8    00000000
00000000`00a9febc    00000000
00000000`00a9fec0    00000000
00000000`00a9fec4    00000000
00000000`00a9fec8    00000000
00000000`00a9fecc    00000000
00000000`00a9fed0    00000000
00000000`00a9fed4    00000000
00000000`00a9fed8    00000000
00000000`00a9fedc    00a9fea8
00000000`00a9fee0    00000000
00000000`00a9fee4    00a9fefc
00000000`00a9fee8    775dd0b0    ntdll_77560000!_except_handler4
00000000`00a9feec    e46c1acb
00000000`00a9fef0    00000000
00000000`00a9fef4    00a9ff04
00000000`00a9fef8    775c8e4d    ntdll_77560000!_RtlUserThreadStart+0x1b
00000000`00a9fefc    ffffffff
00000000`00a9ff00    775f8ca9    ntdll_77560000!FinalExceptionHandlerPad41
00000000`00a9ff04    00000000
00000000`00a9ff08    00000000
00000000`00a9ff0c    01036e40    wordpad!wWinMainCRTStartup
00000000`00a9ff10    008b4000
00000000`00a9ff14    00000000
00000000`00a9ff18    00000000
00000000`00a9ff1c    00000000
00000000`00a9ff20    00000000
00000000`00a9ff24    00000000
00000000`00a9ff28    00000000
00000000`00a9ff2c    00000000
00000000`00a9ff30    00000000
00000000`00a9ff34    00000000
00000000`00a9ff38    00000000
00000000`00a9ff3c    00000000
00000000`00a9ff40    00000000
00000000`00a9ff44    00000000
00000000`00a9ff48    00000000
00000000`00a9ff4c    00000000
00000000`00a9ff50    00000000
00000000`00a9ff54    00000000
00000000`00a9ff58    00000000
00000000`00a9ff5c    00000000
00000000`00a9ff60    00000000
00000000`00a9ff64    00000000
00000000`00a9ff68    00000000
00000000`00a9ff6c    00000000
00000000`00a9ff70    00000000
00000000`00a9ff74    00000000
00000000`00a9ff78    00000000
00000000`00a9ff7c    00000000
00000000`00a9ff80    00000000
00000000`00a9ff84    00000000
00000000`00a9ff88    00000000
```

```
00000000`00a9ff8c   00000000
00000000`00a9ff90   00000000
00000000`00a9ff94   00000000
00000000`00a9ff98   00000000
00000000`00a9ff9c   00000000
00000000`00a9ffa0   00000000
00000000`00a9ffa4   00000000
00000000`00a9ffa8   00000000
00000000`00a9ffac   00000000
00000000`00a9ffb0   00000000
00000000`00a9ffb4   00000000
00000000`00a9ffb8   00000000
00000000`00a9ffbc   00000000
00000000`00a9ffc0   00000000
00000000`00a9ffc4   00000000
00000000`00a9ffc8   00000000
00000000`00a9ffcc   00000000
00000000`00a9ffd0   00000000
00000000`00a9ffd4   00000000
00000000`00a9ffd8   00000000
00000000`00a9ffdc   00000000
00000000`00a9ffe0   00000000
00000000`00a9ffe4   00000000
00000000`00a9ffe8   00000000
00000000`00a9ffec   00000000
00000000`00a9fff0   00000000
00000000`00a9fff4   00000000
00000000`00a9fff8   00000000
00000000`00a9fffc   00000000
00000000`00aa0000   78746341
```

Note: We get this tentative 32-bit stack trace:

```
00000000`00a9f9f8   USER32!UserCallWinProcCheckWow+0x4aa
00000000`00a9fae8   USER32!CallWindowProcW+0x7f
00000000`00a9fb20   UIRibbon!WndBridge::RawWndProc+0x10b
00000000`00a9fb60   atlthunk!AtlThunk_0x00+0x3a
00000000`00a9fb80   USER32!_InternalCallWinProc+0x2a
00000000`00a9fbac   USER32!UserCallWinProcCheckWow+0x4aa
00000000`00a9fc9c   USER32!DispatchClientMessage+0xea
00000000`00a9fd00   USER32!__fnDWORD+0x3f
00000000`00a9fd3c   ntdll_77560000!KiUserCallbackDispatcher+0x4c
00000000`00a9fdb0   MFC42u!CWinThread::PumpMessage+0x15
00000000`00a9fde8   MFC42u!AfxWinMain+0xa2
00000000`00a9fe00   wordpad!__wmainCRTStartup+0x153
00000000`00a9fe90   KERNEL32!BaseThreadInitThunk+0x19
00000000`00a9fea0   ntdll_77560000!__RtlUserThreadStart+0x2b
00000000`00a9fef8   ntdll_77560000!_RtlUserThreadStart+0x1b
```

9.   However, this reconstructed stack trace may be a union of the current stack trace and some past stack trace by continuity of saved EBP values. We need to find the current value of EIP, EBP, and ESP pointers to get the correct stack trace. These are available in the second TLS slot of the native TEB:

```
1: kd> dt nt!_TEB 008b5000
   +0x000 NtTib            : _NT_TIB
   +0x038 EnvironmentPointer : (null)
   +0x040 ClientId         : _CLIENT_ID
```

```
+0x050 ActiveRpcHandle    : (null)
+0x058 ThreadLocalStoragePointer : (null)
+0x060 ProcessEnvironmentBlock : 0x00000000`008b3000 _PEB
+0x068 LastErrorValue    : 0
+0x06c CountOfOwnedCriticalSections : 0
+0x070 CsrClientThread   : (null)
+0x078 Win32ThreadInfo   : 0x00000000`00001bb0 Void
+0x080 User32Reserved    : [26] 0
+0x0e8 UserReserved      : [5] 0
+0x100 WOW32Reserved     : (null)
+0x108 CurrentLocale     : 0x1809
+0x10c FpSoftwareStatusRegister : 0
+0x110 ReservedForDebuggerInstrumentation : [16] (null)
+0x190 SystemReserved1   : [30] (null)
+0x280 PlaceholderCompatibilityMode : 0 ''
+0x281 PlaceholderHydrationAlwaysExplicit : 0 ''
+0x282 PlaceholderReserved : [10]  ""
+0x28c ProxiedProcessId  : 0
+0x290 _ActivationStack  : _ACTIVATION_CONTEXT_STACK
+0x2b8 WorkingOnBehalfTicket : [8]  ""
+0x2c0 ExceptionCode     : 0n0
+0x2c4 Padding0          : [4]  ""
+0x2c8 ActivationContextStackPointer : 0x00000000`008b5290 _ACTIVATION_CONTEXT_STACK
+0x2d0 InstrumentationCallbackSp : 0
+0x2d8 InstrumentationCallbackPreviousPc : 0
+0x2e0 InstrumentationCallbackPreviousSp : 0
+0x2e8 TxFsContext       : 0xfffe
+0x2ec InstrumentationCallbackDisabled : 0 ''
+0x2ed UnalignedLoadStoreExceptions : 0 ''
+0x2ee Padding1          : [2]  ""
+0x2f0 GdiTebBatch       : _GDI_TEB_BATCH
+0x7d8 RealClientId      : _CLIENT_ID
+0x7e8 GdiCachedProcessHandle : (null)
+0x7f0 GdiClientPID      : 0
+0x7f4 GdiClientTID      : 0
+0x7f8 GdiThreadLocalInfo : (null)
+0x800 Win32ClientInfo   : [62] 0x388
+0x9f0 glDispatchTable   : [233] (null)
+0x1138 glReserved1      : [29] 0
+0x1220 glReserved2      : (null)
+0x1228 glSectionInfo    : (null)
+0x1230 glSection        : (null)
+0x1238 glTable          : (null)
+0x1240 glCurrentRC      : (null)
+0x1248 glContext        : (null)
+0x1250 LastStatusValue  : 0xc0000008
+0x1254 Padding2         : [4]  ""
+0x1258 StaticUnicodeString : _UNICODE_STRING ""
+0x1268 StaticUnicodeBuffer : [261]  ""
+0x1472 Padding3         : [6]  ""
+0x1478 DeallocationStack : 0x00000000`00a20000 Void
+0x1480 TlsSlots         : [64] (null)
+0x1680 TlsLinks         : _LIST_ENTRY [ 0x00000000`00000000 - 0x00000000`00000000 ]
+0x1690 Vdm             : (null)
+0x1698 ReservedForNtRpc : (null)
+0x16a0 DbgSsReserved    : [2] (null)
+0x16b0 HardErrorMode    : 0
+0x16b4 Padding4         : [4]  ""
+0x16b8 Instrumentation  : [11] (null)
```

```
+0x1710 ActivityId          : _GUID {00000000-0000-0000-0000-000000000000}
+0x1720 SubProcessTag       : (null)
+0x1728 PerflibData         : (null)
+0x1730 EtwTraceData        : (null)
+0x1738 WinSockData         : (null)
+0x1740 GdiBatchCount       : 0
+0x1744 CurrentIdealProcessor : _PROCESSOR_NUMBER
+0x1744 IdealProcessorValue : 0x1010000
+0x1744 ReservedPad0        : 0 ''
+0x1745 ReservedPad1        : 0 ''
+0x1746 ReservedPad2        : 0x1 ''
+0x1747 IdealProcessor      : 0x1 ''
+0x1748 GuaranteedStackBytes : 0
+0x174c Padding5            : [4]  ""
+0x1750 ReservedForPerf     : (null)
+0x1758 ReservedForOle      : (null)
+0x1760 WaitingOnLoaderLock : 0
+0x1764 Padding6            : [4]  ""
+0x1768 SavedPriorityState  : (null)
+0x1770 ReservedForCodeCoverage : 0
+0x1778 ThreadPoolData      : (null)
+0x1780 TlsExpansionSlots   : (null)
+0x1788 ChpeV2CpuAreaInfo   : (null)
+0x1790 Unused              : (null)
+0x1798 MuiGeneration       : 0
+0x179c IsImpersonating     : 0
+0x17a0 NlsCache            : (null)
+0x17a8 pShimData           : (null)
+0x17b0 HeapData            : 0x9daf0000
+0x17b4 Padding7            : [4]  ""
+0x17b8 CurrentTransactionHandle : (null)
+0x17c0 ActiveFrame         : (null)
+0x17c8 FlsData             : (null)
+0x17d0 PreferredLanguages  : (null)
+0x17d8 UserPrefLanguages   : (null)
+0x17e0 MergedPrefLanguages : (null)
+0x17e8 MuiImpersonation    : 1
+0x17ec CrossTebFlags       : 0
+0x17ec SpareCrossTebBits   : 0y0000000000000000 (0)
+0x17ee SameTebFlags        : 0x420
+0x17ee SafeThunkCall       : 0y0
+0x17ee InDebugPrint        : 0y0
+0x17ee HasFiberData        : 0y0
+0x17ee SkipThreadAttach    : 0y0
+0x17ee WerInShipAssertCode : 0y0
+0x17ee RanProcessInit      : 0y1
+0x17ee ClonedThread        : 0y0
+0x17ee SuppressDebugMsg    : 0y0
+0x17ee DisableUserStackWalk : 0y0
+0x17ee RtlExceptionAttached : 0y0
+0x17ee InitialThread       : 0y1
+0x17ee SessionAware        : 0y0
+0x17ee LoadOwner           : 0y0
+0x17ee LoaderWorker        : 0y0
+0x17ee SkipLoaderInit      : 0y0
+0x17ee SkipFileAPIBrokering : 0y0
+0x17f0 TxnScopeEnterCallback : (null)
+0x17f8 TxnScopeExitCallback : (null)
+0x1800 TxnScopeContext     : (null)
```

```
+0x1808 LockCount           : 0
+0x180c WowTebOffset        : 0n8192
+0x1810 ResourceRetValue    : (null)
+0x1818 ReservedForWdf      : (null)
+0x1820 ReservedForCrt      : 0
+0x1828 EffectiveContainerId : _GUID {00000000-0000-0000-0000-000000000000}
+0x1838 LastSleepCounter    : 0
+0x1840 SpinCallCount       : 0
+0x1844 Padding8            : [4]  ""
+0x1848 ExtendedFeatureDisableMask : 0
```

```
1: kd> dp 008b5000+0x1480+8 L1
00000000`008b6488  00000000`00a5fd20
```

```
1: kd> dd 00000000`00a5fd20
00000000`00a5fd20  014c0003 0001003f 00000000 00000000
00000000`00a5fd30  00000000 00000000 00000000 00000000
00000000`00a5fd40  0000027f 00000000 0000ffff 00000000
00000000`00a5fd50  00000000 00000000 00000000 00a9fd38
00000000`00a5fd60  00000000 775d6f90 00000000 00000000
00000000`00a5fd70  00000000 00000000 00000000 00000000
00000000`00a5fd80  00000000 00000000 00000000 00000000
00000000`00a5fd90  00000000 00000000 00000000 00000000
```

```
1: kd> lmi m ntdll*
Browse full module list
start               end                 module name
00000000`77560000 00000000`77709000   ntdll_77560000 # (pdb symbols)        ntdll.dll
00007ffe`5af80000 00007ffe`5b189000   ntdll   # (pdb symbols)        ntdll.dll
```

```
1: kd> dt ntdll_77560000!_CONTEXT 00000000`00a5fd20+4
+0x000 ContextFlags        : 0x1003f
+0x004 Dr0                 : 0
+0x008 Dr1                 : 0
+0x00c Dr2                 : 0
+0x010 Dr3                 : 0
+0x014 Dr6                 : 0
+0x018 Dr7                 : 0
+0x01c FloatSave           : _FLOATING_SAVE_AREA
+0x08c SegGs               : 0x2b
+0x090 SegFs               : 0x53
+0x094 SegEs               : 0x2b
+0x098 SegDs               : 0x2b
+0x09c Edi                 : 0x10493fc
+0x0a0 Esi                 : 0x10493fc
+0x0a4 Ebx                 : 0x10493c8
+0x0a8 Edx                 : 0
+0x0ac Ecx                 : 0
+0x0b0 Eax                 : 0
+0x0b4 Ebp                 : 0xa9fdac
+0x0b8 Eip                 : 0x768210cc
+0x0bc SegCs               : 0x23
+0x0c0 EFlags              : 0x206
+0x0c4 Esp                 : 0xa9fd74
+0x0c8 SegSs               : 0x2b
+0x0cc ExtendedRegisters   : [512]  "???"
```

Note: ESP and EBP register values help find where to cut the reconstructed stack trace. The EIP register value helps find the currently executing function, and the ESP register value helps find the previous caller.

```
00000000`00a9f9f8   USER32!UserCallWinProcCheckWow+0x4aa
00000000`00a9fae8   USER32!CallWindowProcW+0x7f
00000000`00a9fb20   UIRibbon!WndBridge::RawWndProc+0x10b
00000000`00a9fb60   atlthunk!AtlThunk_0x00+0x3a
00000000`00a9fb80   USER32!_InternalCallWinProc+0x2a
00000000`00a9fbac   USER32!UserCallWinProcCheckWow+0x4aa
00000000`00a9fc9c   USER32!DispatchClientMessage+0xea
00000000`00a9fd00   USER32!__fnDWORD+0x3f
00000000`00a9fd3c   ntdll_77560000!KiUserCallbackDispatcher+0x4c
================================================================
00000000`00a9fdac   00a9fde4
00000000`00a9fdb0   75238f35 MFC42u!CWinThread::PumpMessage+0x15
        a9fd74
================================================================
00000000`00a9fdb0   MFC42u!CWinThread::PumpMessage+0x15
00000000`00a9fde8   MFC42u!AfxWinMain+0xa2
00000000`00a9fe00   wordpad!__wmainCRTStartup+0x153
00000000`00a9fe90   KERNEL32!BaseThreadInitThunk+0x19
00000000`00a9fea0   ntdll_77560000!__RtlUserThreadStart+0x2b
00000000`00a9fef8   ntdll_77560000!_RtlUserThreadStart+0x1b
```

```
1: kd> dds a9fd74 L1
00000000`00a9fd74   758e0200 USER32!GetMessageW+0x30
```

```
1: kd> ln 0x768210cc
Browse module
Set bu breakpoint

(00000000`768210c0)   win32u!NtUserGetMessage+0xc   |   (00000000`768210d0)   win32u!NtUserMessageCall
```

```
1: kd> ub 0x768210cc
win32u!NtUserInvalidateRect:
00000000`768210b0 b803100c00       mov     eax,0C1003h
00000000`768210b5 ba606c8276       mov     edx,offset win32u!Wow64SystemServiceCall
(00000000`76826c60)
00000000`768210ba ffd2             call    rdx
00000000`768210bc c20c00           ret     0Ch
00000000`768210bf 90               nop
win32u!NtUserGetMessage:
00000000`768210c0 b804100000       mov     eax,1004h
00000000`768210c5 ba606c8276       mov     edx,offset win32u!Wow64SystemServiceCall
(00000000`76826c60)
00000000`768210ca ffd2             call    rdx
```

Note: Together we can glue these pieces together:

```
00000000`00a9f9f8   win32u!NtUserGetMessage+0xc
00000000`00a9fd74   USER32!GetMessageW+0x30
00000000`00a9fdb0   MFC42u!CWinThread::PumpMessage+0x15
00000000`00a9fde8   MFC42u!AfxWinMain+0xa2
00000000`00a9fe00   wordpad!__wmainCRTStartup+0x153
00000000`00a9fe90   KERNEL32!BaseThreadInitThunk+0x19
00000000`00a9fea0   ntdll_77560000!__RtlUserThreadStart+0x2b
00000000`00a9fef8   ntdll_77560000!_RtlUserThreadStart+0x1b
```

10.   Finally, since we know EBP, ESP, and EIP register values, we can use the extended version of the **k** command with hints when the ordinary one failed:

```
1: kd> .thread /w ffffbe0c8beda080
Implicit thread is now ffffbe0c`8beda080
x86 context set
```

```
1: kd:x86> .reload
Loading Kernel Symbols
...............................................................
...............................................................
...............................................................
..
Loading User Symbols
.......
Loading unloaded module list
........
Loading Wow64 Symbols
...............................................................
....

************* Symbol Loading Error Summary **************
Module name            Error
SharedUserData         No error - symbol load deferred

You can troubleshoot most symbol related issues by turning on symbol loading diagnostics (!sym
noisy) and repeating the command that caused symbols to be loaded.
You should also verify that your symbol search path (.sympath) is correct.
```

```
1: kd:x86> k=0xa9fdac 0xa9fd74 0x768210cc
 # ChildEBP          RetAddr
00 00a9fd70 758e0200     win32u!NtUserGetMessage+0xc
01 00a9fdac 75238f35     USER32!GetMessageW+0x30
02 00a9fdc8 75238fe3     CWinThread::PumpMessage+0x15
03 00a9fde4 7520a242     MFC42u!CWinThread::Run+0x63
04 00a9fdfc 01036d0c     MFC42u!AfxWinMain+0xa2
05 00a9fe8c 75eb6739     wordpad!__wmainCRTStartup+0x153
06 00a9fe9c 775c8e7f     KERNEL32!BaseThreadInitThunk+0x19
07 00a9fef4 775c8e4d     ntdll_77560000!__RtlUserThreadStart+0x2b
08 00a9ff04 00000000     ntdll_77560000!_RtlUserThreadStart+0x1b
```

11.   We close logging before exiting WinDbg:

```
1: kd> .logclose
Closing open log file C:\AdvWMDA-Dumps\x64\C1B.log
```

Exercise C2

- **Goal:** Learn how to assemble code and evaluate expressions; recognize byte ordering conventions; search memory for specific values

- **Patterns:** Value References; Foreign Stack

- \AdvWMDA-Dumps\Exercise-C2-Memory-Search.pdf

Exercise C2: Memory Search

Goal: Learn how to assemble code and evaluate expressions; recognize byte ordering conventions; search memory for specific values.

Patterns: Value References; Foreign Stack.

1.   Launch WinDbg.

2.   Open \AdvWMDA-Dumps\x64\MEMORY-Normal.DMP

3.   We get the dump file loaded (the output should be the same as in the previous exercise).

4.   We open a log file:

```
1: kd> .logopen C:\AdvWMDA-Dumps\x64\C2.log
Opened log file 'C:\AdvWMDA-Dumps\x64\C2.log'
```

5.   We check nonpaged pool consumption:

```
1: kd> !poolused 2
..
Sorting by NonPaged Pool Consumed
```

Tag	NonPaged Allocs	Used	Paged Allocs	Used	
ConT	588	9375744	0	0	UNKNOWN pooltag 'ConT', please update pooltag.txt
Thre	2190	5886208	0	0	Thread objects , Binary: nt!ps
EtwB	97	5632256	11	241664	Etw Buffer , Binary: nt!etw
File	11435	4551600	0	0	File objects
NtxF	9810	3610080	0	0	FCB_NONPAGED NtfsFcbNonpagedDataLookasideList , Binary: ntfs.sys
EtwR	15211	3358304	0	0	Etw KM RegEntry , Binary: nt!etw
FMsl	12296	2557568	0	0	STREAM_LIST_CTRL structure , Binary: fltmgr.sys
Cont	42	2412688	0	0	Contiguous physical memory allocations for device drivers
Vad	15046	2407360	0	0	Mm virtual address descriptors , Binary: nt!mm
AmlH	4	2097152	0	0	ACPI AMLI Pooltags
MmCa	5661	2018464	0	0	Mm control areas for mapped files , Binary: nt!mm
ALPC	3349	1993840	0	0	ALPC port objects , Binary: nt!alpc
Even	14763	1903072	0	0	Event objects
smNp	415	1699840	0	0	ReadyBoost store node pool allocations , Binary: nt!store or rdyboost.sys
MmPb	3	1617920	0	0	Paging file bitmaps , Binary: nt!mm
Pool	6	1482752	0	0	Pool tables, etc.
MmCi	2167	1355232	0	0	Mm control areas for images , Binary: nt!mm
Ahci	42	1278144	0	0	UNKNOWN pooltag 'Ahci', please update pooltag.txt
ViSh	801	1218176	138	4416	Video scheduler , Binary: dxgkrnl.sys
[...]					
ahgt	3	1248	0	0	UNKNOWN pooltag 'ahgt', please update pooltag.txt
LSfR	9	1248	9	24144	SMB2 rfssequence table and rfs64table , Binary: srv2.sys
ExEH	11	1232	3	336	UNKNOWN pooltag 'ExEH', please update pooltag.txt
FMfn	4	1216	26058	11745920	NAME_CACHE_NODE structure , Binary: fltmgr.sys
Nb05	4	1216	0	0	NetBT client element , Binary: netbt.sys
UMD~	25	1200	0	0	UMDF pool allocation , Binary: WUDFRd.sys
I4ua	5	1200	0	0	IPv4 Local Unicast Addresses , Binary: tcpip.sys
vmmp	9	1200	0	0	UNKNOWN pooltag 'vmmp', please update pooltag.txt
TcTx	9	1168	0	0	TCP Transmit , Binary: tcpip.sys
[...]					
Nv4f	1	528	0	0	UNKNOWN pooltag 'Nv4f', please update pooltag.txt
AlP6	1	528	0	0	ALE peer IPv6 address , Binary: tcpip.sys
InSA	1	528	0	0	UNKNOWN pooltag 'InSA', please update pooltag.txt
AlSP	1	528	0	0	ALE secure socket policy , Binary: tcpip.sys
IPjp	1	528	0	0	UNKNOWN pooltag 'IPjp', please update pooltag.txt
[...]					

Note: Suppose we are interested in drivers that allocated memory with *vmmp* and *InSA* pool tags.

6. Pool tags are usually pushed to stack or moved to registers before calling pool allocation functions. So, to understand how to find pool tags in memory and see how it looks in the binary code, we now try assembling the **push 12345678** instruction as an example using the **a** command:

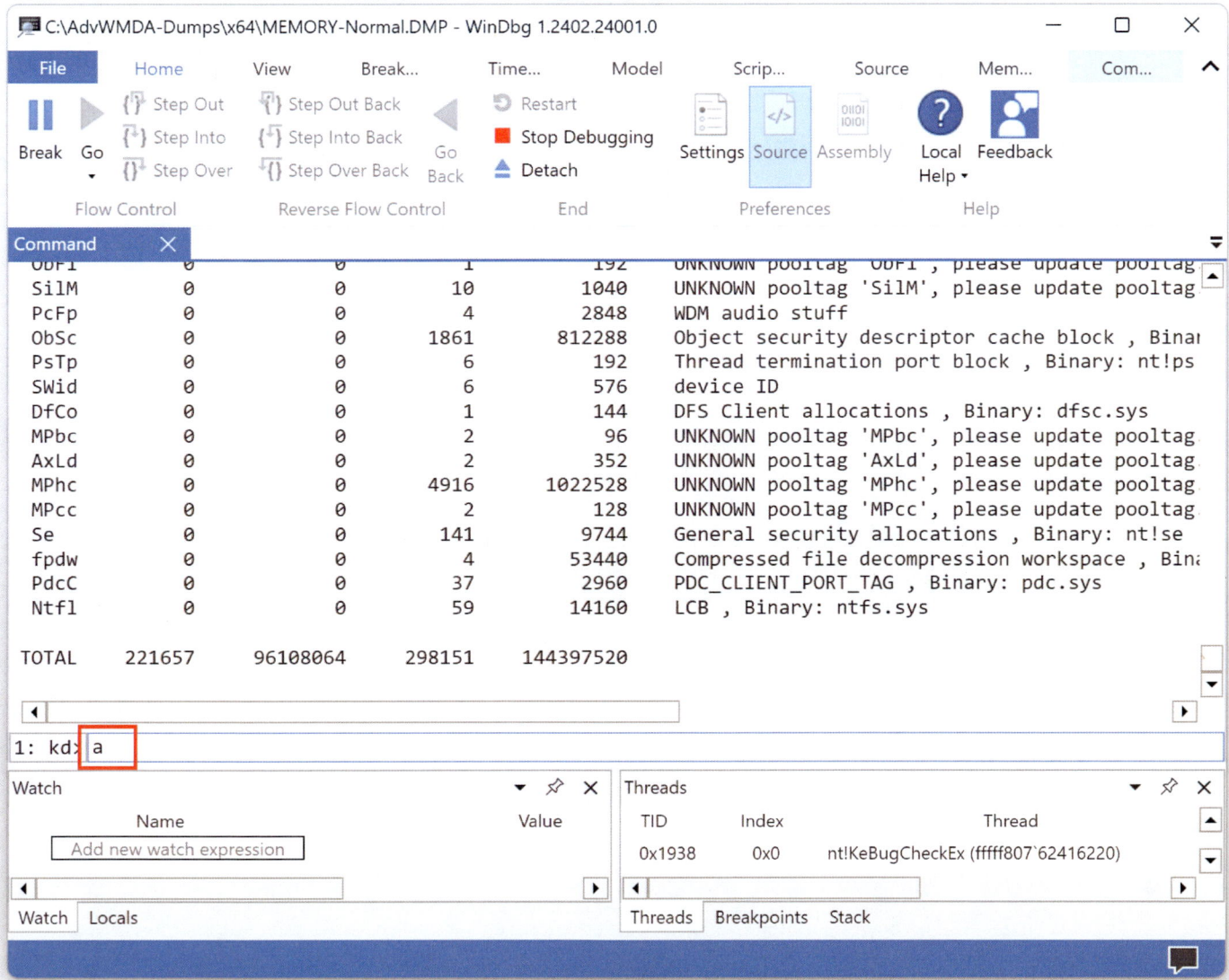

The prompt changes from **1: kd>** to **Input>**

C:\AdvWMDA-Dumps\x64\MEMORY-Normal.DMP - WinDbg 1.2402.24001.0

File | Home | View | Break... | Time... | Model | Scrip... | Source | Mem... | Com...

Step Out | Step Out Back | Restart | Settings | Source | Assembly | Local Help | Feedback
Break | Go | Step Into | Step Into Back | Go | Stop Debugging
Step Over | Step Over Back | Go Back | Detach

Flow Control | Reverse Flow Control | End | Preferences | Help

Command ✕

SilM	0	0	10	1040	UNKNOWN pooltag 'SilM', please update pooltag
PcFp	0	0	4	2848	WDM audio stuff
ObSc	0	0	1861	812288	Object security descriptor cache block , Binar
PsTp	0	0	6	192	Thread termination port block , Binary: nt!ps
SWid	0	0	6	576	device ID
DfCo	0	0	1	144	DFS Client allocations , Binary: dfsc.sys
MPbc	0	0	2	96	UNKNOWN pooltag 'MPbc', please update pooltag
AxLd	0	0	2	352	UNKNOWN pooltag 'AxLd', please update pooltag
MPhc	0	0	4916	1022528	UNKNOWN pooltag 'MPhc', please update pooltag
MPcc	0	0	2	128	UNKNOWN pooltag 'MPcc', please update pooltag
Se	0	0	141	9744	General security allocations , Binary: nt!se
fpdw	0	0	4	53440	Compressed file decompression workspace , Bina
PdcC	0	0	37	2960	PDC_CLIENT_PORT_TAG , Binary: pdc.sys
Ntfl	0	0	59	14160	LCB , Binary: ntfs.sys

```
TOTAL    221657    96108064    298151    144397520
1: kd> a
fffff807`62416220
```

Input>

Watch 📌 ✕

Name	Value
Add new watch expression	

Watch | Locals

Threads 📌 ✕

TID	Index	Thread
0x1938	0x0	nt!KeBugCheckEx (fffff807`62416220)

Threads | Breakpoints | Stack

We enter the assembly instruction:

```
C:\AdvWMDA-Dumps\x64\MEMORY-Normal.DMP - WinDbg 1.2402.24001.0          —   □   ✕
```

File | Home | View | Break... | Time... | Model | Scrip... | Source | Mem... | Com... | ^

▌▌ Break	▶ Go	⌐} Step Out	⊤} Step Out Back	◀ Go Back	↺ Restart	Settings	Source	Assembly	? Local Help ▾	Feedback
{↓} Step Into	{↑} Step Into Back	■ Stop Debugging
{}↓ Step Over	⊤{} Step Over Back	▲ Detach

Flow Control | Reverse Flow Control | End | Preferences | Help

Command   ✕

```
  PcFp         0          0          4        2848   WDM audio stuff
  ObSc         0          0       1861      812288   Object security descriptor cache block , Binaı
  PsTp         0          0          6         192   Thread termination port block , Binary: nt!ps
  SWid         0          0          6         576   device ID
  DfCo         0          0          1         144   DFS Client allocations , Binary: dfsc.sys
  MPbc         0          0          2          96   UNKNOWN pooltag 'MPbc', please update pooltag
  AxLd         0          0          2         352   UNKNOWN pooltag 'AxLd', please update pooltag
  MPhc         0          0       4916     1022528   UNKNOWN pooltag 'MPhc', please update pooltag
  MPcc         0          0          2         128   UNKNOWN pooltag 'MPcc', please update pooltag
  Se           0          0        141        9744   General security allocations , Binary: nt!se
  fpdw         0          0          4       53440   Compressed file decompression workspace , Binı
  PdcC         0          0         37        2960   PDC_CLIENT_PORT_TAG , Binary: pdc.sys
  Ntfl         0          0         59       14160   LCB , Binary: ntfs.sys

TOTAL      221657   96108064     298151   144397520
1: kd> a
fffff807`62416220 push 12345678
fffff807`62416225
◀                                                                           ▶
```

Input>

Watch   ▾ 📌 ✕ | **Threads**   ▾ 📌 ✕
| Name | Value | | TID | Index | Thread |
| Add new watch expression | | | 0x1938 | 0x0 | nt!KeBugCheckEx (fffff807`62416220) |
◀   ▶ | ◀   ▶

Watch | Locals | | Threads | Breakpoints | Stack

Then we press <Enter> again:

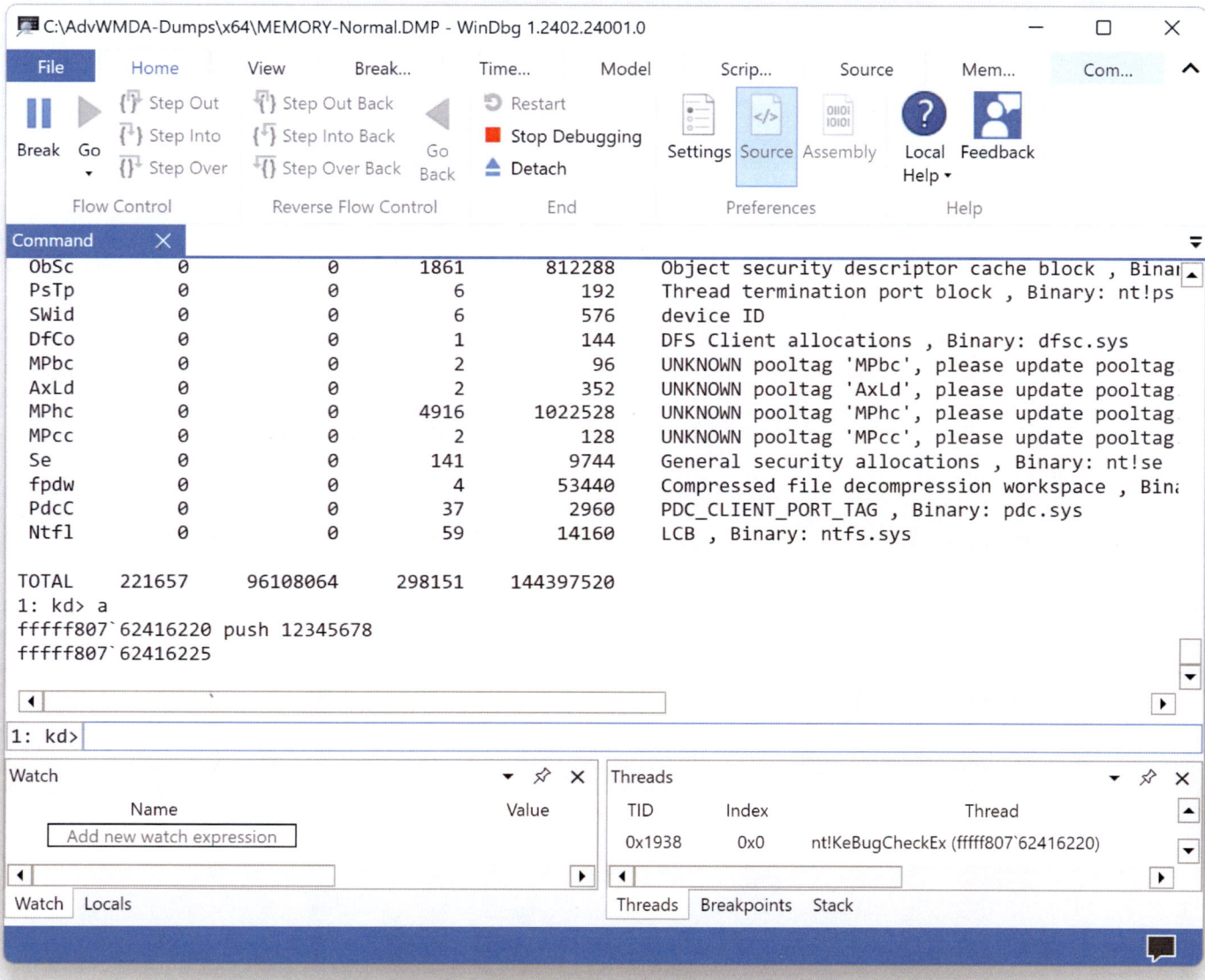

Note: At the address fffff807`62416220, we should have our instruction in a binary form:

```
1: kd> .asm- no_code_bytes
Assembly options: <default>
```

```
1: kd> u fffff807`62416220
nt!KeBugCheckEx:
fffff807`62416220 6878563412          push    12345678h
fffff807`62416225 4889542410          mov     qword ptr [rsp+10h],rdx
fffff807`6241622a 4c89442418          mov     qword ptr [rsp+18h],r8
fffff807`6241622f 4c894c2420          mov     qword ptr [rsp+20h],r9
fffff807`62416234 9c                  pushfq
fffff807`62416235 4883ec30            sub     rsp,30h
fffff807`62416239 fa                  cli
fffff807`6241623a 65488b0c2520000000  mov     rcx,qword ptr gs:[20h]
```

Note: The layout of the number in memory is 78563412 because we have a little-endian byte ordering convention. The least significant byte **78** in the number 12345**678** is at the lower byte address in the instruction stream 68**78**563412. 68 is the opcode for *push imm* instruction.

7.   Pool allocations with tags are done using *ExAllocatePoolWithTag* or *ExAllocatePoolWithTagPriority* functions, where a 4-byte pool tag is a function parameter that could be passed either via the stack (push) or a register (mov). Let's now determine pool tag binary equivalents corresponding to their memory layout:

```
1: kd> ? 'vmmp'
Evaluate expression: 1986882928 = 00000000`766d6d70
```

```
1: kd> ? 'InSA'
Evaluate expression: 1231967041 = 00000000`496e5341
```

8.   We now search every module for such values. The command to search virtual memory is **s.** So if we want to find 12345678 (78 56 34 12 as a byte stream) in the memory region RIP – RIP+100, we use this command (RIP is a CPU register pointing to the next instruction to execute, in our case fffff807`62416220):

```
1: kd> s-b fffff807`62416220 fffff807`62416220+100 78 56 34 12
fffff807`62416221  78 56 34 12 48 89 54 24-10 4c 89 44 24 18 4c 89  xV4.H.T$.L.D$.L.
```

```
1: kd> dc fffff807`62416221 L1
fffff807`62416221  12345678                                         xV4.
```

```
1: kd> db fffff807`62416221 L4
fffff807`62416221  78 56 34 12                                      xV4.
```

Note: If we search for double word values, we shouldn't forget to respect the alignment boundary:

```
1: kd> s-d fffff807`62416220 fffff807`62416220+100 12345678
```

```
1: kd> s-d fffff807`62416220+1 fffff807`62416220+100 12345678
fffff807`62416221  12345678 24548948 44894c10 894c1824  xV4.H.T$.L.D$.L.
```

9.   To find code that uses the chosen pool tags above, we repeat the memory byte search for every module:

```
1: kd> !for_each_module "s-b @#Base @#End 76 6d 6d 70"
fffff807`68b612a8  76 6d 6d 70 ff 15 96 1d-00 00 33 c0 48 8b 5c 24  vmmp......3.H.\$
fffff807`68b61402  76 6d 6d 70 ff 15 3c 1c-00 00 48 83 c4 28 c3 cc  vmmp..<...H..(..
fffff807`68b61429  76 6d 6d 70 ff 15 0d 1c-00 00 48 85 c0 74 07 48  vmmp......H..t.H
fffff807`68b61491  76 6d 6d 70 49 8b ce ff-15 aa 1b 00 00 33 ff eb  vmmpI........3..
fffff807`68b614e3  76 6d 6d 70 49 8b ce ff-15 58 1b 00 00 48 8b 5c  vmmpI....X...H.\
fffff807`68b9013c  76 6d 6d 70 ff 15 22 30-01 00 33 c0 48 8b 5c 24  vmmp.."0..3.H.\$
fffff807`68b9020e  76 6d 6d 70 ff 15 50 2f-01 00 48 83 c4 28 c3 cc  vmmp..P/..H..(..
fffff807`68b90235  76 6d 6d 70 ff 15 49 30-01 00 48 85 c0 74 07 48  vmmp..I0..H..t.H
fffff807`68b9029d  76 6d 6d 70 49 8b ce ff-15 be 2e 01 00 33 ff eb  vmmpI........3..
fffff807`68b902ef  76 6d 6d 70 49 8b ce ff-15 6c 2e 01 00 48 8b 5c  vmmpI....l...H.\
```

```
1: kd> !for_each_module "s-b @#Base @#End 'v' 'm' 'm' 'p'"
fffff807`68b612a8  76 6d 6d 70 ff 15 96 1d-00 00 33 c0 48 8b 5c 24  vmmp......3.H.\$
fffff807`68b61402  76 6d 6d 70 ff 15 3c 1c-00 00 48 83 c4 28 c3 cc  vmmp..<...H..(..
fffff807`68b61429  76 6d 6d 70 ff 15 0d 1c-00 00 48 85 c0 74 07 48  vmmp......H..t.H
fffff807`68b61491  76 6d 6d 70 49 8b ce ff-15 aa 1b 00 00 33 ff eb  vmmpI........3..
fffff807`68b614e3  76 6d 6d 70 49 8b ce ff-15 58 1b 00 00 48 8b 5c  vmmpI....X...H.\
fffff807`68b9013c  76 6d 6d 70 ff 15 22 30-01 00 33 c0 48 8b 5c 24  vmmp.."0..3.H.\$
```

```
fffff807`68b9020e   76 6d 6d 70 ff 15 50 2f-01 00 48 83 c4 28 c3 cc   vmmp..P/..H..(..
fffff807`68b90235   76 6d 6d 70 ff 15 49 30-01 00 48 85 c0 74 07 48   vmmp..I0..H..t.H
fffff807`68b9029d   76 6d 6d 70 49 8b ce ff-15 be 2e 01 00 33 ff eb   vmmpI........3..
fffff807`68b902ef   76 6d 6d 70 49 8b ce ff-15 6c 2e 01 00 48 8b 5c   vmmpI....l...H.\
```

```
1: kd> !for_each_module "s-b @#Base @#End 'I' 'n' 'S' 'A'"
fffff807`675d8e0d   49 6e 53 41 4c 8b 15 e0-a7 17 00 e8 03 26 49 fb   InSAL........&I.
fffff807`6764a3a7   49 6e 53 41 4c 8b 15 36-92 10 00 e8 59 0c 42 fb   InSAL..6....Y.B.
```

10.   Let's now check module load addresses to see which modules correspond to our search results (we use 'o' to display only loaded modules):

```
1: kd> lmko
start             end               module name
ffffbc92`8dc40000 ffffbc92`8dcea000 win32k      (deferred)
ffffbc92`8e110000 ffffbc92`8e451000 win32kbase   (deferred)
ffffbc92`8e6d0000 ffffbc92`8ea82000 win32kfull    (deferred)
ffffbc92`8ea90000 ffffbc92`8ead3000 cdd        (deferred)
fffff807`608f0000 fffff807`60c73000 mcupdate_GenuineIntel    (deferred)
fffff807`60ca0000 fffff807`60ca6000 hal        (deferred)
fffff807`60cb0000 fffff807`60cbb000 kd         (deferred)
fffff807`60cc0000 fffff807`60ce8000 tm         (deferred)
fffff807`60cf0000 fffff807`60d5c000 CLFS       (deferred)
fffff807`60d60000 fffff807`60d7a000 PSHED      (deferred)
fffff807`60d80000 fffff807`60d8b000 BOOTVID    (deferred)
fffff807`60d90000 fffff807`60db9000 ksecdd     (deferred)
fffff807`60dc0000 fffff807`60dce000 cmimcext   (deferred)
fffff807`60dd0000 fffff807`60de4000 werkernel   (deferred)
fffff807`60df0000 fffff807`60dfc000 ntosext    (deferred)
fffff807`60e00000 fffff807`60e38000 wcifs      (deferred)
fffff807`60e40000 fffff807`60ec5000 cldflt     (deferred)
fffff807`60ed0000 fffff807`60eea000 storqosflt    (deferred)
fffff807`60ef0000 fffff807`60f1a000 bindflt    (deferred)
fffff807`60f20000 fffff807`60f38000 lltdio     (deferred)
fffff807`60f40000 fffff807`60f58000 mslldp     (deferred)
fffff807`60f60000 fffff807`60f7b000 rspndr     (deferred)
fffff807`60f80000 fffff807`60f9d000 wanarp     (deferred)
fffff807`60fa0000 fffff807`61003000 msquic     (deferred)
fffff807`61010000 fffff807`611ae000 HTTP       (deferred)
fffff807`611b0000 fffff807`611d7000 bowser     (deferred)
fffff807`611e0000 fffff807`61277000 mrxsmb     (deferred)
fffff807`61280000 fffff807`6129b000 mpsdrv     (deferred)
fffff807`612a0000 fffff807`612e9000 mrxsmb20   (deferred)
fffff807`612f0000 fffff807`61304000 mmcss      (deferred)
fffff807`61310000 fffff807`6131a000 vmmemctl   (deferred)
fffff807`61320000 fffff807`6137a000 srvnet     (deferred)
fffff807`61380000 fffff807`613d3000 mrxsmb10   (deferred)
fffff807`613e0000 fffff807`614ae000 srv2       (deferred)
fffff807`614b0000 fffff807`614d8000 Ndu        (deferred)
fffff807`614e0000 fffff807`615ae000 peauth     (deferred)
fffff807`615b0000 fffff807`615c4000 tcpipreg   (deferred)
fffff807`615d0000 fffff807`615ed000 rassstp    (deferred)
fffff807`615f0000 fffff807`6160d000 NDProxy    (deferred)
fffff807`61610000 fffff807`6163b000 vmhgfs     (deferred)
fffff807`61640000 fffff807`61653000 condrv     (deferred)
fffff807`61660000 fffff807`61688000 AgileVpn   (deferred)
fffff807`61690000 fffff807`616b0000 rasl2tp    (deferred)
```

```
fffff807`616c0000 fffff807`616e1000    raspptp      (deferred)
fffff807`616f0000 fffff807`6170c000    raspppoe     (deferred)
fffff807`61710000 fffff807`6171f000    ndistapi     (deferred)
fffff807`61720000 fffff807`6175b000    ndiswan      (deferred)
fffff807`61760000 fffff807`6177a000    WdNisDrv     (deferred)
fffff807`61780000 fffff807`61788000    myfault      (deferred)
fffff807`61ba0000 fffff807`61c22000    dxgmms1      (deferred)
fffff807`61c30000 fffff807`61c4c000    monitor      (deferred)
fffff807`61c50000 fffff807`61d54000    dxgmms2      (deferred)
fffff807`61d60000 fffff807`61db4000    WUDFRd       (deferred)
fffff807`61dc0000 fffff807`61deb000    luafv        (deferred)
fffff807`62000000 fffff807`63047000    nt           (pdb symbols)
C:\ProgramData\dbg\sym\ntkrnlmp.pdb\BF8CAE58DB897A8B8E09080F577B7ECD1\ntkrnlmp.pdb
fffff807`66200000 fffff807`66312000    clipsp       (deferred)
fffff807`66320000 fffff807`66393000    FLTMGR       (deferred)
fffff807`663a0000 fffff807`66403000    msrpc        (deferred)
fffff807`66410000 fffff807`664f4000    CI           (deferred)
fffff807`66500000 fffff807`665bc000    cng          (deferred)
fffff807`665c0000 fffff807`66693000    Wdf01000     (deferred)
fffff807`666a0000 fffff807`666b4000    WDFLDR       (deferred)
fffff807`666c0000 fffff807`666cd000    PRM          (deferred)
fffff807`666d0000 fffff807`666f6000    acpiex       (deferred)
fffff807`66700000 fffff807`66712000    WppRecorder    (deferred)
fffff807`66720000 fffff807`6673b000    SgrmAgent     (deferred)
fffff807`66740000 fffff807`6680c000    ACPI         (deferred)
fffff807`66810000 fffff807`6681c000    WMILIB       (deferred)
fffff807`66820000 fffff807`6682b000    msisadrv     (deferred)
fffff807`66830000 fffff807`668b2000    pci          (deferred)
fffff807`668c0000 fffff807`66912000    tpm          (deferred)
fffff807`66940000 fffff807`669b3000    intelpep     (deferred)
fffff807`669c0000 fffff807`669d7000    WindowsTrustedRT    (deferred)
fffff807`669e0000 fffff807`669f0000    IntelPMT     (deferred)
fffff807`66a00000 fffff807`66a0b000    WindowsTrustedRTProxy    (deferred)
fffff807`66a10000 fffff807`66a24000    pcw          (deferred)
fffff807`66a30000 fffff807`66a47000    vdrvroot     (deferred)
fffff807`66a50000 fffff807`66a7f000    pdc          (deferred)
fffff807`66a80000 fffff807`66a97000    CEA          (deferred)
fffff807`66aa0000 fffff807`66ad2000    partmgr      (deferred)
fffff807`66ae0000 fffff807`66baf000    spaceport    (deferred)
fffff807`66bb0000 fffff807`66bcb000    volmgr       (deferred)
fffff807`66bd0000 fffff807`66bdb000    intelide     (deferred)
fffff807`66be0000 fffff807`66bf3000    PCIIDEX      (deferred)
fffff807`66c00000 fffff807`66c63000    volmgrx      (deferred)
fffff807`66c70000 fffff807`66c88000    vsock        (deferred)
fffff807`66c90000 fffff807`66cac000    vmci         (deferred)
fffff807`66cb0000 fffff807`66cce000    mountmgr     (deferred)
fffff807`66cd0000 fffff807`66cef000    lsi_sas      (deferred)
fffff807`66cf0000 fffff807`66dd0000    storport     (deferred)
fffff807`66de0000 fffff807`66ded000    atapi        (deferred)
fffff807`66df0000 fffff807`66e2c000    ataport      (deferred)
fffff807`66e30000 fffff807`66e61000    storahci     (deferred)
fffff807`66e70000 fffff807`66e92000    EhStorClass    (deferred)
fffff807`66ea0000 fffff807`66ebb000    fileinfo     (deferred)
fffff807`66ec0000 fffff807`66f03000    Wof          (deferred)
fffff807`66f10000 fffff807`66f7c000    WdFilter     (deferred)
fffff807`66f80000 fffff807`67294000    Ntfs         (deferred)
fffff807`672a0000 fffff807`672ad000    Fs_Rec       (deferred)
fffff807`672b0000 fffff807`67431000    ndis         (deferred)
fffff807`67440000 fffff807`674db000    NETIO        (deferred)
```

```
fffff807`674e0000 fffff807`67513000   ksecpkg      (deferred)
fffff807`67520000 fffff807`67836000   tcpip        (deferred)
fffff807`67840000 fffff807`678c1000   fwpkclnt     (deferred)
fffff807`678d0000 fffff807`67900000   wfplwfs      (deferred)
fffff807`67910000 fffff807`679e0000   fvevol       (deferred)
fffff807`679f0000 fffff807`679fb000   volume       (deferred)
fffff807`67a00000 fffff807`67a73000   volsnap      (deferred)
fffff807`67a80000 fffff807`67acf000   rdyboost     (deferred)
fffff807`67ad0000 fffff807`67af6000   mup          (deferred)
fffff807`67b00000 fffff807`67b12000   iorate       (deferred)
fffff807`67b40000 fffff807`67b5c000   disk         (deferred)
fffff807`67b60000 fffff807`67bcf000   CLASSPNP     (deferred)
fffff807`68060000 fffff807`68090000   cdrom        (deferred)
fffff807`680a0000 fffff807`680b5000   filecrypt    (deferred)
fffff807`680c0000 fffff807`680ce000   tbs          (deferred)
fffff807`680d0000 fffff807`680da000   Null         (deferred)
fffff807`680e0000 fffff807`680ea000   Beep         (deferred)
fffff807`680f0000 fffff807`68100000   vmrawdsk     (deferred)
fffff807`68110000 fffff807`68580000   dxgkrnl      (deferred)
fffff807`68590000 fffff807`685ae000   watchdog     (deferred)
fffff807`685b0000 fffff807`685c5000   BasicDisplay (deferred)
fffff807`685d0000 fffff807`685e1000   BasicRender  (deferred)
fffff807`685f0000 fffff807`6860c000   Npfs         (deferred)
fffff807`68610000 fffff807`68621000   Msfs         (deferred)
fffff807`68630000 fffff807`68655000   CimFS        (deferred)
fffff807`68660000 fffff807`68683000   tdx          (deferred)
fffff807`68690000 fffff807`686a0000   TDI          (deferred)
fffff807`686b0000 fffff807`6870a000   netbt        (deferred)
fffff807`68710000 fffff807`68723000   afunix       (deferred)
fffff807`68730000 fffff807`687d4000   afd          (deferred)
fffff807`687e0000 fffff807`687fa000   vwififlt     (deferred)
fffff807`68800000 fffff807`6882b000   pacer        (deferred)
fffff807`68830000 fffff807`68843000   ndiscap      (deferred)
fffff807`68850000 fffff807`68864000   netbios      (deferred)
fffff807`68870000 fffff807`68925000   Vid          (deferred)
fffff807`68930000 fffff807`68955000   winhvr       (deferred)
fffff807`68990000 fffff807`689b3000   crashdmp     (deferred)
fffff807`689e0000 fffff807`689fd000   dump_dumpfve (deferred)
fffff807`68a00000 fffff807`68a53000   ahcache      (deferred)
fffff807`68a60000 fffff807`68a73000   CompositeBus (deferred)
fffff807`68a80000 fffff807`68a8e000   kdnic        (deferred)
fffff807`68a90000 fffff807`68aa6000   umbus        (deferred)
fffff807`68ab0000 fffff807`68ad6000   i8042prt     (deferred)
fffff807`68ae0000 fffff807`68af4000   kbdclass     (deferred)
fffff807`68b00000 fffff807`68b09000   vmmouse      (deferred)
fffff807`68b10000 fffff807`68b24000   mouclass     (deferred)
fffff807`68b30000 fffff807`68b4d000   serial       (deferred)
fffff807`68b50000 fffff807`68b5f000   serenum      (deferred)
fffff807`68b60000 fffff807`68b6a000   vm3dmp_loader (deferred)
fffff807`68b70000 fffff807`68bbb000   vm3dmp       (deferred)
fffff807`68bc0000 fffff807`68bd1000   usbuhci      (deferred)
fffff807`68be0000 fffff807`68bff000   dump_lsi_sas (deferred)
fffff807`68c00000 fffff807`68c7a000   rdbss        (deferred)
fffff807`68c80000 fffff807`68c92000   nsiproxy     (deferred)
fffff807`68ca0000 fffff807`68caf000   npsvctrig    (deferred)
fffff807`68cb0000 fffff807`68cc0000   mssmbios     (deferred)
fffff807`68cd0000 fffff807`68cda000   gpuenergydrv (deferred)
fffff807`68ce0000 fffff807`68d0c000   dfsc         (deferred)
fffff807`68d10000 fffff807`68d36000   bthpan       (deferred)
```

```
fffff807`68d40000 fffff807`68dac000   fastfat       (deferred)
fffff807`68db0000 fffff807`68dc8000   bam           (deferred)
fffff807`69000000 fffff807`69081000   ks            (deferred)
fffff807`69090000 fffff807`690aa000   usbehci       (deferred)
fffff807`690b0000 fffff807`69143000   e1i68x64      (deferred)
fffff807`69150000 fffff807`691ee000   USBXHCI       (deferred)
fffff807`691f0000 fffff807`69236000   ucx01000      (deferred)
fffff807`69240000 fffff807`6924b000   vmgencounter    (deferred)
fffff807`69250000 fffff807`69261000   CmBatt        (deferred)
fffff807`69270000 fffff807`692e9000   USBPORT       (deferred)
fffff807`692f0000 fffff807`6931c000   HDAudBus      (deferred)
fffff807`69320000 fffff807`69391000   portcls       (deferred)
fffff807`693a0000 fffff807`693c1000   drmk          (deferred)
fffff807`693d0000 fffff807`693e8000   BATTC         (deferred)
fffff807`69400000 fffff807`6947f000   HdAudio       (deferred)
fffff807`69480000 fffff807`6948f000   ksthunk       (deferred)
fffff807`69490000 fffff807`69538000   UsbHub3       (deferred)
fffff807`69540000 fffff807`69574000   usbccgp       (deferred)
fffff807`69580000 fffff807`69592000   hidusb        (deferred)
fffff807`695a0000 fffff807`695e3000   HIDCLASS      (deferred)
fffff807`695f0000 fffff807`69603000   HIDPARSE      (deferred)
fffff807`69610000 fffff807`69620000   mouhid        (deferred)
fffff807`69630000 fffff807`69639000   vmusbmouse    (deferred)
fffff807`69640000 fffff807`6965d000   BTHUSB        (deferred)
fffff807`69660000 fffff807`69836000   BTHport       (deferred)
fffff807`69840000 fffff807`6987c000   rfcomm        (deferred)
fffff807`69880000 fffff807`698a2000   BthEnum       (deferred)
fffff807`698c0000 fffff807`698cf000   dump_diskdump   (deferred)
fffff807`698d0000 fffff807`6991c000   intelppm      (deferred)
fffff807`69920000 fffff807`6992d000   NdisVirtualBus   (deferred)
fffff807`69930000 fffff807`6993c000   swenum        (deferred)
fffff807`69940000 fffff807`6994f000   rdpbus        (deferred)
fffff807`69950000 fffff807`699d4000   usbhub        (deferred)
fffff807`699e0000 fffff807`699ee000   USBD          (deferred)
```

Note: We can also use the **ln** command to find the nearest module addresses:

```
1: kd> ln fffff807`68b612a8
Browse module
Set bu breakpoint

Unable to load image \SystemRoot\system32\DRIVERS\vm3dmp_loader.sys, Win32 error 0n2

1: kd> ln fffff807`68b9013c
Browse module
Set bu breakpoint

Unable to load image \SystemRoot\system32\DRIVERS\vm3dmp.sys, Win32 error 0n2

1: kd> ln fffff807`675d8e0d
Browse module
Set bu breakpoint

(fffff807`675d8de0)   tcpip!InetStartModule+0x2d   |   (fffff807`675d8e70)
tcpip!IppStartBatching
```

11. We now check a sample search address:

```
1: kd> u fffff807`675d8e0d
tcpip!InetStartModule+0x2d:
fffff807`675d8e0d 496e            outs    dx,byte ptr [rsi]
fffff807`675d8e0f 53              push    rbx
fffff807`675d8e10 41              ???
fffff807`675d8e11 4c8b15e0a71700  mov     r10,qword ptr [tcpip!_imp_ExAllocatePool2
(fffff807`677535f8)]
fffff807`675d8e18 e8032649fb      call    nt!ExAllocatePool2 (fffff807`62a6b420)
fffff807`675d8e1d 48890524041600  mov     qword ptr [tcpip!InetSockAddrStorage
(fffff807`67739248)],rax
fffff807`675d8e24 488b051d041600  mov     rax,qword ptr [tcpip!InetSockAddrStorage
(fffff807`67739248)]
fffff807`675d8e2b 4885c0          test    rax,rax
```

```
1: kd> u fffff807`675d8e0d-1
tcpip!InetStartModule+0x2c:
fffff807`675d8e0c b8496e5341      mov     eax,41536E49h
fffff807`675d8e11 4c8b15e0a71700  mov     r10,qword ptr [tcpip!_imp_ExAllocatePool2
(fffff807`677535f8)]
fffff807`675d8e18 e8032649fb      call    nt!ExAllocatePool2 (fffff807`62a6b420)
fffff807`675d8e1d 48890524041600  mov     qword ptr [tcpip!InetSockAddrStorage
(fffff807`67739248)],rax
fffff807`675d8e24 488b051d041600  mov     rax,qword ptr [tcpip!InetSockAddrStorage
(fffff807`67739248)]
fffff807`675d8e2b 4885c0          test    rax,rax
fffff807`675d8e2e 7431            je      tcpip!InetStartModule+0x81 (fffff807`675d8e61)
fffff807`675d8e30 4c8d0581001600  lea     r8,[tcpip!InetStartedModules (fffff807`67738eb8)]
```

```
1: kd> .formats 41536E49h
Evaluate expression:
  Hex:      00000000`41536e49
  Decimal:  1095986761
  Octal:    0000000000010124667111
  Binary:   00000000 00000000 00000000 00000000 01000001 01010011 01101110 01001001
  Chars:    ....ASnI
  Time:     Fri Sep 24 01:46:01 2004
  Float:    low 13.2144 high 0
  Double:   5.41489e-315
```

12. We can also look for ASCII and UNICODE strings in the found driver and on the current thread raw stack:

```
1: kd> lmo m vm3dmp
Browse full module list
start             end               module name
fffff807`68b70000 fffff807`68bbb000  vm3dmp     (deferred)
```

```
1: kd> s-sa fffff807`68b70000 fffff807`68bbb000
fffff807`68b7004d  "!This program cannot be run in D"
fffff807`68b7006d  "OS mode."
fffff807`68b700e8  "RichW"
fffff807`68b70200  ".text"
fffff807`68b70227  "h.rdata"
fffff807`68b7024f  "H.data"
fffff807`68b70278  ".pdata"
fffff807`68b7029f  "Htext"
fffff807`68b702c7  "(data"
```

```
ffffff807`68b702ef    "HPAGE"
ffffff807`68b70317    "`INIT"
ffffff807`68b7033f    "b.rsrc"
ffffff807`68b70367    "B.reloc"
[...]
ffffff807`68bb71c0    "Modeset enabled, types available"
ffffff807`68bb71e0    ":%s%s%s"
ffffff807`68bb71f0    "No modeset types available."
ffffff807`68bb7210    "Modeset disabled."
ffffff807`68bb7230    "svga.wddm.forcePreemption"
ffffff807`68bb7250    "svga.wddm.directFlip"
ffffff807`68bb7270    "svga.wddm.errorFailingColorFill"
ffffff807`68bb7290    "svga.wddm.allowInactiveMonitors"
ffffff807`68bb72b0    "svga.wddm.disableDevTap"
ffffff807`68bb72d0    "svga.devtap.noMultimon"
ffffff807`68bb72f0    "svga.wddm.enableVSync"
ffffff807`68bb7310    "WDDM Aperture memory %I64uKB."
ffffff807`68bb7330    "enabled"
ffffff807`68bb7340    "disabled"
ffffff807`68bb7350    "WDDM VSync is %s."
ffffff807`68bb7370    "WDDM VSync Flip is %s."
ffffff807`68bb7390    "svga.wddm.enableDWMVSync"
ffffff807`68bb73b0    "WDDM VSync Flip for DWM is %s."
ffffff807`68bb73d0    "%d monitors active"
ffffff807`68bb73f0    "WDDM Error: failed to start the "
ffffff807`68bb7410    "device"
ffffff807`68bb7420    "TDR detected, display adapter re"
ffffff807`68bb7440    "set."
ffffff807`68bb7450    "svga.wddm.enableDX11DDI"
ffffff807`68bb7470    "svga.wddm.enable10_1FeatureLevel"
ffffff807`68bb74a0    "svga.wddm.fakeMSAAQualityLevels"
ffffff807`68bb74c0    "svga.wddm.enableDX9msaa"
ffffff807`68bb74e0    "svga.wddm.enableMSQualityResolve"
ffffff807`68bb7500    "d"

1: kd> s-su ffffff807`68b70000 ffffff807`68bbb000
[...]
ffffff807`68ba4bb8    "HardwareInformation.ChipType"
ffffff807`68ba4c00    "VMware Virtual SVGA 3D Graphics "
ffffff807`68ba4c40    "Adapter"
ffffff807`68ba4c50    "HardwareInformation.DacType"
ffffff807`68ba4c88    "n/a"
ffffff807`68ba4c90    "HardwareInformation.MemorySize"
ffffff807`68ba4ce0    "HardwareInformation.AdapterStrin"
ffffff807`68ba4d20    "g"
ffffff807`68ba4d28    "VMware SVGA 3D"
ffffff807`68ba4d48    "HardwareInformation.BiosString"
ffffff807`68ba4d88    "ActiveMonitors"
ffffff807`68ba4da8    "Flags"
ffffff807`68ba4db8    "Width"
ffffff807`68ba4dc8    "Height"
[...]

1: kd> !thread -1 3f
THREAD ffffbe0c8974f080  Cid 243c.1938  Teb: 00000034f5f84000 Win32Thread: ffffbe0c8cccb2a0 RUNNING on processor 1
IRP List:
    ffffbe0c8ac38d00: (0006,0118) Flags: 00060000  Mdl: 00000000
Not impersonating
DeviceMap                   ffff800eda519d60
Owning Process              ffffbe0c8c2cd0c0      Image:      notmyfault64.exe
```

```
Attached Process        N/A           Image:       N/A
Wait Start TickCount     29786         Ticks: 1 (0:00:00.015)
Context Switch Count     1701          IdealProcessor: 1
UserTime                00:00:00.015
KernelTime              00:00:00.125
Unable to load image C:\Work\notmyfault64.exe, Win32 error 0n2
Win32 Start Address notmyfault64 (0x00007ff72c045b0c)
Stack Init ffffa28c9d8d8fb0 Current ffffa28c9d8d82e0
Base ffffa28c9d8d9000 Limit ffffa28c9d8d3000 Call 0000000000000000
Priority 12 BasePriority 8 PriorityDecrement 2 IoPriority 2 PagePriority 5
Child-SP          RetAddr           Call Site
ffffa28c`9d8d8688 fffff807`62428da9 nt!KeBugCheckEx
ffffa28c`9d8d8690 fffff807`62424f00 nt!KiBugCheckDispatch+0x69
ffffa28c`9d8d87d0 fffff807`61781530 nt!KiPageFault+0x440 (TrapFrame @ ffffa28c`9d8d87d0)
ffffa28c`9d8d8960 fffff807`61781e2d myfault+0x1530
ffffa28c`9d8d8990 fffff807`61781f88 myfault+0x1e2d
ffffa28c`9d8d8ae0 fffff807`62303115 myfault+0x1f88
ffffa28c`9d8d8b20 fffff807`6276bbf2 nt!IofCallDriver+0x55
ffffa28c`9d8d8b60 fffff807`6276b9d2 nt!IopSynchronousServiceTail+0x1d2
ffffa28c`9d8d8c10 fffff807`6276ad36 nt!IopXxxControlFile+0xc82
ffffa28c`9d8d8d40 fffff807`62428775 nt!NtDeviceIoControlFile+0x56
ffffa28c`9d8d8db0 00007ffe`5b023834 nt!KiSystemServiceCopyEnd+0x25 (TrapFrame @ ffffa28c`9d8d8e20)
00000034`f5d2eb88 00007ffe`58a33ffb ntdll!NtDeviceIoControlFile+0x14
00000034`f5d2eb90 00007ffe`5a2d5f91 KERNELBASE!DeviceIoControl+0x6b
00000034`f5d2ec00 00007ff7`2c0426ce KERNEL32!DeviceIoControlImplementation+0x81
00000034`f5d2ec50 00007ffe`5901484b notmyfault64+0x26ce
00000034`f5d2ed50 00007ffe`5a2d5f91 USER32!UserCallDlgProcCheckWow+0x14b
00000034`f5d2ee30 00007ffe`590597c9 USER32!DefDlgProcWorker+0xcb
00000034`f5d2eef0 00007ffe`59011c4c USER32!DefDlgProcA+0x39
00000034`f5d2ef30 00007ffe`5901179c USER32!UserCallWinProcCheckWow+0x33c
00000034`f5d2f0a0 00007ffe`59024b4d USER32!DispatchClientMessage+0x9c
00000034`f5d2f100 00007ffe`5b0276a4 USER32!_fnDWORD+0x3d
00000034`f5d2f160 00007ffe`58d81434 ntdll!KiUserCallbackDispatcherContinue (TrapFrame @ 00000034`f5d2f028)
00000034`f5d2f1e8 00007ffe`590108cf win32u!NtUserMessageCall+0x14
00000034`f5d2f1f0 00007ffe`59010737 USER32!SendMessageWorker+0x12f
00000034`f5d2f290 00007ffe`444750bf USER32!SendMessageW+0x137
00000034`f5d2f2f0 00007ffe`444a8822 COMCTL32!Button_ReleaseCapture+0xbb
00000034`f5d2f320 00007ffe`59011c4c COMCTL32!Button_WndProc+0x802
00000034`f5d2f430 00007ffe`59010ea6 USER32!UserCallWinProcCheckWow+0x33c
00000034`f5d2f5a0 00007ffe`59016084 USER32!DispatchMessageWorker+0x2a6
00000034`f5d2f620 00007ffe`44455f9f USER32!IsDialogMessageW+0x104
00000034`f5d2f680 00007ffe`44455e48 COMCTL32!Prop_IsDialogMessage+0x4b
00000034`f5d2f6c0 00007ffe`44455abd COMCTL32!_RealPropertySheet+0x2c0
00000034`f5d2f790 00007ffe`44520953 COMCTL32!_PropertySheet+0x49
00000034`f5d2f7c0 00007ff7`2c043415 COMCTL32!PropertySheetA+0x53
00000034`f5d2f860 00007ff7`2c045c68 notmyfault64+0x3415
00000034`f5d2fa90 00007ffe`5a2d54e0 notmyfault64+0x5c68
00000034`f5d2fad0 00007ffe`5af8485b KERNEL32!BaseThreadInitThunk+0x10
00000034`f5d2fb00 00000000`00000000 ntdll!RtlUserThreadStart+0x2b
```

Note: We can now search for ASCII fragments in the kernel raw stack region:

```
1: kd> s-sa ffffa28c9d8d3000 ffffa28c9d8d9000
ffffa28c`9d8d3000  "$0H"
ffffa28c`9d8d3004  "\$("
ffffa28c`9d8d3008  "D$ "
ffffa28c`9d8d3011  "L$TH"
ffffa28c`9d8d3064  "ID$T"
ffffa28c`9d8d30a1  "A_A^_^["
ffffa28c`9d8d3176  "u7H"
ffffa28c`9d8d31b0  "U0H"
ffffa28c`9d8d31cb  "tID"
ffffa28c`9d8d31cf  "E0H"
[...]
```

13.   The **!findthreads** extension command can be used for searching memory locations referencing a thread address, addresses from the thread stack region, and thread IRPs, devices, and modules:

```
1: kd> !findthreads -v -t ffffbe0c8974f080
```

Added criterion for THREAD 0xffffbe0c8974f080
  Added criterion for THREAD STACK 0xffffa28c9d8d82e0
  Added criterion for IRP 0xffffbe0c8ac38d00
    Added criterion for IRP STACK LOCATION 0xffffbe0c8ac38dd0
      Added criterion for DEVICE 0xffffbe0c8b78b4e0
        Added criterion for DEVICE EXTENSION 0x0
        Added criterion for MODULE myfault(0xfffff80761780000)
  Added criterion for MODULE ntdll(0x7ffe5af80000)
  Added criterion for MODULE KERNELBASE(0x7ffe58a00000)
  Added criterion for MODULE KERNEL32(0x7ffe5a2c0000)
  Added criterion for MODULE notmyfault64(0x7ff72c040000)
  Added criterion for MODULE USER32(0x7ffe59000000)
  Added criterion for MODULE win32u(0x7ffe58d80000)
  Added criterion for MODULE COMCTL32(0x7ffe44420000)

Found 19 threads matching the search criteria

Found 35 criteria matches for THREAD 0xffffbe0c8974f080, PROCESS 0xffffbe0c8c2cd0c0
  Kernel stack location 0xffffa28c9d8d86b0 references MODULE myfault(0xfffff80761780000)
  Kernel stack location 0xffffa28c9d8d8798 references IRP 0xffffbe0c8ac38d00
  Kernel stack location 0xffffa28c9d8d87a0 references IRP 0xffffbe0c8ac38d00
  Kernel stack location 0xffffa28c9d8d87a8 references IRP 0xffffbe0c8ac38d00
  Kernel stack location 0xffffa28c9d8d87b0 references DEVICE 0xffffbe0c8b78b4e0
  Kernel stack location 0xffffa28c9d8d87d0 references THREAD STACK 0xffffa28c9d8d82e0
  Kernel stack location 0xffffa28c9d8d87d8 references THREAD STACK 0xffffa28c9d8d82e0
  Kernel stack location 0xffffa28c9d8d88f8 references IRP 0xffffbe0c8ac38d00
  Kernel stack location 0xffffa28c9d8d8908 references DEVICE 0xffffbe0c8b78b4e0
  Kernel stack location 0xffffa28c9d8d8910 references IRP 0xffffbe0c8ac38d00
  Kernel stack location 0xffffa28c9d8d8918 references IRP 0xffffbe0c8ac38d00
  Kernel stack location 0xffffa28c9d8d8928 references THREAD STACK 0xffffa28c9d8d82e0
  Kernel stack location 0xffffa28c9d8d8938 references MODULE myfault(0xfffff80761780000)
  Kernel stack location 0xffffa28c9d8d8950 references THREAD STACK 0xffffa28c9d8d82e0
  Kernel stack location 0xffffa28c9d8d8980 references IRP 0xffffbe0c8ac38d00
  Kernel stack location 0xffffa28c9d8d8988 references MODULE myfault(0xfffff80761780000)
  Kernel stack location 0xffffa28c9d8d8a18 references THREAD STACK 0xffffa28c9d8d82e0
  Kernel stack location 0xffffa28c9d8d8a30 references THREAD STACK 0xffffa28c9d8d82e0
  Kernel stack location 0xffffa28c9d8d8a40 references THREAD STACK 0xffffa28c9d8d82e0
  Kernel stack location 0xffffa28c9d8d8ad8 references MODULE myfault(0xfffff80761780000)
  Kernel stack location 0xffffa28c9d8d8ae0 references THREAD STACK 0xffffa28c9d8d82e0
  Kernel stack location 0xffffa28c9d8d8b20 references IRP 0xffffbe0c8ac38d00
  Kernel stack location 0xffffa28c9d8d8b50 references IRP 0xffffbe0c8ac38d00
  Kernel stack location 0xffffa28c9d8d8b68 references IRP 0xffffbe0c8ac38d00
  Kernel stack location 0xffffa28c9d8d8b70 references THREAD STACK 0xffffa28c9d8d82e0
  Kernel stack location 0xffffa28c9d8d8c00 references THREAD STACK 0xffffa28c9d8d82e0
  Kernel stack location 0xffffa28c9d8d8c18 references THREAD STACK 0xffffa28c9d8d82e0
  Kernel stack location 0xffffa28c9d8d8c28 references IRP 0xffffbe0c8ac38d00
  Kernel stack location 0xffffa28c9d8d8c30 references THREAD STACK 0xffffa28c9d8d82e0
  Kernel stack location 0xffffa28c9d8d8ca0 references DEVICE 0xffffbe0c8b78b4e0
  Kernel stack location 0xffffa28c9d8d8ca8 references IRP 0xffffbe0c8ac38d00
  Kernel stack location 0xffffa28c9d8d8cc0 references THREAD 0xffffbe0c8974f080
  Kernel stack location 0xffffa28c9d8d8d20 references THREAD STACK 0xffffa28c9d8d82e0
  Kernel stack location 0xffffa28c9d8d8d30 references THREAD 0xffffbe0c8974f080
  Kernel stack location 0xffffa28c9d8d8db0 references THREAD STACK 0xffffa28c9d8d82e0

  ffffa28c9d8d8680 nt!KeBugCheckEx+0
  ffffa28c9d8d87c0 nt!KiBugCheckDispatch+69
  ffffa28c9d8d8950 nt!KiPageFault+440
  ffffa28c9d8d8980 myfault+1530
  ffffa28c9d8d8ad0 myfault+1e2d
  ffffa28c9d8d8b10 myfault+1f88
  ffffa28c9d8d8b50 nt!IofCallDriver+55

```
ffffa28c9d8d8c00 nt!IopSynchronousServiceTail+1d2
ffffa28c9d8d8d30 nt!IopXxxControlFile+c82
ffffa28c9d8d8da0 nt!NtDeviceIoControlFile+56
00000034f5d2eb78 nt!KiSystemServiceCopyEnd+25
00000034f5d2eb80 ntdll!NtDeviceIoControlFile+14
00000034f5d2ebf0 KERNELBASE!DeviceIoControl+6b
00000034f5d2ec40 KERNEL32!DeviceIoControlImplementation+81
00000034f5d2ed40 notmyfault64+26ce
00000034f5d2ee20 USER32!UserCallDlgProcCheckWow+14b
00000034f5d2eee0 USER32!DefDlgProcWorker+cb
00000034f5d2ef20 USER32!DefDlgProcA+39
00000034f5d2f090 USER32!UserCallWinProcCheckWow+33c
00000034f5d2f0f0 USER32!DispatchClientMessage+9c
00000034f5d2f150 USER32!_fnDWORD+3d
00000034f5d2f1d8 ntdll!KiUserCallbackDispatcherContinue+0
00000034f5d2f1e0 win32u!NtUserMessageCall+14
00000034f5d2f280 USER32!SendMessageWorker+12f
00000034f5d2f2e0 USER32!SendMessageW+137
00000034f5d2f310 COMCTL32!Button_ReleaseCapture+bb
00000034f5d2f420 COMCTL32!Button_WndProc+802
00000034f5d2f590 USER32!UserCallWinProcCheckWow+33c
00000034f5d2f610 USER32!DispatchMessageWorker+2a6
00000034f5d2f670 USER32!IsDialogMessageW+104
00000034f5d2f6b0 COMCTL32!Prop_IsDialogMessage+4b
00000034f5d2f780 COMCTL32!_RealPropertySheet+2c0
00000034f5d2f7b0 COMCTL32!_PropertySheet+49
00000034f5d2f850 COMCTL32!PropertySheetA+53
00000034f5d2fa80 notmyfault64+3415
00000034f5d2fac0 notmyfault64+5c68
00000034f5d2faf0 KERNEL32!BaseThreadInitThunk+10
00000034f5d2fb70 ntdll!RtlUserThreadStart+2b

Found 9 criteria matches for THREAD 0xffffbe0c8a6020c0, PROCESS 0xffffbe0c89a42080
  Kernel stack location 0xffffa28c9eeae540 references IRP 0xffffbe0c8ac38d00
  Kernel stack location 0xffffa28c9eeae558 references IRP 0xffffbe0c8ac38d00
  Kernel stack location 0xffffa28c9eeae6d0 references IRP 0xffffbe0c8ac38d00
  Kernel stack location 0xffffa28c9eeae6e0 references IRP 0xffffbe0c8ac38d00
  Kernel stack location 0xffffa28c9eeae6e8 references IRP 0xffffbe0c8ac38d00
  Kernel stack location 0xffffa28c9eeae6f8 references IRP 0xffffbe0c8ac38d00
  Kernel stack location 0xffffa28c9eeae770 references IRP 0xffffbe0c8ac38d00
  Kernel stack location 0xffffa28c9eeae820 references IRP 0xffffbe0c8ac38d00
  Kernel stack location 0xffffa28c9eeae8e8 references IRP 0xffffbe0c8ac38d00


  ffffa28c9eeae660 nt!KiSwapContext+76
  ffffa28c9eeae740 nt!KiSwapThread+3a7
  ffffa28c9eeae7e0 nt!KiCommitThreadWait+159
  ffffa28c9eeae890 nt!KeRemoveQueueEx+2b6
  ffffa28c9eeae9b0 nt!IoRemoveIoCompletion+98
  ffffa28c9eeaea60 nt!NtRemoveIoCompletion+13d
  000000056fdffc18 nt!KiSystemServiceCopyEnd+25
  000000056fdffc18 ntdll!NtRemoveIoCompletion+14

[...]

Found 1 criteria matches for THREAD 0xffffbe0c888b8040, PROCESS 0xffffbe0c89a42080
  Kernel stack location 0xffffa28c9ce766a8 references IRP 0xffffbe0c8ac38d00


  ffffa28c9ce764d0 nt!KiSwapContext+76
  ffffa28c9ce765b0 nt!KiSwapThread+3a7
  ffffa28c9ce76650 nt!KiCommitThreadWait+159
  ffffa28c9ce76700 nt!KeRemoveQueueEx+2b6
  ffffa28c9ce76820 nt!IoRemoveIoCompletion+98
  ffffa28c9ce76a60 nt!NtWaitForWorkViaWorkerFactory+39c
```

```
       000000056faff508 nt!KiSystemServiceCopyEnd+25
       000000056faff508 ntdll!NtWaitForWorkViaWorkerFactory+14


   Found 1 criteria matches for THREAD 0xffffbe0c8b121080, PROCESS 0xffffbe0c8b4d80c0
    Kernel stack location 0xffffa28c9e59c880 references THREAD STACK 0xffffa28c9d8d82e0


       ffffa28c9e59c8c0 nt!KiSwapContext+76
       ffffa28c9e59c9a0 nt!KiSwapThread+3a7
       ffffa28c9e59ca40 nt!KiCommitThreadWait+159
       ffffa28c9e59caa0 nt!KeWaitForAlertByThreadId+c4
       ffffa28c9e59cad0 nt!NtWaitForAlertByThreadId+30
       000000ae693ffb08 nt!KiSystemServiceCopyEnd+25
       000000ae693ffb08 ntdll!NtWaitForAlertByThreadId+14
```

[...]

```
1: kd> !thread 0xffffbe0c8b121080 3f
THREAD ffffbe0c8b121080  Cid 0f0c.2338  Teb: 000000ae593c2000 Win32Thread: ffffbe0c8b64dc20 WAIT: (WrAlertByThreadId)
UserMode Non-Alertable
    000009b400090718  NotificationEvent
Not impersonating
DeviceMap              ffff800eda518d20
Owning Process         ffffbe0c8b4d80c0       Image:         msedge.exe
Attached Process       N/A             Image:       N/A
Wait Start TickCount   29358           Ticks: 429 (0:00:00:06.703)
Context Switch Count   4186            IdealProcessor: 1
UserTime               00:00:00.953
KernelTime             00:00:00.421
Unable to load image C:\Program Files (x86)\Microsoft\Edge\Application\97.0.1072.76\msedge.dll, Win32 error 0n2
Win32 Start Address msedge!ChromeMain (0x00007ffe217c8380)
Stack Init ffffa28c9e59cc70 Current ffffa28c9e59c750
Base ffffa28c9e59d000 Limit ffffa28c9e597000 Call 0000000000000000
Priority 9  BasePriority 8  IoPriority 2  PagePriority 5
...
```

```
1: kd> dps 0xffffa28c9e59c880 L1
ffffa28c`9e59c880   ffffa28c`9d8d8860
```

```
1: kd> !thread ffffbe0c8974f080 3f
THREAD ffffbe0c8974f080  Cid 243c.1938  Teb: 00000034f5f84000 Win32Thread: ffffbe0c8cccb2a0 RUNNING on processor 1
IRP List:
    ffffbe0c8ac38d00: (0006,0118) Flags: 00060000  Mdl: 00000000
Not impersonating
DeviceMap              ffff800eda519d60
Owning Process         ffffbe0c8c2cd0c0       Image:         notmyfault64.exe
Attached Process       N/A             Image:       N/A
Wait Start TickCount   29786           Ticks: 1 (0:00:00:00.015)
Context Switch Count   1701            IdealProcessor: 1
UserTime               00:00:00.015
KernelTime             00:00:00.125
Unable to load image C:\Work\notmyfault64.exe, Win32 error 0n2
Win32 Start Address notmyfault64 (0x00007ff72c045b0c)
Stack Init ffffa28c9d8d8fb0 Current ffffa28c9d8d82e0
Base ffffa28c9d8d9000 Limit ffffa28c9d8d3000 Call 0000000000000000
...
```

Note: We see that the thread 0xffffbe0c8b121080 kernel stack contains a value from the thread ffffbe0c8974f080 kernel stack address range.

14.   We close logging before exiting WinDbg:


```
1: kd> .logclose
Closing open log file C:\AdvWMDA-Dumps\x64\C2.log
```

A Crash Dump Course in
Unified Modeling Language

Part I

© 2024 Software Diagnostics Services

For this edition, I added a brief tutorial for the relevant UML diagrams we use to explain linked lists later.

Classes and Objects

```
                Class
+fieldPublic  : typeA
-fieldPrivate : typeB
+methodPublic()
-methodPrivate()
```

```
  ObjectA : Class              ObjectB : Class
fieldPublic = value1         fieldPublic = value3
fieldPrivate = value2        fieldPrivate = value4
```

If you are familiar with object-oriented programming, you may know the distinction between classes and objects. Classes describe the structure (fields) and behavior (methods) of similar objects (we can also say they have the same type). Objects are specific instances of a particular class (we can also say objects are of a particular class type) having specific values for fields (object state). '+' means that an object's internal state structure and behavior (public) are accessible from outside by other objects of the same or different class. '-' means that an object's internal state and behavior (private) can only be accessible from inside the same object.

Data Types as Classes

```
           DT
+fieldA : typeA
+fieldB : typeB
```

```
   ObjectA : DT
fieldA = value1
FieldB = value2
```

```
   ObjectB : DT
fieldA = value3
fieldB = value4
```

We can call classes with public fields without associated methods data types (or structures).

Memory as Objects

```
0: kd> dt nt!_DISPATCHER_HEADER
   +0x000 Lock              : Int4B
   +0x000 LockNV            : Int4B
   +0x000 Type              : UChar
   +0x001 Signalling        : UChar
   +0x002 Size              : UChar
   +0x003 Reserved1         : UChar
   +0x000 TimerType         : Uchar
...

0: kd> dt nt!_DISPATCHER_HEADER ffffbe0c89120080
   +0x000 Lock              : 0n3
   +0x000 LockNV            : 0n3
   +0x000 Type              : 0x3 ''
   +0x001 Signalling        : 0 ''
   +0x002 Size              : 0 ''
   +0x003 Reserved1         : 0 ''
   +0x000 TimerType         : 0x3 ''
...
```

We can interpret memory region with a starting address as an instance of some data type. Please note that '+' here denotes positive byte offsets from the beginning of the structure in memory instead of public access in UML class diagrams.

Aggregation

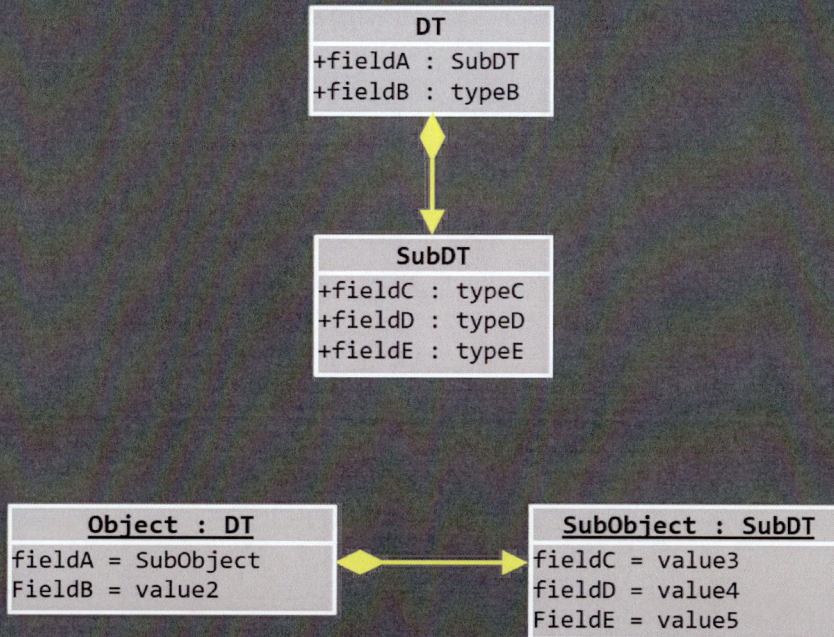

Data types can be aggregated into bigger data types; for example, a field may be of a non-trivial data type. We show aggregation as a filled diamond where the optional arrow points to the direction of a subtype or an object that is now a part of the bigger object. The lifetime of subobjects is the same as the objects they are in.

Aggregation in Memory

```
0: kd> dt nt!_EPROCESS
   +0x000 Pcb                : _KPROCESS
   +0x438 ProcessLock        : _EX_PUSH_LOCK
   +0x440 UniqueProcessId    : Ptr64 Void
   +0x448 ActiveProcessLinks : _LIST_ENTRY
   +0x458 RundownProtect     : _EX_RUNDOWN_REF
   +0x460 Flags2             : Uint4B
...

0: kd> dt nt!_KPROCESS
   +0x000 Header             : _DISPATCHER_HEADER
   +0x018 ProfileListHead    : _LIST_ENTRY
   +0x028 DirectoryTableBase : Uint8B
   +0x030 ThreadListHead     : _LIST_ENTRY
   +0x040 ProcessLock        : Uint4B
   +0x044 ProcessTimerDelay  : Uint4B
   +0x048 DeepFreezeStartTime : Uint8B
   +0x050 Affinity           : _KAFFINITY_EX
...
```

Aggregated data types are laid out sequentially in memory with accumulated offsets. Here, we see an example of the Pcb field of the _KPROCESS data type as a part of the bigger _EPROCESS structure. The _KPROCESS structure also aggregates the _DISPATCHER_HEADER structure. Both _KPROCESS and _DISPATCHER_HEADER structures start at the offset 0 from the _EPROCESS starting address and, therefore, have the same starting address.

Composition

```
                          ┌──────────────────────┐
                          │          DT          │
                          ├──────────────────────┤
                          │ +fieldA : SubDT *    │
                          │ +fieldB : typeB      │
                          └──────────────────────┘
                                    │
                                    ◇
                                    │
                                    ▼
                          ┌──────────────────────┐
                          │         SubDT        │
                          ├──────────────────────┤
                          │ +fieldC : typeC      │
                          │ +fieldD : typeD      │
                          │ +fieldE : typeE      │
                          └──────────────────────┘


┌──────────────────────┐                  ┌──────────────────────────┐
│     Object : DT      │                  │   SubObject : SubDT      │
├──────────────────────┤                  ├──────────────────────────┤
│ fieldA = &SubObject  │◇───────────▶     │ fieldC = value3          │
│ FieldB = value2      │                  │ fieldD = value4          │
└──────────────────────┘                  │ FieldE = value5          │
                                          └──────────────────────────┘
```

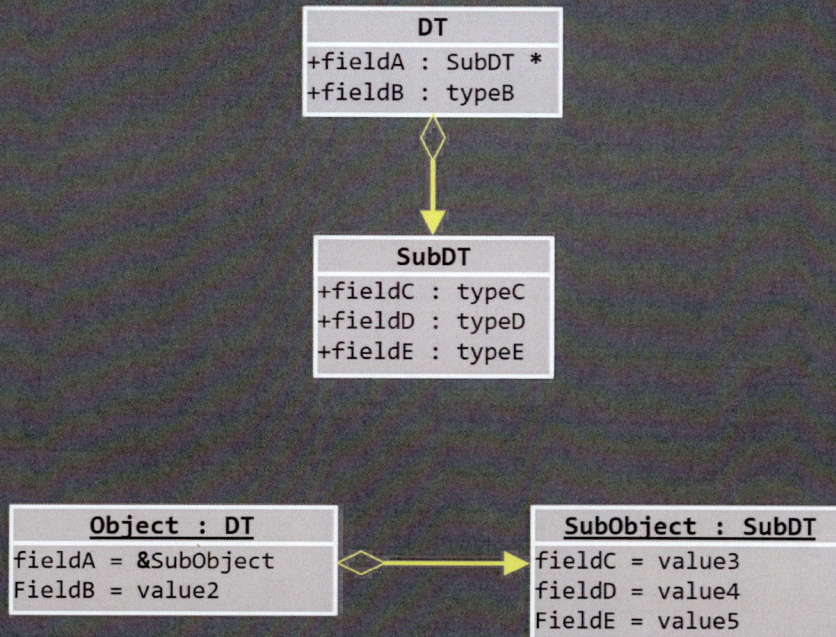

Instead of aggregation we can have composition, when a data type references another data type that has an independent lifetime. We depict such relationships with hollow diamonds with arrows pointing toward referenced data types. Following C and C++, we specify the subtype as a pointer data type (*) with objects containing addresses (&).

Composition in Memory

```
0: kd> dt nt!_EPROCESS
...
   +0x548 OwnerProcessId   : Uint8B
   +0x550 Peb              : Ptr64 _PEB
   +0x558 Session          : Ptr64 _MM_SESSION_SPACE
   +0x560 Spare1           : Ptr64 Void
...

0: kd> dt nt!_EPROCESS ffffbe0c89120080
   +0x548 OwnerProcessId   : 0x2b4
   +0x550 Peb              : 0x0000005b`47b81000 _PEB
   +0x558 Session          : 0xffffbe0c`87efbaa0 _MM_SESSION_SPACE
   +0x560 Spare1           : (null)
...

0: kd> dt nt!_PEB 0x0000005b`47b81000
   +0x000 InheritedAddressSpace : 0 ''
   +0x001 ReadImageFileExecOptions : 0 ''
   +0x002 BeingDebugged    : 0 ''
...
```

In WinDbg output, we see Ptr64 data types in data type definitions and addresses, adding only 8-byte offsets in interpreted memory regions.

Linked List

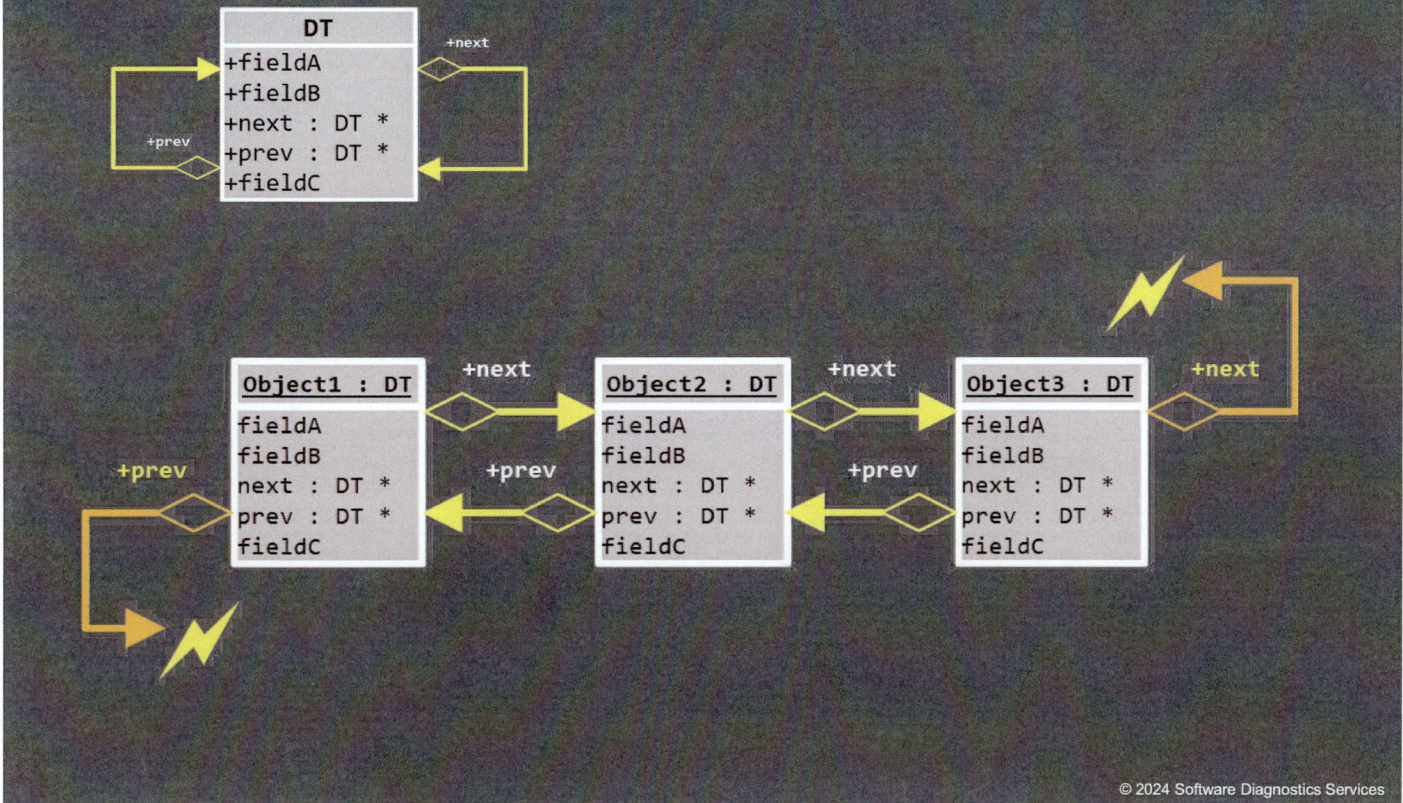

© 2024 Software Diagnostics Services

The usual terminology here is **linked list** vs. **double linked list**. In Windows kernel parlance, the corresponding terminology is **single linked list** vs. **linked list**. One of the solutions to link objects in memory is to put the *next* and *prev* fields in every data structure, type, or class.

Note: If you feel uncomfortable with this diagram and the next two diagrams, please revisit them after the exercise. Hollow diamond shape arrows mean a pointer reference.

_LIST_ENTRY

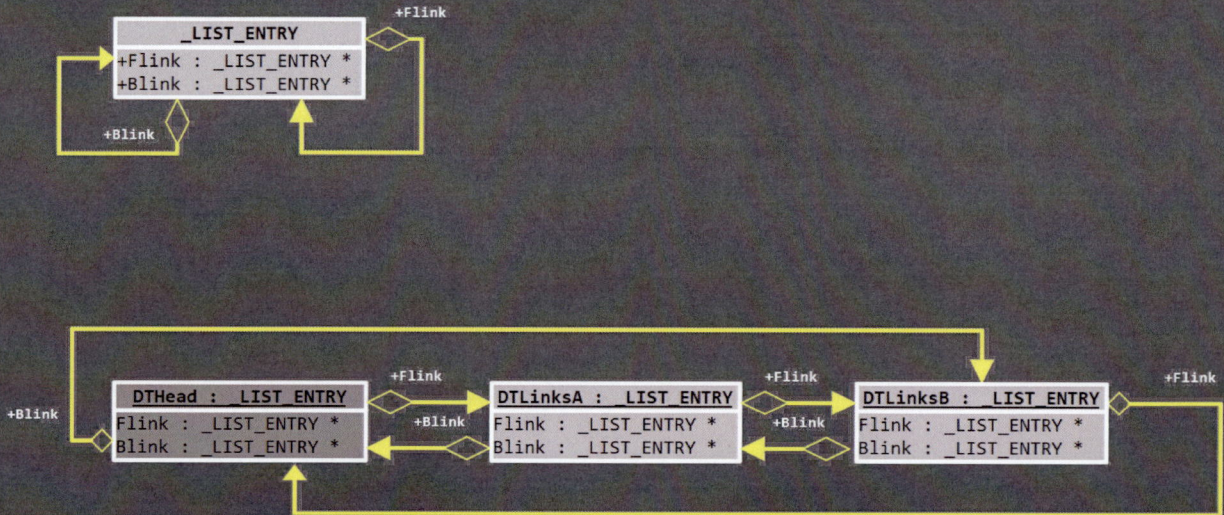

The better solution is to have the *next* and *prev* structure or class fields be abstracted into a separate _LIST_ENTRY data type. It allows standardizing linked list manipulation API as having parameters of _LIST_ENTRY type.

Linked Data Structures

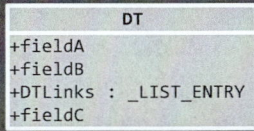

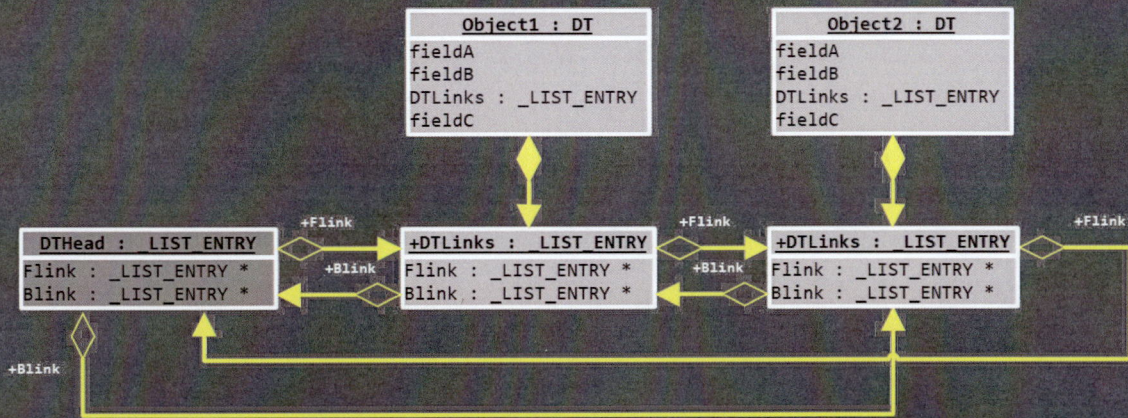

Any custom structure can embed _LIST_ENTRY structure as its field. And, therefore, a programmer can use linked list manipulation API by passing a custom structure _LIST_ENTRY address (usually a structure address plus _LIST_ENTRY offset). Conversely, if we have an address of a _LIST_ENTRY, we can get a custom structure address by subtracting _LIST_ENTRY offset. We would see that during the exercise.

Diamond-filled arrows (from DT to _LIST_ENTRY) depict embedded objects (substructure fields) in this context.

Exercise C3A

- **Goal:** Learn how to navigate linked lists

- **Patterns:** Structure Field Collection

- \AdvWMDA-Dumps\Exercise-C3A-Linked-Lists.pdf

Exercise C3A: Linked Lists

Goal: Learn how to navigate linked lists.

Patterns: Structure Field Collection.

1.   Launch WinDbg.

2.   Open \AdvWMDA-Dumps\x64\MEMORY-Normal.DMP

3.   We get the dump file loaded (the output should be the same as in the previous exercise).

4.   We open a log file:

```
1: kd> .logopen C:\AdvWMDA-Dumps\x64\C3A.log
Opened log file 'C:\AdvWMDA-Dumps\x64\C3A.log'
```

5.   We check the system variable **nt!PsActiveProcessHead**:

```
1: kd> dp nt!PsActiveProcessHead L1
fffff807`62c1bfa0   ffffbe0c`840eb488
```

Note: This is a pointer to a double-linked list. Its structure _LIST_ENTRY is embedded into the _EPROCESS structure:

```
1: kd> dt _LIST_ENTRY
nt!_LIST_ENTRY
   +0x000 Flink           : Ptr64 _LIST_ENTRY
   +0x008 Blink           : Ptr64 _LIST_ENTRY
```

Note: Notice that the *nt* symbol file was picked up first during the symbol search. Sometimes, *ntdll* may be picked. Such search might also be slow, so we advise using an explicit symbol naming such as *nt!_EPROCESS*. Also, sometimes, we should be careful and specify the module name explicitly as there could be differences, especially in the case of 32-bit and 64-bit versions of the same structures as we saw for the _CONTEXT structure in Exercise C1B.

```
1: kd> dt nt!_EPROCESS
   +0x000 Pcb             : _KPROCESS
   +0x438 ProcessLock     : _EX_PUSH_LOCK
   +0x440 UniqueProcessId : Ptr64 Void
   +0x448 ActiveProcessLinks : _LIST_ENTRY
   +0x458 RundownProtect  : _EX_RUNDOWN_REF
   +0x460 Flags2          : Uint4B
   +0x460 JobNotReallyActive : Pos 0, 1 Bit
   +0x460 AccountingFolded : Pos 1, 1 Bit
   +0x460 NewProcessReported : Pos 2, 1 Bit
   +0x460 ExitProcessReported : Pos 3, 1 Bit
   +0x460 ReportCommitChanges : Pos 4, 1 Bit
   +0x460 LastReportMemory : Pos 5, 1 Bit
   +0x460 ForceWakeCharge  : Pos 6, 1 Bit
   +0x460 CrossSessionCreate : Pos 7, 1 Bit
   +0x460 NeedsHandleRundown : Pos 8, 1 Bit
   +0x460 RefTraceEnabled  : Pos 9, 1 Bit
   +0x460 PicoCreated     : Pos 10, 1 Bit
   +0x460 EmptyJobEvaluated : Pos 11, 1 Bit
```

131

```
+0x460 DefaultPagePriority : Pos 12, 3 Bits
+0x460 PrimaryTokenFrozen : Pos 15, 1 Bit
+0x460 ProcessVerifierTarget : Pos 16, 1 Bit
+0x460 RestrictSetThreadContext : Pos 17, 1 Bit
+0x460 AffinityPermanent : Pos 18, 1 Bit
+0x460 AffinityUpdateEnable : Pos 19, 1 Bit
+0x460 PropagateNode     : Pos 20, 1 Bit
+0x460 ExplicitAffinity : Pos 21, 1 Bit
+0x460 ProcessExecutionState : Pos 22, 2 Bits
+0x460 EnableReadVmLogging : Pos 24, 1 Bit
+0x460 EnableWriteVmLogging : Pos 25, 1 Bit
+0x460 FatalAccessTerminationRequested : Pos 26, 1 Bit
+0x460 DisableSystemAllowedCpuSet : Pos 27, 1 Bit
+0x460 ProcessStateChangeRequest : Pos 28, 2 Bits
+0x460 ProcessStateChangeInProgress : Pos 30, 1 Bit
+0x460 InPrivate         : Pos 31, 1 Bit
+0x464 Flags             : Uint4B
+0x464 CreateReported    : Pos 0, 1 Bit
+0x464 NoDebugInherit    : Pos 1, 1 Bit
+0x464 ProcessExiting    : Pos 2, 1 Bit
+0x464 ProcessDelete     : Pos 3, 1 Bit
+0x464 ManageExecutableMemoryWrites : Pos 4, 1 Bit
+0x464 VmDeleted         : Pos 5, 1 Bit
+0x464 OutswapEnabled    : Pos 6, 1 Bit
+0x464 Outswapped        : Pos 7, 1 Bit
+0x464 FailFastOnCommitFail : Pos 8, 1 Bit
+0x464 Wow64VaSpace4Gb   : Pos 9, 1 Bit
+0x464 AddressSpaceInitialized : Pos 10, 2 Bits
+0x464 SetTimerResolution : Pos 12, 1 Bit
+0x464 BreakOnTermination : Pos 13, 1 Bit
+0x464 DeprioritizeViews : Pos 14, 1 Bit
+0x464 WriteWatch        : Pos 15, 1 Bit
+0x464 ProcessInSession  : Pos 16, 1 Bit
+0x464 OverrideAddressSpace : Pos 17, 1 Bit
+0x464 HasAddressSpace   : Pos 18, 1 Bit
+0x464 LaunchPrefetched  : Pos 19, 1 Bit
+0x464 Background        : Pos 20, 1 Bit
+0x464 VmTopDown         : Pos 21, 1 Bit
+0x464 ImageNotifyDone   : Pos 22, 1 Bit
+0x464 PdeUpdateNeeded   : Pos 23, 1 Bit
+0x464 VdmAllowed        : Pos 24, 1 Bit
+0x464 ProcessRundown    : Pos 25, 1 Bit
+0x464 ProcessInserted   : Pos 26, 1 Bit
+0x464 DefaultIoPriority : Pos 27, 3 Bits
+0x464 ProcessSelfDelete : Pos 30, 1 Bit
+0x464 SetTimerResolutionLink : Pos 31, 1 Bit
+0x468 CreateTime        : _LARGE_INTEGER
+0x470 ProcessQuotaUsage : [2] Uint8B
+0x480 ProcessQuotaPeak  : [2] Uint8B
+0x490 PeakVirtualSize   : Uint8B
+0x498 VirtualSize       : Uint8B
+0x4a0 SessionProcessLinks : _LIST_ENTRY
+0x4b0 ExceptionPortData : Ptr64 Void
+0x4b0 ExceptionPortValue : Uint8B
+0x4b0 ExceptionPortState : Pos 0, 3 Bits
+0x4b8 Token             : _EX_FAST_REF
+0x4c0 MmReserved        : Uint8B
+0x4c8 AddressCreationLock : _EX_PUSH_LOCK
+0x4d0 PageTableCommitmentLock : _EX_PUSH_LOCK
```

```
+0x4d8 RotateInProgress : Ptr64 _ETHREAD
+0x4e0 ForkInProgress    : Ptr64 _ETHREAD
+0x4e8 CommitChargeJob   : Ptr64 _EJOB
+0x4f0 CloneRoot         : _RTL_AVL_TREE
+0x4f8 NumberOfPrivatePages : Uint8B
+0x500 NumberOfLockedPages : Uint8B
+0x508 Win32Process      : Ptr64 Void
+0x510 Job               : Ptr64 _EJOB
+0x518 SectionObject     : Ptr64 Void
+0x520 SectionBaseAddress : Ptr64 Void
+0x528 Cookie            : Uint4B
+0x530 WorkingSetWatch   : Ptr64 _PAGEFAULT_HISTORY
+0x538 Win32WindowStation : Ptr64 Void
+0x540 InheritedFromUniqueProcessId : Ptr64 Void
+0x548 OwnerProcessId    : Uint8B
+0x550 Peb               : Ptr64 _PEB
+0x558 Session           : Ptr64 _MM_SESSION_SPACE
+0x560 Spare1            : Ptr64 Void
+0x568 QuotaBlock        : Ptr64 _EPROCESS_QUOTA_BLOCK
+0x570 ObjectTable       : Ptr64 _HANDLE_TABLE
+0x578 DebugPort         : Ptr64 Void
+0x580 WoW64Process      : Ptr64 _EWOW64PROCESS
+0x588 DeviceMap         : _EX_FAST_REF
+0x590 EtwDataSource     : Ptr64 Void
+0x598 PageDirectoryPte  : Uint8B
+0x5a0 ImageFilePointer  : Ptr64 _FILE_OBJECT
+0x5a8 ImageFileName     : [15] UChar
+0x5b7 PriorityClass     : UChar
+0x5b8 SecurityPort      : Ptr64 Void
+0x5c0 SeAuditProcessCreationInfo : _SE_AUDIT_PROCESS_CREATION_INFO
+0x5c8 JobLinks          : _LIST_ENTRY
+0x5d8 HighestUserAddress : Ptr64 Void
+0x5e0 ThreadListHead    : _LIST_ENTRY
+0x5f0 ActiveThreads     : Uint4B
+0x5f4 ImagePathHash     : Uint4B
+0x5f8 DefaultHardErrorProcessing : Uint4B
+0x5fc LastThreadExitStatus : Int4B
+0x600 PrefetchTrace     : _EX_FAST_REF
+0x608 LockedPagesList   : Ptr64 Void
+0x610 ReadOperationCount : _LARGE_INTEGER
+0x618 WriteOperationCount : _LARGE_INTEGER
+0x620 OtherOperationCount : _LARGE_INTEGER
+0x628 ReadTransferCount : _LARGE_INTEGER
+0x630 WriteTransferCount : _LARGE_INTEGER
+0x638 OtherTransferCount : _LARGE_INTEGER
+0x640 CommitChargeLimit : Uint8B
+0x648 CommitCharge      : Uint8B
+0x650 CommitChargePeak  : Uint8B
+0x680 Vm                : _MMSUPPORT_FULL
+0x7c0 MmProcessLinks    : _LIST_ENTRY
+0x7d0 ModifiedPageCount : Uint4B
+0x7d4 ExitStatus        : Int4B
+0x7d8 VadRoot           : _RTL_AVL_TREE
+0x7e0 VadHint           : Ptr64 Void
+0x7e8 VadCount          : Uint8B
+0x7f0 VadPhysicalPages  : Uint8B
+0x7f8 VadPhysicalPagesLimit : Uint8B
+0x800 AlpcContext       : _ALPC_PROCESS_CONTEXT
+0x820 TimerResolutionLink : _LIST_ENTRY
```

```
+0x830 TimerResolutionStackRecord : Ptr64 _PO_DIAG_STACK_RECORD
+0x838 RequestedTimerResolution : Uint4B
+0x83c SmallestTimerResolution : Uint4B
+0x840 ExitTime        : _LARGE_INTEGER
+0x848 InvertedFunctionTable : Ptr64 _INVERTED_FUNCTION_TABLE
+0x850 InvertedFunctionTableLock : _EX_PUSH_LOCK
+0x858 ActiveThreadsHighWatermark : Uint4B
+0x85c LargePrivateVadCount : Uint4B
+0x860 ThreadListLock  : _EX_PUSH_LOCK
+0x868 WnfContext      : Ptr64 Void
+0x870 ServerSilo      : Ptr64 _EJOB
+0x878 SignatureLevel  : UChar
+0x879 SectionSignatureLevel : UChar
+0x87a Protection      : _PS_PROTECTION
+0x87b HangCount       : Pos 0, 3 Bits
+0x87b GhostCount      : Pos 3, 3 Bits
+0x87b PrefilterException : Pos 6, 1 Bit
+0x87c Flags3          : Uint4B
+0x87c Minimal         : Pos 0, 1 Bit
+0x87c ReplacingPageRoot : Pos 1, 1 Bit
+0x87c Crashed         : Pos 2, 1 Bit
+0x87c JobVadsAreTracked : Pos 3, 1 Bit
+0x87c VadTrackingDisabled : Pos 4, 1 Bit
+0x87c AuxiliaryProcess : Pos 5, 1 Bit
+0x87c SubsystemProcess : Pos 6, 1 Bit
+0x87c IndirectCpuSets : Pos 7, 1 Bit
+0x87c RelinquishedCommit : Pos 8, 1 Bit
+0x87c HighGraphicsPriority : Pos 9, 1 Bit
+0x87c CommitFailLogged : Pos 10, 1 Bit
+0x87c ReserveFailLogged : Pos 11, 1 Bit
+0x87c SystemProcess   : Pos 12, 1 Bit
+0x87c HideImageBaseAddresses : Pos 13, 1 Bit
+0x87c AddressPolicyFrozen : Pos 14, 1 Bit
+0x87c ProcessFirstResume : Pos 15, 1 Bit
+0x87c ForegroundExternal : Pos 16, 1 Bit
+0x87c ForegroundSystem : Pos 17, 1 Bit
+0x87c HighMemoryPriority : Pos 18, 1 Bit
+0x87c EnableProcessSuspendResumeLogging : Pos 19, 1 Bit
+0x87c EnableThreadSuspendResumeLogging : Pos 20, 1 Bit
+0x87c SecurityDomainChanged : Pos 21, 1 Bit
+0x87c SecurityFreezeComplete : Pos 22, 1 Bit
+0x87c VmProcessorHost : Pos 23, 1 Bit
+0x87c VmProcessorHostTransition : Pos 24, 1 Bit
+0x87c AltSyscall      : Pos 25, 1 Bit
+0x87c TimerResolutionIgnore : Pos 26, 1 Bit
+0x87c DisallowUserTerminate : Pos 27, 1 Bit
+0x87c EnableProcessRemoteExecProtectVmLogging : Pos 28, 1 Bit
+0x87c EnableProcessLocalExecProtectVmLogging : Pos 29, 1 Bit
+0x880 DeviceAsid      : Int4B
+0x888 SvmData         : Ptr64 Void
+0x890 SvmProcessLock  : _EX_PUSH_LOCK
+0x898 SvmLock         : Uint8B
+0x8a0 SvmProcessDeviceListHead : _LIST_ENTRY
+0x8b0 LastFreezeInterruptTime : Uint8B
+0x8b8 DiskCounters    : Ptr64 _PROCESS_DISK_COUNTERS
+0x8c0 PicoContext     : Ptr64 Void
+0x8c8 EnclaveTable    : Ptr64 Void
+0x8d0 EnclaveNumber   : Uint8B
+0x8d8 EnclaveLock     : _EX_PUSH_LOCK
```

```
+0x8e0 HighPriorityFaultsAllowed : Uint4B
+0x8e8 EnergyContext      : Ptr64 _PO_PROCESS_ENERGY_CONTEXT
+0x8f0 VmContext          : Ptr64 Void
+0x8f8 SequenceNumber     : Uint8B
+0x900 CreateInterruptTime : Uint8B
+0x908 CreateUnbiasedInterruptTime : Uint8B
+0x910 TotalUnbiasedFrozenTime : Uint8B
+0x918 LastAppStateUpdateTime : Uint8B
+0x920 LastAppStateUptime : Pos 0, 61 Bits
+0x920 LastAppState       : Pos 61, 3 Bits
+0x928 SharedCommitCharge : Uint8B
+0x930 SharedCommitLock   : _EX_PUSH_LOCK
+0x938 SharedCommitLinks  : _LIST_ENTRY
+0x948 AllowedCpuSets     : Uint8B
+0x950 DefaultCpuSets     : Uint8B
+0x948 AllowedCpuSetsIndirect : Ptr64 Uint8B
+0x950 DefaultCpuSetsIndirect : Ptr64 Uint8B
+0x958 DiskIoAttribution  : Ptr64 Void
+0x960 DxgProcess         : Ptr64 Void
+0x968 Win32KFilterSet    : Uint4B
+0x96c Machine            : Uint2B
+0x96e Spare0             : Uint2B
+0x970 ProcessTimerDelay  : _PS_INTERLOCKED_TIMER_DELAY_VALUES
+0x978 KTimerSets         : Uint4B
+0x97c KTimer2Sets        : Uint4B
+0x980 ThreadTimerSets    : Uint4B
+0x988 VirtualTimerListLock : Uint8B
+0x990 VirtualTimerListHead : _LIST_ENTRY
+0x9a0 WakeChannel        : _WNF_STATE_NAME
+0x9a0 WakeInfo           : _PS_PROCESS_WAKE_INFORMATION
+0x9d0 MitigationFlags    : Uint4B
+0x9d0 MitigationFlagsValues : <unnamed-tag>
+0x9d4 MitigationFlags2   : Uint4B
+0x9d4 MitigationFlags2Values : <unnamed-tag>
+0x9d8 PartitionObject    : Ptr64 Void
+0x9e0 SecurityDomain     : Uint8B
+0x9e8 ParentSecurityDomain : Uint8B
+0x9f0 CoverageSamplerContext : Ptr64 Void
+0x9f8 MmHotPatchContext  : Ptr64 Void
+0xa00 IdealProcessorAssignmentBlock : _KE_IDEAL_PROCESSOR_ASSIGNMENT_BLOCK
+0xb18 DynamicEHContinuationTargetsTree : _RTL_AVL_TREE
+0xb20 DynamicEHContinuationTargetsLock : _EX_PUSH_LOCK
+0xb28 DynamicEnforcedCetCompatibleRanges : _PS_DYNAMIC_ENFORCED_ADDRESS_RANGES
+0xb38 DisabledComponentFlags : Uint4B
+0xb3c PageCombineSequence : Int4B
+0xb40 EnableOptionalXStateFeaturesLock : _EX_PUSH_LOCK
```

6.   We now get the address of the first process structure by subtracting the *ActiveProcessLinks* field offset from the value *PsActiveProcessHead* address points to (**poi** command):

```
1: kd> dt nt!_EPROCESS poi(nt!PsActiveProcessHead)-0x448
   +0x000 Pcb                : _KPROCESS
   +0x438 ProcessLock        : _EX_PUSH_LOCK
   +0x440 UniqueProcessId    : 0x00000000`00000004 Void
   +0x448 ActiveProcessLinks : _LIST_ENTRY [ 0xffffbe0c`841364c8 - 0xfffff807`62c1bfa0 ]
   +0x458 RundownProtect     : _EX_RUNDOWN_REF
   +0x460 Flags2             : 0xd000
   +0x460 JobNotReallyActive : 0y0
   +0x460 AccountingFolded   : 0y0
```

```
+0x460 NewProcessReported : 0y0
+0x460 ExitProcessReported : 0y0
+0x460 ReportCommitChanges : 0y0
+0x460 LastReportMemory : 0y0
+0x460 ForceWakeCharge  : 0y0
+0x460 CrossSessionCreate : 0y0
+0x460 NeedsHandleRundown : 0y0
+0x460 RefTraceEnabled  : 0y0
+0x460 PicoCreated      : 0y0
+0x460 EmptyJobEvaluated : 0y0
+0x460 DefaultPagePriority : 0y101
+0x460 PrimaryTokenFrozen : 0y1
+0x460 ProcessVerifierTarget : 0y0
+0x460 RestrictSetThreadContext : 0y0
+0x460 AffinityPermanent : 0y0
+0x460 AffinityUpdateEnable : 0y0
+0x460 PropagateNode    : 0y0
+0x460 ExplicitAffinity : 0y0
+0x460 ProcessExecutionState : 0y00
+0x460 EnableReadVmLogging : 0y0
+0x460 EnableWriteVmLogging : 0y0
+0x460 FatalAccessTerminationRequested : 0y0
+0x460 DisableSystemAllowedCpuSet : 0y0
+0x460 ProcessStateChangeRequest : 0y00
+0x460 ProcessStateChangeInProgress : 0y0
+0x460 InPrivate        : 0y0
+0x464 Flags            : 0x14840c00
+0x464 CreateReported   : 0y0
+0x464 NoDebugInherit   : 0y0
+0x464 ProcessExiting   : 0y0
+0x464 ProcessDelete    : 0y0
+0x464 ManageExecutableMemoryWrites : 0y0
+0x464 VmDeleted        : 0y0
+0x464 OutswapEnabled   : 0y0
+0x464 Outswapped       : 0y0
+0x464 FailFastOnCommitFail : 0y0
+0x464 Wow64VaSpace4Gb  : 0y0
+0x464 AddressSpaceInitialized : 0y11
+0x464 SetTimerResolution : 0y0
+0x464 BreakOnTermination : 0y0
+0x464 DeprioritizeViews : 0y0
+0x464 WriteWatch       : 0y0
+0x464 ProcessInSession : 0y0
+0x464 OverrideAddressSpace : 0y0
+0x464 HasAddressSpace  : 0y1
+0x464 LaunchPrefetched : 0y0
+0x464 Background       : 0y0
+0x464 VmTopDown        : 0y0
+0x464 ImageNotifyDone  : 0y0
+0x464 PdeUpdateNeeded  : 0y1
+0x464 VdmAllowed       : 0y0
+0x464 ProcessRundown   : 0y0
+0x464 ProcessInserted  : 0y1
+0x464 DefaultIoPriority : 0y010
+0x464 ProcessSelfDelete : 0y0
+0x464 SetTimerResolutionLink : 0y0
+0x468 CreateTime       : _LARGE_INTEGER 0x01d81e1a`13a38448
+0x470 ProcessQuotaUsage : [2] 0x110
+0x480 ProcessQuotaPeak : [2] 0x110
+0x490 PeakVirtualSize  : 0xf1a000
+0x498 VirtualSize      : 0x3e7000
+0x4a0 SessionProcessLinks : _LIST_ENTRY [ 0x00000000`00000000 - 0x00000000`00000000 ]
+0x4b0 ExceptionPortData : (null)
+0x4b0 ExceptionPortValue : 0
+0x4b0 ExceptionPortState : 0y000
```

```
+0x4b8 Token             : _EX_FAST_REF
+0x4c0 MmReserved        : 0
+0x4c8 AddressCreationLock : _EX_PUSH_LOCK
+0x4d0 PageTableCommitmentLock : _EX_PUSH_LOCK
+0x4d8 RotateInProgress  : (null)
+0x4e0 ForkInProgress    : (null)
+0x4e8 CommitChargeJob   : (null)
+0x4f0 CloneRoot         : _RTL_AVL_TREE
+0x4f8 NumberOfPrivatePages : 0x14
+0x500 NumberOfLockedPages : 0
+0x508 Win32Process      : (null)
+0x510 Job               : (null)
+0x518 SectionObject     : (null)
+0x520 SectionBaseAddress : (null)
+0x528 Cookie            : 0xec9a6c71
+0x530 WorkingSetWatch   : (null)
+0x538 Win32WindowStation : (null)
+0x540 InheritedFromUniqueProcessId : (null)
+0x548 OwnerProcessId    : 2
+0x550 Peb               : (null)
+0x558 Session           : (null)
+0x560 Spare1            : (null)
+0x568 QuotaBlock        : 0xfffff807`62c5a380 _EPROCESS_QUOTA_BLOCK
+0x570 ObjectTable       : 0xffff800e`d4820c80 _HANDLE_TABLE
+0x578 DebugPort         : (null)
+0x580 WoW64Process      : (null)
+0x588 DeviceMap         : _EX_FAST_REF
+0x590 EtwDataSource     : (null)
+0x598 PageDirectoryPte  : 0
+0x5a0 ImageFilePointer  : (null)
+0x5a8 ImageFileName     : [15] "System"
+0x5b7 PriorityClass     : 0x2 ''
+0x5b8 SecurityPort      : (null)
+0x5c0 SeAuditProcessCreationInfo : _SE_AUDIT_PROCESS_CREATION_INFO
+0x5c8 JobLinks          : _LIST_ENTRY [ 0x00000000`00000000 - 0x00000000`00000000 ]
+0x5d8 HighestUserAddress : 0x00007fff`ffff0000 Void
+0x5e0 ThreadListHead    : _LIST_ENTRY [ 0xffffbe0c`841cd5b8 - 0xffffbe0c`8c0dd578 ]
+0x5f0 ActiveThreads     : 0x88
+0x5f4 ImagePathHash     : 0
+0x5f8 DefaultHardErrorProcessing : 5
+0x5fc LastThreadExitStatus : 0n0
+0x600 PrefetchTrace     : _EX_FAST_REF
+0x608 LockedPagesList   : (null)
+0x610 ReadOperationCount : _LARGE_INTEGER 0x1d
+0x618 WriteOperationCount : _LARGE_INTEGER 0x3b
+0x620 OtherOperationCount : _LARGE_INTEGER 0x51c
+0x628 ReadTransferCount : _LARGE_INTEGER 0x33e8
+0x630 WriteTransferCount : _LARGE_INTEGER 0x1a5d23f
+0x638 OtherTransferCount : _LARGE_INTEGER 0x4a96
+0x640 CommitChargeLimit : 0
+0x648 CommitCharge      : 0xb
+0x650 CommitChargePeak  : 0x10
+0x680 Vm                : _MMSUPPORT_FULL
+0x7c0 MmProcessLinks    : _LIST_ENTRY [ 0xffffbe0c`84136840 - 0xfffff807`62d332c0 ]
+0x7d0 ModifiedPageCount : 0xc98e
+0x7d4 ExitStatus        : 0n259
+0x7d8 VadRoot           : _RTL_AVL_TREE
+0x7e0 VadHint           : 0xffffbe0c`840a16f0 Void
+0x7e8 VadCount          : 6
+0x7f0 VadPhysicalPages  : 0
+0x7f8 VadPhysicalPagesLimit : 0
+0x800 AlpcContext       : _ALPC_PROCESS_CONTEXT
+0x820 TimerResolutionLink : _LIST_ENTRY [ 0x00000000`00000000 - 0x00000000`00000000 ]
+0x830 TimerResolutionStackRecord : (null)
+0x838 RequestedTimerResolution : 0
```

```
+0x83c SmallestTimerResolution : 0
+0x840 ExitTime          : _LARGE_INTEGER 0x0
+0x848 InvertedFunctionTable : (null)
+0x850 InvertedFunctionTableLock : _EX_PUSH_LOCK
+0x858 ActiveThreadsHighWatermark : 0x88
+0x85c LargePrivateVadCount : 0
+0x860 ThreadListLock    : _EX_PUSH_LOCK
+0x868 WnfContext         : 0xffff800e`d48b52e0 Void
+0x870 ServerSilo        : (null)
+0x878 SignatureLevel    : 0x1e ''
+0x879 SectionSignatureLevel : 0x1c ''
+0x87a Protection        : _PS_PROTECTION
+0x87b HangCount         : 0y000
+0x87b GhostCount        : 0y000
+0x87b PrefilterException : 0y0
+0x87c Flags3            : 0x405080
+0x87c Minimal           : 0y0
+0x87c ReplacingPageRoot : 0y0
+0x87c Crashed           : 0y0
+0x87c JobVadsAreTracked : 0y0
+0x87c VadTrackingDisabled : 0y0
+0x87c AuxiliaryProcess  : 0y0
+0x87c SubsystemProcess  : 0y0
+0x87c IndirectCpuSets   : 0y1
+0x87c RelinquishedCommit : 0y0
+0x87c HighGraphicsPriority : 0y0
+0x87c CommitFailLogged  : 0y0
+0x87c ReserveFailLogged : 0y0
+0x87c SystemProcess     : 0y1
+0x87c HideImageBaseAddresses : 0y0
+0x87c AddressPolicyFrozen : 0y1
+0x87c ProcessFirstResume : 0y0
+0x87c ForegroundExternal : 0y0
+0x87c ForegroundSystem  : 0y0
+0x87c HighMemoryPriority : 0y0
+0x87c EnableProcessSuspendResumeLogging : 0y0
+0x87c EnableThreadSuspendResumeLogging : 0y0
+0x87c SecurityDomainChanged : 0y0
+0x87c SecurityFreezeComplete : 0y1
+0x87c VmProcessorHost   : 0y0
+0x87c VmProcessorHostTransition : 0y0
+0x87c AltSyscall        : 0y0
+0x87c TimerResolutionIgnore : 0y0
+0x87c DisallowUserTerminate : 0y0
+0x87c EnableProcessRemoteExecProtectVmLogging : 0y0
+0x87c EnableProcessLocalExecProtectVmLogging : 0y0
+0x880 DeviceAsid        : 0n0
+0x888 SvmData           : (null)
+0x890 SvmProcessLock    : _EX_PUSH_LOCK
+0x898 SvmLock           : 0
+0x8a0 SvmProcessDeviceListHead : _LIST_ENTRY [ 0xffffbe0c`840eb8e0 - 0xffffbe0c`840eb8e0 ]
+0x8b0 LastFreezeInterruptTime : 0
+0x8b8 DiskCounters      : 0xffffbe0c`840ebbc0 _PROCESS_DISK_COUNTERS
+0x8c0 PicoContext       : (null)
+0x8c8 EnclaveTable      : (null)
+0x8d0 EnclaveNumber     : 0
+0x8d8 EnclaveLock       : _EX_PUSH_LOCK
+0x8e0 HighPriorityFaultsAllowed : 0
+0x8e8 EnergyContext     : 0xffffbe0c`840ebbe8 _PO_PROCESS_ENERGY_CONTEXT
+0x8f0 VmContext         : (null)
+0x8f8 SequenceNumber    : 1
+0x900 CreateInterruptTime : 0x89eae9f
+0x908 CreateUnbiasedInterruptTime : 0x89eae9f
+0x910 TotalUnbiasedFrozenTime : 0
+0x918 LastAppStateUpdateTime : 0
```

```
+0x920 LastAppStateUptime : 0y0000000000000000000000000000000000000000000000000000000000000000 (0)
+0x920 LastAppState       : 0y000
+0x928 SharedCommitCharge : 0x4a
+0x930 SharedCommitLock   : _EX_PUSH_LOCK
+0x938 SharedCommitLinks  : _LIST_ENTRY [ 0xffff800e`d71a16b8 - 0xffff800e`d4cfba78 ]
+0x948 AllowedCpuSets     : 0xffffbe0c`840ebdc8
+0x950 DefaultCpuSets     : 0xffffbe0c`840ebec8
+0x948 AllowedCpuSetsIndirect : 0xffffbe0c`840ebdc8  -> 3
+0x950 DefaultCpuSetsIndirect : 0xffffbe0c`840ebec8  -> 0
+0x958 DiskIoAttribution  : (null)
+0x960 DxgProcess         : 0xffff800e`d4ef4a40 Void
+0x968 Win32KFilterSet    : 0
+0x96c Machine            : 0x8664
+0x96e Spare0             : 0
+0x970 ProcessTimerDelay  : _PS_INTERLOCKED_TIMER_DELAY_VALUES
+0x978 KTimerSets         : 0
+0x97c KTimer2Sets        : 0
+0x980 ThreadTimerSets    : 0
+0x988 VirtualTimerListLock : 0
+0x990 VirtualTimerListHead : _LIST_ENTRY [ 0xffffbe0c`840eb9d0 - 0xffffbe0c`840eb9d0 ]
+0x9a0 WakeChannel        : _WNF_STATE_NAME
+0x9a0 WakeInfo           : _PS_PROCESS_WAKE_INFORMATION
+0x9d0 MitigationFlags    : 0x40000060
+0x9d0 MitigationFlagsValues : <unnamed-tag>
+0x9d4 MitigationFlags2   : 0x40002000
+0x9d4 MitigationFlags2Values : <unnamed-tag>
+0x9d8 PartitionObject    : 0xffffbe0c`840bf960 Void
+0x9e0 SecurityDomain     : 0
+0x9e8 ParentSecurityDomain : 0
+0x9f0 CoverageSamplerContext : (null)
+0x9f8 MmHotPatchContext  : (null)
+0xa00 IdealProcessorAssignmentBlock : _KE_IDEAL_PROCESSOR_ASSIGNMENT_BLOCK
+0xb18 DynamicEHContinuationTargetsTree : _RTL_AVL_TREE
+0xb20 DynamicEHContinuationTargetsLock : _EX_PUSH_LOCK
+0xb28 DynamicEnforcedCetCompatibleRanges : _PS_DYNAMIC_ENFORCED_ADDRESS_RANGES
+0xb38 DisabledComponentFlags : 0
+0xb3c PageCombineSequence : 0n1
+0xb40 EnableOptionalXStateFeaturesLock : _EX_PUSH_LOCK
```

Note: This is the **System** process. We can get the next links by using **-r1** (shows substructures one level deep) with the previous command:

```
1: kd> dt -r1 nt!_EPROCESS poi(nt!PsActiveProcessHead)-0x448
   +0x000 Pcb                : _KPROCESS
      +0x000 Header          : _DISPATCHER_HEADER
      +0x018 ProfileListHead : _LIST_ENTRY [ 0xffffbe0c`840eb058 - 0xffffbe0c`840eb058 ]
      +0x028 DirectoryTableBase : 0x1ae002
      +0x030 ThreadListHead  : _LIST_ENTRY [ 0xffffbe0c`841cd378 - 0xffffbe0c`8c0dd338 ]
      +0x040 ProcessLock     : 0
      +0x044 ProcessTimerDelay : 0
      +0x048 DeepFreezeStartTime : 0
      +0x050 Affinity        : _KAFFINITY_EX
      +0x158 ReadyListHead   : _LIST_ENTRY [ 0xffffbe0c`840eb198 - 0xffffbe0c`840eb198 ]
      +0x168 SwapListEntry   : _SINGLE_LIST_ENTRY
      +0x170 ActiveProcessors : _KAFFINITY_EX
      +0x278 AutoAlignment   : 0y1
      +0x278 DisableBoost    : 0y0
      +0x278 DisableQuantum  : 0y0
      +0x278 DeepFreeze      : 0y0
      +0x278 TimerVirtualization : 0y0
      +0x278 CheckStackExtents : 0y0
      +0x278 CacheIsolationEnabled : 0y0
      +0x278 PpmPolicy       : 0y0000
      +0x278 VaSpaceDeleted  : 0y0
      +0x278 MultiGroup      : 0y0
      +0x278 ReservedFlags   : 0y0000000000000000000 (0)
      +0x278 ProcessFlags    : 0n1
```

```
   +0x27c ActiveGroupsMask : 1
   +0x280 BasePriority    : 8 ''
   +0x281 QuantumReset    : 6 ''
   +0x282 Visited         : 0 ''
   +0x283 Flags           : _KEXECUTE_OPTIONS
   +0x284 ThreadSeed      : [32] 0
   +0x2c4 IdealProcessor  : [32] 0
   +0x304 IdealNode       : [32] 0
   +0x344 IdealGlobalNode : 0
   +0x346 Spare1          : 0
   +0x348 StackCount      : _KSTACK_COUNT
   +0x350 ProcessListEntry : _LIST_ENTRY [ 0xffffbe0c`841363d0 - 0xfffff807`62c2bba0 ]
   +0x360 CycleTime       : 0x00000004`a5a12c9f
   +0x368 ContextSwitches : 0xd81e
   +0x370 SchedulingGroup : (null)
   +0x378 FreezeCount     : 0
   +0x37c KernelTime      : 0x205
   +0x380 UserTime        : 0
   +0x384 ReadyTime       : 0x38
   +0x388 UserDirectoryTableBase : 0x00000001`00200001
   +0x390 AddressPolicy   : 0x1 ''
   +0x391 Spare2          : [71]  ""
   +0x3d8 InstrumentationCallback : (null)
   +0x3e0 SecureState     : <unnamed-tag>
   +0x3e8 KernelWaitTime  : 0xaad4
   +0x3f0 UserWaitTime    : 0
   +0x3f8 LastRebalanceQpc : 0
   +0x400 PerProcessorCycleTimes : (null)
   +0x408 ExtendedFeatureDisableMask : 0
   +0x410 PrimaryGroup    : 0
   +0x412 Spare3          : [3] 0
   +0x418 UserCetLogging  : (null)
   +0x420 EndPadding      : [3] 0
 +0x438 ProcessLock       : _EX_PUSH_LOCK
   +0x000 Locked          : 0y0
   +0x000 Waiting         : 0y0
   +0x000 Waking          : 0y0
   +0x000 MultipleShared  : 0y0
   +0x000 Shared          : 0y000000000000000000000000000000000000000000000000000000000000000 (0)
   +0x000 Value           : 0
   +0x000 Ptr             : (null)
 +0x440 UniqueProcessId   : 0x00000000`00000004 Void
 +0x448 ActiveProcessLinks : _LIST_ENTRY [ 0xffffbe0c`841364c8 - 0xfffff807`62c1bfa0 ]
   +0x000 Flink           : 0xffffbe0c`841364c8 _LIST_ENTRY [ 0xffffbe0c`8780f488 - 0xffffbe0c`840eb488 ]
   +0x008 Blink           : 0xffffff807`62c1bfa0 _LIST_ENTRY [ 0xffffbe0c`840eb488 - 0xffffbe0c`8bfb1508 ]
[...]
```

Note: Blink points to the address of the **nt!PsActiveProcessHead** value. We can now get the second process from the list (**Flink**):

```
1: kd> ? poi(nt!PsActiveProcessHead)
Evaluate expression: -72514012269432 = ffffbe0c`840eb488
```

```
1: kd> dt -r1 nt!_EPROCESS 0xffffbe0c`841364c8-0x448
   +0x000 Pcb             : _KPROCESS
   +0x000 Header          : _DISPATCHER_HEADER
   +0x018 ProfileListHead : _LIST_ENTRY [ 0xffffbe0c`84136098 - 0xffffbe0c`84136098 ]
   +0x028 DirectoryTableBase : 0xfe0c002
   +0x030 ThreadListHead  : _LIST_ENTRY [ 0xffffbe0c`84138378 - 0xffffbe0c`87f2e378 ]
   +0x040 ProcessLock     : 0
   +0x044 ProcessTimerDelay : 0
   +0x048 DeepFreezeStartTime : 0
   +0x050 Affinity        : _KAFFINITY_EX
   +0x158 ReadyListHead   : _LIST_ENTRY [ 0xffffbe0c`841361d8 - 0xffffbe0c`841361d8 ]
   +0x168 SwapListEntry   : _SINGLE_LIST_ENTRY
   +0x170 ActiveProcessors : _KAFFINITY_EX
   +0x278 AutoAlignment   : 0y1
   +0x278 DisableBoost    : 0y0
   +0x278 DisableQuantum  : 0y0
   +0x278 DeepFreeze      : 0y0
   +0x278 TimerVirtualization : 0y0
```

```
   +0x278 CheckStackExtents : 0y0
   +0x278 CacheIsolationEnabled : 0y0
   +0x278 PpmPolicy         : 0y0000
   +0x278 VaSpaceDeleted    : 0y0
   +0x278 MultiGroup        : 0y0
   +0x278 ReservedFlags     : 0y0000000000000000000 (0)
   +0x278 ProcessFlags      : 0n1
   +0x27c ActiveGroupsMask  : 1
   +0x280 BasePriority      : 8 ''
   +0x281 QuantumReset      : 6 ''
   +0x282 Visited           : 0 ''
   +0x283 Flags             : _KEXECUTE_OPTIONS
   +0x284 ThreadSeed        : [32] 0
   +0x2c4 IdealProcessor    : [32] 0
   +0x304 IdealNode         : [32] 0
   +0x344 IdealGlobalNode   : 0
   +0x346 Spare1            : 0
   +0x348 StackCount        : _KSTACK_COUNT
   +0x350 ProcessListEntry  : _LIST_ENTRY [ 0xffffbe0c`8780f390 - 0xffffbe0c`840eb390 ]
   +0x360 CycleTime         : 0x6add0fdf
   +0x368 ContextSwitches   : 0x22e
   +0x370 SchedulingGroup   : (null)
   +0x378 FreezeCount       : 0
   +0x37c KernelTime        : 0x2f
   +0x380 UserTime          : 0
   +0x384 ReadyTime         : 0xa
   +0x388 UserDirectoryTableBase : 1
   +0x390 AddressPolicy     : 0x1 ''
   +0x391 Spare2            : [71]  ""
   +0x3d8 InstrumentationCallback : (null)
   +0x3e0 SecureState       : <unnamed-tag>
   +0x3e8 KernelWaitTime    : 0x4e
   +0x3f0 UserWaitTime      : 0
   +0x3f8 LastRebalanceQpc  : 0x00000001`14d49fe6
   +0x400 PerProcessorCycleTimes : 0x00000000`00008000 Void
   +0x408 ExtendedFeatureDisableMask : 0
   +0x410 PrimaryGroup      : 0
   +0x412 Spare3            : [3] 0
   +0x418 UserCetLogging    : (null)
   +0x420 EndPadding        : [3] 0
+0x438 ProcessLock          : _EX_PUSH_LOCK
   +0x000 Locked            : 0y0
   +0x000 Waiting           : 0y0
   +0x000 Waking            : 0y0
   +0x000 MultipleShared    : 0y0
   +0x000 Shared            : 0y0000000000000000000000000000000000000000000000000000000000000 (0)
   +0x000 Value             : 0
   +0x000 Ptr               : (null)
+0x440 UniqueProcessId      : 0x00000000`00000064 Void
+0x448 ActiveProcessLinks   : _LIST_ENTRY [ 0xffffbe0c`8780f488 - 0xffffbe0c`840eb488 ]
   +0x000 Flink             : 0xffffbe0c`8780f488 _LIST_ENTRY [ 0xffffbe0c`87f2b4c8 - 0xffffbe0c`841364c8 ]
   +0x008 Blink             : 0xffffbe0c`840eb488 _LIST_ENTRY [ 0xffffbe0c`841364c8 - 0xfffff807`62c1bfa0 ]
+0x458 RundownProtect       : _EX_RUNDOWN_REF
   +0x000 Count             : 0
   +0x000 Ptr               : (null)
+0x460 Flags2               : 0xd000
+0x460 JobNotReallyActive   : 0y0
+0x460 AccountingFolded     : 0y0
+0x460 NewProcessReported   : 0y0
+0x460 ExitProcessReported  : 0y0
+0x460 ReportCommitChanges  : 0y0
+0x460 LastReportMemory     : 0y0
+0x460 ForceWakeCharge      : 0y0
+0x460 CrossSessionCreate   : 0y0
+0x460 NeedsHandleRundown   : 0y0
[...]
   +0x590 EtwDataSource     : (null)
   +0x598 PageDirectoryPte  : 0
   +0x5a0 ImageFilePointer  : (null)
   +0x5a8 ImageFileName     : [15]  "Registry"
   +0x5b7 PriorityClass     : 0x2 ''
   +0x5b8 SecurityPort      : (null)
[...]
```

```
1: kd> dt -r1 nt!_EPROCESS 0xffffbe0c`8780f488-0x448
   +0x000 Pcb              : _KPROCESS
      +0x000 Header            : _DISPATCHER_HEADER
      +0x018 ProfileListHead   : _LIST_ENTRY [ 0xffffbe0c`8780f058 - 0xffffbe0c`8780f058 ]
      +0x028 DirectoryTableBase : 0x00000001`22311002
      +0x030 ThreadListHead    : _LIST_ENTRY [ 0xffffbe0c`87810338 - 0xffffbe0c`89fb5338 ]
      +0x040 ProcessLock       : 0
      +0x044 ProcessTimerDelay : 0
      +0x048 DeepFreezeStartTime : 0
      +0x050 Affinity          : _KAFFINITY_EX
      +0x158 ReadyListHead     : _LIST_ENTRY [ 0xffffbe0c`8780f198 - 0xffffbe0c`8780f198 ]
      +0x168 SwapListEntry     : _SINGLE_LIST_ENTRY
      +0x170 ActiveProcessors  : _KAFFINITY_EX
      +0x278 AutoAlignment     : 0y0
      +0x278 DisableBoost      : 0y0
      +0x278 DisableQuantum    : 0y0
      +0x278 DeepFreeze        : 0y0
      +0x278 TimerVirtualization : 0y0
      +0x278 CheckStackExtents : 0y1
      +0x278 CacheIsolationEnabled : 0y0
      +0x278 PpmPolicy         : 0y0000
      +0x278 VaSpaceDeleted    : 0y0
      +0x278 MultiGroup        : 0y0
      +0x278 ReservedFlags     : 0y0000000000000000000 (0)
      +0x278 ProcessFlags      : 0n32
      +0x27c ActiveGroupsMask  : 1
      +0x280 BasePriority      : 11 ''
      +0x281 QuantumReset      : 6 ''
      +0x282 Visited           : 0 ''
      +0x283 Flags             : _KEXECUTE_OPTIONS
      +0x284 ThreadSeed        : [32] 0
      +0x2c4 IdealProcessor    : [32] 0
      +0x304 IdealNode         : [32] 0
      +0x344 IdealGlobalNode   : 0
      +0x346 Spare1            : 0
      +0x348 StackCount        : _KSTACK_COUNT
      +0x350 ProcessListEntry  : _LIST_ENTRY [ 0xffffbe0c`87f2b3d0 - 0xffffbe0c`841363d0 ]
      +0x360 CycleTime         : 0
      +0x368 ContextSwitches   : 0
      +0x370 SchedulingGroup   : (null)
      +0x378 FreezeCount       : 0
      +0x37c KernelTime        : 0
      +0x380 UserTime          : 0
      +0x384 ReadyTime         : 0
      +0x388 UserDirectoryTableBase : 1
      +0x390 AddressPolicy     : 0x1 ''
      +0x391 Spare2            : [71] ""
      +0x3d8 InstrumentationCallback : (null)
      +0x3e0 SecureState       : <unnamed-tag>
      +0x3e8 KernelWaitTime    : 0
      +0x3f0 UserWaitTime      : 0
      +0x3f8 LastRebalanceQpc  : 0x00000001`14d49ff8
      +0x400 PerProcessorCycleTimes : 0x00000000`00008020 Void
      +0x408 ExtendedFeatureDisableMask : 0
      +0x410 PrimaryGroup      : 0
      +0x412 Spare3            : [3] 0
      +0x418 UserCetLogging    : (null)
      +0x420 EndPadding        : [3] 0
   +0x438 ProcessLock      : _EX_PUSH_LOCK
      +0x000 Locked            : 0y0
      +0x000 Waiting           : 0y0
      +0x000 Waking            : 0y0
      +0x000 MultipleShared    : 0y0
      +0x000 Shared            : 0y0000000000000000000000000000000000000000000000000000000000000 (0)
      +0x000 Value             : 0
      +0x000 Ptr               : (null)
   +0x440 UniqueProcessId  : 0x00000000`00000168 Void
   +0x448 ActiveProcessLinks : _LIST_ENTRY [ 0xffffbe0c`87f2b4c8 - 0xffffbe0c`841364c8 ]
      +0x000 Flink             : 0xffffbe0c`87f2b4c8 _LIST_ENTRY [ 0xffffbe0c`887d44c8 - 0xffffbe0c`8780f488 ]
      +0x008 Blink             : 0xffffbe0c`841364c8 _LIST_ENTRY [ 0xffffbe0c`8780f488 - 0xffffbe0c`840eb488 ]
   +0x458 RundownProtect   : _EX_RUNDOWN_REF
      +0x000 Count             : 0
      +0x000 Ptr               : (null)
```

```
    +0x460 Flags2            : 0xd000
    +0x460 JobNotReallyActive : 0y0
    +0x460 AccountingFolded  : 0y0
    +0x460 NewProcessReported : 0y0
    +0x460 ExitProcessReported : 0y0
    +0x460 ReportCommitChanges : 0y0
    +0x460 LastReportMemory  : 0y0
    +0x460 ForceWakeCharge   : 0y0
    +0x460 CrossSessionCreate : 0y0
    +0x460 NeedsHandleRundown : 0y0
[...]
    +0x590 EtwDataSource     : 0xffffbe0c`87afd8d0 Void
    +0x598 PageDirectoryPte  : 0
    +0x5a0 ImageFilePointer  : 0xffffbe0c`87815510 _FILE_OBJECT
        +0x000 Type            : 0n5
        +0x002 Size            : 0n216
        +0x008 DeviceObject    : 0xffffbe0c`84df6870 _DEVICE_OBJECT
        +0x010 Vpb             : 0xffffbe0c`84da05e0 _VPB
        +0x018 FsContext       : 0xffff800e`d70f4b10 Void
        +0x020 FsContext2      : 0xffff800e`d70f4d88 Void
        +0x028 SectionObjectPointer : 0xffffbe0c`87816c78 _SECTION_OBJECT_POINTERS
        +0x030 PrivateCacheMap : (null)
        +0x038 FinalStatus     : 0n0
        +0x040 RelatedFileObject : (null)
        +0x048 LockOperation   : 0 ''
        +0x049 DeletePending   : 0 ''
        +0x04a ReadAccess      : 0x1 ''
        +0x04b WriteAccess     : 0 ''
        +0x04c DeleteAccess    : 0 ''
        +0x04d SharedRead      : 0x1 ''
        +0x04e SharedWrite     : 0 ''
        +0x04f SharedDelete    : 0x1 ''
        +0x050 Flags           : 0x44442
        +0x058 FileName        : _UNICODE_STRING "\Windows\System32\smss.exe"
        +0x068 CurrentByteOffset : _LARGE_INTEGER 0x0
        +0x070 Waiters         : 0
        +0x074 Busy            : 0
        +0x078 LastLock        : (null)
        +0x080 Lock            : _KEVENT
        +0x098 Event           : _KEVENT
        +0x0b0 CompletionContext : (null)
        +0x0b8 IrpListLock     : 0
        +0x0c0 IrpList         : _LIST_ENTRY [ 0xffffbe0c`878155d0 - 0xffffbe0c`878155d0 ]
        +0x0d0 FileObjectExtension : (null)
    +0x5a8 ImageFileName     : [15] "smss.exe"
    +0x5b7 PriorityClass     : 0x2 ''
    +0x5b8 SecurityPort      : (null)
[...]
```

Note: This is *smss.exe* process. So we can now navigate the process list manually. Next, we learn how to do that using special WinDbg commands.

7.   The command **dl** shows all double link list pointers. For example, if we want to see all forward pointers we can use this command variant:

```
1: kd> dl nt!PsActiveProcessHead 100 1
fffff807`62c1bfa0  ffffbe0c`840eb488
ffffbe0c`840eb488  ffffbe0c`841364c8
ffffbe0c`841364c8  ffffbe0c`8780f488
ffffbe0c`8780f488  ffffbe0c`87f2b4c8
ffffbe0c`87f2b4c8  ffffbe0c`887d44c8
ffffbe0c`887d44c8  ffffbe0c`88884508
ffffbe0c`88884508  ffffbe0c`888c9548
ffffbe0c`888c9548  ffffbe0c`888cb508
ffffbe0c`888cb508  ffffbe0c`888dc4c8
ffffbe0c`888dc4c8  ffffbe0c`889b1608
ffffbe0c`889b1608  ffffbe0c`889af608
```

143

```
fffffbe0c`889af608    fffffbe0c`889ae4c8
fffffbe0c`889ae4c8    fffffbe0c`89013508
fffffbe0c`89013508    fffffbe0c`889c74c8
fffffbe0c`889c74c8    fffffbe0c`89102508
fffffbe0c`89102508    fffffbe0c`891204c8
fffffbe0c`891204c8    fffffbe0c`891a04c8
fffffbe0c`891a04c8    fffffbe0c`8919e4c8
fffffbe0c`8919e4c8    fffffbe0c`891a8508
fffffbe0c`891a8508    fffffbe0c`891b9508
fffffbe0c`891b9508    fffffbe0c`891c64c8
fffffbe0c`891c64c8    fffffbe0c`892094c8
fffffbe0c`892094c8    fffffbe0c`892414c8
fffffbe0c`892414c8    fffffbe0c`89255508
fffffbe0c`89255508    fffffbe0c`892b64c8
fffffbe0c`892b64c8    fffffbe0c`893484c8
fffffbe0c`893484c8    fffffbe0c`8934d4c8
fffffbe0c`8934d4c8    fffffbe0c`893624c8
fffffbe0c`893624c8    fffffbe0c`893bc4c8
fffffbe0c`893bc4c8    fffffbe0c`893bf4c8
fffffbe0c`893bf4c8    fffffbe0c`893634c8
fffffbe0c`893634c8    fffffbe0c`894074c8
fffffbe0c`894074c8    fffffbe0c`8940a4c8
fffffbe0c`8940a4c8    fffffbe0c`841ba4c8
fffffbe0c`841ba4c8    fffffbe0c`841b04c8
fffffbe0c`841b04c8    fffffbe0c`841854c8
fffffbe0c`841854c8    fffffbe0c`841ed4c8
fffffbe0c`841ed4c8    fffffbe0c`841354c8
fffffbe0c`841354c8    fffffbe0c`894964c8
fffffbe0c`894964c8    fffffbe0c`89534508
fffffbe0c`89534508    fffffbe0c`895384c8
fffffbe0c`895384c8    fffffbe0c`895964c8
fffffbe0c`895964c8    fffffbe0c`895b3488
fffffbe0c`895b3488    fffffbe0c`895cc4c8
fffffbe0c`895cc4c8    fffffbe0c`895df4c8
fffffbe0c`895df4c8    fffffbe0c`8963c4c8
fffffbe0c`8963c4c8    fffffbe0c`896b14c8
fffffbe0c`896b14c8    fffffbe0c`896d2508
fffffbe0c`896d2508    fffffbe0c`897304c8
fffffbe0c`897304c8    fffffbe0c`89745508
fffffbe0c`89745508    fffffbe0c`897284c8
fffffbe0c`897284c8    fffffbe0c`897da4c8
fffffbe0c`897da4c8    fffffbe0c`897ed508
fffffbe0c`897ed508    fffffbe0c`897dc508
fffffbe0c`897dc508    fffffbe0c`898954c8
fffffbe0c`898954c8    fffffbe0c`89a074c8
fffffbe0c`89a074c8    fffffbe0c`89a064c8
fffffbe0c`89a064c8    fffffbe0c`890424c8
fffffbe0c`890424c8    fffffbe0c`89a0a4c8
fffffbe0c`89a0a4c8    fffffbe0c`89a8e508
fffffbe0c`89a8e508    fffffbe0c`89a964c8
fffffbe0c`89a964c8    fffffbe0c`89aa64c8
fffffbe0c`89aa64c8    fffffbe0c`89aa94c8
fffffbe0c`89aa94c8    fffffbe0c`89aaa4c8
fffffbe0c`89aaa4c8    fffffbe0c`89a424c8
fffffbe0c`89a424c8    fffffbe0c`89ac1508
fffffbe0c`89ac1508    fffffbe0c`89aae4c8
fffffbe0c`89aae4c8    fffffbe0c`899e8508
fffffbe0c`899e8508    fffffbe0c`89c304c8
fffffbe0c`89c304c8    fffffbe0c`89cf84c8
```

```
fffffbe0c`89cf84c8    fffffbe0c`89e84508
fffffbe0c`89e84508    fffffbe0c`89f5e4c8
fffffbe0c`89f5e4c8    fffffbe0c`8a054508
fffffbe0c`8a054508    fffffbe0c`8a0cb4c8
fffffbe0c`8a0cb4c8    fffffbe0c`8a232508
fffffbe0c`8a232508    fffffbe0c`898c1508
fffffbe0c`898c1508    fffffbe0c`8a334508
fffffbe0c`8a334508    fffffbe0c`8a0c44c8
fffffbe0c`8a0c44c8    fffffbe0c`8a3374c8
fffffbe0c`8a3374c8    fffffbe0c`8a0714c8
fffffbe0c`8a0714c8    fffffbe0c`8a402508
fffffbe0c`8a402508    fffffbe0c`8a43b4c8
fffffbe0c`8a43b4c8    fffffbe0c`8a4544c8
fffffbe0c`8a4544c8    fffffbe0c`8a4554c8
fffffbe0c`8a4554c8    fffffbe0c`8a4f84c8
fffffbe0c`8a4f84c8    fffffbe0c`8a4f74c8
fffffbe0c`8a4f74c8    fffffbe0c`8a4ef508
fffffbe0c`8a4ef508    fffffbe0c`8a4e94c8
fffffbe0c`8a4e94c8    fffffbe0c`8a6c14c8
fffffbe0c`8a6c14c8    fffffbe0c`8a7294c8
fffffbe0c`8a7294c8    fffffbe0c`8a854508
fffffbe0c`8a854508    fffffbe0c`8a8594c8
fffffbe0c`8a8594c8    fffffbe0c`8a924508
fffffbe0c`8a924508    fffffbe0c`8a9824c8
fffffbe0c`8a9824c8    fffffbe0c`8aa02508
fffffbe0c`8aa02508    fffffbe0c`8a55b508
fffffbe0c`8a55b508    fffffbe0c`8aaa0508
fffffbe0c`8aaa0508    fffffbe0c`8ab524c8
fffffbe0c`8ab524c8    fffffbe0c`8aa374c8
fffffbe0c`8aa374c8    fffffbe0c`8ac074c8
fffffbe0c`8ac074c8    fffffbe0c`8acd64c8
fffffbe0c`8acd64c8    fffffbe0c`8ad944c8
fffffbe0c`8ad944c8    fffffbe0c`8ae6f4c8
fffffbe0c`8ae6f4c8    fffffbe0c`8ae724c8
fffffbe0c`8ae724c8    fffffbe0c`8ae76508
fffffbe0c`8ae76508    fffffbe0c`8aeeb508
fffffbe0c`8aeeb508    fffffbe0c`8ac8e4c8
fffffbe0c`8ac8e4c8    fffffbe0c`8af24508
fffffbe0c`8af24508    fffffbe0c`8ac984c8
fffffbe0c`8ac984c8    fffffbe0c`841204c8
fffffbe0c`841204c8    fffffbe0c`8aee14c8
fffffbe0c`8aee14c8    fffffbe0c`8aedd4c8
fffffbe0c`8aedd4c8    fffffbe0c`8b208508
fffffbe0c`8b208508    fffffbe0c`8ad844c8
fffffbe0c`8ad844c8    fffffbe0c`8af554c8
fffffbe0c`8af554c8    fffffbe0c`8b49a4c8
fffffbe0c`8b49a4c8    fffffbe0c`8b4e9508
fffffbe0c`8b4e9508    fffffbe0c`8b402508
fffffbe0c`8b402508    fffffbe0c`8b4174c8
fffffbe0c`8b4174c8    fffffbe0c`8b37b4c8
fffffbe0c`8b37b4c8    fffffbe0c`8b4b24c8
fffffbe0c`8b4b24c8    fffffbe0c`8b0924c8
fffffbe0c`8b0924c8    fffffbe0c`876f24c8
fffffbe0c`876f24c8    fffffbe0c`8b4d64c8
fffffbe0c`8b4d64c8    fffffbe0c`89a02508
fffffbe0c`89a02508    fffffbe0c`8b5e6508
fffffbe0c`8b5e6508    fffffbe0c`8b887508
fffffbe0c`8b887508    fffffbe0c`8b4b6508
fffffbe0c`8b4b6508    fffffbe0c`876f84c8
```

145

```
ffffbe0c`876f84c8    ffffbe0c`892bc4c8
ffffbe0c`892bc4c8    ffffbe0c`89a9b4c8
ffffbe0c`89a9b4c8    ffffbe0c`8b3d54c8
ffffbe0c`8b3d54c8    ffffbe0c`8b4d8508
ffffbe0c`8b4d8508    ffffbe0c`8ad81508
ffffbe0c`8ad81508    ffffbe0c`8b0d6508
ffffbe0c`8b0d6508    ffffbe0c`8cce9508
ffffbe0c`8cce9508    ffffbe0c`8b2244c8
ffffbe0c`8b2244c8    ffffbe0c`8b696508
ffffbe0c`8b696508    ffffbe0c`8b396508
ffffbe0c`8b396508    ffffbe0c`8b5b3508
ffffbe0c`8b5b3508    ffffbe0c`8af46508
ffffbe0c`8af46508    ffffbe0c`8b0e2508
ffffbe0c`8b0e2508    ffffbe0c`87021508
ffffbe0c`87021508    ffffbe0c`87648508
ffffbe0c`87648508    ffffbe0c`84caf4c8
ffffbe0c`84caf4c8    ffffbe0c`8b5384c8
ffffbe0c`8b5384c8    ffffbe0c`8be62508
ffffbe0c`8be62508    ffffbe0c`8bed84c8
ffffbe0c`8bed84c8    ffffbe0c`84c99508
ffffbe0c`84c99508    ffffbe0c`8be76508
ffffbe0c`8be76508    ffffbe0c`8a7a64c8
ffffbe0c`8a7a64c8    ffffbe0c`8b3184c8
ffffbe0c`8b3184c8    ffffbe0c`8c9d34c8
ffffbe0c`8c9d34c8    ffffbe0c`8b3174c8
ffffbe0c`8b3174c8    ffffbe0c`877ec4c8
ffffbe0c`877ec4c8    ffffbe0c`8c2de508
ffffbe0c`8c2de508    ffffbe0c`8c576508
ffffbe0c`8c576508    ffffbe0c`8c2cd508
ffffbe0c`8c2cd508    ffffbe0c`8bfb1508
ffffbe0c`8bfb1508    fffff807`62c1bfa0
```

Note: We specified to list at most 100 elements, and we see the list loops on itself. We can again examine any element by subtracting the list structure offset:

```
1: kd> dt nt!_EPROCESS ffffbe0c`8bfb1508-0x448
   +0x000 Pcb              : _KPROCESS
   +0x438 ProcessLock      : _EX_PUSH_LOCK
   +0x440 UniqueProcessId  : 0x00000000`00002434 Void
   +0x448 ActiveProcessLinks : _LIST_ENTRY [ 0xfffff807`62c1bfa0 - 0xffffbe0c`8c2cd508 ]
   +0x458 RundownProtect   : _EX_RUNDOWN_REF
   +0x460 Flags2           : 0xd094
   +0x460 JobNotReallyActive : 0y0
   +0x460 AccountingFolded : 0y0
   +0x460 NewProcessReported : 0y1
   +0x460 ExitProcessReported : 0y0
   +0x460 ReportCommitChanges : 0y1
   +0x460 LastReportMemory : 0y0
   +0x460 ForceWakeCharge  : 0y0
   +0x460 CrossSessionCreate : 0y1
   +0x460 NeedsHandleRundown : 0y0
   +0x460 RefTraceEnabled  : 0y0
   +0x460 PicoCreated      : 0y0
   +0x460 EmptyJobEvaluated : 0y0
   +0x460 DefaultPagePriority : 0y101
   +0x460 PrimaryTokenFrozen : 0y1
[...]
   +0x598 PageDirectoryPte : 0
```

```
    +0x5a0 ImageFilePointer : 0xffffbe0c`8bf609c0 _FILE_OBJECT
    +0x5a8 ImageFileName    : [15] "SearchHost.exe"
    +0x5b7 PriorityClass    : 0x2 ''
    +0x5b8 SecurityPort     : (null)
[...]
```

Note: We see that *SearchHost.exe* process is the last process in the list. If we want to display both forward and backward links we use this command variant:

```
1: kd> dl nt!PsActiveProcessHead 100 2
fffff807`62c1bfa0  ffffbe0c`840eb488 ffffbe0c`8bfb1508
ffffbe0c`840eb488  ffffbe0c`841364c8 fffff807`62c1bfa0
ffffbe0c`841364c8  ffffbe0c`8780f488 ffffbe0c`840eb488
ffffbe0c`8780f488  ffffbe0c`87f2b4c8 ffffbe0c`841364c8
ffffbe0c`87f2b4c8  ffffbe0c`887d44c8 ffffbe0c`8780f488
ffffbe0c`887d44c8  ffffbe0c`88884508 ffffbe0c`87f2b4c8
ffffbe0c`88884508  ffffbe0c`888c9548 ffffbe0c`887d44c8
ffffbe0c`888c9548  ffffbe0c`888cb508 ffffbe0c`88884508
ffffbe0c`888cb508  ffffbe0c`888dc4c8 ffffbe0c`888c9548
ffffbe0c`888dc4c8  ffffbe0c`889b1608 ffffbe0c`888cb508
ffffbe0c`889b1608  ffffbe0c`889af608 ffffbe0c`888dc4c8
ffffbe0c`889af608  ffffbe0c`889ae4c8 ffffbe0c`889b1608
ffffbe0c`889ae4c8  ffffbe0c`89013508 ffffbe0c`889af608
ffffbe0c`89013508  ffffbe0c`889c74c8 ffffbe0c`889ae4c8
ffffbe0c`889c74c8  ffffbe0c`89102508 ffffbe0c`89013508
ffffbe0c`89102508  ffffbe0c`891204c8 ffffbe0c`889c74c8
ffffbe0c`891204c8  ffffbe0c`891a04c8 ffffbe0c`89102508
ffffbe0c`891a04c8  ffffbe0c`8919e4c8 ffffbe0c`891204c8
ffffbe0c`8919e4c8  ffffbe0c`891a8508 ffffbe0c`891a04c8
ffffbe0c`891a8508  ffffbe0c`891b9508 ffffbe0c`8919e4c8
ffffbe0c`891b9508  ffffbe0c`891c64c8 ffffbe0c`891a8508
ffffbe0c`891c64c8  ffffbe0c`892094c8 ffffbe0c`891b9508
ffffbe0c`892094c8  ffffbe0c`892414c8 ffffbe0c`891c64c8
ffffbe0c`892414c8  ffffbe0c`89255508 ffffbe0c`892094c8
ffffbe0c`89255508  ffffbe0c`892b64c8 ffffbe0c`892414c8
ffffbe0c`892b64c8  ffffbe0c`893484c8 ffffbe0c`89255508
ffffbe0c`893484c8  ffffbe0c`8934d4c8 ffffbe0c`892b64c8
ffffbe0c`8934d4c8  ffffbe0c`893624c8 ffffbe0c`893484c8
ffffbe0c`893624c8  ffffbe0c`893bc4c8 ffffbe0c`8934d4c8
ffffbe0c`893bc4c8  ffffbe0c`893bf4c8 ffffbe0c`893624c8
ffffbe0c`893bf4c8  ffffbe0c`893634c8 ffffbe0c`893bc4c8
ffffbe0c`893634c8  ffffbe0c`894074c8 ffffbe0c`893bf4c8
ffffbe0c`894074c8  ffffbe0c`8940a4c8 ffffbe0c`893634c8
ffffbe0c`8940a4c8  ffffbe0c`841ba4c8 ffffbe0c`894074c8
ffffbe0c`841ba4c8  ffffbe0c`841b04c8 ffffbe0c`8940a4c8
ffffbe0c`841b04c8  ffffbe0c`841854c8 ffffbe0c`841ba4c8
ffffbe0c`841854c8  ffffbe0c`841ed4c8 ffffbe0c`841b04c8
ffffbe0c`841ed4c8  ffffbe0c`841354c8 ffffbe0c`841854c8
ffffbe0c`841354c8  ffffbe0c`894964c8 ffffbe0c`841ed4c8
ffffbe0c`894964c8  ffffbe0c`89534508 ffffbe0c`841354c8
ffffbe0c`89534508  ffffbe0c`895384c8 ffffbe0c`894964c8
ffffbe0c`895384c8  ffffbe0c`895964c8 ffffbe0c`89534508
ffffbe0c`895964c8  ffffbe0c`895b3488 ffffbe0c`895384c8
ffffbe0c`895b3488  ffffbe0c`895cc4c8 ffffbe0c`895964c8
ffffbe0c`895cc4c8  ffffbe0c`895df4c8 ffffbe0c`895b3488
ffffbe0c`895df4c8  ffffbe0c`8963c4c8 ffffbe0c`895cc4c8
ffffbe0c`8963c4c8  ffffbe0c`896b14c8 ffffbe0c`895df4c8
```

```
ffffbe0c`896b14c8    ffffbe0c`896d2508    ffffbe0c`8963c4c8
ffffbe0c`896d2508    ffffbe0c`897304c8    ffffbe0c`896b14c8
ffffbe0c`897304c8    ffffbe0c`89745508    ffffbe0c`896d2508
ffffbe0c`89745508    ffffbe0c`897284c8    ffffbe0c`897304c8
ffffbe0c`897284c8    ffffbe0c`897da4c8    ffffbe0c`89745508
ffffbe0c`897da4c8    ffffbe0c`897ed508    ffffbe0c`897284c8
ffffbe0c`897ed508    ffffbe0c`897dc508    ffffbe0c`897da4c8
ffffbe0c`897dc508    ffffbe0c`898954c8    ffffbe0c`897ed508
ffffbe0c`898954c8    ffffbe0c`89a074c8    ffffbe0c`897dc508
ffffbe0c`89a074c8    ffffbe0c`89a064c8    ffffbe0c`898954c8
ffffbe0c`89a064c8    ffffbe0c`890424c8    ffffbe0c`89a074c8
ffffbe0c`890424c8    ffffbe0c`89a0a4c8    ffffbe0c`89a064c8
ffffbe0c`89a0a4c8    ffffbe0c`89a8e508    ffffbe0c`890424c8
ffffbe0c`89a8e508    ffffbe0c`89a964c8    ffffbe0c`89a0a4c8
ffffbe0c`89a964c8    ffffbe0c`89aa64c8    ffffbe0c`89a8e508
ffffbe0c`89aa64c8    ffffbe0c`89aa94c8    ffffbe0c`89a964c8
ffffbe0c`89aa94c8    ffffbe0c`89aaa4c8    ffffbe0c`89aa64c8
ffffbe0c`89aaa4c8    ffffbe0c`89a424c8    ffffbe0c`89aa94c8
ffffbe0c`89a424c8    ffffbe0c`89ac1508    ffffbe0c`89aaa4c8
ffffbe0c`89ac1508    ffffbe0c`89aae4c8    ffffbe0c`89a424c8
ffffbe0c`89aae4c8    ffffbe0c`899e8508    ffffbe0c`89ac1508
ffffbe0c`899e8508    ffffbe0c`89c304c8    ffffbe0c`89aae4c8
ffffbe0c`89c304c8    ffffbe0c`89cf84c8    ffffbe0c`899e8508
ffffbe0c`89cf84c8    ffffbe0c`89e84508    ffffbe0c`89c304c8
ffffbe0c`89e84508    ffffbe0c`89f5e4c8    ffffbe0c`89cf84c8
ffffbe0c`89f5e4c8    ffffbe0c`8a054508    ffffbe0c`89e84508
ffffbe0c`8a054508    ffffbe0c`8a0cb4c8    ffffbe0c`89f5e4c8
ffffbe0c`8a0cb4c8    ffffbe0c`8a232508    ffffbe0c`8a054508
ffffbe0c`8a232508    ffffbe0c`898c1508    ffffbe0c`8a0cb4c8
ffffbe0c`898c1508    ffffbe0c`8a334508    ffffbe0c`8a232508
ffffbe0c`8a334508    ffffbe0c`8a0c44c8    ffffbe0c`898c1508
ffffbe0c`8a0c44c8    ffffbe0c`8a3374c8    ffffbe0c`8a334508
ffffbe0c`8a3374c8    ffffbe0c`8a0714c8    ffffbe0c`8a0c44c8
ffffbe0c`8a0714c8    ffffbe0c`8a402508    ffffbe0c`8a3374c8
ffffbe0c`8a402508    ffffbe0c`8a43b4c8    ffffbe0c`8a0714c8
ffffbe0c`8a43b4c8    ffffbe0c`8a4544c8    ffffbe0c`8a402508
ffffbe0c`8a4544c8    ffffbe0c`8a4554c8    ffffbe0c`8a43b4c8
ffffbe0c`8a4554c8    ffffbe0c`8a4f84c8    ffffbe0c`8a4544c8
ffffbe0c`8a4f84c8    ffffbe0c`8a4f74c8    ffffbe0c`8a4554c8
ffffbe0c`8a4f74c8    ffffbe0c`8a4ef508    ffffbe0c`8a4f84c8
ffffbe0c`8a4ef508    ffffbe0c`8a4e94c8    ffffbe0c`8a4f74c8
ffffbe0c`8a4e94c8    ffffbe0c`8a6c14c8    ffffbe0c`8a4ef508
ffffbe0c`8a6c14c8    ffffbe0c`8a7294c8    ffffbe0c`8a4e94c8
ffffbe0c`8a7294c8    ffffbe0c`8a854508    ffffbe0c`8a6c14c8
ffffbe0c`8a854508    ffffbe0c`8a8594c8    ffffbe0c`8a7294c8
ffffbe0c`8a8594c8    ffffbe0c`8a924508    ffffbe0c`8a854508
ffffbe0c`8a924508    ffffbe0c`8a9824c8    ffffbe0c`8a8594c8
ffffbe0c`8a9824c8    ffffbe0c`8aa02508    ffffbe0c`8a924508
ffffbe0c`8aa02508    ffffbe0c`8a55b508    ffffbe0c`8a9824c8
ffffbe0c`8a55b508    ffffbe0c`8aaa0508    ffffbe0c`8aa02508
ffffbe0c`8aaa0508    ffffbe0c`8ab524c8    ffffbe0c`8a55b508
ffffbe0c`8ab524c8    ffffbe0c`8aa374c8    ffffbe0c`8aaa0508
ffffbe0c`8aa374c8    ffffbe0c`8ac074c8    ffffbe0c`8ab524c8
ffffbe0c`8ac074c8    ffffbe0c`8acd64c8    ffffbe0c`8aa374c8
ffffbe0c`8acd64c8    ffffbe0c`8ad944c8    ffffbe0c`8ac074c8
ffffbe0c`8ad944c8    ffffbe0c`8ae6f4c8    ffffbe0c`8acd64c8
ffffbe0c`8ae6f4c8    ffffbe0c`8ae724c8    ffffbe0c`8ad944c8
ffffbe0c`8ae724c8    ffffbe0c`8ae76508    ffffbe0c`8ae6f4c8
ffffbe0c`8ae76508    ffffbe0c`8aeeb508    ffffbe0c`8ae724c8
```

```
fffffbe0c`8aeeb508    fffffbe0c`8ac8e4c8    fffffbe0c`8ae76508
fffffbe0c`8ac8e4c8    fffffbe0c`8af24508    fffffbe0c`8aeeb508
fffffbe0c`8af24508    fffffbe0c`8ac984c8    fffffbe0c`8ac8e4c8
fffffbe0c`8ac984c8    fffffbe0c`841204c8    fffffbe0c`8af24508
fffffbe0c`841204c8    fffffbe0c`8aee14c8    fffffbe0c`8ac984c8
fffffbe0c`8aee14c8    fffffbe0c`8aedd4c8    fffffbe0c`841204c8
fffffbe0c`8aedd4c8    fffffbe0c`8b208508    fffffbe0c`8aee14c8
fffffbe0c`8b208508    fffffbe0c`8ad844c8    fffffbe0c`8aedd4c8
fffffbe0c`8ad844c8    fffffbe0c`8af554c8    fffffbe0c`8b208508
fffffbe0c`8af554c8    fffffbe0c`8b49a4c8    fffffbe0c`8ad844c8
fffffbe0c`8b49a4c8    fffffbe0c`8b4e9508    fffffbe0c`8af554c8
fffffbe0c`8b4e9508    fffffbe0c`8b402508    fffffbe0c`8b49a4c8
fffffbe0c`8b402508    fffffbe0c`8b4174c8    fffffbe0c`8b4e9508
fffffbe0c`8b4174c8    fffffbe0c`8b37b4c8    fffffbe0c`8b402508
fffffbe0c`8b37b4c8    fffffbe0c`8b4b24c8    fffffbe0c`8b4174c8
fffffbe0c`8b4b24c8    fffffbe0c`8b0924c8    fffffbe0c`8b37b4c8
fffffbe0c`8b0924c8    fffffbe0c`876f24c8    fffffbe0c`8b4b24c8
fffffbe0c`876f24c8    fffffbe0c`8b4d64c8    fffffbe0c`8b0924c8
fffffbe0c`8b4d64c8    fffffbe0c`89a02508    fffffbe0c`876f24c8
fffffbe0c`89a02508    fffffbe0c`8b5e6508    fffffbe0c`8b4d64c8
fffffbe0c`8b5e6508    fffffbe0c`8b887508    fffffbe0c`89a02508
fffffbe0c`8b887508    fffffbe0c`8b4b6508    fffffbe0c`8b5e6508
fffffbe0c`8b4b6508    fffffbe0c`876f84c8    fffffbe0c`8b887508
fffffbe0c`876f84c8    fffffbe0c`892bc4c8    fffffbe0c`8b4b6508
fffffbe0c`892bc4c8    fffffbe0c`89a9b4c8    fffffbe0c`876f84c8
fffffbe0c`89a9b4c8    fffffbe0c`8b3d54c8    fffffbe0c`892bc4c8
fffffbe0c`8b3d54c8    fffffbe0c`8b4d8508    fffffbe0c`89a9b4c8
fffffbe0c`8b4d8508    fffffbe0c`8ad81508    fffffbe0c`8b3d54c8
fffffbe0c`8ad81508    fffffbe0c`8b0d6508    fffffbe0c`8b4d8508
fffffbe0c`8b0d6508    fffffbe0c`8cce9508    fffffbe0c`8ad81508
fffffbe0c`8cce9508    fffffbe0c`8b2244c8    fffffbe0c`8b0d6508
fffffbe0c`8b2244c8    fffffbe0c`8b696508    fffffbe0c`8cce9508
fffffbe0c`8b696508    fffffbe0c`8b396508    fffffbe0c`8b2244c8
fffffbe0c`8b396508    fffffbe0c`8b5b3508    fffffbe0c`8b696508
fffffbe0c`8b5b3508    fffffbe0c`8af46508    fffffbe0c`8b396508
fffffbe0c`8af46508    fffffbe0c`8b0e2508    fffffbe0c`8b5b3508
fffffbe0c`8b0e2508    fffffbe0c`87021508    fffffbe0c`8af46508
fffffbe0c`87021508    fffffbe0c`87648508    fffffbe0c`8b0e2508
fffffbe0c`87648508    fffffbe0c`84caf4c8    fffffbe0c`87021508
fffffbe0c`84caf4c8    fffffbe0c`8b5384c8    fffffbe0c`87648508
fffffbe0c`8b5384c8    fffffbe0c`8be62508    fffffbe0c`84caf4c8
fffffbe0c`8be62508    fffffbe0c`8bed84c8    fffffbe0c`8b5384c8
fffffbe0c`8bed84c8    fffffbe0c`84c99508    fffffbe0c`8be62508
fffffbe0c`84c99508    fffffbe0c`8be76508    fffffbe0c`8bed84c8
fffffbe0c`8be76508    fffffbe0c`8a7a64c8    fffffbe0c`84c99508
fffffbe0c`8a7a64c8    fffffbe0c`8b3184c8    fffffbe0c`8be76508
fffffbe0c`8b3184c8    fffffbe0c`8c9d34c8    fffffbe0c`8a7a64c8
fffffbe0c`8c9d34c8    fffffbe0c`8b3174c8    fffffbe0c`8b3184c8
fffffbe0c`8b3174c8    fffffbe0c`877ec4c8    fffffbe0c`8c9d34c8
fffffbe0c`877ec4c8    fffffbe0c`8c2de508    fffffbe0c`8b3174c8
fffffbe0c`8c2de508    fffffbe0c`8c576508    fffffbe0c`877ec4c8
fffffbe0c`8c576508    fffffbe0c`8c2cd508    fffffbe0c`8c2de508
fffffbe0c`8c2cd508    fffffbe0c`8bfb1508    fffffbe0c`8c576508
fffffbe0c`8bfb1508    fffff807`62c1bfa0    fffffbe0c`8c2cd508
```

8.   If we want to execute a command per each linked list element, we use the **!list** command (the **@$extret**
variable contains the address of the current list element):

```
1: kd> !list -t nt!_LIST_ENTRY.Flink -x "dt nt!_EPROCESS @$extret-448" poi(nt!PsActiveProcessHead)
   +0x000 Pcb                 : _KPROCESS
   +0x438 ProcessLock         : _EX_PUSH_LOCK
   +0x440 UniqueProcessId     : 0x00000000`00000004 Void
   +0x448 ActiveProcessLinks  : _LIST_ENTRY [ 0xffffbe0c`841364c8 - 0xfffff807`62c1bfa0 ]
   +0x458 RundownProtect      : _EX_RUNDOWN_REF
   +0x460 Flags2              : 0xd000
   +0x460 JobNotReallyActive  : 0y0
   +0x460 AccountingFolded    : 0y0
   +0x460 NewProcessReported  : 0y0
   +0x460 ExitProcessReported : 0y0
   +0x460 ReportCommitChanges : 0y0
   +0x460 LastReportMemory    : 0y0
   +0x460 ForceWakeCharge     : 0y0
   +0x460 CrossSessionCreate  : 0y0
   +0x460 NeedsHandleRundown  : 0y0
   +0x460 RefTraceEnabled     : 0y0
   +0x460 PicoCreated         : 0y0
   +0x460 EmptyJobEvaluated   : 0y0
   +0x460 DefaultPagePriority : 0y101
   +0x460 PrimaryTokenFrozen  : 0y1
   +0x460 ProcessVerifierTarget : 0y0
   +0x460 RestrictSetThreadContext : 0y0
   +0x460 AffinityPermanent   : 0y0
   +0x460 AffinityUpdateEnable : 0y0
   +0x460 PropagateNode       : 0y0
   +0x460 ExplicitAffinity    : 0y0
   +0x460 ProcessExecutionState : 0y00
   +0x460 EnableReadVmLogging : 0y0
   +0x460 EnableWriteVmLogging : 0y0
   +0x460 FatalAccessTerminationRequested : 0y0
   +0x460 DisableSystemAllowedCpuSet : 0y0
   +0x460 ProcessStateChangeRequest : 0y00
   +0x460 ProcessStateChangeInProgress : 0y0
   +0x460 InPrivate           : 0y0
   +0x464 Flags               : 0x14840c00
   +0x464 CreateReported      : 0y0
   +0x464 NoDebugInherit      : 0y0
   +0x464 ProcessExiting      : 0y0
   +0x464 ProcessDelete       : 0y0
   +0x464 ManageExecutableMemoryWrites : 0y0
   +0x464 VmDeleted           : 0y0
   +0x464 OutswapEnabled      : 0y0
   +0x464 Outswapped          : 0y0
   +0x464 FailFastOnCommitFail : 0y0
   +0x464 Wow64VaSpace4Gb     : 0y0
   +0x464 AddressSpaceInitialized : 0y11
   +0x464 SetTimerResolution  : 0y0
   +0x464 BreakOnTermination  : 0y0
   +0x464 DeprioritizeViews   : 0y0
   +0x464 WriteWatch          : 0y0
   +0x464 ProcessInSession    : 0y0
   +0x464 OverrideAddressSpace : 0y0
   +0x464 HasAddressSpace     : 0y1
   +0x464 LaunchPrefetched    : 0y0
   +0x464 Background          : 0y0
   +0x464 VmTopDown           : 0y0
   +0x464 ImageNotifyDone     : 0y0
   +0x464 PdeUpdateNeeded     : 0y1
   +0x464 VdmAllowed          : 0y0
   +0x464 ProcessRundown      : 0y0
   +0x464 ProcessInserted     : 0y1
   +0x464 DefaultIoPriority   : 0y010
   +0x464 ProcessSelfDelete   : 0y0
   +0x464 SetTimerResolutionLink : 0y0
```

```
+0x468 CreateTime          : _LARGE_INTEGER 0x01d81e1a`13a38448
+0x470 ProcessQuotaUsage   : [2] 0x110
+0x480 ProcessQuotaPeak    : [2] 0x110
+0x490 PeakVirtualSize     : 0xf1a000
+0x498 VirtualSize         : 0x3e7000
+0x4a0 SessionProcessLinks : _LIST_ENTRY [ 0x00000000`00000000 - 0x00000000`00000000 ]
+0x4b0 ExceptionPortData   : (null)
+0x4b0 ExceptionPortValue  : 0
+0x4b0 ExceptionPortState  : 0y000
+0x4b8 Token               : _EX_FAST_REF
+0x4c0 MmReserved          : 0
+0x4c8 AddressCreationLock : _EX_PUSH_LOCK
+0x4d0 PageTableCommitmentLock : _EX_PUSH_LOCK
+0x4d8 RotateInProgress    : (null)
+0x4e0 ForkInProgress      : (null)
+0x4e8 CommitChargeJob     : (null)
+0x4f0 CloneRoot           : _RTL_AVL_TREE
+0x4f8 NumberOfPrivatePages : 0x14
+0x500 NumberOfLockedPages : 0
+0x508 Win32Process        : (null)
+0x510 Job                 : (null)
+0x518 SectionObject       : (null)
+0x520 SectionBaseAddress  : (null)
+0x528 Cookie              : 0xec9a6c71
+0x530 WorkingSetWatch     : (null)
+0x538 Win32WindowStation  : (null)
+0x540 InheritedFromUniqueProcessId : (null)
+0x548 OwnerProcessId      : 2
+0x550 Peb                 : (null)
+0x558 Session             : (null)
+0x560 Spare1              : (null)
+0x568 QuotaBlock          : 0xfffff807`62c5a380 _EPROCESS_QUOTA_BLOCK
+0x570 ObjectTable         : 0xffff800e`d4820c80 _HANDLE_TABLE
+0x578 DebugPort           : (null)
+0x580 WoW64Process        : (null)
+0x588 DeviceMap           : _EX_FAST_REF
+0x590 EtwDataSource       : (null)
+0x598 PageDirectoryPte    : 0
+0x5a0 ImageFilePointer    : (null)
+0x5a8 ImageFileName       : [15]  "System"
+0x5b7 PriorityClass       : 0x2 ''
+0x5b8 SecurityPort        : (null)
+0x5c0 SeAuditProcessCreationInfo : _SE_AUDIT_PROCESS_CREATION_INFO
+0x5c8 JobLinks            : _LIST_ENTRY [ 0x00000000`00000000 - 0x00000000`00000000 ]
+0x5d8 HighestUserAddress  : 0x00007fff`ffff0000 Void
+0x5e0 ThreadListHead      : _LIST_ENTRY [ 0xffffbe0c`841cd5b8 - 0xffffbe0c`8c0dd578 ]
+0x5f0 ActiveThreads       : 0x88
+0x5f4 ImagePathHash       : 0
+0x5f8 DefaultHardErrorProcessing : 5
+0x5fc LastThreadExitStatus : 0n0
+0x600 PrefetchTrace       : _EX_FAST_REF
+0x608 LockedPagesList     : (null)
+0x610 ReadOperationCount  : _LARGE_INTEGER 0x1d
+0x618 WriteOperationCount : _LARGE_INTEGER 0x3b
+0x620 OtherOperationCount : _LARGE_INTEGER 0x51c
+0x628 ReadTransferCount   : _LARGE_INTEGER 0x33e8
+0x630 WriteTransferCount  : _LARGE_INTEGER 0x1a5d23f
+0x638 OtherTransferCount  : _LARGE_INTEGER 0x4a96
+0x640 CommitChargeLimit   : 0
+0x648 CommitCharge        : 0xb
+0x650 CommitChargePeak    : 0x10
+0x680 Vm                  : _MMSUPPORT_FULL
+0x7c0 MmProcessLinks      : _LIST_ENTRY [ 0xffffbe0c`84136840 - 0xfffff807`62d332c0 ]
+0x7d0 ModifiedPageCount   : 0xc98e
+0x7d4 ExitStatus          : 0n259
```

```
+0x7d8 VadRoot             : _RTL_AVL_TREE
+0x7e0 VadHint             : 0xffffbe0c`840a16f0 Void
+0x7e8 VadCount            : 6
+0x7f0 VadPhysicalPages    : 0
+0x7f8 VadPhysicalPagesLimit : 0
+0x800 AlpcContext         : _ALPC_PROCESS_CONTEXT
+0x820 TimerResolutionLink : _LIST_ENTRY [ 0x00000000`00000000 - 0x00000000`00000000 ]
+0x830 TimerResolutionStackRecord : (null)
+0x838 RequestedTimerResolution : 0
+0x83c SmallestTimerResolution : 0
+0x840 ExitTime            : _LARGE_INTEGER 0x0
+0x848 InvertedFunctionTable : (null)
+0x850 InvertedFunctionTableLock : _EX_PUSH_LOCK
+0x858 ActiveThreadsHighWatermark : 0x88
+0x85c LargePrivateVadCount : 0
+0x860 ThreadListLock      : _EX_PUSH_LOCK
+0x868 WnfContext          : 0xffff800e`d48b52e0 Void
+0x870 ServerSilo          : (null)
+0x878 SignatureLevel      : 0x1e ''
+0x879 SectionSignatureLevel : 0x1c ''
+0x87a Protection          : _PS_PROTECTION
+0x87b HangCount           : 0y000
+0x87b GhostCount          : 0y000
+0x87b PrefilterException  : 0y0
+0x87c Flags3              : 0x405080
+0x87c Minimal             : 0y0
+0x87c ReplacingPageRoot   : 0y0
+0x87c Crashed             : 0y0
+0x87c JobVadsAreTracked   : 0y0
+0x87c VadTrackingDisabled : 0y0
+0x87c AuxiliaryProcess    : 0y0
+0x87c SubsystemProcess    : 0y0
+0x87c IndirectCpuSets     : 0y1
+0x87c RelinquishedCommit  : 0y0
+0x87c HighGraphicsPriority : 0y0
+0x87c CommitFailLogged    : 0y0
+0x87c ReserveFailLogged   : 0y0
+0x87c SystemProcess       : 0y1
+0x87c HideImageBaseAddresses : 0y0
+0x87c AddressPolicyFrozen : 0y1
+0x87c ProcessFirstResume  : 0y0
+0x87c ForegroundExternal  : 0y0
+0x87c ForegroundSystem    : 0y0
+0x87c HighMemoryPriority  : 0y0
+0x87c EnableProcessSuspendResumeLogging : 0y0
+0x87c EnableThreadSuspendResumeLogging : 0y0
+0x87c SecurityDomainChanged : 0y0
+0x87c SecurityFreezeComplete : 0y1
+0x87c VmProcessorHost     : 0y0
+0x87c VmProcessorHostTransition : 0y0
+0x87c AltSyscall          : 0y0
+0x87c TimerResolutionIgnore : 0y0
+0x87c DisallowUserTerminate : 0y0
+0x87c EnableProcessRemoteExecProtectVmLogging : 0y0
+0x87c EnableProcessLocalExecProtectVmLogging : 0y0
+0x880 DeviceAsid          : 0n0
+0x888 SvmData             : (null)
+0x890 SvmProcessLock      : _EX_PUSH_LOCK
+0x898 SvmLock             : 0
+0x8a0 SvmProcessDeviceListHead : _LIST_ENTRY [ 0xffffbe0c`840eb8e0 - 0xffffbe0c`840eb8e0 ]
+0x8b0 LastFreezeInterruptTime : 0
+0x8b8 DiskCounters        : 0xffffbe0c`840ebbc0 _PROCESS_DISK_COUNTERS
+0x8c0 PicoContext         : (null)
+0x8c8 EnclaveTable        : (null)
+0x8d0 EnclaveNumber       : 0
```

```
   +0x8d8 EnclaveLock         : _EX_PUSH_LOCK
   +0x8e0 HighPriorityFaultsAllowed : 0
   +0x8e8 EnergyContext       : 0xffffbe0c`840ebbe8 _PO_PROCESS_ENERGY_CONTEXT
   +0x8f0 VmContext           : (null)
   +0x8f8 SequenceNumber      : 1
   +0x900 CreateInterruptTime : 0x89eae9f
   +0x908 CreateUnbiasedInterruptTime : 0x89eae9f
   +0x910 TotalUnbiasedFrozenTime : 0
   +0x918 LastAppStateUpdateTime : 0
   +0x920 LastAppStateUptime : 0y0000000000000000000000000000000000000000000000000000000000000 (0)
   +0x920 LastAppState        : 0y000
   +0x928 SharedCommitCharge : 0x4a
   +0x930 SharedCommitLock : _EX_PUSH_LOCK
   +0x938 SharedCommitLinks : _LIST_ENTRY [ 0xffff800e`d71a16b8 - 0xffff800e`d4cfba78 ]
   +0x948 AllowedCpuSets      : 0xffffbe0c`840ebdc8
   +0x950 DefaultCpuSets      : 0xffffbe0c`840ebec8
   +0x948 AllowedCpuSetsIndirect : 0xffffbe0c`840ebdc8  -> 3
   +0x950 DefaultCpuSetsIndirect : 0xffffbe0c`840ebec8  -> 0
   +0x958 DiskIoAttribution : (null)
   +0x960 DxgProcess          : 0xffff800e`d4ef4a40 Void
   +0x968 Win32KFilterSet     : 0
   +0x96c Machine             : 0x8664
   +0x96e Spare0              : 0
   +0x970 ProcessTimerDelay : _PS_INTERLOCKED_TIMER_DELAY_VALUES
   +0x978 KTimerSets          : 0
   +0x97c KTimer2Sets         : 0
   +0x980 ThreadTimerSets     : 0
   +0x988 VirtualTimerListLock : 0
   +0x990 VirtualTimerListHead : _LIST_ENTRY [ 0xffffbe0c`840eb9d0 - 0xffffbe0c`840eb9d0 ]
   +0x9a0 WakeChannel         : _WNF_STATE_NAME
   +0x9a0 WakeInfo            : _PS_PROCESS_WAKE_INFORMATION
   +0x9d0 MitigationFlags     : 0x40000060
   +0x9d0 MitigationFlagsValues : <unnamed-tag>
   +0x9d4 MitigationFlags2 : 0x40002000
   +0x9d4 MitigationFlags2Values : <unnamed-tag>
   +0x9d8 PartitionObject     : 0xffffbe0c`840bf960 Void
   +0x9e0 SecurityDomain      : 0
   +0x9e8 ParentSecurityDomain : 0
   +0x9f0 CoverageSamplerContext : (null)
   +0x9f8 MmHotPatchContext : (null)
   +0xa00 IdealProcessorAssignmentBlock : _KE_IDEAL_PROCESSOR_ASSIGNMENT_BLOCK
   +0xb18 DynamicEHContinuationTargetsTree : _RTL_AVL_TREE
   +0xb20 DynamicEHContinuationTargetsLock : _EX_PUSH_LOCK
   +0xb28 DynamicEnforcedCetCompatibleRanges : _PS_DYNAMIC_ENFORCED_ADDRESS_RANGES
   +0xb38 DisabledComponentFlags : 0
   +0xb3c PageCombineSequence : 0n1
   +0xb40 EnableOptionalXStateFeaturesLock : _EX_PUSH_LOCK

[...]

dt nt!_EPROCESS @$extret-448
   +0x000 Pcb                 : _KPROCESS
   +0x438 ProcessLock         : _EX_PUSH_LOCK
   +0x440 UniqueProcessId     : 0x00000000`00002434 Void
   +0x448 ActiveProcessLinks : _LIST_ENTRY [ 0xfffff807`62c1bfa0 - 0xffffbe0c`8c2cd508 ]
   +0x458 RundownProtect      : _EX_RUNDOWN_REF
   +0x460 Flags2              : 0xd094
   +0x460 JobNotReallyActive : 0y0
   +0x460 AccountingFolded   : 0y0
   +0x460 NewProcessReported : 0y1
   +0x460 ExitProcessReported : 0y0
   +0x460 ReportCommitChanges : 0y1
   +0x460 LastReportMemory   : 0y0
   +0x460 ForceWakeCharge    : 0y0
   +0x460 CrossSessionCreate : 0y1
```

```
+0x460 NeedsHandleRundown : 0y0
+0x460 RefTraceEnabled    : 0y0
+0x460 PicoCreated        : 0y0
+0x460 EmptyJobEvaluated  : 0y0
+0x460 DefaultPagePriority : 0y101
+0x460 PrimaryTokenFrozen : 0y1
+0x460 ProcessVerifierTarget : 0y0
+0x460 RestrictSetThreadContext : 0y0
+0x460 AffinityPermanent  : 0y0
+0x460 AffinityUpdateEnable : 0y0
+0x460 PropagateNode      : 0y0
+0x460 ExplicitAffinity   : 0y0
+0x460 ProcessExecutionState : 0y00
+0x460 EnableReadVmLogging : 0y0
+0x460 EnableWriteVmLogging : 0y0
+0x460 FatalAccessTerminationRequested : 0y0
+0x460 DisableSystemAllowedCpuSet : 0y0
+0x460 ProcessStateChangeRequest : 0y00
+0x460 ProcessStateChangeInProgress : 0y0
+0x460 InPrivate          : 0y0
+0x464 Flags              : 0x944d8c01
+0x464 CreateReported     : 0y1
+0x464 NoDebugInherit     : 0y0
+0x464 ProcessExiting     : 0y0
+0x464 ProcessDelete      : 0y0
+0x464 ManageExecutableMemoryWrites : 0y0
+0x464 VmDeleted          : 0y0
+0x464 OutswapEnabled     : 0y0
+0x464 Outswapped         : 0y0
+0x464 FailFastOnCommitFail : 0y0
+0x464 Wow64VaSpace4Gb    : 0y0
+0x464 AddressSpaceInitialized : 0y11
+0x464 SetTimerResolution : 0y0
+0x464 BreakOnTermination : 0y0
+0x464 DeprioritizeViews  : 0y0
+0x464 WriteWatch         : 0y1
+0x464 ProcessInSession   : 0y1
+0x464 OverrideAddressSpace : 0y0
+0x464 HasAddressSpace    : 0y1
+0x464 LaunchPrefetched   : 0y1
+0x464 Background         : 0y0
+0x464 VmTopDown          : 0y0
+0x464 ImageNotifyDone    : 0y1
+0x464 PdeUpdateNeeded    : 0y0
+0x464 VdmAllowed         : 0y0
+0x464 ProcessRundown     : 0y0
+0x464 ProcessInserted    : 0y1
+0x464 DefaultIoPriority  : 0y010
+0x464 ProcessSelfDelete  : 0y0
+0x464 SetTimerResolutionLink : 0y1
+0x468 CreateTime         : _LARGE_INTEGER 0x01d81e1b`18b4a49c
+0x470 ProcessQuotaUsage  : [2] 0x154d0
+0x480 ProcessQuotaPeak   : [2] 0x1fe90
+0x490 PeakVirtualSize    : 0x00000209`46bb3000
+0x498 VirtualSize        : 0x00000209`468d3000
+0x4a0 SessionProcessLinks : _LIST_ENTRY [ 0xffffbe0c`87efbab0 - 0xffffbe0c`8c2cd560 ]
+0x4b0 ExceptionPortData  : 0xffffbe0c`87ce4d30 Void
+0x4b0 ExceptionPortValue : 0xffffbe0c`87ce4d30
+0x4b0 ExceptionPortState : 0y000
+0x4b8 Token              : _EX_FAST_REF
+0x4c0 MmReserved         : 0
+0x4c8 AddressCreationLock : _EX_PUSH_LOCK
+0x4d0 PageTableCommitmentLock : _EX_PUSH_LOCK
+0x4d8 RotateInProgress   : (null)
+0x4e0 ForkInProgress     : (null)
```

```
+0x4e8 CommitChargeJob  : 0xffffbe0c`8b4bd060 _EJOB
+0x4f0 CloneRoot        : _RTL_AVL_TREE
+0x4f8 NumberOfPrivatePages : 0x4727
+0x500 NumberOfLockedPages : 0xd99
+0x508 Win32Process     : 0xffffbcc6`4293c280 Void
+0x510 Job              : 0xffffbe0c`8b4bd060 _EJOB
+0x518 SectionObject    : 0xffff800e`dec2fb70 Void
+0x520 SectionBaseAddress : 0x00007ff6`6dd00000 Void
+0x528 Cookie           : 0x3d982939
+0x530 WorkingSetWatch  : (null)
+0x538 Win32WindowStation : 0x00000000`00000208 Void
+0x540 InheritedFromUniqueProcessId : 0x00000000`00000354 Void
+0x548 OwnerProcessId   : 0x356
+0x550 Peb              : 0x0000008e`61c8c000 _PEB
+0x558 Session          : 0xffffbe0c`87efbaa0 _MM_SESSION_SPACE
+0x560 Spare1           : (null)
+0x568 QuotaBlock       : 0xffffbe0c`8900b580 _EPROCESS_QUOTA_BLOCK
+0x570 ObjectTable      : 0xffff800e`dff94180 _HANDLE_TABLE
+0x578 DebugPort        : (null)
+0x580 WoW64Process     : (null)
+0x588 DeviceMap        : _EX_FAST_REF
+0x590 EtwDataSource    : 0xffffbe0c`8c46d250 Void
+0x598 PageDirectoryPte : 0
+0x5a0 ImageFilePointer : 0xffffbe0c`8bf609c0 _FILE_OBJECT
+0x5a8 ImageFileName    : [15]  "SearchHost.exe"
+0x5b7 PriorityClass    : 0x2 ''
+0x5b8 SecurityPort     : (null)
+0x5c0 SeAuditProcessCreationInfo : _SE_AUDIT_PROCESS_CREATION_INFO
+0x5c8 JobLinks         : _LIST_ENTRY [ 0xffffbe0c`8b4bd088 - 0xffffbe0c`8b4bd088 ]
+0x5d8 HighestUserAddress : 0x00007fff`ffff0000 Void
+0x5e0 ThreadListHead   : _LIST_ENTRY [ 0xffffbe0c`841d45b8 - 0xffffbe0c`8c1165b8 ]
+0x5f0 ActiveThreads    : 0x42
+0x5f4 ImagePathHash    : 0xc75e5e6e
+0x5f8 DefaultHardErrorProcessing : 0
+0x5fc LastThreadExitStatus : 0n0
+0x600 PrefetchTrace    : _EX_FAST_REF
+0x608 LockedPagesList  : (null)
+0x610 ReadOperationCount : _LARGE_INTEGER 0x0
+0x618 WriteOperationCount : _LARGE_INTEGER 0x0
+0x620 OtherOperationCount : _LARGE_INTEGER 0x3e
+0x628 ReadTransferCount : _LARGE_INTEGER 0x0
+0x630 WriteTransferCount : _LARGE_INTEGER 0x0
+0x638 OtherTransferCount : _LARGE_INTEGER 0x8298
+0x640 CommitChargeLimit : 0
+0x648 CommitCharge     : 0x4d87
+0x650 CommitChargePeak : 0x52b9
+0x680 Vm               : _MMSUPPORT_FULL
+0x7c0 MmProcessLinks   : _LIST_ENTRY [ 0xfffff807`62c50698 - 0xffffbe0c`8c2cd880 ]
+0x7d0 ModifiedPageCount : 0x38e
+0x7d4 ExitStatus       : 0n259
+0x7d8 VadRoot          : _RTL_AVL_TREE
+0x7e0 VadHint          : 0xffffbe0c`8c407b40 Void
+0x7e8 VadCount         : 0x24f
+0x7f0 VadPhysicalPages : 0
+0x7f8 VadPhysicalPagesLimit : 0
+0x800 AlpcContext      : _ALPC_PROCESS_CONTEXT
+0x820 TimerResolutionLink : _LIST_ENTRY [ 0xffffbe0c`8a9828a0 - 0xfffff807`62c15a80 ]
+0x830 TimerResolutionStackRecord : 0xffff800e`dc1cd490 _PO_DIAG_STACK_RECORD
+0x838 RequestedTimerResolution : 0
+0x83c SmallestTimerResolution : 0x9c40
+0x840 ExitTime         : _LARGE_INTEGER 0x0
+0x848 InvertedFunctionTable : 0xffff800e`e046b000 _INVERTED_FUNCTION_TABLE
+0x850 InvertedFunctionTableLock : _EX_PUSH_LOCK
+0x858 ActiveThreadsHighWatermark : 0x42
+0x85c LargePrivateVadCount : 0
```

```
+0x860 ThreadListLock       : _EX_PUSH_LOCK
+0x868 WnfContext           : 0xffff800e`dec2d500 Void
+0x870 ServerSilo           : (null)
+0x878 SignatureLevel       : 0x8 ''
+0x879 SectionSignatureLevel : 0 ''
+0x87a Protection           : _PS_PROTECTION
+0x87b HangCount            : 0y000
+0x87b GhostCount           : 0y000
+0x87b PrefilterException   : 0y0
+0x87c Flags3               : 0x440c008
+0x87c Minimal              : 0y0
+0x87c ReplacingPageRoot    : 0y0
+0x87c Crashed              : 0y0
+0x87c JobVadsAreTracked    : 0y1
+0x87c VadTrackingDisabled  : 0y0
+0x87c AuxiliaryProcess     : 0y0
+0x87c SubsystemProcess     : 0y0
+0x87c IndirectCpuSets      : 0y0
+0x87c RelinquishedCommit   : 0y0
+0x87c HighGraphicsPriority : 0y0
+0x87c CommitFailLogged     : 0y0
+0x87c ReserveFailLogged    : 0y0
+0x87c SystemProcess        : 0y0
+0x87c HideImageBaseAddresses : 0y0
+0x87c AddressPolicyFrozen  : 0y1
+0x87c ProcessFirstResume   : 0y1
+0x87c ForegroundExternal   : 0y0
+0x87c ForegroundSystem     : 0y0
+0x87c HighMemoryPriority   : 0y0
+0x87c EnableProcessSuspendResumeLogging : 0y0
+0x87c EnableThreadSuspendResumeLogging : 0y0
+0x87c SecurityDomainChanged : 0y0
+0x87c SecurityFreezeComplete : 0y1
+0x87c VmProcessorHost      : 0y0
+0x87c VmProcessorHostTransition : 0y0
+0x87c AltSyscall           : 0y0
+0x87c TimerResolutionIgnore : 0y1
+0x87c DisallowUserTerminate : 0y0
+0x87c EnableProcessRemoteExecProtectVmLogging : 0y0
+0x87c EnableProcessLocalExecProtectVmLogging : 0y0
+0x880 DeviceAsid           : 0n0
+0x888 SvmData              : (null)
+0x890 SvmProcessLock       : _EX_PUSH_LOCK
+0x898 SvmLock              : 0
+0x8a0 SvmProcessDeviceListHead : _LIST_ENTRY [ 0xffffbe0c`8bfb1960 - 0xffffbe0c`8bfb1960 ]
+0x8b0 LastFreezeInterruptTime : 0
+0x8b8 DiskCounters         : 0xffffbe0c`8bfb1c40 _PROCESS_DISK_COUNTERS
+0x8c0 PicoContext          : (null)
+0x8c8 EnclaveTable         : (null)
+0x8d0 EnclaveNumber        : 0
+0x8d8 EnclaveLock          : _EX_PUSH_LOCK
+0x8e0 HighPriorityFaultsAllowed : 0
+0x8e8 EnergyContext        : 0xffffbe0c`8bfb1c68 _PO_PROCESS_ENERGY_CONTEXT
+0x8f0 VmContext            : (null)
+0x8f8 SequenceNumber       : 0x121
+0x900 CreateInterruptTime  : 0x00000001`0daf77b8
+0x908 CreateUnbiasedInterruptTime : 0x00000001`0daf77b8
+0x910 TotalUnbiasedFrozenTime : 0
+0x918 LastAppStateUpdateTime : 0x00000001`0daf77b8
+0x920 LastAppStateUptime   : 0y00000000000000000000000000000000000000000000000000000000000000 (0)
+0x920 LastAppState         : 0y000
+0x928 SharedCommitCharge   : 0x123e
+0x930 SharedCommitLock     : _EX_PUSH_LOCK
+0x938 SharedCommitLinks    : _LIST_ENTRY [ 0xffff800e`de335f58 - 0xffff800e`e0516d58 ]
+0x948 AllowedCpuSets       : 0
```

```
+0x950 DefaultCpuSets     : 0
+0x948 AllowedCpuSetsIndirect : (null)
+0x950 DefaultCpuSetsIndirect : (null)
+0x958 DiskIoAttribution : (null)
+0x960 DxgProcess         : 0xffff800e`dffd6b30 Void
+0x968 Win32KFilterSet    : 0
+0x96c Machine            : 0x8664
+0x96e Spare0             : 0
+0x970 ProcessTimerDelay : _PS_INTERLOCKED_TIMER_DELAY_VALUES
+0x978 KTimerSets         : 0x223
+0x97c KTimer2Sets        : 0
+0x980 ThreadTimerSets    : 0x1fd
+0x988 VirtualTimerListLock : 0
+0x990 VirtualTimerListHead : _LIST_ENTRY [ 0xffffbe0c`8c3e61a0 - 0xffffbe0c`8709fc90 ]
+0x9a0 WakeChannel        : _WNF_STATE_NAME
+0x9a0 WakeInfo           : _PS_PROCESS_WAKE_INFORMATION
+0x9d0 MitigationFlags    : 0x39
+0x9d0 MitigationFlagsValues : <unnamed-tag>
+0x9d4 MitigationFlags2 : 0x40000000
+0x9d4 MitigationFlags2Values : <unnamed-tag>
+0x9d8 PartitionObject    : 0xffffbe0c`840bf960 Void
+0x9e0 SecurityDomain     : 0x00000001`000000ef
+0x9e8 ParentSecurityDomain : 0
+0x9f0 CoverageSamplerContext : (null)
+0x9f8 MmHotPatchContext : (null)
+0xa00 IdealProcessorAssignmentBlock : _KE_IDEAL_PROCESSOR_ASSIGNMENT_BLOCK
+0xb18 DynamicEHContinuationTargetsTree : _RTL_AVL_TREE
+0xb20 DynamicEHContinuationTargetsLock : _EX_PUSH_LOCK
+0xb28 DynamicEnforcedCetCompatibleRanges : _PS_DYNAMIC_ENFORCED_ADDRESS_RANGES
+0xb38 DisabledComponentFlags : 0
+0xb3c PageCombineSequence : 0n1
+0xb40 EnableOptionalXStateFeaturesLock : _EX_PUSH_LOCK
```

Note: Another command variant starting from the address of the first _EPROCESS structure instead of its link address:

```
1: kd> !list -t nt!_EPROCESS.ActiveProcessLinks.Flink -x "dt nt!_EPROCESS" poi(nt!PsActiveProcessHead)-448
dt nt!_EPROCESS 0xffffbe0c840eb040
   +0x000 Pcb                : _KPROCESS
   +0x438 ProcessLock        : _EX_PUSH_LOCK
   +0x440 UniqueProcessId    : 0x00000000`00000004 Void
   +0x448 ActiveProcessLinks : _LIST_ENTRY [ 0xffffbe0c`841364c8 - 0xfffff807`62c1bfa0 ]
   +0x458 RundownProtect     : _EX_RUNDOWN_REF
   +0x460 Flags2             : 0xd000
   +0x460 JobNotReallyActive : 0y0
   +0x460 AccountingFolded   : 0y0
   +0x460 NewProcessReported : 0y0
   +0x460 ExitProcessReported : 0y0
   +0x460 ReportCommitChanges : 0y0
   +0x460 LastReportMemory   : 0y0
   +0x460 ForceWakeCharge    : 0y0
   +0x460 CrossSessionCreate : 0y0
   +0x460 NeedsHandleRundown : 0y0
   +0x460 RefTraceEnabled    : 0y0
   +0x460 PicoCreated        : 0y0
   +0x460 EmptyJobEvaluated  : 0y0
   +0x460 DefaultPagePriority : 0y101
   +0x460 PrimaryTokenFrozen : 0y1
   +0x460 ProcessVerifierTarget : 0y0
   +0x460 RestrictSetThreadContext : 0y0
   +0x460 AffinityPermanent  : 0y0
   +0x460 AffinityUpdateEnable : 0y0
   +0x460 PropagateNode      : 0y0
```

```
+0x460 ExplicitAffinity : 0y0
+0x460 ProcessExecutionState : 0y00
+0x460 EnableReadVmLogging : 0y0
+0x460 EnableWriteVmLogging : 0y0
+0x460 FatalAccessTerminationRequested : 0y0
+0x460 DisableSystemAllowedCpuSet : 0y0
+0x460 ProcessStateChangeRequest : 0y00
+0x460 ProcessStateChangeInProgress : 0y0
+0x460 InPrivate          : 0y0
+0x464 Flags              : 0x14840c00
+0x464 CreateReported     : 0y0
+0x464 NoDebugInherit     : 0y0
+0x464 ProcessExiting     : 0y0
+0x464 ProcessDelete      : 0y0
+0x464 ManageExecutableMemoryWrites : 0y0
+0x464 VmDeleted          : 0y0
+0x464 OutswapEnabled     : 0y0
+0x464 Outswapped         : 0y0
+0x464 FailFastOnCommitFail : 0y0
+0x464 Wow64VaSpace4Gb    : 0y0
+0x464 AddressSpaceInitialized : 0y11
+0x464 SetTimerResolution : 0y0
+0x464 BreakOnTermination : 0y0
+0x464 DeprioritizeViews  : 0y0
+0x464 WriteWatch         : 0y0
+0x464 ProcessInSession   : 0y0
+0x464 OverrideAddressSpace : 0y0
+0x464 HasAddressSpace    : 0y1
+0x464 LaunchPrefetched   : 0y0
+0x464 Background         : 0y0
+0x464 VmTopDown          : 0y0
+0x464 ImageNotifyDone    : 0y0
+0x464 PdeUpdateNeeded    : 0y1
+0x464 VdmAllowed         : 0y0
+0x464 ProcessRundown     : 0y0
+0x464 ProcessInserted    : 0y1
+0x464 DefaultIoPriority  : 0y010
+0x464 ProcessSelfDelete  : 0y0
+0x464 SetTimerResolutionLink : 0y0
+0x468 CreateTime         : _LARGE_INTEGER 0x01d81e1a`13a38448
+0x470 ProcessQuotaUsage  : [2] 0x110
+0x480 ProcessQuotaPeak   : [2] 0x110
+0x490 PeakVirtualSize    : 0xf1a000
+0x498 VirtualSize        : 0x3e7000
+0x4a0 SessionProcessLinks : _LIST_ENTRY [ 0x00000000`00000000 - 0x00000000`00000000 ]
+0x4b0 ExceptionPortData  : (null)
+0x4b0 ExceptionPortValue : 0
+0x4b0 ExceptionPortState : 0y000
+0x4b8 Token              : _EX_FAST_REF
+0x4c0 MmReserved         : 0
+0x4c8 AddressCreationLock : _EX_PUSH_LOCK
+0x4d0 PageTableCommitmentLock : _EX_PUSH_LOCK
+0x4d8 RotateInProgress   : (null)
+0x4e0 ForkInProgress     : (null)
+0x4e8 CommitChargeJob    : (null)
+0x4f0 CloneRoot          : _RTL_AVL_TREE
+0x4f8 NumberOfPrivatePages : 0x14
+0x500 NumberOfLockedPages : 0
+0x508 Win32Process       : (null)
+0x510 Job                : (null)
+0x518 SectionObject      : (null)
+0x520 SectionBaseAddress : (null)
+0x528 Cookie             : 0xec9a6c71
+0x530 WorkingSetWatch    : (null)
+0x538 Win32WindowStation : (null)
```

```
+0x540 InheritedFromUniqueProcessId : (null)
+0x548 OwnerProcessId    : 2
+0x550 Peb               : (null)
+0x558 Session           : (null)
+0x560 Spare1            : (null)
+0x568 QuotaBlock        : 0xfffff807`62c5a380 _EPROCESS_QUOTA_BLOCK
+0x570 ObjectTable       : 0xffff800e`d4820c80 _HANDLE_TABLE
+0x578 DebugPort         : (null)
+0x580 WoW64Process      : (null)
+0x588 DeviceMap         : _EX_FAST_REF
+0x590 EtwDataSource     : (null)
+0x598 PageDirectoryPte  : 0
+0x5a0 ImageFilePointer  : (null)
+0x5a8 ImageFileName     : [15] "System"
+0x5b7 PriorityClass     : 0x2 ''
+0x5b8 SecurityPort      : (null)
+0x5c0 SeAuditProcessCreationInfo : _SE_AUDIT_PROCESS_CREATION_INFO
+0x5c8 JobLinks          : _LIST_ENTRY [ 0x00000000`00000000 - 0x00000000`00000000 ]
+0x5d8 HighestUserAddress : 0x00007fff`ffff0000 Void
+0x5e0 ThreadListHead    : _LIST_ENTRY [ 0xffffbe0c`841cd5b8 - 0xffffbe0c`8c0dd578 ]
+0x5f0 ActiveThreads     : 0x88
+0x5f4 ImagePathHash     : 0
+0x5f8 DefaultHardErrorProcessing : 5
+0x5fc LastThreadExitStatus : 0n0
+0x600 PrefetchTrace     : _EX_FAST_REF
+0x608 LockedPagesList   : (null)
+0x610 ReadOperationCount : _LARGE_INTEGER 0x1d
+0x618 WriteOperationCount : _LARGE_INTEGER 0x3b
+0x620 OtherOperationCount : _LARGE_INTEGER 0x51c
+0x628 ReadTransferCount : _LARGE_INTEGER 0x33e8
+0x630 WriteTransferCount : _LARGE_INTEGER 0x1a5d23f
+0x638 OtherTransferCount : _LARGE_INTEGER 0x4a96
+0x640 CommitChargeLimit : 0
+0x648 CommitCharge      : 0xb
+0x650 CommitChargePeak  : 0x10
+0x680 Vm                : _MMSUPPORT_FULL
+0x7c0 MmProcessLinks    : _LIST_ENTRY [ 0xffffbe0c`84136840 - 0xfffff807`62d332c0 ]
+0x7d0 ModifiedPageCount : 0xc98e
+0x7d4 ExitStatus        : 0n259
+0x7d8 VadRoot           : _RTL_AVL_TREE
+0x7e0 VadHint           : 0xffffbe0c`840a16f0 Void
+0x7e8 VadCount          : 6
+0x7f0 VadPhysicalPages  : 0
+0x7f8 VadPhysicalPagesLimit : 0
+0x800 AlpcContext       : _ALPC_PROCESS_CONTEXT
+0x820 TimerResolutionLink : _LIST_ENTRY [ 0x00000000`00000000 - 0x00000000`00000000 ]
+0x830 TimerResolutionStackRecord : (null)
+0x838 RequestedTimerResolution : 0
+0x83c SmallestTimerResolution : 0
+0x840 ExitTime          : _LARGE_INTEGER 0x0
+0x848 InvertedFunctionTable : (null)
+0x850 InvertedFunctionTableLock : _EX_PUSH_LOCK
+0x858 ActiveThreadsHighWatermark : 0x88
+0x85c LargePrivateVadCount : 0
+0x860 ThreadListLock    : _EX_PUSH_LOCK
+0x868 WnfContext        : 0xffff800e`d48b52e0 Void
+0x870 ServerSilo        : (null)
+0x878 SignatureLevel    : 0x1e ''
+0x879 SectionSignatureLevel : 0x1c ''
+0x87a Protection        : _PS_PROTECTION
+0x87b HangCount         : 0y000
+0x87b GhostCount        : 0y000
+0x87b PrefilterException : 0y0
+0x87c Flags3            : 0x405080
+0x87c Minimal           : 0y0
```

```
+0x87c ReplacingPageRoot : 0y0
+0x87c Crashed          : 0y0
+0x87c JobVadsAreTracked : 0y0
+0x87c VadTrackingDisabled : 0y0
+0x87c AuxiliaryProcess : 0y0
+0x87c SubsystemProcess : 0y0
+0x87c IndirectCpuSets  : 0y1
+0x87c RelinquishedCommit : 0y0
+0x87c HighGraphicsPriority : 0y0
+0x87c CommitFailLogged : 0y0
+0x87c ReserveFailLogged : 0y0
+0x87c SystemProcess    : 0y1
+0x87c HideImageBaseAddresses : 0y0
+0x87c AddressPolicyFrozen : 0y1
+0x87c ProcessFirstResume : 0y0
+0x87c ForegroundExternal : 0y0
+0x87c ForegroundSystem : 0y0
+0x87c HighMemoryPriority : 0y0
+0x87c EnableProcessSuspendResumeLogging : 0y0
+0x87c EnableThreadSuspendResumeLogging : 0y0
+0x87c SecurityDomainChanged : 0y0
+0x87c SecurityFreezeComplete : 0y1
+0x87c VmProcessorHost  : 0y0
+0x87c VmProcessorHostTransition : 0y0
+0x87c AltSyscall       : 0y0
+0x87c TimerResolutionIgnore : 0y0
+0x87c DisallowUserTerminate : 0y0
+0x87c EnableProcessRemoteExecProtectVmLogging : 0y0
+0x87c EnableProcessLocalExecProtectVmLogging : 0y0
+0x880 DeviceAsid       : 0n0
+0x888 SvmData          : (null)
+0x890 SvmProcessLock   : _EX_PUSH_LOCK
+0x898 SvmLock          : 0
+0x8a0 SvmProcessDeviceListHead : _LIST_ENTRY [ 0xffffbe0c`840eb8e0 - 0xffffbe0c`840eb8e0 ]
+0x8b0 LastFreezeInterruptTime : 0
+0x8b8 DiskCounters     : 0xffffbe0c`840ebbc0 _PROCESS_DISK_COUNTERS
+0x8c0 PicoContext      : (null)
+0x8c8 EnclaveTable     : (null)
+0x8d0 EnclaveNumber    : 0
+0x8d8 EnclaveLock      : _EX_PUSH_LOCK
+0x8e0 HighPriorityFaultsAllowed : 0
+0x8e8 EnergyContext    : 0xffffbe0c`840ebbe8 _PO_PROCESS_ENERGY_CONTEXT
+0x8f0 VmContext        : (null)
+0x8f8 SequenceNumber   : 1
+0x900 CreateInterruptTime : 0x89eae9f
+0x908 CreateUnbiasedInterruptTime : 0x89eae9f
+0x910 TotalUnbiasedFrozenTime : 0
+0x918 LastAppStateUpdateTime : 0
+0x920 LastAppStateUptime : 0y0000000000000000000000000000000000000000000000000000000000000000 (0)
+0x920 LastAppState     : 0y000
+0x928 SharedCommitCharge : 0x4a
+0x930 SharedCommitLock : _EX_PUSH_LOCK
+0x938 SharedCommitLinks : _LIST_ENTRY [ 0xffff800e`d71a16b8 - 0xffff800e`d4cfba78 ]
+0x948 AllowedCpuSets   : 0xffffbe0c`840ebdc8
+0x950 DefaultCpuSets   : 0xffffbe0c`840ebec8
+0x948 AllowedCpuSetsIndirect : 0xffffbe0c`840ebdc8  -> 3
+0x950 DefaultCpuSetsIndirect : 0xffffbe0c`840ebec8  -> 0
+0x958 DiskIoAttribution : (null)
+0x960 DxgProcess       : 0xffff800e`d4ef4a40 Void
+0x968 Win32KFilterSet  : 0
+0x96c Machine          : 0x8664
+0x96e Spare0           : 0
+0x970 ProcessTimerDelay : _PS_INTERLOCKED_TIMER_DELAY_VALUES
+0x978 KTimerSets       : 0
+0x97c KTimer2Sets      : 0
```

```
+0x980 ThreadTimerSets   : 0
+0x988 VirtualTimerListLock : 0
+0x990 VirtualTimerListHead : _LIST_ENTRY [ 0xffffbe0c`840eb9d0 - 0xffffbe0c`840eb9d0 ]
+0x9a0 WakeChannel      : _WNF_STATE_NAME
+0x9a0 WakeInfo         : _PS_PROCESS_WAKE_INFORMATION
+0x9d0 MitigationFlags  : 0x40000060
+0x9d0 MitigationFlagsValues : <unnamed-tag>
+0x9d4 MitigationFlags2 : 0x40002000
+0x9d4 MitigationFlags2Values : <unnamed-tag>
+0x9d8 PartitionObject  : 0xffffbe0c`840bf960 Void
+0x9e0 SecurityDomain   : 0
+0x9e8 ParentSecurityDomain : 0
+0x9f0 CoverageSamplerContext : (null)
+0x9f8 MmHotPatchContext : (null)
+0xa00 IdealProcessorAssignmentBlock : _KE_IDEAL_PROCESSOR_ASSIGNMENT_BLOCK
+0xb18 DynamicEHContinuationTargetsTree : _RTL_AVL_TREE
+0xb20 DynamicEHContinuationTargetsLock : _EX_PUSH_LOCK
+0xb28 DynamicEnforcedCetCompatibleRanges : _PS_DYNAMIC_ENFORCED_ADDRESS_RANGES
+0xb38 DisabledComponentFlags : 0
+0xb3c PageCombineSequence : 0n1
+0xb40 EnableOptionalXStateFeaturesLock : _EX_PUSH_LOCK

[...]

dt nt!_EPROCESS 0xffffbe0c8bfb10c0
+0x000 Pcb                  : _KPROCESS
+0x438 ProcessLock          : _EX_PUSH_LOCK
+0x440 UniqueProcessId      : 0x00000000`00002434 Void
+0x448 ActiveProcessLinks   : _LIST_ENTRY [ 0xfffff807`62c1bfa0 - 0xffffbe0c`8c2cd508 ]
+0x458 RundownProtect       : _EX_RUNDOWN_REF
+0x460 Flags2               : 0xd094
+0x460 JobNotReallyActive   : 0y0
+0x460 AccountingFolded     : 0y0
+0x460 NewProcessReported   : 0y1
+0x460 ExitProcessReported  : 0y0
+0x460 ReportCommitChanges  : 0y1
+0x460 LastReportMemory     : 0y0
+0x460 ForceWakeCharge      : 0y0
+0x460 CrossSessionCreate   : 0y1
+0x460 NeedsHandleRundown   : 0y0
+0x460 RefTraceEnabled      : 0y0
+0x460 PicoCreated          : 0y0
+0x460 EmptyJobEvaluated    : 0y0
+0x460 DefaultPagePriority  : 0y101
+0x460 PrimaryTokenFrozen   : 0y1
+0x460 ProcessVerifierTarget : 0y0
+0x460 RestrictSetThreadContext : 0y0
+0x460 AffinityPermanent    : 0y0
+0x460 AffinityUpdateEnable : 0y0
+0x460 PropagateNode        : 0y0
+0x460 ExplicitAffinity     : 0y0
+0x460 ProcessExecutionState : 0y00
+0x460 EnableReadVmLogging  : 0y0
+0x460 EnableWriteVmLogging : 0y0
+0x460 FatalAccessTerminationRequested : 0y0
+0x460 DisableSystemAllowedCpuSet : 0y0
+0x460 ProcessStateChangeRequest : 0y00
+0x460 ProcessStateChangeInProgress : 0y0
+0x460 InPrivate            : 0y0
+0x464 Flags                : 0x944d8c01
+0x464 CreateReported       : 0y1
+0x464 NoDebugInherit       : 0y0
+0x464 ProcessExiting       : 0y0
+0x464 ProcessDelete        : 0y0
+0x464 ManageExecutableMemoryWrites : 0y0
```

```
+0x464 VmDeleted          : 0y0
+0x464 OutswapEnabled     : 0y0
+0x464 Outswapped         : 0y0
+0x464 FailFastOnCommitFail : 0y0
+0x464 Wow64VaSpace4Gb    : 0y0
+0x464 AddressSpaceInitialized : 0y11
+0x464 SetTimerResolution : 0y0
+0x464 BreakOnTermination : 0y0
+0x464 DeprioritizeViews  : 0y0
+0x464 WriteWatch         : 0y1
+0x464 ProcessInSession   : 0y1
+0x464 OverrideAddressSpace : 0y0
+0x464 HasAddressSpace    : 0y1
+0x464 LaunchPrefetched   : 0y1
+0x464 Background         : 0y0
+0x464 VmTopDown          : 0y0
+0x464 ImageNotifyDone    : 0y1
+0x464 PdeUpdateNeeded    : 0y0
+0x464 VdmAllowed         : 0y0
+0x464 ProcessRundown     : 0y0
+0x464 ProcessInserted    : 0y1
+0x464 DefaultIoPriority  : 0y010
+0x464 ProcessSelfDelete  : 0y0
+0x464 SetTimerResolutionLink : 0y1
+0x468 CreateTime         : _LARGE_INTEGER 0x01d81e1b`18b4a49c
+0x470 ProcessQuotaUsage  : [2] 0x154d0
+0x480 ProcessQuotaPeak   : [2] 0x1fe90
+0x490 PeakVirtualSize    : 0x00000209`46bb3000
+0x498 VirtualSize        : 0x00000209`468d3000
+0x4a0 SessionProcessLinks : _LIST_ENTRY [ 0xffffbe0c`87efbab0 - 0xffffbe0c`8c2cd560 ]
+0x4b0 ExceptionPortData  : 0xffffbe0c`87ce4d30 Void
+0x4b0 ExceptionPortValue : 0xffffbe0c`87ce4d30
+0x4b0 ExceptionPortState : 0y000
+0x4b8 Token              : _EX_FAST_REF
+0x4c0 MmReserved         : 0
+0x4c8 AddressCreationLock : _EX_PUSH_LOCK
+0x4d0 PageTableCommitmentLock : _EX_PUSH_LOCK
+0x4d8 RotateInProgress   : (null)
+0x4e0 ForkInProgress     : (null)
+0x4e8 CommitChargeJob    : 0xffffbe0c`8b4bd060 _EJOB
+0x4f0 CloneRoot          : _RTL_AVL_TREE
+0x4f8 NumberOfPrivatePages : 0x4727
+0x500 NumberOfLockedPages : 0xd99
+0x508 Win32Process       : 0xffffbcc6`4293c280 Void
+0x510 Job                : 0xffffbe0c`8b4bd060 _EJOB
+0x518 SectionObject      : 0xffff800e`dec2fb70 Void
+0x520 SectionBaseAddress : 0x00007ff6`6dd00000 Void
+0x528 Cookie             : 0x3d982939
+0x530 WorkingSetWatch    : (null)
+0x538 Win32WindowStation : 0x00000000`00000208 Void
+0x540 InheritedFromUniqueProcessId : 0x00000000`00000354 Void
+0x548 OwnerProcessId     : 0x356
+0x550 Peb                : 0x0000008e`61c8c000 _PEB
+0x558 Session            : 0xffffbe0c`87efbaa0 _MM_SESSION_SPACE
+0x560 Spare1             : (null)
+0x568 QuotaBlock         : 0xffffbe0c`8900b580 _EPROCESS_QUOTA_BLOCK
+0x570 ObjectTable        : 0xffff800e`dff94180 _HANDLE_TABLE
+0x578 DebugPort          : (null)
+0x580 WoW64Process       : (null)
+0x588 DeviceMap          : _EX_FAST_REF
+0x590 EtwDataSource      : 0xffffbe0c`8c46d250 Void
+0x598 PageDirectoryPte   : 0
+0x5a0 ImageFilePointer   : 0xffffbe0c`8bf609c0 _FILE_OBJECT
+0x5a8 ImageFileName      : [15] "SearchHost.exe"
+0x5b7 PriorityClass      : 0x2 ''
```

```
+0x5b8 SecurityPort        : (null)
+0x5c0 SeAuditProcessCreationInfo : _SE_AUDIT_PROCESS_CREATION_INFO
+0x5c8 JobLinks            : _LIST_ENTRY [ 0xffffbe0c`8b4bd088 - 0xffffbe0c`8b4bd088 ]
+0x5d8 HighestUserAddress : 0x00007fff`ffff0000 Void
+0x5e0 ThreadListHead      : _LIST_ENTRY [ 0xffffbe0c`841d45b8 - 0xffffbe0c`8c1165b8 ]
+0x5f0 ActiveThreads       : 0x42
+0x5f4 ImagePathHash       : 0xc75e5e6e
+0x5f8 DefaultHardErrorProcessing : 0
+0x5fc LastThreadExitStatus : 0n0
+0x600 PrefetchTrace       : _EX_FAST_REF
+0x608 LockedPagesList     : (null)
+0x610 ReadOperationCount  : _LARGE_INTEGER 0x0
+0x618 WriteOperationCount : _LARGE_INTEGER 0x0
+0x620 OtherOperationCount : _LARGE_INTEGER 0x3e
+0x628 ReadTransferCount   : _LARGE_INTEGER 0x0
+0x630 WriteTransferCount  : _LARGE_INTEGER 0x0
+0x638 OtherTransferCount  : _LARGE_INTEGER 0x8298
+0x640 CommitChargeLimit   : 0
+0x648 CommitCharge        : 0x4d87
+0x650 CommitChargePeak    : 0x52b9
+0x680 Vm                  : _MMSUPPORT_FULL
+0x7c0 MmProcessLinks      : _LIST_ENTRY [ 0xfffff807`62c50698 - 0xffffbe0c`8c2cd880 ]
+0x7d0 ModifiedPageCount   : 0x38e
+0x7d4 ExitStatus          : 0n259
+0x7d8 VadRoot             : _RTL_AVL_TREE
+0x7e0 VadHint             : 0xffffbe0c`8c407b40 Void
+0x7e8 VadCount            : 0x24f
+0x7f0 VadPhysicalPages    : 0
+0x7f8 VadPhysicalPagesLimit : 0
+0x800 AlpcContext         : _ALPC_PROCESS_CONTEXT
+0x820 TimerResolutionLink : _LIST_ENTRY [ 0xffffbe0c`8a9828a0 - 0xfffff807`62c15a80 ]
+0x830 TimerResolutionStackRecord : 0xffff800e`dc1cd490 _PO_DIAG_STACK_RECORD
+0x838 RequestedTimerResolution : 0
+0x83c SmallestTimerResolution : 0x9c40
+0x840 ExitTime            : _LARGE_INTEGER 0x0
+0x848 InvertedFunctionTable : 0xffff800e`e046b000 _INVERTED_FUNCTION_TABLE
+0x850 InvertedFunctionTableLock : _EX_PUSH_LOCK
+0x858 ActiveThreadsHighWatermark : 0x42
+0x85c LargePrivateVadCount : 0
+0x860 ThreadListLock      : _EX_PUSH_LOCK
+0x868 WnfContext          : 0xffff800e`dec2d500 Void
+0x870 ServerSilo          : (null)
+0x878 SignatureLevel      : 0x8 ''
+0x879 SectionSignatureLevel : 0 ''
+0x87a Protection          : _PS_PROTECTION
+0x87b HangCount           : 0y000
+0x87b GhostCount          : 0y000
+0x87b PrefilterException  : 0y0
+0x87c Flags3              : 0x440c008
+0x87c Minimal             : 0y0
+0x87c ReplacingPageRoot   : 0y0
+0x87c Crashed             : 0y0
+0x87c JobVadsAreTracked   : 0y1
+0x87c VadTrackingDisabled : 0y0
+0x87c AuxiliaryProcess    : 0y0
+0x87c SubsystemProcess    : 0y0
+0x87c IndirectCpuSets     : 0y0
+0x87c RelinquishedCommit  : 0y0
+0x87c HighGraphicsPriority : 0y0
+0x87c CommitFailLogged    : 0y0
+0x87c ReserveFailLogged   : 0y0
+0x87c SystemProcess       : 0y0
+0x87c HideImageBaseAddresses : 0y0
+0x87c AddressPolicyFrozen : 0y1
+0x87c ProcessFirstResume  : 0y1
```

```
+0x87c ForegroundExternal : 0y0
+0x87c ForegroundSystem : 0y0
+0x87c HighMemoryPriority : 0y0
+0x87c EnableProcessSuspendResumeLogging : 0y0
+0x87c EnableThreadSuspendResumeLogging : 0y0
+0x87c SecurityDomainChanged : 0y0
+0x87c SecurityFreezeComplete : 0y1
+0x87c VmProcessorHost : 0y0
+0x87c VmProcessorHostTransition : 0y0
+0x87c AltSyscall        : 0y0
+0x87c TimerResolutionIgnore : 0y1
+0x87c DisallowUserTerminate : 0y0
+0x87c EnableProcessRemoteExecProtectVmLogging : 0y0
+0x87c EnableProcessLocalExecProtectVmLogging : 0y0
+0x880 DeviceAsid        : 0n0
+0x888 SvmData           : (null)
+0x890 SvmProcessLock    : _EX_PUSH_LOCK
+0x898 SvmLock           : 0
+0x8a0 SvmProcessDeviceListHead : _LIST_ENTRY [ 0xffffbe0c`8bfb1960 - 0xffffbe0c`8bfb1960 ]
+0x8b0 LastFreezeInterruptTime : 0
+0x8b8 DiskCounters      : 0xffffbe0c`8bfb1c40 _PROCESS_DISK_COUNTERS
+0x8c0 PicoContext       : (null)
+0x8c8 EnclaveTable      : (null)
+0x8d0 EnclaveNumber     : 0
+0x8d8 EnclaveLock       : _EX_PUSH_LOCK
+0x8e0 HighPriorityFaultsAllowed : 0
+0x8e8 EnergyContext     : 0xffffbe0c`8bfb1c68 _PO_PROCESS_ENERGY_CONTEXT
+0x8f0 VmContext         : (null)
+0x8f8 SequenceNumber    : 0x121
+0x900 CreateInterruptTime : 0x00000001`0daf77b8
+0x908 CreateUnbiasedInterruptTime : 0x00000001`0daf77b8
+0x910 TotalUnbiasedFrozenTime : 0
+0x918 LastAppStateUpdateTime : 0x00000001`0daf77b8
+0x920 LastAppStateUptime : 0y0000000000000000000000000000000000000000000000000000000000000 (0)
+0x920 LastAppState      : 0y000
+0x928 SharedCommitCharge : 0x123e
+0x930 SharedCommitLock : _EX_PUSH_LOCK
+0x938 SharedCommitLinks : _LIST_ENTRY [ 0xffff800e`de335f58 - 0xffff800e`e0516d58 ]
+0x948 AllowedCpuSets    : 0
+0x950 DefaultCpuSets    : 0
+0x948 AllowedCpuSetsIndirect : (null)
+0x950 DefaultCpuSetsIndirect : (null)
+0x958 DiskIoAttribution : (null)
+0x960 DxgProcess        : 0xffff800e`dffd6b30 Void
+0x968 Win32KFilterSet   : 0
+0x96c Machine           : 0x8664
+0x96e Spare0            : 0
+0x970 ProcessTimerDelay : _PS_INTERLOCKED_TIMER_DELAY_VALUES
+0x978 KTimerSets        : 0x223
+0x97c KTimer2Sets       : 0
+0x980 ThreadTimerSets   : 0x1fd
+0x988 VirtualTimerListLock : 0
+0x990 VirtualTimerListHead : _LIST_ENTRY [ 0xffffbe0c`8c3e61a0 - 0xffffbe0c`8709fc90 ]
+0x9a0 WakeChannel       : _WNF_STATE_NAME
+0x9a0 WakeInfo          : _PS_PROCESS_WAKE_INFORMATION
+0x9d0 MitigationFlags   : 0x39
+0x9d0 MitigationFlagsValues : <unnamed-tag>
+0x9d4 MitigationFlags2 : 0x40000000
+0x9d4 MitigationFlags2Values : <unnamed-tag>
+0x9d8 PartitionObject   : 0xffffbe0c`840bf960 Void
+0x9e0 SecurityDomain    : 0x00000001`000000ef
+0x9e8 ParentSecurityDomain : 0
+0x9f0 CoverageSamplerContext : (null)
+0x9f8 MmHotPatchContext : (null)
+0xa00 IdealProcessorAssignmentBlock : _KE_IDEAL_PROCESSOR_ASSIGNMENT_BLOCK
```

```
+0xb18 DynamicEHContinuationTargetsTree : _RTL_AVL_TREE
+0xb20 DynamicEHContinuationTargetsLock : _EX_PUSH_LOCK
+0xb28 DynamicEnforcedCetCompatibleRanges : _PS_DYNAMIC_ENFORCED_ADDRESS_RANGES
+0xb38 DisabledComponentFlags : 0
+0xb3c PageCombineSequence : 0n1
+0xb40 EnableOptionalXStateFeaturesLock : _EX_PUSH_LOCK
```

9.   Yet another method is to use the **dt** command variant for linked lists:

```
1: kd> dt nt!_EPROCESS -l ActiveProcessLinks.Flink poi(nt!PsActiveProcessHead)-448
ActiveProcessLinks.Flink at 0xffffbe0c`840eb040
---------------------------------------------
   +0x000 Pcb              : _KPROCESS
   +0x438 ProcessLock      : _EX_PUSH_LOCK
   +0x440 UniqueProcessId  : 0x00000000`00000004 Void
   +0x448 ActiveProcessLinks : [ 0xffffbe0c`841364c8 - 0xfffff807`62c1bfa0 ]
      +0x000 Flink          : 0xffffbe0c`841364c8 _LIST_ENTRY [ 0xffffbe0c`8780f488 - 0xffffbe0c`840eb488 ]
      +0x008 Blink          : 0xfffff807`62c1bfa0 _LIST_ENTRY [ 0xffffbe0c`840eb488 - 0xffffbe0c`8bfb1508 ]
   +0x458 RundownProtect   : _EX_RUNDOWN_REF
   +0x460 Flags2           : 0xd000
   +0x460 JobNotReallyActive : 0y0
   +0x460 AccountingFolded : 0y0
   +0x460 NewProcessReported : 0y0
   +0x460 ExitProcessReported : 0y0
   +0x460 ReportCommitChanges : 0y0
   +0x460 LastReportMemory : 0y0
   +0x460 ForceWakeCharge  : 0y0
   +0x460 CrossSessionCreate : 0y0
   +0x460 NeedsHandleRundown : 0y0
   +0x460 RefTraceEnabled  : 0y0
   +0x460 PicoCreated      : 0y0
   +0x460 EmptyJobEvaluated : 0y0
   +0x460 DefaultPagePriority : 0y101
   +0x460 PrimaryTokenFrozen : 0y1
   +0x460 ProcessVerifierTarget : 0y0
   +0x460 RestrictSetThreadContext : 0y0
   +0x460 AffinityPermanent : 0y0
   +0x460 AffinityUpdateEnable : 0y0
   +0x460 PropagateNode    : 0y0
   +0x460 ExplicitAffinity : 0y0
   +0x460 ProcessExecutionState : 0y00
   +0x460 EnableReadVmLogging : 0y0
   +0x460 EnableWriteVmLogging : 0y0
   +0x460 FatalAccessTerminationRequested : 0y0
   +0x460 DisableSystemAllowedCpuSet : 0y0
   +0x460 ProcessStateChangeRequest : 0y00
   +0x460 ProcessStateChangeInProgress : 0y0
   +0x460 InPrivate        : 0y0
   +0x464 Flags            : 0x14840c00
   +0x464 CreateReported   : 0y0
   +0x464 NoDebugInherit   : 0y0
   +0x464 ProcessExiting   : 0y0
   +0x464 ProcessDelete    : 0y0
   +0x464 ManageExecutableMemoryWrites : 0y0
   +0x464 VmDeleted        : 0y0
   +0x464 OutswapEnabled   : 0y0
   +0x464 Outswapped       : 0y0
   +0x464 FailFastOnCommitFail : 0y0
   +0x464 Wow64VaSpace4Gb  : 0y0
   +0x464 AddressSpaceInitialized : 0y11
   +0x464 SetTimerResolution : 0y0
   +0x464 BreakOnTermination : 0y0
   +0x464 DeprioritizeViews : 0y0
   +0x464 WriteWatch       : 0y0
   +0x464 ProcessInSession : 0y0
   +0x464 OverrideAddressSpace : 0y0
   +0x464 HasAddressSpace  : 0y1
   +0x464 LaunchPrefetched : 0y0
   +0x464 Background       : 0y0
   +0x464 VmTopDown        : 0y0
   +0x464 ImageNotifyDone  : 0y0
```

```
+0x464 PdeUpdateNeeded   : 0y1
+0x464 VdmAllowed        : 0y0
+0x464 ProcessRundown    : 0y0
+0x464 ProcessInserted   : 0y1
+0x464 DefaultIoPriority : 0y010
+0x464 ProcessSelfDelete : 0y0
+0x464 SetTimerResolutionLink : 0y0
+0x468 CreateTime        : _LARGE_INTEGER 0x01d81e1a`13a38448
+0x470 ProcessQuotaUsage : [2] 0x110
+0x480 ProcessQuotaPeak  : [2] 0x110
+0x490 PeakVirtualSize   : 0xf1a000
+0x498 VirtualSize       : 0x3e7000
+0x4a0 SessionProcessLinks : _LIST_ENTRY [ 0x00000000`00000000 - 0x00000000`00000000 ]
+0x4b0 ExceptionPortData : (null)
+0x4b0 ExceptionPortValue : 0
+0x4b0 ExceptionPortState : 0y000
+0x4b8 Token             : _EX_FAST_REF
+0x4c0 MmReserved        : 0
+0x4c8 AddressCreationLock : _EX_PUSH_LOCK
+0x4d0 PageTableCommitmentLock : _EX_PUSH_LOCK
+0x4d8 RotateInProgress  : (null)
+0x4e0 ForkInProgress    : (null)
+0x4e8 CommitChargeJob   : (null)
+0x4f0 CloneRoot         : _RTL_AVL_TREE
+0x4f8 NumberOfPrivatePages : 0x14
+0x500 NumberOfLockedPages : 0
+0x508 Win32Process      : (null)
+0x510 Job               : (null)
+0x518 SectionObject     : (null)
+0x520 SectionBaseAddress : (null)
+0x528 Cookie            : 0xec9a6c71
+0x530 WorkingSetWatch   : (null)
+0x538 Win32WindowStation : (null)
+0x540 InheritedFromUniqueProcessId : (null)
+0x548 OwnerProcessId    : 2
+0x550 Peb               : (null)
+0x558 Session           : (null)
+0x560 Spare1            : (null)
+0x568 QuotaBlock        : 0xfffff807`62c5a380 _EPROCESS_QUOTA_BLOCK
+0x570 ObjectTable       : 0xffff800e`d4820c80 _HANDLE_TABLE
+0x578 DebugPort         : (null)
+0x580 WoW64Process      : (null)
+0x588 DeviceMap         : _EX_FAST_REF
+0x590 EtwDataSource     : (null)
+0x598 PageDirectoryPte  : 0
+0x5a0 ImageFilePointer  : (null)
+0x5a8 ImageFileName     : [15]  "System"
+0x5b7 PriorityClass     : 0x2 ''
+0x5b8 SecurityPort      : (null)
+0x5c0 SeAuditProcessCreationInfo : _SE_AUDIT_PROCESS_CREATION_INFO
+0x5c8 JobLinks          : _LIST_ENTRY [ 0x00000000`00000000 - 0x00000000`00000000 ]
+0x5d8 HighestUserAddress : 0x00007fff`ffff0000 Void
+0x5e0 ThreadListHead    : _LIST_ENTRY [ 0xffffbe0c`841cd5b8 - 0xffffbe0c`8c0dd578 ]
+0x5f0 ActiveThreads     : 0x88
+0x5f4 ImagePathHash     : 0
+0x5f8 DefaultHardErrorProcessing : 5
+0x5fc LastThreadExitStatus : 0n0
+0x600 PrefetchTrace     : _EX_FAST_REF
+0x608 LockedPagesList   : (null)
+0x610 ReadOperationCount : _LARGE_INTEGER 0x1d
+0x618 WriteOperationCount : _LARGE_INTEGER 0x3b
+0x620 OtherOperationCount : _LARGE_INTEGER 0x51c
+0x628 ReadTransferCount : _LARGE_INTEGER 0x33e8
+0x630 WriteTransferCount : _LARGE_INTEGER 0x1a5d23f
+0x638 OtherTransferCount : _LARGE_INTEGER 0x4a96
+0x640 CommitChargeLimit : 0
+0x648 CommitCharge      : 0xb
+0x650 CommitChargePeak  : 0x10
+0x680 Vm                : _MMSUPPORT_FULL
+0x7c0 MmProcessLinks    : _LIST_ENTRY [ 0xffffbe0c`84136840 - 0xfffff807`62d332c0 ]
+0x7d0 ModifiedPageCount : 0xc98e
+0x7d4 ExitStatus        : 0n259
+0x7d8 VadRoot           : _RTL_AVL_TREE
+0x7e0 VadHint           : 0xffffbe0c`840a16f0 Void
```

166

```
+0x7e8 VadCount          : 6
+0x7f0 VadPhysicalPages  : 0
+0x7f8 VadPhysicalPagesLimit : 0
+0x800 AlpcContext       : _ALPC_PROCESS_CONTEXT
+0x820 TimerResolutionLink : _LIST_ENTRY [ 0x00000000`00000000 - 0x00000000`00000000 ]
+0x830 TimerResolutionStackRecord : (null)
+0x838 RequestedTimerResolution : 0
+0x83c SmallestTimerResolution : 0
+0x840 ExitTime          : _LARGE_INTEGER 0x0
+0x848 InvertedFunctionTable : (null)
+0x850 InvertedFunctionTableLock : _EX_PUSH_LOCK
+0x858 ActiveThreadsHighWatermark : 0x88
+0x85c LargePrivateVadCount : 0
+0x860 ThreadListLock    : _EX_PUSH_LOCK
+0x868 WnfContext        : 0xffff800e`d48b52e0 Void
+0x870 ServerSilo        : (null)
+0x878 SignatureLevel    : 0x1e ''
+0x879 SectionSignatureLevel : 0x1c ''
+0x87a Protection        : _PS_PROTECTION
+0x87b HangCount         : 0y000
+0x87b GhostCount        : 0y000
+0x87b PrefilterException : 0y0
+0x87c Flags3            : 0x405080
+0x87c Minimal           : 0y0
+0x87c ReplacingPageRoot : 0y0
+0x87c Crashed           : 0y0
+0x87c JobVadsAreTracked : 0y0
+0x87c VadTrackingDisabled : 0y0
+0x87c AuxiliaryProcess  : 0y0
+0x87c SubsystemProcess  : 0y0
+0x87c IndirectCpuSets   : 0y1
+0x87c RelinquishedCommit : 0y0
+0x87c HighGraphicsPriority : 0y0
+0x87c CommitFailLogged  : 0y0
+0x87c ReserveFailLogged : 0y0
+0x87c SystemProcess     : 0y1
+0x87c HideImageBaseAddresses : 0y0
+0x87c AddressPolicyFrozen : 0y1
+0x87c ProcessFirstResume : 0y0
+0x87c ForegroundExternal : 0y0
+0x87c ForegroundSystem  : 0y0
+0x87c HighMemoryPriority : 0y0
+0x87c EnableProcessSuspendResumeLogging : 0y0
+0x87c EnableThreadSuspendResumeLogging : 0y0
+0x87c SecurityDomainChanged : 0y0
+0x87c SecurityFreezeComplete : 0y1
+0x87c VmProcessorHost   : 0y0
+0x87c VmProcessorHostTransition : 0y0
+0x87c AltSyscall        : 0y0
+0x87c TimerResolutionIgnore : 0y0
+0x87c DisallowUserTerminate : 0y0
+0x87c EnableProcessRemoteExecProtectVmLogging : 0y0
+0x87c EnableProcessLocalExecProtectVmLogging : 0y0
+0x880 DeviceAsid        : 0n0
+0x888 SvmData           : (null)
+0x890 SvmProcessLock    : _EX_PUSH_LOCK
+0x898 SvmLock           : 0
+0x8a0 SvmProcessDeviceListHead : _LIST_ENTRY [ 0xffffbe0c`840eb8e0 - 0xffffbe0c`840eb8e0 ]
+0x8b0 LastFreezeInterruptTime : 0
+0x8b8 DiskCounters      : 0xffffbe0c`840ebbc0 _PROCESS_DISK_COUNTERS
+0x8c0 PicoContext       : (null)
+0x8c8 EnclaveTable      : (null)
+0x8d0 EnclaveNumber     : 0
+0x8d8 EnclaveLock       : _EX_PUSH_LOCK
+0x8e0 HighPriorityFaultsAllowed : 0
+0x8e8 EnergyContext     : 0xffffbe0c`840ebbe8 _PO_PROCESS_ENERGY_CONTEXT
+0x8f0 VmContext         : (null)
+0x8f8 SequenceNumber    : 1
+0x900 CreateInterruptTime : 0x89eae9f
+0x908 CreateUnbiasedInterruptTime : 0x89eae9f
+0x910 TotalUnbiasedFrozenTime : 0
+0x918 LastAppStateUpdateTime : 0
+0x920 LastAppStateUptime : 0y00000000000000000000000000000000000000000000000000000000000000 (0)
+0x920 LastAppState      : 0y000
```

```
   +0x928 SharedCommitCharge : 0x4a
   +0x930 SharedCommitLock : _EX_PUSH_LOCK
   +0x938 SharedCommitLinks : _LIST_ENTRY [ 0xffff800e`d71a16b8 - 0xffff800e`d4cfba78 ]
   +0x948 AllowedCpuSets   : 0xffffbe0c`840ebdc8
   +0x950 DefaultCpuSets   : 0xffffbe0c`840ebec8
   +0x948 AllowedCpuSetsIndirect : 0xffffbe0c`840ebdc8  -> 3
   +0x950 DefaultCpuSetsIndirect : 0xffffbe0c`840ebec8  -> 0
   +0x958 DiskIoAttribution : (null)
   +0x960 DxgProcess       : 0xffff800e`d4ef4a40 Void
   +0x968 Win32KFilterSet  : 0
   +0x96c Machine          : 0x8664
   +0x96e Spare0           : 0
   +0x970 ProcessTimerDelay : _PS_INTERLOCKED_TIMER_DELAY_VALUES
   +0x978 KTimerSets       : 0
   +0x97c KTimer2Sets      : 0
   +0x980 ThreadTimerSets  : 0
   +0x988 VirtualTimerListLock : 0
   +0x990 VirtualTimerListHead : _LIST_ENTRY [ 0xffffbe0c`840eb9d0 - 0xffffbe0c`840eb9d0 ]
   +0x9a0 WakeChannel      : _WNF_STATE_NAME
   +0x9a0 WakeInfo         : _PS_PROCESS_WAKE_INFORMATION
   +0x9d0 MitigationFlags  : 0x40000060
   +0x9d0 MitigationFlagsValues : <unnamed-tag>
   +0x9d4 MitigationFlags2 : 0x40002000
   +0x9d4 MitigationFlags2Values : <unnamed-tag>
   +0x9d8 PartitionObject  : 0xffffbe0c`840bf960 Void
   +0x9e0 SecurityDomain   : 0
   +0x9e8 ParentSecurityDomain : 0
   +0x9f0 CoverageSamplerContext : (null)
   +0x9f8 MmHotPatchContext : (null)
   +0xa00 IdealProcessorAssignmentBlock : _KE_IDEAL_PROCESSOR_ASSIGNMENT_BLOCK
   +0xb18 DynamicEHContinuationTargetsTree : _RTL_AVL_TREE
   +0xb20 DynamicEHContinuationTargetsLock : _EX_PUSH_LOCK
   +0xb28 DynamicEnforcedCetCompatibleRanges : _PS_DYNAMIC_ENFORCED_ADDRESS_RANGES
   +0xb38 DisabledComponentFlags : 0
   +0xb3c PageCombineSequence : 0n1
   +0xb40 EnableOptionalXStateFeaturesLock : _EX_PUSH_LOCK

[...]


ActiveProcessLinks.Flink at 0xffffbe0c`8bfb10c0
-------------------------------------------
   +0x000 Pcb              : _KPROCESS
   +0x438 ProcessLock      : _EX_PUSH_LOCK
   +0x440 UniqueProcessId  : 0x00000000`00002434 Void
   +0x448 ActiveProcessLinks : [ 0xfffff807`62c1bfa0 - 0xffffbe0c`8c2cd508 ]
      +0x000 Flink         : 0xfffff807`62c1bfa0 _LIST_ENTRY [ 0xffffbe0c`840eb488 - 0xffffbe0c`8bfb1508 ]
      +0x008 Blink         : 0xffffbe0c`8c2cd508 _LIST_ENTRY [ 0xffffbe0c`8bfb1508 - 0xffffbe0c`8c576508 ]
   +0x458 RundownProtect   : _EX_RUNDOWN_REF
   +0x460 Flags2           : 0xd094
   +0x460 JobNotReallyActive : 0y0
   +0x460 AccountingFolded : 0y0
   +0x460 NewProcessReported : 0y1
   +0x460 ExitProcessReported : 0y0
   +0x460 ReportCommitChanges : 0y1
   +0x460 LastReportMemory : 0y0
   +0x460 ForceWakeCharge  : 0y0
   +0x460 CrossSessionCreate : 0y1
   +0x460 NeedsHandleRundown : 0y0
   +0x460 RefTraceEnabled  : 0y0
   +0x460 PicoCreated      : 0y0
   +0x460 EmptyJobEvaluated : 0y0
   +0x460 DefaultPagePriority : 0y101
   +0x460 PrimaryTokenFrozen : 0y1
   +0x460 ProcessVerifierTarget : 0y0
   +0x460 RestrictSetThreadContext : 0y0
   +0x460 AffinityPermanent : 0y0
   +0x460 AffinityUpdateEnable : 0y0
   +0x460 PropagateNode    : 0y0
   +0x460 ExplicitAffinity : 0y0
   +0x460 ProcessExecutionState : 0y00
   +0x460 EnableReadVmLogging : 0y0
   +0x460 EnableWriteVmLogging : 0y0
   +0x460 FatalAccessTerminationRequested : 0y0
   +0x460 DisableSystemAllowedCpuSet : 0y0
```

```
+0x460 ProcessStateChangeRequest : 0y00
+0x460 ProcessStateChangeInProgress : 0y0
+0x460 InPrivate        : 0y0
+0x464 Flags            : 0x944d8c01
+0x464 CreateReported   : 0y1
+0x464 NoDebugInherit   : 0y0
+0x464 ProcessExiting   : 0y0
+0x464 ProcessDelete    : 0y0
+0x464 ManageExecutableMemoryWrites : 0y0
+0x464 VmDeleted        : 0y0
+0x464 OutswapEnabled   : 0y0
+0x464 Outswapped       : 0y0
+0x464 FailFastOnCommitFail : 0y0
+0x464 Wow64VaSpace4Gb  : 0y0
+0x464 AddressSpaceInitialized : 0y11
+0x464 SetTimerResolution : 0y0
+0x464 BreakOnTermination : 0y0
+0x464 DeprioritizeViews : 0y0
+0x464 WriteWatch       : 0y1
+0x464 ProcessInSession : 0y1
+0x464 OverrideAddressSpace : 0y0
+0x464 HasAddressSpace  : 0y1
+0x464 LaunchPrefetched : 0y1
+0x464 Background       : 0y0
+0x464 VmTopDown        : 0y0
+0x464 ImageNotifyDone  : 0y1
+0x464 PdeUpdateNeeded  : 0y0
+0x464 VdmAllowed       : 0y0
+0x464 ProcessRundown   : 0y0
+0x464 ProcessInserted  : 0y1
+0x464 DefaultIoPriority : 0y010
+0x464 ProcessSelfDelete : 0y0
+0x464 SetTimerResolutionLink : 0y1
+0x468 CreateTime       : _LARGE_INTEGER 0x01d81e1b`18b4a49c
+0x470 ProcessQuotaUsage : [2] 0x154d0
+0x480 ProcessQuotaPeak : [2] 0x1fe90
+0x490 PeakVirtualSize  : 0x00000209`46bb3000
+0x498 VirtualSize      : 0x00000209`468d3000
+0x4a0 SessionProcessLinks : _LIST_ENTRY [ 0xffffbe0c`87efbab0 - 0xffffbe0c`8c2cd560 ]
+0x4b0 ExceptionPortData : 0xffffbe0c`87ce4d30 Void
+0x4b0 ExceptionPortValue : 0xffffbe0c`87ce4d30
+0x4b0 ExceptionPortState : 0y000
+0x4b8 Token            : _EX_FAST_REF
+0x4c0 MmReserved       : 0
+0x4c8 AddressCreationLock : _EX_PUSH_LOCK
+0x4d0 PageTableCommitmentLock : _EX_PUSH_LOCK
+0x4d8 RotateInProgress : (null)
+0x4e0 ForkInProgress   : (null)
+0x4e8 CommitChargeJob  : 0xffffbe0c`8b4bd060 _EJOB
+0x4f0 CloneRoot        : _RTL_AVL_TREE
+0x4f8 NumberOfPrivatePages : 0x4727
+0x500 NumberOfLockedPages : 0xd99
+0x508 Win32Process     : 0xffffbcc6`4293c280 Void
+0x510 Job              : 0xffffbe0c`8b4bd060 _EJOB
+0x518 SectionObject    : 0xffff800e`dec2fb70 Void
+0x520 SectionBaseAddress : 0x00007ff6`6dd00000 Void
+0x528 Cookie           : 0x3d982939
+0x530 WorkingSetWatch  : (null)
+0x538 Win32WindowStation : 0x00000000`00000208 Void
+0x540 InheritedFromUniqueProcessId : 0x00000000`00000354 Void
+0x548 OwnerProcessId   : 0x356
+0x550 Peb              : 0x0000008e`61c8c000 _PEB
+0x558 Session          : 0xffffbe0c`87efbaa0 _MM_SESSION_SPACE
+0x560 Spare1           : (null)
+0x568 QuotaBlock       : 0xffffbe0c`8900b580 _EPROCESS_QUOTA_BLOCK
+0x570 ObjectTable      : 0xffff800e`dff94180 _HANDLE_TABLE
+0x578 DebugPort        : (null)
+0x580 WoW64Process     : (null)
+0x588 DeviceMap        : _EX_FAST_REF
+0x590 EtwDataSource    : 0xffffbe0c`8c46d250 Void
+0x598 PageDirectoryPte : 0
+0x5a0 ImageFilePointer : 0xffffbe0c`8bf609c0 _FILE_OBJECT
+0x5a8 ImageFileName    : [15] "SearchHost.exe"
+0x5b7 PriorityClass    : 0x2 ''
```

```
+0x5b8 SecurityPort      : (null)
+0x5c0 SeAuditProcessCreationInfo : _SE_AUDIT_PROCESS_CREATION_INFO
+0x5c8 JobLinks          : _LIST_ENTRY [ 0xffffbe0c`8b4bd088 - 0xffffbe0c`8b4bd088 ]
+0x5d8 HighestUserAddress : 0x00007fff`ffff0000 Void
+0x5e0 ThreadListHead    : _LIST_ENTRY [ 0xffffbe0c`841d45b8 - 0xffffbe0c`8c1165b8 ]
+0x5f0 ActiveThreads     : 0x42
+0x5f4 ImagePathHash     : 0xc75e5e6e
+0x5f8 DefaultHardErrorProcessing : 0
+0x5fc LastThreadExitStatus : 0n0
+0x600 PrefetchTrace     : _EX_FAST_REF
+0x608 LockedPagesList   : (null)
+0x610 ReadOperationCount : _LARGE_INTEGER 0x0
+0x618 WriteOperationCount : _LARGE_INTEGER 0x0
+0x620 OtherOperationCount : _LARGE_INTEGER 0x3e
+0x628 ReadTransferCount : _LARGE_INTEGER 0x0
+0x630 WriteTransferCount : _LARGE_INTEGER 0x0
+0x638 OtherTransferCount : _LARGE_INTEGER 0x8298
+0x640 CommitChargeLimit : 0
+0x648 CommitCharge      : 0x4d87
+0x650 CommitChargePeak  : 0x52b9
+0x680 Vm                : _MMSUPPORT_FULL
+0x7c0 MmProcessLinks    : _LIST_ENTRY [ 0xffffff807`62c50698 - 0xffffbe0c`8c2cd880 ]
+0x7d0 ModifiedPageCount : 0x38e
+0x7d4 ExitStatus        : 0n259
+0x7d8 VadRoot           : _RTL_AVL_TREE
+0x7e0 VadHint           : 0xffffbe0c`8c407b40 Void
+0x7e8 VadCount          : 0x24f
+0x7f0 VadPhysicalPages  : 0
+0x7f8 VadPhysicalPagesLimit : 0
+0x800 AlpcContext       : _ALPC_PROCESS_CONTEXT
+0x820 TimerResolutionLink : _LIST_ENTRY [ 0xffffbe0c`8a9828a0 - 0xffffff807`62c15a80 ]
+0x830 TimerResolutionStackRecord : 0xffff800e`dc1cd490 _PO_DIAG_STACK_RECORD
+0x838 RequestedTimerResolution : 0
+0x83c SmallestTimerResolution : 0x9c40
+0x840 ExitTime          : _LARGE_INTEGER 0x0
+0x848 InvertedFunctionTable : 0xffff800e`e046b000 _INVERTED_FUNCTION_TABLE
+0x850 InvertedFunctionTableLock : _EX_PUSH_LOCK
+0x858 ActiveThreadsHighWatermark : 0x42
+0x85c LargePrivateVadCount : 0
+0x860 ThreadListLock    : _EX_PUSH_LOCK
+0x868 WnfContext        : 0xffff800e`dec2d500 Void
+0x870 ServerSilo        : (null)
+0x878 SignatureLevel    : 0x8 ''
+0x879 SectionSignatureLevel : 0 ''
+0x87a Protection        : _PS_PROTECTION
+0x87b HangCount         : 0y000
+0x87b GhostCount        : 0y000
+0x87b PrefilterException : 0y0
+0x87c Flags3            : 0x440c008
+0x87c Minimal           : 0y0
+0x87c ReplacingPageRoot : 0y0
+0x87c Crashed           : 0y0
+0x87c JobVadsAreTracked : 0y1
+0x87c VadTrackingDisabled : 0y0
+0x87c AuxiliaryProcess  : 0y0
+0x87c SubsystemProcess  : 0y0
+0x87c IndirectCpuSets   : 0y0
+0x87c RelinquishedCommit : 0y0
+0x87c HighGraphicsPriority : 0y0
+0x87c CommitFailLogged  : 0y0
+0x87c ReserveFailLogged : 0y0
+0x87c SystemProcess     : 0y0
+0x87c HideImageBaseAddresses : 0y0
+0x87c AddressPolicyFrozen : 0y1
+0x87c ProcessFirstResume : 0y1
+0x87c ForegroundExternal : 0y0
+0x87c ForegroundSystem  : 0y0
+0x87c HighMemoryPriority : 0y0
+0x87c EnableProcessSuspendResumeLogging : 0y0
+0x87c EnableThreadSuspendResumeLogging : 0y0
+0x87c SecurityDomainChanged : 0y0
+0x87c SecurityFreezeComplete : 0y1
+0x87c VmProcessorHost   : 0y0
+0x87c VmProcessorHostTransition : 0y0
```

```
+0x87c AltSyscall        : 0y0
+0x87c TimerResolutionIgnore : 0y1
+0x87c DisallowUserTerminate : 0y0
+0x87c EnableProcessRemoteExecProtectVmLogging : 0y0
+0x87c EnableProcessLocalExecProtectVmLogging : 0y0
+0x880 DeviceAsid        : 0n0
+0x888 SvmData           : (null)
+0x890 SvmProcessLock    : _EX_PUSH_LOCK
+0x898 SvmLock           : 0
+0x8a0 SvmProcessDeviceListHead : _LIST_ENTRY [ 0xffffbe0c`8bfb1960 - 0xffffbe0c`8bfb1960 ]
+0x8b0 LastFreezeInterruptTime : 0
+0x8b8 DiskCounters      : 0xffffbe0c`8bfb1c40 _PROCESS_DISK_COUNTERS
+0x8c0 PicoContext       : (null)
+0x8c8 EnclaveTable      : (null)
+0x8d0 EnclaveNumber     : 0
+0x8d8 EnclaveLock       : _EX_PUSH_LOCK
+0x8e0 HighPriorityFaultsAllowed : 0
+0x8e8 EnergyContext     : 0xffffbe0c`8bfb1c68 _PO_PROCESS_ENERGY_CONTEXT
+0x8f0 VmContext         : (null)
+0x8f8 SequenceNumber    : 0x121
+0x900 CreateInterruptTime : 0x00000001`0daf77b8
+0x908 CreateUnbiasedInterruptTime : 0x00000001`0daf77b8
+0x910 TotalUnbiasedFrozenTime : 0
+0x918 LastAppStateUpdateTime : 0x00000001`0daf77b8
+0x920 LastAppStateUptime : 0y00000000000000000000000000000000000000000000000000000000000000 (0)
+0x920 LastAppState      : 0y000
+0x928 SharedCommitCharge : 0x123e
+0x930 SharedCommitLock  : _EX_PUSH_LOCK
+0x938 SharedCommitLinks : _LIST_ENTRY [ 0xffff800e`de335f58 - 0xffff800e`e0516d58 ]
+0x948 AllowedCpuSets    : 0
+0x950 DefaultCpuSets    : 0
+0x948 AllowedCpuSetsIndirect : (null)
+0x950 DefaultCpuSetsIndirect : (null)
+0x958 DiskIoAttribution : (null)
+0x960 DxgProcess        : 0xffff800e`dffd6b30 Void
+0x968 Win32KFilterSet   : 0
+0x96c Machine           : 0x8664
+0x96e Spare0            : 0
+0x970 ProcessTimerDelay : _PS_INTERLOCKED_TIMER_DELAY_VALUES
+0x978 KTimerSets        : 0x223
+0x97c KTimer2Sets       : 0
+0x980 ThreadTimerSets   : 0x1fd
+0x988 VirtualTimerListLock : 0
+0x990 VirtualTimerListHead : _LIST_ENTRY [ 0xffffbe0c`8c3e61a0 - 0xffffbe0c`8709fc90 ]
+0x9a0 WakeChannel       : _WNF_STATE_NAME
+0x9a0 WakeInfo          : _PS_PROCESS_WAKE_INFORMATION
+0x9d0 MitigationFlags   : 0x39
+0x9d0 MitigationFlagsValues : <unnamed-tag>
+0x9d4 MitigationFlags2  : 0x40000000
+0x9d4 MitigationFlags2Values : <unnamed-tag>
+0x9d8 PartitionObject   : 0xffffbe0c`840bf960 Void
+0x9e0 SecurityDomain    : 0x00000001`000000ef
+0x9e8 ParentSecurityDomain : 0
+0x9f0 CoverageSamplerContext : (null)
+0x9f8 MmHotPatchContext : (null)
+0xa00 IdealProcessorAssignmentBlock : _KE_IDEAL_PROCESSOR_ASSIGNMENT_BLOCK
+0xb18 DynamicEHContinuationTargetsTree : _RTL_AVL_TREE
+0xb20 DynamicEHContinuationTargetsLock : _EX_PUSH_LOCK
+0xb28 DynamicEnforcedCetCompatibleRanges : _PS_DYNAMIC_ENFORCED_ADDRESS_RANGES
+0xb38 DisabledComponentFlags : 0
+0xb3c PageCombineSequence : 0n1
+0xb40 EnableOptionalXStateFeaturesLock : _EX_PUSH_LOCK
```

10.   If we want to dump some field from linked structures, we can add the field name to the **dt** command:

```
1: kd> !list -t nt!_EPROCESS.ActiveProcessLinks.Flink -x "dt nt!_EPROCESS ImageFileName"
poi(nt!PsActiveProcessHead)-448
   +0x5a8 ImageFileName : [15]  "System"

   +0x5a8 ImageFileName : [15]  "Registry"
```

171

```
+0x5a8 ImageFileName : [15] "smss.exe"

+0x5a8 ImageFileName : [15] "csrss.exe"

+0x5a8 ImageFileName : [15] "wininit.exe"

+0x5a8 ImageFileName : [15] "csrss.exe"

+0x5a8 ImageFileName : [15] "services.exe"

+0x5a8 ImageFileName : [15] "lsass.exe"

+0x5a8 ImageFileName : [15] "winlogon.exe"

+0x5a8 ImageFileName : [15] "fontdrvhost.ex"

+0x5a8 ImageFileName : [15] "fontdrvhost.ex"

+0x5a8 ImageFileName : [15] "svchost.exe"

+0x5a8 ImageFileName : [15] "WUDFHost.exe"

+0x5a8 ImageFileName : [15] "svchost.exe"

+0x5a8 ImageFileName : [15] "svchost.exe"

+0x5a8 ImageFileName : [15] "dwm.exe"

+0x5a8 ImageFileName : [15] "svchost.exe"

+0x5a8 ImageFileName : [15] "svchost.exe"

+0x5a8 ImageFileName : [15] "svchost.exe"

+0x5a8 ImageFileName : [15] "svchost.exe"

+0x5a8 ImageFileName : [15] "svchost.exe"

+0x5a8 ImageFileName : [15] "svchost.exe"

+0x5a8 ImageFileName : [15] "svchost.exe"

+0x5a8 ImageFileName : [15] "svchost.exe"

+0x5a8 ImageFileName : [15] "svchost.exe"

+0x5a8 ImageFileName : [15] "svchost.exe"

+0x5a8 ImageFileName : [15] "svchost.exe"

+0x5a8 ImageFileName : [15] "svchost.exe"

+0x5a8 ImageFileName : [15] "svchost.exe"

+0x5a8 ImageFileName : [15] "svchost.exe"

+0x5a8 ImageFileName : [15] "svchost.exe"

+0x5a8 ImageFileName : [15] "svchost.exe"

+0x5a8 ImageFileName : [15] "svchost.exe"
```

```
+0x5a8 ImageFileName : [15]    "svchost.exe"

+0x5a8 ImageFileName : [15]    "svchost.exe"

+0x5a8 ImageFileName : [15]    "svchost.exe"

+0x5a8 ImageFileName : [15]    "svchost.exe"

+0x5a8 ImageFileName : [15]    "svchost.exe"

+0x5a8 ImageFileName : [15]    "svchost.exe"

+0x5a8 ImageFileName : [15]    "svchost.exe"

+0x5a8 ImageFileName : [15]    "MemCompression"

+0x5a8 ImageFileName : [15]    "svchost.exe"

+0x5a8 ImageFileName : [15]    "svchost.exe"

+0x5a8 ImageFileName : [15]    "svchost.exe"

+0x5a8 ImageFileName : [15]    "svchost.exe"

+0x5a8 ImageFileName : [15]    "svchost.exe"

+0x5a8 ImageFileName : [15]    "svchost.exe"

+0x5a8 ImageFileName : [15]    "svchost.exe"

+0x5a8 ImageFileName : [15]    "svchost.exe"

+0x5a8 ImageFileName : [15]    "svchost.exe"

+0x5a8 ImageFileName : [15]    "spoolsv.exe"

+0x5a8 ImageFileName : [15]    "svchost.exe"

+0x5a8 ImageFileName : [15]    "svchost.exe"

+0x5a8 ImageFileName : [15]    "svchost.exe"

+0x5a8 ImageFileName : [15]    "svchost.exe"

+0x5a8 ImageFileName : [15]    "svchost.exe"

+0x5a8 ImageFileName : [15]    "svchost.exe"

+0x5a8 ImageFileName : [15]    "svchost.exe"

+0x5a8 ImageFileName : [15]    "svchost.exe"

+0x5a8 ImageFileName : [15]    "svchost.exe"

+0x5a8 ImageFileName : [15]    "VGAuthService."

+0x5a8 ImageFileName : [15]    "vmtoolsd.exe"

+0x5a8 ImageFileName : [15]    "MsMpEng.exe"

+0x5a8 ImageFileName : [15]    "svchost.exe"

+0x5a8 ImageFileName : [15]    "svchost.exe"
```

173

```
+0x5a8 ImageFileName : [15]    "svchost.exe"

+0x5a8 ImageFileName : [15]    "dllhost.exe"

+0x5a8 ImageFileName : [15]    "AggregatorHost"

+0x5a8 ImageFileName : [15]    "svchost.exe"

+0x5a8 ImageFileName : [15]    "msdtc.exe"

+0x5a8 ImageFileName : [15]    "svchost.exe"

+0x5a8 ImageFileName : [15]    "WmiPrvSE.exe"

+0x5a8 ImageFileName : [15]    "sihost.exe"

+0x5a8 ImageFileName : [15]    "svchost.exe"

+0x5a8 ImageFileName : [15]    "svchost.exe"

+0x5a8 ImageFileName : [15]    "taskhostw.exe"

+0x5a8 ImageFileName : [15]    "taskhostw.exe"

+0x5a8 ImageFileName : [15]    "svchost.exe"

+0x5a8 ImageFileName : [15]    "MsMpEngCP.exe"

+0x5a8 ImageFileName : [15]    "svchost.exe"

+0x5a8 ImageFileName : [15]    "userinit.exe"

+0x5a8 ImageFileName : [15]    "explorer.exe"

+0x5a8 ImageFileName : [15]    "svchost.exe"

+0x5a8 ImageFileName : [15]    "svchost.exe"

+0x5a8 ImageFileName : [15]    "svchost.exe"

+0x5a8 ImageFileName : [15]    "WmiPrvSE.exe"

+0x5a8 ImageFileName : [15]    "NisSrv.exe"

+0x5a8 ImageFileName : [15]    "svchost.exe"

+0x5a8 ImageFileName : [15]    "SearchIndexer."

+0x5a8 ImageFileName : [15]    "svchost.exe"

+0x5a8 ImageFileName : [15]    "svchost.exe"

+0x5a8 ImageFileName : [15]    "SearchHost.exe"

+0x5a8 ImageFileName : [15]    "StartMenuExper"

+0x5a8 ImageFileName : [15]    "svchost.exe"

+0x5a8 ImageFileName : [15]    "RuntimeBroker."

+0x5a8 ImageFileName : [15]    "svchost.exe"

+0x5a8 ImageFileName : [15]    "RuntimeBroker."

+0x5a8 ImageFileName : [15]    "svchost.exe"
```

```
  +0x5a8 ImageFileName : [15]  "dllhost.exe"

[...]

  +0x5a8 ImageFileName : [15]  "msedge.exe"

  +0x5a8 ImageFileName : [15]  "msedge.exe"

  +0x5a8 ImageFileName : [15]  "msedge.exe"

  +0x5a8 ImageFileName : [15]  "msedge.exe"

  +0x5a8 ImageFileName : [15]  "msedge.exe"

  +0x5a8 ImageFileName : [15]  "msedge.exe"

  +0x5a8 ImageFileName : [15]  "identity_helpe"

  +0x5a8 ImageFileName : [15]  "msedge.exe"

  +0x5a8 ImageFileName : [15]  "msedge.exe"

  +0x5a8 ImageFileName : [15]  "MiniSearchHost"

  +0x5a8 ImageFileName : [15]  "Notepad.exe"

  +0x5a8 ImageFileName : [15]  "dllhost.exe"

  +0x5a8 ImageFileName : [15]  "CalculatorApp."

  +0x5a8 ImageFileName : [15]  "RuntimeBroker."

  +0x5a8 ImageFileName : [15]  "wordpad.exe"

  +0x5a8 ImageFileName : [15]  "splwow64.exe"

  +0x5a8 ImageFileName : [15]  "svchost.exe"

  +0x5a8 ImageFileName : [15]  "svchost.exe"

  +0x5a8 ImageFileName : [15]  "LINQPad7.exe"

  +0x5a8 ImageFileName : [15]  "LINQPad7.Query"

  +0x5a8 ImageFileName : [15]  "cmd.exe"

  +0x5a8 ImageFileName : [15]  "conhost.exe"

  +0x5a8 ImageFileName : [15]  "Taskmgr.exe"

  +0x5a8 ImageFileName : [15]  "audiodg.exe"

  +0x5a8 ImageFileName : [15]  "TabTip.exe"

  +0x5a8 ImageFileName : [15]  "notmyfault64.e"

  +0x5a8 ImageFileName : [15]  "SearchHost.exe"
```

11.   We can also validate any list by using the **!validatelist** command:

```
1: kd> !validatelist nt!PsActiveProcessHead
Found list end after 159 entries
```

Note: Let's check a random data value to see if the command detects anything wrong:

```
1: kd> !validatelist nt!PsActiveProcessHead+100
Failed to read entry at address 0000000000000000 got from fffff80762c1c0a0
```

12.   We can also use the MEX extension **foreachitem** command for linked list navigation:

```
1: kd> .load C:\AdvWMDA-Dumps\x64\mex
Mex External 3.0.0.7172 Loaded!
```

```
1: kd> !mex.foreachitem -nohead nt!PsActiveProcessHead -o 448 -x "dt nt!_EPROCESS ImageFileName"
```

```
Item #1 @ 0xffffbe0c840eb040
nt!_EPROCESS
   +0x5a8 ImageFileName : [15]  "System"


Item #2 @ 0xffffbe0c84136080
nt!_EPROCESS
   +0x5a8 ImageFileName : [15]  "Registry"


Item #3 @ 0xffffbe0c8780f040
nt!_EPROCESS
   +0x5a8 ImageFileName : [15]  "smss.exe"


Item #4 @ 0xffffbe0c87f2b080
nt!_EPROCESS
   +0x5a8 ImageFileName : [15]  "csrss.exe"


Item #5 @ 0xffffbe0c887d4080
nt!_EPROCESS
   +0x5a8 ImageFileName : [15]  "wininit.exe"


Item #6 @ 0xffffbe0c888840c0
nt!_EPROCESS
   +0x5a8 ImageFileName : [15]  "csrss.exe"


Item #7 @ 0xffffbe0c888c9100
nt!_EPROCESS
   +0x5a8 ImageFileName : [15]  "services.exe"


Item #8 @ 0xffffbe0c888cb0c0
nt!_EPROCESS
   +0x5a8 ImageFileName : [15]  "lsass.exe"


Item #9 @ 0xffffbe0c888dc080
nt!_EPROCESS
   +0x5a8 ImageFileName : [15]  "winlogon.exe"
[...]

Item #150 @ 0xffffbe0c8be760c0
nt!_EPROCESS
   +0x5a8 ImageFileName : [15]  "svchost.exe"
```

```
Item #151 @ 0xffffbe0c8a7a6080
nt!_EPROCESS
   +0x5a8 ImageFileName : [15]  "LINQPad7.exe"


Item #152 @ 0xffffbe0c8b318080
nt!_EPROCESS
   +0x5a8 ImageFileName : [15]  "LINQPad7.Query"


Item #153 @ 0xffffbe0c8c9d3080
nt!_EPROCESS
   +0x5a8 ImageFileName : [15]  "cmd.exe"


Item #154 @ 0xffffbe0c8b317080
nt!_EPROCESS
   +0x5a8 ImageFileName : [15]  "conhost.exe"


Item #155 @ 0xffffbe0c877ec080
nt!_EPROCESS
   +0x5a8 ImageFileName : [15]  "Taskmgr.exe"


Item #156 @ 0xffffbe0c8c2de0c0
nt!_EPROCESS
   +0x5a8 ImageFileName : [15]  "audiodg.exe"


Item #157 @ 0xffffbe0c8c5760c0
nt!_EPROCESS
   +0x5a8 ImageFileName : [15]  "TabTip.exe"


Item #158 @ 0xffffbe0c8c2cd0c0
nt!_EPROCESS
   +0x5a8 ImageFileName : [15]  "notmyfault64.e"


Item #159 @ 0xffffbe0c8bfb10c0
nt!_EPROCESS
   +0x5a8 ImageFileName : [15]  "SearchHost.exe"
```

13.   We close logging before exiting WinDbg:

```
1: kd> .logclose
Closing open log file C:\AdvWMDA-Dumps\x64\C3A.log
```

Exercise C3B

- **Goal:** Learn how to navigate session processes using linked lists

- **Patterns:** Debugger Bug

- \AdvWMDA-Dumps\Exercise-C3B-Session-Processes.pdf

Exercise C3B: Linked Lists, Additional Example

Goal: Learn how to navigate session processes using linked lists.

Patterns: Debugger Bug.

1.   Launch WinDbg.

2.   Open \AdvWMDA-Dumps\x64\MEMORY-Normal.DMP

3.   We get the dump file loaded (the output should be the same as in the previous exercise).

4.   We open a log file:

```
1: kd> .logopen C:\AdvWMDA-Dumps\x64\C3B.log
Opened log file 'C:\AdvWMDA-Dumps\x64\C3B.log'
```

5.   The current version of WinDbg (and WinDbg from Windows SDK) has a broken command that is supposed to list session processes:

```
1: kd> !sprocess 1
Dumping Session 1
```

Note: We try to implement this command through other means.

6.   Get the address of a session structure:

```
1: kd> !vm 5
Page File: \??\C:\pagefile.sys
  Current:    4456448 Kb  Free Space:    4398516 Kb
  Minimum:    4456448 Kb  Maximum:       7704060 Kb
Page File: \??\C:\swapfile.sys
  Current:     262144 Kb  Free Space:     234936 Kb
  Minimum:     262144 Kb  Maximum:       6163248 Kb
No Name for Paging File
  Current:   11897160 Kb  Free Space:   11546468 Kb
  Minimum:   11897160 Kb  Maximum:      11897160 Kb

Physical Memory:          1048275 (    4193100 Kb)
Available Pages:           282130 (    1128520 Kb)
ResAvail Pages:            844344 (    3377376 Kb)
Locked IO Pages:                0 (          0 Kb)
Free System PTEs:      4294988039 (17179952156 Kb)

******* 487232 kernel stack PTE allocations have failed ******


******* 1 kernel stack growth attempts have failed ******

Modified Pages:              5252 (      21008 Kb)
Modified PF Pages:           4824 (      19296 Kb)
Modified No Write Pages:       13 (         52 Kb)
```

```
NonPagedPool Usage:            130 (         520 Kb)
NonPagedPoolNx Usage:        23519 (       94076 Kb)
NonPagedPool Max:       4294967296 (17179869184 Kb)
PagedPool Usage:             38539 (      154156 Kb)
PagedPool Maximum:      4294967296 (17179869184 Kb)
Processor Commit:              401 (        1604 Kb)
Session Commit:              14595 (       58380 Kb)
Shared Commit:              104010 (      416040 Kb)
Special Pool:                    0 (           0 Kb)
Kernel Stacks:               13356 (       53424 Kb)
Pages For MDLs:               2343 (        9372 Kb)
ContigMem Pages:              2364 (        9456 Kb)
Pages For AWE:                   0 (           0 Kb)
NonPagedPool Commit:         25015 (      100060 Kb)
PagedPool Commit:            38539 (      154156 Kb)
Driver Commit:               13452 (       53808 Kb)
Boot Commit:                  4775 (       19100 Kb)
PFN Array Commit:            13317 (       53268 Kb)
SmallNonPagedPtesCommit:       158 (         632 Kb)
SlabAllocatorPages:           4608 (       18432 Kb)
System PageTables:             960 (        3840 Kb)
ProcessLockedFilePages:         16 (          64 Kb)
Pagefile Hash Pages:            78 (         312 Kb)
Sum System Commit:          233379 (      933516 Kb)
Total Private:              578643 (     2314572 Kb)
Misc/Transient Commit:         887 (        3548 Kb)
Committed pages:            812909 (     3251636 Kb)
Commit limit:              2162387 (     8649548 Kb)

Terminal Server Memory Usage By Session:


Session ID 0 @ ffffbe0c84f52010:
Paged Pool Usage:      2392 Kb
NonPaged Usage:          64 Kb
Commit Usage:          2760 Kb

Session ID 1 @ ffffbe0c87efbaa0:
Paged Pool Usage:     55092 Kb
NonPaged Usage:         212 Kb
Commit Usage:         55620 Kb

Session Summary
Paged Pool Usage:     57484 Kb
NonPaged Usage:         276 Kb
Commit Usage:         58380 Kb
```

7.   If you forgot the structure name you can always guess it:

```
1: kd> dt nt!*SESSION*
         ntkrnlmp!_ETW_SESSION_PERF_COUNTERS
         ntkrnlmp!_ETW_SESSION_PERF_COUNTERS
         ntkrnlmp!_SEP_LOGON_SESSION_REFERENCES
         ntkrnlmp!_IO_SESSION_STATE
         ntkrnlmp!_MM_SESSION_SPACE
         ntkrnlmp!_MM_SESSION_SPACE_FLAGS
         ntkrnlmp!_EX_HEAP_SESSION_STATE
         ntkrnlmp!_MI_SESSION_DRIVER_UNLOAD
```

```
          ntkrnlmp!_MI_SESSION_STATE
          ntkrnlmp!_PS_TRUSTLET_TKSESSION_ID
          ntkrnlmp!_PS_TRUSTLET_TKSESSION_ID
          ntkrnlmp!_SESSION_LOWBOX_MAP
          ntkrnlmp!_MI_PER_SESSION_PROTOS
fffff80762253db8   ntkrnlmp!MiMarkSessionDeletePending
fffff8076265ee28   ntkrnlmp!MiDereferenceSessionFinal
fffff8076221db10   ntkrnlmp!MiUpdateSessionPxeMaster
fffff80762b2b32c   ntkrnlmp!InitSkuSessionParameters
fffff8076279b138   ntkrnlmp!MiSessionCreateInternal
fffff807628252e8   ntkrnlmp!CreateTlgAggregateSession
fffff807627f2094   ntkrnlmp!PopSleepstudyCaptureSessionStatistics
fffff80762665ec0   ntkrnlmp!SepSetLogonSessionToken
fffff80762b2ba14   ntkrnlmp!MiInitializeSessionIds
fffff807622078e8   ntkrnlmp!MiSessionUnlinkProcess
fffff8076279b074   ntkrnlmp!MiGetNewSessionId
fffff80762b26c58   ntkrnlmp!MiAssignSessionRanges
fffff80762803a0c   ntkrnlmp!SshpAlpcOpenTraceSessionUnsafe
fffff807626fee78   ntkrnlmp!EtwpClearSessionAndUnreferenceEntry
fffff8076282c994   ntkrnlmp!SepGetLogonSessionAccountInfo
fffff807625906dc   ntkrnlmp!MiLockAndSelectSessionAttachProcess
fffff807627f030c   ntkrnlmp!SshSessionManagerTraceCsExitReason
fffff80762694d8c   ntkrnlmp!SepCreateLogonSessionTrack
fffff8076279dbd4   ntkrnlmp!PopDiagTraceSessionState
fffff80762260e3c   ntkrnlmp!MiReferenceOwningSession
fffff8076279b450   ntkrnlmp!PopDiagTraceSessionStates
fffff8076284a108   ntkrnlmp!ExIsMultiSessionSku
fffff80762661114   ntkrnlmp!MiReleaseProcessReferenceToSessionDataPage
fffff8076283b290   ntkrnlmp!PopSleepstudyRegisterSessionCallback
fffff8076269f444   ntkrnlmp!SepUpdateLogonSessionTrack
fffff80762253590   ntkrnlmp!MmIsSessionInCurrentServerSilo
fffff8076220fd58   ntkrnlmp!SepLinkLogonSessions
fffff807626bec34   ntkrnlmp!PspAttachSession
fffff80762253e28   ntkrnlmp!MiUnlinkSessionWorkingSet
fffff807622537b4   ntkrnlmp!MmSessionSetUnloadAddress
fffff807626c5b00   ntkrnlmp!AddDecodeGuidToSessions
fffff807622e6650   ntkrnlmp!MmGetSessionById
fffff807622533e0   ntkrnlmp!MiInsertSessionWorkingSet
fffff80762274510   ntkrnlmp!MmDetachSession
fffff807627dd840   ntkrnlmp!RtlIsMultiSessionSku
fffff8076273e51c   ntkrnlmp!PspBindProcessSessionToJob
fffff8076224be50   ntkrnlmp!MiUpdatePerSessionProto
fffff807622745b0   ntkrnlmp!MmAttachSession
fffff80762253d70   ntkrnlmp!IoGetRequestorSessionId
fffff80762229b84   ntkrnlmp!ExInitializeSessionHeapManager
fffff80762210188   ntkrnlmp!SepDeReferenceLogonSessionDirect
fffff80762742e08   ntkrnlmp!SepReferenceLogonSessionSilo
fffff807622722f8   ntkrnlmp!MiGetNextSession
fffff807626c67a8   ntkrnlmp!MiDeleteSessionDriverProtos
fffff8076224e8f8   ntkrnlmp!SepDuplicateLogonSessionReference
fffff807628493a0   ntkrnlmp!SeRegisterLogonSessionTerminatedRoutineEx
fffff80762680f1c   ntkrnlmp!MiSessionObjectCreate
fffff80762680b8c   ntkrnlmp!MiInitializeSessionGlobals
fffff80762209bd8   ntkrnlmp!MiSessionInsertImage
fffff807627aa5a0   ntkrnlmp!RtlSetConsoleSessionForegroundProcessId
fffff807626c6a24   ntkrnlmp!MiReleaseSessionDriverCharges
fffff8076266ed6c   ntkrnlmp!AlpcpPortQueryServerSessionInfo
fffff807627f22b8   ntkrnlmp!PopSleepstudyStartNextSession
fffff8076224fc78   ntkrnlmp!MiReleaseSessionVa
```

```
fffff8076279b38c    ntkrnlmp!PopSessionConnected
fffff80762223558    ntkrnlmp!ExGetSessionPoolTagInfo
fffff80762209274    ntkrnlmp!MiSessionRemoveImage
fffff80762271a70    ntkrnlmp!ExpHpCompactSessionPools
fffff80762208f9c    ntkrnlmp!MmIsSessionExecutionValid
fffff807622334fc    ntkrnlmp!MiAttachSessionGlobal
fffff8076224322c    ntkrnlmp!MiObtainSessionVa
fffff807627f266c    ntkrnlmp!SshpSendSessionData
fffff80762697230    ntkrnlmp!MmCommitSessionMappedView
fffff8076267abc0    ntkrnlmp!ExGetSessionPoolTagInformation
fffff8076236598c    ntkrnlmp!SessionIsInteractive
fffff80762860217    ntkrnlmp!NtOpenSession$filt$0
fffff80762364f18    ntkrnlmp!MiMarkSessionMasterProcess
fffff80762668eb8    ntkrnlmp!SeSetSessionIdToken
fffff8076279c6d0    ntkrnlmp!PopDiagTraceSessionStateCounted
fffff8076279d7dc    ntkrnlmp!PopAdaptiveGetConsoleSessionState
fffff8076279d714    ntkrnlmp!PopAdaptiveGetSessionStateUnsafe
fffff8076267dac0    ntkrnlmp!SepDeleteLogonSessionTrack
fffff807626b96a0    ntkrnlmp!MiCreatePerSessionProtos
fffff807626ce6a4    ntkrnlmp!ExCallSessionCallBack
fffff8076267d72a4   ntkrnlmp!EtwpSendSessionNotification
fffff807623b0c34    ntkrnlmp!WheapCheckForAndReportErrorsFromPreviousSession
fffff80762210350    ntkrnlmp!MmGetSessionObjectById
fffff807622079f0    ntkrnlmp!MiDetachProcessFromSession
fffff807622099c4    ntkrnlmp!MiUnlinkProcessFromSession
fffff807626c0570    ntkrnlmp!PnpInitializeSessionId
fffff80762224650    ntkrnlmp!SepDeleteSessionLowboxEntries
fffff8076224bf0c    ntkrnlmp!MiDeletePerSessionProtos
fffff80762680dd8    ntkrnlmp!MiSessionCreate
fffff8076267b550    ntkrnlmp!NtNotifyChangeSession
fffff8076265f3d0    ntkrnlmp!EtwpTrackDebugIdForSession
fffff8076267ae60    ntkrnlmp!MmAcquireSessionPoolRundown
fffff8076267d8b0    ntkrnlmp!SepDeReferenceLogonSession
fffff8076267dca8    ntkrnlmp!SepDeleteLogonSessionClaims
fffff807626b97e8    ntkrnlmp!MiAllocatePerSessionProtos
fffff80762a2e918    ntkrnlmp!DestroyAggregateSession
```

8.   When we explore the structure, we see the process list there, which we suppose to be a process list head:

```
1: kd> dt nt!_MM_SESSION_SPACE ffffbe0c87efbaa0
   +0x000 ReferenceCount          : 0n57
   +0x004 u                       : <unnamed-tag>
   +0x008 SessionId               : 1
   +0x00c ProcessReferenceToSession : 0n64
   +0x010 ProcessList             : _LIST_ENTRY [ 0xffffbe0c`88884560 - 0xffffbe0c`8bfb1560 ]
   +0x020 NonPagablePages         : 0x35
   +0x028 CommittedPages          : 0x3651
   +0x030 PagedPoolStart          : 0xffffbcc6`40000000 Void
   +0x038 PagedPoolEnd            : 0xffffbce6`3fffffff Void
   +0x040 SessionObject           : 0xffffbe0c`87cea1a0 Void
   +0x048 SessionObjectHandle     : 0xffffffff`8000070c Void
   +0x050 ImageTree               : _RTL_AVL_TREE
   +0x058 LocaleId                : 0x1809
   +0x05c AttachCount             : 0
   +0x060 AttachGate              : _KGATE
   +0x078 WsListEntry             : _LIST_ENTRY [ 0xfffff807`62c534c0 - 0xffffbe0c`84f52088 ]
   +0x088 WsTreeEntry             : _RTL_BALANCED_NODE
   +0x0a0 PagedPoolInfo           : _MM_PAGED_POOL_INFO
```

```
+0x0b8 CombineDomain      : 0x00000001`00000005
+0x0c0 Vm                 : _MMSUPPORT_FULL
+0x200 WorkingSetList     : _MMWSL_INSTANCE
+0x240 AggregateSessionWs : _MMSUPPORT_AGGREGATION
+0x260 HeapState          : 0xffffbe0c`8881e000 Void
+0x268 DriverUnload       : _MI_SESSION_DRIVER_UNLOAD
+0x270 TopLevelPteLockBits : [32] 0
+0x2f0 SessionVaLock      : _EX_PUSH_LOCK
+0x2f8 DynamicVaBitMap    : _RTL_BITMAP_EX
+0x308 DynamicVaHint      : 0x1a
+0x310 PageTables         : [1] _MMPTE
+0x318 PoolBigEntriesInUse : 0n996
+0x31c PagedPoolPdeCount  : 0n43
+0x320 DynamicSessionPdeCount : 0x2b
+0x328 PoolTrackTableExpansion : 0xffffbe0c`84e9c000 Void
+0x330 PoolTrackTableExpansionSize : 0xcc
+0x338 PoolTrackBigPages  : 0xffffbe0c`84352000 Void
+0x340 PoolTrackBigPagesSize : 0x800
+0x348 PermittedFaultsTree : _RTL_AVL_TREE
+0x350 IoState            : 6 ( IoSessionStateLoggedOn )
+0x354 IoStateSequence    : 7
+0x358 IoNotificationEvent : _KEVENT
+0x370 ServerSilo         : (null)
+0x378 CreateTime         : 0x13594d32
+0x380 PoolTags           : 0xffffbe0c`88880000 Void
```

9.   We can now use any method we learned in Exercise C3A to list processes.

```
1: kd> !validatelist ffffbe0c87efbaa0+0x10
Found list end after 63 entries
```

Note: The previous offset 0x448 for _EPROCESS.*ActiveProcessLinks* structure does not work. Here, the list structure pointers are embedded in a different place: _EPROCESS.*SessionProcessLinks*.

```
1: kd> dt nt!_EPROCESS
    +0x000 Pcb                : _KPROCESS
    +0x438 ProcessLock        : _EX_PUSH_LOCK
    +0x440 UniqueProcessId    : Ptr64 Void
    +0x448 ActiveProcessLinks : _LIST_ENTRY
    +0x458 RundownProtect     : _EX_RUNDOWN_REF
    +0x460 Flags2             : Uint4B
    +0x460 JobNotReallyActive : Pos 0, 1 Bit
    +0x460 AccountingFolded   : Pos 1, 1 Bit
    +0x460 NewProcessReported : Pos 2, 1 Bit
    +0x460 ExitProcessReported : Pos 3, 1 Bit
    +0x460 ReportCommitChanges : Pos 4, 1 Bit
    +0x460 LastReportMemory   : Pos 5, 1 Bit
    +0x460 ForceWakeCharge    : Pos 6, 1 Bit
    +0x460 CrossSessionCreate : Pos 7, 1 Bit
    +0x460 NeedsHandleRundown : Pos 8, 1 Bit
    +0x460 RefTraceEnabled    : Pos 9, 1 Bit
    +0x460 PicoCreated        : Pos 10, 1 Bit
    +0x460 EmptyJobEvaluated  : Pos 11, 1 Bit
    +0x460 DefaultPagePriority : Pos 12, 3 Bits
    +0x460 PrimaryTokenFrozen : Pos 15, 1 Bit
    +0x460 ProcessVerifierTarget : Pos 16, 1 Bit
    +0x460 RestrictSetThreadContext : Pos 17, 1 Bit
    +0x460 AffinityPermanent  : Pos 18, 1 Bit
```

```
+0x460 AffinityUpdateEnable : Pos 19, 1 Bit
+0x460 PropagateNode    : Pos 20, 1 Bit
+0x460 ExplicitAffinity : Pos 21, 1 Bit
+0x460 ProcessExecutionState : Pos 22, 2 Bits
+0x460 EnableReadVmLogging : Pos 24, 1 Bit
+0x460 EnableWriteVmLogging : Pos 25, 1 Bit
+0x460 FatalAccessTerminationRequested : Pos 26, 1 Bit
+0x460 DisableSystemAllowedCpuSet : Pos 27, 1 Bit
+0x460 ProcessStateChangeRequest : Pos 28, 2 Bits
+0x460 ProcessStateChangeInProgress : Pos 30, 1 Bit
+0x460 InPrivate        : Pos 31, 1 Bit
+0x464 Flags            : Uint4B
+0x464 CreateReported   : Pos 0, 1 Bit
+0x464 NoDebugInherit   : Pos 1, 1 Bit
+0x464 ProcessExiting   : Pos 2, 1 Bit
+0x464 ProcessDelete    : Pos 3, 1 Bit
+0x464 ManageExecutableMemoryWrites : Pos 4, 1 Bit
+0x464 VmDeleted        : Pos 5, 1 Bit
+0x464 OutswapEnabled   : Pos 6, 1 Bit
+0x464 Outswapped       : Pos 7, 1 Bit
+0x464 FailFastOnCommitFail : Pos 8, 1 Bit
+0x464 Wow64VaSpace4Gb  : Pos 9, 1 Bit
+0x464 AddressSpaceInitialized : Pos 10, 2 Bits
+0x464 SetTimerResolution : Pos 12, 1 Bit
+0x464 BreakOnTermination : Pos 13, 1 Bit
+0x464 DeprioritizeViews : Pos 14, 1 Bit
+0x464 WriteWatch       : Pos 15, 1 Bit
+0x464 ProcessInSession : Pos 16, 1 Bit
+0x464 OverrideAddressSpace : Pos 17, 1 Bit
+0x464 HasAddressSpace  : Pos 18, 1 Bit
+0x464 LaunchPrefetched : Pos 19, 1 Bit
+0x464 Background       : Pos 20, 1 Bit
+0x464 VmTopDown        : Pos 21, 1 Bit
+0x464 ImageNotifyDone  : Pos 22, 1 Bit
+0x464 PdeUpdateNeeded  : Pos 23, 1 Bit
+0x464 VdmAllowed       : Pos 24, 1 Bit
+0x464 ProcessRundown   : Pos 25, 1 Bit
+0x464 ProcessInserted  : Pos 26, 1 Bit
+0x464 DefaultIoPriority : Pos 27, 3 Bits
+0x464 ProcessSelfDelete : Pos 30, 1 Bit
+0x464 SetTimerResolutionLink : Pos 31, 1 Bit
+0x468 CreateTime       : _LARGE_INTEGER
+0x470 ProcessQuotaUsage : [2] Uint8B
+0x480 ProcessQuotaPeak : [2] Uint8B
+0x490 PeakVirtualSize  : Uint8B
+0x498 VirtualSize      : Uint8B
+0x4a0 SessionProcessLinks : _LIST_ENTRY
+0x4b0 ExceptionPortData : Ptr64 Void
+0x4b0 ExceptionPortValue : Uint8B
+0x4b0 ExceptionPortState : Pos 0, 3 Bits
+0x4b8 Token            : _EX_FAST_REF
+0x4c0 MmReserved       : Uint8B
+0x4c8 AddressCreationLock : _EX_PUSH_LOCK
+0x4d0 PageTableCommitmentLock : _EX_PUSH_LOCK
+0x4d8 RotateInProgress : Ptr64 _ETHREAD
+0x4e0 ForkInProgress   : Ptr64 _ETHREAD
+0x4e8 CommitChargeJob  : Ptr64 _EJOB
+0x4f0 CloneRoot        : _RTL_AVL_TREE
+0x4f8 NumberOfPrivatePages : Uint8B
```

```
+0x500 NumberOfLockedPages : Uint8B
+0x508 Win32Process      : Ptr64 Void
+0x510 Job               : Ptr64 _EJOB
+0x518 SectionObject     : Ptr64 Void
+0x520 SectionBaseAddress : Ptr64 Void
+0x528 Cookie            : Uint4B
+0x530 WorkingSetWatch   : Ptr64 _PAGEFAULT_HISTORY
+0x538 Win32WindowStation : Ptr64 Void
+0x540 InheritedFromUniqueProcessId : Ptr64 Void
+0x548 OwnerProcessId    : Uint8B
+0x550 Peb               : Ptr64 _PEB
+0x558 Session           : Ptr64 _MM_SESSION_SPACE
+0x560 Spare1            : Ptr64 Void
+0x568 QuotaBlock        : Ptr64 _EPROCESS_QUOTA_BLOCK
+0x570 ObjectTable       : Ptr64 _HANDLE_TABLE
+0x578 DebugPort         : Ptr64 Void
+0x580 WoW64Process      : Ptr64 _EWOW64PROCESS
+0x588 DeviceMap         : _EX_FAST_REF
+0x590 EtwDataSource     : Ptr64 Void
+0x598 PageDirectoryPte  : Uint8B
+0x5a0 ImageFilePointer  : Ptr64 _FILE_OBJECT
+0x5a8 ImageFileName     : [15] UChar
+0x5b7 PriorityClass     : UChar
+0x5b8 SecurityPort      : Ptr64 Void
+0x5c0 SeAuditProcessCreationInfo : _SE_AUDIT_PROCESS_CREATION_INFO
+0x5c8 JobLinks          : _LIST_ENTRY
+0x5d8 HighestUserAddress : Ptr64 Void
+0x5e0 ThreadListHead    : _LIST_ENTRY
+0x5f0 ActiveThreads     : Uint4B
+0x5f4 ImagePathHash     : Uint4B
+0x5f8 DefaultHardErrorProcessing : Uint4B
+0x5fc LastThreadExitStatus : Int4B
+0x600 PrefetchTrace     : _EX_FAST_REF
+0x608 LockedPagesList   : Ptr64 Void
+0x610 ReadOperationCount : _LARGE_INTEGER
+0x618 WriteOperationCount : _LARGE_INTEGER
+0x620 OtherOperationCount : _LARGE_INTEGER
+0x628 ReadTransferCount : _LARGE_INTEGER
+0x630 WriteTransferCount : _LARGE_INTEGER
+0x638 OtherTransferCount : _LARGE_INTEGER
+0x640 CommitChargeLimit : Uint8B
+0x648 CommitCharge      : Uint8B
+0x650 CommitChargePeak  : Uint8B
+0x680 Vm                : _MMSUPPORT_FULL
+0x7c0 MmProcessLinks    : _LIST_ENTRY
+0x7d0 ModifiedPageCount : Uint4B
+0x7d4 ExitStatus        : Int4B
+0x7d8 VadRoot           : _RTL_AVL_TREE
+0x7e0 VadHint           : Ptr64 Void
+0x7e8 VadCount          : Uint8B
+0x7f0 VadPhysicalPages  : Uint8B
+0x7f8 VadPhysicalPagesLimit : Uint8B
+0x800 AlpcContext       : _ALPC_PROCESS_CONTEXT
+0x820 TimerResolutionLink : _LIST_ENTRY
+0x830 TimerResolutionStackRecord : Ptr64 _PO_DIAG_STACK_RECORD
+0x838 RequestedTimerResolution : Uint4B
+0x83c SmallestTimerResolution : Uint4B
+0x840 ExitTime          : _LARGE_INTEGER
+0x848 InvertedFunctionTable : Ptr64 _INVERTED_FUNCTION_TABLE
```

```
+0x850 InvertedFunctionTableLock : _EX_PUSH_LOCK
+0x858 ActiveThreadsHighWatermark : Uint4B
+0x85c LargePrivateVadCount : Uint4B
+0x860 ThreadListLock    : _EX_PUSH_LOCK
+0x868 WnfContext        : Ptr64 Void
+0x870 ServerSilo        : Ptr64 _EJOB
+0x878 SignatureLevel    : UChar
+0x879 SectionSignatureLevel : UChar
+0x87a Protection        : _PS_PROTECTION
+0x87b HangCount         : Pos 0, 3 Bits
+0x87b GhostCount        : Pos 3, 3 Bits
+0x87b PrefilterException : Pos 6, 1 Bit
+0x87c Flags3            : Uint4B
+0x87c Minimal           : Pos 0, 1 Bit
+0x87c ReplacingPageRoot : Pos 1, 1 Bit
+0x87c Crashed           : Pos 2, 1 Bit
+0x87c JobVadsAreTracked : Pos 3, 1 Bit
+0x87c VadTrackingDisabled : Pos 4, 1 Bit
+0x87c AuxiliaryProcess  : Pos 5, 1 Bit
+0x87c SubsystemProcess  : Pos 6, 1 Bit
+0x87c IndirectCpuSets   : Pos 7, 1 Bit
+0x87c RelinquishedCommit : Pos 8, 1 Bit
+0x87c HighGraphicsPriority : Pos 9, 1 Bit
+0x87c CommitFailLogged  : Pos 10, 1 Bit
+0x87c ReserveFailLogged : Pos 11, 1 Bit
+0x87c SystemProcess     : Pos 12, 1 Bit
+0x87c HideImageBaseAddresses : Pos 13, 1 Bit
+0x87c AddressPolicyFrozen : Pos 14, 1 Bit
+0x87c ProcessFirstResume : Pos 15, 1 Bit
+0x87c ForegroundExternal : Pos 16, 1 Bit
+0x87c ForegroundSystem  : Pos 17, 1 Bit
+0x87c HighMemoryPriority : Pos 18, 1 Bit
+0x87c EnableProcessSuspendResumeLogging : Pos 19, 1 Bit
+0x87c EnableThreadSuspendResumeLogging : Pos 20, 1 Bit
+0x87c SecurityDomainChanged : Pos 21, 1 Bit
+0x87c SecurityFreezeComplete : Pos 22, 1 Bit
+0x87c VmProcessorHost   : Pos 23, 1 Bit
+0x87c VmProcessorHostTransition : Pos 24, 1 Bit
+0x87c AltSyscall        : Pos 25, 1 Bit
+0x87c TimerResolutionIgnore : Pos 26, 1 Bit
+0x87c DisallowUserTerminate : Pos 27, 1 Bit
+0x87c EnableProcessRemoteExecProtectVmLogging : Pos 28, 1 Bit
+0x87c EnableProcessLocalExecProtectVmLogging : Pos 29, 1 Bit
+0x880 DeviceAsid        : Int4B
+0x888 SvmData           : Ptr64 Void
+0x890 SvmProcessLock    : _EX_PUSH_LOCK
+0x898 SvmLock           : Uint8B
+0x8a0 SvmProcessDeviceListHead : _LIST_ENTRY
+0x8b0 LastFreezeInterruptTime : Uint8B
+0x8b8 DiskCounters      : Ptr64 _PROCESS_DISK_COUNTERS
+0x8c0 PicoContext       : Ptr64 Void
+0x8c8 EnclaveTable      : Ptr64 Void
+0x8d0 EnclaveNumber     : Uint8B
+0x8d8 EnclaveLock       : _EX_PUSH_LOCK
+0x8e0 HighPriorityFaultsAllowed : Uint4B
+0x8e8 EnergyContext     : Ptr64 _PO_PROCESS_ENERGY_CONTEXT
+0x8f0 VmContext         : Ptr64 Void
+0x8f8 SequenceNumber    : Uint8B
+0x900 CreateInterruptTime : Uint8B
```

```
+0x908 CreateUnbiasedInterruptTime : Uint8B
+0x910 TotalUnbiasedFrozenTime : Uint8B
+0x918 LastAppStateUpdateTime : Uint8B
+0x920 LastAppStateUptime : Pos 0, 61 Bits
+0x920 LastAppState       : Pos 61, 3 Bits
+0x928 SharedCommitCharge : Uint8B
+0x930 SharedCommitLock : _EX_PUSH_LOCK
+0x938 SharedCommitLinks : _LIST_ENTRY
+0x948 AllowedCpuSets    : Uint8B
+0x950 DefaultCpuSets    : Uint8B
+0x948 AllowedCpuSetsIndirect : Ptr64 Uint8B
+0x950 DefaultCpuSetsIndirect : Ptr64 Uint8B
+0x958 DiskIoAttribution : Ptr64 Void
+0x960 DxgProcess        : Ptr64 Void
+0x968 Win32KFilterSet   : Uint4B
+0x96c Machine           : Uint2B
+0x96e Spare0            : Uint2B
+0x970 ProcessTimerDelay : _PS_INTERLOCKED_TIMER_DELAY_VALUES
+0x978 KTimerSets        : Uint4B
+0x97c KTimer2Sets       : Uint4B
+0x980 ThreadTimerSets   : Uint4B
+0x988 VirtualTimerListLock : Uint8B
+0x990 VirtualTimerListHead : _LIST_ENTRY
+0x9a0 WakeChannel       : _WNF_STATE_NAME
+0x9a0 WakeInfo          : _PS_PROCESS_WAKE_INFORMATION
+0x9d0 MitigationFlags   : Uint4B
+0x9d0 MitigationFlagsValues : <unnamed-tag>
+0x9d4 MitigationFlags2  : Uint4B
+0x9d4 MitigationFlags2Values : <unnamed-tag>
+0x9d8 PartitionObject   : Ptr64 Void
+0x9e0 SecurityDomain    : Uint8B
+0x9e8 ParentSecurityDomain : Uint8B
+0x9f0 CoverageSamplerContext : Ptr64 Void
+0x9f8 MmHotPatchContext : Ptr64 Void
+0xa00 IdealProcessorAssignmentBlock : _KE_IDEAL_PROCESSOR_ASSIGNMENT_BLOCK
+0xb18 DynamicEHContinuationTargetsTree : _RTL_AVL_TREE
+0xb20 DynamicEHContinuationTargetsLock : _EX_PUSH_LOCK
+0xb28 DynamicEnforcedCetCompatibleRanges : _PS_DYNAMIC_ENFORCED_ADDRESS_RANGES
+0xb38 DisabledComponentFlags : Uint4B
+0xb3c PageCombineSequence : Int4B
+0xb40 EnableOptionalXStateFeaturesLock : _EX_PUSH_LOCK
```

```
1: kd> !list -t nt!_EPROCESS.SessionProcessLinks.Flink -x "dt nt!_EPROCESS ImageFileName"
poi(ffffbe0c87efbaa0+0x10)-0x4a0
   +0x5a8 ImageFileName : [15]  "csrss.exe"

   +0x5a8 ImageFileName : [15]  "winlogon.exe"

   +0x5a8 ImageFileName : [15]  "fontdrvhost.ex"

   +0x5a8 ImageFileName : [15]  "dwm.exe"

   +0x5a8 ImageFileName : [15]  "sihost.exe"

   +0x5a8 ImageFileName : [15]  "svchost.exe"

   +0x5a8 ImageFileName : [15]  "svchost.exe"

   +0x5a8 ImageFileName : [15]  "taskhostw.exe"
```

```
+0x5a8 ImageFileName : [15] "taskhostw.exe"

+0x5a8 ImageFileName : [15] "userinit.exe"

+0x5a8 ImageFileName : [15] "explorer.exe"

+0x5a8 ImageFileName : [15] "svchost.exe"

+0x5a8 ImageFileName : [15] "SearchHost.exe"

+0x5a8 ImageFileName : [15] "StartMenuExper"

+0x5a8 ImageFileName : [15] "RuntimeBroker."

+0x5a8 ImageFileName : [15] "svchost.exe"

+0x5a8 ImageFileName : [15] "RuntimeBroker."

+0x5a8 ImageFileName : [15] "dllhost.exe"

+0x5a8 ImageFileName : [15] "YourPhone.exe"

+0x5a8 ImageFileName : [15] "ctfmon.exe"

+0x5a8 ImageFileName : [15] "TabTip.exe"

+0x5a8 ImageFileName : [15] "RuntimeBroker."

+0x5a8 ImageFileName : [15] "smartscreen.ex"

+0x5a8 ImageFileName : [15] "SecurityHealth"

+0x5a8 ImageFileName : [15] "vmtoolsd.exe"

+0x5a8 ImageFileName : [15] "TextInputHost."

+0x5a8 ImageFileName : [15] "ApplicationFra"

+0x5a8 ImageFileName : [15] "vm3dservice.ex"

+0x5a8 ImageFileName : [15] "OneDrive.exe"

+0x5a8 ImageFileName : [15] "msedge.exe"

+0x5a8 ImageFileName : [15] "Cortana.exe"

+0x5a8 ImageFileName : [15] "RuntimeBroker."

+0x5a8 ImageFileName : [15] "svchost.exe"

+0x5a8 ImageFileName : [15] "svchost.exe"

+0x5a8 ImageFileName : [15] "Win32Bridge.Se"

+0x5a8 ImageFileName : [15] "SystemSettings"

+0x5a8 ImageFileName : [15] "UserOOBEBroker"
```

```
+0x5a8 ImageFileName : [15]  "svchost.exe"

+0x5a8 ImageFileName : [15]  "msedge.exe"

+0x5a8 ImageFileName : [15]  "msedge.exe"

+0x5a8 ImageFileName : [15]  "msedge.exe"

+0x5a8 ImageFileName : [15]  "msedge.exe"

+0x5a8 ImageFileName : [15]  "msedge.exe"

+0x5a8 ImageFileName : [15]  "msedge.exe"

+0x5a8 ImageFileName : [15]  "identity_helpe"

+0x5a8 ImageFileName : [15]  "msedge.exe"

+0x5a8 ImageFileName : [15]  "msedge.exe"

+0x5a8 ImageFileName : [15]  "MiniSearchHost"

+0x5a8 ImageFileName : [15]  "Notepad.exe"

+0x5a8 ImageFileName : [15]  "dllhost.exe"

+0x5a8 ImageFileName : [15]  "CalculatorApp."

+0x5a8 ImageFileName : [15]  "RuntimeBroker."

+0x5a8 ImageFileName : [15]  "wordpad.exe"

+0x5a8 ImageFileName : [15]  "splwow64.exe"

+0x5a8 ImageFileName : [15]  "svchost.exe"

+0x5a8 ImageFileName : [15]  "LINQPad7.exe"

+0x5a8 ImageFileName : [15]  "LINQPad7.Query"

+0x5a8 ImageFileName : [15]  "cmd.exe"

+0x5a8 ImageFileName : [15]  "conhost.exe"

+0x5a8 ImageFileName : [15]  "Taskmgr.exe"

+0x5a8 ImageFileName : [15]  "TabTip.exe"

+0x5a8 ImageFileName : [15]  "notmyfault64.e"

+0x5a8 ImageFileName : [15]  "SearchHost.exe"

1: kd> !list -t nt!_EPROCESS.SessionProcessLinks.Flink -x "!process @$extret 0"
poi(ffffbe0c87efbaa0+0x10)-0x4a0
PROCESS ffffbe0c888840c0
    SessionId: 1  Cid: 0250    Peb: 7a7a825000  ParentCid: 023c
    DirBase: 134473002  ObjectTable: ffff800ed7356bc0  HandleCount: 477.
    Image: csrss.exe
```

```
PROCESS ffffbe0c888dc080
    SessionId: 1  Cid: 02b4    Peb: c208de5000  ParentCid: 023c
    DirBase: 138de6002  ObjectTable: ffff800ed87e05c0  HandleCount: 282.
    Image: winlogon.exe


PROCESS ffffbe0c889b11c0
    SessionId: 1  Cid: 0340    Peb: 2bd6122000  ParentCid: 02b4
    DirBase: 12fe08002  ObjectTable: ffff800ed88f44c0  HandleCount:  39.
    Image: fontdrvhost.exe


PROCESS ffffbe0c89120080
    SessionId: 1  Cid: 0310    Peb: 5b47b81000  ParentCid: 02b4
    DirBase: 139d66002  ObjectTable: ffff800ed8a93380  HandleCount: 1446.
    Image: dwm.exe

[...]

PROCESS ffffbe0c8b318080
    SessionId: 1  Cid: 2478    Peb: bee717e000  ParentCid: 1260
    DirBase: 73abe002  ObjectTable: ffff800edffa1500  HandleCount: 330.
    Image: LINQPad7.Query.exe


PROCESS ffffbe0c8c9d3080
    SessionId: 1  Cid: 2560    Peb: de04a58000  ParentCid: 1070
    DirBase: 3bce9002  ObjectTable: ffff800edffa9f00  HandleCount:  70.
    Image: cmd.exe


PROCESS ffffbe0c8b317080
    SessionId: 1  Cid: 2568    Peb: 1f882d7000  ParentCid: 2560
    DirBase: ba786002  ObjectTable: ffff800edff98680  HandleCount: 260.
    Image: conhost.exe


PROCESS ffffbe0c877ec080
    SessionId: 1  Cid: 2678    Peb: 21216b8000  ParentCid: 1070
    DirBase: 65669002  ObjectTable: ffff800edff8e300  HandleCount: 711.
    Image: Taskmgr.exe


PROCESS ffffbe0c8c5760c0
    SessionId: 1  Cid: 25ac    Peb: 46f82c5000  ParentCid: 0748
    DirBase: 6ee6d002  ObjectTable: 00000000  HandleCount:   0.
    Image: TabTip.exe


PROCESS ffffbe0c8c2cd0c0
    SessionId: 1  Cid: 243c    Peb: 34f5f83000  ParentCid: 1070
    DirBase: 12ea72002  ObjectTable: ffff800edff979c0  HandleCount: 176.
    Image: notmyfault64.exe

PROCESS ffffbe0c8bfb10c0
    SessionId: 1  Cid: 2434    Peb: 8e61c8c000  ParentCid: 0354
    DirBase: 09014002  ObjectTable: ffff800edff94180  HandleCount: 1383.
    Image: SearchHost.exe
```

14.   We saw that the number of session 1 processes is 63. Let's check the number of session 0 processes and the number of processes in the active process list:

```
1: kd> !vm 5
Page File: \??\C:\pagefile.sys
  Current:    4456448 Kb  Free Space:    4398516 Kb
  Minimum:    4456448 Kb  Maximum:       7704060 Kb
Page File: \??\C:\swapfile.sys
  Current:     262144 Kb  Free Space:     234936 Kb
  Minimum:     262144 Kb  Maximum:       6163248 Kb
No Name for Paging File
  Current:   11897160 Kb  Free Space:   11546468 Kb
  Minimum:   11897160 Kb  Maximum:      11897160 Kb


Physical Memory:           1048275 (    4193100 Kb)
Available Pages:            282130 (    1128520 Kb)
ResAvail Pages:             844344 (    3377376 Kb)
Locked IO Pages:                 0 (          0 Kb)
Free System PTEs:       4294988039 (17179952156 Kb)


******* 487232 kernel stack PTE allocations have failed ******


******* 1 kernel stack growth attempts have failed ******

Modified Pages:               5252 (      21008 Kb)
Modified PF Pages:            4824 (      19296 Kb)
Modified No Write Pages:        13 (         52 Kb)
NonPagedPool Usage:            130 (        520 Kb)
NonPagedPoolNx Usage:        23519 (      94076 Kb)
NonPagedPool Max:       4294967296 (17179869184 Kb)
PagedPool Usage:             38539 (     154156 Kb)
PagedPool Maximum:      4294967296 (17179869184 Kb)
Processor Commit:              401 (       1604 Kb)
Session Commit:              14595 (      58380 Kb)
Shared Commit:              104010 (     416040 Kb)
Special Pool:                    0 (          0 Kb)
Kernel Stacks:               13356 (      53424 Kb)
Pages For MDLs:               2343 (       9372 Kb)
ContigMem Pages:              2364 (       9456 Kb)
Pages For AWE:                   0 (          0 Kb)
NonPagedPool Commit:         25015 (     100060 Kb)
PagedPool Commit:            38539 (     154156 Kb)
Driver Commit:               13452 (      53808 Kb)
Boot Commit:                  4775 (      19100 Kb)
PFN Array Commit:            13317 (      53268 Kb)
SmallNonPagedPtesCommit:       158 (        632 Kb)
SlabAllocatorPages:           4608 (      18432 Kb)
System PageTables:             960 (       3840 Kb)
ProcessLockedFilePages:         16 (         64 Kb)
Pagefile Hash Pages:            78 (        312 Kb)
Sum System Commit:          233379 (     933516 Kb)
Total Private:              578643 (    2314572 Kb)
Misc/Transient Commit:         887 (       3548 Kb)
Committed pages:            812909 (    3251636 Kb)
Commit limit:              2162387 (    8649548 Kb)


Terminal Server Memory Usage By Session:
```

191

```
Session ID 0 @ ffffbe0c84f52010:
Paged Pool Usage:        2392 Kb
NonPaged Usage:            64 Kb
Commit Usage:            2760 Kb

Session ID 1 @ ffffbe0c87efbaa0:
Paged Pool Usage:       55092 Kb
NonPaged Usage:           212 Kb
Commit Usage:           55620 Kb

Session Summary
Paged Pool Usage:       57484 Kb
NonPaged Usage:           276 Kb
Commit Usage:           58380 Kb
```

```
1: kd> !validatelist ffffbe0c84f52010+10
Found list end after 92 entries
```

```
1: kd> !validatelist nt!PsActiveProcessHead
Found list end after 159 entries
```

Note: 63 + 92 = 155. There are also 4 processes that do not belong to any session: System, Registry, *smss.exe*, and MemCompression. Therefore, the numbers look correct.

15.   We close logging before exiting WinDbg:

```
1: kd> .logclose
Closing open log file C:\AdvWMDA-Dumps\x64\C3B.log
```

Exercise C4A

- **Goal:** Learn how to create scripts to extend WinDbg functionality (via built-in scripting)

- **Patterns:** Spiking Thread; Thread Waiting Time

- \AdvWMDA-Dumps\Exercise-C4A-Scripting.pdf

Exercise Ç4A: WinDbg Built-in Scripting

Goal: Learn how to create scripts to extend WinDbg functionality (via built-in scripting).

Patterns: Spiking Thread; Thread Waiting Time.

1.   Launch WinDbg.

2.   Open \AdvWMDA-Dumps\x64\MEMORY-Normal.DMP

3.   We get the dump file loaded (the output should be the same as in the previous exercise).

4.   We open a log file:

```
1: kd> .logopen C:\AdvWMDA-Dumps\x64\C4A.log
Opened log file 'C:\AdvWMDA-Dumps\x64\C4A.log'
```

5.   Our goal for this exercise is to emulate the functionality of the **!runaway** WinDbg command to show threads that spent time in the kernel and user modes greater than a certain amount. But first, we learn various time formatting commands. We display the current thread _ETHREAD and _KTHREAD thread structures:

```
1: kd> !thread -1 0
THREAD ffffbe0c8974f080  Cid 243c.1938  Teb: 00000034f5f84000 Win32Thread: ffffbe0c8cccb2a0 RUNNING on processor 1
```

```
1: kd> dt nt!_ETHREAD ffffbe0c8974f080
   +0x000 Tcb                : _KTHREAD
   +0x480 CreateTime         : _LARGE_INTEGER 0x01d81e1b`14d10996
   +0x488 ExitTime           : _LARGE_INTEGER 0xffffbe0c`8974f508
   +0x488 KeyedWaitChain     : _LIST_ENTRY [ 0xffffbe0c`8974f508 - 0xffffbe0c`8974f508 ]
   +0x498 PostBlockList      : _LIST_ENTRY [ 0x00000000`00000000 - 0x00007ffe`5af84830 ]
   +0x498 ForwardLinkShadow  : (null)
   +0x4a0 StartAddress       : 0x00007ffe`5af84830 Void
   +0x4a8 TerminationPort    : (null)
   +0x4a8 ReaperLink         : (null)
   +0x4a8 KeyedWaitValue     : (null)
   +0x4b0 ActiveTimerListLock : 0
   +0x4b8 ActiveTimerListHead : _LIST_ENTRY [ 0xffffbe0c`8974f538 - 0xffffbe0c`8974f538 ]
   +0x4c8 Cid                : _CLIENT_ID
   +0x4d8 KeyedWaitSemaphore : _KSEMAPHORE
   +0x4d8 AlpcWaitSemaphore  : _KSEMAPHORE
   +0x4f8 ClientSecurity     : _PS_CLIENT_SECURITY_CONTEXT
   +0x500 IrpList            : _LIST_ENTRY [ 0xffffbe0c`8ac38d20 - 0xffffbe0c`8ac38d20 ]
   +0x510 TopLevelIrp        : 0
   +0x518 DeviceToVerify     : (null)
   +0x520 Win32StartAddress  : 0x00007ff7`2c045b0c Void
   +0x528 ChargeOnlySession  : (null)
   +0x530 LegacyPowerObject  : (null)
   +0x538 ThreadListEntry    : _LIST_ENTRY [ 0xffffbe0c`8b5e05b8 - 0xffffbe0c`8c2cd6a0 ]
   +0x548 RundownProtect     : _EX_RUNDOWN_REF
   +0x550 ThreadLock         : _EX_PUSH_LOCK
   +0x558 ReadClusterSize    : 7
   +0x55c MmLockOrdering     : 0n0
   +0x560 CrossThreadFlags   : 0x5402
   +0x560 Terminated         : 0y0
   +0x560 ThreadInserted     : 0y1
   +0x560 HideFromDebugger   : 0y0
   +0x560 ActiveImpersonationInfo : 0y0
   +0x560 HardErrorsAreDisabled : 0y0
   +0x560 BreakOnTermination : 0y0
   +0x560 SkipCreationMsg    : 0y0
   +0x560 SkipTerminationMsg : 0y0
```

```
+0x560 CopyTokenOnOpen   : 0y0
+0x560 ThreadIoPriority  : 0y010
+0x560 ThreadPagePriority : 0y101
+0x560 RundownFail       : 0y0
+0x560 UmsForceQueueTermination : 0y0
+0x560 IndirectCpuSets   : 0y0
+0x560 DisableDynamicCodeOptOut : 0y0
+0x560 ExplicitCaseSensitivity : 0y0
+0x560 PicoNotifyExit    : 0y0
+0x560 DbgWerUserReportActive : 0y0
+0x560 ForcedSelfTrimActive : 0y0
+0x560 SamplingCoverage  : 0y0
+0x560 ReservedCrossThreadFlags : 0y00000000 (0)
+0x564 SameThreadPassiveFlags : 0
+0x564 ActiveExWorker    : 0y0
+0x564 MemoryMaker       : 0y0
+0x564 StoreLockThread   : 0y00
+0x564 ClonedThread      : 0y0
+0x564 KeyedEventInUse   : 0y0
+0x564 SelfTerminate     : 0y0
+0x564 RespectIoPriority : 0y0
+0x564 ActivePageLists   : 0y0
+0x564 SecureContext     : 0y0
+0x564 ZeroPageThread    : 0y0
+0x564 WorkloadClass     : 0y0
+0x564 ReservedSameThreadPassiveFlags : 0y00000000000000000000 (0)
+0x568 SameThreadApcFlags : 0
+0x568 OwnsProcessAddressSpaceExclusive : 0y0
+0x568 OwnsProcessAddressSpaceShared : 0y0
+0x568 HardFaultBehavior : 0y0
+0x568 StartAddressInvalid : 0y0
+0x568 EtwCalloutActive  : 0y0
+0x568 SuppressSymbolLoad : 0y0
+0x568 Prefetching       : 0y0
+0x568 OwnsVadExclusive  : 0y0
+0x569 SystemPagePriorityActive : 0y0
+0x569 SystemPagePriority : 0y000
+0x569 AllowUserWritesToExecutableMemory : 0y0
+0x569 AllowKernelWritesToExecutableMemory : 0y0
+0x569 OwnsVadShared     : 0y0
+0x569 SessionAttachActive : 0y0
+0x56a PasidMsrValid     : 0y0
+0x56c CacheManagerActive : 0 ''
+0x56d DisablePageFaultClustering : 0 ''
+0x56e ActiveFaultCount  : 0 ''
+0x56f LockOrderState    : 0 ''
+0x570 PerformanceCountLowReserved : 0
+0x574 PerformanceCountHighReserved : 0n0
+0x578 AlpcMessageId     : 0
+0x580 AlpcMessage       : (null)
+0x580 AlpcReceiveAttributeSet : 0
+0x588 AlpcWaitListEntry : _LIST_ENTRY [ 0x00000000`00000000 - 0x00000000`00000000 ]
+0x598 ExitStatus        : 0n0
+0x59c CacheManagerCount : 0
+0x5a0 IoBoostCount      : 0
+0x5a4 IoQoSBoostCount   : 0
+0x5a8 IoQoSThrottleCount : 0
+0x5ac KernelStackReference : 1
+0x5b0 BoostList         : _LIST_ENTRY [ 0xffffbe0c`8974f630 - 0xffffbe0c`8974f630 ]
+0x5c0 DeboostList       : _LIST_ENTRY [ 0xffffbe0c`8974f640 - 0xffffbe0c`8974f640 ]
+0x5d0 BoostListLock     : 0
+0x5d8 IrpListLock       : 0
+0x5e0 ReservedForSynchTracking : (null)
+0x5e8 CmCallbackListHead : _SINGLE_LIST_ENTRY
+0x5f0 ActivityId        : (null)
+0x5f8 SeLearningModeListHead : _SINGLE_LIST_ENTRY
+0x600 VerifierContext   : (null)
+0x608 AdjustedClientToken : (null)
+0x610 WorkOnBehalfThread : (null)
+0x618 PropertySet       : _PS_PROPERTY_SET
+0x630 PicoContext       : (null)
+0x638 UserFsBase        : 0
+0x640 UserGsBase        : 0
+0x648 EnergyValues      : 0xffffbe0c`8974f970 _THREAD_ENERGY_VALUES
```

```
+0x650 SelectedCpuSets    : 0
+0x650 SelectedCpuSetsIndirect : (null)
+0x658 Silo               : 0xffffffff`ffffffffd _EJOB
+0x660 ThreadName         : (null)
+0x668 SetContextState    : (null)
+0x670 LastExpectedRunTime : 0x32e2b
+0x674 HeapData           : 0x63b40000
+0x678 OwnerEntryListHead : _LIST_ENTRY [ 0xffffbe0c`8974f6f8 - 0xffffbe0c`8974f6f8 ]
+0x688 DisownedOwnerEntryListLock : 0
+0x690 DisownedOwnerEntryListHead : _LIST_ENTRY [ 0xffffbe0c`8974f710 - 0xffffbe0c`8974f710 ]
+0x6a0 LockEntries        : [6] _KLOCK_ENTRY
+0x8e0 CmThreadInfo       : (null)
+0x8e8 FlsData            : 0xffff800e`d9886b90 Void
```

```
1: kd> dt nt!_KTHREAD ffffbe0c8974f080
```

```
+0x000 Header             : _DISPATCHER_HEADER
+0x018 SListFaultAddress  : (null)
+0x020 QuantumTarget      : 0x1d56dd65
+0x028 InitialStack       : 0xffffffa28c`9d8d8fb0 Void
+0x030 StackLimit         : 0xffffffa28c`9d8d3000 Void
+0x038 StackBase          : 0xffffffa28c`9d8d9000 Void
+0x040 ThreadLock         : 0
+0x048 CycleTime          : 0x15c62c09
+0x050 CurrentRunTime     : 0x3c3bda
+0x054 ExpectedRunTime    : 0x5486d
+0x058 KernelStack        : 0xffffffa28c`9d8d82e0 Void
+0x060 StateSaveArea      : 0xffffffa28c`9fc22cc0 _XSAVE_FORMAT
+0x068 SchedulingGroup    : (null)
+0x070 WaitRegister       : _KWAIT_STATUS_REGISTER
+0x071 Running            : 0x1 ''
+0x072 Alerted            : [2]  ""
+0x074 AutoBoostActive    : 0y1
+0x074 ReadyTransition    : 0y0
+0x074 WaitNext           : 0y0
+0x074 SystemAffinityActive : 0y0
+0x074 Alertable          : 0y0
+0x074 UserStackWalkActive : 0y0
+0x074 ApcInterruptRequest : 0y0
+0x074 QuantumEndMigrate  : 0y0
+0x074 Spare1             : 0y0
+0x074 TimerActive        : 0y0
+0x074 SystemThread       : 0y0
+0x074 ProcessDetachActive : 0y0
+0x074 CalloutActive      : 0y0
+0x074 ScbReadyQueue      : 0y0
+0x074 ApcQueueable       : 0y1
+0x074 ReservedStackInUse : 0y0
+0x074 Spare2             : 0y0
+0x074 TimerSuspended     : 0y0
+0x074 SuspendedWaitMode  : 0y0
+0x074 SuspendSchedulerApcWait : 0y0
+0x074 CetUserShadowStack : 0y0
+0x074 BypassProcessFreeze : 0y0
+0x074 CetKernelShadowStack : 0y0
+0x074 StateSaveAreaDecoupled : 0y0
+0x074 IsolationWidth     : 0y0
+0x074 Reserved           : 0y0000000 (0)
+0x074 MiscFlags          : 0n16385
+0x078 UserIdealProcessorFixed : 0y0
+0x078 ThreadFlagsSpare   : 0y0
+0x078 AutoAlignment      : 0y0
+0x078 DisableBoost       : 0y0
+0x078 AlertedByThreadId  : 0y0
+0x078 QuantumDonation    : 0y0
+0x078 EnableStackSwap    : 0y1
+0x078 GuiThread          : 0y1
+0x078 DisableQuantum     : 0y0
+0x078 ChargeOnlySchedulingGroup : 0y0
+0x078 DeferPreemption    : 0y0
+0x078 QueueDeferPreemption : 0y0
+0x078 ForceDeferSchedule : 0y0
+0x078 SharedReadyQueueAffinity : 0y1
+0x078 FreezeCount        : 0y0
```

```
+0x078 TerminationApcRequest : 0y0
+0x078 AutoBoostEntriesExhausted : 0y1
+0x078 KernelStackResident : 0y1
+0x078 TerminateRequestReason : 0y00
+0x078 ProcessStackCountDecremented : 0y0
+0x078 RestrictedGuiThread : 0y0
+0x078 VpBackingThread   : 0y0
+0x078 EtwStackTraceCrimsonApcDisabled : 0y0
+0x078 EtwStackTraceApcInserted : 0y00000000 (0)
+0x078 ThreadFlags       : 0n204992
+0x07c Tag               : 0 ''
+0x07d SystemHeteroCpuPolicy : 0 ''
+0x07e UserHeteroCpuPolicy : 0y0001000 (0x8)
+0x07e ExplicitSystemHeteroCpuPolicy : 0y0
+0x07f RunningNonRetpolineCode : 0y0
+0x07f SpecCtrlSpare     : 0y0000000 (0)
+0x07f SpecCtrl          : 0 ''
+0x080 SystemCallNumber : 7
+0x084 ReadyTime         : 0xd
+0x088 FirstArgument     : 0x00000000`00000200 Void
+0x090 TrapFrame         : 0xffffa28c`9d8d8e20 _KTRAP_FRAME
+0x098 ApcState          : _KAPC_STATE
+0x098 ApcStateFill      : [43]  "???"
+0x0c3 Priority          : 12 ''
+0x0c4 UserIdealProcessor : 1
+0x0c8 WaitStatus        : 0n0
+0x0d0 WaitBlockList     : 0xffffbe0c`8974f1c0 _KWAIT_BLOCK
+0x0d8 WaitListEntry     : _LIST_ENTRY [ 0x00000000`00000000 - 0xffffff807`604eeee0 ]
+0x0d8 SwapListEntry     : _SINGLE_LIST_ENTRY
+0x0e8 Queue             : 0xffffbe0c`8b61a500 _DISPATCHER_HEADER
+0x0f0 Teb               : 0x00000034`f5f84000 Void
+0x0f8 RelativeTimerBias : 0
+0x100 Timer             : _KTIMER
+0x140 WaitBlock         : [4] _KWAIT_BLOCK
+0x140 WaitBlockFill4    : [20]  "???"
+0x154 ContextSwitches   : 0x6a5
+0x140 WaitBlockFill5    : [68]  "???"
+0x184 State             : 0x2 ''
+0x185 Spare13           : 0 ''
+0x186 WaitIrql          : 0 ''
+0x187 WaitMode          : 0 ''
+0x140 WaitBlockFill6    : [116]  "???"
+0x1b4 WaitTime          : 0x745a
+0x140 WaitBlockFill7    : [164]  "???"
+0x1e4 KernelApcDisable  : 0n-1
+0x1e6 SpecialApcDisable : 0n0
+0x1e4 CombinedApcDisable : 0xffff
+0x140 WaitBlockFill8    : [40]  "???"
+0x168 ThreadCounters    : (null)
+0x140 WaitBlockFill9    : [88]  "???"
+0x198 XStateSave        : (null)
+0x140 WaitBlockFill10   : [136]  "???"
+0x1c8 Win32Thread       : 0xffffbe0c`8cccb2a0 Void
+0x140 WaitBlockFill11   : [176]  "???"
+0x1f0 Spare18           : 0
+0x1f8 Spare19           : 0
+0x200 ThreadFlags2      : 0n0
+0x200 BamQosLevel       : 0y00000000 (0)
+0x200 ThreadFlags2Reserved : 0y0000000000000000000000000 (0)
+0x204 HgsFeedbackClass : 0 ''
+0x205 Spare21           : [3]  ""
+0x208 QueueListEntry    : _LIST_ENTRY [ 0xffffbe0c`8b61a530 - 0xffffbe0c`8b61a530 ]
+0x218 NextProcessor     : 1
+0x218 NextProcessorNumber : 0y000000000000000000000000000000001 (0x1)
+0x218 SharedReadyQueue : 0y0
+0x21c QueuePriority     : 0n0
+0x220 Process           : 0xffffbe0c`8c2cd0c0 _KPROCESS
+0x228 UserAffinity      : 0xffffbe0c`8974fa48 _KAFFINITY_EX
+0x230 UserAffinityPrimaryGroup : 0
+0x232 PreviousMode      : 1 ''
+0x233 BasePriority      : 8 ''
+0x234 PriorityDecrement : 2 ''
+0x234 ForegroundBoost   : 0y0010
+0x234 UnusualBoost      : 0y0000
```

197

```
+0x235 Preempted            : 0 ''
+0x236 AdjustReason         : 0 ''
+0x237 AdjustIncrement      : 0 ''
+0x238 AffinityVersion      : 0x18
+0x240 Affinity             : 0xffffbe0c`8974fa38 _KAFFINITY_EX
+0x248 AffinityPrimaryGroup : 0
+0x24a ApcStateIndex        : 0 ''
+0x24b WaitBlockCount       : 0x1 ''
+0x24c IdealProcessor       : 1
+0x250 NpxState             : 5
+0x258 SavedApcState        : _KAPC_STATE
+0x258 SavedApcStateFill    : [43] "???"
+0x283 WaitReason           : 0x1b ''
+0x284 SuspendCount         : 0 ''
+0x285 Saturation           : 0 ''
+0x286 SListFaultCount      : 0
+0x288 SchedulerApc         : _KAPC
+0x288 SchedulerApcFill0    : [1] "??????"
+0x289 ResourceIndex        : 0x1 ''
+0x288 SchedulerApcFill1    : [3] "???"
+0x28b QuantumReset         : 0x12 ''
+0x288 SchedulerApcFill2    : [4] "???"
+0x28c KernelTime           : 8
+0x288 SchedulerApcFill3    : [64] "???"
+0x2c8 WaitPrcb             : (null)
+0x288 SchedulerApcFill4    : [72] "???"
+0x2d0 LegoData             : (null)
+0x288 SchedulerApcFill5    : [83] "???"
+0x2db CallbackNestingLevel : 0x1 ''
+0x2dc UserTime             : 1
+0x2e0 SuspendEvent         : _KEVENT
+0x2f8 ThreadListEntry      : _LIST_ENTRY [ 0xffffbe0c`8b5e0378 - 0xffffbe0c`8c2cd0f0 ]
+0x308 MutantListHead       : _LIST_ENTRY [ 0xffffbe0c`8974f388 - 0xffffbe0c`8974f388 ]
+0x318 AbEntrySummary       : 0x3e '>'
+0x319 AbWaitEntryCount     : 0 ''
+0x31a FreezeFlags          : 0 ''
+0x31a FreezeCount2         : 0y0
+0x31a FreezeNormal         : 0y0
+0x31a FreezeDeep           : 0y0
+0x31b SystemPriority       : 0 ''
+0x31c SecureThreadCookie   : 0
+0x320 Spare22              : (null)
+0x328 PropagateBoostsEntry : _SINGLE_LIST_ENTRY
+0x330 IoSelfBoostsEntry    : _SINGLE_LIST_ENTRY
+0x338 PriorityFloorCounts  : [32] ""
+0x358 PriorityFloorSummary : 0
+0x35c AbCompletedIoBoostCount : 0n0
+0x360 AbCompletedIoQoSBoostCount : 0n0
+0x364 KeReferenceCount     : 0n0
+0x366 AbOrphanedEntrySummary : 0 ''
+0x367 AbOwnedEntryCount    : 0 ''
+0x368 ForegroundLossTime   : 0x70b8
+0x370 GlobalForegroundListEntry : _LIST_ENTRY [ 0x00000000`00000001 - 0x00000000`00000000 ]
+0x370 ForegroundDpcStackListEntry : _SINGLE_LIST_ENTRY
+0x378 InGlobalForegroundList : 0
+0x380 ReadOperationCount   : 0n1
+0x388 WriteOperationCount  : 0n4
+0x390 OtherOperationCount  : 0n276
+0x398 ReadTransferCount    : 0n60
+0x3a0 WriteTransferCount   : 0n50784
+0x3a8 OtherTransferCount   : 0n6486
+0x3b0 QueuedScb            : (null)
+0x3b8 ThreadTimerDelay     : 0
+0x3bc ThreadFlags3         : 0n0
+0x3bc ThreadFlags3Reserved : 0y00000000 (0)
+0x3bc PpmPolicy            : 0y000
+0x3bc ThreadFlags3Reserved2 : 0y00000000000000000000 (0)
+0x3c0 TracingPrivate       : [1] 0
+0x3c8 SchedulerAssist      : (null)
+0x3d0 AbWaitObject         : (null)
+0x3d8 ReservedPreviousReadyTimeValue : 0
+0x3e0 KernelWaitTime       : 0x83
+0x3e8 UserWaitTime         : 0x442
+0x3f0 GlobalUpdateVpThreadPriorityListEntry : _LIST_ENTRY [ 0x00000000`00000001 - 0x00000000`00000000 ]
```

```
+0x3f0 UpdateVpThreadPriorityDpcStackListEntry : _SINGLE_LIST_ENTRY
+0x3f8 InGlobalUpdateVpThreadPriorityList : 0
+0x400 SchedulerAssistPriorityFloor : 0n0
+0x404 RealtimePriorityFloor : 0n32
+0x408 KernelShadowStack : (null)
+0x410 KernelShadowStackInitial : (null)
+0x418 KernelShadowStackBase : (null)
+0x420 KernelShadowStackLimit : _KERNEL_SHADOW_STACK_LIMIT
+0x428 ExtendedFeatureDisableMask : 0
+0x430 HgsFeedbackStartTime : 0
+0x438 HgsFeedbackCycles : 0
+0x440 HgsInvalidFeedbackCount : 0
+0x444 HgsLowerPerfClassFeedbackCount : 0
+0x448 HgsHigherPerfClassFeedbackCount : 0
+0x44c Spare27         : 0
+0x450 SystemAffinityTokenListHead : _SINGLE_LIST_ENTRY
+0x458 IptSaveArea     : (null)
+0x460 EndPadding      : [4] 0
```

Note: We see the thread create time value **0x01d81e1b`14d10996** and Kernel(User)Time values **0x8(0x1)**. For the first one, we use the **!filetime** command that converts 64-bit values representing the number of 100-nanosecond intervals since January 1, 1601, into a readable format:

```
1: kd> !filetime 0x01d81e1b`14d10996
 2/10/2022 01:11:06.962 (GMT Standard Time)
```

Note: We compare the thread creation time with the memory dump creation time to see how long it had existed:

```
1: kd> .time
Debug session time: Thu Feb 10 01:11:26.439 2022 (UTC + 0:00)
System Uptime: 0 days 0:07:45.422
```

Note: The other 2 values are in processor ticks, and we use the **!whattime** extension command for conversion:

```
1: kd> !whattime 8
8 Ticks in Standard Time: 00.125s
```

```
1: kd> !whattime 1
1 Ticks in Standard Time: 00.015s
```

6.   We compare kernel and user times data with the output of the **!thread** command:

```
1: kd> !thread -1 3f
THREAD ffffbe0c8974f080  Cid 243c.1938  Teb: 00000034f5f84000 Win32Thread: ffffbe0c8cccb2a0 RUNNING on processor 1
IRP List:
    ffffbe0c8ac38d00: (0006,0118) Flags: 00060000  Mdl: 00000000
Not impersonating
DeviceMap             ffff800eda519d60
Owning Process        ffffbe0c8c2cd0c0       Image:         notmyfault64.exe
Attached Process      N/A             Image:         N/A
Wait Start TickCount  29786           Ticks: 1 (0:00:00:00.015)
Context Switch Count  1701            IdealProcessor: 1
UserTime              00:00:00.015
KernelTime            00:00:00.125
Unable to load image C:\Work\notmyfault64.exe, Win32 error 0n2
Win32 Start Address notmyfault64 (0x00007ff72c045b0c)
Stack Init ffffa28c9d8d8fb0 Current ffffa28c9d8d82e0
Base ffffa28c9d8d9000 Limit ffffa28c9d8d3000 Call 0000000000000000
Priority 12 BasePriority 8 PriorityDecrement 2 IoPriority 2 PagePriority 5
Unable to load image \??\C:\WINDOWS\system32\drivers\myfault.sys, Win32 error 0n2
Child-SP          RetAddr              Call Site
ffffa28c`9d8d8688 fffff807`62428da9    nt!KeBugCheckEx
ffffa28c`9d8d8690 fffff807`62424f00    nt!KiBugCheckDispatch+0x69
ffffa28c`9d8d87d0 fffff807`61781530    nt!KiPageFault+0x440 (TrapFrame @ ffffa28c`9d8d87d0)
ffffa28c`9d8d8960 fffff807`61781e2d    myfault+0x1530
ffffa28c`9d8d8990 fffff807`61781f88    myfault+0x1e2d
```

```
ffffa28c`9d8d8ae0 fffff807`62303115     myfault+0x1f88
ffffa28c`9d8d8b20 fffff807`6276bbf2     nt!IofCallDriver+0x55
ffffa28c`9d8d8b60 fffff807`6276b9d2     nt!IopSynchronousServiceTail+0x1d2
ffffa28c`9d8d8c10 fffff807`6276ad36     nt!IopXxxControlFile+0xc82
ffffa28c`9d8d8d40 fffff807`62428775     nt!NtDeviceIoControlFile+0x56
ffffa28c`9d8d8db0 00007ffe`5b023834     nt!KiSystemServiceCopyEnd+0x25 (TrapFrame @ ffffa28c`9d8d8e20)
00000034`f5d2eb88 00007ffe`58a33ffb     ntdll!NtDeviceIoControlFile+0x14
00000034`f5d2eb90 00007ffe`5a2d5f91     KERNELBASE!DeviceIoControl+0x6b
00000034`f5d2ec00 00007ff7`2c0426ce     KERNEL32!DeviceIoControlImplementation+0x81
00000034`f5d2ec50 00007ffe`5901484b     notmyfault64+0x26ce
00000034`f5d2ed50 00007ffe`5901409b     USER32!UserCallDlgProcCheckWow+0x14b
00000034`f5d2ee30 00007ffe`590597c9     USER32!DefDlgProcWorker+0xcb
00000034`f5d2eef0 00007ffe`59011c4c     USER32!DefDlgProcA+0x39
00000034`f5d2ef30 00007ffe`5901179c     USER32!UserCallWinProcCheckWow+0x33c
00000034`f5d2f0a0 00007ffe`59024b4d     USER32!DispatchClientMessage+0x9c
00000034`f5d2f100 00007ffe`5b0276a4     USER32!_fnDWORD+0x3d
00000034`f5d2f160 00007ffe`58d81434     ntdll!KiUserCallbackDispatcherContinue (TrapFrame @ 00000034`f5d2f028)
00000034`f5d2f1e8 00007ffe`590108cf     win32u!NtUserMessageCall+0x14
00000034`f5d2f1f0 00007ffe`59010737     USER32!SendMessageWorker+0x12f
00000034`f5d2f290 00007ffe`444750bf     USER32!SendMessageW+0x137
00000034`f5d2f2f0 00007ffe`444a8822     COMCTL32!Button_ReleaseCapture+0xbb
00000034`f5d2f320 00007ffe`59011c4c     COMCTL32!Button_WndProc+0x802
00000034`f5d2f430 00007ffe`59010ea6     USER32!UserCallWinProcCheckWow+0x33c
00000034`f5d2f5a0 00007ffe`59016084     USER32!DispatchMessageWorker+0x2a6
00000034`f5d2f620 00007ffe`44455f9f     USER32!IsDialogMessageW+0x104
00000034`f5d2f680 00007ffe`44455e48     COMCTL32!Prop_IsDialogMessage+0x4b
00000034`f5d2f6c0 00007ffe`44455abd     COMCTL32!_RealPropertySheet+0x2c0
00000034`f5d2f790 00007ffe`44520953     COMCTL32!_PropertySheet+0x49
00000034`f5d2f7c0 00007ff7`2c043415     COMCTL32!PropertySheetA+0x53
00000034`f5d2f860 00007ff7`2c045c68     notmyfault64+0x3415
00000034`f5d2fa90 00007ffe`5a2d54e0     notmyfault64+0x5c68
00000034`f5d2fad0 00007ffe`5af8485b     KERNEL32!BaseThreadInitThunk+0x10
00000034`f5d2fb00 00000000`00000000     ntdll!RtlUserThreadStart+0x2b
```

7.   To implement our script, we use the **!for_each_thread** command to navigate all threads in the system (**@#Thread** variable contains the address of the current thread structure).

```
1: kd> !for_each_thread "dt nt!_KTHREAD UserTime @#Thread"
   +0x2dc UserTime : 0
   +0x2dc UserTime : 0
   +0x2dc UserTime : 0
   +0x2dc UserTime : 0
[...]
   +0x2dc UserTime : 4
   +0x2dc UserTime : 2
   +0x2dc UserTime : 2
   +0x2dc UserTime : 0
   +0x2dc UserTime : 1
   +0x2dc UserTime : 0
   +0x2dc UserTime : 0
   +0x2dc UserTime : 0
   +0x2dc UserTime : 3
   +0x2dc UserTime : 0x31
   +0x2dc UserTime : 0x151
   +0x2dc UserTime : 0x23
   +0x2dc UserTime : 0
   +0x2dc UserTime : 0x51
   +0x2dc UserTime : 0
   +0x2dc UserTime : 0
   +0x2dc UserTime : 0
   +0x2dc UserTime : 0
   +0x2dc UserTime : 0
   +0x2dc UserTime : 0x1b
   +0x2dc UserTime : 0
   +0x2dc UserTime : 0x11
```

```
    +0x2dc UserTime : 0
    +0x2dc UserTime : 0
    +0x2dc UserTime : 0
    +0x2dc UserTime : 0x12
    +0x2dc UserTime : 0
    +0x2dc UserTime : 0
    +0x2dc UserTime : 0
    +0x2dc UserTime : 1
    +0x2dc UserTime : 0
[...]
```

8.   We see user time in ticks, but we don't know which thread it corresponds to, so we extend our script:

```
1: kd> !for_each_thread "dt nt!_KTHREAD UserTime @#Thread; dp @#Thread L1"
    +0x2dc UserTime : 0
ffffbe0c`841cd080  00000000`00200006
    +0x2dc UserTime : 0
ffffbe0c`84145080  00000000`00200006
    +0x2dc UserTime : 0
ffffbe0c`841bc080  00000000`00200006
    +0x2dc UserTime : 0
ffffbe0c`84189080  00000000`00200006
    +0x2dc UserTime : 0
ffffbe0c`84097480  00000000`00200006
    +0x2dc UserTime : 0
ffffbe0c`840af080  00000000`00200006
    +0x2dc UserTime : 0
ffffbe0c`8420c140  00000000`00200006
    +0x2dc UserTime : 0
ffffbe0c`84167080  00000000`00280006
[...]
    +0x2dc UserTime : 1
ffffbe0c`8b4d9040  00000000`00a00006
    +0x2dc UserTime : 0
ffffbe0c`8b5da040  00000000`00a00006
    +0x2dc UserTime : 0
ffffbe0c`8b53f040  00000000`00a00006
    +0x2dc UserTime : 0
ffffbe0c`8c889080  00000000`00a00006
    +0x2dc UserTime : 3
ffffbe0c`89121080  00000000`00a00006
    +0x2dc UserTime : 0x31
ffffbe0c`8918e080  00000000`00a00006
    +0x2dc UserTime : 0x151
ffffbe0c`89190080  00000000`00a00006
    +0x2dc UserTime : 0x23
ffffbe0c`8919d040  00000000`00a00006
    +0x2dc UserTime : 0
ffffbe0c`892130c0  00000000`00a00006
    +0x2dc UserTime : 0x51
ffffbe0c`891d4080  00000000`00a00006
    +0x2dc UserTime : 0
ffffbe0c`89211080  00000000`00a00006
    +0x2dc UserTime : 0
ffffbe0c`89210080  00000000`00a00006
    +0x2dc UserTime : 0
ffffbe0c`89281080  00000000`00a00006
    +0x2dc UserTime : 0
```

```
 fffffbe0c`8927d080  00000000`00a00006
   +0x2dc UserTime : 0
fffffbe0c`89279080  00000000`00a00006
   +0x2dc UserTime : 0x1b
fffffbe0c`89278080  00000000`00a00006
   +0x2dc UserTime : 0
fffffbe0c`892c9080  00000000`00a00006
   +0x2dc UserTime : 0x11
fffffbe0c`892c7040  00000000`00a00006
   +0x2dc UserTime : 0
fffffbe0c`89337080  00000000`00a00006
[...]
```

Note: We can now use the **!thread** command to check the thread:

```
1: kd> !thread ffffbe0c`89190080 3f
THREAD ffffbe0c89190080  Cid 0310.0428  Teb: 0000005b47b8e000 Win32Thread: ffffbe0c89099e10 RUNNING on processor 0
Not impersonating
DeviceMap                 ffff800ed8b27090
Owning Process            ffffbe0c89120080       Image:          dwm.exe
Attached Process          N/A             Image:          N/A
Wait Start TickCount      29786           Ticks: 1 (0:00:00.015)
Context Switch Count      19997           IdealProcessor: 1
UserTime                  00:00:05.265
KernelTime                00:00:03.625
Win32 Start Address dwmcore!CConnection::CompositionThreadEntryPoint (0x00007ffe54eece90)
Stack Init ffffa28c9d2cac70 Current ffffa28c9d2c9ee0
Base ffffa28c9d2cb000 Limit ffffa28c9d2c5000 Call 0000000000000000
Priority 15 BasePriority 15 PriorityDecrement 0 IoPriority 2 PagePriority 5
Child-SP          RetAddr           Call Site
0000005b`47eff318 00007ffe`552d22e4  CoreMessaging!AlpcClientConnection::PendingPortCheck
0000005b`47eff320 00007ffe`552aae27  CoreMessaging!`CFlat::DelegateImpl<System::Action,0,void
__cdecl(void),void,0>::Bind<CFlat::SmartPtr<Microsoft::CoreUI::Messaging::CrossProcessReceivePort$AlpcReceiveSource>,&Microsoft::CoreUI::Messaging::CrossProce
ssReceivePort$AlpcReceiveSource::ScheduleReceiveIfNeeded>'::`2'::Thunk::Invoke+0x24
0000005b`47eff350 00007ffe`552ca6f6  CoreMessaging!CFlat::DelegateImpl<System::Action,0,void __cdecl(void),void,0>::MulticastInvoke+0x47
0000005b`47eff380 00007ffe`552ff321  CoreMessaging!Microsoft::CoreUI::Dispatch::EventLoop::CallYieldCheckHandler+0xa2
0000005b`47eff3b0 00007ffe`552aa4bd  CoreMessaging!Microsoft::CoreUI::Dispatch::Dispatcher::PeekNextItem+0x26355
0000005b`47eff3e0 00007ffe`552a70ba  CoreMessaging!Microsoft::CoreUI::Dispatch::EventLoop::Callback_RunCoreLoop+0x1ed
0000005b`47eff4a0 00007ffe`552d280e  CoreMessaging!Microsoft::CoreUI::Dispatch::Win32EventLoopBridge::Callback_Run+0x41a
0000005b`47eff550 00007ffe`55290dcf  CoreMessaging!Microsoft::CoreUI::Dispatch::EventLoop::Callback_Run+0xae
0000005b`47eff590 00007ffe`54e698c9  CoreMessaging!Microsoft::CoreUI::IExportMessageLoopExtensions::ExportAdapter$::Run+0x19f
0000005b`47eff600 00007ffe`54e6999b  dwmcore!CComposition::ProcessBatches+0xb1
0000005b`47eff640 00007ffe`54e691c2  dwmcore!CComposition::PreRender+0x77
0000005b`47eff6d0 00007ffe`54e682c7  dwmcore!CComposition::ProcessComposition+0x4a
0000005b`47eff770 00007ffe`54e67876  dwmcore!CPartitionVerticalBlankScheduler::Render+0x5b
0000005b`47eff7d0 00007ffe`54e6684f  dwmcore!CPartitionVerticalBlankScheduler::ProcessFrame+0x102
0000005b`47eff870 00007ffe`54eed3a6  dwmcore!CPartitionVerticalBlankScheduler::ScheduleAndProcessFrame+0x8f
0000005b`47eff990 00007ffe`54eed2d6  dwmcore!CConnection::MainCompositionThreadLoop+0xba
0000005b`47effa00 00007ffe`5a2d54e0  dwmcore!CConnection::RunCompositionThread+0xfa
0000005b`47effa30 00007ffe`5af8485b  KERNEL32!BaseThreadInitThunk+0x10
0000005b`47effa60 00000000`00000000  ntdll!RtlUserThreadStart+0x2b
```

9.   Let's now check the pseudo-registers functionality. We need these to keep the last largest value of the *UserTime* field. We count the number of threads:

```
1: kd> r $t0 = 0
```

```
1: kd> !for_each_thread "r $t0 = @$t0 + 1"
```

```
1: kd> ? @$t0
Evaluate expression: 2105 = 00000000`00000839
```

Note: When we want to get the value from a variable, we append **@** to its name, for example, **@$t0**. Otherwise, a script runs much longer, checking every symbol file, and might finally fail.

10.   We know from the _KTHREAD structure that the *UserTime* field has the offset 0x2dc. We use the following algorithm: for each thread, we check the field value; if it is greater than the one we saved, we replace it and remember the current thread information. The **$t0** register holds the last saved ticks value. We, therefore, need to zero it before:

```
1: kd> r $t0 = 0
```

```
1: kd> ? @$t0
Evaluate expression: 0 = 00000000`00000000
```

11.   Now we try to dump every thread structure field value using this sample code:

```
1: kd> !for_each_thread "dd @#Thread +0x2dc L1"
ffffbe0c`841cd35c  00000000
ffffbe0c`8414535c  00000000
ffffbe0c`841bc35c  00000000
ffffbe0c`8418935c  00000000
ffffbe0c`8409775c  00000000
ffffbe0c`840af35c  00000000
ffffbe0c`8420c41c  00000000
ffffbe0c`8416735c  00000000
ffffbe0c`841de35c  00000000
ffffbe0c`8415635c  00000000
ffffbe0c`8412335c  00000000
ffffbe0c`841ef35c  00000000
ffffbe0c`8420235c  00000000
ffffbe0c`8412d35c  00000000
[...]
ffffbe0c`8b37e35c  00000000
ffffbe0c`8b79535c  00000001
ffffbe0c`8910459c  00000000
ffffbe0c`8911031c  00000000
ffffbe0c`8911135c  00000004
ffffbe0c`8911c31c  00000002
ffffbe0c`8927e35c  00000002
ffffbe0c`89def31c  00000000
ffffbe0c`8b4d931c  00000001
ffffbe0c`8b5da31c  00000000
ffffbe0c`8b53f31c  00000000
ffffbe0c`8c88935c  00000000
ffffbe0c`8912135c  00000003
ffffbe0c`8918e35c  00000031
ffffbe0c`8919035c  00000151
ffffbe0c`8919d31c  00000023
ffffbe0c`8921339c  00000000
ffffbe0c`891d435c  00000051
ffffbe0c`8921135c  00000000
ffffbe0c`8921035c  00000000
ffffbe0c`8928135c  00000000
ffffbe0c`8927d35c  00000000
ffffbe0c`8927935c  00000000
ffffbe0c`8927835c  0000001b
ffffbe0c`892c935c  00000000
ffffbe0c`892c731c  00000011
[...]
```

Note: We used the **dd** command because the field size is 4 bytes:

```
1: kd> dt nt!_KTHREAD UserTime
   +0x2dc UserTime : Uint4B
```

12.   The **poi** operator can be used to get the stored value at a specified address. We also need to either hardcode the field offset or use C++ expression macros:

```
1: kd> !for_each_thread "? poi( @#Thread +0x2dc )"
Evaluate expression: 1688849860263936 = 00060000`00000000
Evaluate expression: 1688849860263936 = 00060000`00000000
Evaluate expression: 1688849860263936 = 00060000`00000000
Evaluate expression: 1688849860263936 = 00060000`00000000
Evaluate expression: 1688849860263936 = 00060000`00000000
[...]
Evaluate expression: 1688849860263936 = 00060000`00000000
Evaluate expression: 1688849860263936 = 00060000`00000000
Evaluate expression: 1688849860263936 = 00060000`00000000
Evaluate expression: 1688849860263939 = 00060000`00000003
Evaluate expression: 1688849860263985 = 00060000`00000031
Evaluate expression: 1688849860264273 = 00060000`00000151
Evaluate expression: 1688849860263971 = 00060000`00000023
Evaluate expression: 1688849860263936 = 00060000`00000000
Evaluate expression: 1688849860264017 = 00060000`00000051
Evaluate expression: 1688849860263936 = 00060000`00000000
Evaluate expression: 1688849860263936 = 00060000`00000000
Evaluate expression: 1688849860263936 = 00060000`00000000
Evaluate expression: 1688849860263936 = 00060000`00000000
Evaluate expression: 1688849860263936 = 00060000`00000000
Evaluate expression: 1688849860263963 = 00060000`0000001b
Evaluate expression: 1688849860263936 = 00060000`00000000
Evaluate expression: 1688849860263953 = 00060000`00000011
Evaluate expression: 1688849860263936 = 00060000`00000000
Evaluate expression: 1688849860263936 = 00060000`00000000
Evaluate expression: 1688849860263936 = 00060000`00000000
Evaluate expression: 1688849860263954 = 00060000`00000012
Evaluate expression: 1688849860263936 = 00060000`00000000
Evaluate expression: 1688849860263936 = 00060000`00000000
Evaluate expression: 1688849860263936 = 00060000`00000000
Evaluate expression: 1688849860263937 = 00060000`00000001
[...]

1: kd> !for_each_thread "? poi( @#Thread + @@c++(#FIELD_OFFSET(nt!_KTHREAD, UserTime)) )"
Evaluate expression: 1688849860263936 = 00060000`00000000
Evaluate expression: 1688849860263936 = 00060000`00000000
Evaluate expression: 1688849860263936 = 00060000`00000000
Evaluate expression: 1688849860263936 = 00060000`00000000
Evaluate expression: 1688849860263936 = 00060000`00000000
[...]
Evaluate expression: 1688849860263938 = 00060000`00000002
Evaluate expression: 1688849860263938 = 00060000`00000002
Evaluate expression: 1688849860263936 = 00060000`00000000
Evaluate expression: 1688849860263937 = 00060000`00000001
Evaluate expression: 1688849860263936 = 00060000`00000000
Evaluate expression: 1688849860263936 = 00060000`00000000
Evaluate expression: 1688849860263936 = 00060000`00000000
Evaluate expression: 1688849860263939 = 00060000`00000003
Evaluate expression: 1688849860263985 = 00060000`00000031
Evaluate expression: 1688849860264273 = 00060000`00000151
Evaluate expression: 1688849860263971 = 00060000`00000023
Evaluate expression: 1688849860263936 = 00060000`00000000
Evaluate expression: 1688849860264017 = 00060000`00000051
Evaluate expression: 1688849860263936 = 00060000`00000000
```

```
Evaluate expression: 1688849860263936 = 00060000`00000000
Evaluate expression: 1688849860263936 = 00060000`00000000
Evaluate expression: 1688849860263936 = 00060000`00000000
Evaluate expression: 1688849860263936 = 00060000`00000000
Evaluate expression: 1688849860263963 = 00060000`0000001b
Evaluate expression: 1688849860263936 = 00060000`00000000
[...]
```

Note: The **$t1** register holds the current field value:

```
1: kd> !for_each_thread "r $t1 = poi( @#Thread + @@c++(#FIELD_OFFSET(nt!_KTHREAD, UserTime)) )"
```

13.   We now add comparison and save the largest value:

```
1: kd> !for_each_thread "r $t1 = poi( @#Thread + @@c++(#FIELD_OFFSET(nt!_KTHREAD, UserTime)) );
.if (@$t1 > @$t0) {r $t0 = @$t1}"
```

```
1: kd> ? @$t0
Evaluate expression: 1688849860264918 = 00060000`000003d6
```

14.   Now we save thread information for the latest largest found value in the **$t2** register (we shouldn't forget to zero our **$t0** register) and display it after the script finishes:

```
1: kd> r $t0 = 0
```

```
1: kd> !for_each_thread "r $t1 = poi( @#Thread + @@c++(#FIELD_OFFSET(nt!_KTHREAD, UserTime)) );
.if (@$t1 > @$t0) {r $t0 = @$t1; r $t2 = @#Thread}"
```

```
1: kd> !thread @$t2 3f
THREAD ffffbe0c8aef9080  Cid 1e7c.1e80  Teb: 000000a05f77c000 Win32Thread: ffffbe0c8a9945d0 WAIT:
(UserRequest) UserMode Alertable
    ffffbe0c8a357850  NotificationEvent
    ffffbe0c8a356810  SynchronizationEvent
    ffffbe0c8aba1460  NotificationEvent
    ffffbe0c8aba22e0  Semaphore Limit 0x10
    ffffbe0c89f99be0  SynchronizationEvent
    ffffbe0c8afcbf88  NotificationEvent
    ffffbe0c8aba57e0  SynchronizationEvent
    ffffbe0c890adf18  NotificationEvent
    ffffbe0c8aaecd08  NotificationEvent
    ffffbe0c8b098600  QueueObject
IRP List:
    ffffbe0c8b3ecaa0: (0006,0478) Flags: 00060000  Mdl: 00000000
    ffffbe0c897a6aa0: (0006,0478) Flags: 00060000  Mdl: 00000000
    ffffbe0c8927aaa0: (0006,0478) Flags: 00060000  Mdl: 00000000
Not impersonating
DeviceMap                 ffff800eda518d20
Owning Process            ffffbe0c8aedd080      Image:         vmtoolsd.exe
Attached Process          N/A          Image:         N/A
Wait Start TickCount      29786        Ticks: 1 (0:00:00:00.015)
Context Switch Count      24970        IdealProcessor: 1
UserTime                  00:00:15.343
KernelTime                00:00:03.203
Unable to load image C:\Program Files\VMware\VMware Tools\vmtoolsd.exe, Win32 error 0n2
Win32 Start Address vmtoolsd (0x00007ff688488580)
Stack Init ffffa28c9fa3ec70 Current ffffa28c9fa3d740
Base ffffa28c9fa3f000 Limit ffffa28c9fa39000 Call 0000000000000000
Priority 8 BasePriority 8 PriorityDecrement 0 IoPriority 2 PagePriority 5
Unable to load image C:\Program Files\VMware\VMware Tools\glib-2.0.dll, Win32 error 0n2
Child-SP          RetAddr           Call Site
ffffa28c`9fa3d780 fffff807`623327f7     nt!KiSwapContext+0x76
```

```
ffffa28c`9fa3d8c0 fffff807`623346a9     nt!KiSwapThread+0x3a7
ffffa28c`9fa3d9a0 fffff807`6228ed51     nt!KiCommitThreadWait+0x159
ffffa28c`9fa3da40 fffff807`627702c5     nt!KeWaitForMultipleObjects+0x2b1
ffffa28c`9fa3db40 ffffbc92`8e81b5ee     nt!ObWaitForMultipleObjects+0x2d5
ffffa28c`9fa3e040 ffffbc92`8e6f2346     win32kfull!xxxMsgWaitForMultipleObjectsEx+0xda
ffffa28c`9fa3e0f0 ffffbc92`8dc47420     win32kfull!NtUserMsgWaitForMultipleObjectsEx+0x406
ffffa28c`9fa3ea30 fffff807`62428775     win32k!NtUserMsgWaitForMultipleObjectsEx+0x20
ffffa28c`9fa3ea70 00007ffe`58d8abf4     nt!KiSystemServiceCopyEnd+0x25 (TrapFrame @ ffffa28c`9fa3eae0)
000000a0`5f8ff4e8 00007ffe`5901d1ee     win32u!NtUserMsgWaitForMultipleObjectsEx+0x14
000000a0`5f8ff4f0 00007ffe`49c61b48     USER32!RealMsgWaitForMultipleObjectsEx+0x1e
000000a0`5f8ff530 0000026c`64343590     glib_2_0!g_pattern_match_simple+0x138
000000a0`5f8ff538 0000026c`64352020     0x0000026c`64343590
000000a0`5f8ff540 00000000`00000029     0x0000026c`64352020
000000a0`5f8ff548 0000026c`6425c6d0     0x29
000000a0`5f8ff550 0000026c`00000002     0x0000026c`6425c6d0
000000a0`5f8ff558 000000a0`5f8ff768     0x0000026c`00000002
000000a0`5f8ff560 00000000`00000009     0x000000a0`5f8ff768
000000a0`5f8ff568 00000000`00000001     0x9
000000a0`5f8ff570 00000000`00000064     0x1
000000a0`5f8ff578 00000000`00000064     0x64
000000a0`5f8ff580 0000026c`64159990     0x64
000000a0`5f8ff588 00007ffe`49c61f54     0x0000026c`64159990
000000a0`5f8ff590 00000000`0000000a     glib_2_0!g_poll+0x184
000000a0`5f8ff598 000000a0`5f8ff5c0     0xa
000000a0`5f8ff5a0 0000026c`641598f0     0x000000a0`5f8ff5c0
000000a0`5f8ff5a8 00000000`00000000     0x0000026c`641598f0
[...]
```

15.   We repeat the same script for the *KernelTime* field:

```
1: kd> r $t0 = 0
```

```
1: kd> !for_each_thread "r $t1 = poi( @#Thread + @@c++(#FIELD_OFFSET(nt!_KTHREAD, KernelTime))
); .if (@$t1 > @$t0) {r $t0 = @$t1; r $t2 = @#Thread}"
```

```
1: kd> !thread @$t2 3f
THREAD ffffbe0c8aef9080  Cid 1e7c.1e80  Teb: 000000a05f77c000 Win32Thread: ffffbe0c8a9945d0
WAIT: (UserRequest) UserMode Alertable
    ffffbe0c8a357850  NotificationEvent
    ffffbe0c8a356810  SynchronizationEvent
    ffffbe0c8aba1460  NotificationEvent
    ffffbe0c8aba22e0  Semaphore Limit 0x10
    ffffbe0c89f99be0  SynchronizationEvent
    ffffbe0c8afcbf88  NotificationEvent
    ffffbe0c8aba57e0  SynchronizationEvent
    ffffbe0c890adf18  NotificationEvent
    ffffbe0c8aaecd08  NotificationEvent
    ffffbe0c8b098600  QueueObject
IRP List:
    ffffbe0c8b3ecaa0: (0006,0478) Flags: 00060000  Mdl: 00000000
    ffffbe0c897a6aa0: (0006,0478) Flags: 00060000  Mdl: 00000000
    ffffbe0c8927aaa0: (0006,0478) Flags: 00060000  Mdl: 00000000
Not impersonating
DeviceMap               ffff800eda518d20
Owning Process          ffffbe0c8aedd080      Image:          vmtoolsd.exe
Attached Process        N/A                   Image:          N/A
Wait Start TickCount    29786                 Ticks: 1 (0:00:00:00.015)
Context Switch Count    24970                 IdealProcessor: 1
UserTime                00:00:15.343
KernelTime              00:00:03.203
[...]
```

Note: Did you notice the strange result? It seems to be the largest kernel time is about 3 seconds. This result happened because we used **poi,** which gets a 64-bit value where the high 32-bit part is garbage. Instead, we now use the **dwo** operator, which gives us the required 32-bit field value:

```
1: kd> r $t0 = 0

1: kd> !for_each_thread "r $t1 = dwo( @#Thread + @@c++(#FIELD_OFFSET(nt!_KTHREAD, KernelTime)) ) ); .if (@$t1 > @$t0) {r $t0 = @$t1; r $t2 = @#Thread}"

1: kd> !thread @$t2 3f
THREAD ffffbe0c8412f080  Cid 0004.0050  Teb: 0000000000000000 Win32Thread: 0000000000000000
WAIT: (WrFreePage) KernelMode Non-Alertable
    fffff80762c55028  NotificationEvent
    ffffbe0c84083458  SynchronizationEvent
Not impersonating
DeviceMap                  ffff800ed4822520
Owning Process             ffffbe0c840eb040       Image:         System
Attached Process           N/A             Image:        N/A
Wait Start TickCount       28809           Ticks: 978 (0:00:00:15.281)
Context Switch Count       12783           IdealProcessor: 1
UserTime                   00:00:00.000
KernelTime                 00:00:19.359
Win32 Start Address nt!MiZeroLargePageThread (0xfffff807623be690)
Stack Init ffffa28c9caa5c70 Current ffffa28c9caa5590
Base ffffa28c9caa6000 Limit ffffa28c9caa0000 Call 0000000000000000
Priority 0 BasePriority 0 PriorityDecrement 0 IoPriority 2 PagePriority 5
Child-SP          RetAddr               Call Site
ffffa28c`9caa55d0 fffff807`623327f7     nt!KiSwapContext+0x76
ffffa28c`9caa5710 fffff807`623346a9     nt!KiSwapThread+0x3a7
ffffa28c`9caa57f0 fffff807`6228ed51     nt!KiCommitThreadWait+0x159
ffffa28c`9caa5890 fffff807`62342c19     nt!KeWaitForMultipleObjects+0x2b1
ffffa28c`9caa5990 fffff807`62342128     nt!MiReadyToZeroNextLargePage+0x179
ffffa28c`9caa5a90 fffff807`623be75d     nt!MiZeroLargePages+0xa8
ffffa28c`9caa5b60 fffff807`622478f5     nt!MiZeroLargePageThread+0xcd
ffffa28c`9caa5bf0 fffff807`6241a2d4     nt!PspSystemThreadStartup+0x55
ffffa28c`9caa5c40 00000000`00000000     nt!KiStartSystemThread+0x34
```

16.   We now run the corrected version of the script for *UserTime*:

```
1: kd> r $t0 = 0

1: kd> !for_each_thread "r $t1 = dwo( @#Thread + @@c++(#FIELD_OFFSET(nt!_KTHREAD, UserTime)) ); .if (@$t1 > @$t0) {r $t0 = @$t1; r $t2 = @#Thread}"

1: kd> !thread @$t2 3f
THREAD ffffbe0c8aef9080  Cid 1e7c.1e80  Teb: 000000a05f77c000 Win32Thread: ffffbe0c8a9945d0
WAIT: (UserRequest) UserMode Alertable
    ffffbe0c8a357850  NotificationEvent
    ffffbe0c8a356810  SynchronizationEvent
    ffffbe0c8aba1460  NotificationEvent
    ffffbe0c8aba22e0  Semaphore Limit 0x10
    ffffbe0c89f99be0  SynchronizationEvent
    ffffbe0c8afcbf88  NotificationEvent
    ffffbe0c8aba57e0  SynchronizationEvent
    ffffbe0c890adf18  NotificationEvent
    ffffbe0c8aaecd08  NotificationEvent
    ffffbe0c8b098600  QueueObject
```

```
IRP List:
    ffffbe0c8b3ecaa0: (0006,0478) Flags: 00060000  Mdl: 00000000
    ffffbe0c897a6aa0: (0006,0478) Flags: 00060000  Mdl: 00000000
    ffffbe0c8927aaa0: (0006,0478) Flags: 00060000  Mdl: 00000000
Not impersonating
DeviceMap                 ffff800eda518d20
Owning Process            ffffbe0c8aedd080        Image:          vmtoolsd.exe
Attached Process          N/A          Image:          N/A
Wait Start TickCount      29786        Ticks: 1 (0:00:00:00.015)
Context Switch Count      24970        IdealProcessor: 1
UserTime                  00:00:15.343
KernelTime                00:00:03.203
[...]
```

17.   Finally, we save both scripts in a *.wds* file. We can load and run them from the file:

```
1: kd> $$><C:\AdvWMDA-Dumps\x64\Scripts\krunaway.wds
[...]
```

18.   Please check the *"Two WinDbg Scripts That Changed the World"* article at the end of the book for a possible further development of our script (reprinted from Memory Dump Analysis Anthology, Volume 7). In addition, the WinDbg.org site contains similar scripts in the *WinDbg Scripts* section. The scripts from the article can also be found in the *\AdvWMDA-Dumps\x64\Scripts* folder.

19.   We close logging before exiting WinDbg:

```
1: kd> .logclose
Closing open log file C:\AdvWMDA-Dumps\x64\C4A.log
```

Exercise C4B

- **Goal:** Learn how to create scripts to extend WinDbg functionality (via JavaScript scripting)

- \AdvWMDA-Dumps\Exercise-C4B-Scripting.pdf

Exercise C4B: WinDbg JavaScript Scripting

Goal: Learn how to create scripts to extend WinDbg functionality (via JavaScript scripting).

1. Launch WinDbg.

2. Open \AdvWMDA-Dumps\x64\MEMORY-Normal.DMP

3. We get the dump file loaded (the output should be the same as in the previous exercise).

4. We open a log file:

```
1: kd> .logopen C:\AdvWMDA-Dumps\x64\C4B.log
Opened log file 'C:\AdvWMDA-Dumps\x64\C4B.log'
```

5. Our goal for this exercise is to emulate the functionality of the **!runaway** WinDbg command using JavaScript WinDbg scripting. We use the knowledge about _ETHREAD and _KTHREAD structures gained from the previous Exercise C4A. Familiarity with JavaScript is assumed. However, if you are familiar with modern programming languages such as Java, C# (or C and C++), you have very little difficulty understanding and modifying the scripts. WinDbg documentation[3] has much additional information not covered in this exercise.

6. We load JavaScript provider:

```
1: kd> .load jsprovider.dll
```

7. We write the following JavaScript function and save it as *krunaway.js* in the *\AdvWMDA-Dumps\x64\Scripts* folder:

```
function listThreadTimes()
{
    for (var p of host.namespace.Debugger.Sessions.First().Processes)
    {
        host.diagnostics.debugLog(p + ":\n");

        for (var t of p.Threads)
        {
            host.diagnostics.debugLog(t.KernelObject.Tcb.KernelTime + " " + t.KernelObject.Tcb.UserTime +
"\n");
        }
    }
}
```

8. We then load the script and execute the function:

```
1: kd> .scriptload C:\AdvWMDA-Dumps\x64\Scripts\krunaway.js
JavaScript script successfully loaded from 'C:\AdvWMDA-Dumps\x64\Scripts\krunaway.js'

1: kd> dx Debugger.State.Scripts.krunaway.Contents.listThreadTimes()
Idle:
14707 0
```

---

[3] https://docs.microsoft.com/en-us/windows-hardware/drivers/debugger/javascript-debugger-scripting

```
13542 0
0 0
0 0
System:
0 0
0 0
1 0
0 0
1 0
68 0
4 0
0 0
0 0
181 0
1 0
0 0
0 0
49 0
1239 0
1 0
9 0
[...]
0 0
0 1
svchost.exe:
0 0
1 0
4 4
4 2
1 2
1 0
2 1
0 0
0 0
0 0
dwm.exe:
15 3
50 49
232 337
4 35
10 0
46 81
26 0
0 0
0 0
0 0
1 0
11 27
1 0
4 17
2 0
0 0
0 0
3 18
0 0
0 0
svchost.exe:
1 0
1 1
```

```
0 0
0 0
0 0
0 0
svchost.exe:
0 1
5 1
2 0
0 0
[...]
0 0
0 1
0 0
0 1
0 0
0 0
0 0
0 0
0 1
0 1
0 0
2 1
0 0
0 0
0 0
1 0
0 0
0 0
0 0
0 0
Debugger.State.Scripts.krunaway.Contents.listThreadTimes()
```

Note: We add an "improved" function to print the *ImageFileName* field just to show that an unsigned character array has to be converted to a JavaScript string (in the earlier versions of the scripting engine, *Idle* and *System* process names were not shown) and also to print thread IDs in hex:

```
function listThreadTimesEx()
{
    for (var p of host.namespace.Debugger.Sessions.First().Processes)
    {
        var imageName = "";

        for (var c of p.KernelObject.ImageFileName)
        {
            if (!c) break;
            imageName += String.fromCharCode(c);
        }

        host.diagnostics.debugLog(imageName + "\n");

        for (var t of p.Threads)
        {
            host.diagnostics.debugLog(t.Id.toString(16) + ": " + t.KernelObject.Tcb.KernelTime + " " +
                                        t.KernelObject.Tcb.UserTime + "\n");
        }
    }
}
```

9.   We reload our script and execute the new function:

```
1: kd> .scriptlist
Command Loaded Scripts:
    NatVis script from 'C:\Program Files (x86)\Windows
Kits\10\Debuggers\x64\Visualizers\atlmfc.natvis'
    NatVis script from 'C:\Program Files (x86)\Windows
Kits\10\Debuggers\x64\Visualizers\ObjectiveC.natvis'
    NatVis script from 'C:\Program Files (x86)\Windows
Kits\10\Debuggers\x64\Visualizers\concurrency.natvis'
    NatVis script from 'C:\Program Files (x86)\Windows
Kits\10\Debuggers\x64\Visualizers\cpp_rest.natvis'
    NatVis script from 'C:\Program Files (x86)\Windows
Kits\10\Debuggers\x64\Visualizers\Kernel.natvis'
    NatVis script from 'C:\Program Files (x86)\Windows
Kits\10\Debuggers\x64\Visualizers\stl.natvis'
    NatVis script from 'C:\Program Files (x86)\Windows
Kits\10\Debuggers\x64\Visualizers\Windows.Data.Json.natvis'
    NatVis script from 'C:\Program Files (x86)\Windows
Kits\10\Debuggers\x64\Visualizers\Windows.Devices.Geolocation.natvis'
    NatVis script from 'C:\Program Files (x86)\Windows
Kits\10\Debuggers\x64\Visualizers\Windows.Devices.Sensors.natvis'
    NatVis script from 'C:\Program Files (x86)\Windows
Kits\10\Debuggers\x64\Visualizers\Windows.Media.natvis'
    NatVis script from 'C:\Program Files (x86)\Windows
Kits\10\Debuggers\x64\Visualizers\windows.natvis'
    NatVis script from 'C:\Program Files (x86)\Windows
Kits\10\Debuggers\x64\Visualizers\winrt.natvis'
    JavaScript script from 'C:\AdvWMDA-Dumps\x64\Scripts\krunaway.js'
Other Clients' Scripts:
    <None Loaded>

1: kd> .scriptunload C:\AdvWMDA-Dumps\x64\Scripts\krunaway.js
JavaScript script unloaded from 'C:\AdvWMDA-Dumps\x64\Scripts\krunaway.js'

1: kd> .scriptlist
Command Loaded Scripts:
    NatVis script from 'C:\Program Files (x86)\Windows
Kits\10\Debuggers\x64\Visualizers\atlmfc.natvis'
    NatVis script from 'C:\Program Files (x86)\Windows
Kits\10\Debuggers\x64\Visualizers\ObjectiveC.natvis'
    NatVis script from 'C:\Program Files (x86)\Windows
Kits\10\Debuggers\x64\Visualizers\concurrency.natvis'
    NatVis script from 'C:\Program Files (x86)\Windows
Kits\10\Debuggers\x64\Visualizers\cpp_rest.natvis'
    NatVis script from 'C:\Program Files (x86)\Windows
Kits\10\Debuggers\x64\Visualizers\Kernel.natvis'
    NatVis script from 'C:\Program Files (x86)\Windows
Kits\10\Debuggers\x64\Visualizers\stl.natvis'
    NatVis script from 'C:\Program Files (x86)\Windows
Kits\10\Debuggers\x64\Visualizers\Windows.Data.Json.natvis'
    NatVis script from 'C:\Program Files (x86)\Windows
Kits\10\Debuggers\x64\Visualizers\Windows.Devices.Geolocation.natvis'
    NatVis script from 'C:\Program Files (x86)\Windows
Kits\10\Debuggers\x64\Visualizers\Windows.Devices.Sensors.natvis'
    NatVis script from 'C:\Program Files (x86)\Windows
Kits\10\Debuggers\x64\Visualizers\Windows.Media.natvis'
```

```
    NatVis script from 'C:\Program Files (x86)\Windows
Kits\10\Debuggers\x64\Visualizers\windows.natvis'
    NatVis script from 'C:\Program Files (x86)\Windows
Kits\10\Debuggers\x64\Visualizers\winrt.natvis'
Other Clients' Scripts:
    <None Loaded>
```

```
1: kd> .scriptload C:\AdvWMDA-Dumps\x64\Scripts\krunaway.js
JavaScript script successfully loaded from 'C:\AdvWMDA-Dumps\x64\Scripts\krunaway.js'
```

```
1: kd> dx Debugger.State.Scripts.krunaway.Contents.listThreadTimesEx()
Idle
0: 14707 0
0: 13542 0
2c: 0 0
34: 0 0
System
c: 0 0
10: 0 0
14: 1 0
18: 0 0
1c: 1 0
20: 68 0
24: 4 0
28: 0 0
30: 0 0
38: 181 0
3c: 1 0
40: 0 0
44: 0 0
4c: 49 0
50: 1239 0
54: 1 0
58: 9 0
5c: 0 0
60: 0 0
6c: 57 0
[...]
19dc: 2 6
1dd8: 0 0
c44: 0 1
svchost.exe
1b0: 0 0
1f0: 1 0
240: 4 4
2d0: 4 2
54c: 1 2
1b68: 1 0
4cc: 2 1
22c8: 0 0
26d4: 0 0
26a4: 0 0
dwm.exe
288: 15 3
420: 50 49
428: 232 337
448: 4 35
510: 10 0
514: 46 81
```

```
518: 26 0
51c: 0 0
53c: 0 0
550: 0 0
564: 1 0
568: 11 27
56c: 1 0
574: 4 17
5e0: 2 0
66c: 0 0
171c: 0 0
1720: 3 18
744: 0 0
27f0: 0 0
svchost.exe
450: 1 0
500: 1 1
520: 0 0
[...]
```

10.   We now add another function that lists thread times greater than some tick value (we also add code to skip the Idle process since it always has high CPU consumption values because its idle threads are executed if there are no other real threads to execute):

```
function findThreadTimesGreaterThan(ticks)
{
    for (var p of host.namespace.Debugger.Sessions.First().Processes)
    {
        var imageName = "";

        for (var c of p.KernelObject.ImageFileName)
        {
            if (!c) break;
            imageName += String.fromCharCode(c);
        }

        if (imageName == "Idle") continue;

        host.diagnostics.debugLog(imageName + "\n");

        for (var t of p.Threads)
        {
            if (t.KernelObject.Tcb.KernelTime > ticks || t.KernelObject.Tcb.UserTime > ticks)
            {
                host.diagnostics.debugLog(t.Id.toString(16) + ": " + t.KernelObject.Tcb.KernelTime + " "
                                          + t.KernelObject.Tcb.UserTime + "\n");
            }
        }
    }
}
```

```
1: kd> .scriptunload C:\AdvWMDA-Dumps\x64\Scripts\krunaway.js
JavaScript script unloaded from 'C:\AdvWMDA-Dumps\x64\Scripts\krunaway.js'

1: kd> .scriptload C:\AdvWMDA-Dumps\x64\Scripts\krunaway.js
JavaScript script successfully loaded from 'C:\AdvWMDA-Dumps\x64\Scripts\krunaway.js'

1: kd> dx Debugger.State.Scripts.krunaway.Contents.findThreadTimesGreaterThan(200)
System
50: 1239 0
```

215

1f8: 235 0
Registry
smss.exe
csrss.exe
wininit.exe
csrss.exe
services.exe
lsass.exe
winlogon.exe
fontdrvhost.ex
fontdrvhost.ex
svchost.exe
WUDFHost.exe
svchost.exe
svchost.exe
dwm.exe
428: 232 337
svchost.exe
svchost.exe
svchost.exe
svchost.exe
svchost.exe
svchost.exe
svchost.exe
svchost.exe
svchost.exe
svchost.exe
svchost.exe
svchost.exe
svchost.exe
svchost.exe
svchost.exe
svchost.exe
svchost.exe
svchost.exe
svchost.exe
svchost.exe
svchost.exe
svchost.exe
svchost.exe
8d0: 171 406
svchost.exe
svchost.exe
MemCompression
8f8: 232 0
svchost.exe
svchost.exe
svchost.exe
svchost.exe
svchost.exe
svchost.exe
svchost.exe
svchost.exe
svchost.exe
spoolsv.exe
svchost.exe
svchost.exe
svchost.exe

```
svchost.exe
svchost.exe
svchost.exe
svchost.exe
svchost.exe
svchost.exe
VGAuthService.
vmtoolsd.exe
MsMpEng.exe
13c8:  92 213
svchost.exe
svchost.exe
svchost.exe
dllhost.exe
AggregatorHost
svchost.exe
msdtc.exe
svchost.exe
WmiPrvSE.exe
sihost.exe
svchost.exe
svchost.exe
taskhostw.exe
taskhostw.exe
svchost.exe
MsMpEngCP.exe
13e4:  101 937
1634:  56 390
svchost.exe
userinit.exe
explorer.exe
14f0:  231 138
svchost.exe
svchost.exe
svchost.exe
WmiPrvSE.exe
NisSrv.exe
svchost.exe
SearchIndexer.
svchost.exe
svchost.exe
SearchHost.exe
191c:  53 222
StartMenuExper
svchost.exe
RuntimeBroker.
svchost.exe
RuntimeBroker.
svchost.exe
dllhost.exe
svchost.exe
YourPhone.exe
ctfmon.exe
svchost.exe
TabTip.exe
WmiApSrv.exe
RuntimeBroker.
smartscreen.ex
SecurityHealth
```

```
SecurityHealth
vmtoolsd.exe
1e80: 205 982
ApplicationFra
TextInputHost.
vm3dservice.ex
OneDrive.exe
msedge.exe
Cortana.exe
RuntimeBroker.
svchost.exe
svchost.exe
svchost.exe
svchost.exe
svchost.exe
Win32Bridge.Se
SystemSettings
svchost.exe
UserOOBEBroker
SgrmBroker.exe
svchost.exe
svchost.exe
svchost.exe
msedge.exe
msedge.exe
msedge.exe
794: 299 277
msedge.exe
msedge.exe
msedge.exe
identity_helpe
msedge.exe
18e4: 59 232
msedge.exe
MiniSearchHost
Notepad.exe
dllhost.exe
CalculatorApp.
RuntimeBroker.
wordpad.exe
splwow64.exe
svchost.exe
svchost.exe
LINQPad7.exe
LINQPad7.Query
cmd.exe
conhost.exe
Taskmgr.exe
audiodg.exe
TabTip.exe
notmyfault64.e
SearchHost.exe
Debugger.State.Scripts.krunaway.Contents.findThreadTimesGreaterThan(200)
```

11.   We add another function that, in addition to the previous functionality, also prints stack traces:

```
function findThreadTimesGreaterThanWithStackTrace(ticks)
{
    for (var p of host.namespace.Debugger.Sessions.First().Processes)
    {
        var imageName = "";

        for (var c of p.KernelObject.ImageFileName)
        {
            if (!c) break;
            imageName += String.fromCharCode(c);
        }

        if (imageName == "Idle") continue;

        host.diagnostics.debugLog(imageName + "\n");

        for (var t of p.Threads)
        {
            if (t.KernelObject.Tcb.KernelTime > ticks || t.KernelObject.Tcb.UserTime > ticks)
            {
                host.diagnostics.debugLog(t.KernelObject.Tcb.KernelTime + " " +
t.KernelObject.Tcb.UserTime + "\n");
                for (var st of t.Stack.Frames)
                {
                    host.diagnostics.debugLog(st.toString() + "\n");
                }
            }
        }
    }
}
```

```
1: kd> .scriptunload C:\AdvWMDA-Dumps\x64\Scripts\krunaway.js
JavaScript script unloaded from 'C:\AdvWMDA-Dumps\x64\Scripts\krunaway.js'

1: kd> .scriptload C:\AdvWMDA-Dumps\x64\Scripts\krunaway.js
JavaScript script successfully loaded from 'C:\AdvWMDA-Dumps\x64\Scripts\krunaway.js'

1: kd> dx
Debugger.State.Scripts.krunaway.Contents.findThreadTimesGreaterThanWithStackTrace(200)
System
50: 1239 0
nt!KiSwapContext + 0x76
nt!KiSwapThread + 0x3a7
nt!KiCommitThreadWait + 0x159
nt!KeWaitForMultipleObjects + 0x2b1
nt!MiReadyToZeroNextLargePage + 0x179
nt!MiZeroLargePages + 0xa8
nt!MiZeroLargePageThread + 0xcd
nt!PspSystemThreadStartup + 0x55
nt!KiStartSystemThread + 0x34
1f8: 235 0
nt!KiSwapContext + 0x76
nt!KiSwapThread + 0x3a7
nt!KiCommitThreadWait + 0x159
nt!KeWaitForMultipleObjects + 0x2b1
nt!MiModifiedPageWriter + 0x112
nt!PspSystemThreadStartup + 0x55
nt!KiStartSystemThread + 0x34
Registry
smss.exe
csrss.exe
wininit.exe
```

```
csrss.exe
services.exe
lsass.exe
winlogon.exe
fontdrvhost.ex
fontdrvhost.ex
svchost.exe
WUDFHost.exe
svchost.exe
svchost.exe
dwm.exe
428: 232 337
CoreMessaging!AlpcClientConnection::PendingPortCheck
svchost.exe
svchost.exe
svchost.exe
svchost.exe
svchost.exe
svchost.exe
svchost.exe
svchost.exe
svchost.exe
svchost.exe
svchost.exe
svchost.exe
svchost.exe
svchost.exe
svchost.exe
svchost.exe
svchost.exe
svchost.exe
svchost.exe
svchost.exe
svchost.exe
8d0: 171 406
nt!KiSwapContext + 0x76
nt!KiSwapThread + 0x3a7
nt!KiCommitThreadWait + 0x159
nt!KeWaitForMultipleObjects + 0x2b1
nt!ObWaitForMultipleObjects + 0x2d5
nt!NtWaitForMultipleObjects + 0x119
nt!KiSystemServiceCopyEnd + 0x25
ntdll!NtWaitForMultipleObjects + 0x14
svchost.exe
svchost.exe
MemCompression
8f8: 232 0
nt!KiSwapContext + 0x76
nt!KiSwapThread + 0x3a7
nt!KiCommitThreadWait + 0x159
nt!KeWaitForSingleObject + 0x234
nt!SMKM_STORE_MGR<SM_TRAITS>::SmCompressCtxWorkerThread + 0xd5
nt!PspSystemThreadStartup + 0x55
nt!KiStartSystemThread + 0x34
svchost.exe
svchost.exe
svchost.exe
svchost.exe
svchost.exe
svchost.exe
svchost.exe
svchost.exe
```

```
svchost.exe
spoolsv.exe
svchost.exe
svchost.exe
svchost.exe
svchost.exe
svchost.exe
svchost.exe
svchost.exe
svchost.exe
svchost.exe
VGAuthService.
vmtoolsd.exe
MsMpEng.exe
13c8: 92 213
nt!KiSwapContext + 0x76
nt!KiSwapThread + 0x3a7
nt!KiCommitThreadWait + 0x159
nt!KeRemoveQueueEx + 0x2b6
nt!IoRemoveIoCompletion + 0x98
nt!NtWaitForWorkViaWorkerFactory + 0x39c
nt!KiSystemServiceCopyEnd + 0x25
ntdll!NtWaitForWorkViaWorkerFactory + 0x14
svchost.exe
svchost.exe
svchost.exe
dllhost.exe
AggregatorHost
svchost.exe
msdtc.exe
svchost.exe
WmiPrvSE.exe
sihost.exe
svchost.exe
svchost.exe
taskhostw.exe
taskhostw.exe
svchost.exe
MsMpEngCP.exe
13e4: 101 937
nt!KiSwapContext + 0x76
nt!KiSwapThread + 0x3a7
nt!KiCommitThreadWait + 0x159
nt!KeRemoveQueueEx + 0x2b6
nt!IoRemoveIoCompletion + 0x98
nt!NtWaitForWorkViaWorkerFactory + 0x39c
nt!KiSystemServiceCopyEnd + 0x25
ntdll!NtWaitForWorkViaWorkerFactory + 0x14
1634: 56 390
nt!KiSwapContext + 0x76
nt!KiSwapThread + 0x3a7
nt!KiCommitThreadWait + 0x159
nt!KeRemoveQueueEx + 0x2b6
nt!IoRemoveIoCompletion + 0x98
nt!NtWaitForWorkViaWorkerFactory + 0x39c
nt!KiSystemServiceCopyEnd + 0x25
ntdll!NtWaitForWorkViaWorkerFactory + 0x14
svchost.exe
userinit.exe
explorer.exe
14f0: 231 138
nt!KxDispatchInterrupt + 0x151
nt!KiDpcInterruptBypass + 0x25
nt!KiInterruptDispatchNoLockNoEtw + 0xb1
nt!KiSystemServiceUser + 0xbb
```

ntdll!NtTraceControl + 0x14
svchost.exe
svchost.exe
svchost.exe
WmiPrvSE.exe
NisSrv.exe
svchost.exe
SearchIndexer.
svchost.exe
svchost.exe
SearchHost.exe
191c: 53 222
nt!KiSwapContext + 0x76
nt!KiSwapThread + 0x3a7
nt!KiCommitThreadWait + 0x159
nt!KeWaitForMultipleObjects + 0x2b1
nt!ObWaitForMultipleObjects + 0x2d5
win32kfull!xxxMsgWaitForMultipleObjectsEx + 0xda
win32kfull!NtUserMsgWaitForMultipleObjectsEx + 0x406
win32k!NtUserMsgWaitForMultipleObjectsEx + 0x20
nt!KiSystemServiceCopyEnd + 0x25
win32u!NtUserMsgWaitForMultipleObjectsEx + 0x14
StartMenuExper
svchost.exe
RuntimeBroker.
svchost.exe
RuntimeBroker.
svchost.exe
dllhost.exe
svchost.exe
YourPhone.exe
ctfmon.exe
svchost.exe
TabTip.exe
WmiApSrv.exe
RuntimeBroker.
smartscreen.ex
SecurityHealth
SecurityHealth
vmtoolsd.exe
1e80: 205 982
nt!KiSwapContext + 0x76
nt!KiSwapThread + 0x3a7
nt!KiCommitThreadWait + 0x159
nt!KeWaitForMultipleObjects + 0x2b1
nt!ObWaitForMultipleObjects + 0x2d5
win32kfull!xxxMsgWaitForMultipleObjectsEx + 0xda
win32kfull!NtUserMsgWaitForMultipleObjectsEx + 0x406
win32k!NtUserMsgWaitForMultipleObjectsEx + 0x20
nt!KiSystemServiceCopyEnd + 0x25
win32u!NtUserMsgWaitForMultipleObjectsEx + 0x14
ApplicationFra
TextInputHost.
vm3dservice.ex
OneDrive.exe
msedge.exe
Cortana.exe
RuntimeBroker.
svchost.exe
svchost.exe
svchost.exe
svchost.exe
svchost.exe
Win32Bridge.Se
SystemSettings

```
svchost.exe
UserOOBEBroker
SgrmBroker.exe
svchost.exe
svchost.exe
svchost.exe
msedge.exe
msedge.exe
msedge.exe
794: 299 277
nt!KiSwapContext + 0x76
nt!KiSwapThread + 0x3a7
nt!KiCommitThreadWait + 0x159
nt!KeWaitForSingleObject + 0x234
nt!KeWaitForMultipleObjects + 0x540
nt!ObWaitForMultipleObjects + 0x2d5
win32kfull!xxxMsgWaitForMultipleObjectsEx + 0xda
win32kfull!NtUserMsgWaitForMultipleObjectsEx + 0x406
win32k!NtUserMsgWaitForMultipleObjectsEx + 0x20
nt!KiSystemServiceCopyEnd + 0x25
win32u!NtUserMsgWaitForMultipleObjectsEx + 0x14
msedge.exe
msedge.exe
msedge.exe
identity_helpe
msedge.exe
18e4: 59 232
nt!KiSwapContext + 0x76
nt!KiSwapThread + 0x3a7
nt!KiCommitThreadWait + 0x159
nt!KeWaitForSingleObject + 0x234
nt!ObWaitForSingleObject + 0xbb
nt!NtWaitForSingleObject + 0x6a
nt!KiSystemServiceCopyEnd + 0x25
ntdll!NtWaitForSingleObject + 0x14
msedge.exe
MiniSearchHost
Notepad.exe
dllhost.exe
CalculatorApp.
RuntimeBroker.
wordpad.exe
splwow64.exe
svchost.exe
svchost.exe
LINQPad7.exe
LINQPad7.Query
cmd.exe
conhost.exe
Taskmgr.exe
audiodg.exe
TabTip.exe
notmyfault64.e
SearchHost.exe
Debugger.State.Scripts.krunaway.Contents.findThreadTimesGreaterThanWithStackTrace(200)
```

Note: We see that user space stack traces are truncated, most likely because no process context was set. Although it is possible to execute WinDbg commands inside JavaScript, commands that change process context seem put the **dx** command into an infinite loop, and WinDbg hangs. Therefore, we use an alternative approach in the next step.

12.   We add a generator function (function*) that returns found thread objects that can be further inspected by **dx -r2** command:

223

```
function *findThreadTimesGreaterThanEx(ticks)
{
    for (var p of host.namespace.Debugger.Sessions.First().Processes)
    {
        var imageName = "";

        for (var c of p.KernelObject.ImageFileName)
        {
            if (!c) break;
            imageName += String.fromCharCode(c);
        }

        if (imageName == "Idle") continue;

        host.diagnostics.debugLog(imageName + "\n");

        for (var t of p.Threads)
        {
            if (t.KernelObject.Tcb.KernelTime > ticks || t.KernelObject.Tcb.UserTime > ticks)
            {
                yield t;
            }
        }
    }
}
```

```
1: kd> .scriptunload C:\AdvWMDA-Dumps\x64\Scripts\krunaway.js
JavaScript script unloaded from 'C:\AdvWMDA-Dumps\x64\Scripts\krunaway.js'
```

```
1: kd> .scriptload C:\AdvWMDA-Dumps\x64\Scripts\krunaway.js
JavaScript script successfully loaded from 'C:\AdvWMDA-Dumps\x64\Scripts\krunaway.js'
```

```
1: kd> dx -r2 Debugger.State.Scripts.krunaway.Contents.findThreadTimesGreaterThanEx(200)
```

```
Debugger.State.Scripts.krunaway.Contents.findThreadTimesGreaterThanEx(200)                   : [object Generator]
System
    [0x0]              : nt!KiSwapContext+0x76 (fffff807`6241dce6)  [Switch To]
        KernelObject     [Type: _ETHREAD]
        Id               : 0x50
        Stack
        Registers
        Environment
    [0x1]              : nt!KiSwapContext+0x76 (fffff807`6241dce6)  [Switch To]
        KernelObject     [Type: _ETHREAD]
        Id               : 0x1f8
        Stack
        Registers
        Environment
Registry
smss.exe
csrss.exe
wininit.exe
csrss.exe
services.exe
lsass.exe
winlogon.exe
fontdrvhost.ex
fontdrvhost.ex
svchost.exe
WUDFHost.exe
svchost.exe
svchost.exe
dwm.exe
    [0x2]              : CoreMessaging!AlpcClientConnection::PendingPortCheck (00007ffe`552d2700)  [Switch To]
        KernelObject     [Type: _ETHREAD]
        Id               : 0x428
        Stack
```

224

```
                Registers
                Environment
svchost.exe
svchost.exe
svchost.exe
svchost.exe
svchost.exe
svchost.exe
svchost.exe
svchost.exe
svchost.exe
svchost.exe
svchost.exe
svchost.exe
svchost.exe
svchost.exe
svchost.exe
svchost.exe
svchost.exe
svchost.exe
svchost.exe
svchost.exe
svchost.exe
svchost.exe
    [0x3]              : nt!KiSwapContext+0x76 (fffff807`6241dce6)  [Switch To]
        KernelObject    [Type: _ETHREAD]
        Id              : 0x8d0
        Stack
        Registers
        Environment
svchost.exe
svchost.exe
MemCompression
    [0x4]              : nt!KiSwapContext+0x76 (fffff807`6241dce6)  [Switch To]
        KernelObject    [Type: _ETHREAD]
        Id              : 0x8f8
        Stack
        Registers
        Environment
svchost.exe
svchost.exe
svchost.exe
svchost.exe
svchost.exe
svchost.exe
svchost.exe
svchost.exe
svchost.exe
spoolsv.exe
svchost.exe
svchost.exe
svchost.exe
svchost.exe
svchost.exe
svchost.exe
svchost.exe
svchost.exe
svchost.exe
VGAuthService.
vmtoolsd.exe
MsMpEng.exe
    [0x5]              : nt!KiSwapContext+0x76 (fffff807`6241dce6)  [Switch To]
        KernelObject    [Type: _ETHREAD]
        Id              : 0x13c8
        Stack
        Registers
        Environment
svchost.exe
svchost.exe
svchost.exe
dllhost.exe
AggregatorHost
```

```
svchost.exe
msdtc.exe
svchost.exe
WmiPrvSE.exe
sihost.exe
svchost.exe
svchost.exe
taskhostw.exe
taskhostw.exe
svchost.exe
MsMpEngCP.exe
    [0x6]               : nt!KiSwapContext+0x76 (fffff807`6241dce6)  [Switch To]
        KernelObject    [Type: _ETHREAD]
        Id              : 0x13e4
        Stack
        Registers
        Environment
    [0x7]               : nt!KiSwapContext+0x76 (fffff807`6241dce6)  [Switch To]
        KernelObject    [Type: _ETHREAD]
        Id              : 0x1634
        Stack
        Registers
        Environment
svchost.exe
userinit.exe
explorer.exe
    [0x8]               : nt!KxDispatchInterrupt+0x151 (fffff807`6241df31)  [Switch To]
        KernelObject    [Type: _ETHREAD]
        Id              : 0x14f0
        Stack
        Registers
        Environment
svchost.exe
svchost.exe
svchost.exe
WmiPrvSE.exe
NisSrv.exe
svchost.exe
SearchIndexer.
svchost.exe
svchost.exe
SearchHost.exe
    [0x9]               : nt!KiSwapContext+0x76 (fffff807`6241dce6)  [Switch To]
        KernelObject    [Type: _ETHREAD]
        Id              : 0x191c
        Stack
        Registers
        Environment
StartMenuExper
svchost.exe
RuntimeBroker.
svchost.exe
RuntimeBroker.
svchost.exe
dllhost.exe
svchost.exe
YourPhone.exe
ctfmon.exe
svchost.exe
TabTip.exe
WmiApSrv.exe
RuntimeBroker.
smartscreen.ex
SecurityHealth
SecurityHealth
vmtoolsd.exe
    [0xa]               : nt!KiSwapContext+0x76 (fffff807`6241dce6)  [Switch To]
        KernelObject    [Type: _ETHREAD]
        Id              : 0x1e80
        Stack
        Registers
        Environment
ApplicationFra
TextInputHost.
```

```
vm3dservice.ex
OneDrive.exe
msedge.exe
Cortana.exe
RuntimeBroker.
svchost.exe
svchost.exe
svchost.exe
svchost.exe
svchost.exe
Win32Bridge.Se
SystemSettings
svchost.exe
UserOOBEBroker
SgrmBroker.exe
svchost.exe
svchost.exe
svchost.exe
msedge.exe
msedge.exe
msedge.exe
        [0xb]           : nt!KiSwapContext+0x76 (fffff807`6241dce6)  [Switch To]
            KernelObject    [Type: _ETHREAD]
            Id              : 0x794
            Stack
            Registers
            Environment
msedge.exe
msedge.exe
msedge.exe
identity_helpe
msedge.exe
        [0xc]           : nt!KiSwapContext+0x76 (fffff807`6241dce6)  [Switch To]
            KernelObject    [Type: _ETHREAD]
            Id              : 0x18e4
            Stack
            Registers
            Environment
msedge.exe
MiniSearchHost
Notepad.exe
dllhost.exe
CalculatorApp.
RuntimeBroker.
wordpad.exe
splwow64.exe
svchost.exe
svchost.exe
LINQPad7.exe
LINQPad7.Query
cmd.exe
conhost.exe
Taskmgr.exe
audiodg.exe
TabTip.exe
notmyfault64.e
SearchHost.exe
```

Note: Since we know thread IDs, we can inspect individual threads:

```
1: kd> !thread -t 0x428 3f
THREAD ffffbe0c89190080  Cid 0310.0428  Teb: 0000005b47b8e000 Win32Thread: ffffbe0c89099e10 RUNNING on processor 0
Not impersonating
DeviceMap               ffff800ed8b27090
Owning Process          ffffbe0c89120080      Image:         dwm.exe
Attached Process        N/A            Image:        N/A
Wait Start TickCount    29786          Ticks: 1 (0:00:00:00.015)
Context Switch Count    19997          IdealProcessor: 1
UserTime                00:00:05.265
KernelTime              00:00:03.625
Win32 Start Address dwmcore!CConnection::CompositionThreadEntryPoint (0x00007ffe54eece90)
Stack Init ffffa28c9d2cac70 Current ffffa28c9d2c9ee0
Base ffffa28c9d2cb000 Limit ffffa28c9d2c5000 Call 0000000000000000
Priority 15 BasePriority 15 PriorityDecrement 0 IoPriority 2 PagePriority 5
```

```
Child-SP          RetAddr           Call Site
0000005b`47eff318 00007ffe`552d22e4 CoreMessaging!AlpcClientConnection::PendingPortCheck
0000005b`47eff320 00007ffe`552aae27 CoreMessaging!`CFlat::DelegateImpl<System::Action,0,void
__cdecl(void),void,0>::Bind<CFlat::SmartPtr<Microsoft::CoreUI::Messaging::CrossProcessReceivePort$AlpcReceiveSource>,&Microsoft::CoreUI
::Messaging::CrossProcessReceivePort$AlpcReceiveSource::ScheduleReceiveIfNeeded>'::`2'::Thunk::Invoke+0x24
0000005b`47eff350 00007ffe`552ca6f6 CoreMessaging!CFlat::DelegateImpl<System::Action,0,void
__cdecl(void),void,0>::MulticastInvoke+0x47
0000005b`47eff380 00007ffe`552ff321 CoreMessaging!Microsoft::CoreUI::Dispatch::EventLoop::CallYieldCheckHandler+0xa2
0000005b`47eff3b0 00007ffe`552aa4bd CoreMessaging!Microsoft::CoreUI::Dispatch::Dispatcher::PeekNextItem+0x26355
0000005b`47eff3e0 00007ffe`552a70ba CoreMessaging!Microsoft::CoreUI::Dispatch::EventLoop::Callback_RunCoreLoop+0x1ed
0000005b`47eff4a0 00007ffe`552d280e CoreMessaging!Microsoft::CoreUI::Dispatch::Win32EventLoopBridge::Callback_Run+0x41a
0000005b`47eff550 00007ffe`55290dcf CoreMessaging!Microsoft::CoreUI::Dispatch::EventLoop::Callback_Run+0xae
0000005b`47eff590 00007ffe`54e698c9 CoreMessaging!Microsoft::CoreUI::IExportMessageLoopExtensions::ExportAdapter$::Run+0x19f
0000005b`47eff600 00007ffe`54e6999b dwmcore!CComposition::ProcessBatches+0xb1
0000005b`47eff640 00007ffe`54e691c2 dwmcore!CComposition::PreRender+0x77
0000005b`47eff6d0 00007ffe`54e682c7 dwmcore!CComposition::ProcessComposition+0x4a
0000005b`47eff770 00007ffe`54e67876 dwmcore!CPartitionVerticalBlankScheduler::Render+0x5b
0000005b`47eff7d0 00007ffe`54e6684f dwmcore!CPartitionVerticalBlankScheduler::ProcessFrame+0x102
0000005b`47eff870 00007ffe`54eed3a6 dwmcore!CPartitionVerticalBlankScheduler::ScheduleAndProcessFrame+0x8f
0000005b`47eff990 00007ffe`54eed2d6 dwmcore!CConnection::MainCompositionThreadLoop+0xba
0000005b`47effa00 00007ffe`5a2d54e0 dwmcore!CConnection::RunCompositionThread+0xfa
0000005b`47effa30 00007ffe`5af8485b KERNEL32!BaseThreadInitThunk+0x10
0000005b`47effa60 00000000`00000000 ntdll!RtlUserThreadStart+0x2b
```

20.   We close logging before exiting WinDbg:

```
1: kd> .logclose
Closing open log file C:\AdvWMDA-Dumps\x64\C4B.log
```

Exercise C5

- **Goal:** Learn how to inspect the registry

- \AdvWMDA-Dumps\Exercise-C5-Registry.pdf

Exercise C5: Registry

Goal: Learn how to inspect the registry.

1.   Launch WinDbg.

2.   Open \AdvWMDA-Dumps\x64\MEMORY-Normal.DMP

3.   We get the dump file loaded (the output should be the same as in the previous exercise).

4.   We open a log file:

```
1: kd> .logopen C:\AdvWMDA-Dumps\x64\C5.log
Opened log file 'C:\AdvWMDA-Dumps\x64\C5.log'
```

5.   We check registry hives using the **!reg hivelist** command:

```
1: kd> !reg
```

```
reg <command>      <params>        - Registry extensions
    querykey|q      <FullKeyPath>  - Dump subkeys and values
    keyinfo         <HiveAddr> <KnodeAddr> - Dump subkeys and values, given knode
    kcb        <Address>       - Dump registry key-control-blocks
    knode      <Address>       - Dump registry key-node struct
    kbody      <Address>       - Dump registry key-body struct
    kvalue     <Address>       - Dump registry key-value struct
    valuelist  <HiveAddr> <KnodeAddr> - Dumps list of values for a particular knode
    subkeylist <HiveAddr> <KnodeAddr> - Dumps list of subkeys for a particular knode
    baseblock  <HiveAddr>      - Dump the baseblock for the specified hive
    seccache   <HiveAddr>       - Dump the security cache for the specified hive
    hashindex  <HiveAddr> <conv_key>  - Find the hash entry given a Kcb ConvKey
    openkeys   <HiveAddr|0>    - Dump the keys opened inside the specified hive
    openhandles <HiveAddr|0>   - Dump the handles opened inside the specified hive
    findkcb    <FullKeyPath>   - Find the kcb for the corresponding path
    hivelist                   - Displays the list of the hives in the system
    viewlist   <HiveAddr>      - Dump the pinned/mapped view list for the specified hive
    freebins   <HiveAddr>      - Dump the free bins for the specified hive
    freecells  <BinAddr>       - Dump the free cells in the specified bin
    dirtyvector<HiveAddr>      - Dump the dirty vector for the specified hive
    cellindex  <HiveAddr> <cellindex> - Finds the VA for a specified cell index
    freehints  <HiveAddr> <Storage> <Display> - Dumps freehint info
    translist  <RmAddr|0>      - Displays the list of active transactions in this RM
    uowlist    <TransAddr>     - Displays the list of UoW attached to this transaction
    locktable  <KcbAddr|ThreadAddr> - Displays relevant LOCK table content
    convkey    <KeyPath>       - Displays hash keys for a key path input
    postblocklist              - Displays the list of threads which have 1 or more postblocks posted
    notifylist                 - Displays the list of notify blocks in the system
    ixlock     <LockAddr>      - Dumps ownership of an intent lock
    finalize   <conv_key>      - Finalizes the specified path or component hash
    dumppool   [s|r]           - Dump registry allocated paged pool
        s - Save list of registry pages to temporary file
        r - Restore list of registry pages from temp. file
```

```
1: kd> !reg hivelist
```

```
----------------------------------------------------------------------------------------------------------------------------------------------------------------
|   HiveAddr      |Stable Length|   Stable Map    |Volatile Length|   Volatile Map   |MappedViews|PinnedViews|U(Cnt)|   BaseBlock     |   FileName
----------------------------------------------------------------------------------------------------------------------------------------------------------------
| ffff800ed4896000 |     2000 | ffff800ed4896128 |     1000 | ffff800ed48963a0 | ffff800ed48c6000 | <UNKNOWN>
| ffff800ed487d000 |    da8000 | ffff800ed48cd000 |    39000 | ffff800ed487d3a0 | ffff800ed48cc000 | SYSTEM
| ffff800ed48f3000 |    24000 | ffff800ed48f3128 |    11000 | ffff800ed48f33a0 | ffff800ed4916000 | <UNKNOWN>
| ffff800ed750b000 |     8000 | ffff800ed750b128 |     1000 | ffff800ed750b3a0 | ffff800ed752f000 | <UNKNOWN>
| ffff800ed74d2000 |    64000 | ffff800ed74d2128 |     1000 | ffff800ed74d23a0 | ffff800ed752e000 | temRoot\System32\Config\DEFAULT
| ffff800ed750f000 |     f000 | ffff800ed750f128 |        0 | 0000000000000000 | ffff800ed7802000 | <UNKNOWN>
| ffff800ed76d8000 |  4c32000 | ffff800ed772e000 |   2bd000 | ffff800eda406000 | ffff800ed7806000 | emRoot\System32\Config\SOFTWARE
| ffff800ed8370000 |     a000 | ffff800ed8370128 |        0 | 0000000000000000 | ffff800ed83e0000 | kVolume2\EFI\Microsoft\Boot\BCD
| ffff800ed896e000 |    32000 | ffff800ed896e128 |        0 | 0000000000000000 | ffff800ed894e000 | rofiles\LocalService\NTUSER.DAT
| ffff800ed8991000 |    35000 | ffff800ed8991128 |     1000 | ffff800ed89913a0 | ffff800ed899c000 | files\NetworkService\NTUSER.DAT
| ffff800ed8c52000 |    57000 | ffff800ed8c52128 |        0 | 0000000000000000 | ffff800ed8c4a000 | \SystemRoot\System32\Config\BBI
| ffff800eda75b000 |   25d000 | ffff800eda4f4000 |        0 | 0000000000000000 | ffff800eda46c000 | \AppCompat\Programs\Amcache.hve
| ffff800eda9cb000 |   19b000 | ffff800eda9cb128 |     5000 | ffff800eda9cb3a0 | ffff800eda466000 | \??\C:\Users\dumpa\ntuser.dat
| ffff800eda97d000 |   548000 | ffff800eda9fd000 |        0 | 0000000000000000 | ffff800eda8ff000 | \Microsoft\Windows\UsrClass.dat
| ffff800edb35f000 |    64000 | ffff800edb35f128 |        0 | 0000000000000000 | ffff800edb387000 | 5n1h2txyewy\ActivationStore.dat
| ffff800edb891000 |    11000 | ffff800edb891128 |        0 | 0000000000000000 | ffff800edb87a000 | <UNKNOWN>
| ffff800edbb62000 |     a000 | ffff800edbb62128 |        0 | 0000000000000000 | ffff800edbbcd000 | <UNKNOWN>
| ffff800edb9e5000 |     c000 | ffff800edb9e5128 |        0 | 0000000000000000 | ffff800edbbce000 | 1h2txyewy\Settings\settings.dat
| ffff800edbd94000 |     1000 | ffff800edbd94128 |        0 | 0000000000000000 | ffff800edbda3000 | 1h2txyewy\Settings\settings.dat
| ffff800edc695000 |    5f000 | ffff800edc695128 |        0 | 0000000000000000 | ffff800ed91f3000 | <UNKNOWN>
| ffff800edc6d1000 |    20000 | ffff800edc6d1128 |        0 | 0000000000000000 | ffff800edd1fe000 | yb3d8bbwe\Settings\settings.dat
| ffff800edd198000 |    1d000 | ffff800edd198128 |        0 | 0000000000000000 | ffff800edc0d1000 | ekyb3d8bbwe\ActivationStore.dat
| ffff800edcf4b000 |     2000 | ffff800edcf4b128 |        0 | 0000000000000000 | ffff800edc04b000 | yb3d8bbwe\Settings\settings.dat
| ffff800edd80a000 |     e000 | ffff800edd80a128 |        0 | 0000000000000000 | ffff800edd975000 | ekyb3d8bbwe\ActivationStore.dat
| ffff800eddac1000 |    99000 | ffff800eddac1128 |        0 | 0000000000000000 | ffff800ede380000 | timization\State\dosvcState.dat
| ffff800ed4f87000 |     2000 | ffff800ed4f87128 |        0 | 0000000000000000 | ffff800ede6ff000 | 5n1h2txyewy\ActivationStore.dat
| ffff800edee42000 |     1000 | ffff800edee42128 |        0 | 0000000000000000 | ffff800edd9fe000 | <UNKNOWN>
| ffff800edee57000 |     1000 | ffff800edee57128 |        0 | 0000000000000000 | ffff800edd9ff000 | e\SystemAppData\Helium\User.dat
| ffff800edee59000 |     1000 | ffff800edee59128 |        0 | 0000000000000000 | ffff800edd6eb000 | mAppData\Helium\UserClasses.dat
| ffff800edeeaa000 |     1000 | ffff800edeeaa128 |        0 | 0000000000000000 | ffff800edc982000 | ache\e9285a6adf7bf45a_COM15.dat
| ffff800edeeac000 |     1000 | ffff800edeeac128 |        0 | 0000000000000000 | ffff800edc982000 | lium\Cache\e9285a6adf7bf45a.dat
| ffff800edef62000 |     7000 | ffff800edef62128 |        0 | 0000000000000000 | ffff800edd4d1000 | ekyb3d8bbwe\ActivationStore.dat
| ffff800edef90000 |     e000 | ffff800edef90128 |        0 | 0000000000000000 | ffff800ede1ff000 | ekyb3d8bbwe\ActivationStore.dat
| ffff800edef6d000 |     1000 | ffff800edef6d128 |        0 | 0000000000000000 | ffff800ede6fe000 | yb3d8bbwe\Settings\settings.dat
----------------------------------------------------------------------------------------------------------------------------------------------------------------
```

6.   Then we can choose a hive and check its more detailed structure:

```
1: kd> dt nt!_CM*
          ntkrnlmp!_CM_RESOURCE_LIST
          ntkrnlmp!_CM_FULL_RESOURCE_DESCRIPTOR
          ntkrnlmp!_CM_PARTIAL_RESOURCE_LIST
          ntkrnlmp!_CM_PARTIAL_RESOURCE_DESCRIPTOR
          ntkrnlmp!_CM_KEY_CONTROL_BLOCK
          ntkrnlmp!_CM_KEY_BODY
          ntkrnlmp!_CM_KEY_NODE
          ntkrnlmp!_CM_NAME_CONTROL_BLOCK
          ntkrnlmp!_CM_KEY_VALUE
          ntkrnlmp!_CMP_COPY_TYPE
          ntkrnlmp!_CMHIVE
          ntkrnlmp!_CM_LOAD_FAILURE_TYPE
          ntkrnlmp!_CM_KCB_UOW
          ntkrnlmp!_CM_TRANS
          ntkrnlmp!_CMP_FAILURE_INJECTION_POINT
          ntkrnlmp!_CMP_VOLUME_CONTEXT
          ntkrnlmp!_CMP_VOLUME_MANAGER
          ntkrnlmp!_CM_INTENT_LOCK
          ntkrnlmp!_CM_NAME_HASH
          ntkrnlmp!_CM_KEY_SECURITY_CACHE_ENTRY
          ntkrnlmp!_CM_PATH_HASH
          ntkrnlmp!_CM_KCB_LAYER_INFO
          ntkrnlmp!_CM_RM
          ntkrnlmp!_CM_KEY_REFERENCE
          ntkrnlmp!_CMSI_RW_LOCK
          ntkrnlmp!_CM_UOW_SET_VALUE_KEY_DATA
          ntkrnlmp!_CM_DIRTY_VECTOR_LOG
          ntkrnlmp!_CM_TRANS_PTR
          ntkrnlmp!_CM_KEY_HASH
```

```
           ntkrnlmp!_CM_UOW_SET_VALUE_LIST_DATA
           ntkrnlmp!_CM_UOW_KEY_STATE_MODIFICATION
           ntkrnlmp!_CM_DIRTY_VECTOR_OPERATION
           ntkrnlmp!_CM_DIRTY_VECTOR_LOG_ENTRY
           ntkrnlmp!_CMP_DISCARD_AND_REPLACE_KCB_CONTEXT
           ntkrnlmp!_CM_KEY_SECURITY_CACHE
           ntkrnlmp!_CM_INDEX_HINT_BLOCK
           ntkrnlmp!_CM_KEY_HASH_TABLE_ENTRY
           ntkrnlmp!_CM_PARSE_DEBUG_INFO
           ntkrnlmp!_CM_UOW_SET_SD_DATA
           ntkrnlmp!_CM_INDEX
           ntkrnlmp!_CMSI_PROCESS_TUPLE
           ntkrnlmp!_CM_NOTIFY_BLOCK
           ntkrnlmp!_CM_KEY_SECURITY
           ntkrnlmp!_CM_SHARE_DISPOSITION
           ntkrnlmp!_CM_KEY_INDEX
           ntkrnlmp!_CM_COMPONENT_HASH
           ntkrnlmp!_CM_BIG_DATA
           ntkrnlmp!_CM_FAST_LEAF_HINT
```

```
1: kd> dt nt!_CMHIVE ffff800eda9cb000
   +0x000 Hive            : _HHIVE
   +0x608 FileHandles     : [6] 0xffffffff`80001bfc Void
   +0x638 NotifyList      : _LIST_ENTRY [ 0xffff800e`d91aec20 - 0x00000000`00000000 ]
   +0x648 HiveList        : _LIST_ENTRY [ 0xffff800e`da97d648 - 0xffff800e`da75b648 ]
   +0x658 PreloadedHiveList : _LIST_ENTRY [ 0xffff800e`da9cb658 - 0xffff800e`da9cb658 ]
   +0x668 HiveRundown     : _EX_RUNDOWN_REF
   +0x670 KcbCacheTable   : 0xffff800e`da968000 _CM_KEY_HASH_TABLE_ENTRY
   +0x678 KcbCacheTableSize : 0x200
   +0x680 DeletedKcbTable : 0xffff800e`da20fb30 _CM_KEY_HASH_TABLE_ENTRY
   +0x688 DeletedKcbTableSize : 0x20
   +0x68c Identity        : 0x13
   +0x690 HiveLock        : _CMSI_RW_LOCK
   +0x698 FlushDirtyVector : _RTL_BITMAP
   +0x6a8 FlushDirtyVectorSize : 0x19c
   +0x6b0 FlushLogEntryOffsetArray : (null)
   +0x6b8 FlushLogEntryOffsetArrayCount : 0
   +0x6bc FlushLogEntrySize : 0
   +0x6c0 FlushHiveTruncated : 0
   +0x6c4 FlushBaseBlockDirty : 0 ''
   +0x6c8 CapturedUnreconciledVector : _RTL_BITMAP
   +0x6d8 CapturedUnreconciledVectorSize : 0x19c
   +0x6e0 UnreconciledOffsetArray : (null)
   +0x6e8 UnreconciledOffsetArrayCount : 0
   +0x6f0 UnreconciledBaseBlock : (null)
   +0x6f8 SecurityLock    : _EX_PUSH_LOCK
   +0x700 LastShrinkHiveSize : 0x19b000
   +0x708 ActualFileSize  : _LARGE_INTEGER 0x1c0000
   +0x710 LogFileSizes    : [2] _LARGE_INTEGER 0x96000
   +0x720 FileFullPath    : _UNICODE_STRING ""
   +0x730 FileUserName    : _UNICODE_STRING "\??\C:\Users\dumpa\ntuser.dat"
   +0x740 HiveRootPath    : _UNICODE_STRING "\REGISTRY\USER\S-1-5-21-3407489871-1359576761-456439074-1001"
   +0x750 SecurityCount   : 0xc1
   +0x754 SecurityCacheSize : 0xc7
   +0x758 SecurityHitHint : 0n59
   +0x760 SecurityCache   : 0xffff800e`da97e300 _CM_KEY_SECURITY_CACHE_ENTRY
   +0x768 SecurityHash    : [64] _LIST_ENTRY [ 0xffff800e`da56f5c8 - 0xffff800e`da56f5c8 ]
   +0xb68 UnloadEventCount : 0
   +0xb70 UnloadEventArray : (null)
   +0xb78 RootKcb         : (null)
   +0xb80 Frozen          : 0 ''
   +0xb88 DirtyVectorLog  : _CM_DIRTY_VECTOR_LOG
   +0x1010 Flags          : 9
   +0x1018 TrustClassEntry : _LIST_ENTRY [ 0xffff800e`dee5a018 - 0xffff800e`dee58018 ]
   +0x1028 DirtyTime      : 0x00000001`073dab51
   +0x1030 UnreconciledTime : 0xce85108c
   +0x1038 CmRm           : 0xffff800e`da2ddd60 _CM_RM
   +0x1040 CmRmInitFailPoint : 0
```

```
+0x1044 CmRmInitFailStatus : 0n0
+0x1048 CreatorOwner    : (null)
+0x1050 RundownThread   : (null)
+0x1058 LastWriteTime   : _LARGE_INTEGER 0x01d817d1`85b9e512
+0x1060 FlushQueue      : _HIVE_WRITE_WAIT_QUEUE
+0x1070 ReconcileQueue  : _HIVE_WRITE_WAIT_QUEUE
+0x1080 FlushFlags      : 1
+0x1080 PrimaryFilePurged : 0y1
+0x1080 DiskFileBad     : 0y0
+0x1084 PrimaryFileSizeBeforeLastFlush : 0
+0x1088 ReferenceCount  : 0n1
+0x108c UnloadHistoryIndex : 0n0
+0x1090 UnloadHistory   : [128] 0
+0x1290 BootStart       : 0
+0x1294 UnaccessedStart : 0
+0x1298 UnaccessedEnd   : 0
+0x129c LoadedKeyCount  : 0x1058
+0x12a0 HandleClosePending : 0
+0x12a8 HandleClosePendingEvent : _EX_PUSH_LOCK
+0x12b0 FinalFlushSucceeded : 0 ''
+0x12b8 VolumeContext   : 0xffff800e`d7161c70 _CMP_VOLUME_CONTEXT
+0x12c0 LateUnloadWorkItemState : 0
+0x12c8 LateUnloadFinishedEvent : _EX_PUSH_LOCK
+0x12d0 LateUnloadWorkItem : 0xffffbe0c`89c5d4d0 _WORK_QUEUE_ITEM
```

7.   Let's view how many registry notifications do exist in the system:

```
1: kd> !reg notifylist

Hive: ffff800ed4896000

[...]

Hive: ffff800eda9cb000
Notify ffff800ed91aec20 Kcb ffff800ed9811610 PostBlockNumber 1
Notify ffff800ede70fa40 Kcb ffff800edce257a0 PostBlockNumber 1
Notify ffff800eda241a10 Kcb ffff800eda5730d0 PostBlockNumber 1
Notify ffff800edb19ad30 Kcb ffff800eda57c910 PostBlockNumber 1
Notify ffff800edb1a4a40 Kcb ffff800eda583210 PostBlockNumber 1
Notify ffff800edb1ac8b0 Kcb ffff800eda580570 PostBlockNumber 1
Notify ffff800edb1b6240 Kcb ffff800eda57c910 PostBlockNumber 1
Notify ffff800edbc2a450 Kcb ffff800eda57c910 PostBlockNumber 1
Notify ffff800edbc2a990 Kcb ffff800edbb6f320 PostBlockNumber 1
Notify ffff800ed91af320 Kcb ffff800eda28b860 PostBlockNumber 1
Notify ffff800ed91aede0 Kcb ffff800eda28a600 PostBlockNumber 1
Notify ffff800edc165830 Kcb ffff800eda57c910 PostBlockNumber 1
Notify ffff800eda623600 Kcb ffff800eda57c910 PostBlockNumber 1
Notify ffff800edd8be820 Kcb ffff800eda57c910 PostBlockNumber 1
Notify ffff800edd8b0f90 Kcb ffff800eda583210 PostBlockNumber 1
Notify ffff800edc17e180 Kcb ffff800eda57c910 PostBlockNumber 1
Notify ffff800edef08260 Kcb ffff800eda57c910 PostBlockNumber 1
Notify ffff800ee02bb4e0 Kcb ffff800eda57c910 PostBlockNumber 1
Notify ffff800edb1a5140 Kcb ffff800eda5830c0 PostBlockNumber 1
Notify ffff800edb1b5830 Kcb ffff800edb45f320 PostBlockNumber 1
Notify ffff800edb1b54b0 Kcb ffff800edbb68630 PostBlockNumber 1
Notify ffff800edbc29ce0 Kcb ffff800edb45f320 PostBlockNumber 1
Notify ffff800edbc2a140 Kcb ffff800edbb68630 PostBlockNumber 1
Notify ffff800edbc2d2b0 Kcb ffff800edbb73760 PostBlockNumber 1
Notify ffff800ed91aed00 Kcb ffff800edbb7ca60 PostBlockNumber 1
Notify ffff800edc163ae0 Kcb ffff800edbb7fc40 PostBlockNumber 1
Notify ffff800edc16a290 Kcb ffff800edb45f320 PostBlockNumber 1
Notify ffff800edc16ad10 Kcb ffff800edbb68630 PostBlockNumber 1
Notify ffff800edc16e970 Kcb ffff800edbb7f1c0 PostBlockNumber 1
```

```
Notify ffff800edc170650 Kcb ffff800edb45f320 PostBlockNumber 1
Notify ffff800edc170880 Kcb ffff800edbb68630 PostBlockNumber 1
Notify ffff800edd0060b0 Kcb ffff800edcec5bf0 PostBlockNumber 1
Notify ffff800edd014eb0 Kcb ffff800edb45f320 PostBlockNumber 1
Notify ffff800edd015310 Kcb ffff800edbb68630 PostBlockNumber 1
Notify ffff800edd00f420 Kcb ffff800edb45f320 PostBlockNumber 1
[...]

Hive: ffff800edef90000

Hive: ffff800edef6d000
```

Note: We can now check the key notification block and key control blocks for a selected notification:

```
1: kd> dt nt!_CM_NOTIFY_BLOCK ffff800edd00f420
   +0x000 HiveList          : _LIST_ENTRY [ 0xffff800e`dd00f7a0 - 0xffff800e`dd015310 ]
   +0x010 PostList          : _LIST_ENTRY [ 0xffff800e`de4c9420 - 0xffff800e`de4c9420 ]
   +0x020 KeyControlBlock   : 0xffff800e`db45f320 _CM_KEY_CONTROL_BLOCK
   +0x028 KeyBody           : 0xffff800e`debc0810 _CM_KEY_BODY
   +0x030 Filter            : 0y000000000000000000000000000101 (0x5)
   +0x030 WatchTree         : 0y0
   +0x030 NotifyPending     : 0y0
   +0x038 SubjectContext    : _SECURITY_SUBJECT_CONTEXT
```

```
1: kd> dt nt!_CM_KEY_CONTROL_BLOCK 0xffff800e`db45f320
   +0x000 RefCount          : 9
   +0x008 ExtFlags          : 0y0000000000000000 (0)
   +0x008 Freed             : 0y0
   +0x008 Discarded         : 0y0
   +0x008 HiveUnloaded      : 0y0
   +0x008 Decommissioned    : 0y0
   +0x008 SpareExtFlag      : 0y0
   +0x008 TotalLevels       : 0y0000000110 (0x6)
   +0x010 KeyHash           : _CM_KEY_HASH
   +0x010 ConvKey           : _CM_PATH_HASH
   +0x018 NextHash          : (null)
   +0x020 KeyHive           : 0xffff800e`da9cb000 _HHIVE
   +0x028 KeyCell           : 0x310
   +0x030 KcbPushlock       : _EX_PUSH_LOCK
   +0x038 Owner             : (null)
   +0x038 SharedCount       : 0n0
   +0x040 DelayedDeref      : 0y0
   +0x040 DelayedClose      : 0y0
   +0x040 Parking           : 0y0
   +0x041 LayerSemantics    : 0 ''
   +0x042 LayerHeight       : 0n0
   +0x044 Spare1            : 0
   +0x048 ParentKcb         : 0xffff800e`da5730d0 _CM_KEY_CONTROL_BLOCK
   +0x050 NameBlock         : 0xffff800e`db96df90 _CM_NAME_CONTROL_BLOCK
   +0x058 CachedSecurity    : 0xffff800e`da0dfb40 _CM_KEY_SECURITY_CACHE
   +0x060 ValueList         : _CHILD_LIST
   +0x068 LinkTarget        : (null)
   +0x070 IndexHint         : 0x00000000`00000001 _CM_INDEX_HINT_BLOCK
   +0x070 HashKey           : 1
   +0x070 SubKeyCount       : 1
   +0x078 KeyBodyListHead   : _LIST_ENTRY [ 0xffff800e`dd1c22e0 - 0xffff800e`dffb92c0 ]
   +0x078 ClonedListEntry   : _LIST_ENTRY [ 0xffff800e`dd1c22e0 - 0xffff800e`dffb92c0 ]
   +0x088 KeyBodyArray      : [4] 0xffff800e`dba27c90 _CM_KEY_BODY
   +0x0a8 KcbLastWriteTime  : _LARGE_INTEGER 0x01d7d815`cecd248a
   +0x0b0 KcbMaxNameLen     : 0xa
   +0x0b2 KcbMaxValueNameLen : 0x24
   +0x0b4 KcbMaxValueDataLen : 0xc
   +0x0b8 KcbUserFlags      : 0y0000
```

```
+0x0b8 KcbVirtControlFlags : 0y0000
+0x0b8 KcbDebug          : 0y00000000 (0)
+0x0b8 Flags             : 0y0000000000100000 (0x20)
+0x0bc Spare3            : 0
+0x0c0 LayerInfo         : 0xffff800e`db537310 _CM_KCB_LAYER_INFO
+0x0c8 RealKeyName       : (null)
+0x0d0 KCBUoWListHead    : _LIST_ENTRY [ 0xffff800e`db45f3f0 - 0xffff800e`db45f3f0 ]
+0x0e0 DelayQueueEntry   : _LIST_ENTRY [ 0xffff800e`db45f400 - 0xffff800e`db45f400 ]
+0x0e0 Stolen            : 0xffff800e`db45f400  ""
+0x0f0 TransKCBOwner     : (null)
+0x0f8 KCBLock           : _CM_INTENT_LOCK
+0x108 KeyLock           : _CM_INTENT_LOCK
+0x118 TransValueCache   : _CHILD_LIST
+0x120 TransValueListOwner : (null)
+0x128 FullKCBName       : (null)
+0x128 FullKCBNameStale  : 0y0
+0x128 Reserved          : 0y000000000000000000000000000000000000000000000000000000000000000 (0)
+0x130 SequenceNumber    : 0
```

```
1: kd> !reg kcb 0xffff800e`db45f320
```

```
Key            : \REGISTRY\USER\S-1-5-21-3407489871-1359576761-456439074-1001\CONTROL
PANEL\INTERNATIONAL\USER PROFILE
RefCount       : 0x0000000000000009
Flags          : CompressedName,
ExtFlags       :
Parent         : 0xffff800eda5730d0
KeyHive        : 0xffff800eda9cb000
KeyCell        : 0x310 [cell index]
TotalLevels    : 6
LayerHeight    : 0
MaxNameLen     : 0xa
MaxValueNameLen : 0x24
MaxValueDataLen : 0xc
LastWriteTime  : 0x 1d7d815:0xcecd248a
KeyBodyListHead : 0xffff800edd1c22e0 0xffff800edffb92c0
SubKeyCount    : 1
Owner          : 0x0000000000000000
KCBLock        : 0xffff800edb45f418
KeyLock        : 0xffff800edb45f428
```

Note: The PID of the process to receive notifications can be found by examining the key body structure:

```
1: kd> dt nt!_CM_KEY_BODY 0xffff800e`dba27c90
   +0x000 Type           : 0x6b793032
   +0x008 KeyControlBlock : 0xffff800e`db45f320 _CM_KEY_CONTROL_BLOCK
   +0x010 NotifyBlock    : 0xffff800e`db1b5830 _CM_NOTIFY_BLOCK
   +0x018 ProcessID      : 0x00000000`0000049c Void
   +0x020 KeyBodyList    : _LIST_ENTRY [ 0xffff800e`dba27cb0 - 0xffff800e`dba27cb0 ]
   +0x030 Flags          : 0y0000000001000000 (0x40)
   +0x030 HandleTags     : 0y0000000000000000 (0)
   +0x038 Trans          : _CM_TRANS_PTR
   +0x040 KtmUow         : (null)
   +0x048 ContextListHead : _LIST_ENTRY [ 0xffff800e`dba27cd8 - 0xffff800e`dba27cd8 ]
   +0x058 EnumerationResumeContext : (null)
   +0x060 RestrictedAccessMask : 0xffffffff
   +0x064 LastSearchedIndex : 0
   +0x068 LockedMemoryMdls : (null)
```

```
1: kd> !reg kbody 0xffff800e`dba27c90

Type        : KEY_BODY_TYPE
KCB         : ffff800edb45f320
NotifyBlock : ffff800edb1b5830
KeyBodyList : 0xffff800edba27cb0 0xffff800edba27cb0
```

Note: We see that in the raw structure, we can find the PID and then check it:

```
1: kd> !process 49c 0
Searching for Process with Cid == 49c
PROCESS ffffbe0c8a982080
    SessionId: 1  Cid: 049c    Peb: 4040cc8000  ParentCid: 0354
DeepFreeze
    DirBase: b394b002  ObjectTable: ffff800edb3e18c0  HandleCount: 1450.
    Image: SearchHost.exe
```

8.   We can inspect individual registry keys, subkeys, and their values using the MEX extension:

```
1: kd> .load C:\AdvWMDA-Dumps\x64\mex
Mex External 3.0.0.7172 Loaded!
```

```
1: kd> !mex.mreg -p "\REGISTRY\USER\S-1-5-21-3407489871-1359576761-456439074-1001\CONTROL
PANEL\INTERNATIONAL\USER PROFILE"
```

```
Found KCB = ffff800edb45f320 :: \REGISTRY\USER\S-1-5-21-3407489871-1359576761-456439074-
1001\CONTROL PANEL\INTERNATIONAL\USER PROFILE

Hive        ffff800eda9cb000
KeyNode     0000021dff911314

[SubKeyAddr]           [SubKeyName]
21dff911e64              en-IE

 Use '!reg keyinfo ffff800eda9cb000 <SubKeyAddr>' to dump the subkey details

[ValueType]            [ValueName]              [ValueData]
REG_MULTI_SZ           Languages                en-IE\0
REG_DWORD              ShowAutoCorrection       1
REG_DWORD              ShowTextPrediction       1
REG_DWORD              ShowCasing               1
REG_DWORD              ShowShiftLock            1
```

```
1: kd> !reg keyinfo ffff800eda9cb000 21dff911e64
```

```
KeyPath       \REGISTRY\USER\S-1-5-21-3407489871-1359576761-456439074-1001\Control
Panel\International\User Profile\en-IE

[ValueType]            [ValueName]              [ValueData]
REG_SZ                 CachedLanguageName       @Winlangdb.dll,-1113
REG_DWORD              1809:00000809            1
REG_DWORD              1809:00001809            2
```

9.   We close logging before exiting WinDbg:

```
1: kd> .logclose
Closing open log file C:\AdvWMDA-Dumps\x64\C5.log
```

Exercise C6

- **Goal:** Learn how to inspect module (including system/kernel) variables and check them with extension command output; dump arrays

- **Patterns:** Module Variable; Regular Data

- \AdvWMDA-Dumps\Exercise-C6-ModuleVariables.pdf

Exercise C6: Module Variables

Goal: Learn how to inspect module (including system/kernel) variables and check them with extension command output; dump arrays.

Patterns: Module Variable; Regular Data

1.   Launch WinDbg.

2.   Open \AdvWMDA-Dumps\x64\MEMORY-Normal.DMP

3.   We get the dump file loaded (the output should be the same as in the previous exercise).

4.   We open a log file:

```
1: kd> .logopen C:\AdvWMDA-Dumps\x64\C6.log
Opened log file 'C:\AdvWMDA-Dumps\x64\C6.log'
```

5.   We can list exported names using the **x** command and use wildcards if necessary:

```
1: kd> x nt!Mm*
fffff807`62776410 nt!MmFreeVirtualMemory (void)
fffff807`62256080 nt!MmAllocatePartitionNodePagesForMdlEx (void)
fffff807`62274ab0 nt!MmQueryMemoryListInformation (void)
fffff807`62845a48 nt!MmInitializeHandBuiltProcess (void)
fffff807`62260bd0 nt!MmOnlySystemCacheViewsPresent (void)
fffff807`6234ee80 nt!MmQueryWorkingSetInformation (void)
fffff807`628492cc nt!MmInitializeHandBuiltProcess2 (void)
fffff807`6279eb98 nt!MmFlushVirtualMemory (void)
[...]
fffff807`629681f0 nt!MmAllocateMemoryRanges (MmAllocateMemoryRanges)
fffff807`6259583c nt!MmGetSessionObjectByProcess (MmGetSessionObjectByProcess)
fffff807`622495a0 nt!MmMdlPagesAreZero (MmMdlPagesAreZero)
fffff807`62d051b0 nt!MmRegistryState = <no type information>
fffff807`62202ba0 nt!MmGetHighestPhysicalPage (MmGetHighestPhysicalPage)
fffff807`6258f878 nt!MmSnapTriageDumpInformation (MmSnapTriageDumpInformation)
fffff807`6258f750 nt!MmMapMemoryDumpMdl (MmMapMemoryDumpMdl)
fffff807`62387cc0 nt!MmMapMemoryDumpMdlEx (MmMapMemoryDumpMdlEx)
fffff807`62388068 nt!MmMapMemoryDumpMdlEx2 (MmMapMemoryDumpMdlEx2)
fffff807`6297c7d8 nt!MmGetSectionStrongImageReference (MmGetSectionStrongImageReference)
fffff807`6280a990 nt!MmGetChannelInformation (MmGetChannelInformation)
fffff807`626badf0 nt!MmMapViewInSessionSpaceEx (MmMapViewInSessionSpaceEx)
fffff807`6259380c nt!MmTrimFilePagesFromWorkingSets (MmTrimFilePagesFromWorkingSets)
fffff807`6286b00a nt!MmSectionToSectionObjectPointers (MmSectionToSectionObjectPointers)
fffff807`6224937 0 nt!MmSetAddressRangeModified (MmSetAddressRangeModified)
fffff807`6297830c nt!MmSelectVsmEnclaveByAddress (MmSelectVsmEnclaveByAddress)
fffff807`62252444 nt!MmDeterminePoolType (MmDeterminePoolType)
fffff807`62976194 nt!MmDeleteShadowMapping (MmDeleteShadowMapping)
fffff807`6226ee08 nt!MmGetAvailablePages (MmGetAvailablePages)
fffff807`62277270 nt!MmIsThisAnNtAsSystem (MmIsThisAnNtAsSystem)
fffff807`6296b410 nt!MmGetIoSessionState (MmGetIoSessionState)
fffff807`62b4f15c nt!MmMarkHypercallPageRetpolineBit (MmMarkHypercallPageRetpolineBit)
fffff807`62d69150 nt!MmVerifyDriverBufferLength = <no type information>
fffff807`622129f0 nt!MmFreePagesFromMdl (MmFreePagesFromMdl)
fffff807`62a7e60c nt!MmCheckMapIoSpace (MmCheckMapIoSpace)
fffff807`62774ab0 nt!MmHardFaultBytesRequired (MmHardFaultBytesRequired)
fffff807`62d06bb0 nt!MmSessionObjectType = <no type information>
fffff807`6297cfec nt!MmMapProtectedKernelPage (MmMapProtectedKernelPage)
fffff807`62967918 nt!MmLockPhysicalPagesByVa (MmLockPhysicalPagesByVa)
[...]
```

Note: There are functions as well as exported variables. For example:

```
1: kd> u fffff807`62277270
nt!MmIsThisAnNtAsSystem:
fffff807`62277270 8a0566dfa800    mov     al,byte ptr [nt!MmRegistryState+0x2c (fffff807`62d051dc)]
fffff807`62277276 c3              ret
fffff807`62277277 cc              int     3
fffff807`62277278 cc              int     3
fffff807`62277279 cc              int     3
fffff807`6227727a cc              int     3
fffff807`6227727b cc              int     3
fffff807`6227727c cc              int     3
```

```
1: kd> db nt!MmRegistryState
fffff807`62d051b0  01 00 00 00 00 00 00 00-00 00 00 00 00 00 00 00  ................
fffff807`62d051c0  00 00 00 00 00 00 00 00-00 00 00 00 00 01 00 00  ................
fffff807`62d051d0  00 00 00 00 00 8d 27 00-00 00 00 00 00 00 00 00  ......'.........
fffff807`62d051e0  00 10 00 00 00 00 00 00-00 00 01 00 00 00 00 00  ................
fffff807`62d051f0  00 20 00 00 00 00 00 00-00 00 10 00 00 00 00 00  . ..............
fffff807`62d05200  00 00 00 00 00 00 00 00-00 00 00 00 00 00 00 00  ................
fffff807`62d05210  00 00 00 00 00 00 00 00-00 00 00 00 00 00 00 00  ................
fffff807`62d05220  00 00 00 00 00 00 00 00-00 f0 87 4b 00 00 00 00  ...........K....
```

6.   Let's check a paged pool variable:

```
1: kd> x nt!Mm*PagedPool*
fffff807`622f3d80 nt!MmBuildMdlForNonPagedPool (void)
fffff807`627f0c10 nt!MmLockPreChargedPagedPool (MmLockPreChargedPagedPool)
fffff807`62d069e4 nt!MmProtectFreedNonPagedPool = <no type information>
fffff807`62d06cc0 nt!MmSizeOfPagedPoolInBytes = <no type information>
fffff807`62805a00 nt!MmObtainChargesToLockPagedPool (MmObtainChargesToLockPagedPool)
fffff807`627e9350 nt!MmUnlockPreChargedPagedPool (MmUnlockPreChargedPagedPool)
fffff807`6296a130 nt!MmReturnChargesToLockPagedPool (MmReturnChargesToLockPagedPool)
fffff807`62254138 nt!MmGetPagedPoolCommitPointer (MmGetPagedPoolCommitPointer)
fffff807`62596b94 nt!MmIsNonPagedPoolNx (MmIsNonPagedPoolNx)
fffff807`62232758 nt!MmGetMaximumNonPagedPoolInBytes (MmGetMaximumNonPagedPoolInBytes)
```

```
1: kd> dp fffff807`62d06cc0 L1
fffff807`62d06cc0   00001000`00000000
```

```
1: kd> ? poi(fffff807`62d06cc0)
Evaluate expression: 17592186044416 = 00001000`00000000
```

Note: We convert the first number to Kb and the number of pages and then compare it to the output of the **!vm** command:

```
1: kd> ? 0n17592186044416 / 0n1024
Evaluate expression: 17179869184 = 00000004`00000000
```

```
1: kd> ? 0n17179869184 / 4
Evaluate expression: 4294967296 = 00000001`00000000
```

```
1: kd> ? 0n17592186044416 / 0n4096
Evaluate expression: 4294967296 = 00000001`00000000
```

```
1: kd> !vm
```

[...]

```
Modified Pages:                    5252 (       21008 Kb)
Modified PF Pages:                 4824 (       19296 Kb)
Modified No Write Pages:             13 (          52 Kb)
NonPagedPool Usage:                 130 (         520 Kb)
NonPagedPoolNx Usage:             23519 (       94076 Kb)
NonPagedPool Max:            4294967296 (17179869184 Kb)
PagedPool Usage:                  38539 (      154156 Kb)
PagedPool Maximum:           4294967296 (17179869184 Kb)
Processor Commit:                   401 (        1604 Kb)
Session Commit:                   14595 (       58380 Kb)
Shared Commit:                   104010 (      416040 Kb)
Special Pool:                         0 (           0 Kb)
Kernel Stacks:                    13356 (       53424 Kb)
Pages For MDLs:                    2343 (        9372 Kb)
ContigMem Pages:                   2364 (        9456 Kb)
Pages For AWE:                        0 (           0 Kb)
NonPagedPool Commit:              25015 (      100060 Kb)
PagedPool Commit:                 38539 (      154156 Kb)
Driver Commit:                    13452 (       53808 Kb)
Boot Commit:                       4775 (       19100 Kb)
PFN Array Commit:                 13317 (       53268 Kb)
SmallNonPagedPtesCommit:            158 (         632 Kb)
SlabAllocatorPages:                4608 (       18432 Kb)
System PageTables:                  960 (        3840 Kb)
ProcessLockedFilePages:              16 (          64 Kb)
Pagefile Hash Pages:                 78 (         312 Kb)
Sum System Commit:               233379 (      933516 Kb)
Total Private:                   578643 (     2314572 Kb)
Misc/Transient Commit:              887 (        3548 Kb)
Committed pages:                 812909 (     3251636 Kb)
Commit limit:                   2162387 (     8649548 Kb)
```

[...]

7.   We now check another module variable name from *mrxsmb*:

```
1: kd> dp mrxsmb!SmbCeContext
fffff807`61235980  00000000`00120012 ffffbe0c`87cb0cd0
fffff807`61235990  00000000`0020001e ffffbe0c`87cb0ca0
fffff807`612359a0  00000000`002c002c ffff800e`d954b710
fffff807`612359b0  00000000`00280028 ffff800e`d954b1d0
fffff807`612359c0  00000000`08200820 ffff800e`d96cb01c
fffff807`612359d0  00000000`00000000 00000000`00000000
fffff807`612359e0  00000000`00000000 00000001`ffffc800
fffff807`612359f0  00000000`00000000 00000000`00000000
```

Note: We see the regular pattern that points to the _UNICODE_STRING structure. We also see there are 5 such structures:

```
1: kd> dt nt!_UNICODE_STRING
nt!_UNICODE_STRING
   +0x000 Length          : Uint2B
   +0x002 MaximumLength   : Uint2B
   +0x008 Buffer          : Ptr64 Wchar
```

```
1: kd> dS mrxsmb!SmbCeContext
ffffbe0c`87cb0cd0  "WORKGROUP"
```

```
1: kd> dt -a5 nt!_UNICODE_STRING fffff807`61235980
nt!_UNICODE_STRING
[0] @ fffff807`61235980
---------------------------------------------
 "WORKGROUP"
   +0x000 Length           : 0x12
   +0x002 MaximumLength    : 0x12
   +0x008 Buffer           : 0xffffbe0c`87cb0cd0  "WORKGROUP"

[1] @ fffff807`61235990
---------------------------------------------
 "DESKTOP-OGPC0LO"
   +0x000 Length           : 0x1e
   +0x002 MaximumLength    : 0x20
   +0x008 Buffer           : 0xffffbe0c`87cb0ca0  "DESKTOP-OGPC0LO"

[2] @ fffff807`612359a0
---------------------------------------------
 "Windows 10 Home 22000"
   +0x000 Length           : 0x2c
   +0x002 MaximumLength    : 0x2c
   +0x008 Buffer           : 0xffff800e`d954b710  "Windows 10 Home 22000"

[3] @ fffff807`612359b0
---------------------------------------------
 "Windows 10 Home 6.3"
   +0x000 Length           : 0x28
   +0x002 MaximumLength    : 0x28
   +0x008 Buffer           : 0xffff800e`d954b1d0  "Windows 10 Home 6.3"

[4] @ fffff807`612359c0
---------------------------------------------
 "\Device\NetBT_Tcpip6_{93123211-9629-4E04-82F0-EA2E4F221468}"
   +0x000 Length           : 0x820
   +0x002 MaximumLength    : 0x820
   +0x008 Buffer           : 0xffff800e`d96cb01c  "\Device\NetBT_Tcpip6_{93123211-9629-4E04-
82F0-EA2E4F221468}"

1: kd> dS fffff807`61235990
ffffbe0c`87cb0ca0  "DESKTOP-OGPC0LO"
```

Note: MS Debugging Extension has a command for this purpose:

```
1: kd> .load C:\AdvWMDA-Dumps\x64\mex
Mex External 3.0.0.7172 Loaded!
```

```
1: kd> !mex.computername
Computer Name: DESKTOP-OGPC0LO
```

8.   We close logging before exiting WinDbg:

```
1: kd> .logclose
Closing open log file C:\AdvWMDA-Dumps\x64\C6.log
```

Exercise C7

- **Goal:** Learn how to inspect various system (kernel) objects

- **Patterns:** System Object

- \AdvWMDA-Dumps\Exercise-C7-SystemObjects.pdf

Goal: Learn how to inspect various system (kernel) objects.

Patterns: System Object.

1.   Launch WinDbg.

2.   Open \AdvWMDA-Dumps\x64\MEMORY-Normal.DMP

3.   We get the dump file loaded (the output should be the same as in the previous exercise).

4.   We open a log file:

```
1: kd> .logopen C:\AdvWMDA-Dumps\x64\C7.log
Opened log file 'C:\AdvWMDA-Dumps\x64\C7.log'
```

5.   We can list all system objects, for example, kernel objects such as events, and check whether they are signaled:

```
1: kd> !object \
Object: ffff800ed4841d20  Type: (ffffbe0c840c6d20) Directory
    ObjectHeader: ffff800ed4841cf0 (new version)
    HandleCount: 0  PointerCount: 58
    Directory Object: 00000000  Name: \

    Hash Address          Type                      Name
    ---- -------          ----                      ----
    01   ffffbe0c87026080 Job
Container_Microsoft.WindowsNotepad_10.2103.6.0_x64__8wekyb3d8bbwe-S-1-5-21-3407489871-1359576761-
456439074-1001
         ffffbe0c87d5e990 Mutant                    PendingRenameMutex
         ffff800ed4838ac0 Directory                 ObjectTypes
    02   ffffbe0c8922d390 FilterConnectionPort      storqosfltport
    03   ffffbe0c84993bb0 FilterConnectionPort      MicrosoftMalwareProtectionRemoteIoPortWD
    05   ffff800ed487cd70 SymbolicLink              SystemRoot
    06   ffff800ed71812a0 Directory                 Sessions
         ffffbe0c849938f0 FilterConnectionPort      MicrosoftMalwareProtectionVeryLowIoPortWD
    07   ffffbe0c84074600 ALPC Port                 SleepstudyControlPort
    08   ffff800ed481de00 Directory                 ArcName
    09   ffffbe0c8922dd30 FilterConnectionPort      WcifsPort
         ffff800ed493a920 Directory                 NLS
    10   ffffbe0c89710260 Event                     LanmanServerAnnounceEvent
         ffffbe0c8958cb20 ALPC Port                 ThemeApiPort
         ffff800ed7182ce0 Directory                 Windows
         ffff800ed4854960 Directory                 GLOBAL??
    11   ffff800ed7182560 Directory                 RPC Control
         ffffbe0c84a93070 ALPC Port                 PdcPort
    13   ffffbe0c87c80760 Event                     EFSInitEvent
    14   ffff800ed701fbc0 SymbolicLink              Dfs
         ffffbe0c849d6d50 Device                    clfs
    15   ffffbe0c84883eb0 Event                     CsrSbSyncEvent
         ffffbe0c84f51280 ALPC Port                 SeRmCommandPort
    16   ffff800ed48365e0 SymbolicLink              DosDevices
    17   ffff800ed7182b00 Directory                 KnownDlls32
    18   ffff800ed4873f50 Key                       \REGISTRY
    19   ffffbe0c84895430 Event                     DSYSDBG.Debug.Trace.Memory.294
         ffff800ed83820c0 Directory                 BaseNamedObjects
```

```
    20  ffff800ed74ad0f0 Section                Win32kCrossSessionGlobals
        ffffbe0c84099d10 ALPC Port              PowerPort
    21  ffffbe0c89022b20 ALPC Port              SmSsWinStationApiPort
        ffffbe0c84882fb0 Event                  UniqueInteractiveSessionIdEvent
        ffff800ed493aae0 Directory              UMDFCommunicationPorts
    22  ffff800ed7182740 Directory              KnownDlls
        ffffbe0c84f4c290 Device                 FatCdrom
        ffffbe0c84f4c060 Device                 Fat
        ffffbe0c841cdb40 ALPC Port              PowerMonitorPort
    23  ffffbe0c849b9de0 Device                 Ntfs
        ffff800ed49395e0 Directory              FileSystem
        ffff800ed483ae60 Directory              KernelObjects
    24  ffffbe0c84994290 FilterConnectionPort   MicrosoftMalwareProtectionControlPortWD
    26  ffffbe0c888e15d0 ALPC Port              SeLsaCommandPort
        ffff800ed483fe60 Directory              Callback
    28  ffffbe0c8922d9c0 FilterConnectionPort   BindFltPort
        ffff800ed48f85b0 Directory              DriverStore
        ffff800ed4856a60 Directory              Security
    30  ffffbe0c84993160 FilterConnectionPort   MicrosoftMalwareProtectionAsyncPortWD
        ffff800ed480d620 Directory              Device
    32  ffff800ed4d702b0 SymbolicLink           DriverData
    34  ffffbe0c84d6bdf0 ALPC Port              SmApiPort
    35  ffffbe0c8922d230 FilterConnectionPort   CLDMSGPORT
        ffffbe0c84994550 FilterConnectionPort   MicrosoftMalwareProtectionPortWD
        ffff800ed4836c70 SymbolicLink           OSDataRoot
    36  ffffbe0c84896970 Event                  SAM_SERVICE_STARTED
        ffff800ed493aca0 Directory              Driver
        ffff800ed48b8410 SymbolicLink           DriverStores

1: kd> !object \KernelObjects
Object: ffff800ed483ae60  Type: (ffffbe0c840c6d20) Directory
    ObjectHeader: ffff800ed483ae30 (new version)
    HandleCount: 0  PointerCount: 22
    Directory Object: ffff800ed4841d20  Name: KernelObjects

    Hash Address          Type                 Name
    ---- -------          ----                 ----
    00  ffff800ed4832420 SymbolicLink          MemoryErrors
    02  ffffbe0c840a7220 Event                 LowNonPagedPoolCondition
    04  ffffbe0c87cea1a0 Session               Session1
    05  ffffbe0c840a7720 Event                 SuperfetchScenarioNotify
        ffffbe0c840a7fa0 Event                 SuperfetchParametersChanged
    09  ffffbe0c8a84f870 Event                 SuperfetchTracesReady
    10  ffff800ed4832660 SymbolicLink          PhysicalMemoryChange
    12  ffff800ed480dc70 SymbolicLink          HighCommitCondition
    13  ffffbe0c840acf00 Mutant                BcdSyncMutant
    14  ffff800ed4836d10 SymbolicLink          HighMemoryCondition
        ffffbe0c840a7a20 Event                 HighNonPagedPoolCondition
    17  ffffbe0c840bf960 Partition             MemoryPartition0
    21  ffff800ed487c6e0 KeyedEvent            CritSecOutOfMemoryEvent
    22  ffffbe0c840a7820 Event                 SystemErrorPortReady
    23  ffff800ed483db00 SymbolicLink          MaximumCommitCondition
    25  ffff800ed4832150 SymbolicLink          LowCommitCondition
    26  ffffbe0c840a7320 Event                 HighPagedPoolCondition
    28  ffff800ed483dd00 SymbolicLink          LowMemoryCondition
    32  ffffbe0c87cead50 Session               Session0
        ffffbe0c840a7420 Event                 LowPagedPoolCondition
    34  ffffbe0c840a70a0 Event                 PrefetchTracesReady

1: kd> !object ffffbe0c840a7220
Object: ffffbe0c840a7220  Type: (ffffbe0c840eac40) Event
    ObjectHeader: ffffbe0c840a71f0 (new version)
```

```
    HandleCount: 1  PointerCount: 32772
    Directory Object: ffff800ed483ae60  Name: LowNonPagedPoolCondition
```

Note: The number of pointer counts to the object usually doesn't reflect the number of real references:

```
1: kd> !trueref ffffbe0c840a7220
ffffbe0c840a7220: HandleCount: 1 PointerCount: 32772 RealPointerCount: 5
```

Note: Each object is prepended by the **header** followed by an object body (**object address**):

```
1: kd> dt nt!_OBJECT_HEADER ffffbe0c840a71f0
   +0x000 PointerCount        : 0n32772
   +0x008 HandleCount         : 0n1
   +0x008 NextToFree          : 0x00000000`00000001 Void
   +0x010 Lock                : _EX_PUSH_LOCK
   +0x018 TypeIndex           : 0xf7 ''
   +0x019 TraceFlags          : 0 ''
   +0x019 DbgRefTrace         : 0y0
   +0x019 DbgTracePermanent   : 0y0
   +0x01a InfoMask            : 0x2 ''
   +0x01b Flags               : 0x2 ''
   +0x01b NewObject           : 0y0
   +0x01b KernelObject        : 0y1
   +0x01b KernelOnlyAccess    : 0y0
   +0x01b ExclusiveObject     : 0y0
   +0x01b PermanentObject     : 0y0
   +0x01b DefaultSecurityQuota : 0y0
   +0x01b SingleHandleEntry   : 0y0
   +0x01b DeletedInline       : 0y0
   +0x01c Reserved            : 0
   +0x020 ObjectCreateInfo    : 0x00000000`00000001 _OBJECT_CREATE_INFORMATION
   +0x020 QuotaBlockCharged   : 0x00000000`00000001 Void
   +0x028 SecurityDescriptor  : 0xffff800e`d483222f Void
   +0x030 Body                : _QUAD
```

```
1: kd> ? ffffbe0c840a71f0 +0x030
Evaluate expression: -72514012548576 = ffffbe0c`840a7220
```

Note: The *Body* field corresponds to some structure. In our case, it is _KEVENT. Synchronization structures usually contain _DISPATCHER_HEADER structure:

```
1: kd> dt nt!_KEVENT ffffbe0c`840a7220
nt!_KEVENT
   +0x000 Header              : _DISPATCHER_HEADER
```

```
1: kd> dt nt!_DISPATCHER_HEADER ffffbe0c`840a7220
nt!_DISPATCHER_HEADER
   +0x000 Lock                : 0n393216
   +0x000 LockNV              : 0n393216
   +0x000 Type                : 0 ''
   +0x001 Signalling          : 0 ''
   +0x002 Size                : 0x6 ''
   +0x003 Reserved1           : 0 ''
   +0x000 TimerType           : 0 ''
   +0x001 TimerControlFlags   : 0 ''
   +0x001 Absolute            : 0y0
   +0x001 Wake                : 0y0
```

245

```
+0x001 EncodedTolerableDelay : 0y000000 (0)
+0x002 Hand              : 0x6 ''
+0x003 TimerMiscFlags    : 0 ''
+0x003 Index             : 0y000000 (0)
+0x003 Inserted          : 0y0
+0x003 Expired           : 0y0
+0x000 Timer2Type        : 0 ''
+0x001 Timer2Flags       : 0 ''
+0x001 Timer2Inserted    : 0y0
+0x001 Timer2Expiring    : 0y0
+0x001 Timer2CancelPending : 0y0
+0x001 Timer2SetPending  : 0y0
+0x001 Timer2Running     : 0y0
+0x001 Timer2Disabled    : 0y0
+0x001 Timer2ReservedFlags : 0y00
+0x002 Timer2ComponentId : 0x6 ''
+0x003 Timer2RelativeId  : 0 ''
+0x000 QueueType         : 0 ''
+0x001 QueueControlFlags : 0 ''
+0x001 Abandoned         : 0y0
+0x001 DisableIncrement  : 0y0
+0x001 QueueReservedControlFlags : 0y000000 (0)
+0x002 QueueSize         : 0x6 ''
+0x003 QueueReserved     : 0 ''
+0x000 ThreadType        : 0 ''
+0x001 ThreadReserved    : 0 ''
+0x002 ThreadControlFlags : 0x6 ''
+0x002 CycleProfiling    : 0y0
+0x002 CounterProfiling  : 0y1
+0x002 GroupScheduling   : 0y1
+0x002 AffinitySet       : 0y0
+0x002 Tagged            : 0y0
+0x002 EnergyProfiling   : 0y0
+0x002 SchedulerAssist   : 0y0
+0x002 ThreadReservedControlFlags : 0y0
+0x003 DebugActive       : 0 ''
+0x003 ActiveDR7         : 0y0
+0x003 Instrumented      : 0y0
+0x003 Minimal           : 0y0
+0x003 Reserved4         : 0y00
+0x003 AltSyscall        : 0y0
+0x003 Emulation         : 0y0
+0x003 Reserved5         : 0y0
+0x000 MutantType        : 0 ''
+0x001 MutantSize        : 0 ''
+0x002 DpcActive         : 0x6 ''
+0x003 MutantReserved    : 0 ''
+0x004 SignalState       : 0n0
+0x008 WaitListHead      : _LIST_ENTRY [ 0xffffa28c`9dd41b10 - 0xffffa28c`9dd41b10 ]
```

Note: *LowNonPagedPoolCondition* event is non-signaled (*SignalState* is 0). Let's look at another event:

```
1: kd> !object ffffbe0c840a7a20
Object: ffffbe0c840a7a20  Type: (ffffbe0c840eac40) Event
    ObjectHeader: ffffbe0c840a79f0 (new version)
    HandleCount: 1  PointerCount: 32773
    Directory Object: ffff800ed483ae60  Name: HighNonPagedPoolCondition
```

```
1: kd> !trueref ffffbe0c840a7a20
ffffbe0c840a7a20: HandleCount: 1 PointerCount: 32773 RealPointerCount: 6

1: kd> dt nt!_DISPATCHER_HEADER ffffbe0c840a7a20
   +0x000 Lock                 : 0n393216
   +0x000 LockNV               : 0n393216
   +0x000 Type                 : 0 ''
   +0x001 Signalling           : 0 ''
   +0x002 Size                 : 0x6 ''
   +0x003 Reserved1            : 0 ''
   +0x000 TimerType            : 0 ''
   +0x001 TimerControlFlags    : 0 ''
   +0x001 Absolute             : 0y0
   +0x001 Wake                 : 0y0
   +0x001 EncodedTolerableDelay : 0y000000 (0)
   +0x002 Hand                 : 0x6 ''
   +0x003 TimerMiscFlags       : 0 ''
   +0x003 Index                : 0y000000 (0)
   +0x003 Inserted             : 0y0
   +0x003 Expired              : 0y0
   +0x000 Timer2Type           : 0 ''
   +0x001 Timer2Flags          : 0 ''
   +0x001 Timer2Inserted       : 0y0
   +0x001 Timer2Expiring       : 0y0
   +0x001 Timer2CancelPending  : 0y0
   +0x001 Timer2SetPending     : 0y0
   +0x001 Timer2Running        : 0y0
   +0x001 Timer2Disabled       : 0y0
   +0x001 Timer2ReservedFlags  : 0y00
   +0x002 Timer2ComponentId    : 0x6 ''
   +0x003 Timer2RelativeId     : 0 ''
   +0x000 QueueType            : 0 ''
   +0x001 QueueControlFlags    : 0 ''
   +0x001 Abandoned            : 0y0
   +0x001 DisableIncrement     : 0y0
   +0x001 QueueReservedControlFlags : 0y000000 (0)
   +0x002 QueueSize            : 0x6 ''
   +0x003 QueueReserved        : 0 ''
   +0x000 ThreadType           : 0 ''
   +0x001 ThreadReserved       : 0 ''
   +0x002 ThreadControlFlags   : 0x6 ''
   +0x002 CycleProfiling       : 0y0
   +0x002 CounterProfiling     : 0y1
   +0x002 GroupScheduling      : 0y1
   +0x002 AffinitySet          : 0y0
   +0x002 Tagged               : 0y0
   +0x002 EnergyProfiling      : 0y0
   +0x002 SchedulerAssist      : 0y0
   +0x002 ThreadReservedControlFlags : 0y0
   +0x003 DebugActive          : 0 ''
   +0x003 ActiveDR7            : 0y0
   +0x003 Instrumented         : 0y0
   +0x003 Minimal              : 0y0
   +0x003 Reserved4            : 0y00
   +0x003 AltSyscall           : 0y0
   +0x003 Emulation            : 0y0
   +0x003 Reserved5            : 0y0
   +0x000 MutantType           : 0 ''
   +0x001 MutantSize           : 0 ''
```

```
    +0x002 DpcActive          : 0x6 ''
    +0x003 MutantReserved     : 0 ''
    +0x004 SignalState        : 0n1
    +0x008 WaitListHead       : _LIST_ENTRY [ 0xffffbe0c`840a7a28 - 0xffffbe0c`840a7a28 ]
```

Note: We see that *HighNonPagedPoolCondition* is signaled, but *LowNonPagedPoolCondition* is not. From that, we conclude that there is plenty of memory available. You may have also noticed that the **!object** command works faster with numerical addresses than with object names.

6.   We can also inspect any other event, for example:

```
1: kd> !object ffffbe0c84896970
Object: ffffbe0c84896970  Type: (ffffbe0c840eac40) Event
    ObjectHeader: ffffbe0c84896940 (new version)
    HandleCount: 1  PointerCount: 32769
    Directory Object: ffff800ed4841d20  Name: SAM_SERVICE_STARTED
```

```
1: kd> !trueref ffffbe0c84896970
ffffbe0c84896970: HandleCount: 1 PointerCount: 32769 RealPointerCount: 2
```

```
1: kd> dt nt!_DISPATCHER_HEADER ffffbe0c84896970
    +0x000 Lock               : 0n393216
    +0x000 LockNV             : 0n393216
    +0x000 Type               : 0 ''
    +0x001 Signalling         : 0 ''
    +0x002 Size               : 0x6 ''
    +0x003 Reserved1          : 0 ''
    +0x000 TimerType          : 0 ''
    +0x001 TimerControlFlags  : 0 ''
    +0x001 Absolute           : 0y0
    +0x001 Wake               : 0y0
    +0x001 EncodedTolerableDelay : 0y000000 (0)
    +0x002 Hand               : 0x6 ''
    +0x003 TimerMiscFlags     : 0 ''
    +0x003 Index              : 0y000000 (0)
    +0x003 Inserted           : 0y0
    +0x003 Expired            : 0y0
    +0x000 Timer2Type         : 0 ''
    +0x001 Timer2Flags        : 0 ''
    +0x001 Timer2Inserted     : 0y0
    +0x001 Timer2Expiring     : 0y0
    +0x001 Timer2CancelPending : 0y0
    +0x001 Timer2SetPending   : 0y0
    +0x001 Timer2Running      : 0y0
    +0x001 Timer2Disabled     : 0y0
    +0x001 Timer2ReservedFlags : 0y00
    +0x002 Timer2ComponentId  : 0x6 ''
    +0x003 Timer2RelativeId   : 0 ''
    +0x000 QueueType          : 0 ''
    +0x001 QueueControlFlags  : 0 ''
    +0x001 Abandoned          : 0y0
    +0x001 DisableIncrement   : 0y0
    +0x001 QueueReservedControlFlags : 0y000000 (0)
    +0x002 QueueSize          : 0x6 ''
    +0x003 QueueReserved      : 0 ''
    +0x000 ThreadType         : 0 ''
    +0x001 ThreadReserved     : 0 ''
```

```
   +0x002 ThreadControlFlags : 0x6 ''
   +0x002 CycleProfiling    : 0y0
   +0x002 CounterProfiling  : 0y1
   +0x002 GroupScheduling   : 0y1
   +0x002 AffinitySet       : 0y0
   +0x002 Tagged            : 0y0
   +0x002 EnergyProfiling   : 0y0
   +0x002 SchedulerAssist   : 0y0
   +0x002 ThreadReservedControlFlags : 0y0
   +0x003 DebugActive       : 0 ''
   +0x003 ActiveDR7         : 0y0
   +0x003 Instrumented      : 0y0
   +0x003 Minimal           : 0y0
   +0x003 Reserved4         : 0y00
   +0x003 AltSyscall        : 0y0
   +0x003 Emulation         : 0y0
   +0x003 Reserved5         : 0y0
   +0x000 MutantType        : 0 ''
   +0x001 MutantSize        : 0 ''
   +0x002 DpcActive         : 0x6 ''
   +0x003 MutantReserved    : 0 ''
   +0x004 SignalState       : 0n1
   +0x008 WaitListHead      : _LIST_ENTRY [ 0xffffbe0c`84896978 - 0xffffbe0c`84896978 ]
```

```
1: kd> !object \Sessions
Object: ffff800ed71812a0  Type: (ffffbe0c840c6d20) Directory
    ObjectHeader: ffff800ed7181270 (new version)
    HandleCount: 1  PointerCount: 5
    Directory Object: ffff800ed4841d20  Name: Sessions

    Hash Address           Type                    Name
    ---- -------           ----                    ----
     11  ffff800ed8383560 Directory               0
     12  ffff800ed87d01a0 Directory               1
     21  ffff800ed8383740 Directory               BNOLINKS
```

```
1: kd> !object \Sessions\1
Object: ffff800ed87d01a0  Type: (ffffbe0c840c6d20) Directory
    ObjectHeader: ffff800ed87d0170 (new version)
    HandleCount: 1  PointerCount: 32772
    Directory Object: ffff800ed71812a0  Name: 1

    Hash Address           Type                    Name
    ---- -------           ----                    ----
     06  ffff800ed87cf480 Directory               AppContainerNamedObjects
     10  ffff800ed87cf2a0 Directory               Windows
     16  ffff800ed87d0560 Directory               DosDevices
     19  ffff800ed87d0740 Directory               BaseNamedObjects
```

```
1: kd> !object \Sessions\1\BaseNamedObjects
Object: ffff800ed87d0740  Type: (ffffbe0c840c6d20) Directory
    ObjectHeader: ffff800ed87d0710 (new version)
    HandleCount: 49  PointerCount: 1590293
    Directory Object: ffff800ed87d01a0  Name: BaseNamedObjects

    Hash Address          Type                   Name
    ---- -------          ----                   ----
     00  ffffbe0c8ccb5a20 Mutant                 SM0:9276:304:WilStaging_02
         ffffbe0c8ccb49a0 Mutant                 WmiApRpl_Perf_Library_Lock_PID_2678
         ffffbe0c8ccb5420 Mutant                 usbhub_Perf_Library_Lock_PID_2678
```

```
       ffffbe0c8ccb52a0 Mutant                    TermService_Perf_Library_Lock_PID_2678
       ffffbe0c8ccb45e0 Mutant                    PerfProc_Perf_Library_Lock_PID_2678
       ffffbe0c8ccb37a0 Mutant                    LSM_Perf_Library_Lock_PID_2678
       ffffbe0c8c228350 Semaphore                 SM0:4704:304:WilStaging_02_p0h
       ffffbe0c8bc72d30 Event                     HasFacadeAnimations.4208.2384
       ffffbe0c8b818f50 Event                     SubscribedContent-88000165
       ffffbe0c8b134e50 Semaphore                 SM0:7928:120:WilError_03_p0h
       ffffbe0c8b133190 Event                     PageNavigationComplete.4208.7972
       ffffbe0c897ac100 Semaphore                 SM0:7672:120:WilError_03_p0h
       ffffbe0c8a0d82c0 Semaphore                 SM0:7024:304:WilStaging_02_p0h
       ffffbe0c8ad12590 Event                     RootVisualReset.4208.5320
       ffffbe0c8ab18d70 Mutant                    SM0:6396:304:WilStaging_02
       ffffbe0c8a36b670 Semaphore                 SM0:4208:120:WilError_03_p0h
       ffffbe0c8a355eb0 Semaphore                 SM0:4612:120:WilError_03_p0h
 01    ffffbe0c8bc80ed0 Event                     BrushTransitionsComplete.4208.10044
       ffffbe0c8bc94e30 Event                     Global_FormChanged{A587A07B-B872-48CE-8D30-522121ABD913}
       ffffbe0c89c7dca0 Semaphore                 SM0:6948:120:WilError_03_p0h
       ffffbe0c8bb06ab0 Semaphore                 SM0:2108:120:WilError_03_p0h
       ffffbe0c8b834110 Semaphore                 SM0:8148:304:WilStaging_02_p0h
       ffffbe0c8b13e3b0 Semaphore                 CDP_CALLBACK_FBCB67B7-138F-BCED-D98F-DF4A012045DB
       ffffbe0c8ab20e70 Mutant                    SM0:7672:304:WilStaging_02
       ffffbe0c8a81fc10 Event                     HasFacadeAnimations.4208.5968
       ffffbe0c8a182870 Mutant                    CDPUserSvc_Ready_db7a3b24-68b7-4c2e-8335-533dd99ee0f6_S-1-5-21-
3407489871-1359576761-456439074-1001
       ffffbe0c8a178130 Mutant                    SM0:4448:304:WilStaging_02
       ffffbe0c88981310 Mutant                    SM0:692:120:WilError_03
       ffffbe0c848942b0 Event                     {773F1B9A-35B9-4E95-83A0-A210F2DE3B37}-request
 02    ffffbe0c8ccb5960 Mutant                    SM0:9276:120:WilError_03
       ffff800edf79fb90 Section                   1260HWNDInterface:20642
       ffffbe0c8b84fa50 Semaphore                 SM0:6356:120:WilError_03_p0h
       ffffbe0c8ad41430 Semaphore                 SM0:7672:304:WilStaging_02_p0h
       ffffbe0c8a820610 Event                     KeyboardInputReceived.4208.5968
       ffffbe0c8a8148b0 Semaphore                 CDP_CALLBACK_86282810-79B7-48F3-5C99-A0A069A73BEE
       ffffbe0c8a182c30 Mutant                    SM0:4816:120:WilError_03
 03    ffffbe0c8b852750 Semaphore                 SM0:6948:304:WilStaging_02_p0h
       ffffbe0c8bb386f0 Event                     RootVisualReset.4208.5964
       ffffbe0c8bb14390 Event                     HasBuildTreeWorks.9128.9168
       ffffbe0c8bb10150 Semaphore                 SM0:9128:304:WilStaging_02_p0
       ffffbe0c8b0f17b0 Mutant                    SM0:5008:304:WilStaging_02
       ffffbe0c8b131d90 Event                     KeyboardInputReceived.4208.7972
       ffffbe0c8b131390 Event                     RootVisualReset.4208.7972
[...]
       ffffbe0c8ab19130 Mutant                    MSCTF.CtfServerMutexDefault1
[...]
```

```
1: kd> !trueref ffff800ed87d0740
ffff800ed87d0740: HandleCount: 49 PointerCount: 1590293 RealPointerCount: 621
```

```
1: kd> dt nt!_KMUTANT ffffbe0c8ab19130
nt!_KMUTANT
   +0x000 Header          : _DISPATCHER_HEADER
   +0x018 MutantListEntry : _LIST_ENTRY [ 0xffffbe0c`8ae543c8 - 0xffffbe0c`8ab19b08 ]
   +0x028 OwnerThread     : 0xffffbe0c`8ae540c0 _KTHREAD
   +0x030 MutantFlags     : 0 ''
   +0x030 Abandoned       : 0y0
   +0x030 Spare1          : 0y0000000 (0)
   +0x030 Abandoned2      : 0y0
   +0x030 AbEnabled       : 0y0
   +0x030 Spare2          : 0y000000 (0)
   +0x031 ApcDisable      : 0 ''
```

7.   We close logging before exiting WinDbg:

```
1: kd> .logclose
Closing open log file C:\AdvWMDA-Dumps\x64\C7.log
```

Exercise C8

- ◎ **Goal:** Learn how to inspect network protocols and adapters

- ◎ **Patterns:** Disconnected Network Adapter

- ◎ \AdvWMDA-Dumps\Exercise-C8-Network.pdf

Goal: Learn how to inspect network protocols and adapters.

Patterns: Disconnected Network Adapter.

1.   Launch WinDbg.

2.   Open \AdvWMDA-Dumps\x64\MEMORY-Normal.DMP

3.   We get the dump file loaded (the output should be the same as in the previous exercise).

4.   We open a log file:

```
1: kd> .logopen C:\AdvWMDA-Dumps\x64\C8.log
Opened log file 'C:\AdvWMDA-Dumps\x64\C8.log'
```

5.   We can inspect network protocols and adapters:

```
1: kd> !ndiskd.protocol
ffffbe0c89ce8aa0 - NDISWANLEGACY

ffffbe0c89ce6aa0 - NDISWAN
  ffffbe0c89cf4720 - WAN Miniport (PPPOE)
  ffffbe0c896cb720 - WAN Miniport (SSTP)
  ffffbe0c89adfae0 - WAN Miniport (IKEv2)
  ffffbe0c897d2a80 - WAN Miniport (L2TP)
  ffffbe0c89ceeaa0 - WAN Miniport (PPTP)

ffffbe0c89cb8940 - RASPPPOE

ffffbe0c899bcaa0 - NDPROXY
  ffffbe0c897d25b0 - WAN Miniport (PPPOE)
  ffffbe0c89ce0a50 - WAN Miniport (PPPOE)
  ffffbe0c89ae0aa0 - WAN Miniport (PPTP)
  ffffbe0c89ae1aa0 - WAN Miniport (PPTP)
  ffffbe0c89ae3aa0 - WAN Miniport (L2TP)
  ffffbe0c89ae4aa0 - WAN Miniport (L2TP)
  ffffbe0c89ae6aa0 - WAN Miniport (IKEv2)
  ffffbe0c89ae7aa0 - WAN Miniport (IKEv2)
  ffffbe0c89aeaaa0 - WAN Miniport (SSTP)
  ffffbe0c89aebaa0 - WAN Miniport (SSTP)

ffffbe0c896ca270 - WANARPV6
  ffffbe0c89cf7010 - WAN Miniport (IPv6)

ffffbe0c896ea7d0 - WANARP
  ffffbe0c89cf78a0 - WAN Miniport (IP)

ffffbe0c896eb420 - RSPNDR
  ffffbe0c89650010 - Intel(R) 82574L Gigabit Network Connection
  ffffbe0c89650460 - Bluetooth Device (Personal Area Network)

ffffbe0c896e9a40 - MSLLDP
```

252

```
ffffbe0c89653b10 - Intel(R) 82574L Gigabit Network Connection

ffffbe0c896e9010 - LLTDIO
  ffffbe0c89651010 - Intel(R) 82574L Gigabit Network Connection
  ffffbe0c896508b0 - Bluetooth Device (Personal Area Network)

ffffbe0c84f3a670 - RDMANDK

ffffbe0c84d90620 - TCPIP6TUNNEL

ffffbe0c84db7660 - TCPIPTUNNEL

ffffbe0c849da3c0 - TCPIP6
  ffffbe0c87da0460 - Bluetooth Device (Personal Area Network)
  ffffbe0c87c53af0 - Intel(R) 82574L Gigabit Network Connection

ffffbe0c849da010 - TCPIP
  ffffbe0c87da0010 - Bluetooth Device (Personal Area Network)
  ffffbe0c87c6ab40 - Intel(R) 82574L Gigabit Network Connection
```

```
1: kd> !ndiskd.protocol ffffbe0c849da010

PROTOCOL

    TCPIP

    Ndis handle          ffffbe0c849da010
    Ndis API version     v6.40
    Driver context       fffff8076772b4d0
    Driver version       v0.0
    Reference count      3
    Flags                [No flags set]
    Driver image         tcpip.sys


BINDINGS

    Open              Miniport          Miniport Name
    ffffbe0c87da0010  ffffbe0c87dce1a0  Bluetooth Device (Personal Area Network)
    ffffbe0c87c6ab40  ffffbe0c8784a1a0  Intel(R) 82574L Gigabit Network Connection


HANDLERS

    Protocol handler                    Function pointer     Symbol (if available)
    BindAdapterHandlerEx                fffff807675b7160     tcpip!FlBindAdapter
    UnbindAdapterHandlerEx              fffff807675a6170     tcpip!FlUnbindAdapter
    OpenAdapterCompleteHandlerEx        fffff807676d1010     tcpip!FlOpenAdapterComplete
    CloseAdapterCompleteHandlerEx       fffff807675a7fb0     tcpip!FlCloseAdapterComplete
    NetPnPEventHandler                  fffff807675b8e10     tcpip!Fl48PnpEvent
    UninstallHandler                    [None]
    SendNetBufferListsCompleteHandler   fffff80767523d50
tcpip!FlSendNetBufferListChainComplete
    ReceiveNetBufferListsHandler        fffff80767522460     tcpip!FlReceiveNetBufferListChain
    StatusHandlerEx                     fffff807675b91d0     tcpip!FlStatus
    OidRequestCompleteHandler           fffff80767535350     tcpip!FlDirectRequestComplete
    DirectOidRequestCompleteHandler     fffff80767535350     tcpip!FlDirectRequestComplete
```

```
1: kd> !ndiskd.mopen ffffbe0c87c6ab40
```

OPEN

```
     Ndis handle         ffffbe0c87c6ab40
     Flags               USE_MULTICAST_LIST
     References          1                   Show detail
     Source              1
     Datapath state      Running

     Protocol            ffffbe0c849da010 - TCPIP
     Protocol context    ffffbe0c87c6b010

     Miniport            ffffbe0c8784a1a0 - Intel(R) 82574L Gigabit Network Connection
     Miniport context    ffffbe0c878bc000
```

RECEIVE PATH

```
     Packet filter       DIRECTED, MULTICAST, BROADCAST
     Frame Type(s)       0x0800, 0x0806
     Multicast address list 01-00-5e-00-00-01  See all on miniport
                         01-00-5e-7f-ff-fa
                         01-00-5e-00-00-fb
                         01-00-5e-00-00-fc
```

```
1: kd> !ndiskd.netadapter ffffbe0c8784a1a0
```

MINIPORT

```
     Intel(R) 82574L Gigabit Network Connection

     Ndis handle         ffffbe0c8784a1a0
     Ndis API version    v6.50
     Adapter context     ffffbe0c878bc000
     Driver              ffffbe0c8782c9c0 - e1i68x64   v12.18
     Network interface   ffffbe0c84d758a0

     Media type          802.3
     Device instance     PCI\VEN_8086&DEV_10D3&SUBSYS_07D015AD&REV_00\000C29FFFF52AFA200
     Device object       ffffbe0c8784a050    More information
     MAC address         00-0c-29-52-af-a2
```

STATE

```
     Miniport            Running
     Device PnP          Started              Show state history
     Datapath            Normal
     Interface           Up
     Media               Connected
     Power               D0
     References          0n13                 Show detail
     Total resets        0
     Pending OID         None
     Flags               BUS_MASTER, 64BIT_DMA, SG_DMA, DEFAULT_PORT_ACTIVATED,
                         SUPPORTS_MEDIA_SENSE, DOES_NOT_DO_LOOPBACK,
                         MEDIA_CONNECTED
     PnP flags           PM_SUPPORTED, DEVICE_POWER_ENABLED,
```

```
            DEVICE_POWER_WAKE_ENABLE, RECEIVED_START,
            HARDWARE_DEVICE, WAKE_CAPABLE
```

BINDINGS

```
    Protocol list      Driver            Open              Context
    Filter list        Driver            Module            Context
```

Some binding data appears to be paged out. Retrying to display bindings
with less detail.

BINDINGS

```
    Protocol list      Driver            Open              Context
    MSLLDP             ffffbe0c896e9a40  ffffbe0c89653b10  ffffbe0c8409f260
    RSPNDR             ffffbe0c896eb420  ffffbe0c89650010  ffffbe0c896ed010
    LLTDIO             ffffbe0c896e9010  ffffbe0c89651010  ffffbe0c896ce920
    TCPIP              ffffbe0c849da010  ffffbe0c87c6ab40  ffffbe0c87c6b010
    TCPIP6             ffffbe0c849da3c0  ffffbe0c87c53af0  ffffbe0c87c54010

    Filter list        Driver            Module            Context
    WFP 802.3 MAC Layer LightWeight Filter-0000
                       ffffbe0c84975d70  ffffbe0c87c52050  ffffbe0c87c52b60
    QoS Packet Scheduler-0000
                       ffffbe0c84f3fd80  ffffbe0c87c4a410  ffffbe0c879feab0
    WFP Native MAC Layer LightWeight Filter-0000
                       ffffbe0c84974d70  ffffbe0c87c094e0  ffffbe0c87c4a010
```


MORE INFORMATION

```
    Driver handlers                Task offloads
    Power management               PM protocol offloads
    Pending OIDs                   Timers
    Pending NBLs
    Wake-on-LAN (WoL)              Packet filter
    Receive queues                 Receive filtering
    RSS                            NIC switch
    Hardware resources             Selective suspend
    NDIS ports                     WMI guids
```

Note: We see normal operation. Here's an example of disconnection:

```
    Datapath           DIVERTED_BECAUSE_MEDIA_DISCONNECTED
    Media              MediaDisconnected
```

Note: Microsoft Debugging Extension has additional debugging commands for networking, but most do not work for this Windows 11 memory dump due to the absence of symbols, module variables, or changed structures.

```
1: kd> .load C:\AdvWMDA-Dumps\x64\mex
Mex External 3.0.0.7172 Loaded!
```

```
1: kd> !mex.help -cat 'Networking'

Command         Description                                                                    Category
==============  ==============================================================================  ==========
afd             Afd Command Help                                                                Networking
dhcp            Displays information for the DHCP server process                                Networking
dnsclient (!dnsc) Displays the DNS client cache, and includes many other features for the DNS Client service. Networking
ip              Converts an address into an IP address format                                   Networking
mup             Displays info for the Multiple UNC Provider (MUP)                               Networking
ncsi            Displays Network Connectivity Status Indicator (NCSI) configuration             Networking
net             Net Command Help                                                                Networking
pingtrack       Pingtrack command                                                               Networking
rasmans         Displays the rasmans!ConnectionBlockList                                        Networking
srvnet          Displays info on SRVNET                                                         Networking
tcpip    (!tcp) TCP/IP - Gets TCP and UDP ports from Kernel Memory                              Networking
winnsi          winnsi Command Help                                                             Networking
```

6.   We close logging before exiting WinDbg:

```
1: kd> .logclose
```
Closing open log file C:\AdvWMDA-Dumps\x64\C8.log

A Crash Dump Course in Unified Modeling Language

Part II

In the previous part of the UML tutorial, we introduced class and object diagrams. In this part, we look at component diagrams and how component interfaces may be implemented in both C++ and C.

Components and Interfaces

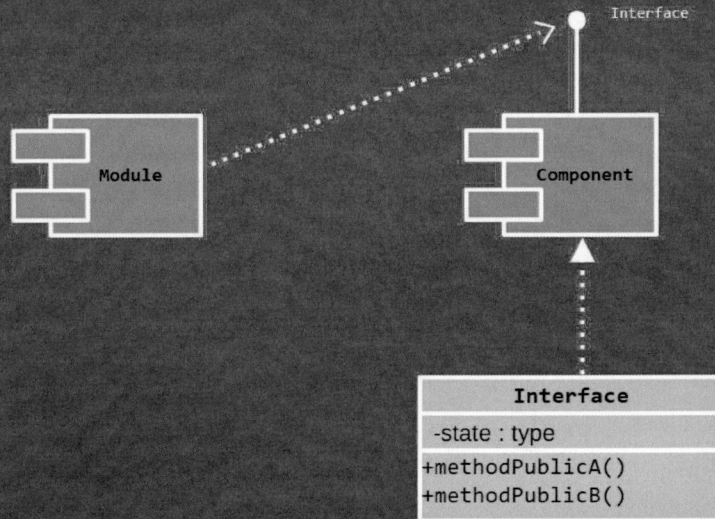

A component is something persistent that can be deployed and loaded, for example, a DLL or driver. It provides one or several distinct interfaces, a set of methods to call, which can be implemented by classes (C++) or just sets of functions (C).

Classes and Objects (C++)

```cpp
class Interface // it can also be a struct Interface
{
public:
    void method();
private:
    int state;
};

Interface ObjectA, ObjectB;

void Interface::method(/* Interface *this */)
{
    state = 0; // this->state = 0;
}

void foo()
{
    ObjectA.method();
}
```

Let's see how an interface can be implemented in an object-oriented language, C++. Interface methods need to differentiate between objects if they access state, which is separate for each object. This differentiation is done by an implicit parameter – a pointer to an object data.

Objects and Methods (C)

```c
struct Interface
{
    int state;
};

void method(struct Interface *obj);

struct Interface ObjectA, ObjectB;

void method(struct Interface *obj)
{
    obj->state = 0;
}

void foo()
{
    method(&ObjectA);
}
```

In C, object differentiation is done explicitly by an object pointer parameter.

Classes and Objects Analogy (C)

```c
struct Object
{
    int state;
};

struct Interface
{
    void (*method)(struct Object *obj);
};

void method(struct Object *obj)
{
    obj->state = 0;
}

struct Interface ClassA = {&method}; struct Object ObjectA, ObjectB;

void foo()
{
    ClassA.method(&ObjectA);
}
```

In C, it is also possible to represent classes as structures that contain pointers to object methods. We see this analogy when we discuss drivers and devices.

A Crash Dump Course in Windows Internals

Device Driver

- A pluggable component for a device or several devices

- Creates device objects and symbolic links to them

- Provides entry points for I/O operations including IOCTL interface (I/O Control - used for any purpose)

- Implemented as a C structure with data and pointers to functions

- Class analogy

Dispatch

Driver

IOCTL

Driver(Init, Unload)

\Driver\<Name>

\FileSystem\<Name>

Consider device drivers as DLLs but for the kernel space. They use the same PE format and import and export functions from other modules. A device driver is a class for device objects.

Device Driver Example

```
3: kd> !drvobj \Driver\Beep 3
Driver object (ffffe000ea9309c0) is for:
 \Driver\Beep
Driver Extension List: (id , addr)

Device Object list:
ffffe000eac2c990

DriverEntry:    fffff801c02e6000        Beep!GsDriverEntry
DriverStartIo:  fffff801c02e16c0        Beep!BeepStartIo
DriverUnload:   fffff801c02e1760        Beep!BeepUnload
AddDevice:      00000000

Dispatch routines:
[00] IRP_MJ_CREATE                      fffff801c02e1430        Beep!BeepOpen
[01] IRP_MJ_CREATE_NAMED_PIPE           fffff8014875ad94        nt!IopInvalidDeviceRequest
[02] IRP_MJ_CLOSE                       fffff801c02e1150        Beep!BeepClose
[03] IRP_MJ_READ                        fffff8014875ad94        nt!IopInvalidDeviceRequest
[04] IRP_MJ_WRITE                       fffff8014875ad94        nt!IopInvalidDeviceRequest
[05] IRP_MJ_QUERY_INFORMATION           fffff8014875ad94        nt!IopInvalidDeviceRequest
[…]
[0c] IRP_MJ_DIRECTORY_CONTROL           fffff8014875ad94        nt!IopInvalidDeviceRequest
[0d] IRP_MJ_FILE_SYSTEM_CONTROL         fffff8014875ad94        nt!IopInvalidDeviceRequest
[0e] IRP_MJ_DEVICE_CONTROL              fffff801c02e1200        Beep!BeepDeviceControl
[0f] IRP_MJ_INTERNAL_DEVICE_CONTROL     fffff8014875ad94        nt!IopInvalidDeviceRequest
[10] IRP_MJ_SHUTDOWN                    fffff8014875ad94        nt!IopInvalidDeviceRequest
[11] IRP_MJ_LOCK_CONTROL                fffff8014875ad94        nt!IopInvalidDeviceRequest
[…]
[1b] IRP_MJ_PNP                         fffff8014875ad94        nt!IopInvalidDeviceRequest
```

In addition to exported functions, device drivers have a mandatory array of function pointers to call for certain requests such as device control, read, and write. The *IopInvalidDeviceRequest* function is used to catch unsupported requests. For example, the *Beep* device doesn't support read and write but supports open, close, and control requests.

264

Devices

- Represents physical or logical device (**\Device\MousePad**)

- Target of an I/O operation

- Name: **\Device\<Name>** or **\FileSystem\<Name>**

- Implemented as a C structure

- Object analogy

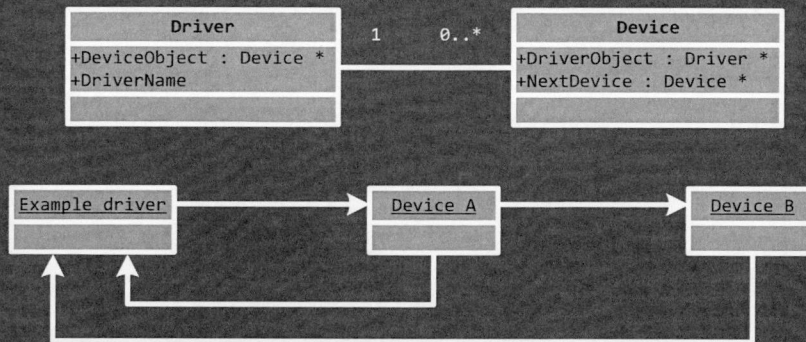

A device driver can create several devices (objects) all linked together, pointing back to its driver.

I/O Manager

⊚ Provides an interface between drivers and OS

⊚ Defines a detailed framework and specification for device drivers

⊚ Provides support functions to drivers

⊚ Packet-driven architecture: each I/O operation is described by IRP (I/O Request Packet) structure

I/O requests, such as reading and writing to a device, are implemented by a packet-driven architecture. Upon such a request, I/O Manager (a loosely defined component in kernel space) allocates a structure to describe a request, including pointers to buffers for device data and then passes it through the device driver stack (for example, file system -> volume -> disk array -> disk).

Big Picture

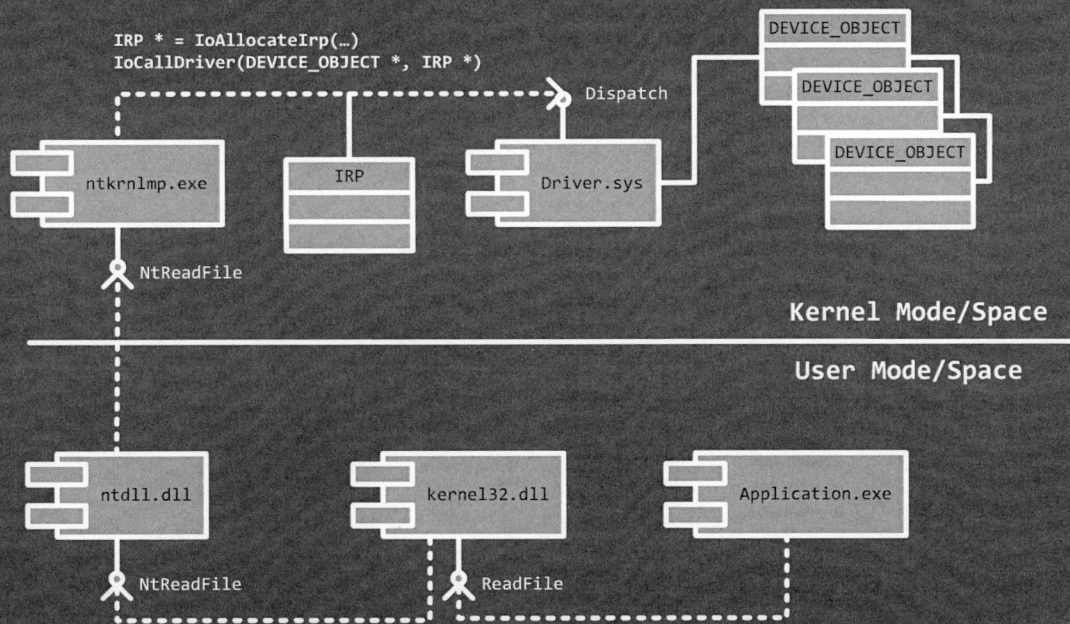

```
IRP * = IoAllocateIrp(…)
IoCallDriver(DEVICE_OBJECT *, IRP *)
```

Dispatch

DEVICE_OBJECT
DEVICE_OBJECT
DEVICE_OBJECT

ntkrnlmp.exe   IRP   Driver.sys

NtReadFile

Kernel Mode/Space

User Mode/Space

ntdll.dll   kernel32.dll   Application.exe

NtReadFile   ReadFile

This big picture describes a read request from *Application.exe*. Notice that an IRP is created and passed to *Driver.sys* code. The appropriate device is represented as a pointer to a device object. This implementation is similar to a class, an object, and *this* pointer in C++.

IRP Communication

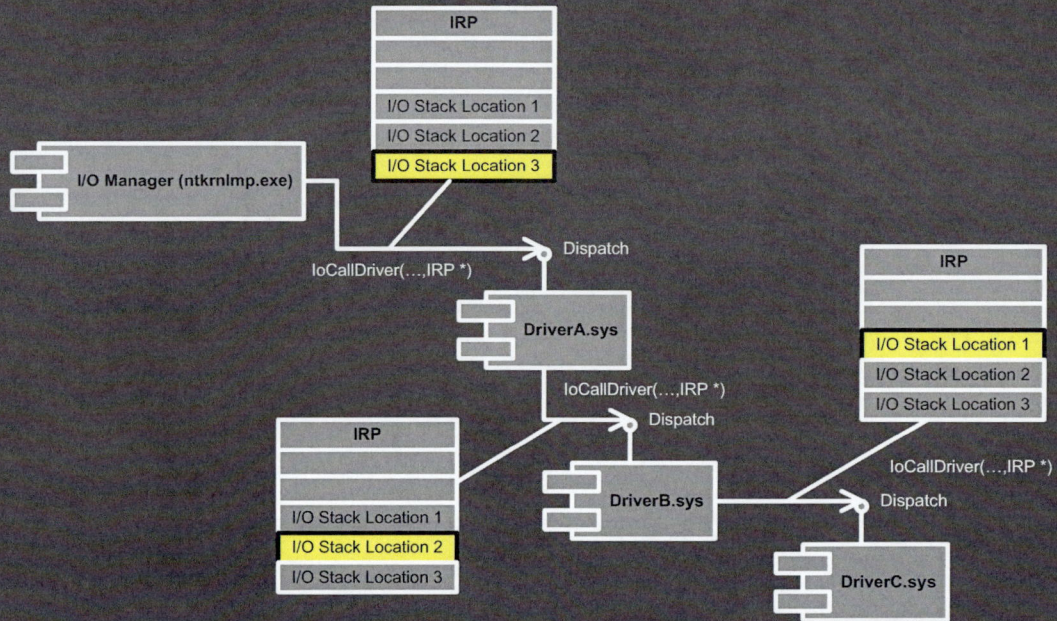

Each I/O Request Packet (IRP) contains a stack at the end of its structure to keep track of the current device driver in the device driver stack. It is implemented similarly to a thread stack: its pointer (slot index) is decremented from bottom to top.

Exercise C9

- **Goal:** Learn how to inspect IRP, file, device, and driver objects

- **Patterns:** Stack Trace (I/O Requests); Stack Trace (I/O Devices)

- \AdvWMDA-Dumps\Exercise-C9-Device-Drivers.pdf

Exercise C9: Device Drivers

Goal: Learn how to inspect IRP, file, device, and driver objects.

Patterns: Stack Trace (I/O Requests); Stack Trace (I/O Devices).

1.   Launch WinDbg.

2.   Open \AdvWMDA-Dumps\x64\MEMORY-Normal.DMP

3.   We get the dump file loaded (the output should be the same as in the previous exercise).

4.   We open a log file:

```
1: kd> .logopen C:\AdvWMDA-Dumps\x64\C9.log
Opened log file 'C:\AdvWMDA-Dumps\x64\C9.log'
```

5.   We list threads from all processes to find a suitable I/O request:

```
1: kd> !process 0 3f

[...]

        THREAD ffffbe0c8b511080  Cid 2434.1cd0  Teb: 0000008e61ced000 Win32Thread: ffffbe0c8cce48e0 WAIT:
(UserRequest) UserMode Non-Alertable
            ffffbe0c8b34fae0  SynchronizationEvent
            ffffbe0c8cc40280  QueueObject
        IRP List:
            ffffbe0c8beddaa0: (0006,0478) Flags: 00060000  Mdl: 00000000
        Not impersonating
        DeviceMap                 ffff800eda518d20
        Owning Process            ffffbe0c8bfb10c0        Image:        SearchHost.exe
        Attached Process          N/A          Image:        N/A
        Wait Start TickCount      29430        Ticks: 357 (0:00:00:05.578)
        Context Switch Count      52           IdealProcessor: 1
        UserTime                  00:00:00.000
        KernelTime                00:00:00.046
        Win32 Start Address edgehtml!CExecFT::StaticThreadProc (0x00007ffe34c7ee60)
        Stack Init ffffa28ca06f4c70 Current ffffa28ca06f3740
        Base ffffa28ca06f5000 Limit ffffa28ca06ef000 Call 0000000000000000
        Priority 9 BasePriority 8 PriorityDecrement 0 IoPriority 2 PagePriority 5
        Child-SP          RetAddr               Call Site
        ffffa28c`a06f3780 fffff807`623327f7     nt!KiSwapContext+0x76
        ffffa28c`a06f38c0 fffff807`623346a9     nt!KiSwapThread+0x3a7
        ffffa28c`a06f39a0 fffff807`6228ed51     nt!KiCommitThreadWait+0x159
        ffffa28c`a06f3a40 fffff807`627702c5     nt!KeWaitForMultipleObjects+0x2b1
        ffffa28c`a06f3b40 ffffbc92`8e81b5ee     nt!ObWaitForMultipleObjects+0x2d5
        ffffa28c`a06f4040 ffffbc92`8e6f2346     win32kfull!xxxMsgWaitForMultipleObjectsEx+0xda
        ffffa28c`a06f40f0 ffffbc92`8dc47420     win32kfull!NtUserMsgWaitForMultipleObjectsEx+0x406
        ffffa28c`a06f4a30 fffff807`62428775     win32k!NtUserMsgWaitForMultipleObjectsEx+0x20
        ffffa28c`a06f4a70 00007ffe`58d8abf4     nt!KiSystemServiceCopyEnd+0x25 (TrapFrame @ ffffa28c`a06f4ae0)
        0000008e`65c9f928 00007ffe`5901d1ee     win32u!NtUserMsgWaitForMultipleObjectsEx+0x14
        0000008e`65c9f930 00007ffe`5a7298b6     user32!RealMsgWaitForMultipleObjectsEx+0x1e
        0000008e`65c9f970 00007ffe`5a72c215     combase!CCliModalLoop::BlockFn+0x196
[onecore\com\combase\dcomrem\callctrl.cxx @ 2156]
        0000008e`65c9fa20 00007ffe`5a73d6a0     combase!ClassicSTAThreadWaitForHandles+0xa5
[onecore\com\combase\dcomrem\classicsta.cpp @ 54]
        0000008e`65c9fb40 00007ffe`34b5556a     combase!CoWaitForMultipleHandles+0x80
[onecore\com\combase\dcomrem\sync.cxx @ 123]
        0000008e`65c9fb80 00007ffe`34c8f308     edgehtml!CDwnTaskExec::ThreadExec+0x14a
        0000008e`65c9fbf0 00007ffe`34c7ef10     edgehtml!CStorageTaskExec::ThreadExec+0x28
        0000008e`65c9fc20 00007ffe`34c7ee98     edgehtml!CExecFT::ThreadProc+0x54
```

```
0000008e`65c9fc50 00007ffe`5a2d54e0     edgehtml!CExecFT::StaticThreadProc+0x38
0000008e`65c9fc80 00007ffe`5af8485b     KERNEL32!BaseThreadInitThunk+0x10
0000008e`65c9fcb0 00000000`00000000     ntdll!RtlUserThreadStart+0x2b
```

[...]

Note: It is also possible to use the **!irpfind** command to search for a suitable I/O request. For the current WinDbg version, it takes a long time to search it tries to load symbol and module files for various drivers.

```
1: kd> !irpfind

Scanning large pool allocation table for tag 0x3f707249 (Irp?) (ffffbe0c86240000 : ffffbe0c86340000)

   Irp             [ Thread ]          irpStack: (Mj,Mn)  DevObj         [Driver]          MDL Process
ffffbe0c84a30a60 [0000000000000000] Irp is complete (CurrentLocation 7 > StackCount 6)
ffffbe0c84a2cae0 [0000000000000000] Irp is complete (CurrentLocation 7 > StackCount 6)
ffffbe0c87de60d0 [0000000000000000] Irp is complete (CurrentLocation 19 > StackCount 18)
ffffbe0c8bfc44b0 [ffffbe0c8a85b080] irpStack: ( d, 0)  ffffbe0c849ceaf0 [ \FileSystem\Npfs]
ffffbe0c899c9a50 [0000000000000000] Irp is complete (CurrentLocation 16 > StackCount 15)
ffffbe0c84a0a960 [0000000000000000] Irp is complete (CurrentLocation 7 > StackCount 6)
ffffbe0c87dea660 [ffffbe0c89971040] irpStack: ( d, 0)  ffffbe0c84c92030 [ \FileSystem\Ntfs]
ffffbe0c84a1f960 [0000000000000000] Irp is complete (CurrentLocation 7 > StackCount 6)
[...]

Searching nonpaged pool (ffffbe0000000000 : ffffce0000000000) for tag 0x3f707249 (Irp?)

ffffbe0c84075aa0 [ffffbe0c8a596080] irpStack: ( c, 2)  ffffbe0c84c92030 [ \FileSystem\Ntfs]
ffffbe0c840ae010 [ffffbe0c89211080] irpStack: ( 3, 0)  ffffbe0c87cdb5f0 [ \Driver\mouclass]
ffffbe0c840c22b0 [0000000000000000] Irp is complete (CurrentLocation 2 > StackCount 1)
ffffbe0c840c23e0 [ffffbe0c89765040] irpStack: ( e, 0)  ffffbe0c84149d80 [ \Driver\DeviceApi]
ffffbe0c840c2510 [0000000000000000] Irp is complete (CurrentLocation 2 > StackCount 1)
ffffbe0c840c2770 [ffffbe0c89788080] irpStack: ( e, 0)  ffffbe0c84149d80 [ \Driver\DeviceApi]
ffffbe0c840c28a0 [ffffbe0c89ac6080] irpStack: ( e, 0)  ffffbe0c899bbaf0 [ \Driver\RasSstp]
ffffbe0c840c2b00 [0000000000000000] Irp is complete (CurrentLocation 2 > StackCount 1)
ffffbe0c840c2d60 [ffffbe0c8988a040] irpStack: ( e, 0)  ffffbe0c84149d80 [ \Driver\DeviceApi]
ffffbe0c840c2e90 [0000000000000000] Irp is complete (CurrentLocation 2 > StackCount 1)
ffffbe0c840dae70 [0000000000000000] Irp is complete (CurrentLocation 3 > StackCount 2)
ffffbe0c84117020 [0000000000000000] Irp is complete (CurrentLocation 43 > StackCount 42)
ffffbe0c8413e020 [0000000000000000] Irp is complete (CurrentLocation 43 > StackCount 42)
ffffbe0c84140020 [0000000000000000] Irp is complete (CurrentLocation 43 > StackCount 42)
ffffbe0c84142020 [0000000000000000] Irp is complete (CurrentLocation 43 > StackCount 42)
ffffbe0c84147020 [0000000000000000] Irp is complete (CurrentLocation 43 > StackCount 42)
ffffbe0c84152aa0 [ffffbe0c8a349080] irpStack: ( e, 6)  ffffbe0c84f36530 [ \Driver\AFD] 0xffffbe0c8a43b080
ffffbe0c8415baa0 [ffffbe0c8a41f080] irpStack: ( e,20)  ffffbe0c84f36530 [ \Driver\AFD] 0xffffbe0c8a43b080
ffffbe0c84163e00 [ffffbe0c8958b080] irpStack: ( e,20)  ffffbe0c84f36530 [ \Driver\AFD] 0xffffbe0c841ed080
ffffbe0c84165e00 [ffffbe0c897e9080] irpStack: ( d, 0)  ffffbe0c849ceaf0 [ \FileSystem\Npfs]
ffffbe0c8416eaa0 [ffffbe0c8a349080] irpStack: ( e, 6)  ffffbe0c84f36530 [ \Driver\AFD] 0xffffbe0c8a43b080
ffffbe0c8417eab0 [0000000000000000] Irp is complete (CurrentLocation 6 > StackCount 5)
ffffbe0c841d8aa0 [ffffbe0c8a596080] irpStack: ( c, 2)  ffffbe0c84c92030 [ \FileSystem\Ntfs]
ffffbe0c841dfe00 [ffffbe0c89a70080] irpStack: ( d, 0)  ffffbe0c849ceaf0 [ \FileSystem\Npfs]
ffffbe0c845fe3e0 [0000000000000000] Irp is complete (CurrentLocation 2 > StackCount 1)
ffffbe0c845fe510 [ffffbe0c89be9080] irpStack: ( e, 0)  ffffbe0c84c82d40 [ \Driver\Beep]
ffffbe0c845fec30 [0000000000000000] Irp is complete (CurrentLocation 2 > StackCount 1)
ffffbe0c8496ab80 [0000000000000000] Irp is complete (CurrentLocation 12 > StackCount 11)
ffffbe0c849728a0 [0000000000000000] Irp is complete (CurrentLocation 12 > StackCount 11)
[...]
ffffbe0c8bed26a0 [ffffbe0c8a4f9080] irpStack: ( 3, 0)  ffffbe0c849ceaf0 [ \FileSystem\Npfs]
ffffbe0c8beddaa0 [ffffbe0c8b511080] irpStack: ( c, 2)  ffffbe0c84c92030 [ \FileSystem\Ntfs]
ffffbe0c8bfe9010 [ffffbe0c888f0080] irpStack: ( 3, 0)  ffffbe0c87802c00 [ \Driver\kbdclass]
ffffbe0c8bfe93d0 [ffffbe0c89fbd040] irpStack: ( 3, 0)  ffffbe0c849ceaf0 [ \FileSystem\Npfs]
ffffbe0c8c07f6a0 [ffffbe0c88822080] irpStack: ( 3, 0)  ffffbe0c849ceaf0 [ \FileSystem\Npfs]
ffffbe0c8c0a64e0 [0000000000000000] Irp is complete (CurrentLocation 3 > StackCount 2) 0x0000000000000000
ffffbe0c8c0aa4e0 [ffffbe0c8ae48080] irpStack: ( c, 2)  ffffbe0c84c92030 [ \FileSystem\Ntfs]
ffffbe0c8c0ac4e0 [ffffbe0c8b541080] irpStack: ( c, 2)  ffffbe0c84c92030 [ \FileSystem\Ntfs]
ffffbe0c8c19b8b0 [ffffbe0c898cb080] irpStack: ( 3, 0)  ffffbe0c849ceaf0 [ \FileSystem\Npfs]
ffffbe0c8c2ecdd0 [ffffbe0c8a51c080] irpStack: ( e, 5)  ffffbe0c84f36530 [ \Driver\AFD] 0xffffbe0c8a982080
ffffbe0c8c424b30 [ffffbe0c88822080] irpStack: ( e, 6)  ffffbe0c84f36530 [ \Driver\AFD] 0xffffbe0c8b4d80c0
ffffbe0c8c42f4e0 [0000000000000000] Irp is complete (CurrentLocation 3 > StackCount 2) 0x0000000000000000
ffffbe0c8c935050 [ffffbe0c840e0040] irpStack: ( d, 0)  ffffbe0c84c92030 [ \FileSystem\Ntfs] 0x0000000000000000
ffffbe0c8ccf2b00 [ffffbe0c8a97b080] irpStack: ( d, 0)  ffffbe0c84c92030 [ \FileSystem\Ntfs] 0xffffbe0c8a8540c0
```

6.   We inspect the I/O request packet (IRP):

```
1: kd> !irp ffffbe0c8beddaa0
Irp is active with 12 stacks 11 is current (= 0xffffbe0c8bedde40)
 No Mdl: No System Buffer: Thread ffffbe0c8b511080:  Irp stack trace.
     cmd  flg cl Device   File     Completion-Context
 [N/A(0), N/A(0)]
            0  0 00000000 00000000 00000000-00000000

                            Args: 00000000 00000000 00000000 00000000
 [N/A(0), N/A(0)]
            0  0 00000000 00000000 00000000-00000000

                            Args: 00000000 00000000 00000000 00000000
 [N/A(0), N/A(0)]
            0  0 00000000 00000000 00000000-00000000

                            Args: 00000000 00000000 00000000 00000000
 [N/A(0), N/A(0)]
            0  0 00000000 00000000 00000000-00000000

                            Args: 00000000 00000000 00000000 00000000
 [N/A(0), N/A(0)]
            0  0 00000000 00000000 00000000-00000000

                            Args: 00000000 00000000 00000000 00000000
 [N/A(0), N/A(0)]
            0  0 00000000 00000000 00000000-00000000

                            Args: 00000000 00000000 00000000 00000000
 [N/A(0), N/A(0)]
            0  0 00000000 00000000 00000000-00000000

                            Args: 00000000 00000000 00000000 00000000
 [N/A(0), N/A(0)]
            0  0 00000000 00000000 00000000-00000000

                            Args: 00000000 00000000 00000000 00000000
 [N/A(0), N/A(0)]
            0  0 00000000 00000000 00000000-00000000

                            Args: 00000000 00000000 00000000 00000000
 [N/A(0), N/A(0)]
            0  0 00000000 00000000 00000000-00000000

                            Args: 00000000 00000000 00000000 00000000
>[IRP_MJ_DIRECTORY_CONTROL(c), N/A(2)]
            0 e1 ffffbe0c84c92030 ffffbe0c84e301d0 fffff80766325400-ffffbe0c8be6a010 Success Error Cancel pending
              \FileSystem\Ntfs  FLTMGR!FltpPassThroughCompletion
                            Args: 00000020 00000001 00000000 00000000
 [IRP_MJ_DIRECTORY_CONTROL(c), N/A(2)]
            0  0 ffffbe0c84dc08d0 ffffbe0c84e301d0 00000000-00000000
              \FileSystem\FltMgr
                            Args: 00000020 00000001 00000000 00000000

Irp Extension present at 0xffffbe0c8bedded0:
```

Note: Each IRP has to travel from a device driver to a device driver, and this path is kept in the IRP stack trace that is right after the IRP structure in memory:

```
1: kd> dt nt!_IRP
   +0x000 Type                    : Int2B
   +0x002 Size                    : Uint2B
   +0x004 AllocationProcessorNumber : Uint2B
   +0x006 Reserved                : Uint2B
   +0x008 MdlAddress              : Ptr64 _MDL
   +0x010 Flags                   : Uint4B
   +0x018 AssociatedIrp           : <unnamed-tag>
```

```
    +0x020 ThreadListEntry    : _LIST_ENTRY
    +0x030 IoStatus           : _IO_STATUS_BLOCK
    +0x040 RequestorMode      : Char
    +0x041 PendingReturned    : UChar
    +0x042 StackCount         : Char
    +0x043 CurrentLocation    : Char
    +0x044 Cancel             : UChar
    +0x045 CancelIrql         : UChar
    +0x046 ApcEnvironment     : Char
    +0x047 AllocationFlags    : UChar
    +0x048 UserIosb           : Ptr64 _IO_STATUS_BLOCK
    +0x048 IoRingContext      : Ptr64 Void
    +0x050 UserEvent          : Ptr64 _KEVENT
    +0x058 Overlay            : <unnamed-tag>
    +0x068 CancelRoutine      : Ptr64     void
    +0x070 UserBuffer         : Ptr64 Void
    +0x078 Tail               : <unnamed-tag>


1: kd> dt nt!_IRP ffffbe0c8beddaa0
    +0x000 Type               : 0n6
    +0x002 Size               : 0x478
    +0x004 AllocationProcessorNumber : 1
    +0x006 Reserved           : 0
    +0x008 MdlAddress         : (null)
    +0x010 Flags              : 0x60000
    +0x018 AssociatedIrp      : <unnamed-tag>
    +0x020 ThreadListEntry    : _LIST_ENTRY [ 0xffffbe0c`8b511580 - 0xffffbe0c`8b511580 ]
    +0x030 IoStatus           : _IO_STATUS_BLOCK
    +0x040 RequestorMode      : 1 ''
    +0x041 PendingReturned    : 0 ''
    +0x042 StackCount         : 12 ''
    +0x043 CurrentLocation    : 11 ''
    +0x044 Cancel             : 0 ''
    +0x045 CancelIrql         : 0 ''
    +0x046 ApcEnvironment     : 0 ''
    +0x047 AllocationFlags    : 0x4 ''
    +0x048 UserIosb           : 0x00007ffe`58d29060 _IO_STATUS_BLOCK
    +0x048 IoRingContext      : 0x00007ffe`58d29060 Void
    +0x050 UserEvent          : (null)
    +0x058 Overlay            : <unnamed-tag>
    +0x068 CancelRoutine      : 0xfffff807`62242d20     void   nt!FsRtlCancelNotify+0
    +0x070 UserBuffer         : 0x00007ffe`58d29040 Void
    +0x078 Tail               : <unnamed-tag>
```

Note: The IRP stack is an array of _IO_STACK_LOCATION structures:

```
1: kd> dt nt!_IO_STACK_LOCATION
    +0x000 MajorFunction      : UChar
    +0x001 MinorFunction      : UChar
    +0x002 Flags              : UChar
    +0x003 Control            : UChar
    +0x008 Parameters         : <unnamed-tag>
    +0x028 DeviceObject       : Ptr64 _DEVICE_OBJECT
    +0x030 FileObject         : Ptr64 _FILE_OBJECT
    +0x038 CompletionRoutine  : Ptr64     long
    +0x040 Context            : Ptr64 Void
```

Note: First, we manually dump the current 11th (0n10 as 0-based) stack location. We know the IRP address, so we must add its size and then index it by stack location structure size:

```
1: kd> ?? sizeof(nt!_IRP)
unsigned int64 0xd0
```

```
1: kd> ?? sizeof(nt!_IO_STACK_LOCATION)
unsigned int64 0x48
```

```
1: kd> dt nt!_IO_STACK_LOCATION ffffbe0c8beddaa0+d0+0n10*48
   +0x000 MajorFunction    : 0xc ''
   +0x001 MinorFunction    : 0x2 ''
   +0x002 Flags            : 0 ''
   +0x003 Control          : 0xe1 ''
   +0x008 Parameters       : <unnamed-tag>
   +0x028 DeviceObject     : 0xffffbe0c`84c92030 _DEVICE_OBJECT
   +0x030 FileObject       : 0xffffbe0c`84e301d0 _FILE_OBJECT
   +0x038 CompletionRoutine : 0xfffff807`66325400     long  FLTMGR!FltpPassThroughCompletion+0
   +0x040 Context          : 0xffffbe0c`8be6a010 Void
```

Note: We can then use the **-a** option to dump 12 array elements (add the **-c** option for compact one-line output):

```
1: kd> dt -a12 nt!_IO_STACK_LOCATION ffffbe0c8beddaa0+d0
[0] @ ffffbe0c`8beddb70
---------------------------------------------
   +0x000 MajorFunction    : 0 ''
   +0x001 MinorFunction    : 0 ''
   +0x002 Flags            : 0 ''
   +0x003 Control          : 0 ''
   +0x008 Parameters       : <unnamed-tag>
   +0x028 DeviceObject     : (null)
   +0x030 FileObject       : (null)
   +0x038 CompletionRoutine : (null)
   +0x040 Context          : (null)

[1] @ ffffbe0c`8beddbb8
---------------------------------------------
   +0x000 MajorFunction    : 0 ''
   +0x001 MinorFunction    : 0 ''
   +0x002 Flags            : 0 ''
   +0x003 Control          : 0 ''
   +0x008 Parameters       : <unnamed-tag>
   +0x028 DeviceObject     : (null)
   +0x030 FileObject       : (null)
   +0x038 CompletionRoutine : (null)
   +0x040 Context          : (null)

[2] @ ffffbe0c`8beddc00
---------------------------------------------
   +0x000 MajorFunction    : 0 ''
   +0x001 MinorFunction    : 0 ''
   +0x002 Flags            : 0 ''
   +0x003 Control          : 0 ''
   +0x008 Parameters       : <unnamed-tag>
   +0x028 DeviceObject     : (null)
   +0x030 FileObject       : (null)
   +0x038 CompletionRoutine : (null)
   +0x040 Context          : (null)

[3] @ ffffbe0c`8beddc48
---------------------------------------------
```

```
    +0x000 MajorFunction     : 0 ''
    +0x001 MinorFunction     : 0 ''
    +0x002 Flags             : 0 ''
    +0x003 Control           : 0 ''
    +0x008 Parameters        : <unnamed-tag>
    +0x028 DeviceObject      : (null)
    +0x030 FileObject        : (null)
    +0x038 CompletionRoutine : (null)
    +0x040 Context           : (null)

[4] @ ffffbe0c`8beddc90
-------------------------------------------------
    +0x000 MajorFunction     : 0 ''
    +0x001 MinorFunction     : 0 ''
    +0x002 Flags             : 0 ''
    +0x003 Control           : 0 ''
    +0x008 Parameters        : <unnamed-tag>
    +0x028 DeviceObject      : (null)
    +0x030 FileObject        : (null)
    +0x038 CompletionRoutine : (null)
    +0x040 Context           : (null)

[5] @ ffffbe0c`8beddcd8
-------------------------------------------------
    +0x000 MajorFunction     : 0 ''
    +0x001 MinorFunction     : 0 ''
    +0x002 Flags             : 0 ''
    +0x003 Control           : 0 ''
    +0x008 Parameters        : <unnamed-tag>
    +0x028 DeviceObject      : (null)
    +0x030 FileObject        : (null)
    +0x038 CompletionRoutine : (null)
    +0x040 Context           : (null)

[6] @ ffffbe0c`8beddd20
-------------------------------------------------
    +0x000 MajorFunction     : 0 ''
    +0x001 MinorFunction     : 0 ''
    +0x002 Flags             : 0 ''
    +0x003 Control           : 0 ''
    +0x008 Parameters        : <unnamed-tag>
    +0x028 DeviceObject      : (null)
    +0x030 FileObject        : (null)
    +0x038 CompletionRoutine : (null)
    +0x040 Context           : (null)

[7] @ ffffbe0c`8beddd68
-------------------------------------------------
    +0x000 MajorFunction     : 0 ''
    +0x001 MinorFunction     : 0 ''
    +0x002 Flags             : 0 ''
    +0x003 Control           : 0 ''
    +0x008 Parameters        : <unnamed-tag>
    +0x028 DeviceObject      : (null)
    +0x030 FileObject        : (null)
    +0x038 CompletionRoutine : (null)
    +0x040 Context           : (null)

[8] @ ffffbe0c`8bedddb0
-------------------------------------------------
    +0x000 MajorFunction     : 0 ''
    +0x001 MinorFunction     : 0 ''
    +0x002 Flags             : 0 ''
    +0x003 Control           : 0 ''
    +0x008 Parameters        : <unnamed-tag>
```

```
    +0x028 DeviceObject      : (null)
    +0x030 FileObject        : (null)
    +0x038 CompletionRoutine : (null)
    +0x040 Context           : (null)

[9] @ ffffbe0c`8bedddf8
------------------------------------------------
    +0x000 MajorFunction     : 0 ''
    +0x001 MinorFunction     : 0 ''
    +0x002 Flags             : 0 ''
    +0x003 Control           : 0 ''
    +0x008 Parameters        : <unnamed-tag>
    +0x028 DeviceObject      : (null)
    +0x030 FileObject        : (null)
    +0x038 CompletionRoutine : (null)
    +0x040 Context           : (null)

[10] @ ffffbe0c`8bedde40
------------------------------------------------
    +0x000 MajorFunction     : 0xc ''
    +0x001 MinorFunction     : 0x2 ''
    +0x002 Flags             : 0 ''
    +0x003 Control           : 0xe1 ''
    +0x008 Parameters        : <unnamed-tag>
    +0x028 DeviceObject      : 0xffffbe0c`84c92030 _DEVICE_OBJECT
    +0x030 FileObject        : 0xffffbe0c`84e301d0 _FILE_OBJECT
    +0x038 CompletionRoutine : 0xfffff807`66325400     long  FLTMGR!FltpPassThroughCompletion+0
    +0x040 Context           : 0xffffbe0c`8be6a010 Void

[11] @ ffffbe0c`8bedde88
------------------------------------------------
    +0x000 MajorFunction     : 0xc ''
    +0x001 MinorFunction     : 0x2 ''
    +0x002 Flags             : 0 ''
    +0x003 Control           : 0 ''
    +0x008 Parameters        : <unnamed-tag>
    +0x028 DeviceObject      : 0xffffbe0c`84dc08d0 _DEVICE_OBJECT
    +0x030 FileObject        : 0xffffbe0c`84e301d0 _FILE_OBJECT
    +0x038 CompletionRoutine : (null)
    +0x040 Context           : (null)
```

```
1: kd> dt -ca12 nt!_IO_STACK_LOCATION ffffbe0c8beddaa0+d0
[0] @ ffffbe0c`8beddb70 +0x000 MajorFunction 0 ''  +0x001 MinorFunction 0 ''  +0x002 Flags 0 ''  +0x003 Control 0 ''  +0x008 Parameters <unnamed-tag>  +0x028 DeviceObject (null)  +0x030
FileObject (null)  +0x038 CompletionRoutine (null)  +0x040 Context (null)
[1] @ ffffbe0c`8beddbb8 +0x000 MajorFunction 0 ''  +0x001 MinorFunction 0 ''  +0x002 Flags 0 ''  +0x003 Control 0 ''  +0x008 Parameters <unnamed-tag>  +0x028 DeviceObject (null)  +0x030
FileObject (null)  +0x038 CompletionRoutine (null)  +0x040 Context (null)
[2] @ ffffbe0c`8beddc00 +0x000 MajorFunction 0 ''  +0x001 MinorFunction 0 ''  +0x002 Flags 0 ''  +0x003 Control 0 ''  +0x008 Parameters <unnamed-tag>  +0x028 DeviceObject (null)  +0x030
FileObject (null)  +0x038 CompletionRoutine (null)  +0x040 Context (null)
[3] @ ffffbe0c`8beddc48 +0x000 MajorFunction 0 ''  +0x001 MinorFunction 0 ''  +0x002 Flags 0 ''  +0x003 Control 0 ''  +0x008 Parameters <unnamed-tag>  +0x028 DeviceObject (null)  +0x030
FileObject (null)  +0x038 CompletionRoutine (null)  +0x040 Context (null)
[4] @ ffffbe0c`8beddc90 +0x000 MajorFunction 0 ''  +0x001 MinorFunction 0 ''  +0x002 Flags 0 ''  +0x003 Control 0 ''  +0x008 Parameters <unnamed-tag>  +0x028 DeviceObject (null)  +0x030
FileObject (null)  +0x038 CompletionRoutine (null)  +0x040 Context (null)
[5] @ ffffbe0c`8beddcd8 +0x000 MajorFunction 0 ''  +0x001 MinorFunction 0 ''  +0x002 Flags 0 ''  +0x003 Control 0 ''  +0x008 Parameters <unnamed-tag>  +0x028 DeviceObject (null)  +0x030
FileObject (null)  +0x038 CompletionRoutine (null)  +0x040 Context (null)
[6] @ ffffbe0c`8beddd20 +0x000 MajorFunction 0 ''  +0x001 MinorFunction 0 ''  +0x002 Flags 0 ''  +0x003 Control 0 ''  +0x008 Parameters <unnamed-tag>  +0x028 DeviceObject (null)  +0x030
FileObject (null)  +0x038 CompletionRoutine (null)  +0x040 Context (null)
[7] @ ffffbe0c`8beddd68 +0x000 MajorFunction 0 ''  +0x001 MinorFunction 0 ''  +0x002 Flags 0 ''  +0x003 Control 0 ''  +0x008 Parameters <unnamed-tag>  +0x028 DeviceObject (null)  +0x030
FileObject (null)  +0x038 CompletionRoutine (null)  +0x040 Context (null)
[8] @ ffffbe0c`8bedddb0 +0x000 MajorFunction 0 ''  +0x001 MinorFunction 0 ''  +0x002 Flags 0 ''  +0x003 Control 0 ''  +0x008 Parameters <unnamed-tag>  +0x028 DeviceObject (null)  +0x030
FileObject (null)  +0x038 CompletionRoutine (null)  +0x040 Context (null)
[9] @ ffffbe0c`8bedddf8 +0x000 MajorFunction 0 ''  +0x001 MinorFunction 0 ''  +0x002 Flags 0 ''  +0x003 Control 0 ''  +0x008 Parameters <unnamed-tag>  +0x028 DeviceObject (null)  +0x030
FileObject (null)  +0x038 CompletionRoutine (null)  +0x040 Context (null)
[10] @ ffffbe0c`8bedde40 +0x000 MajorFunction 0xc ''  +0x001 MinorFunction 0x2 ''  +0x002 Flags 0 ''  +0x003 Control 0xe1 ''  +0x008 Parameters <unnamed-tag>  +0x028 DeviceObject
0xffffbe0c`84c92030 _DEVICE_OBJECT  +0x030 FileObject 0xffffbe0c`84e301d0 _FILE_OBJECT  +0x038 CompletionRoutine 0xfffff807`66325400 long FLTMGR!FltpPassThroughCompletion+0  +0x040
Context 0xffffbe0c`8be6a010 Void
[11] @ ffffbe0c`8bedde88 +0x000 MajorFunction 0xc ''  +0x001 MinorFunction 0x2 ''  +0x002 Flags 0 ''  +0x003 Control 0 ''  +0x008 Parameters <unnamed-tag>  +0x028 DeviceObject
0xffffbe0c`84dc08d0 _DEVICE_OBJECT  +0x030 FileObject 0xffffbe0c`84e301d0 _FILE_OBJECT  +0x038 CompletionRoutine (null)  +0x040 Context (null)
```

7.   We now inspect a file object associated with IRP either using a special command or a data structure:

```
1: kd> !fileobj 0xffffbe0c`84e301d0
```

\Users\dumpa\AppData\Local\Packages\MicrosoftWindows.Client.CBS_cw5n1h2txyewy\AC\Microsoft\Internet
Explorer\DOMStore\252T5R3S

Device Object: 0xffffbe0c84df6870   \Driver\volmgr

```
Vpb: 0xffffbe0c84da05e0
Access: Read SharedRead SharedWrite SharedDelete

Flags:  0x40000
        Handle Created

FsContext: 0xffff800edba0f170FsContext2: 0xffff800edfd68b10
CurrentByteOffset: 0
```

```
1: kd> dt nt!_FILE_OBJECT 0xffffbe0c`84e301d0
   +0x000 Type             : 0n5
   +0x002 Size             : 0n216
   +0x008 DeviceObject     : 0xffffbe0c`84df6870 _DEVICE_OBJECT
   +0x010 Vpb              : 0xffffbe0c`84da05e0 _VPB
   +0x018 FsContext        : 0xffff800e`dba0f170 Void
   +0x020 FsContext2       : 0xffff800e`dfd68b10 Void
   +0x028 SectionObjectPointer : (null)
   +0x030 PrivateCacheMap  : (null)
   +0x038 FinalStatus      : 0n0
   +0x040 RelatedFileObject : (null)
   +0x048 LockOperation    : 0 ''
   +0x049 DeletePending    : 0 ''
   +0x04a ReadAccess       : 0x1 ''
   +0x04b WriteAccess      : 0 ''
   +0x04c DeleteAccess     : 0 ''
   +0x04d SharedRead       : 0x1 ''
   +0x04e SharedWrite      : 0x1 ''
   +0x04f SharedDelete     : 0x1 ''
   +0x050 Flags            : 0x40000
   +0x058 FileName         : _UNICODE_STRING
"\Users\dumpa\AppData\Local\Packages\MicrosoftWindows.Client.CBS_cw5n1h2txyewy\AC\Microsoft\Internet
Explorer\DOMStore\252T5R3S"
   +0x068 CurrentByteOffset : _LARGE_INTEGER 0x0
   +0x070 Waiters          : 0
   +0x074 Busy             : 0
   +0x078 LastLock         : (null)
   +0x080 Lock             : _KEVENT
   +0x098 Event            : _KEVENT
   +0x0b0 CompletionContext : (null)
   +0x0b8 IrpListLock      : 0
   +0x0c0 IrpList          : _LIST_ENTRY [ 0xffffbe0c`84e30290 - 0xffffbe0c`84e30290 ]
   +0x0d0 FileObjectExtension : (null)
```

8.   From a file object, we can navigate to a device object:

```
1: kd> !devobj 0xffffbe0c`84df6870
Device object (ffffbe0c84df6870) is for:
 HarddiskVolume4 \Driver\volmgr DriverObject ffffbe0c84a94df0
Current Irp 00000000 RefCount 10134 Type 00000007 Flags 00001150
Vpb 0xffffbe0c84da05e0 SecurityDescriptor ffff800ed4de4d60 DevExt ffffbe0c84df69c0 DevObjExt ffffbe0c84df6b88 Dope ffffbe0c84da03b0 DevNode ffffbe0c84963010
ExtensionFlags (0000000000)
Characteristics (0x00060000)  FILE_DEVICE_ALLOW_APPCONTAINER_TRAVERSAL, FILE_PORTABLE_DEVICE
AttachedDevice (Upper) ffffbe0c84c8b030 \Driver\fvevol
Device queue is not busy.
```

```
1: kd> dt nt!_DEVICE_OBJECT 0xffffbe0c`84df6870
   +0x000 Type             : 0n3
   +0x002 Size             : 0x318
   +0x004 ReferenceCount   : 0n10134
   +0x008 DriverObject     : 0xffffbe0c`84a94df0 _DRIVER_OBJECT
   +0x010 NextDevice       : 0xffffbe0c`84df5870 _DEVICE_OBJECT
   +0x018 AttachedDevice   : 0xffffbe0c`84c8b030 _DEVICE_OBJECT
   +0x020 CurrentIrp       : (null)
   +0x028 Timer            : (null)
   +0x030 Flags            : 0x1150
   +0x034 Characteristics  : 0x60000
```

```
+0x038 Vpb                    : 0xffffbe0c`84da05e0 _VPB
+0x040 DeviceExtension        : 0xffffbe0c`84df69c0 Void
+0x048 DeviceType             : 7
+0x04c StackSize              : 5 ''
+0x050 Queue                  : <unnamed-tag>
+0x098 AlignmentRequirement   : 0
+0x0a0 DeviceQueue            : _KDEVICE_QUEUE
+0x0c8 Dpc                    : _KDPC
+0x108 ActiveThreadCount      : 0
+0x110 SecurityDescriptor     : 0xffff800e`d4de4d60 Void
+0x118 DeviceLock             : _KEVENT
+0x130 SectorSize             : 0x200
+0x132 Spare1                 : 1
+0x138 DeviceObjectExtension  : 0xffffbe0c`84df6b88 _DEVOBJ_EXTENSION
+0x140 Reserved               : (null)
```

Note: This device has a corresponding device node in a device tree:

```
1: kd> !devnode ffffbe0c84963010
DevNode 0xffffbe0c84963010 for PDO 0xffffbe0c84df6870
  Parent 0xffffbe0c84202ae0   Sibling 0xffffbe0c849629a0   Child 0000000000
  InstancePath is "STORAGE\Volume\{ce84e2de-e778-11e7-b1ce-806e6f6e6963}#0000000026700000"
  ServiceName is "volume"
  TargetDeviceNotify List - f 0xffff800ed4e73510  b 0xffff800ed72e3610
  State = DeviceNodeStarted (0x30a)
  Previous State = DeviceNodeStartPostWork (0x309)
  StateHistory[06] = DeviceNodeStartPostWork (0x309)
  StateHistory[05] = DeviceNodeStartCompletion (0x308)
  StateHistory[04] = DeviceNodeStartPending (0x307)
  StateHistory[03] = DeviceNodeResourcesAssigned (0x306)
  StateHistory[02] = DeviceNodeDriversAdded (0x305)
  StateHistory[01] = DeviceNodeInitialized (0x304)
  StateHistory[00] = DeviceNodeUninitialized (0x301)
  StateHistory[19] = Unknown State (0x0)
  StateHistory[18] = Unknown State (0x0)
  StateHistory[17] = Unknown State (0x0)
  StateHistory[16] = Unknown State (0x0)
  StateHistory[15] = Unknown State (0x0)
  StateHistory[14] = Unknown State (0x0)
  StateHistory[13] = Unknown State (0x0)
  StateHistory[12] = Unknown State (0x0)
  StateHistory[11] = Unknown State (0x0)
  StateHistory[10] = Unknown State (0x0)
  StateHistory[09] = Unknown State (0x0)
  StateHistory[08] = Unknown State (0x0)
  StateHistory[07] = Unknown State (0x0)
  Flags (0x24000130)  DNF_ENUMERATED, DNF_IDS_QUERIED,
                      DNF_NO_RESOURCE_REQUIRED, DNF_NO_LOWER_DEVICE_FILTERS,
                      DNF_NO_UPPER_DEVICE_FILTERS
  UserFlags (0x0000000a)  DNUF_DONT_SHOW_IN_UI, DNUF_NOT_DISABLEABLE
  CapabilityFlags (0x000002c0)  UniqueID, SilentInstall,
                                SurpriseRemovalOK
  DisableableDepends = 1 (including self)
```

9.   From a device object, we can navigate to a driver object:

```
1: kd> !drvobj 0xffffbe0c`84a94df0
Driver object (ffffbe0c84a94df0) is for:
 \Driver\volmgr

Driver Extension List: (id , addr)

Device Object list:
ffffbe0c84df7870   ffffbe0c84df6870   ffffbe0c84df5870   ffffbe0c84df4870
ffffbe0c84df3b90   ffffbe0c84a95af0
```

Note: There can be several device objects for each driver object. The driver object points to the first one, and then the *NextDevice* field in the _DEVICE_OBJECT structure points to the next one in the list.

```
1: kd> dt nt!_DRIVER_OBJECT 0xffffbe0c`84a94df0
   +0x000 Type            : 0n4
   +0x002 Size            : 0n336
   +0x008 DeviceObject    : 0xffffbe0c`84df7870 _DEVICE_OBJECT
   +0x010 Flags           : 0x12
   +0x018 DriverStart     : 0xfffff807`66bb0000 Void
   +0x020 DriverSize      : 0x1b000
   +0x028 DriverSection   : 0xffffbe0c`84086050 Void
   +0x030 DriverExtension : 0xffffbe0c`84a94f40 _DRIVER_EXTENSION
   +0x038 DriverName      : _UNICODE_STRING "\Driver\volmgr"
   +0x048 HardwareDatabase : 0xfffff807`62d3d700 _UNICODE_STRING "\REGISTRY\MACHINE\HARDWARE\DESCRIPTION\SYSTEM"
   +0x050 FastIoDispatch  : (null)
   +0x058 DriverInit      : 0xfffff807`66bc7010     long volmgr!GsDriverEntry+0
   +0x060 DriverStartIo   : (null)
   +0x068 DriverUnload    : 0xfffff807`66bc5e70     void volmgr!VmUnload+0
   +0x070 MajorFunction   : [28] 0xfffff807`66bb1390     long volmgr!VmCreate+0
```

Note: We can also list driver dispatch functions:

```
1: kd> !drvobj 0xffffbe0c`84a94df0 3
Driver object (ffffbe0c84a94df0) is for:
 \Driver\volmgr

Driver Extension List: (id , addr)

Device Object list:
ffffbe0c84df7870   ffffbe0c84df6870   ffffbe0c84df5870   ffffbe0c84df4870
ffffbe0c84df3b90   ffffbe0c84a95af0

DriverEntry:   fffff80766bc7010  volmgr!GsDriverEntry
DriverStartIo: 00000000
DriverUnload:  fffff80766bc5e70  volmgr!VmUnload
AddDevice:     00000000

Dispatch routines:
[00] IRP_MJ_CREATE                     fffff80766bb1390    volmgr!VmCreate
[01] IRP_MJ_CREATE_NAMED_PIPE          fffff80762233c40    nt!IopInvalidDeviceRequest
[02] IRP_MJ_CLOSE                      fffff80762233c40    nt!IopInvalidDeviceRequest
[03] IRP_MJ_READ                       fffff80766bb1010    volmgr!VmReadWrite
[04] IRP_MJ_WRITE                      fffff80766bb1010    volmgr!VmReadWrite
[05] IRP_MJ_QUERY_INFORMATION          fffff80762233c40    nt!IopInvalidDeviceRequest
[06] IRP_MJ_SET_INFORMATION            fffff80762233c40    nt!IopInvalidDeviceRequest
[07] IRP_MJ_QUERY_EA                   fffff80762233c40    nt!IopInvalidDeviceRequest
[08] IRP_MJ_SET_EA                     fffff80762233c40    nt!IopInvalidDeviceRequest
[09] IRP_MJ_FLUSH_BUFFERS             fffff80766bb1250    volmgr!VmFlushBuffers
[0a] IRP_MJ_QUERY_VOLUME_INFORMATION   fffff80762233c40    nt!IopInvalidDeviceRequest
[0b] IRP_MJ_SET_VOLUME_INFORMATION     fffff80762233c40    nt!IopInvalidDeviceRequest
```

```
[0c] IRP_MJ_DIRECTORY_CONTROL          fffff80762233c40    nt!IopInvalidDeviceRequest
[0d] IRP_MJ_FILE_SYSTEM_CONTROL        fffff80762233c40    nt!IopInvalidDeviceRequest
[0e] IRP_MJ_DEVICE_CONTROL             fffff80766bb15d0    volmgr!VmDeviceControl
[0f] IRP_MJ_INTERNAL_DEVICE_CONTROL    fffff80766bb23f0    volmgr!VmInternalDeviceControl
[10] IRP_MJ_SHUTDOWN                   fffff80766bb5790    volmgr!VmShutdown
[11] IRP_MJ_LOCK_CONTROL              fffff80762233c40    nt!IopInvalidDeviceRequest
[12] IRP_MJ_CLEANUP                    fffff80766bb11f0    volmgr!VmCleanup
[13] IRP_MJ_CREATE_MAILSLOT            fffff80762233c40    nt!IopInvalidDeviceRequest
[14] IRP_MJ_QUERY_SECURITY             fffff80762233c40    nt!IopInvalidDeviceRequest
[15] IRP_MJ_SET_SECURITY               fffff80762233c40    nt!IopInvalidDeviceRequest
[16] IRP_MJ_POWER                      fffff80766bb2230    volmgr!VmPower
[17] IRP_MJ_SYSTEM_CONTROL             fffff80766bb1500    volmgr!VmWmi
[18] IRP_MJ_DEVICE_CHANGE              fffff80762233c40    nt!IopInvalidDeviceRequest
[19] IRP_MJ_QUERY_QUOTA                fffff80762233c40    nt!IopInvalidDeviceRequest
[1a] IRP_MJ_SET_QUOTA                  fffff80762233c40    nt!IopInvalidDeviceRequest
[1b] IRP_MJ_PNP                        fffff80766bbd450    volmgr!VmPnp
```

Note: We can also get this list manually:

```
1: kd> dps 0xffffbe0c`84a94df0+70 L0n28
ffffbe0c`84a94e60  fffff807`66bb1390 volmgr!VmCreate
ffffbe0c`84a94e68  fffff807`62233c40 nt!IopInvalidDeviceRequest
ffffbe0c`84a94e70  fffff807`62233c40 nt!IopInvalidDeviceRequest
ffffbe0c`84a94e78  fffff807`66bb1010 volmgr!VmReadWrite
ffffbe0c`84a94e80  fffff807`66bb1010 volmgr!VmReadWrite
ffffbe0c`84a94e88  fffff807`62233c40 nt!IopInvalidDeviceRequest
ffffbe0c`84a94e90  fffff807`62233c40 nt!IopInvalidDeviceRequest
ffffbe0c`84a94e98  fffff807`62233c40 nt!IopInvalidDeviceRequest
ffffbe0c`84a94ea0  fffff807`62233c40 nt!IopInvalidDeviceRequest
ffffbe0c`84a94ea8  fffff807`66bb1250 volmgr!VmFlushBuffers
ffffbe0c`84a94eb0  fffff807`62233c40 nt!IopInvalidDeviceRequest
ffffbe0c`84a94eb8  fffff807`62233c40 nt!IopInvalidDeviceRequest
ffffbe0c`84a94ec0  fffff807`62233c40 nt!IopInvalidDeviceRequest
ffffbe0c`84a94ec8  fffff807`62233c40 nt!IopInvalidDeviceRequest
ffffbe0c`84a94ed0  fffff807`66bb15d0 volmgr!VmDeviceControl
ffffbe0c`84a94ed8  fffff807`66bb23f0 volmgr!VmInternalDeviceControl
ffffbe0c`84a94ee0  fffff807`66bb5790 volmgr!VmShutdown
ffffbe0c`84a94ee8  fffff807`62233c40 nt!IopInvalidDeviceRequest
ffffbe0c`84a94ef0  fffff807`66bb11f0 volmgr!VmCleanup
ffffbe0c`84a94ef8  fffff807`62233c40 nt!IopInvalidDeviceRequest
ffffbe0c`84a94f00  fffff807`62233c40 nt!IopInvalidDeviceRequest
ffffbe0c`84a94f08  fffff807`62233c40 nt!IopInvalidDeviceRequest
ffffbe0c`84a94f10  fffff807`66bb2230 volmgr!VmPower
ffffbe0c`84a94f18  fffff807`66bb1500 volmgr!VmWmi
ffffbe0c`84a94f20  fffff807`62233c40 nt!IopInvalidDeviceRequest
ffffbe0c`84a94f28  fffff807`62233c40 nt!IopInvalidDeviceRequest
ffffbe0c`84a94f30  fffff807`62233c40 nt!IopInvalidDeviceRequest
ffffbe0c`84a94f38  fffff807`66bbd450 volmgr!VmPnp
```

10.   We see the presence of **AttachedDevice** in the device object structure output above, so we examine the device stack for our initial device object:

```
1: kd> !devstack 0xffffbe0c`84df6870
  !DevObj           !DrvObj            !DevExt           ObjectName
  ffffbe0c84c8d040  \Driver\volsnap    ffffbe0c84c8d190
  ffffbe0c849ddd60  \Driver\volume     ffffbe0c849ddeb0
  ffffbe0c84c85600  \Driver\rdyboost   ffffbe0c84c85750
```

```
  ffffbe0c84c82600    \Driver\iorate        ffffbe0c84c82750
  ffffbe0c84c8b030    \Driver\fvevol        ffffbe0c84c8b180
> ffffbe0c84df6870    \Driver\volmgr        ffffbe0c84df69c0   HarddiskVolume4
!DevNode ffffbe0c84963010 :
  DeviceInst is "STORAGE\Volume\{ce84e2de-e778-11e7-b1ce-806e6f6e6963}#0000000026700000"
  ServiceName is "volume"
```

Note: Compared to thread stack trace or I/O stack, the device stack is shown from top to bottom:

```
0: kd> !devobj ffffbe0c84c8b030
Device object (ffffbe0c84c8b030) is for:
  \Driver\fvevol DriverObject ffffbe0c849e1cd0
Current Irp 00000000 RefCount 0 Type 00000007 Flags 00000010
SecurityDescriptor ffff800ed4c19be0 DevExt ffffbe0c84c8b180 DevObjExt ffffbe0c84c8c540
ExtensionFlags (0x00000800)  DOE_DEFAULT_SD_PRESENT
Characteristics (0x00040100)  FILE_DEVICE_SECURE_OPEN, FILE_PORTABLE_DEVICE
AttachedDevice (Upper) ffffbe0c84c82600 \Driver\iorate
AttachedTo (Lower) ffffbe0c84df6870 \Driver\volmgr
Device queue is not busy.
```

11.   Drivers and devices can be listed from the object directory:

```
1: kd> !object \Driver
Object: ffff800ed493aca0  Type: (ffffbe0c840c6d20) Directory
    ObjectHeader: ffff800ed493ac70 (new version)
    HandleCount: 0  PointerCount: 130
    Directory Object: ffff800ed4841d20  Name: Driver

    Hash Address          Type              Name
    ---- -------          ----              ----
    00  ffffbe0c849e1cd0 Driver            fvevol
        ffffbe0c84bd6b80 Driver            vdrvroot
    01  ffffbe0c89c67e20 Driver            PptpMiniport
        ffffbe0c87823de0 Driver            usbuhci
        ffffbe0c84f35d70 Driver            GpuEnergyDrv
        ffffbe0c84eafe30 Driver            NetBT
        ffffbe0c84076e30 Driver            acpiex
        ffffbe0c84119e30 Driver            Wdf01000
    02  ffffbe0c8b5cee30 Driver            MYFAULT
        ffffbe0c89fbde30 Driver            WdNisDrv
        ffffbe0c89803e00 Driver            mpsdrv
        ffffbe0c84971e00 Driver            storahci
    03  ffffbe0c89884e00 Driver            ndproxy
        ffffbe0c897f8370 Driver            MMCSS
        ffffbe0c89421e20 Driver            lltdio
        ffffbe0c87d4caf0 Driver            BthEnum
        ffffbe0c84cd8060 Driver            bam
        ffffbe0c84df8e30 Driver            Psched
        ffffbe0c84df7530 Driver            BasicRender
        ffffbe0c84deccd0 Driver            disk
    04  ffffbe0c8972d9e0 Driver            HTTP
    05  ffffbe0c84f353d0 Driver            WscVReg
    06  ffffbe0c87dd2e30 Driver            monitor
        ffffbe0c87811370 Driver            usbehci
        ffffbe0c84f3b300 Driver            ahcache
        ffffbe0c84eb8150 Driver            VMRawDsk
        ffffbe0c84dd7e40 Driver            iorate
        ffffbe0c84bd4d50 Driver            pcw
    07  ffffbe0c8782e060 Driver            Ucx01000
        ffffbe0c87805310 Driver            USBXHCI
        ffffbe0c84a93790 Driver            partmgr
    08  ffffbe0c89a93c00 Driver            PEAUTH
```

```
        ffffbe0c89425e20 Driver                    MsLldp
        ffffbe0c87aef310 Driver                    e1i68x64
        ffffbe0c84f3ec90 Driver                    Vid
        ffffbe0c8412fe30 Driver                    ACPI_HAL
09      ffffbe0c84a93d80 Driver                    spaceport
10      ffffbe0c89ba7df0 Driver                    Rasl2tp
        ffffbe0c87c6e060 Driver                    HidUsb
        ffffbe0c84f3d080 Driver                    vwififlt
11      ffffbe0c8923be30 Driver                    condrv
        ffffbe0c849ca630 Driver                    DXGKrnl
        ffffbe0c8413ed80 Driver                    PnpManager
12      ffffbe0c849c4e30 Driver                    Null
        ffffbe0c84a98270 Driver                    vsock
        ffffbe0c8412de30 Driver                    intelpep
        ffffbe0c84115e30 Driver                    PRM
13      ffffbe0c89bb1060 Driver                    RasAgileVpn
        ffffbe0c8923ae30 Driver                    wanarp
        ffffbe0c84142d80 Driver                    SoftwareDevice
14      ffffbe0c87d55e50 Driver                    RFCOMM
        ffffbe0c87af0530 Driver                    Serenum
        ffffbe0c8411de30 Driver                    CLFS
        ffffbe0c84186b00 Driver                    WindowsTrustedRTProxy
15      ffffbe0c84f51060 Driver                    Serial
        ffffbe0c84f37750 Driver                    NdisCap
        ffffbe0c84bcb9f0 Driver                    KSecDD
        ffffbe0c84a94df0 Driver                    volmgr
        ffffbe0c84147d80 Driver                    DeviceApi
16      ffffbe0c89880e00 Driver                    VMMemCtl
        ffffbe0c87aef530 Driver                    umbus
        ffffbe0c84131e30 Driver                    CNG
17      ffffbe0c87e0ae30 Driver                    Win32k
        ffffbe0c87af77b0 Driver                    i8042prt
        ffffbe0c84f48dc0 Driver                    npsvctrig
        ffffbe0c849e28f0 Driver                    volume
        ffffbe0c84983af0 Driver                    KSecPkg
        ffffbe0c84bcabd0 Driver                    TPM
18      ffffbe0c84f4daf0 Driver                    mouclass
19      ffffbe0c8486ac90 Driver                    msisadrv
        ffffbe0c84180e30 Driver                    IntelPMT
20      ffffbe0c89a3ae00 Driver                    Ndu
        ffffbe0c87af2e00 Driver                    kbdclass
21      ffffbe0c87cc4e30 Driver                    mouhid
        ffffbe0c849e2b00 Driver                    volsnap
22      ffffbe0c84f40e20 Driver                    nsiproxy
        ffffbe0c84113e30 Driver                    WMIxWDM
23      ffffbe0c89882e00 Driver                    RasSstp
        ffffbe0c8942be20 Driver                    MsQuic
        ffffbe0c87d30e00 Driver                    BthPan
        ffffbe0c8498ed40 Driver                    tdx
        ffffbe0c84a9cb10 Driver                    vmci
24      ffffbe0c87d37e00 Driver                    BTHUSB
        ffffbe0c84175e30 Driver                    WindowsTrustedRT
25      ffffbe0c89a6a380 Driver                    RasPppoe
        ffffbe0c87811600 Driver                    HDAudBus
        ffffbe0c84df1290 Driver                    BasicDisplay
26      ffffbe0c87870e20 Driver                    rdpbus
27      ffffbe0c84a92bc0 Driver                    pdc
28      ffffbe0c87d8a7f0 Driver                    rspndr
        ffffbe0c87cc9530 Driver                    vmusbmouse
29      ffffbe0c87940c20 Driver                    HdAudAddService
        ffffbe0c84f3f750 Driver                    mssmbios
        ffffbe0c84a98060 Driver                    volmgrx
        ffffbe0c8486ec90 Driver                    pci
30      ffffbe0c8787eda0 Driver                    NdisVirtualBus
        ffffbe0c87852e10 Driver                    CmBatt
```

```
        ffffbe0c84cdfb70 Driver                vm3dmp_loader
        ffffbe0c87af37b0 Driver                kdnic
        ffffbe0c84977ba0 Driver                cdrom
        ffffbe0c84b3ba20 Driver                NDIS
    31  ffffbe0c87852940 Driver                swenum
    32  ffffbe0c878b4d30 Driver                usbhub
        ffffbe0c849e2d10 Driver                rdyboost
        ffffbe0c84d82e30 Driver                WFPLWFS
        ffffbe0c84983d00 Driver                Tcpip
        ffffbe0c84138e30 Driver                SgrmAgent
    33  ffffbe0c87b87540 Driver                USBHUB3
        ffffbe0c87826df0 Driver                intelppm
        ffffbe0c8782b140 Driver                gencounter
        ffffbe0c8413ce30 Driver                Beep
        ffffbe0c84961dd0 Driver                atapi
    34  ffffbe0c89c98e20 Driver                NdisTapi
        ffffbe0c87c49dc0 Driver                usbccgp
        ffffbe0c84f3de00 Driver                AFD
        ffffbe0c84a9e4a0 Driver                mountmgr
        ffffbe0c84a96060 Driver                intelide
    35  ffffbe0c89a983b0 Driver                tcpipreg
        ffffbe0c87d47e00 Driver                BTHPORT
        ffffbe0c87940e30 Driver                ksthunk
        ffffbe0c87af9cd0 Driver                vmmouse
        ffffbe0c84f36ca0 Driver                afunix
    36  ffffbe0c891d1e00 Driver                NdisWan
        ffffbe0c87e2de30 Driver                WudfRd
        ffffbe0c84f362e0 Driver                vm3dmp
        ffffbe0c87af6530 Driver                CompositeBus
        ffffbe0c84973dc0 Driver                EhStorClass
        ffffbe0c84a9ea60 Driver                LSI_SAS
        ffffbe0c8417cb00 Driver                ACPI
```

```
1: kd> !object \FileSystem
Object: ffff800ed49395e0  Type: (ffffbe0c840c6d20) Directory
    ObjectHeader: ffff800ed49395b0 (new version)
    HandleCount: 0  PointerCount: 38
    Directory Object: ffff800ed4841d20  Name: FileSystem

    Hash Address          Type                 Name
    ---- -------          ----                 ----
    02  ffffbe0c89043e30 Driver                mrxsmb10
        ffffbe0c89427e20 Driver                mrxsmb
    03  ffffbe0c89804e00 Driver                mrxsmb20
        ffffbe0c8416ae50 Driver                storqosflt
    04  ffffbe0c84168e50 Driver                bindflt
        ffffbe0c89345e30 Driver                luafv
        ffffbe0c8494ddc0 Driver                CimFS
        ffffbe0c849c3d90 Driver                Wof
    06  ffffbe0c89ac9e00 Driver                vmhgfs
    11  ffffbe0c84189dd0 Driver                rdbss
        ffffbe0c84b3b7e0 Device                CdfsRecognizer
    12  ffffbe0c849dacb0 Device                UdfsDiskRecognizer
        ffffbe0c8418bb00 Device                Fs_Rec
    13  ffffbe0c84949060 Driver                Msfs
    15  ffffbe0c84cd8270 Driver                Dfsc
    17  ffffbe0c89a0cbf0 Driver                srvnet
    19  ffffbe0c84187e50 Driver                wcifs
        ffff800ed4939ea0 Directory             Filters
    21  ffffbe0c897e8e00 Driver                bowser
        ffffbe0c849b7bc0 Driver                FltMgr
    22  ffffbe0c84b3b360 Device                FatCdRomRecognizer
    23  ffffbe0c84a91930 Driver                Ntfs
    24  ffffbe0c8417de50 Driver                CldFlt
        ffffbe0c84df1060 Driver                Npfs
```

```
        ffffbe0c84dd6d80 Driver                     Mup
        ffffbe0c84bd3af0 Driver                     RAW
    25  ffffbe0c849da830 Device                     ReFSRecognizer
        ffffbe0c849c9c90 Driver                     WdFilter
    27  ffffbe0c84f3f2d0 Driver                     fastfat
    28  ffffbe0c849b7dd0 Driver                     FileInfo
    31  ffffbe0c84bcade0 Device                     FatDiskRecognizer
    32  ffffbe0c849daa70 Device                     ReFSv1Recognizer
    33  ffffbe0c89041e30 Driver                     srv2
        ffffbe0c84f3d830 Driver                     NetBIOS
        ffffbe0c84c79b20 Driver                     FileCrypt
        ffffbe0c849d5da0 Device                     ExFatRecognizer
    35  ffffbe0c84b3b5a0 Device                     UdfsCdRomRecognizer
```

```
1: kd> !object \Device
Object: ffff800ed480d620  Type: (ffffbe0c840c6d20) Directory
    ObjectHeader: ffff800ed480d5f0 (new version)
    HandleCount: 2  PointerCount: 65900
    Directory Object: ffff800ed4841d20  Name: Device

    Hash Address          Type                    Name
    ---- -------          ----                    ----
    00  ffffbe0c87dce050 Device                   NDMP2
        ffffbe0c87d81050 Device                   0000007e
        ffffbe0c87825630 Device                   VmGenerationCounter
        ffffbe0c84915c90 Device                   0000006a
        ffffbe0c84b350a0 Device                   NTPNP_PCI0030
        ffffbe0c84b37360 Device                   NTPNP_PCI0002
        ffffbe0c84847c90 Device                   00000058
        ffffbe0c8410ec90 Device                   00000044
        ffffbe0c84204ca0 Device                   00000030
    01  ffff800ed9d09510 SymbolicLink             {6b78f721-544e-40d3-8b3a-2e0bef0c12a5}
        ffff800ed9d06e40 SymbolicLink             {eced6451-fb79-4c57-ae57-7f2a080ae525}
        ffffbe0c899b7520 Device                   0000008e
        ffffbe0c899c8050 Device                   NDMP3
        ffffbe0c87cc9060 Device                   USBPDO-9
        ffffbe0c87cbe060 Device                   0000007a
        ffffbe0c84f4cd40 Device                   gpuenergydrv
        ffffbe0c84a9cd20 Device                   VMCIHostDev
        ffffbe0c84910c90 Device                   00000068
        ffffbe0c84d130a0 Device                   NTPNP_PCI0031
        ffffbe0c84b39360 Device                   NTPNP_PCI0003
        ffffbe0c84843c90 Device                   00000054
        ffffbe0c840d5c90 Device                   00000040
    02  ffffbe0c8b78b4e0 Device                   Myfault
        ffffbe0c8a591910 Device                   wdnisdrv
        ffffbe0c89c24050 Device                   NDMP4
        ffffbe0c891aed30 Device                   0000008a
        ffffbe0c88940d90 Device                   UMDFCtrlDev-4990bad6-8a0d-11ec-b28a-806e6f6e6963
        ffffbe0c87c71060 Device                   00000078
        ffffbe0c87cbbd40 Device                   USBPDO-5
        ffffbe0c87919900 Device                   INTELPRO_{E672CB02-CF89-4A6E-8D8D-3C0313D48C6D}
        ffff800ed4ea9850 SymbolicLink             Ip
        ffffbe0c8490cc90 Device                   00000064
        ffffbe0c849240a0 Device                   NTPNP_PCI0032
        ffffbe0c84832c90 Device                   00000050
        ffffbe0c8416dd30 Device                   MSSGRMAGENTSYS
        ffffbe0c8407a060 Device                   0000000f
    03  ffffbe0c89c2c050 Device                   NDMP5
        ffffbe0c89644d90 Device                   NDProxy
        ffffbe0c8952ae00 Device                   MMCSS
        ffffbe0c893ebe00 Device                   lltdio
        ffffbe0c89159e00 Device                   00000088
        ffffbe0c889b8af0 Device                   UMDFCtrlDev-4990bacb-8a0d-11ec-b28a-806e6f6e6963
        ffffbe0c8790e050 Device                   00000074
```

```
        ffffbe0c878b2050 Device                        USBPDO-1
        ffffbe0c84f3e2f0 Device                        Bam
        ffffbe0c8498d530 Device                        Psched
        ffffbe0c84eaf2a0 Device                        Tcp6
        ffffbe0c84b020a0 Device                        NTPNP_PCI0033
        ffffbe0c84d18360 Device                        NTPNP_PCI0005
        ffffbe0c8485ec90 Device                        00000060
        ffffbe0c848bccd0 Device                        0000001f
        ffffbe0c8411bd40 Device                        0000000b
        ffff800ed48b55b0 Section                       PhysicalMemory
   04   ffffbe0c89fcee00 Device                        00000098
        ffffbe0c89cab050 Device                        NDMP6
        ffff800ed941b960 Directory                     Http
        ffffbe0c887de5c0 Device                        00000084
        ffff800ed4939420 Directory                     cimfs
        ffffbe0c84940050 Device                        RaidPort0
        ffffbe0c84b3c060 Device                        NTPNP_PCI0034
        ffffbe0c84d1a360 Device                        NTPNP_PCI0006
        ffffbe0c841fdca0 Device                        0000002f
        ffffbe0c84857cd0 Device                        0000001b
        ffffbe0c8413ad40 Device                        00000009
   05   ffffbe0c8980be00 Device                        00000094
        ffffbe0c89cdf050 Device                        NDMP7
        ffffbe0c89036d20 Device                        SrvAdmin
        ffffbe0c87cfad20 Device                        00000080
        ffffbe0c87c6d8f0 Device                        NetBT_Tcpip_{E672CB02-CF89-4A6E-8D8D-3C0313D48C6D}
        ffffbe0c87831cb0 Device                        CdRom0
        ffff800ed4eff4f0 SymbolicLink                  Ip6
        ffffbe0c84984050 Device                        RaidPort1
        ffffbe0c84d14060 Device                        NTPNP_PCI0035
[...]
```

12.   We close logging before exiting WinDbg:

```
1: kd> .logclose
Closing open log file C:\AdvWMDA-Dumps\x64\C9.log
```

Exercise C10

- **Goal:** Learn how to inspect storage device queues and file system filter stack traces

- **Patterns:** Disk Packet Buildup; Stack Trace (File System Filters)

- \AdvWMDA-Dumps\Exercise-C10-Storage-File-System-Filters.pdf

Exercise C10: Storage and File System

Goal: Learn how to inspect storage device queues and file system filter stack traces.

Patterns: Disk Packet Buildup; Stack Trace (File System Filters).

1.   Launch WinDbg.

2.   Open \AdvWMDA-Dumps\x64\MEMORY-Normal.DMP

3.   We get the dump file loaded (the output should be the same as in the previous exercise).

4.   We open a log file:

```
1: kd> .logopen C:\AdvWMDA-Dumps\x64\C10.log
Opened log file 'C:\AdvWMDA-Dumps\x64\C10.log'
```

5.   We choose the same thread from the list of threads from the previous exercise (C9.log) obtained by
!process 0 3f command:

```
        THREAD ffffbe0c8b511080  Cid 2434.1cd0  Teb: 0000008e61ced000 Win32Thread: ffffbe0c8cce48e0 WAIT:
(UserRequest) UserMode Non-Alertable
        ffffbe0c8b34fae0  SynchronizationEvent
        ffffbe0c8cc40280  QueueObject
    IRP List:
        ffffbe0c8beddaa0: (0006,0478) Flags: 00060000  Mdl: 00000000
        Not impersonating
        DeviceMap                 ffff800eda518d20
        Owning Process            ffffbe0c8bfb10c0    Image:        SearchHost.exe
        Attached Process          N/A         Image:        N/A
        Wait Start TickCount      29430       Ticks: 357 (0:00:00:05.578)
        Context Switch Count      52          IdealProcessor: 1
        UserTime                  00:00:00.000
        KernelTime                00:00:00.046
        Win32 Start Address edgehtml!CExecFT::StaticThreadProc (0x00007ffe34c7ee60)
        Stack Init ffffa28ca06f4c70 Current ffffa28ca06f3740
        Base ffffa28ca06f5000 Limit ffffa28ca06ef000 Call 0000000000000000
        Priority 9 BasePriority 8 PriorityDecrement 0 IoPriority 2 PagePriority 5
        Child-SP          RetAddr             Call Site
        ffffa28c`a06f3780 fffff807`623327f7   nt!KiSwapContext+0x76
        ffffa28c`a06f38c0 fffff807`623346a9   nt!KiSwapThread+0x3a7
        ffffa28c`a06f39a0 fffff807`6228ed51   nt!KiCommitThreadWait+0x159
        ffffa28c`a06f3a40 fffff807`627702c5   nt!KeWaitForMultipleObjects+0x2b1
        ffffa28c`a06f3b40 ffffbc92`8e81b5ee   nt!ObWaitForMultipleObjects+0x2d5
        ffffa28c`a06f4040 ffffbc92`8e6f2346   win32kfull!xxxMsgWaitForMultipleObjectsEx+0xda
        ffffa28c`a06f40f0 ffffbc92`8dc47420   win32kfull!NtUserMsgWaitForMultipleObjectsEx+0x406
        ffffa28c`a06f4a30 fffff807`62428775   win32k!NtUserMsgWaitForMultipleObjectsEx+0x20
        ffffa28c`a06f4a70 00007ffe`58d8abf4   nt!KiSystemServiceCopyEnd+0x25 (TrapFrame @ ffffa28c`a06f4ae0)
        0000008e`65c9f928 00007ffe`5901d1ee   win32u!NtUserMsgWaitForMultipleObjectsEx+0x14
        0000008e`65c9f930 00007ffe`5a7298b6   user32!RealMsgWaitForMultipleObjectsEx+0x1e
        0000008e`65c9f970 00007ffe`5a72c215   combase!CCliModalLoop::BlockFn+0x196
[onecore\com\combase\dcomrem\callctrl.cxx @ 2156]
        0000008e`65c9fa20 00007ffe`5a73d6a0    combase!ClassicSTAThreadWaitForHandles+0xa5
[onecore\com\combase\dcomrem\classicsta.cpp @ 54]
        0000008e`65c9fb40 00007ffe`34b5556a    combase!CoWaitForMultipleHandles+0x80
[onecore\com\combase\dcomrem\sync.cxx @ 123]
        0000008e`65c9fb80 00007ffe`34c8f308    edgehtml!CDwnTaskExec::ThreadExec+0x14a
        0000008e`65c9fbf0 00007ffe`34c7ef10    edgehtml!CStorageTaskExec::ThreadExec+0x28
        0000008e`65c9fc20 00007ffe`34c7ee98    edgehtml!CExecFT::ThreadProc+0x54
        0000008e`65c9fc50 00007ffe`5a2d54e0    edgehtml!CExecFT::StaticThreadProc+0x38
        0000008e`65c9fc80 00007ffe`5af8485b    KERNEL32!BaseThreadInitThunk+0x10
        0000008e`65c9fcb0 00000000`00000000    ntdll!RtlUserThreadStart+0x2b
```

6. We inspect the I/O request packet (IRP):

```
1: kd> !irp ffffbe0c8beddaa0
Irp is active with 12 stacks 11 is current (= 0xffffbe0c8bedde40)
 No Mdl: No System Buffer: Thread ffffbe0c8b511080:  Irp stack trace.
     cmd  flg cl Device   File     Completion-Context
 [N/A(0), N/A(0)]
            0  0 00000000 00000000 00000000-00000000

                        Args: 00000000 00000000 00000000 00000000
 [N/A(0), N/A(0)]
            0  0 00000000 00000000 00000000-00000000

                        Args: 00000000 00000000 00000000 00000000
 [N/A(0), N/A(0)]
            0  0 00000000 00000000 00000000-00000000

                        Args: 00000000 00000000 00000000 00000000
 [N/A(0), N/A(0)]
            0  0 00000000 00000000 00000000-00000000

                        Args: 00000000 00000000 00000000 00000000
 [N/A(0), N/A(0)]
            0  0 00000000 00000000 00000000-00000000

                        Args: 00000000 00000000 00000000 00000000
 [N/A(0), N/A(0)]
            0  0 00000000 00000000 00000000-00000000

                        Args: 00000000 00000000 00000000 00000000
 [N/A(0), N/A(0)]
            0  0 00000000 00000000 00000000-00000000

                        Args: 00000000 00000000 00000000 00000000
 [N/A(0), N/A(0)]
            0  0 00000000 00000000 00000000-00000000

                        Args: 00000000 00000000 00000000 00000000
 [N/A(0), N/A(0)]
            0  0 00000000 00000000 00000000-00000000

                        Args: 00000000 00000000 00000000 00000000
 [N/A(0), N/A(0)]
            0  0 00000000 00000000 00000000-00000000

                        Args: 00000000 00000000 00000000 00000000
>[IRP_MJ_DIRECTORY_CONTROL(c), N/A(2)]
            0 e1 ffffbe0c84c92030 ffffbe0c84e301d0 fffff80766325400-ffffbe0c8be6a010 Success Error Cancel pending
               \FileSystem\Ntfs  FLTMGR!FltpPassThroughCompletion
                        Args: 00000020 00000001 00000000 00000000
 [IRP_MJ_DIRECTORY_CONTROL(c), N/A(2)]
            0  0 ffffbe0c84dc08d0 ffffbe0c84e301d0 00000000-00000000
               \FileSystem\FltMgr
                        Args: 00000020 00000001 00000000 00000000

Irp Extension present at 0xffffbe0c8bedded0:
```

Note: The presence of the *Filter Manager* (FltMgr) and pending status may point to a possible blocking filter driver (not visible in thread stack traces). We can use the **fltkd** extension to check for that:

```
1: kd> !fltkd.irpctrl ffffbe0c8be6a010

IRP_CTRL: ffffbe0c8be6a010  DIRECTORY_CONTROL (12) [00000001] Irp
Flags                   : [10000004] DontCopyParms FixedAlloc
Irp                     : ffffbe0c8beddaa0
DeviceObject            : ffffbe0c84dc08d0 "\Device\HarddiskVolume4"
FileObject              : ffffbe0c84e301d0
CompletionNodeStack     : ffffbe0c8be6a198   Size=6 Next=1
SyncEvent               : (ffffbe0c8be6a028)
InitiatingInstance      : 0000000000000000
Icc                     : ffffa28ca06f4840
PendingCallbackNode     : ffffffffffffffff
```

288

```
PendingCallbackContext  : 0000000000000000
PendingStatus           : 0x00000000
CallbackData            : (ffffbe0c8be6a0f8)
 Flags                  : [00000001] Irp
 Thread                 : ffffbe0c8b511080
 Iopb                   : ffffbe0c8be6a150
 RequestorMode          : [01] UserMode
 IoStatus.Status        : 0x00000000
 IoStatus.Information    : 0000000000000000
 TagData                : 0000000000000000 *******************************************************************
***                                              ***
***                                              ***
***     Either you specified an unqualified symbol, or your debugger   ***
***     doesn't have full symbol information.  Unqualified symbol      ***
***     resolution is turned off by default. Please either specify a   ***
***     fully qualified symbol module!symbolname, or enable resolution ***
***     of unqualified symbols by typing ".symopt- 100". Note that     ***
***     enabling unqualified symbol resolution with network symbol     ***
***     server shares in the symbol path may cause the debugger to     ***
***     appear to hang for long periods of time when an incorrect      ***
***     symbol name is typed or the network symbol server is down.     ***
***                                              ***
***     For some commands to work properly, your symbol path           ***
***     must point to .pdb files that have full type information.       ***
***                                              ***
***     Certain .pdb files (such as the public OS symbols) do not      ***
***     contain the required information.  Contact the group that      ***
***     provided you with these symbols if you need this command to    ***
***     work.                                    ***
***                                              ***
***     Type referenced: PVOID                   ***
***                                              ***
*****************************************************************

 FilterContext[0]        : 0000000000000000
 FilterContext[1]        : 0000000000000000
 FilterContext[2]        : 0000000000000000
 FilterContext[3]        : 0000000000000000

  Cmd    IrpFl  OpFl  CmpFl  Instance FileObjt Completion-Context  Node Adr
--------  --------- ----- -----  -------- -------- ------------------  --------
 [0,0]   00000000  00    0000   0000000000000000 0000000000000000 0000000000000000-0000000000000000   ffffbe0c8be6a418
             Args: 0000000000000000 0000000000000000 0000000000000000 0000000000000000 0000000000000000 0000000000000000
 [0,0]   00000000  00    0000   0000000000000000 0000000000000000 0000000000000000-0000000000000000   ffffbe0c8be6a398
             Args: 0000000000000000 0000000000000000 0000000000000000 0000000000000000 0000000000000000 0000000000000000
 [0,0]   00000000  00    0000   0000000000000000 0000000000000000 0000000000000000-0000000000000000   ffffbe0c8be6a318
             Args: 0000000000000000 0000000000000000 0000000000000000 0000000000000000 0000000000000000 0000000000000000
 [0,0]   00000000  00    0000   0000000000000000 0000000000000000 0000000000000000-0000000000000000   ffffbe0c8be6a298
             Args: 0000000000000000 0000000000000000 0000000000000000 0000000000000000 0000000000000000 0000000000000000
 [12,2]  00060000  00    0000   ffffbe0c84eab8e0 ffffbe0c84e301d0 fffff80766ea1030-0000000000000000   ffffbe0c8be6a218
          ("FileInfo","FileInfo")  fileinfo!FIPostOperationCommonCallback
             Args: 0000000000000020 0000000000000001 0000000000000000 0000000000000000 00007ffe58d29040 0000000000000000
 [12,2]  00060000  00    0002   ffffbe0c84d6a8a0 ffffbe0c84e301d0 fffff80766f19a50-0000000000000000   ffffbe0c8be6a198
          ("WdFilter","WdFilter Instance")  Unable to load image \SystemRoot\system32\drivers\wd\WdFilter.sys, Win32 error 0n2
WdFilter+0x9a50
             Args: 0000000000000020 0000000000000001 0000000000000000 0000000000000000 00007ffe58d29040 0000000000000000
Working IOPB:
>[12,2]  00060000  00           ffffbe0c84eab8e0 ffffbe0c84e301d0                     ffffbe0c8be6a150
          ("FileInfo","FileInfo")
             Args: 0000000000000020 0000000000000001 0000000000000000 0000000000000000 00007ffe58d29040 0000000000000000
```

Note: We examine the suspected module:

```
1: kd> lmv m FileInfo
Browse full module list
start            end              module name
fffff807`66ea0000 fffff807`66ebb000   fileinfo # (pdb symbols)
C:\WinDbg.Docker.AdvWMDA\mss\fileinfo.pdb\8EB8F56AE9BBC66C8BBC64E5780F9EA51\fileinfo.pdb
    Loaded symbol image file: fileinfo.sys
    Mapped memory image file: C:\WinDbg.Docker.AdvWMDA\mss\fileinfo.sys\0144422D1b000\fileinfo.sys
    Image path: \SystemRoot\System32\drivers\fileinfo.sys
    Image name: fileinfo.sys
    Browse all global symbols  functions  data
    Image was built with /Brepro flag.
    Timestamp:        0144422D (This is a reproducible build file hash, not a timestamp)
    CheckSum:         0002942B
    ImageSize:        0001B000
    Translations:     0000.04b0 0000.04e4 0409.04b0 0409.04e4
```

Information from resource tables:

7.   Virtualized and provisioned systems may have problems with storage. If such a problem occurs, we may observe the queue of disk packets blocking NTFS and other operations. We can inspect the available storage devices and their queues by using the **scsikd** extension (in our case, we don't see any problems; in the case of a problem, we would see Queued Status for Packet and possibly an IRP and associated filename):

`1: kd> !scsikd.classext`

```
IMPORTANT NOTE: Please consider using StorageKD instead of scsikd for your debugging needs for
win8 and above targets
Storage class devices:

* !classext ffffbe0c84c7a060 [1,2] VMware, VMware Virtual S Paging Disk

Usage: !classext <class device> <level [0-2]>

Optical devices, such as DVD drives, can be listed with !wdfkd.wdfdriverinfo cdrom, and further
explored
using the "!wdfkd.wdfdevice <device_handle>" and "!wdfkd.wdfdevicequeues <device_handle>"
commands.
```

`1: kd> !scsikd.classext ffffbe0c84c7a060 2`
```
Storage class device ffffbe0c84c7a060 with extension at ffffbe0c84c7a1b0

Classpnp Internal Information at ffffbe0c84c7b040

    Transfer Packet Engine:
```

Packet	Status	DL Irp	Opcode	Sector/ListId	UL Irp
ffffbe0c840c5570	Free	ffffbe0c840dae70			
ffffbe0c898f5870	Free	ffffbe0c8a561bc0			
ffffbe0c898f6710	Free	ffffbe0c8b974260			
ffffbe0c8749d530	Free	ffffbe0c8b978760			
ffffbe0c8749e570	Free	ffffbe0c8af2f6a0			
ffffbe0c8749d1f0	Free	ffffbe0c8baecaa0			
ffffbe0c879e9d90	Free	ffffbe0c8ae69aa0			
ffffbe0c879e93d0	Free	ffffbe0c8b1d1010			
ffffbe0c898f63d0	Free	ffffbe0c8abe94e0			
ffffbe0c89a8c530	Free	ffffbe0c8be688a0			
ffffbe0c89a8da50	Free	ffffbe0c8be6c010			
ffffbe0c84ed7570	Free	ffffbe0c8c0a64e0			
ffffbe0c840c41f0	Free	ffffbe0c8bfdcc30			
ffffbe0c87135d90	Free	ffffbe0c8c42d9b0			
ffffbe0c87135a50	Free	ffffbe0c8c42f4e0			
ffffbe0c87135090	Free	ffffbe0c8a7b5de0			
ffffbe0c87134050	Free	ffffbe0c8bcb7b20			

```
    Pending Idle Requests: 0x0


    Failed Requests:
```

	Srb	Scsi			
Opcode	Status	Status	Sense Code	Sector/ListId	Time Stamp
------	------	------	----------	---------------	------------
1a	04	02	05 24 00		01:05:32.096

```
1a      04      02      05 24 00                01:05:32.096
1a      04      02      05 24 00                01:05:32.096
1a      04      02      05 24 00                01:05:32.096
1a      04      02      05 24 00                01:05:32.111
1a      04      02      05 24 00                01:05:32.111
1a      04      02      05 24 00                01:05:32.111
1a      04      02      05 24 00                01:05:32.111
1a      04      02      05 24 00                01:05:32.174
1a      04      02      05 24 00                01:05:32.174
1a      04      02      05 24 00                01:05:32.658
1a      04      02      05 24 00                01:05:32.658
1a      04      02      05 24 00                01:05:32.674
1a      04      02      05 24 00                01:05:32.674
1a      04      02      05 24 00                01:05:32.689
1a      04      02      05 24 00                01:05:32.689
```

```
    -- dt classpnp!_CLASS_PRIVATE_FDO_DATA ffffbe0c84c7b040 --

Classpnp External Information at ffffbe0c84c7a1b0

    VMware, VMware Virtual S 1.0

    Minidriver information at ffffbe0c84c7a670
    Attached device object at ffffbe0c84947050
    Physical device object at ffffbe0c84947050

    Media Geometry:

        Bytes in a Sector = 512
        Sectors per Track = 63
        Tracks / Cylinder = 255
        Media Length      = 64424509440 bytes = ~60 GB

    -- dt classpnp!_FUNCTIONAL_DEVICE_EXTENSION ffffbe0c84c7a1b0 --
```

8.   We close logging before exiting WinDbg:

```
1: kd> .logclose
Closing open log file C:\AdvWMDA-Dumps\x64\C10.log
```

Exercise C11

- **Goal:** Learn how to analyze raw stack to mine for missing information manually

- **Patterns:** Wait Chain (Window Messaging); Hidden Parameter; Data Correlation

- \AdvWMDA-Dumps\Exercise-C11-Window-Messaging.pdf

Exercise C11: Window Messaging

Goal: Learn how to analyze raw stack to mine for missing information manually.

Patterns: Wait Chain (Window Messaging); Hidden Parameter; Data Correlation.

1.   Launch WinDbg.

2.   Open \AdvWMDA-Dumps\x64\MEMORY-WM.DMP

3.   We get the dump file loaded:

```
Microsoft (R) Windows Debugger Version 10.0.27553.1004 AMD64
Copyright (c) Microsoft Corporation. All rights reserved.


Loading Dump File [C:\AdvWMDA-Dumps\x64\MEMORY-WM.DMP]
Kernel Bitmap Dump File: Full address space is available


************* Path validation summary **************
Response                        Time (ms)      Location
Deferred                                       srv*
Symbol search path is: srv*
Executable search path is:
Windows 10 Kernel Version 22000 MP (2 procs) Free x64
Product: WinNt, suite: TerminalServer SingleUserTS Personal
Edition build lab: 22000.1.amd64fre.co_release.210604-1628
Kernel base = 0xfffff804`04a00000 PsLoadedModuleList = 0xfffff804`05629bc0
Debug session time: Sat Feb 19 14:26:18.655 2022 (UTC + 0:00)
System Uptime: 0 days 0:06:04.659
Loading Kernel Symbols
...............................................................
...............................................................
...............................................................
..
Loading User Symbols
...................................
Loading unloaded module list
........
For analysis of this file, run !analyze -v
nt!KeBugCheckEx:
fffff804`04e16220 mov     qword ptr [rsp+8],rcx ss:0018:ffffa784`8ee7d680=000000000000000a
```

4.   We open a log file:

```
1: kd> .logopen C:\AdvWMDA-Dumps\x64\C11.log
Opened log file 'C:\AdvWMDA-Dumps\x64\C11.log'
```

5.   First, we get the list of all processes and their stack traces:

```
1: kd> !process 0 3f
```

[...]

Note: We skip the output here as it is very large.

6.   Open the log file *C11.log* in Notepad and search for "USER32!SendMessage". We find these threads:

```
        THREAD ffff8008afcc6080  Cid 20d0.10e8  Teb: 000000aa3c2e9000 Win32Thread: ffff8008b34cab70 WAIT:
(WrUserRequest) UserMode Non-Alertable
          ffff8008b35b9d80  QueueObject
        Not impersonating
        DeviceMap                 ffffbc06b0049df0
        Owning Process            ffff8008ad7ca080      Image:         AppF.exe
        Attached Process          N/A               Image:         N/A
        Wait Start TickCount      22929             Ticks: 409 (0:00:00:06.390)
        Context Switch Count      916               IdealProcessor: 1  NoStackSwap
        UserTime                  00:00:00.015
        KernelTime                00:00:00.062
Unable to load image C:\Work\AppF.exe, Win32 error 0n2
*** WARNING: Unable to verify checksum for AppF.exe
        Win32 Start Address AppF (0x00007ff6074515b8)
        Stack Init ffffa7848cb6bc70 Current ffffa7848cb6aff0
        Base ffffa7848cb6c000 Limit ffffa7848cb66000 Call 0000000000000000
        Priority 10 BasePriority 8 PriorityDecrement 0 IoPriority 2 PagePriority 5
        Child-SP          RetAddr             Call Site
        ffffa784`8cb6b030 fffff804`04d327f7   nt!KiSwapContext+0x76
        ffffa784`8cb6b170 fffff804`04d346a9   nt!KiSwapThread+0x3a7
        ffffa784`8cb6b250 fffff804`04d2e5c4   nt!KiCommitThreadWait+0x159
        ffffa784`8cb6b2f0 fffff804`04c8efe0   nt!KeWaitForSingleObject+0x234
        ffffa784`8cb6b3e0 fffff951`1d3aafd6   nt!KeWaitForMultipleObjects+0x540
        ffffa784`8cb6b4e0 fffff951`1d3aa222   win32kfull!xxxRealSleepThread+0x2c6
        ffffa784`8cb6b600 fffff951`1d3a8efd   win32kfull!xxxInterSendMsgEx+0xd72
        ffffa784`8cb6b770 fffff951`1d400594   win32kfull!xxxSendTransformableMessageTimeout+0x38d
        ffffa784`8cb6b8f0 fffff951`1d3f3da7   win32kfull!xxxWrapSendMessage+0x24
        ffffa784`8cb6b950 fffff951`1d3eaefc   win32kfull!NtUserfnDWORD+0x67
        ffffa784`8cb6b990 fffff951`1bd77305   win32kfull!NtUserMessageCall+0x1bc
        ffffa784`8cb6ba20 fffff804`04e28775   win32k!NtUserMessageCall+0x3d
        ffffa784`8cb6ba70 00007ffe`4b031434   nt!KiSystemServiceCopyEnd+0x25 (TrapFrame @ ffffa784`8cb6bae0)
        000000aa`3c4ff778 00007ffe`4cd608cf   win32u!NtUserMessageCall+0x14
        000000aa`3c4ff780 00007ffe`4cd60737   USER32!SendMessageWorker+0x12f
        000000aa`3c4ff820 00007ff6`0745127e   USER32!SendMessageW+0x137
        000000aa`3c4ff880 00007ffe`4cd61c4c   AppF+0x127e
        000000aa`3c4ff920 00007ffe`4cd60ea6   USER32!UserCallWinProcCheckWow+0x33c
        000000aa`3c4ffa90 00007ff6`074511bd   USER32!DispatchMessageWorker+0x2a6
        000000aa`3c4ffb10 00007ff6`0745154a   AppF+0x11bd
        000000aa`3c4ffc00 00007ffe`4bb954e0   AppF+0x154a
        000000aa`3c4ffc40 00007ffe`4d1c485b   KERNEL32!BaseThreadInitThunk+0x10
        000000aa`3c4ffc70 00000000`00000000   ntdll!RtlUserThreadStart+0x2b

        THREAD ffff8008b0747080  Cid 1060.0a28  Teb: 000000ea3dd90000 Win32Thread: ffff8008b34d5f70 WAIT:
(WrUserRequest) UserMode Non-Alertable
          ffff8008b35bf500  QueueObject
        Not impersonating
        DeviceMap                 ffffbc06b0049df0
        Owning Process            ffff8008b10ed080      Image:         AppG.exe
        Attached Process          N/A               Image:         N/A
        Wait Start TickCount      22929             Ticks: 409 (0:00:00:06.390)
        Context Switch Count      400               IdealProcessor: 1  NoStackSwap
        UserTime                  00:00:00.015
        KernelTime                00:00:00.078
Unable to load image C:\Work\AppG.exe, Win32 error 0n2
*** WARNING: Unable to verify checksum for AppG.exe
        Win32 Start Address AppG (0x00007ff6717b15b8)
        Stack Init ffffa7848ed25fb0 Current ffffa7848ed25330
        Base ffffa7848ed26000 Limit ffffa7848ed20000 Call 0000000000000000
        Priority 10 BasePriority 8 PriorityDecrement 0 IoPriority 2 PagePriority 5
        Child-SP          RetAddr             Call Site
```

```
ffffa784`8ed25370 fffff804`04d327f7     nt!KiSwapContext+0x76
ffffa784`8ed254b0 fffff804`04d346a9     nt!KiSwapThread+0x3a7
ffffa784`8ed25590 fffff804`04d2e5c4     nt!KiCommitThreadWait+0x159
ffffa784`8ed25630 fffff804`04c8efe0     nt!KeWaitForSingleObject+0x234
ffffa784`8ed25720 fffff951`1d3aafd6     nt!KeWaitForMultipleObjects+0x540
ffffa784`8ed25820 fffff951`1d3aa222     win32kfull!xxxRealSleepThread+0x2c6
ffffa784`8ed25940 fffff951`1d3a8efd     win32kfull!xxxInterSendMsgEx+0xd72
ffffa784`8ed25ab0 fffff951`1d400594     win32kfull!xxxSendTransformableMessageTimeout+0x38d
ffffa784`8ed25c30 fffff951`1d3f3da7     win32kfull!xxxWrapSendMessage+0x24
ffffa784`8ed25c90 fffff951`1d3eaefc     win32kfull!NtUserfnDWORD+0x67
ffffa784`8ed25cd0 fffff951`1bd77305     win32kfull!NtUserMessageCall+0x1bc
ffffa784`8ed25d60 fffff804`04e28775     win32k!NtUserMessageCall+0x3d
ffffa784`8ed25db0 00007ffe`4b031434     nt!KiSystemServiceCopyEnd+0x25 (TrapFrame @ ffffa784`8ed25e20)
000000ea`3dbff698 00007ffe`4cd608cf     win32u!NtUserMessageCall+0x14
000000ea`3dbff6a0 00007ffe`4cd60737     USER32!SendMessageWorker+0x12f
000000ea`3dbff740 00007ff6`717b127e     USER32!SendMessageW+0x137
000000ea`3dbff7a0 00007ffe`4cd61c4c     AppG+0x127e
000000ea`3dbff840 00007ffe`4cd6179c     USER32!UserCallWinProcCheckWow+0x33c
000000ea`3dbff9b0 00007ffe`4cd74b4d     USER32!DispatchClientMessage+0x9c
000000ea`3dbffa10 00007ffe`4d2676a4     USER32!_fnDWORD+0x3d
000000ea`3dbffa70 00007ffe`4b031414     ntdll!KiUserCallbackDispatcherContinue (TrapFrame @ 000000ea`3dbff938)
000000ea`3dbffaf8 00007ffe`4cd7464e     win32u!NtUserGetMessage+0x14
000000ea`3dbffb00 00007ff6`717b11d0     USER32!GetMessageW+0x2e
000000ea`3dbffb60 00007ff6`717b154a     AppG+0x11d0
000000ea`3dbffc50 00007ffe`4bb954e0     AppG+0x154a
000000ea`3dbffc90 00007ffe`4d1c485b     KERNEL32!BaseThreadInitThunk+0x10
000000ea`3dbffcc0 00000000`00000000     ntdll!RtlUserThreadStart+0x2b

        THREAD ffff8008ada52080  Cid 2590.2594  Teb: 0000009bcbff5000 Win32Thread: ffff8008b2bd8920 RUNNING on
processor 1
        IRP List:
            ffff8008b0f05120: (0006,0118) Flags: 00060000  Mdl: 00000000
        Not impersonating
        DeviceMap                ffffbc06b004bbf0
        Owning Process           ffff8008b1ae90c0       Image:          notmyfault64.exe
        Attached Process         N/A            Image:          N/A
        Wait Start TickCount     23338          Ticks: 0
        Context Switch Count     623            IdealProcessor: 1
        UserTime                 00:00:00.046
        KernelTime               00:00:00.046
        Win32 Start Address notmyfault64 (0x00007ff765445384)
        Stack Init ffffa7848ee7dfb0 Current ffffa7848f87d3a0
        Base ffffa7848ee7e000 Limit ffffa7848ee78000 Call 0000000000000000
        Priority 12 BasePriority 8 PriorityDecrement 2 IoPriority 2 PagePriority 5
        Child-SP          RetAddr           Call Site
        ffffa784`8ee7d678 fffff804`04e28da9     nt!KeBugCheckEx
        ffffa784`8ee7d680 fffff804`04e24f00     nt!KiBugCheckDispatch+0x69
        ffffa784`8ee7d7c0 fffff804`03c61981     nt!KiPageFault+0x440 (TrapFrame @ ffffa784`8ee7d7c0)
        ffffa784`8ee7d950 fffff804`03c61d3d     myfault+0x1981
        ffffa784`8ee7d980 fffff804`03c61ea1     myfault+0x1d3d
        ffffa784`8ee7dac0 fffff804`04d03115     myfault+0x1ea1
        ffffa784`8ee7db20 fffff804`0516bbf2     nt!IofCallDriver+0x55
        ffffa784`8ee7db60 fffff804`0516b9d2     nt!IopSynchronousServiceTail+0x1d2
        ffffa784`8ee7dc10 fffff804`0516ad36     nt!IopXxxControlFile+0xc82
        ffffa784`8ee7dd40 fffff804`04e28775     nt!NtDeviceIoControlFile+0x56
        ffffa784`8ee7ddb0 00007ffe`4d263834     nt!KiSystemServiceCopyEnd+0x25 (TrapFrame @ ffffa784`8ee7de20)
        0000009b`cc0fedd8 00007ffe`4a893ffb     ntdll!NtDeviceIoControlFile+0x14
        0000009b`cc0fede0 00007ffe`4bb95f91     KERNELBASE!DeviceIoControl+0x6b
        0000009b`cc0fee50 00007ff7`6544342f     KERNEL32!DeviceIoControlImplementation+0x81
        0000009b`cc0feea0 00007ffe`4cd6484b     notmyfault64+0x342f
        0000009b`cc0fefa0 00007ffe`4cd6409b     USER32!UserCallDlgProcCheckWow+0x14b
        0000009b`cc0ff080 00007ffe`4cda97c9     USER32!DefDlgProcWorker+0xcb
        0000009b`cc0ff140 00007ffe`4cd61c4c     USER32!DefDlgProcA+0x39
        0000009b`cc0ff180 00007ffe`4cd6179c     USER32!UserCallWinProcCheckWow+0x33c
        0000009b`cc0ff2f0 00007ffe`4cd74b4d     USER32!DispatchClientMessage+0x9c
        0000009b`cc0ff350 00007ffe`4d2676a4     USER32!_fnDWORD+0x3d
        0000009b`cc0ff3b0 00007ffe`4b031434     ntdll!KiUserCallbackDispatcherContinue (TrapFrame @ 0000009b`cc0ff278)
        0000009b`cc0ff438 00007ffe`4cd608cf     win32u!NtUserMessageCall+0x14
        0000009b`cc0ff440 00007ffe`4cd60737     USER32!SendMessageWorker+0x12f
        0000009b`cc0ff4e0 00007ffe`3c0750bf     USER32!SendMessageW+0x137
        0000009b`cc0ff540 00007ffe`3c0a8822     COMCTL32!Button_ReleaseCapture+0xbb
        0000009b`cc0ff570 00007ffe`4cd61c4c     COMCTL32!Button_WndProc+0x802
        0000009b`cc0ff680 00007ffe`4cd60ea6     USER32!UserCallWinProcCheckWow+0x33c
        0000009b`cc0ff7f0 00007ffe`4cd66084     USER32!DispatchMessageWorker+0x2a6
```

```
0000009b`cc0ff870 00007ffe`3c055f9f     USER32!IsDialogMessageW+0x104
0000009b`cc0ff8d0 00007ffe`3c055e48     COMCTL32!Prop_IsDialogMessage+0x4b
0000009b`cc0ff910 00007ffe`3c055abd     COMCTL32!_RealPropertySheet+0x2c0
0000009b`cc0ff9e0 00007ffe`3c120953     COMCTL32!_PropertySheet+0x49
0000009b`cc0ffa10 00007ff7`65444cd0     COMCTL32!PropertySheetA+0x53
0000009b`cc0ffab0 00007ff7`65445292     notmyfault64+0x4cd0
0000009b`cc0ffd80 00007ffe`4bb954e0     notmyfault64+0x5292
0000009b`cc0ffdc0 00007ffe`4d1c485b     KERNEL32!BaseThreadInitThunk+0x10
0000009b`cc0ffdf0 00000000`00000000     ntdll!RtlUserThreadStart+0x2b
```

Note: We find threads that belong to *notmyfault64.exe* and the two 3rd-party application processes: *AppF* and *AppG*. We would like to know what window handles correspond to *SendMessage* calls for the latter two processes. Although we don't expect to see them as stack-based function parameters in this 64-bit memory dump (according to the x64 calling convention, it should be in the RCX register), we nevertheless hope to see window handles as execution residue that surfaces on verbose stack traces (hidden parameters).

7.   Now we dump all stack traces with 4 parameters using the **!for_each_thread** script and then search for possible window handle values in the form "000x0yyy" or similar in threads from *AppF* and *AppG* processes:

```
1: kd> !for_each_thread ".thread /r /p @#Thread; kv"

[...]

Implicit thread is now ffff8008`afcc6080
Implicit process is now ffff8008`ad7ca080
Loading User Symbols
.............................

************* Symbol Loading Error Summary **************
Module name             Error
vsock                   The system cannot find the file specified
vmci                    The system cannot find the file specified
WdFilter                The system cannot find the file specified
vm3dmp                  The system cannot find the file specified
vmmemctl                The system cannot find the file specified
vmhgfs                  The system cannot find the file specified
myfault                 The system cannot find the file specified

You can troubleshoot most symbol related issues by turning on symbol loading diagnostics (!sym noisy) and repeating the command that caused symbols to be
loaded.
You should also verify that your symbol search path (.sympath) is correct.
    *** Stack trace for last set context - .thread/.cxr resets it
    # Child-SP          RetAddr           : Args to Child                                                           : Call Site
00 ffffa784`8cb6b030 fffff804`04d327f7 : ffffa784`0000000a 00000000`ffffffff 00000000`00000000 ffff8008`b0747158 : nt!KiSwapContext+0x76
01 ffffa784`8cb6b170 fffff804`04d346a9 : ffffa784`8cb6b2f0 00000000`00000000 ffffa784`8cb6b350 00000000`00000006 : nt!KiSwapThread+0x3a7
02 ffffa784`8cb6b250 fffff804`04d2e5c4 : 00000000`00000000 00000000`00000000 00000000`00000000 00000000`00000000 : nt!KiCommitThreadWait+0x159
03 ffffa784`8cb6b2f0 fffff804`04c8efe0 : ffff8008`b35b9d80 fffff951`00000000 00000000`00000001 ffff8008`aa0a4400 : nt!KeWaitForSingleObject+0x234
04 ffffa784`8cb6b3e0 fffff951`1d3aafd6 : fffff906`0086b010 fffff906`0086b010 fffff804`0f5d1150 00000000`00000004 : nt!KeWaitForMultipleObjects+0x540
05 ffffa784`8cb6b4e0 fffff951`1d3aa222 : ffff8008`b35bf500 fffff804`00000000 00000000`00000000 ffff8008`00000000 : win32kfull!xxxRealSleepThread+0x2c6
06 ffffa784`8cb6b600 fffff951`1d3a8efd : fffff804`0f5d1150 00000000`00000001 00000000`00000068 00000000`00000000 : win32kfull!xxxInterSendMsgEx+0xd72
07 ffffa784`8cb6b770 fffff951`1d400594 : fffff804`0f5d1150 fffff951`1c2f3ad8 00000000`00000000 00000000`00000001 : win32kfull!xxxSendTransformableMessageTimeout+0x38d
08 ffffa784`8cb6b8f0 fffff951`1d3f3da7 : 00000000`00000000 fffff951`1c2f5c40 fffff804`0f5d1150 00000000`0005044c : win32kfull!xxxWrapSendMessage+0x24
09 ffffa784`8cb6b950 fffff951`1d3eaefc : fffff804`0f5d1150 00000000`0005044c 000000aa`3c4ff701 00000000`00000000 : win32kfull!NtUserfnDWORD+0x67
0a ffffa784`8cb6b990 fffff804`1bd77305 : ffffa784`8cb6ba88 00000000`0005044c 00000000`00000068 ffff8008`afcc6080 : win32kfull!NtUserMessageCall+0x1bc
0b ffffa784`8cb6ba20 fffff804`04e28775 : 00000000`00000000 00000000`00000000 00000000`00000000 fffff804`0f5cf930 : win32k!NtUserMessageCall+0x3d
0c ffffa784`8cb6ba70 00007ffe`4b031434 : 00007ffe`4cd608cf 00000000`00000003 00000000`000000a1 00000000`00000001 : nt!KiSystemServiceCopyEnd+0x25
(TrapFrame @ ffffa784`8cb6bae0)
0d 000000aa`3c4ff778 00007ffe`4cd608cf : 00000000`00000003 00000000`000000a1 00000000`00000001 00000000`00000005 : win32u!NtUserMessageCall+0x14
0e 000000aa`3c4ff780 00007ffe`4cd60737 : 000000aa`3c4ff810 00000000`00000000 00000000`00000068 00000000`00000000 : USER32!SendMessageWorker+0x12f
Unable to load image C:\Work\AppF.exe, Win32 error 0n2
*** WARNING: Unable to verify checksum for AppF.exe
0f 000000aa`3c4ff820 00007ff6`0745127e : 00000000`00030464 00007ff6`07469d00 00000000`80006010 00000000`00000000 : USER32!SendMessageW+0x137
10 000000aa`3c4ff880 00007ff6`4cd61c4c : 00000000`00000000 00000000`00000001 00000000`00000001 00000000`00000000 : AppF+0x127e
11 000000aa`3c4ff920 00007ff6`4cd60ea6 : 00000000`02010005 00007ff6`07451200 00000000`00030464 00007ffe`00000111 : USER32!UserCallWinProcCheckWow+0x33c
12 000000aa`3c4ffa90 00007ff6`074511bd : 00007ff6`07451200 00000000`0001047a 00000000`00000001 00007ff6`07450000 : USER32!DispatchMessageWorker+0x2a6
13 000000aa`3c4ffb10 00007ff6`0745154a : 00000000`00000001 00000000`00000000 00000000`00000000 00000000`00000000 : AppF+0x11bd
14 000000aa`3c4ffc00 00007ffe`4bb954e0 : 00000000`00000000 00000000`00000000 00000000`00000000 00000000`00000000 : AppF+0x154a
15 000000aa`3c4ffc40 00007ffe`4d1c485b : 00000000`00000000 00000000`00000000 00000000`00000000 00000000`00000000 : KERNEL32!BaseThreadInitThunk+0x10
16 000000aa`3c4ffc70 00000000`00000000 : 00000000`00000000 00000000`00000000 00000000`00000000 00000000`00000000 : ntdll!RtlUserThreadStart+0x2b

[...]

Implicit thread is now ffff8008`b0747080
Implicit process is now ffff8008`b10ed080
Loading User Symbols
.............................

************* Symbol Loading Error Summary **************
Module name             Error
vsock                   The system cannot find the file specified
vmci                    The system cannot find the file specified
WdFilter                The system cannot find the file specified
vm3dmp                  The system cannot find the file specified
vmmemctl                The system cannot find the file specified
```

```
vmhgfs              The system cannot find the file specified
myfault             The system cannot find the file specified

You can troubleshoot most symbol related issues by turning on symbol loading diagnostics (!sym noisy) and repeating the command that caused symbols to be
loaded.
You should also verify that your symbol search path (.sympath) is correct.
  *** Stack trace for last set context - .thread/.cxr resets it
  # Child-SP          RetAddr           : Args to Child                                                                       : Call Site
00 ffffa784`8ed25370 fffff804`04d327f7 : 00000000`00000009 00000000`ffffffff 00000000`00000000 fffff8008`b11ed158 : nt!KiSwapContext+0x76
01 ffffa784`8ed254b0 fffff804`04d346a9 : ffffa784`00000014 00000000`00000000 ffffa784`8ed25690 00000000`00000000 : nt!KiSwapThread+0x3a7
02 ffffa784`8ed25590 fffff804`04d2e5c4 : 00000000`00000000 00000000`00000000 00000000`00000000 00000000`00000000 : nt!KiCommitThreadWait+0x159
03 ffffa784`8ed25630 fffff804`04c8efe0 : fffff8008`b35bf500 fffff951`0000000d 00000000`00000001 fffff8008`aa0a4400 : nt!KeWaitForSingleObject+0x234
04 ffffa784`8ed25720 fffff951`1d3aafd6 : fffff906`022d67a0 fffff906`022d67a0 fffff804`0f5d22a0 00000000`00000008 : nt!KeWaitForMultipleObjects+0x540
05 ffffa784`8ed25820 fffff951`1d3aa222 : fffff8008`b35c3cc0 fffff804`00000000 00000000`00000000 fffff8008`00000000 : win32kfull!xxxRealSleepThread+0x2c6
06 ffffa784`8ed25940 fffff951`1d3a8efd : fffff804`0f5d22a0 fffff804`00000068 00000000`00000000 00000000`00000000 : win32kfull!xxxInterSendMsgEx+0xd72
07 ffffa784`8ed25ab0 fffff951`1d400594 : fffff804`0f5d22a0 fffff951`1c2f3ad8 00000000`00000000 00000000`00000001 :
win32kfull!xxxSendTransformableMessageTimeout+0x38d
08 ffffa784`8ed25c30 fffff951`1d3f3da7 : 00000000`00000000 fffff951`1c2f5c40 fffff804`0f5d22a0 00000000`00080478 : win32kfull!xxxWrapSendMessage+0x24
09 ffffa784`8ed25c90 fffff951`1d3eaefc : fffff804`0f5d22a0 00000000`00080478 000000ea`3dbff601 fffff804`0516dfc1 : win32kfull!NtUserfnDWORD+0x67
0a ffffa784`8ed25cd0 fffff951`1bd77305 : ffffa784`8ed25dc8 00000000`00080478 00000000`00000068 fffff8008`b0747080 : win32kfull!NtUserMessageCall+0x1bc
0b ffffa784`8ed25d60 fffff804`04e28775 : 00000000`00000000 00000000`00000000 00000000`00000000 00000000`00000001 : win32k!NtUserMessageCall+0x3d
0c ffffa784`8ed25db0 00007ffe`4b031434 : 00007ffe`4cd608cf 000000ea`3dbff760 00007ffe`4749bc92 000002e5`414a5a30 : nt!KiSystemServiceCopyEnd+0x25
(TrapFrame @ ffffa784`8ed25e20)
0d 000000ea`3dbff698 00007ffe`4cd608cf : 000000ea`3dbff760 00007ffe`4749bc92 000002e5`414a5a30 000002e5`414a0800 : win32u!NtUserMessageCall+0x14
0e 000000ea`3dbff6a0 00007ffe`4cd60737 : 000000ea`3dbff730 00000000`00000000 00000000`00000068 00000000`00000000 : USER32!SendMessageWorker+0x12f
Unable to load image C:\Work\AppG.exe, Win32 error 0n2
*** WARNING: Unable to verify checksum for AppG.exe
0f 000000ea`3dbff740 00007ff6`717b127e : 00000000`0005044c 00007ff6`717c9d00 00000000`80006010 00000000`00000000 : USER32!SendMessageW+0x137
10 000000ea`3dbff7a0 00007ffe`4cd61c4c : 000002e5`41460000 00000000`00000001 00000000`00000001 00000000`00000000 : AppG+0x127e
11 000000ea`3dbff840 00007ffe`4cd6179c : 00000000`00000000 00007ff6`717b1200 00000000`0005044c 00000000`00000111 : USER32!UserCallWinProcCheckWow+0x33c
12 000000ea`3dbff9b0 00007ffe`4cd74b4d : 00000000`00000000 00000000`00000000 00000000`00000068 00000000`00000a28 : USER32!DispatchClientMessage+0x9c
13 000000ea`3dbffa10 00007ffe`4d2676a4 : 00000000`00000000 00000000`00000000 00000000`00000070 ffffffff`ffffffff : USER32!_fnDWORD+0x3d
14 000000ea`3dbffa70 00007ffe`4b031414 : 00007ffe`4cd7464e 00000000`00007f45 00000000`00036207 00007ff6`00000001 : ntdll!KiUserCallbackDispatcherContinue
(TrapFrame @ 000000ea`3dbff938)
15 000000ea`3dbffaf8 00007ffe`4cd7464e : 00000000`00007f45 00000000`00036207 00007ff6`00000001 00007ffe`00000001 : win32u!NtUserGetMessage+0x14
16 000000ea`3dbffb00 00007ff6`717b11d0 : 00007ff6`717b0000 00000000`000104a9 00000000`00000001 00007ff6`717b0000 : USER32!GetMessageW+0x2e
17 000000ea`3dbffb60 00007ff6`717b154a : 00000000`00000001 00000000`00000000 00000000`00000000 00000000`00000000 : AppG+0x11d0
18 000000ea`3dbffc50 00007ffe`4bb954e0 : 00000000`00000000 00000000`00000000 00000000`00000000 00000000`00000000 : AppG+0x154a
19 000000ea`3dbffc90 00007ffe`4d1c485b : 00000000`00000000 00000000`00000000 00000000`00000000 00000000`00000000 : KERNEL32!BaseThreadInitThunk+0x10
1a 000000ea`3dbffcc0 00000000`00000000 : 00000000`00000000 00000000`00000000 00000000`00000000 00000000`00000000 : ntdll!RtlUserThreadStart+0x2b

[...]
```

Note: We notice the similarity between the **0005044c** pattern of 3 values in *AppF* and the **00080478** pattern of 3 values in *AppG*. One value of **0005044c** is also seen in *AppG*. So we search for **00080478** in the log and find one on the *AppH* thread stack:

```
Implicit thread is now ffff8008`b01f1280
Implicit process is now ffff8008`b36f6080
Loading User Symbols
...........................

************* Symbol Loading Error Summary **************
Module name         Error
vsock               The system cannot find the file specified
vmci                The system cannot find the file specified
WdFilter            The system cannot find the file specified
vm3dmp              The system cannot find the file specified
vmmemctl            The system cannot find the file specified
vmhgfs              The system cannot find the file specified
myfault             The system cannot find the file specified

You can troubleshoot most symbol related issues by turning on symbol loading diagnostics (!sym noisy) and repeating the command that caused symbols to be
loaded.
You should also verify that your symbol search path (.sympath) is correct.
  *** Stack trace for last set context - .thread/.cxr resets it
  # Child-SP          RetAddr           : Args to Child                                                                       : Call Site
00 ffffa784`8e2d8790 fffff804`04d327f7 : 00000000`00000009 00000000`ffffffff 00000000`00000000 fffff8008`b0454158 : nt!KiSwapContext+0x76
01 ffffa784`8e2d88d0 fffff804`04d346a9 : 00000000`00000002 fffff804`04cd4dac ffffa784`8e2d8ab0 00000000`00000000 : nt!KiSwapThread+0x3a7
02 ffffa784`8e2d89b0 fffff804`04d2e5c4 : ffffa784`00000000 00000000`00000000 00000000`00000000 fffff8008`00000000 : nt!KiCommitThreadWait+0x159
03 ffffa784`8e2d8a50 fffff804`04c8efe0 : fffff8008`b35c3cc0 fffff951`0000000d 00000000`00000001 fffff8008`aa0a4400 : nt!KeWaitForSingleObject+0x234
04 ffffa784`8e2d8b40 fffff951`1d3aafd6 : fffff906`022a9050 fffff906`022a9050 00000000`00000000 00007ff7`06530000 : nt!KeWaitForMultipleObjects+0x540
05 ffffa784`8e2d8c40 fffff951`1d3aac3f : fffff906`022a9050 fffff906`00000000 00000000`00000001 00000000`00000000 : win32kfull!xxxRealSleepThread+0x2c6
06 ffffa784`8e2d8d60 fffff951`1d331864 : fffff8008`b01f1280 ffffa784`8e2d8ea0 00000182`a4810130 00000000`00000020 : win32kfull!xxxSleepThread2+0xb3
07 ffffa784`8e2d8db0 fffff951`1bd79562 : fffff8008`b01f1280 ffffa784`8e2d8ea0 00000000`00000000 00000182`a4810130 : win32kfull!NtUserWaitMessage+0x44
08 ffffa784`8e2d8df0 fffff804`04e28775 : 00000182`a480c140 00007ffe`00000000 00000000`00000111 ffffa784`8e2d8ea0 : win32k!NtUserWaitMessage+0x16
09 ffffa784`8e2d8e20 00007ffe`4b0314d4 : 00007ffe`4cd864cc 00000000`00080478 00000182`a4810130 00000000`00070494 : nt!KiSystemServiceCopyEnd+0x25
(TrapFrame @ ffffa784`8e2d8e20)
0a 00000030`17aff748 00007ffe`4cd864cc : 00000000`00080478 00000182`a4810130 00000000`00070494 00000182`a4810130 : win32u!NtUserWaitMessage+0x14
0b 00000030`17aff750 00007ffe`4cda924b : 00007ff7`00000001 00000000`00000478 00000000`00000000 00000000`00000000 : USER32!DialogBox2+0x254
0c 00000030`17aff7f0 00007ffe`4cd9fa48 : 00007ff7`06557d60 00000000`00080478 00007ff7`065312c0 00007ff7`06530000 : USER32!InternalDialogBox+0x14b
0d 00000030`17aff850 00007ffe`4cd9fc4d : ffffffff`ffffffff 00000000`00000000 00000000`00080478 00007ff7`065312c0 00000182`a42a5b80 : USER32!DialogBoxIndirectParamAorW+0x58
Unable to load image C:\Work\AppH.exe, Win32 error 0n2
*** WARNING: Unable to verify checksum for AppH.exe
0e 00000030`17aff890 00007ff7`06531276 : 00000000`00080478 00007ff7`06549d00 00000000`00000000 00000000`00000000 : USER32!DialogBoxParamW+0x7d
0f 00000030`17aff8d0 00007ffe`4cd61c4c : 00000000`00080478 00000000`00000001 00000000`00000001 00000000`00000000 : AppH+0x1276
10 00000030`17aff970 00007ffe`4cd6179c : 00000000`00000000 00007ff7`06531200 00000000`00080478 00000000`00000111 : USER32!UserCallWinProcCheckWow+0x33c
11 00000030`17affae0 00007ffe`4cd74b4d : 00000000`00000000 00000000`00000000 00000000`00000068 00007ffe`00001e00 : USER32!DispatchClientMessage+0x9c
12 00000030`17affb40 00007ffe`4d2676a4 : 00000000`00000000 00000000`00000000 00000000`00000070 ffffffff`ffffffff : USER32!_fnDWORD+0x3d
13 00000030`17affba0 00007ffe`4b031414 : 00007ffe`4cd7464e 00000000`00007f34 00000000`0003711a 00007ff7`00000001 : ntdll!KiUserCallbackDispatcherContinue
(TrapFrame @ 00000030`17affa68)
14 00000030`17affc28 00007ffe`4cd7464e : 00000000`00007f34 00000000`0003711a 00007ff7`00000001 00007ffe`00000001 : win32u!NtUserGetMessage+0x14
15 00000030`17affc30 00007ff7`065311d0 : 00007ff7`06530000 00000000`000104c9 00000000`00000001 00007ff7`06530000 : USER32!GetMessageW+0x2e
16 00000030`17affc90 00007ff7`0653151a : 00000000`00000001 00000000`00000000 00000000`00000000 00000000`00000000 : AppH+0x11d0
```

```
17 00000030`17affd80 00007ffe`4bb954e0  : 00000000`00000000 00000000`00000000 00000000`00000000 00000000`00000000 : AppH+0x151a
18 00000030`17affdc0 00007ffe`4d1c485b  : 00000000`00000000 00000000`00000000 00000000`00000000 00000000`00000000 : KERNEL32!BaseThreadInitThunk+0x10
19 00000030`17affdf0 00000000`00000000  : 00000000`00000000 00000000`00000000 00000000`00000000 00000000`00000000 : ntdll!RtlUserThreadStart+0x2b
```

Note: We link all these values into a wait chain: the *AppF* thread window sent a message to the *AppG* window, and the latter sent a message to the *AppH* thread window, which is blocked, showing a dialog box.

8.　　　If we expect the 00080478 window handle to be a recipient of a message in the *AppH,* we should find it around *GetMessage* calls in thread raw stack data survived as execution residue:

```
1: kd> .thread /r /p ffff8008`b01f1280
Implicit thread is now ffff8008`b01f1280
Implicit process is now ffff8008`b36f6080
Loading User Symbols
..............................

************* Symbol Loading Error Summary **************
Module name             Error
vsock                   The system cannot find the file specified
vmci                    The system cannot find the file specified
WdFilter                The system cannot find the file specified
vm3dmp                  The system cannot find the file specified
vmmemctl                The system cannot find the file specified
vmhgfs                  The system cannot find the file specified
myfault                 The system cannot find the file specified

You can troubleshoot most symbol related issues by turning on symbol loading diagnostics (!sym
noisy) and repeating the command that caused symbols to be loaded.
You should also verify that your symbol search path (.sympath) is correct.
```

```
1: kd> !teb
TEB at 0000003017943000
    ExceptionList:        0000000000000000
    StackBase:            0000003017b00000
    StackLimit:           0000003017afb000
    SubSystemTib:         0000000000000000
    FiberData:            0000000000001e00
    ArbitraryUserPointer: 0000000000000000
    Self:                 0000003017943000
    EnvironmentPointer:   0000000000000000
    ClientId:             0000000000001cb8 . 0000000000001e00
    RpcHandle:            0000000000000000
    Tls Storage:          00000182a4267670
    PEB Address:          0000003017942000
    LastErrorValue:       0
    LastStatusValue:      0
    Count Owned Locks:    0
    HardErrorMode:        0
```

```
1: kd> dps 0000003017afb000 0000003017b00000
[...]
00000030`17affba0  00000000`00000000
00000030`17affba8  00000000`00000000
00000030`17affbb0  00000000`00000070
00000030`17affbb8  ffffffff`ffffffff
00000030`17affbc0  00000030`17affbf8
00000030`17affbc8  00000002`00000030
00000030`17affbd0  00007ffe`4b031414 win32u!NtUserGetMessage+0x14
00000030`17affbd8  00000030`17943800
```

```
00000030`17affbe0  00000000`00000000
00000030`17affbe8  00000030`17affc28
00000030`17affbf0  00000000`00000000
00000030`17affbf8  00000182`a480e8e0
00000030`17affc00  00000000`00000111
00000030`17affc08  00000000`00000068
00000030`17affc10  00000000`00000000
00000030`17affc18  00007ff7`06531200  AppH+0x1200
00000030`17affc20  00007ffe`4d263640  ntdll!NtdllDispatchMessage_W
00000030`17affc28  00007ffe`4cd7464e  USER32!GetMessageW+0x2e
00000030`17affc30  00000000`00007f34
00000030`17affc38  00000000`0003711a
00000030`17affc40  00007ff7`00000001
00000030`17affc48  00007ffe`00000001
00000030`17affc50  00000000`00000001
00000030`17affc58  00000000`00000000
00000030`17affc60  00000000`00000000
00000030`17affc68  00000000`00000000
00000030`17affc70  00000000`00000000
00000030`17affc78  00000000`00000000
00000030`17affc80  00000000`000104c9
[...]
```

Note: Unfortunately, we don't find this value around *GetMessageW*. We try to do a double dereference of the same region to see if it survives as a member of the MSG structure or similar:

```
1: kd> dpp 0000003017afb000 0000003017b00000
[...]
00000030`17affba0  00000000`00000000
00000030`17affba8  00000000`00000000
00000030`17affbb0  00000000`00000070
00000030`17affbb8  ffffffff`ffffffff
00000030`17affbc0  00000030`17affbf8  00000182`a480e8e0
00000030`17affbc8  00000002`00000030
00000030`17affbd0  00007ffe`4b031414  00841f0f`c32ecdc3
00000030`17affbd8  00000030`17943800  00000000`c0000388
00000030`17affbe0  00000000`00000000
00000030`17affbe8  00000030`17affc28  00007ffe`4cd7464e  USER32!GetMessageW+0x2e
00000030`17affbf0  00000000`00000000
00000030`17affbf8  00000182`a480e8e0  00000000`00080478
00000030`17affc00  00000000`00000111
00000030`17affc08  00000000`00000068
00000030`17affc10  00000000`00000000
00000030`17affc18  00007ff7`06531200  000090ec`81485340
00000030`17affc20  00007ffe`4d263640  6666000e`bb2225ff
00000030`17affc28  00007ffe`4cd7464e  9a3d8300`00441f0f
00000030`17affc30  00000000`00007f34
00000030`17affc38  00000000`0003711a
00000030`17affc40  00007ff7`00000001
00000030`17affc48  00007ffe`00000001
00000030`17affc50  00000000`00000001
[...]
```

9.   We close logging before exiting WinDbg:

```
1: kd> .logclose
Closing open log file C:\AdvWMDA-Dumps\x64\C11.log
```

Exercise C12

◉ **Goal:** Learn how to look for signs of past behavior

◉ **Patterns:** Black Box; Historical Information; Rough Stack Trace (Unmanaged Space); Unloaded Module; Past Module

◉ \AdvWMDA-Dumps\Exercise-C12-Past-Behavior.pdf

Exercise C12: Past Behavior

Goal: Learn how to mine for information about past behavior.

Patterns: Black Box; Historical Information; Rough Stack Trace (Unmanaged Space); Unloaded Module; Past Process.

1.	Launch WinDbg.

2.	Open \AdvWMDA-Dumps\x64\MEMORY-WM.DMP

3.	We get the dump file loaded (the output should be the same as in the previous exercise).

4.	We open a log file:

```
1: kd> .logopen C:\AdvWMDA-Dumps\x64\C12.log
Opened log file 'C:\AdvWMDA-Dumps\x64\C12.log'
```

5.	First, we check black box data using these undocumented commands:

```
1: kd> !blackboxpnp
```

```
1: kd> !blackboxntfs

NTFS Blackbox Data

0 Slow I/O Timeout Records Found
0 Oplock Break Timeout Records Found
```

```
1: kd> !blackboxbsd
Version: 192
Product type: 1

Auto advanced boot: FALSE
Advanced boot menu timeout: 30
Last boot succeeded: TRUE
Last boot shutdown: FALSE
Sleep in progrees: FALSE

Power button timestamp: 0
System running: TRUE
Connected standby in progress: FALSE
User shutdown in progress: FALSE
System shutdown in progress: FALSE
Sleep in progress: 0
Connected standby scenario instance id: 0
Connected standby entry reason: 0
Connected standby exit reason: 0
System sleep transitions to on: 0
Last reference time: 0x1d8259bda00b856
Last reference time checksum: 0x4c95de38
Last update boot id: 16

Boot attempt count: 1
Last boot checkpoint: TRUE
```

```
Checksum: 0xa3
Last boot id: 16
Last successful shutdown boot id: 15
Last reported abnormal shutdown boot id: 15

Error info boot id: 0
Error info repeat count: 0
Error info other error count: 0
Error info code: 0
Error info other error count: 0

Power button last press time: 0
Power button cumulative press count: 0
Power button last press boot id: 0First,
Power button last power watchdog stage: 0
Power button watchdog armed: FALSE
Power button shutdown in progress: FALSE
Power button last release time: 0
Power button cumulative release count: 0
Power button last release boot id: 0
Power button error count: 0
Power button current connected standby phase: 0
Power button transition latest checkpoint id: 0
Power button transition latest checkpoint type: 0
Power button transition latest checkpoint sequence number: 0
```

Note: Nothing is worrying here, but in the case of PNP-related faults, we may want to find the associated devices and drivers in the registry, as this example from the problem system shows:

```
2: kd> !blackboxpnp
    PnpActivityId      : {00000000-0000-0000-0000-000000000000}
    PnpActivityTime    : 132804247587428354
    PnpEventInformation: 3
    PnpEventInProgress : 0
    PnpProblemCode     : 24
    PnpVetoType        : 0
    DeviceId           : SW\{96E080C7-143C-11D1-B40F-00A0C9223196}\{3C0D501A-140B-11D1-B40F-00A0C9223196}
    VetoString         :
```

6.   We also check unloaded kernel modules:

```
1: kd> lmk

Unloaded modules:
fffff804`0a640000 fffff804`0a650000   dump_storport.sys
fffff804`0a670000 fffff804`0a690000   dump_lsi_sas.sys
fffff804`0a6b0000 fffff804`0a6ce000   dump_dumpfve.sys
fffff804`0bc00000 fffff804`0bc55000   WUDFRd.sys
fffff804`0af10000 fffff804`0af2f000   dam.sys
fffff804`0af30000 fffff804`0af3f000   KMPDC.sys
fffff804`08fa0000 fffff804`08fb1000   WdBoot.sys
fffff804`0a1a0000 fffff804`0a1b2000   hwpolicy.sys
```

Note: In the problem case, there may be some hints of hardware and associated software usage:

```
Unloaded modules:
fffff804`63100000 fffff804`63111000   MSKSSRV.sys
```

```
fffff804`63100000 fffff804`63126000  MpKslDrv.sys
fffff804`63130000 fffff804`63141000  MSKSSRV.sys
fffff804`63150000 fffff804`6315f000  hiber_storport.sys
fffff804`5f600000 fffff804`5f635000  hiber_stornvme.sys
fffff804`63160000 fffff804`6317e000  hiber_dumpfve.sys
fffff804`630b0000 fffff804`630d2000  Microsoft.Bluetooth.Legacy.LEEnumerator.sys
fffff804`630f0000 fffff804`630fc000  mshidumdf.sys
fffff804`630e0000 fffff804`630ec000  umpass.sys
fffff804`63080000 fffff804`630a7000  bthpan.sys
fffff804`63050000 fffff804`63073000  BthEnum.sys
fffff804`63010000 fffff804`6304d000  rfcomm.sys
fffff804`63320000 fffff804`63352000  SurfaceIntegrationDriver.sys
fffff804`63360000 fffff804`63379000  SurfacePowerMeterDriver.sys
fffff804`62c40000 fffff804`62c51000  MSKSSRV.sys
fffff804`63100000 fffff804`6310f000  hiber_storport.sys
fffff804`63110000 fffff804`63145000  hiber_stornvme.sys
fffff804`63150000 fffff804`6316e000  hiber_dumpfve.sys
fffff804`63330000 fffff804`63362000  SurfaceIntegrationDriver.sys
fffff804`62c40000 fffff804`62c59000  SurfacePowerMeterDriver.sys
fffff804`62fd0000 fffff804`62fe1000  MSKSSRV.sys
fffff804`63120000 fffff804`63169000  iFiHDUSBAudio_x64.sys
fffff804`63170000 fffff804`63181000  iFiHDUSBAudioks_x64.sys
fffff804`46040000 fffff804`460ad000  WdFilter.sys
fffff804`62420000 fffff804`6243b000  WdNisDrv.sys
fffff804`62fd0000 fffff804`62feb000  WdNisDrv.sys
fffff804`63190000 fffff804`631b6000  MpKslDrv.sys
fffff804`631e0000 fffff804`631f1000  MSKSSRV.sys
fffff804`631c0000 fffff804`631d1000  MSKSSRV.sys
fffff804`63100000 fffff804`63111000  MSKSSRV.sys
fffff804`62420000 fffff804`62431000  MSKSSRV.sys
fffff804`632c0000 fffff804`632cf000  hiber_storport.sys
fffff804`632d0000 fffff804`63305000  hiber_stornvme.sys
fffff804`63310000 fffff804`6332e000  hiber_dumpfve.sys
fffff804`631e0000 fffff804`63202000  Microsoft.Bluetooth.Legacy.LEEnumerator.sys
fffff804`63220000 fffff804`6322c000  mshidumdf.sys
fffff804`63210000 fffff804`6321c000  umpass.sys
fffff804`631b0000 fffff804`631d7000  bthpan.sys
fffff804`63180000 fffff804`631a3000  BthEnum.sys
fffff804`63140000 fffff804`6317d000  rfcomm.sys
fffff804`63070000 fffff804`630a2000  SurfaceIntegrationDriver.sys
fffff804`630b0000 fffff804`630c9000  SurfacePowerMeterDriver.sys
fffff804`632a0000 fffff804`632b1000  MSKSSRV.sys
fffff804`630f0000 fffff804`63139000  iFiHDUSBAudio_x64.sys
fffff804`63230000 fffff804`63241000  iFiHDUSBAudioks_x64.sys
fffff804`63280000 fffff804`63291000  MSKSSRV.sys
fffff804`630d0000 fffff804`630e1000  MSKSSRV.sys
fffff804`63250000 fffff804`63276000  MpKslDrv.sys
fffff804`62420000 fffff804`62431000  MSKSSRV.sys
fffff804`62700000 fffff804`6270f000  hiber_storport.sys
```

Note: !irpfind command may also point to other devices and drivers.

7.   We can also mine kernel raw stack regions for traces of module symbolic information using this script:

```
!for_each_thread "!thread @#Thread; r? $t1 = ((nt!_KTHREAD *) @#Thread )->StackLimit; r? $t2 =
((nt!_KTHREAD *) @#Thread )->StackBase; dpS @$t1 @$t2"
```

8. Information about processes executed in the past may be present as control areas of the previously mapped files (even if there are no mapped views at the moment):

```
1: kd> !memusage
Control      Valid Standby Dirty Shared Locked PageTables   name
...
ffff8008ae0b9b50    0    152     0      0      0       0  mapped_file( AppF.exe )
ffff8008ae0b9dd0    0    152     0      0      0       0  mapped_file( AppG.exe )
...
ffff8008af841d00    0    108     0      0      0       0  mapped_file( cleanmgr.exe )
...
ffff8008aae57a30   48     16     0     48     48       0  mapped_file( vcruntime140.dll )
...
ffff8008aff3fd50  112     16     0      0    112       0  mapped_file( AppF.exe )
...
ffff8008b11b5d50   64    432     0      0     64       0  mapped_file( mfc140u.dll )
...
ffff8008b2084690   12      0     0      0     12       0  mapped_file( 71d9e9abf0f8b54f9c664329a458c741.tmp )
...
ffff8008b2a29010  112     16     0      0    112       0  mapped_file( AppG.exe )
...
```

```
1: kd> !ca ffff8008b2084690

ControlArea  @ ffff8008b2084690
  Segment      ffffbc06b2a1db90  Flink      ffff8008b2084698  Blink          ffff8008b2084698
  Section Ref              1  Pfn Ref                 3  Mapped Views                 1
  User Ref                 0  WaitForDel              0  Flush Count                  0
  File Object  ffff8008b20541c0  ModWriteCount         0  System Views                 1
  WritableRefs             0  PartitionId             0
  Flags (8080) File WasPurged

    \Windows\SoftwareDistribution\Download\69821e13ffd54f582fabc2e054ec644d\Metadata\Windows10.0-
KB5010386-x64\$dpx$.tmp\71d9e9abf0f8b54f9c664329a458c741.tmp

Segment @ ffffbc06b2a1db90
  ControlArea      ffff8008b2084690  ExtendInfo    0000000000000000
  Total Ptes               100
  Segment Size          100000  Committed                 0
  Flags (c0000) ProtectionMask

Subsection 1 @ ffff8008b2084710
  ControlArea  ffff8008b2084690  Starting Sector       0  Number Of Sectors  100
  Base Pte     ffffbc06c69a3010  Ptes In Subsect     100  Unused Ptes          0
  Flags                     d  Sector Offset         0  Protection           6
  Accessed
  Flink        ffff8008adbfa648  Blink     ffff8008adbfa648  MappedViews          1
```

Note: We see past Windows update activity, the launch of Disk Clean-up, and the previous launch of *AppH.exe* and *AppG.exe* apps before other instances of the same apps were launched that we analyzed in the previous exercise.

Note: Additionally, we can see what processes a particular DLL is mapped into:

```
1: kd> !ca ffff8008b11b5d50 4

ControlArea  @ ffff8008b11b5d50
  Segment      ffffbc06b295d990  Flink      ffff8008b10b5b20  Blink          ffff8008b10b5b20
  Section Ref              0  Pfn Ref                7c  Mapped Views                 1
  User Ref                 1  WaitForDel              0  Flush Count               5f90
  File Object  ffff8008b106b530  ModWriteCount         0  System Views              e39b
  WritableRefs         40005a  PartitionId             0
```

```
   Flags (a0) Image File

        \Windows\System32\mfc140u.dll

1 mapped view(s):

ffff8008b10b5b20 - VAD ffff8008b10b5ac0, process ffff8008b12c0080  vmtoolsd.exe

1: kd> !ca ffff8008aae57a30 4

ControlArea  @ ffff8008aae57a30
   Segment         ffffbc06af8e2160  Flink       ffff8008b1bb8a40  Blink         ffff8008aface090
   Section Ref              0  Pfn Ref               10  Mapped Views          6
   User Ref                6  WaitForDel             0  Flush Count          7c70
   File Object  ffff8008afa58160  ModWriteCount          0  System Views          c56d
   WritableRefs          400002  PartitionId            0
   Flags (a0) Image File

        \Windows\System32\vcruntime140.dll

6 mapped view(s):

ffff8008b1bb8a40 - VAD ffff8008b1bb89e0, process ffff8008b0461080  explorer.exe
ffff8008b10b3960 - VAD ffff8008b10b3900, process ffff8008b12c0080  vmtoolsd.exe
ffff8008b0c24d00 - VAD ffff8008b0c24ca0, process ffff8008afd6a080  RuntimeBroker.
ffff8008aa8c2b60 - VAD ffff8008aa8c2b00, process ffff8008ae9240c0  winlogon.exe
ffff8008afad1fb0 - VAD ffff8008afad1f50, process ffff8008afa82080  VGAuthService.
ffff8008aface090 - VAD ffff8008aface030, process ffff8008af9ed080  vmtoolsd.exe

1: kd> .process /r /p ffff8008af9ed080
Implicit process is now ffff8008`af9ed080
Loading User Symbols
........................................................
...................

1: kd> !vad ffff8008aface030
VAD             Level        Start           End             Commit
ffff8008aface030  0         7ffe3a900       7ffe3a915        2 Mapped  Exe
EXECUTE_WRITECOPY   \Windows\System32\vcruntime140.dll
...

1: kd> lm m vcr*
Browse full module list
start             end               module name
00007ffe`3a900000 00007ffe`3a916000  VCRUNTIME140   (deferred)
```

9.   We close logging before exiting WinDbg:

```
1: kd> .logclose
Closing open log file C:\AdvWMDA-Dumps\x64\C12.log
```

Warning

Because of the evolving nature of Generative AI LLMs and their differences, the following exercise output may differ from what you get when reproducing the results.

Exercise C13

- **Goal:** Learn how to use a Generative AI LLM as a memory dump analysis assistant

- **Patterns:** Annotated Stack Trace; Disassembly Summary; Region Summary; Coincidental Symbolic Information; Analysis Summary

- \AdvWMDA-Dumps\Exercise-C13-Generative-AI-LLM.pdf

Exercise C13: Generative AI LLM Assistant

Goal: Learn how to use a Generative AI LLM as a memory dump analysis assistant.

Patterns: Annotated Stack Trace; Disassembly Summary; Region Summary; Coincidental Symbolic Information; Analysis Summary.

1.   Launch WinDbg.

2.   Open \AdvWMDA-Dumps\x64\MEMORY-WM.DMP

3.   We get the dump file loaded (the output should be the same as in the previous exercise).

4.   We open a log file:

```
1: kd> .logopen C:\AdvWMDA-Dumps\x64\C13.log
Opened log file 'C:\AdvWMDA-Dumps\x64\C13.log'
```

5.   We use OpenAI ChatGPT-4 (https://chat.openai.com/). Your results may vary depending on the LLM you use and the prompts you choose.

6.   We ask ChatGPT to annotate a stack trace line by line, for example:

```
1: kd> k
# Child-SP          RetAddr            Call Site
00 ffffa784`8ee7d678 fffff804`04e28da9   nt!KeBugCheckEx
01 ffffa784`8ee7d680 fffff804`04e24f00   nt!KiBugCheckDispatch+0x69
02 ffffa784`8ee7d7c0 fffff804`03c61981   nt!KiPageFault+0x440
Unable to load image \??\C:\WINDOWS\system32\drivers\myfault.sys, Win32 error 0n2
03 ffffa784`8ee7d950 fffff804`03c61d3d   myfault+0x1981
04 ffffa784`8ee7d980 fffff804`03c61ea1   myfault+0x1d3d
05 ffffa784`8ee7dac0 fffff804`04d03115   myfault+0x1ea1
06 ffffa784`8ee7db20 fffff804`0516bbf2   nt!IofCallDriver+0x55
07 ffffa784`8ee7db60 fffff804`0516b9d2   nt!IopSynchronousServiceTail+0x1d2
08 ffffa784`8ee7dc10 fffff804`0516ad36   nt!IopXxxControlFile+0xc82
09 ffffa784`8ee7dd40 fffff804`04e28775   nt!NtDeviceIoControlFile+0x56
0a ffffa784`8ee7ddb0 00007ffe`4d263834   nt!KiSystemServiceCopyEnd+0x25
0b 0000009b`cc0fedd8 00007ffe`4a893ffb   ntdll!NtDeviceIoControlFile+0x14
0c 0000009b`cc0fede0 00007ffe`4bb95f91   KERNELBASE!DeviceIoControl+0x6b
0d 0000009b`cc0fee50 00007ff7`6544342f   KERNEL32!DeviceIoControlImplementation+0x81
0e 0000009b`cc0feea0 00007ffe`4cd6484b   notmyfault64+0x342f
0f 0000009b`cc0fefa0 00007ffe`4cd6409b   USER32!UserCallDlgProcCheckWow+0x14b
10 0000009b`cc0ff080 00007ffe`4cda97c9   USER32!DefDlgProcWorker+0xcb
11 0000009b`cc0ff140 00007ffe`4cd61c4c   USER32!DefDlgProcA+0x39
12 0000009b`cc0ff180 00007ffe`4cd6179c   USER32!UserCallWinProcCheckWow+0x33c
13 0000009b`cc0ff2f0 00007ffe`4cd74b4d   USER32!DispatchClientMessage+0x9c
14 0000009b`cc0ff350 00007ffe`4d2676a4   USER32!_fnDWORD+0x3d
15 0000009b`cc0ff3b0 00007ffe`4b031434   ntdll!KiUserCallbackDispatcherContinue
16 0000009b`cc0ff438 00007ffe`4cd608cf   win32u!NtUserMessageCall+0x14
17 0000009b`cc0ff440 00007ffe`4cd60737   USER32!SendMessageWorker+0x12f
18 0000009b`cc0ff4e0 00007ffe`3c0750bf   USER32!SendMessageW+0x137
19 0000009b`cc0ff540 00007ffe`3c0a8822   COMCTL32!Button_ReleaseCapture+0xbb
1a 0000009b`cc0ff570 00007ffe`4cd61c4c   COMCTL32!Button_WndProc+0x802
```

```
1b 0000009b`cc0ff680 00007ffe`4cd60ea6     USER32!UserCallWinProcCheckWow+0x33c
1c 0000009b`cc0ff7f0 00007ffe`4cd66084     USER32!DispatchMessageWorker+0x2a6
1d 0000009b`cc0ff870 00007ffe`3c055f9f     USER32!IsDialogMessageW+0x104
1e 0000009b`cc0ff8d0 00007ffe`3c055e48     COMCTL32!Prop_IsDialogMessage+0x4b
1f 0000009b`cc0ff910 00007ffe`3c055abd     COMCTL32!_RealPropertySheet+0x2c0
20 0000009b`cc0ff9e0 00007ffe`3c120953     COMCTL32!_PropertySheet+0x49
21 0000009b`cc0ffa10 00007ff7`65444cd0     COMCTL32!PropertySheetA+0x53
22 0000009b`cc0ffab0 00007ff7`65445292     notmyfault64+0x4cd0
23 0000009b`cc0ffd80 00007ffe`4bb954e0     notmyfault64+0x5292
24 0000009b`cc0ffdc0 00007ffe`4d1c485b     KERNEL32!BaseThreadInitThunk+0x10
25 0000009b`cc0ffdf0 00000000`00000000     ntdll!RtlUserThreadStart+0x2b
```

We get the following output:

Annotating a stack trace involves explaining what each frame represents, typically indicating the function call chain that led to an error or crash. This particular stack trace seems to indicate a crash on a Windows system. Here's a breakdown of each frame:

1. `nt!KeBugCheckEx`
   - This is the Windows kernel function that displays the blue screen of death (BSOD) and stops the system. It's called when the system encounters a fatal error that it cannot recover from.
2. `nt!KiBugCheckDispatch+0x69`
   - A function that handles the dispatching of bug checks (crashes) after an exception or system failure is detected, leading to `KeBugCheckEx`.
3. `nt!KiPageFault+0x440`
   - Indicates a page fault occurred. A page fault happens when a program accesses a page of memory that is not currently mapped to the physical memory. The `+0x440` indicates the offset within the function where the fault occurred.
4. `myfault+0x1981`
   - A custom driver (likely used for testing purposes given its name `myfault.sys`), which has encountered an issue. The `+0x1981` is the offset from the start of this driver's code in memory where the problem occurred.
5. `myfault+0x1d3d`
   - Another location within the `myfault.sys` driver where an issue has occurred, further indicating that this driver is the source of the problem.
6. `myfault+0x1ea1`
   - Yet another location within the `myfault.sys` driver involved in the error.
7. `nt!IofCallDriver+0x55`
   - A kernel function that forwards a request to a device driver. This suggests that `myfault.sys` was being called as part of a chain of device driver calls.
8. `nt!IopSynchronousServiceTail+0x1d2`
   - This function handles the synchronous part of a device I/O operation, indicating that the crash occurred during such an operation.
9. `nt!IopXxxControlFile+0xc82`
   - Manages device I/O control operations. An I/O control operation was in progress, likely initiated by `myfault.sys`, when the crash occurred.

10. `nt!NtDeviceIoControlFile+0x56`
   - The system service function that applications use to send control codes to drivers. The crash occurred as a result of such a call.
11. `nt!KiSystemServiceCopyEnd+0x25`
   - Marks the end of a system service call. This indicates the transition back from kernel mode to user mode.

Frames 11 through 1d represent calls made from user-space applications and libraries, culminating in the original system call that triggered the chain of events leading to the crash. These frames show the interaction between the Windows kernel, user-mode libraries like **KERNELBASE**, **KERNEL32**, **USER32**, and the **myfault64** application, which likely initiated the faulty operation that caused the crash.

Specifically, it appears that **notmyfault64**, a tool commonly used for deliberately causing system crashes to test Windows dump collection and analysis (part of the Sysinternals Suite), was involved in triggering this crash, as indicated by its presence in frame 0e. The presence of user-mode Windows API calls related to dialog message processing (frames 10 onwards) suggests that the crash was triggered during some form of UI interaction or message handling.

7.   We notice that the user space portion was not fully annotated, so we ask ChatGPT to annotate it line by line by specifying only these lines:

```
0b 0000009b`cc0fedd8 00007ffe`4a893ffb     ntdll!NtDeviceIoControlFile+0x14
0c 0000009b`cc0fede0 00007ffe`4bb95f91     KERNELBASE!DeviceIoControl+0x6b
0d 0000009b`cc0fee50 00007ff7`6544342f     KERNEL32!DeviceIoControlImplementation+0x81
0e 0000009b`cc0feea0 00007ffe`4cd6484b     notmyfault64+0x342f
0f 0000009b`cc0fefa0 00007ffe`4cd6409b     USER32!UserCallDlgProcCheckWow+0x14b
10 0000009b`cc0ff080 00007ffe`4cda97c9     USER32!DefDlgProcWorker+0xcb
11 0000009b`cc0ff140 00007ffe`4cd61c4c     USER32!DefDlgProcA+0x39
12 0000009b`cc0ff180 00007ffe`4cd6179c     USER32!UserCallWinProcCheckWow+0x33c
13 0000009b`cc0ff2f0 00007ffe`4cd74b4d     USER32!DispatchClientMessage+0x9c
14 0000009b`cc0ff350 00007ffe`4d2676a4     USER32!_fnDWORD+0x3d
15 0000009b`cc0ff3b0 00007ffe`4b031434     ntdll!KiUserCallbackDispatcherContinue
16 0000009b`cc0ff438 00007ffe`4cd608cf     win32u!NtUserMessageCall+0x14
17 0000009b`cc0ff440 00007ffe`4cd60737     USER32!SendMessageWorker+0x12f
18 0000009b`cc0ff4e0 00007ffe`3c0750bf     USER32!SendMessageW+0x137
19 0000009b`cc0ff540 00007ffe`3c0a8822     COMCTL32!Button_ReleaseCapture+0xbb
1a 0000009b`cc0ff570 00007ffe`4cd61c4c     COMCTL32!Button_WndProc+0x802
1b 0000009b`cc0ff680 00007ffe`4cd60ea6     USER32!UserCallWinProcCheckWow+0x33c
1c 0000009b`cc0ff7f0 00007ffe`4cd66084     USER32!DispatchMessageWorker+0x2a6
1d 0000009b`cc0ff870 00007ffe`3c055f9f     USER32!IsDialogMessageW+0x104
1e 0000009b`cc0ff8d0 00007ffe`3c055e48     COMCTL32!Prop_IsDialogMessage+0x4b
1f 0000009b`cc0ff910 00007ffe`3c055abd     COMCTL32!_RealPropertySheet+0x2c0
20 0000009b`cc0ff9e0 00007ffe`3c120953     COMCTL32!_PropertySheet+0x49
21 0000009b`cc0ffa10 00007ff7`65444cd0     COMCTL32!PropertySheetA+0x53
22 0000009b`cc0ffab0 00007ff7`65445292     notmyfault64+0x4cd0
23 0000009b`cc0ffd80 00007ffe`4bb954e0     notmyfault64+0x5292
24 0000009b`cc0ffdc0 00007ffe`4d1c485b     KERNEL32!BaseThreadInitThunk+0x10
25 0000009b`cc0ffdf0 00000000`00000000     ntdll!RtlUserThreadStart+0x2b
```

<u>We get the following output:</u>

This portion of the stack trace picks up from a user-mode perspective, detailing how an application interacts with the system, specifically involving device I/O control operations, user interface (UI) dialogs, and message handling. Here's a frame-by-frame annotation:

0b. `ntdll!NtDeviceIoControlFile+0x14`

- A system call into the Windows NT Kernel (ntdll.dll) to perform an I/O control operation on a device. This is often used for low-level device management and communication.

0c. **`KERNELBASE!DeviceIoControl+0x6b`**

- The call to **`DeviceIoControl`** in KERNELBASE.dll, which is a wrapper that applications use to access device drivers via **`NtDeviceIoControlFile`**. The offset indicates the specific part of this function where control is passed to the kernel.

0d. **`KERNEL32!DeviceIoControlImplementation+0x81`**

- The actual implementation of the **`DeviceIoControl`** function within KERNEL32.dll, which abstracts the details of the system call to **`ntdll!NtDeviceIoControlFile`**.

0e. **`notmyfault64+0x342f`**

- This frame points to a specific offset within the **`notmyfault64`** application, indicating where the **`DeviceIoControl`** operation was initiated. **`notmyfault64`** is a tool used for deliberately causing system errors to test crash analysis and recovery procedures.

0f. **`USER32!UserCallDlgProcCheckWow+0x14b`**

- A function within USER32.dll that processes dialog box messages, possibly as part of handling UI interactions in **`notmyfault64`**. The function checks for dialog messages and directs them appropriately, including compatibility layers for older Windows applications ("WOW" stands for Windows on Windows).

10. **`USER32!DefDlgProcWorker+0xcb`**
- This function processes default dialog box procedures if a custom procedure isn't defined by the application.

11. **`USER32!DefDlgProcA+0x39`**
- The ANSI version of the default dialog procedure, which processes messages for dialog boxes that do not have explicit handlers defined by the application.

12. **`USER32!UserCallWinProcCheckWow+0x33c`**

- Invoked to handle window messages, ensuring that messages to windows are processed correctly, including those to dialog boxes, with checks for older application compatibility.

13. `USER32!DispatchClientMessage+0x9c`
   - Dispatches a message to a window procedure, part of the USER32.dll's mechanism for managing UI message passing.

14. `USER32!_fnDWORD+0x3d`
   - Likely a function involved in the processing or marshaling of messages with DWORD parameters in the USER32.dll.

15. `ntdll!KiUserCallbackDispatcherContinue`
   - Part of the ntdll.dll, this function continues the execution of a user-mode callback from the kernel, often involved in message processing or system callbacks.

16. `win32u!NtUserMessageCall+0x14`
   - A system call to the Win32 User subsystem (win32u.dll) for sending messages to window procedures.

17. `USER32!SendMessageWorker+0x12f`
   - Performs the work of sending messages to window procedures, ensuring that the message is delivered and processed.

18. `USER32!SendMessageW+0x137`
   - The wide-character version of `SendMessage`, which sends a message to a window or windows and waits for the process to complete.

19. `COMCTL32!Button_ReleaseCapture+0xbb`
   - A function in the Common Controls library (COMCTL32.dll) that releases the mouse capture from a button control, typically involved in button click event handling.

1a. `COMCTL32!Button_WndProc+0x802`

   - The window procedure for button controls in COMCTL32.dll, handling all messages sent to button controls.

1b. `USER32!UserCallWinProcCheckWow+0x33c`

   - (Repeated) Handles window procedure calls with compatibility checks.

1c. `USER32!DispatchMessageWorker+0x2a6`

   - Processes a message queue, dispatching messages to the appropriate window procedures.

1d. `USER32!IsDialogMessageW+0x104`

- Checks messages to see if they are intended for a dialog box and processes them if so.

1e. `COMCTL32!Prop_IsDialogMessage+0x4b`

- A function in COMCTL32.dll that determines if a message is for a property sheet dialog, a specific type of dialog box used for settings.

1f. `COMCTL32!_RealPropertySheet+0x2c0`

- Handles the implementation details of displaying and operating a property sheet dialog.

20. `COMCTL32!_PropertySheet+0x49`
- A wrapper function that creates and displays a property sheet dialog.

21. `COMCTL32!PropertySheetA+0x53`
- The ANSI version of the `PropertySheet` function, which creates and displays property sheets.

22-23. `notmyfault64+0x4cd0` and `notmyfault64+0x5292`

- Further operations within `notmyfault64`, likely related to UI handling or triggering the fault that leads to crash analysis.

24. `KERNEL32!BaseThreadInitThunk+0x10`
- A standard function that is executed when a new thread is created, marking the transition from kernel initialization of a thread to the execution of thread-specific code.

25. `ntdll!RtlUserThreadStart+0x2b`
- The start function for a new thread in user mode, initiating the execution of the thread's main function.

8.   We ask ChatGPT to summarize this disassembly fragment:

```
1: kd> ub fffff804`0516bbf2
nt!IopSynchronousServiceTail+0x1b1:
fffff804`0516bbd1 cmp       byte ptr [rbx+47h],0
fffff804`0516bbd5 jl        nt!IopSynchronousServiceTail+0x1c7 (fffff804`0516bbe7)
fffff804`0516bbd7 mov       rax,qword ptr [rbx+0C8h]
fffff804`0516bbde test      rax,rax
fffff804`0516bbe1 jne       nt!IopSynchronousServiceTail+0x3a0 (fffff804`0516bdc0)
fffff804`0516bbe7 mov       rdx,rbx
fffff804`0516bbea mov       rcx,r13
fffff804`0516bbed call      nt!IofCallDriver (fffff804`04d030c0
```

This sequence of instructions is part of a routine within the Windows kernel, dealing with handling synchronous I/O operations. Here's a summary of what each instruction does:

1. `cmp byte ptr [rbx+47h],0` - This instruction compares a byte value at the address `rbx+47h` to 0. It's likely checking a status or flag related to an I/O operation or device.
2. `jl nt!IopSynchronousServiceTail+0x1c7 (fffff804`0516bbe7`)` - If the comparison results in a "less than" condition (meaning the byte at `rbx+47h` is negative), the execution jumps to an address offset `+0x1c7` from `IopSynchronousServiceTail`, handling a specific case or error condition.
3. `mov rax,qword ptr [rbx+0C8h]` - Moves a 64-bit value from the address `rbx+0C8h` into the `rax` register. This could be loading a pointer or data related to the current I/O request.
4. `test rax,rax` - Performs a bitwise AND operation on `rax` with itself, setting flags based on the result. This is often used to check if a value (such as a pointer) is null.
5. `jne nt!IopSynchronousServiceTail+0x3a0 (fffff804`0516bdc0`)` - If `rax` is not equal to 0 (indicating the `test` instruction found `rax` to be non-null), execution jumps to an offset `+0x3a0` from `IopSynchronousServiceTail`, presumably to handle a valid or successful case.
6. `mov rdx,rbx` - Moves the value in `rbx` into `rdx`. Since `rdx` is often used as the second argument in function calls, this could be preparing for such a call.
7. `mov rcx,r13` - Moves the value in `r13` into `rcx`, which is typically used as the first argument in function calls on Windows x64. This sets up the first parameter for a subsequent call.
8. `call nt!IofCallDriver (fffff804`04d030c0`)` - Calls the `IofCallDriver` function, passing the values in `rcx` and `rdx` as arguments. This function is responsible for forwarding the I/O request to the appropriate driver.

In summary, these instructions are part of a routine that checks conditions related to an I/O request, potentially branching based on those conditions, and eventually forwards the request to a driver by calling `IofCallDriver`. The checks and branches likely handle different scenarios or states of the I/O operation.

9.　　　We ask ChatGPT to summarize the raw stack region:

```
1: kd> !teb
TEB at 0000009bcbff5000
    ExceptionList:        0000000000000000
    StackBase:            0000009bcc100000
    StackLimit:           0000009bcc0fb000
    SubSystemTib:         0000000000000000
    FiberData:            0000000000001e00
    ArbitraryUserPointer: 0000000000000000
    Self:                 0000009bcbff5000
    EnvironmentPointer:   0000000000000000
    ClientId:             0000000000002590 . 0000000000002594
    RpcHandle:            0000000000000000
    Tls Storage:          000001dd6f001b10
    PEB Address:          0000009bcbff4000
    LastErrorValue:       0
    LastStatusValue:      c0000034
    Count Owned Locks:    0
    HardErrorMode:        0
```

```
1: kd> dpS 0000009bcc0fb000 0000009bcc100000
00007ffe`4d2599f9 ntdll!guard_check_icall+0xd
00007ffe`4d2599f9 ntdll!guard_check_icall+0xd
00007ffe`4d255ea1 ntdll!bsearch+0x81
00007ffe`4d255ea1 ntdll!bsearch+0x81
00007ffe`4d2599f9 ntdll!guard_check_icall+0xd
00007ffe`4d20637d ntdll!RtlpLocateActivationContextSection+0x13d
00007ffe`4d255ea1 ntdll!bsearch+0x81
00007ffe`4d205ea6 ntdll!RtlpFindUnicodeStringInSection+0x1d6
00007ffe`4d20637d ntdll!RtlpLocateActivationContextSection+0x13d
00007ffe`4d22cba0 ntdll!RtlpCompareActivationContextDataTOCEntryById
00007ffe`4d205aa1 ntdll!RtlFindActivationContextSectionString+0xf1
00007ffe`4d1e964d ntdll!RtlpLowFragHeapAllocFromContext+0x1cd
00007ffe`4d1e8c6a ntdll!RtlpAllocateHeapInternal+0x12a
00007ffe`4d2ec280 ntdll!RtlpDosDevicesPrefix
00007ffe`4d2066d8 ntdll!RtlpDosPathNameToRelativeNtPathName+0x2e8
00007ffe`4d1e830a ntdll!RtlpFreeHeapInternal+0x7ca
00007ffe`4d1e7631 ntdll!RtlFreeHeap+0x51
00007ffe`4d20df9d ntdll!LdrpMapResourceFile+0x139
00007ffe`4cd50000 USER32!InternalGetWindow <PERF> (USER32+0x0)
00007ffe`4d2104e2 ntdll!LdrMapAndVerifyResourceFile+0x9a
00007ffe`4d1df4bb ntdll!LdrpSetAlternateResourceModuleHandle+0x46b
00007ffe`4d20f249 ntdll!RtlAppendUnicodeToString+0x69
00007ffe`4d202752 ntdll!LdrLoadAlternateResourceModuleEx+0xad2
00007ffe`4cd50000 USER32!InternalGetWindow <PERF> (USER32+0x0)
00007ffe`4cd50000 USER32!InternalGetWindow <PERF> (USER32+0x0)
00007ffe`4d255ea1 ntdll!bsearch+0x81
00007ffe`4d20637d ntdll!RtlpLocateActivationContextSection+0x13d
00007ffe`4d22cba0 ntdll!RtlpCompareActivationContextDataTOCEntryById
00007ffe`4d20637d ntdll!RtlpLocateActivationContextSection+0x13d
00007ffe`4d205aa1 ntdll!RtlFindActivationContextSectionString+0xf1
00007ffe`4d3142b0 ntdll!_xmm+0x43f0
00007ffe`4d3419ec ntdll!__PchSym_ <PERF> (ntdll+0x1819ec)
00007ffe`4d3142b0 ntdll!_xmm+0x43f0
00007ffe`4d1f518e ntdll!LdrpGetDelayloadExportDll+0xa2
00007ffe`4d1f92d9 ntdll!RtlpxVirtualUnwind+0x1c9
00007ffe`4d1c0000 ntdll!LdrpGetModuleName <PERF> (ntdll+0x0)
00007ffe`4d1f518e ntdll!LdrpGetDelayloadExportDll+0xa2
00007ffe`4d3419ec ntdll!__PchSym_ <PERF> (ntdll+0x1819ec)
00007ffe`4d1f637d ntdll!RtlLookupFunctionEntryForStackWalks+0x145
00007ffe`4b707000 OLEAUT32!__PchSym_ <PERF> (OLEAUT32+0xc7000)
00007ffe`4b661742 OLEAUT32!dllmain_crt_process_attach+0x7a
00007ffe`4d3419ec ntdll!__PchSym_ <PERF> (ntdll+0x1819ec)
00007ffe`4d1f518e ntdll!LdrpGetDelayloadExportDll+0xa2
00007ffe`4d1f6ad7 ntdll!RtlpWalkFrameChain+0x2bf
00007ffe`4d1c0000 ntdll!LdrpGetModuleName <PERF> (ntdll+0x0)
00007ffe`4d1f518e ntdll!LdrpGetDelayloadExportDll+0xa2
00007ffe`4d3419ec ntdll!__PchSym_ <PERF> (ntdll+0x1819ec)
00007ffe`4a8cae40 KERNELBASE!DelayLoadFailureHook
00007ffe`4ccda728 MSCTF!_imp_InputFocusChanged
00007ffe`4d2066d8 ntdll!RtlpDosPathNameToRelativeNtPathName+0x2e8
00007ffe`4ccc50e0 MSCTF!_DELAY_IMPORT_DESCRIPTOR_api_ms_win_core_textinput_client_l1_1_0_dll
00007ffe`4d1e964d ntdll!RtlpLowFragHeapAllocFromContext+0x1cd
00007ffe`4d1fb8ed ntdll!LdrpLoadDllInternal+0xd5
00007ffe`4d2f10f8 ntdll!`string'
00007ffe`4d2f11f8 ntdll!`string'
00007ffe`4d20f7df ntdll!RtlDosPathNameToRelativeNtPathName+0x3b
00007ffe`4d2599f9 ntdll!guard_check_icall+0xd
00007ffe`4d2599f9 ntdll!guard_check_icall+0xd
00007ffe`4d255ea1 ntdll!bsearch+0x81
00007ffe`4d20f767 ntdll!LdrpGetNtPathFromDosPath+0x9b
00007ffe`4d255ed4 ntdll!bsearch+0xb4
00007ffe`4d2599f9 ntdll!guard_check_icall+0xd
00007ffe`4d2599f9 ntdll!guard_check_icall+0xd
00007ffe`4d255ea1 ntdll!bsearch+0x81
00007ffe`4d2599f9 ntdll!guard_check_icall+0xd
00007ffe`4d255ea1 ntdll!bsearch+0x81
00007ffe`4d255ea1 ntdll!bsearch+0x81
00007ffe`4d2599f9 ntdll!guard_check_icall+0xd
00007ffe`4d20637d ntdll!RtlpLocateActivationContextSection+0x13d
00007ffe`4d255ea1 ntdll!bsearch+0x81
00007ffe`4d205ea6 ntdll!RtlpFindUnicodeStringInSection+0x1d6
00007ffe`4cd500f8 USER32!InternalGetWindow <PERF> (USER32+0xf8)
```

315

```
00007ffe`4d20637d ntdll!RtlpLocateActivationContextSection+0x13d
00007ffe`4d1ff7d7 ntdll!LdrpResGetMappingSize+0x177
00007ffe`4d22cba0 ntdll!RtlpCompareActivationContextDataTOCEntryById
00007ffe`4d200cde ntdll!ResourceEntryBinarySearch+0x146
00007ffe`4ce12000 USER32!ext-ms-win32-subsystem-query-l1-1-0_NULL_THUNK_DATA_DLA <PERF> (USER32+0xc2000)
00007ffe`4cd50000 USER32!InternalGetWindow <PERF> (USER32+0x0)
00007ffe`4ce12068 USER32!ext-ms-win32-subsystem-query-l1-1-0_NULL_THUNK_DATA_DLA <PERF> (USER32+0xc2068)
00007ffe`4ce12068 USER32!ext-ms-win32-subsystem-query-l1-1-0_NULL_THUNK_DATA_DLA <PERF> (USER32+0xc2068)
00007ffe`4cd50000 USER32!InternalGetWindow <PERF> (USER32+0x0)
00007ffe`4d200b25 ntdll!LdrpSearchResourceSection_U+0xdc5
00007ffe`4ce12058 USER32!ext-ms-win32-subsystem-query-l1-1-0_NULL_THUNK_DATA_DLA <PERF> (USER32+0xc2058)
00007ffe`4abef737 gdi32full!CreateCompatibleBitmap+0x137
00007ffe`4ce12068 USER32!ext-ms-win32-subsystem-query-l1-1-0_NULL_THUNK_DATA_DLA <PERF> (USER32+0xc2068)
00007ffe`4d1fa436 ntdll!LdrpGetImageSize+0x3a
00007ffe`4d1fc664 ntdll!RtlpImageDirectoryEntryToDataEx+0x64
00007ffe`4d1e977f ntdll!RtlpLowFragHeapAllocFromContext+0x2ff
00007ffe`4d1facae ntdll!LdrpGetFromMUIMemCache+0x166
00007ffe`4d1c6800 ntdll!RtlSetLastWin32Error+0x40
00007ffe`4a8ae63b KERNELBASE!FlsGetValue+0x1b
00007ffe`4cf4daaa msvcrt!getptd_noexit+0x6e
00007ffe`4cf133d2 msvcrt!isleadbyte_l+0x12
00007ffe`4cf62986 msvcrt!write_string+0x4a
00007ffe`4cfa40a0 msvcrt!_initiallocinfo
00007ffe`4cf63466 msvcrt!output_l+0xa96
00007ffe`4d1eb70b ntdll!RtlpAllocateHeap+0x65b
00007ffe`4ccacdf4 MSCTF!`string'+0x44
00007ffe`4cfa40a0 msvcrt!_initiallocinfo
00007ffe`4d1e1d4a ntdll!RtlpFindEntry+0x3a
00007ffe`4d1e6101 ntdll!RtlpFreeHeap+0x481
00007ffe`4abff14b gdi32full!StretchDIBitsImpl+0x35b
00007ffe`4cd6a4d2 USER32!Scale3232+0x162
00007ffe`4d1e830a ntdll!RtlpFreeHeapInternal+0x7ca
00007ffe`4cf5dde0 msvcrt!vsnprintf_l+0x80
00007ffe`4d1e7631 ntdll!RtlFreeHeap+0x51
00007ffe`4d1e1d4a ntdll!RtlpFindEntry+0x3a
00007ffe`4cf5dd51 msvcrt!vsnprintf+0x11
00007ffe`4ccacdb0 MSCTF!`string'
00007ffe`4d1e6101 ntdll!RtlpFreeHeap+0x481
00007ffe`4cbd96ec MSCTF!CicTrace+0x9c
00007ffe`4a8b0ad1 KERNELBASE!InitOnceExecuteOnce+0x21
00007ffe`4d1c6800 ntdll!RtlSetLastWin32Error+0x40
00007ffe`4d1d5c0b ntdll!RtlUnlockHeap+0x3b
00007ffe`4d1d5b76 ntdll!RtlLockHeap+0x46
00007ffe`4d1c6800 ntdll!RtlSetLastWin32Error+0x40
00007ffe`4a8bd8ab KERNELBASE!LocalUnlock+0xab
00007ffe`4d0e330c IMM32!CtfImmTIMCreateInputContext+0x11c
00007ffe`4a8bd8ab KERNELBASE!LocalUnlock+0xab
00007ffe`4d0e3c11 IMM32!ImmUnlockIMC+0x131
00007ffe`4cbd8d9c MSCTF!CIMFUIWindowHandler::ImeUINotifyHandler+0x1cc
00007ffe`4d1fefa7 ntdll!RtlDeactivateActivationContextUnsafeFast+0xc7
00007ffe`4cca23b0 MSCTF!IMCLock::`vftable'
00007ffe`4cbd8898 MSCTF!CIMEUIWindowHandler::ImeUIWndProcWorker+0x1f8
00007ffe`4cd61f1b USER32!UserCallWinProcCheckWow+0x60b
00007ffe`478f2a84 apphelp!Insp_WindowHook+0x74
00007ffe`478f2a10 apphelp!Insp_WindowHook
00007ffe`4cd6dc90 USER32!DispatchHookW+0xd0
00007ffe`4cd61aed USER32!UserCallWinProcCheckWow+0x1dd
00007ffe`4cd61f1b USER32!UserCallWinProcCheckWow+0x60b
00007ffe`4cddcaf8 USER32!fnHkINLPCWPRETSTRUCTW+0x78
00007ffe`4cbd8690 MSCTF!UIWndProc
00007ffe`4cd74b65 USER32!_fnDWORD+0x55
00007ffe`478f2a10 apphelp!Insp_WindowHook
00007ffe`4cde5000 USER32!apfnDispatch
00007ffe`4d2676a4 ntdll!KiUserCallbackDispatcherContinue
00007ffe`4d1fefa7 ntdll!RtlDeactivateActivationContextUnsafeFast+0xc7
00007ffe`4b031434 win32u!NtUserMessageCall+0x14
00007ffe`4d1ffc83 ntdll!RtlActivateActivationContextUnsafeFast+0x93
00007ffe`478f2a10 apphelp!Insp_WindowHook
00007ffe`4d2635e0 ntdll!NtdllHkINLPCWPRETSTRUCT_W
00007ffe`4cd608cf USER32!SendMessageWorker+0x12f
00007ffe`4cbd874f MSCTF!CIMEUIWindowHandler::ImeUIWndProcWorker+0xaf
00007ffe`4cd65265 USER32!SendMessageToUI+0x69
00007ffe`4d1fefa7 ntdll!RtlDeactivateActivationContextUnsafeFast+0xc7
00007ffe`4cd65c6e USER32!ImeNotifyHandler+0x5e
```

316

```
00007ffe`4d0e4cc4 IMM32!CtfImmDispatchDefImeMessage+0x64
00007ffe`3e4b73f5 TextShaping!otlChainingLookup::apply+0x405
00007ffe`4d2599f9 ntdll!guard_check_icall+0xd
00007ffe`4d255ea1 ntdll!bsearch+0x81
00007ffe`4d255ed4 ntdll!bsearch+0xb4
00007ffe`4d2599f9 ntdll!guard_check_icall+0xd
00007ffe`4d20637d ntdll!RtlpLocateActivationContextSection+0x13d
00007ffe`4d255ea1 ntdll!bsearch+0x81
00007ffe`4d20637d ntdll!RtlpLocateActivationContextSection+0x13d
00007ffe`3e4ab411 TextShaping!otlResourceMgr::FeatureVariationsTable+0x21
00007ffe`3e4b373e TextShaping!otlRealizedFeatureVariation::CalculateSubstitutions+0x5e
00007ffe`3e4b73f5 TextShaping!otlChainingLookup::apply+0x405
00007ffe`3e47a60f TextShaping!COtlsClient::GetCache+0x7f
00007ffe`4abfc885 gdi32full!CUspShapingClient::AllocMem+0x35
00007ffe`3e4a0001 TextShaping!LegacyArabicShape+0x5c31
00007ffe`4d1e8c6a ntdll!RtlpAllocateHeapInternal+0x12a
00007ffe`3e4ab411 TextShaping!otlResourceMgr::FeatureVariationsTable+0x21
00007ffe`3e47a533 TextShaping!COtlsClient::AllocMem+0x23
00007ffe`3e4b373e TextShaping!otlRealizedFeatureVariation::CalculateSubstitutions+0x5e
00007ffe`3e47a60f TextShaping!COtlsClient::GetCache+0x7f
00007ffe`3e4ab411 TextShaping!otlResourceMgr::FeatureVariationsTable+0x21
00007ffe`3e47a533 TextShaping!COtlsClient::AllocMem+0x23
00007ffe`3e4b373e TextShaping!otlRealizedFeatureVariation::CalculateSubstitutions+0x5e
00007ffe`3e4ab411 TextShaping!otlResourceMgr::FeatureVariationsTable+0x21
00007ffe`4abfc885 gdi32full!CUspShapingClient::AllocMem+0x35
00007ffe`3e4b373e TextShaping!otlRealizedFeatureVariation::CalculateSubstitutions+0x5e
00007ffe`3e47a60f TextShaping!COtlsClient::GetCache+0x7f
00007ffe`3e4ab411 TextShaping!otlResourceMgr::FeatureVariationsTable+0x21
00007ffe`3e47a533 TextShaping!COtlsClient::AllocMem+0x23
00007ffe`3e4b373e TextShaping!otlRealizedFeatureVariation::CalculateSubstitutions+0x5e
00007ffe`3e47a60f TextShaping!COtlsClient::GetCache+0x7f
00007ffe`4abfc885 gdi32full!CUspShapingClient::AllocMem+0x35
00007ffe`3e47a533 TextShaping!COtlsClient::AllocMem+0x23
00007ffe`4abfc972 gdi32full!CUspShapingClient::FreeMem+0x42
00007ffe`3e47a57f TextShaping!COtlsClient::FreeMem+0x1f
00007ffe`3e4aeec4 TextShaping!ApplyFeatures+0x1b4
00007ffe`3e47a30a TextShaping!COtlsClient::ReleaseOtlTable+0xba
00007ffe`3e47a00f TextShaping!COtlsClient::GetVariationAxisValues+0x1f
00007ffe`3e47a6f8 TextShaping!COtlsClient::Release+0x68
00007ffe`3e4aaeaa TextShaping!otlResourceMgr::detach+0x1fa
00007ffe`4abfc972 gdi32full!CUspShapingClient::FreeMem+0x42
00007ffe`3e490b47 TextShaping!GenericEngineGetGlyphPositions+0x13e7
00007ffe`4abee083 gdi32full!bBatchTextOut+0x2f3
00007ffe`4abeda62 gdi32full!ExtTextOutWImpl+0xf2
00007ffe`4b523b74 GDI32!ExtTextOutW+0x74
00007ffe`4abf72b0 gdi32full!CUspShapingDrawingSurface::GenericGlyphOut+0x360
00007ffe`4abf6f0e gdi32full!CUspShapingDrawingSurface::DrawGlyphs+0xde
00007ffe`3e47850a
TextShaping!ShapingLibraryInternal::CCacheSlot<ShapingLibraryInternal::COMMON_FONT_CACHE_DATA,0,65538>::CCacheSlot<Sha
pingLibraryInternal::COMMON_FONT_CACHE_DATA,0,65538>+0x8a
00007ffe`4abf6e30 gdi32full!CUspShapingDrawingSurface::DrawGlyphs
00007ffe`3e490c37 TextShaping!GenericEngineDrawGlyphs+0xc7
00007ffe`3e4787bc TextShaping!ShapingDrawGlyphs+0x1bc
00007ffe`4abfde1b gdi32full!MoveToExImpl+0x9b
00007ffe`4b523ddc GDI32!SetTextAlign+0x2c
00007ffe`4abf5a88 gdi32full!ShlTextOut+0x948
00007ffe`4ac826c8 gdi32full!CUspShapingDrawingSurface::`vftable'
00007ffe`4ac82728 gdi32full!CUspShapingClient::`vftable'
00007ffe`4ac826d0 gdi32full!CUspShapingFont::`vftable'
00007ffe`4abf9b2e gdi32full!RenderItemNoFallback+0x56e
00007ffe`4abf5017 gdi32full!ScriptTextOut+0x1b7
00007ffe`4abf91d8 gdi32full!RenderItemWithFallback+0xe8
00007ffe`4abf6da2 gdi32full!InternalStringOut+0x142
00007ffe`4abfc3b2 gdi32full!ScriptItemizeCommon+0x102
00007ffe`4abf6c0b gdi32full!ScriptStringOut+0x34b
00007ffe`4abfb152 gdi32full!ScriptStringAnalyse+0x782
00007ffe`4abf816a gdi32full!LpkCharsetDraw+0x65a
00007ffe`47974937 uxtheme!GetDialogColor+0x3f
00007ffe`4abf816a gdi32full!LpkCharsetDraw+0x65a
00007ffe`4abf7aee gdi32full!LpkDrawTextEx+0x5e
00007ffe`4abf0d6c gdi32full!GetLayout+0x6c
00007ffe`4abfd631 gdi32full!ExtSelectClipRgnImpl+0x3f1
00007ffe`4a8b0ad1 KERNELBASE!InitOnceExecuteOnce+0x21
00007ffe`4cd624b5 USER32!_GetWindowLongPtr+0x65
```

317

```
00007ffe`4b521cc8 GDI32!DeleteObject+0x58
00007ffe`4cd623e6 USER32!GetWindowLongPtrW+0xf6
00007ffe`4d1fefa7 ntdll!RtlDeactivateActivationContextUnsafeFast+0xc7
00007ffe`4cd64181 USER32!DefDlgProcWorker+0x1b1
00007ffe`4d1ffc83 ntdll!RtlActivateActivationContextUnsafeFast+0x93
00007ffe`4cd61f1b USER32!UserCallWinProcCheckWow+0x60b
00007ffe`4d1c6800 ntdll!RtlSetLastWin32Error+0x40
00007ffe`478f2a84 apphelp!Insp_WindowHook+0x74
00007ffe`478f2a10 apphelp!Insp_WindowHook
00007ffe`4cd6dc90 USER32!DispatchHookW+0xd0
00007ffe`4cd61aed USER32!UserCallWinProcCheckWow+0x1dd
00007ffe`4cd61f1b USER32!UserCallWinProcCheckWow+0x60b
00007ffe`4cddcaf8 USER32!fnHkINLPCWPRETSTRUCTW+0x78
00007ffe`3c0a8020 COMCTL32!Button_WndProc
00007ffe`4cd74b65 USER32!_fnDWORD+0x55
00007ffe`478f2a10 apphelp!Insp_WindowHook
00007ffe`4cde5000 USER32!apfnDispatch
00007ffe`4d2676a4 ntdll!KiUserCallbackDispatcherContinue
00007ffe`4b031434 win32u!NtUserMessageCall+0x14
00007ffe`478f2a10 apphelp!Insp_WindowHook
00007ffe`4d2635e0 ntdll!NtdllHkINLPCWPRETSTRUCT_W
00007ffe`4cd608cf USER32!SendMessageWorker+0x12f
00007ffe`4a893ffb KERNELBASE!DeviceIoControl+0x6b
00007ffe`4b031434 win32u!NtUserMessageCall+0x14
00007ffe`4cd60737 USER32!SendMessageW+0x137
00007ffe`4bb95f91 KERNEL32!DeviceIoControlImplementation+0x81
00007ffe`4cda99f9 USER32!IsDlgButtonChecked+0x9
00007ff7`6544342f notmyfault64+0x342f
00007ffe`4d1e4922 ntdll!RtlpReAllocateHeap+0x142
00007ffe`4cd63800 USER32!SendOrCallDefWindowProc+0x4c
00007ffe`4cd64a0a USER32!_BeginIfHookedDManipHook+0x36
00007ffe`4d1e7631 ntdll!RtlFreeHeap+0x51
00007ffe`4cd6484b USER32!UserCallDlgProcCheckWow+0x14b
00007ffe`4cd624b5 USER32!_GetWindowLongPtr+0x65
00007ffe`4d2ea06b ntdll!RtlFindLowerBoundInSortedArray+0x63
00007ff7`654432d0 notmyfault64+0x32d0
00007ffe`4d338bf8 ntdll!RtlpFcProcessManager+0x98
00007ffe`4cd647b6 USER32!UserCallDlgProcCheckWow+0xb6
00007ffe`4cd6409b USER32!DefDlgProcWorker+0xcb
00007ff7`654432d0 notmyfault64+0x32d0
00007ffe`4cd624b5 USER32!_GetWindowLongPtr+0x65
00007ffe`4cc2952c MSCTF!wil_RtlStagingConfig_QueryFeatureState+0x110
00007ffe`4cda97c9 USER32!DefDlgProcA+0x39
00007ffe`4d1fefa7 ntdll!RtlDeactivateActivationContextUnsafeFast+0xc7
00007ffe`4cd61c4c USER32!UserCallWinProcCheckWow+0x33c
00007ffe`4a8a4099 KERNELBASE!OpenEventW+0x99
00007ffe`478f2a84 apphelp!Insp_WindowHook+0x74
00007ffe`478f2a10 apphelp!Insp_WindowHook
00007ffe`4d2634d0 ntdll!NtdllDialogWndProc_A
00007ffe`4cd61aed USER32!UserCallWinProcCheckWow+0x1dd
00007ffe`4cd6179c USER32!DispatchClientMessage+0x9c
00007ffe`4d2634d0 ntdll!NtdllDialogWndProc_A
00007ffe`4cd74b4d USER32!_fnDWORD+0x3d
00007ffe`4d2634d0 ntdll!NtdllDialogWndProc_A
00007ffe`4cde5000 USER32!apfnDispatch
00007ffe`4cd61f1b USER32!UserCallWinProcCheckWow+0x60b
00007ffe`4d2676a4 ntdll!KiUserCallbackDispatcherContinue
00007ffe`4b031434 win32u!NtUserMessageCall+0x14
00007ffe`4cddcaf8 USER32!fnHkINLPCWPRETSTRUCTW+0x78
00007ffe`4d2634d0 ntdll!NtdllDialogWndProc_A
00007ffe`4d263640 ntdll!NtdllDispatchMessage_W
00007ffe`4cd608cf USER32!SendMessageWorker+0x12f
00007ffe`4cd74b65 USER32!_fnDWORD+0x55
00007ffe`4cd60737 USER32!SendMessageW+0x137
00007ffe`4b03b2d4 win32u!NtUserReleaseCapture+0x14
00007ffe`3c075120 COMCTL32!Button_NotifyParent+0x30
00007ffe`3c0750bf COMCTL32!Button_ReleaseCapture+0xbb
00007ffe`3c0a8822 COMCTL32!Button_WndProc+0x802
00007ffe`4d1ffc83 ntdll!RtlActivateActivationContextUnsafeFast+0x93
00007ffe`4cddcaf8 USER32!fnHkINLPCWPRETSTRUCTW+0x78
00007ffe`3c0a8020 COMCTL32!Button_WndProc
00007ffe`3c0a8020 COMCTL32!Button_WndProc
00007ffe`4cd61c4c USER32!UserCallWinProcCheckWow+0x33c
00007ffe`3c0a8020 COMCTL32!Button_WndProc
```

```
00007ffe`4cd760fa USER32!CtfHookProcWorker+0x2a
00007ffe`4cde5000 USER32!apfnDispatch
00007ffe`3c0a8020 COMCTL32!Button_WndProc
00007ffe`4cd6d063 USER32!CallHookWithSEH+0x33
00007ffe`4cd61aed USER32!UserCallWinProcCheckWow+0x1dd
00007ffe`4cd51da6 USER32!_fnHkINLPMOUSEHOOKSTRUCTEX+0x36
00007ffe`3c0a8020 COMCTL32!Button_WndProc
00007ffe`4cd60ea6 USER32!DispatchMessageWorker+0x2a6
00007ffe`3c0a8020 COMCTL32!Button_WndProc
00007ffe`4cd66084 USER32!IsDialogMessageW+0x104
00007ffe`3c0a8020 COMCTL32!Button_WndProc
00007ffe`3c055f9f COMCTL32!Prop_IsDialogMessage+0x4b
00007ffe`3c055e48 COMCTL32!_RealPropertySheet+0x2c0
00007ffe`3c057675 COMCTL32!_CreatePropertySheetPage+0x105
00007ff7`65440000 notmyfault64
00007ffe`3c055abd COMCTL32!_PropertySheet+0x49
00007ffe`3c120953 COMCTL32!PropertySheetA+0x53
00007ffe`4c731168 SHELL32!_imp_CommandLineToArgvW
00007ff7`65440000 notmyfault64
00007ff7`65444130 notmyfault64+0x4130
00007ff7`65444cd0 notmyfault64+0x4cd0
00007ff7`65440000 notmyfault64
00007ff7`65440000 notmyfault64
00007ff7`654be290 notmyfault64+0x7e290
00007ff7`65444130 notmyfault64+0x4130
00007ff7`65440000 notmyfault64
00007ff7`654aa730 notmyfault64+0x6a730
00007ff7`654432d0 notmyfault64+0x32d0
00007ff7`65440000 notmyfault64
00007ff7`654aa738 notmyfault64+0x6a738
00007ff7`65443c60 notmyfault64+0x3c60
00007ff7`65440000 notmyfault64
00007ff7`654aa740 notmyfault64+0x6a740
00007ff7`65443df0 notmyfault64+0x3df0
00007ff7`65483c9d notmyfault64+0x43c9d
00007ff7`65445292 notmyfault64+0x5292
00007ffe`4bb954e0 KERNEL32!BaseThreadInitThunk+0x10
00007ffe`4d1c485b ntdll!RtlUserThreadStart+0x2b
????????`????????
```

We get the following output:

This extensive trace details a sequence of operations across various system and application components, mainly within Windows' core libraries (**ntdll**, **USER32**, **KERNELBASE**, **COMCTL32**, **GDI32**, **MSCTF**, **IMM32**, **OLEAUT32**, **SHELL32**, and **win32u**) and an application named **notmyfault64**. The trace reflects a complex interaction between system calls, memory management, UI handling, resource loading, and possibly error handling or security checks. Here's a summarized overview of key operations and themes in this trace:

1. **Security and System Integrity Checks**: Repeated calls to **ntdll!guard_check_icall** suggest security checks related to indirect calls, a feature to prevent exploits like return-oriented programming (ROP).

2. **Memory and Resource Management**: Operations such as **RtlFreeHeap**, **RtlAllocateHeapInternal**, and **LdrpLoadDllInternal** indicate dynamic memory management and DLL loading, essential for handling the application's and system's needs.

3. **UI and Input Handling**: References to **USER32** and **COMCTL32** functions, like **SendMessageW**, **DefDlgProcWorker**, and **Button_WndProc**, point to user interface processing, including window message handling and dialog box management.

319

4. **File and Path Management**: Functions like `RtlpDosPathNameToRelativeNtPathName` and `RtlDosPathNameToRelativeNtPathName` are involved in translating DOS file paths to NT-style paths, essential for file system navigation and access.

5. **Resource Loading and Management**: Calls to `LdrpGetDelayloadExportDll`, `LdrMapAndVerifyResourceFile`, and `LdrpSearchResourceSection_U` indicate loading and accessing various resources, crucial for application functionality and localization.

6. **Activation Contexts and Versioning**: Functions such as `RtlFindActivationContextSectionString` and `RtlpLocateActivationContextSection` are part of managing side-by-side assemblies, enabling applications to specify and use particular versions of shared libraries.

7. **Error Handling and Debugging**: Entries like `RtlpReAllocateHeap`, `RtlSetLastWin32Error`, and various `PERF` (performance) and `DEBUG` markers suggest error management and performance monitoring during the operations.

8. **Custom Application Logic**: The `notmyfault64` application, known for deliberately triggering system crashes for testing purposes, is actively involved, indicated by numerous calls prefixed with its name. This application is executing specific actions that interact deeply with Windows internals.

9. **Text and Drawing Operations**: The presence of `GDI32`, `uxtheme`, and `TextShaping` calls indicates graphics and text rendering activities, likely related to drawing UI elements or processing text input.

Overall, this trace captures a snapshot of intricate system activities involving security measures, memory handling, UI interactions, and application-specific actions, all critical to the functioning of Windows and the involved application.

Note: If you find a symbolic reference of interest, always double-check its return address via the backward disassembly. Valid return addresses have the associated *call* CPU instruction:

```
1: kd> ub 00007ff7`654432d0
notmyfault64+0x32c8:
00007ff7`654432c8 int      3
00007ff7`654432c9 int      3
00007ff7`654432ca int      3
00007ff7`654432cb int      3
00007ff7`654432cc int      3
00007ff7`654432cd int      3
00007ff7`654432ce int      3
00007ff7`654432cf int      3
```

```
1: kd> ub 00007ffe`4cd6409b
USER32!DefDlgProcWorker+0xa6:
00007ffe`4cd64076 lea      rax,[rbp-38h]
00007ffe`4cd6407a mov      rcx,qword ptr [rdi+0E0h]
00007ffe`4cd64081 mov      r9d,esi
00007ffe`4cd64084 mov      qword ptr [rsp+38h],rax
00007ffe`4cd64089 mov      r8,r13
00007ffe`4cd6408c mov      qword ptr [rsp+28h],r14
00007ffe`4cd64091 mov      qword ptr [rsp+20h],r12
00007ffe`4cd64096 call     USER32!UserCallDlgProcCheckWow (00007ffe`4cd64700)
```

Note: <PERF> annotation is about performance-optimized code, not performance monitoring.

10.   We ask ChatGPT to summarize the **!analyze -v** command output:

```
1: kd> !analyze -v
*******************************************************************************
*                                                                             *
*                        Bugcheck Analysis                                    *
*                                                                             *
*******************************************************************************

DRIVER_IRQL_NOT_LESS_OR_EQUAL (d1)
An attempt was made to access a pageable (or completely invalid) address at an
interrupt request level (IRQL) that is too high.  This is usually
caused by drivers using improper addresses.
If kernel debugger is available get stack backtrace.
Arguments:
Arg1: ffffbc06b64895a0, memory referenced
Arg2: 0000000000000002, IRQL
Arg3: 0000000000000000, value 0 = read operation, 1 = write operation
Arg4: fffff80403c61981, address which referenced memory

Debugging Details:
------------------


KEY_VALUES_STRING: 1

    Key  : Analysis.CPU.mSec
    Value: 3077

    Key  : Analysis.Elapsed.mSec
    Value: 6553

    Key  : Analysis.IO.Other.Mb
    Value: 1

    Key  : Analysis.IO.Read.Mb
    Value: 5

    Key  : Analysis.IO.Write.Mb
    Value: 4

    Key  : Analysis.Init.CPU.mSec
    Value: 26733

    Key  : Analysis.Init.Elapsed.mSec
    Value: 52087475

    Key  : Analysis.Memory.CommitPeak.Mb
    Value: 189

    Key  : Bugcheck.Code.KiBugCheckData
    Value: 0xd1

    Key  : Bugcheck.Code.LegacyAPI
    Value: 0xd1

    Key  : Bugcheck.Code.TargetModel
    Value: 0xd1

    Key  : Failure.Bucket
    Value: AV_myfault!unknown_function

    Key  : Failure.Hash
    Value: {9745090a-9bce-ccba-c096-ca6e9ca04c64}

    Key  : Hypervisor.Enlightenments.Value
    Value: 8480

    Key  : Hypervisor.Enlightenments.ValueHex
    Value: 2120

    Key  : Hypervisor.Flags.AnyHypervisorPresent
    Value: 1

    Key  : Hypervisor.Flags.ApicEnlightened
    Value: 0

    Key  : Hypervisor.Flags.ApicVirtualizationAvailable
    Value: 0

    Key  : Hypervisor.Flags.AsyncMemoryHint
    Value: 0

    Key  : Hypervisor.Flags.CoreSchedulerRequested
    Value: 0

    Key  : Hypervisor.Flags.CpuManager
    Value: 0

    Key  : Hypervisor.Flags.DeprecateAutoEoi
```

```
        Value: 0

        Key  : Hypervisor.Flags.DynamicCpuDisabled
        Value: 0

        Key  : Hypervisor.Flags.Epf
        Value: 0

        Key  : Hypervisor.Flags.ExtendedProcessorMasks
        Value: 0

        Key  : Hypervisor.Flags.HardwareMbecAvailable
        Value: 0

[...]

        Key  : Hypervisor.RootFlags.HypervisorDebuggingEnabled
        Value: 0

        Key  : Hypervisor.RootFlags.IsHyperV
        Value: 0

        Key  : Hypervisor.RootFlags.LivedumpEnlightened
        Value: 0

        Key  : Hypervisor.RootFlags.MapDeviceInterrupt
        Value: 0

        Key  : Hypervisor.RootFlags.MceEnlightened
        Value: 0

        Key  : Hypervisor.RootFlags.Nested
        Value: 0

        Key  : Hypervisor.RootFlags.StartLogicalProcessor
        Value: 0

        Key  : Hypervisor.RootFlags.Value
        Value: 0

        Key  : Hypervisor.RootFlags.ValueHex
        Value: 0

        Key  : SecureKernel.HalpHvciEnabled
        Value: 0

        Key  : WER.OS.Branch
        Value: co_release

        Key  : WER.OS.Version
        Value: 10.0.22000.1


BUGCHECK_CODE:  d1

BUGCHECK_P1: ffffbc06b64895a0

BUGCHECK_P2: 2

BUGCHECK_P3: 0

BUGCHECK_P4: fffff80403c61981

FILE_IN_CAB:  MEMORY-WM.DMP

VIRTUAL_MACHINE:  VMware

READ_ADDRESS: unable to get nt!PspSessionIdBitmap
 ffffbc06b64895a0 Paged pool

BLACKBOXBSD: 1 (!blackboxbsd)


BLACKBOXNTFS: 1 (!blackboxntfs)


BLACKBOXWINLOGON: 1

PROCESS_NAME:  notmyfault64.exe

TRAP_FRAME:  ffffa7848ee7d7c0 -- (.trap 0xffffa7848ee7d7c0)
NOTE: The trap frame does not contain all registers.
Some register values may be zeroed or incorrect.
rax=000000000210f204 rbx=0000000000000000 rcx=ffffbc06aa200380
rdx=0000000000000880 rsi=0000000000000000 rdi=0000000000000000
rip=fffff80403c61981 rsp=ffffa7848ee7d950 rbp=ffffa7848ee7dbc1
 r8=ffffbc06b9320aa0  r9=0000000000000000 r10=ffffbc06aa200300
r11=ffffbc06b647e590 r12=0000000000000000 r13=0000000000000000
r14=0000000000000000 r15=0000000000000000
iopl=0         nv up ei ng nz na po nc
myfault+0x1981:
fffff804`03c61981 mov     eax,dword ptr [rbx]     ds:00000000`00000000=????????
Resetting default scope

STACK_TEXT:
ffffa784`8ee7d678 fffff804`04e28da9     : 00000000`0000000a ffffbc06`b64895a0 00000000`00000002 00000000`00000000 : nt!KeBugCheckEx
ffffa784`8ee7d680 fffff804`04e24f00     : ffffa784`8ee7d878 ffffa784`8ee7d7fc ffffbc06`b647e580 fffff804`04cfcba7 : nt!KiBugCheckDispatch+0x69
ffffa784`8ee7d7c0 fffff804`03c61981     : 00000000`00000000 ffff8008`aaed9ef0 00000000`00000000 00000000`00000000 : nt!KiPageFault+0x440
```

```
ffffa784`8ee7d950 fffff804`03c61d3d : ffff8008`0210f204 fffff906`021a0010 00000000`00000000 00000000`00000000 : myfault+0x1981
ffffa784`8ee7d980 fffff804`03c61ea1 : ffff8008`b0f05120 fffff804`050a4524 ffff8008`aa135b00 00000000`00001dc9 : myfault+0x1d3d
ffffa784`8ee7dac0 fffff804`04d03115 : ffff8008`b0f05120 00000000`00000002 00000000`000000f0 00000000`00000000 : myfault+0x1ea1
ffffa784`8ee7db20 fffff804`0516bbf2 : 00000000`00000001 ffff8008`b0f05120 ffffa784`8ee7dbc1 fffff804`04d02ed3 : nt!IofCallDriver+0x55
ffffa784`8ee7db60 fffff804`0516b9d2 : ffff8008`00000000 ffffa784`8ee7dea0 00000000`83360018 ffff8008`b0f05120 : nt!IopSynchronousServiceTail+0x1d2
ffffa784`8ee7dc10 fffff804`0516ad36 : 00000000`00000000 00000000`00000000 00000000`00000000 00000000`00000000 : nt!IopXxxControlFile+0xc82
ffffa784`8ee7dd40 fffff804`04e28775 : 00000000`00000000 00000000`00000000 ffff0cbf`113fcb36 00000000`00070000 : nt!NtDeviceIoControlFile+0x56
ffffa784`8ee7ddb0 00007ffe`4d263834 : 00007ffe`4a893ffb 00000000`0008040a 00000014`00000048 00007ffe`4b031434 : nt!KiSystemServiceCopyEnd+0x25
0000009b`cc0feea0 00007ffe`4a893ffb : 00000000`0008040a 00000014`00000048 00007ffe`4b031434 00000000`00000000 : ntdll!NtDeviceIoControlFile+0x14
0000009b`cc0fede0 00007ffe`4bb95f91 : 00000000`83360018 00000000`00000000 00000000`00000000 00007ffe`4cda99f9 : KERNELBASE!DeviceIoControl+0x6b
0000009b`cc0fee50 00007ff7`6544342f : 00000000`0008050e 0000009b`cc0fef39 0000009b`cc0fef39 00000000`00000000 :
KERNEL32!DeviceIoControlImplementation+0x81
0000009b`cc0feea0 00007ffe`4cd6484b : 00000000`00000001 00000000`00000001 00000000`00000001 00000000`00000002 : notmyfault64+0x342f
0000009b`cc0fefa0 00007ffe`4cd6409b : 00000000`00000000 00007ff7`654432d0 00000000`00000111 000001dd`6f707610 : USER32!UserCallDlgProcCheckWow+0x14b
0000009b`cc0ff080 00007ffe`4cda97c9 : 00000000`00090436 00000000`000000f3 00000000`00090436 00000000`00000000 : USER32!DefDlgProcWorker+0xcb
0000009b`cc0ff140 00007ffe`4cd61c4c : 00000000`00000001 00000000`00000000 00000000`00000001 00000000`00000000 : USER32!DefDlgProcA+0x39
0000009b`cc0ff180 00007ffe`4cd6179c : 00008c36`a8298660 00007ffe`4d2634d0 00000000`0008050e 00007ffe`00000111 : USER32!UserCallWinProcCheckWow+0x33c
0000009b`cc0ff2f0 00007ffe`4cd74b4d : 00000000`00000000 00000000`00000000 00000000`000003f9 00000000`000c0000 : USER32!DispatchClientMessage+0x9c
0000009b`cc0ff350 00007ffe`4d2676a4 : 00000000`00000000 00000000`00000000 00000000`00000000 00000000`00000000 : USER32!_fnDWORD+0x3d
0000009b`cc0ff3b0 00007ffe`4b031434 : 00007ffe`4cd608cf 00000000`00000000 00007ffe`4cd74b65 00000000`00000000 : ntdll!KiUserCallbackDispatcherContinue
0000009b`cc0ff438 00007ffe`4cd608cf : 00000000`00000000 00007ffe`4cd74b65 00000000`00000000 00000000`00000000 : win32u!NtUserMessageCall+0x14
0000009b`cc0ff440 00007ffe`4cd60737 : 00007ffe`4b03b2d4 00000000`00000000 00000000`000003f9 00000000`00090436 : USER32!SendMessageWorker+0x12f
0000009b`cc0ff4e0 00007ffe`3c0750bf : 000001dd`6f057d00 00000000`00000001 00000000`50010001 00000000`00000001 : USER32!SendMessageW+0x137
0000009b`cc0ff540 00007ffe`3c0a8822 : 00000000`00000202 0000009b`cc0ff619 00000000`00000000 00000000`00000000 : COMCTL32!Button_ReleaseCapture+0xbb
0000009b`cc0ff570 00007ffe`4cd61c4c : 00000000`00000000 80000000`00000000 00000000`00000001 00000000`00000000 : COMCTL32!Button_WndProc+0x802
0000009b`cc0ff680 00007ffe`4cd60ea6 : 00000000`00000000 00007ffe`3c0a8020 00000000`00090436 00007ffe`00000202 : USER32!UserCallWinProcCheckWow+0x33c
0000009b`cc0ff7f0 00007ffe`4cd66084 : 00007ffe`3c0a8020 00000000`00000000 000001dd`6f6fbdd0 00000000`00090436 : USER32!DispatchMessageWorker+0x2a6
0000009b`cc0ff870 00007ffe`3c055f9f : 000001dd`6f0162d0 0000009b`cc0ff979 00000000`00000100 00000000`000f03e8 : USER32!IsDialogMessageW+0x104
0000009b`cc0ff8d0 00007ffe`3c055e48 : 000001dd`6efff3c0 0000009b`cc0ff979 00000000`00000000 10057c6b`00000001 : COMCTL32!Prop_IsDialogMessage+0x4b
0000009b`cc0ff910 00007ffe`3c055abd : 0000009b`cc0ffa30 0000009b`cc0ffa30 00000000`83360018 000001dd`6f0162d0 : COMCTL32!_RealPropertySheet+0x2c0
0000009b`cc0ff9e0 00007ffe`3c120953 : 000001dd`6f0162d0 0000009b`cc0ffb10 00007ffe`4c731168 00000000`00000000 : COMCTL32!_PropertySheet+0x49
0000009b`cc0ffa10 00007ff7`65444cd0 : 0000009b`cc0ffbb0 00000000`83360018 00000000`00000000 0000009b`cc0ffbb0 : COMCTL32!PropertySheetA+0x53
0000009b`cc0ffab0 00007ff7`65445292 : 00000000`00000001 00000000`00000001 00000000`00000000 00000000`00000000 : notmyfault64+0x4cd0
0000009b`cc0ffd80 00007ffe`4bb954e0 : 00000000`00000000 00000000`00000000 00000000`00000000 00000000`00000000 : notmyfault64+0x5292
0000009b`cc0ffdc0 00007ffe`4d1c485b : 00000000`00000000 00000000`00000000 00000000`00000000 00000000`00000000 : KERNEL32!BaseThreadInitThunk+0x10
0000009b`cc0ffdf0 00000000`00000000 : 00000000`00000000 00000000`00000000 00000000`00000000 00000000`00000000 : ntdll!RtlUserThreadStart+0x2b

SYMBOL_NAME:  myfault+1981

MODULE_NAME: myfault

IMAGE_NAME:  myfault.sys

STACK_COMMAND:  .cxr; .ecxr ; kb

BUCKET_ID_FUNC_OFFSET:  1981

FAILURE_BUCKET_ID:  AV_myfault!unknown_function

OS_VERSION:  10.0.22000.1

BUILDLAB_STR:  co_release

OSPLATFORM_TYPE:  x64

OSNAME:  Windows 10

FAILURE_ID_HASH:  {9745090a-9bce-ccba-c096-ca6e9ca04c64}

Followup:    MachineOwner
---------
```

<u>We get the following output:</u>

This crash analysis report indicates a DRIVER_IRQL_NOT_LESS_OR_EQUAL error, commonly associated with a driver attempting to access an invalid or pageable memory address at a high interrupt request level (IRQL). This specific type of bug check has a value of 0xD1. The details provided can help identify the root cause of the crash:

- **Error Code (Bugcheck):** 0xD1 indicates a DRIVER_IRQL_NOT_LESS_OR_EQUAL error.
- **Memory Referenced (Arg1):** The problematic memory address being referenced is ffffbc06b64895a0.
- **IRQL (Arg2):** The operation was attempted at IRQL level 2, which is higher than permissible for the operation being performed.
- **Operation Type (Arg3):** A value of 0 suggests a read operation was being performed when the error occurred.

- **Faulting Address (Arg4):** The instruction at address `fffff80403c61981` in the `myfault.sys` driver referenced the memory that caused the fault.

Key Analysis Points:

- **Process Name:** The crash was triggered by `notmyfault64.exe`, which is a tool commonly used to deliberately cause system crashes for testing and educational purposes.
- **Trap Frame:** A detailed trap frame is provided (`ffffa7848ee7d7c0`), but crucially it shows the fault occurring within the `myfault.sys` driver at the offset `+0x1981`.
- **Analysis Keys and Values:** Several key-value pairs provide additional context, such as CPU and I/O metrics during analysis, and environmental specifics like the operating system version (Windows 10, version `10.0.22000.1`), and the indication that a VMware virtual machine was being used.
- **Symbol and Module Name:** The fault is associated with the `myfault+1981` symbol within the `myfault.sys` driver, pointing directly to where the inappropriate memory access occurred.
- **Failure Bucket:** Identified as `AV_myfault!unknown_function`, indicating an Access Violation within the `myfault.sys` driver without specifying the function due to possibly being dynamically generated or not having symbol information available.

Conclusion:

The crash is caused by the `myfault.sys` driver attempting a read operation on a non-accessible memory address at an IRQL that is too high, which is consistent with the behavior of `notmyfault64.exe`, designed to cause crashes. This report is particularly useful for understanding the conditions under which the crash occurred, especially useful in debugging, testing, or educational scenarios to learn about system stability and crash analysis.

Pattern Links

Stack Trace Collection (Unmanaged Space)
Coupled Processes (Weak)
Value References
Spiking Thread
Stack Trace Collection (Predicate)
Invalid Pointer
Disconnected Network Adapter
Stack Trace Collection (I/O Requests)
Wait Chain (Window Messaging)
Hidden Parameter
Wait Chain (ALPC)
Incorrect Stack Trace
Stack Trace (I/O Request)
Stack Trace (File System Filters)
Input Thread
Black Box
Rough Stack Trace (Unmanaged Space)
Zombie Processes
Unloaded Module
Annotated Stack Trace
Analysis Summary
Coincidental Symbolic Information

Passive Thread
Virtualized Process
Module Variable
Thread Waiting Time
Foreign Stack
System Object
Historical Information
Main Thread
Execution Residue
Data Correlation
Coupled Processes (Strong)
Truncated Stack Trace
Stack Trace (I/O Devices)
Disk Packet Buildup
Debugger Bug
Past Process
Memory Data Model
Active Thread
Structure Field Collection
Disassembly Summary
Region Summary

Here are the links to pattern descriptions and additional examples:

http://www.dumpanalysis.org/blog/index.php/crash-dump-analysis-patterns/

(Also available in Memory Dump Analysis Anthology volumes or Encyclopedia of Crash Dump
Analysis Patterns)

Pattern Case Studies

70 multiple pattern case studies:

http://www.dumpanalysis.org/blog/index.php/pattern-cooperation/

Pattern Interaction chapters in Memory Dump Analysis Anthology

Hunting for a Driver

Here are the links to the pattern case studies and the additional example:

http://www.dumpanalysis.org/blog/index.php/pattern-cooperation/

(Also available in Memory Dump Analysis Anthology volumes)

http://www.dumpanalysis.org/blog/index.php/2009/07/06/hunting-for-a-driver/

(Also available in Memory Dump Analysis Anthology, Volume 4, Revised Edition)

Resources

- WinDbg Help / WinDbg.org (quick links)
- DumpAnalysis.org / SoftwareDiagnostics.Institute / PatternDiagnostics.com
- Debugging.TV / YouTube.com/DebuggingTV / YouTube.com/PatternDiagnostics
- UML Distilled, 3rd ed.
- Schaum's Outline of UML, 2nd ed.
- Windows Kernel Programming, 2nd ed.
- Windows Internals, 7th ed.
- Accelerated Windows Memory Dump Analysis, 6th Edition
- Encyclopedia of Crash Dump Analysis Patterns, 3rd Edition
- Memory Dump Analysis Anthology (Diagnomicon)

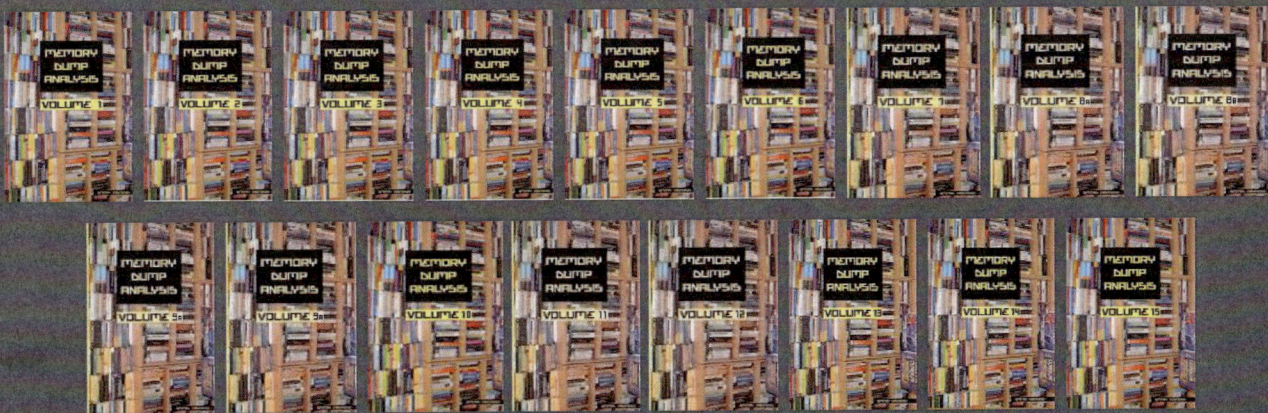

Additional learning and reference resources:

WinDbg quick links
http://WinDbg.org

Software Diagnostics Institute
https://www.dumpanalysis.org

Debugging.TV
http://debugging.tv

Pattern Diagnostics Seminars
https://www.youtube.com/PatternDiagnostics

Software Diagnostics Services
https://www.patterndiagnostics.com

WinDbg images
https://hub.docker.com/r/patterndiagnostics/windbg

Accelerated Windows Memory Dump Analysis, Sixth Edition
https://www.patterndiagnostics.com/accelerated-windows-memory-dump-analysis-book

Encyclopedia of Crash Dump Analysis Patterns, Third Edition
https://www.patterndiagnostics.com/encyclopedia-crash-dump-analysis-patterns

Memory Dump Analysis Anthology (Diagnomicon)
https://www.patterndiagnostics.com/mdaa-volumes

Going Further

More basic/foundational:

- Practical Foundations of Windows Debugging, Disassembling, Reversing
- Accelerated Windows Memory Dump Analysis

Special topics:

- Accelerated Windows Malware Analysis with Memory Dumps
- Accelerated Disassembly, Reconstruction and Reversing
- Accelerated .NET Core Memory Dump Analysis
- Accelerated Windows Debugging[4]
- Extended Windows Memory Dump Analysis (Python scripting)
- Accelerated Windows API for Software Diagnostics
- Accelerated C & C++ for Windows Diagnostics (Memory thinking)

© 2024 Software Diagnostics Services

Accelerated Windows Memory Dump Analysis, Sixth Edition
https://www.patterndiagnostics.com/accelerated-windows-memory-dump-analysis-book

Practical Foundations of Windows Debugging, Disassembling, Reversing, Second Edition:
https://www.patterndiagnostics.com/practical-foundations-windows-debugging-disassembling-reversing

Accelerated .NET Core Memory Dump Analysis, Revised Edition:
https://www.patterndiagnostics.com/accelerated-net-memory-dump-analysis-book

Accelerated Windows Malware Analysis with Memory Dumps, Third Edition:
https://www.patterndiagnostics.com/accelerated-windows-malware-analysis-book

Accelerated Disassembly, Reconstruction and Reversing, Third Edition:
https://www.patterndiagnostics.com/accelerated-disassembly-reconstruction-reversing-book

Accelerated Windows Debugging[4], Fourth Edition:
https://www.patterndiagnostics.com/accelerated-windows-debugging-book

Extended Windows Memory Dump Analysis:

https://www.patterndiagnostics.com/extended-windows-memory-dump-analysis-book

Accelerated Windows API for Software Diagnostics:

https://www.patterndiagnostics.com/accelerated-windows-api-book

Accelerated C & C++ for Windows Diagnostics:

https://www.patterndiagnostics.com/accelerated-c-cpp-windows-diagnostics

Selected Q&A

Q. How to invoke help in WinDbg?

A. Use **.hh** or **.hh** <command>.

Q. In the case of many RDP sessions, do we have one session per RDP connection?

A. Yes, this is the same for Citrix terminal services ICA connections.

Q. Is there a difference between **.process /r /p** and **!process 3f** ?

A. Yes, the former command sets the process as the current process, and the latter merely lists process threads and their stack traces.

Q. Is there any way to get the data of specific registry keys or values from the hive? Let's say I needed to know what was stored in HKCU\Control Panel\Desktop\Wallpaper - how would I find that?

A. I propose a simple memory search for memory dumps based on the fact that registry hive pages were mapped into memory. For example, we can search mapped views for Desktop and Wallpaper either using search commands or by a visual inspection:

```
1: kd> !reg hivelist

-------------------------------------------------------------------------------------------
| HiveAddr |Stable Length|Stable Map|Volatile Length|Volatile Map|MappedViews|PinnedViews|U(Cnt)| BaseBlock | FileName
-------------------------------------------------------------------------------------------
[...]
| fffff88001c6c010 | 7a000  | fffff88001c6c0c0 | 3000  | fffff88001c6c338 | 23  | 0 | 0| fffff88001ca3000 | ??\C:\Users\Training\ntuser.dat
[...]
-------------------------------------------------------------------------------------------

1: kd> !reg viewlist fffff88001c6c010

   0  Pinned Views ; PinViewListHead = fffff88001c6c628 fffff88001c6c628

  23  Mapped Views ; LRUViewListHead = fffff88001c54380 fffff88001967a90

-------------------------------------------------------------------------------------------
| ViewAddr |FileOffset|  Size  |ViewAddress|   Bcb    |   LRUViewList   |   PinViewList   |  UseCount |
-------------------------------------------------------------------------------------------
| fffff88001c54380 |  20000 |  4000 | fffff9800ff20000 | fffffa8000c558f9 | fffff88001c13f00  fffff88001c6c618 | fffff88001c54390  fffff88001c54390 |       0 |
| fffff88001c13f00 |  2c000 |  4000 | fffff9800ff2c000 | fffffa8000c558f9 | fffff88001a5b310  fffff88001c54380 | fffff88001c13f10  fffff88001c13f10 |       0 |
[...]
-------------------------------------------------------------------------------------------

1: kd> dc fffff9800ff2c000 L4000
fffff980`0ff2c000   6e696268 0002b000 00001000 00000000   hbin............
fffff980`0ff2c010   00000000 00000000 00000000 00000000   ................
fffff980`0ff2c020   ffffffa0 00206b6e cec3a124 01cc3ffe   ....nk .$....?..
fffff980`0ff2c030   00000000 0002af60 00000001 00000000   ....`...........
fffff980`0ff2c040   0002b0e8 ffffffff 00000000 ffffffff   ................
[...]
fffff980`0ff39260   00000000 00000000 00000000 00000007   ................
fffff980`0ff39270   6b736544 00706f74 ffffffa8 00206b6e   Desktop.....nk .
fffff980`0ff39280   d4fea656 01cc3ffe 00000000 00038220   V....?...... ...
fffff980`0ff39290   00000000 00000000 ffffffff ffffffff   ................
fffff980`0ff392a0   00000006 00038490 00022498 ffffffff   ..........$.....
fffff980`0ff392b0   00000000 00000000 0000002c 0000004a   ........,...J...
fffff980`0ff392c0   00000000 00000007 656e6547 006c6172   ........General.
fffff980`0ff392d0   ffffffd8 000d6b76 80000004 00000030   ....vk......0...
fffff980`0ff392e0   00000001 00000001 656c6954 6c6c6157   ........TileWall
fffff980`0ff392f0   65706170 00000072 ffffffd8 000e6b76   paper.......vk..
fffff980`0ff39300   80000004 00000032 00000001 00000001   ....2...........
fffff980`0ff39310   6c6c6157 65706170 79745372 0000656c   WallpaperStyle..
fffff980`0ff39320   ffffffd8 00096b76 0000004a 00038348   ....vk..J...H...
fffff980`0ff39330   00000002 00000001 6c6c6157 65706170   ........Wallpape
fffff980`0ff39340   00000072 00000000 ffffffb0 00530025   r...........%.S.
```

```
fffff980`0ff39350    00730079 00650074 0052006d 006f006f    y.s.t.e.m.R.o.o.
fffff980`0ff39360    00250074 0057005c 00620065 0057005c    t.%.\.W.e.b.\.W.
fffff980`0ff39370    006c0061 0070006c 00700061 00720065    a.l.l.p.a.p.e.r.
fffff980`0ff39380    0069005c 0067006d 00340032 006a002e    \.i.m.g.2.4...j.
fffff980`0ff39390    00670070 00000000 fffffffd8 000f6b76    p.g........vk..
fffff980`0ff393a0    0000004a 000383c0 00000002 00000001    J...............
fffff980`0ff393b0    6b636142 61577075 61706c6c 00726570    BackupWallpaper.
fffff980`0ff393c0    ffffffb0 00530025 00730079 00650074    ....%.S.y.s.t.e.
fffff980`0ff393d0    0052006d 006f006f 00250074 0057005c    m.R.o.o.t.%.\.W.
fffff980`0ff393e0    00620065 0057005c 006c0061 0070006c    e.b.\.W.a.l.l.p.
fffff980`0ff393f0    00700061 00720065 0069005c 0067006d    a.p.e.r.\.i.m.g.
fffff980`0ff39400    00340032 006a002e 00670070 00000000    2.4...j.p.g.....
fffff980`0ff39410    fffffffd0 00116b76 00000008 00038440    ....vk......@...
fffff980`0ff39420    00000003 00000001 6c6c6157 65706170    ........Wallpape
fffff980`0ff39430    6c694672 6d695465 00000065 00000000    rFileTime.......
fffff980`0ff39440    fffffff0 148addb4 01c6fe90 00000000    ...............
fffff980`0ff39450    fffffffd0 00166b76 00000008 00038480    ....vk..........
fffff980`0ff39460    00000003 00000001 6c6c6157 65706170    ........Wallpape
fffff980`0ff39470    636f4c72 69466c61 6954656c 0000656d    rLocalFileTime..
fffff980`0ff39480    fffffff0 764f45b4 01c6fe98 00000000    .....EOv........
fffff980`0ff39490    ffffffe0 000382d0 000382f8 00038320    ............ ...
fffff980`0ff394a0    00038398 00038410 00038450 00000000    ........P.......
fffff980`0ff394b0    fffffffd8 000c6b76 80000004 00000039    ....vk......9...
fffff980`0ff394c0    00000001 00000001 75746553 72655670    ........SetupVer
fffff980`0ff394d0    6e6f6973 00000000 ffffff88 00206b6e    sion........nk .
fffff980`0ff394e0    d56c5282 01cc3ffe 00000000 0002b080    .Rl..?..........
fffff980`0ff394f0    00000000 00000000 ffffffff ffffffff    ...............
fffff980`0ff39500    00000002 00000a18 00022498 ffffffff    .........$......
[...]
```

```
1: kd> du /c 90 fffff980`0ff39340+c
fffff980`0ff3934c  "%SystemRoot%\Web\Wallpaper\img24.jpg"
```

You can also try Microsoft Debugging Extension (MEX) **!mreg** command as described in Exercise C5.

Q. How to reconstruct a corrupt stack?

A. Please find this case study for 32-bit systems (also available in Memory Dump Analysis Anthology, Volume 1, Revised Edition, pages 157 - 166):

http://www.dumpanalysis.org/blog/index.php/2007/07/25/reconstructing-stack-trace-manually/

Q. How do we get to know the number of instances or objects of class or structures created in the process memory?

A. If these objects are linked, we can use the **!validatelist** command, like in one of the exercises:

```
0: kd> !validatelist nt!PsActiveProcessHead
Found list end after 48 entries
```

Or, if an object has some signature, we can search memory and count its occurrences.

Q. What other files can we collect besides dumps to get additional information when we are taking the dumps?

A. Various software traces and logs can be useful to see the missing dynamics from static memory dumps. For example, process monitor logs, ETW traces, and window message traces. For the latter, please check **WindowHistory** and **MessageHistory** tools that I wrote:

https://support.citrix.com/article/CTX109235

https://support.citrix.com/article/CTX111068

Please also check this case study for unified software trace and memory dump analysis:
https://www.amazon.com/Debugged-MZ-PE-Software-Tracing/dp/1906717796/

Q. If a process working set becomes high, but its private bytes value is stable, does it show a memory leak?

A. It doesn't necessarily mean a memory leak. The working set is a memory resident portion of committed pages. It may increase for many reasons; for example, when we save a crash dump using Task Manager, all pages need to be brought from a page file. On the other hand, even if we have a memory leak, the working set can be trimmed by OS by paging out increasing memory.

Q. If I want to find a disk symbol link (e.g., c:\), which **!object** shall I check? Is there a way to find all disk symbol links from a dump?

A. You can find them in *\Sessions* directory for each session number or in *\Global ??* if they point to the latter, for example:

```
1: kd> !object \Sessions\0\DosDevices
Object: fffff880014ea830  Type: (fffffa8000c3aad0) Directory
    ObjectHeader: fffff880014ea800 (old version)
    HandleCount: 1  PointerCount: 6
    Directory Object: fffff880014ea5b0  Name: DosDevices

    Hash Address          Type         Name
    ---- -------          ----         ----
     05  fffff880016817b0 Directory    00000000-000003e4
     06  fffff88001861940 Directory    00000000-000003e5
     24  fffff8800167e9f0 Directory    00000000-0001a41b
     31  fffff8800181c170 Directory    00000000-0001a47e

1: kd> !object \Sessions\0\DosDevices\00000000-0001a47e
Object: fffff8800181c170  Type: (fffffa8000c3aad0) Directory
    ObjectHeader: fffff8800181c140 (old version)
    HandleCount: 0  PointerCount: 3
    Directory Object: fffff880014ea830  Name: 00000000-0001a47e

    Hash Address          Type          Name
    ---- -------          ----          ----
     18  fffff880018b2930 SymbolicLink  Global

1: kd> !object \Sessions\0\DosDevices\00000000-0001a47e\Global
Object: fffff880018b2930  Type: (fffffa8000c3a830) SymbolicLink
```

```
    ObjectHeader: fffff880018b2900 (old version)
    HandleCount: 0  PointerCount: 1
    Directory Object: fffff8800181c170  Name: Global
    Target String is '\Global??'

1: kd> !object \Global??
Object: fffff880000056c0  Type: (fffffa8000c3aad0) Directory
    ObjectHeader: fffff88000005690 (old version)
    HandleCount: 1  PointerCount: 145
    Directory Object: fffff880000054b0  Name: GLOBAL??

    Hash Address          Type            Name
    ---- -------          ----            ----
     00  fffff88001819db0 SymbolicLink    D:
[...]
     33  fffff880006fa680 SymbolicLink    C:
[...]

1: kd> !object \Global??\C:
Object: fffff880006fa680  Type: (fffffa8000c3a830) SymbolicLink
    ObjectHeader: fffff880006fa650 (old version)
    HandleCount: 0  PointerCount: 1
    Directory Object: fffff880000056c0  Name: C:
    Target String is '\Device\HarddiskVolume1'
    Drive Letter Index is 3 (C:)

1: kd> !object \Global??\D:
Object: fffff88001819db0  Type: (fffffa8000c3a830) SymbolicLink
    ObjectHeader: fffff88001819d80 (old version)
    HandleCount: 0  PointerCount: 1
    Directory Object: fffff880000056c0  Name: D:
    Target String is '\Device\CdRom0'
    Drive Letter Index is 4 (D:)
```

Q. Are there any TDI-related commands?

A. It looks like TDI is not even mentioned in the current WinDbg documentation at the time of this writing, but there is a good article about TDI: https://codemachine.com/articles/tdi_overview.html

As a side note, there is an extension that integrates WinDbg with Wireshark protocol analyzer: https://code.google.com/archive/p/windbgshark/

Q. Could you please provide an example for **!reg knode** and **!reg kvalue**?

A. Yes, they are simple formatting shortcuts for the **dt** command for _CM_KEY_NODE and _CM_KEY_VALUE structures. For example:

```
1: kd> !reg viewlist fffff88001c6c010

  0  Pinned Views ; PinViewListHead = fffff88001c6c628 fffff88001c6c628

 23  Mapped Views ; LRUViewListHead = fffff88001c54380 fffff88001967a90
---------------------------------------------------------------------------------------------------------------------
| ViewAddr |FileOffset|  Size  |ViewAddress|    Bcb     |      LRUViewList        |       PinViewList        | UseCount |
---------------------------------------------------------------------------------------------------------------------
| fffff88001c54380 |  20000 |  4000 | fffff9800ff20000 | fffffa8000c558f9 | fffff88001c13f00  fffff88001c6c618 | fffff88001c54390  fffff88001c54390 |    0 |
| fffff88001c13f00 |  2c000 |  4000 | fffff9800ff2c000 | fffffa8000c558f9 | fffff88001a5b310  fffff88001c54380 | fffff88001c13f10  fffff88001c13f10 |    0 |
[...]
---------------------------------------------------------------------------------------------------------------------

1: kd> dc fffff9800ff2c000 L4000
```

```
[...]
fffff980`0ff3be20  0003adc0 44534d57 ffffffa8 00206b6e   ....WMSD....nk .
fffff980`0ff3be30  df2601fe 01cc3ffe 00000000 0003adc0   ..&..?..........
fffff980`0ff3be40  00000000 00000000 ffffffff ffffffff   ................
fffff980`0ff3be50  00000003 00032b90 00022498 ffffffff   .....+...$......
fffff980`0ff3be60  00000000 00000000 00000024 0000004e   ........$...N...
fffff980`0ff3be70  00000000 00000007 656e6547 006c6172   ........General.
fffff980`0ff3be80  fffffff0 006e0065 00030000 50545448   ....e.n.....HTTP
fffff980`0ff3be90  ffffffe0 00086b76 0000004e 0003aeb0   ....vk..N.......
fffff980`0ff3bea0  00000001 00000001 71696e55 44496575   ........UniqueID
fffff980`0ff3beb0  ffffffa8 0046007b 00390042 00310039   ....{.F.B.9.9.1.
fffff980`0ff3bec0  00320035 002d0041 00340039 00460034   5.2.A.-.9.4.4.F.
fffff980`0ff3bed0  0034002d 00440044 002d0039 00320042   -.4.D.D.9.-.B.2.
fffff980`0ff3bee0  00390034 0030002d 00330032 00310035   4.9.-.0.2.3.5.1.
fffff980`0ff3bef0  00380045 00390031 00320039 007d0039   E.8.1.9.9.2.9.}.
fffff980`0ff3bf00  00000000 00000000 ffffffd8 000c6b76   ............vk..
fffff980`0ff3bf10  00000020 0003af30 00000001 00000001   ...0...........
fffff980`0ff3bf20  706d6f43 72657475 656d614e 00000000   ComputerName....
fffff980`0ff3bf30  ffffffd8 0048004c 0055002d 0049005a   ....L.H.-.U.Z.I.
fffff980`0ff3bf40  00550059 00370030 00300046 00390032   Y.U.0.7.F.0.2.9.
fffff980`0ff3bf50  0000004f 00000000 ffffffd0 00126b76   O..........vk..
fffff980`0ff3bf60  80000004 701c1547 00000004 00000001   ....G..p........
fffff980`0ff3bf70  756c6f56 6553656d 6c616972 626d754e   VolumeSerialNumb
fffff980`0ff3bf80  00007265 00000000 ffffffa0 00206b6e   er..........nk .
fffff980`0ff3bf90  df5fd2d4 01cc3ffe 00000000 0003adc0   .._..?..........
fffff980`0ff3bfa0  00000000 00000000 ffffffff ffffffff   ................
fffff980`0ff3bfb0  00000004 00031ee0 00022498 ffffffff   .........$......
fffff980`0ff3bfc0  00000000 00000000 00000016 00000094   ................
fffff980`0ff3bfd0  00000000 00000009 656d614e 63617073   ........Namespac
```

```
1: kd> !reg knode fffff980`0ff3be20+4*3

Signature: CM_KEY_NODE_SIGNATURE (kn)
Name                 : General
ParentCell           : 0x3adc0
Security             : 0x22498 [cell index]
Class                : 0xffffffff [cell index]
Flags                : 0x20
MaxNameLen           : 0x0
MaxClassLen          : 0x0
MaxValueNameLen      : 0x24
MaxValueDataLen      : 0x4e
LastWriteTime        : 0x 1cc3ffe:0xdf2601fe
SubKeyCount[Stable  ]: 0x0
SubKeyLists[Stable  ]: 0xffffffff
SubKeyCount[Volatile]: 0x0
SubKeyLists[Volatile]: 0xffffffff
ValueList.Count      : 0x3
ValueList.List       : 0x32b90
```

```
1: kd> !reg kvalue fffff980`0ff3bf00+4*3

Signature: CM_KEY_VALUE_SIGNATURE (kv)
Name       : ComputerName {compressed}
DataLength: 20
Data       : 3af30 [cell index]
Type       : 1
```

The **!reg valuelist** command can list all values for particular hive and node addresses:

```
1: kd> !reg valuelist fffff88001c6c010 fffff980`0ff3be20+4*3
```

```
Dumping ValueList of Key <General> :

[Idx] [ValAddr]        [ValueName]

[    0] fffff9800ff3be94      UniqueID
[    1] fffff9800ff3bf0c      ComputerName
[    2] fffff9800ff3bf5c      VolumeSerialNumber

 Use '!reg kvalue <ValAddr>' to dump the value
```

We can play with the *Data* field:

```
1: kd> !reg kvalue fffff9800ff3be94
```

```
Signature: CM_KEY_VALUE_SIGNATURE (kv)
Name       : UniqueID {compressed}
DataLength: 4e
Data       : 3aeb0  [cell index]
Type       : 1
```

```
1: kd> du fffff9800ff3beb0
```

```
fffff980`0ff3beb0  "⌐.{FB99152A-944F-4DD9-B249-02351"
fffff980`0ff3bef0  "E819929}"
```

```
1: kd> !reg kvalue fffff9800ff3bf0c
```

```
Signature: CM_KEY_VALUE_SIGNATURE (kv)
Name       : ComputerName {compressed}
DataLength: 20
Data       : 3af30  [cell index]
Type       : 1
```

```
1: kd> du fffff9800ff3bf30
fffff980`0ff3bf30  "..LH-UZIYU07F029O"
```

Two WinDbg Scripts That Changed the World

Reprinted from Memory Dump Analysis Anthology, Volume 7, pages 32 – 36.

One of the readers of this Anthology asked whether there was **!runaway WinDbg** command equivalent for kernel and complete memory dumps to diagnose **Spiking Thread** pattern (Volume 1, page 305) faster. So, after some thinking, we gave it a try, especially in the context of WinDbg scripting exercises designed for Advanced Windows Memory Dump Analysis training. As a result, we wrote two scripts initially. Their output is taken from a complete memory dump we used for the Fundamentals of Complete Crash and Hang Memory Dump Analysis presentation[4].

The first one dumps the most CPU consuming threads for user and kernel mode:

```
$$
$$ krunawaymost.wds
$$ Copyright (c) 2011 Software Diagnostics Services
$$ GNU GENERAL PUBLIC LICENSE
$$ http://www.gnu.org/licenses/gpl-3.0.txt
$$
r $t0 = 0
!for_each_thread "r $t1 = dwo( @#Thread + @@c++(#FIELD_OFFSET(nt!_KTHREAD, UserTime)) ); .if (@$t1 > @$t0) {r $t0 = @$t1; r $t2 = @#Thread}"
.echo "The largest UserTime value: "
? @$t0
!thread @$t2 3f
r $t0 = 0
!for_each_thread "r $t1 = dwo( @#Thread + @@c++(#FIELD_OFFSET(nt!_KTHREAD, KernelTime)) ); .if (@$t1 > @$t0) {r $t0 = @$t1; r $t2 = @#Thread}"
.echo "The largest KernelTime value: "
? @$t0
!thread @$t2 3f
```

```
0: kd> $$><c:\Scripts\krunawaymost.wds
The largest UserTime value:
Evaluate expression: 5470 = 00000000`0000155e
THREAD fffffa800451d720 Cid 1418.17fc Teb: 000007fffffdc000 Win32Thread: 0000000000000000 RUNNING on processor 2
Not impersonating
DeviceMap                 fffff8a001ce6b90
Owning Process            fffffa800442ab30       Image:         ApplicationE.exe
Attached Process          N/A          Image:         N/A
Wait Start TickCount      22295        Ticks: 0
Context Switch Count      27960
UserTime                  00:01:25.332
KernelTime                00:00:00.015
*** ERROR: Module load completed but symbols could not be loaded for ApplicationE.exe
Win32 Start Address ApplicationE (0×000000013f0f1578)
Stack Init fffff8800723cc70 Current fffff8800723c960
Base fffff8800723d000 Limit fffff88007237000 Call 0
Priority 8 BasePriority 8 UnusualBoost 0 ForegroundBoost 0 IoPriority 2 PagePriority 5
Child-SP          RetAddr           Call Site
00000000`0021f9e0 00000000`00000000 ApplicationE+0×6cd3


The largest KernelTime value:
Evaluate expression: 187 = 00000000`000000bb
THREAD fffffa80098d7b60 Cid 07bc.0a14 Teb: 000007fffffd7000 Win32Thread: fffff900c2ca0c20 WAIT: (UserRequest) KernelMode Non-Alertable
fffffa8008a4a030 NotificationEvent
Not impersonating
DeviceMap                 fffff8a001ce6b90
Owning Process            fffffa80096beb30       Image:         dwm.exe
Attached Process          N/A          Image:         N/A
Wait Start TickCount      22294        Ticks: 1 (0:00:00.015)
Context Switch Count      15473        LargeStack
UserTime                  00:00:06.801
KernelTime                00:00:02.917
Win32 Start Address dwmcore!CPartitionThread::ThreadMain (0×000007fef8a1f0d8)
Stack Init fffff8800d3d5c70 Current fffff8800d3d5740
Base fffff8800d3d6000 Limit fffff8800d3cf000 Call 0
Priority 15 BasePriority 15 UnusualBoost 0 ForegroundBoost 0 IoPriority 2 PagePriority 5
Child-SP          RetAddr           Call Site
fffff880`0d3d5780 fffff800`02ee6f32 nt!KiSwapContext+0×7a
fffff880`0d3d58c0 fffff800`02ee974f nt!KiCommitThreadWait+0×1d2
fffff880`0d3d5950 fffff880`0fef65b3 nt!KeWaitForSingleObject+0×19f
fffff880`0d3d59f0 fffff960`001fedea dxgkrnl!DxgkWaitForVerticalBlankEvent+0×53f
fffff880`0d3d5ab0 fffff800`02ee0ed3 win32k!NtGdiDdDDIWaitForVerticalBlankEvent+0×12
fffff880`0d3d5ae0 000007fe`ff1d143a nt!KiSystemServiceCopyEnd+0×13 (TrapFrame @ fffff880`0d3d5ae0)
00000000`0287f778 000007fe`f8791da1 GDI32!NtGdiDdDDIWaitForVerticalBlankEvent+0xa
00000000`0287f780 000007fe`f89e1b6e dxgi!CDXGIOutput::WaitForVBlank+0×51
```

---

[4] https://www.dumpanalysis.org/FCMDA-book

```
00000000`0287f7c0 000007fe`f89e1ae9 dwmcore!CD3DDeviceLevel1::WaitForVBlank+0×1f9
00000000`0287f810 000007fe`f89e1a9d dwmcore!CHwDisplayRenderTarget::WaitForVBlank+0×39
00000000`0287f850 000007fe`f89e1a4c dwmcore!CDesktopRenderTarget::WaitForVBlank+0×40
00000000`0287f880 000007fe`f89d3513 dwmcore!CSlaveHWndRenderTarget::WaitForVBlank+0×2c
00000000`0287f8c0 000007fe`f89d3584 dwmcore!CRenderTargetManager::WaitForVBlank+0×7d
00000000`0287f900 000007fe`f89d2661 dwmcore!CPartitionVerticalBlankScheduler::WaitForVBlank+0×7c
00000000`0287f950 000007fe`f8a1f0f4 dwmcore!CPartitionVerticalBlankScheduler::Run+0xe5
00000000`0287f9b0 00000000`7719652d dwmcore!CPartitionThread::ThreadMain+0×1c
00000000`0287f9e0 00000000`772cc521 kernel32!BaseThreadInitThunk+0xd
00000000`0287fa10 00000000`00000000 ntdll!RtlUserThreadStart+0×1d
```

The second script takes two arguments and shows all threads that have *UserTime* and *KernelTime* ticks values greater than these arguments:

```
$$
$$ krunawaygt.wds
$$ Copyright (c) 2011 Software Diagnostics Services
$$ GNU GENERAL PUBLIC LICENSE
$$ http://www.gnu.org/licenses/gpl-3.0.txt
$$
!for_each_thread "r $t1 = dwo( @#Thread + @@c++(#FIELD_OFFSET(nt!_KTHREAD, UserTime)) ); r $t0 = $arg1; .if (@$t1 > @$t0) {!thread @#Thread 3f}"
!for_each_thread "r $t1 = dwo( @#Thread + @@c++(#FIELD_OFFSET(nt!_KTHREAD, KernelTime)) ); r $t0 = $arg2; .if (@$t1 > @$t0) {!thread @#Thread 3f}"
```

Using hints from the previous script run (the largest *UserTime* ticks value is 0x155e) we now get threads that spent more than 0x100 ticks in user mode:

```
0: kd> $$>a<c:\Scripts\krunawaygt.wds 100 100
THREAD fffffa800843e060  Cid 03f4.0658  Teb: 000007fffff90000 Win32Thread: 0000000000000000 WAIT: (WrQueue) UserMode Non-Alertable
    fffffa800843c2c0  QueueObject
Not impersonating
DeviceMap                fffff8a000008aa0
Owning Process           fffffa800916b060       Image:         MsMpEng.exe
Attached Process         N/A            Image:          N/A
Wait Start TickCount     21211          Ticks: 1084 (0:00:00:16.910)
Context Switch Count     6028
UserTime                 00:00:10.140
KernelTime               00:00:00.296
Win32 Start Address msvcrt!endthreadex (0×000007feff5173fc)
Stack Init fffff88009d4bc70 Current fffff88009d4b660
Base fffff88009d4c000 Limit fffff88009d46000 Call 0
Priority 9 BasePriority 8 UnusualBoost 0 ForegroundBoost 0 IoPriority 2 PagePriority 5
*** ERROR: Symbol file could not be found.  Defaulted to export symbols for mprtp.dll -
Child-SP          RetAddr           Call Site
fffff880`09d4b6a0 fffff800`02ee6f32 nt!KiSwapContext+0×7a
fffff880`09d4b7e0 fffff800`02ee9f93 nt!KiCommitThreadWait+0×1d2
fffff880`09d4b870 fffff800`031ca647 nt!KeRemoveQueueEx+0×323
fffff880`09d4b930 fffff800`0319cae5 nt!IoRemoveIoCompletion+0×47
fffff880`09d4b9c0 fffff800`02ee0ed3 nt!NtRemoveIoCompletion+0×145
fffff880`09d4ba70 00000000`772f13aa nt!KiSystemServiceCopyEnd+0×13 (TrapFrame @ fffff880`09d4bae0)
00000000`0209fb08 000007fe`fd9e169d ntdll!ZwRemoveIoCompletion+0xa
00000000`0209fb10 00000000`7718a4e1 KERNELBASE!GetQueuedCompletionStatus+0×39
00000000`0209fb70 00000000`748f2c74 kernel32!GetQueuedCompletionStatusStub+0×11
00000000`0209fbb0 00000000`0045cbc0 mprtp!MpPluginSignatureChange+0×3e170
00000000`0209fbb8 000007fe`fbac25ff 0×45cbc0
00000000`0209fbc0 00000000`00466610 FLTLIB!FilterGetMessage+0×2b
00000000`0209fc20 00000000`00000000 0×466610


THREAD fffffa800845c060  Cid 03f4.065c  Teb: 000007fffff8e000 Win32Thread: 0000000000000000 WAIT: (WrQueue) UserMode Non-Alertable
    fffffa800843c2c0  QueueObject
Not impersonating
DeviceMap                fffff8a000008aa0
Owning Process           fffffa800916b060       Image:         MsMpEng.exe
Attached Process         N/A            Image:          N/A
Wait Start TickCount     21520          Ticks: 775 (0:00:00:12.090)
Context Switch Count     4979
UserTime                 00:00:04.149
KernelTime               00:00:00.156
Win32 Start Address msvcrt!endthreadex (0×000007feff5173fc)
Stack Init fffff88009d52c70 Current fffff88009d52660
Base fffff88009d53000 Limit fffff88009d4d000 Call 0
Priority 8 BasePriority 8 UnusualBoost 0 ForegroundBoost 0 IoPriority 2 PagePriority 5
*** ERROR: Symbol file could not be found.  Defaulted to export symbols for mprtp.dll -
Child-SP          RetAddr           Call Site
fffff880`09d526a0 fffff800`02ee6f32 nt!KiSwapContext+0×7a
fffff880`09d527e0 fffff800`02ee9f93 nt!KiCommitThreadWait+0×1d2
fffff880`09d52870 fffff800`031ca647 nt!KeRemoveQueueEx+0×323
fffff880`09d52930 fffff800`0319cae5 nt!IoRemoveIoCompletion+0×47
fffff880`09d529c0 fffff800`02ee0ed3 nt!NtRemoveIoCompletion+0×145
fffff880`09d52a70 00000000`772f13aa nt!KiSystemServiceCopyEnd+0×13 (TrapFrame @ fffff880`09d52ae0)
00000000`01ccf498 000007fe`fd9e169d ntdll!ZwRemoveIoCompletion+0xa
00000000`01ccf4a0 00000000`7718a4e1 KERNELBASE!GetQueuedCompletionStatus+0×39
00000000`01ccf500 00000000`748f2c74 kernel32!GetQueuedCompletionStatusStub+0×11
00000000`01ccf540 00000000`0045d030 mprtp!MpPluginSignatureChange+0×3e170
00000000`01ccf548 000007fe`fbac25ff 0×45d030
00000000`01ccf550 00000000`004666b0 FLTLIB!FilterGetMessage+0×2b
00000000`01ccf5b0 00000000`00000000 0×4666b0
```

```
THREAD ffffa80092b7060  Cid 03f4.1268  Teb: 000007fffff6a000 Win32Thread: 0000000000000000 WAIT: (WrQueue) UserMode Alertable
    ffffa8009299140  QueueObject
Not impersonating
DeviceMap                   fffff8a000008aa0
Owning Process              ffffa800916b060    Image:          MsMpEng.exe
Attached Process            N/A           Image:         N/A
Wait Start TickCount        7762          Ticks: 14533 (0:00:03:46.716)
Context Switch Count        3297
UserTime                    00:00:06.489
KernelTime                  00:00:00.499
Win32 Start Address ntdll!TppWorkerThread (0×00000000772bfbc0)
Stack Init fffff8800e620c70 Current fffff8800e620680
Base fffff8800e621000 Limit fffff8800e61b000 Call 0
Priority 8 BasePriority 8 UnusualBoost 0 ForegroundBoost 0 IoPriority 2 PagePriority 5
Child-SP          RetAddr           Call Site
fffff880`0e6206c0 fffff800`02ee6f32 nt!KiSwapContext+0×7a
fffff880`0e620800 fffff800`02ee9f93 nt!KiCommitThreadWait+0×1d2
fffff880`0e620890 fffff800`031ca647 nt!KeRemoveQueueEx+0×323
fffff880`0e620950 fffff800`02ecdb36 nt!IoRemoveIoCompletion+0×47
fffff880`0e6209e0 fffff800`02ee0ed3 nt!NtWaitForWorkViaWorkerFactory+0×285
fffff880`0e620ae0 00000000`772f2c1a nt!KiSystemServiceCopyEnd+0×13 (TrapFrame @ fffff880`0e620ae0)
00000000`0540f998 00000000`772bfe0b ntdll!ZwWaitForWorkViaWorkerFactory+0×a
00000000`0540f9a0 00000000`7719652d ntdll!TppWorkerThread+0×2c9
00000000`0540fca0 00000000`772cc521 kernel32!BaseThreadInitThunk+0×d
00000000`0540fcd0 00000000`00000000 ntdll!RtlUserThreadStart+0×1d


THREAD ffffa80098d7b60  Cid 07bc.0a14  Teb: 000007fffffd7000 Win32Thread: fffff900c2ca0c20 WAIT: (UserRequest) KernelMode Non-Alertable
    ffffa8008a4a030  NotificationEvent
Not impersonating
DeviceMap                   fffff8a001ce6b90
Owning Process              ffffa80096beb30    Image:          dwm.exe
Attached Process            N/A           Image:         N/A
Wait Start TickCount        22294         Ticks: 1 (0:00:00:00.015)
Context Switch Count        15473                    LargeStack
UserTime                    00:00:06.801
KernelTime                  00:00:02.917
Win32 Start Address dwmcore!CPartitionThread::ThreadMain (0×000007fef8a1f0d8)
Stack Init fffff8800d3d5c70 Current fffff8800d3d5740
Base fffff8800d3d6000 Limit fffff8800d3cf000 Call 0
Priority 15 BasePriority 15 UnusualBoost 0 ForegroundBoost 0 IoPriority 2 PagePriority 5
Child-SP          RetAddr           Call Site
fffff880`0d3d5780 fffff800`02ee6f32 nt!KiSwapContext+0×7a
fffff880`0d3d58c0 fffff800`02ee974f nt!KiCommitThreadWait+0×1d2
fffff880`0d3d5950 fffff800`0fef65b3 nt!KeWaitForSingleObject+0×19f
fffff880`0d3d59f0 fffff960`001fedea dxgkrnl!DxgkWaitForVerticalBlankEvent+0×53f
fffff880`0d3d5ab0 fffff800`02ee0ed3 win32k!NtGdiDdDDIWaitForVerticalBlankEvent+0×12
fffff880`0d3d5ae0 000007fe`ff1d143a nt!KiSystemServiceCopyEnd+0×13 (TrapFrame @ fffff880`0d3d5ae0)
00000000`0287f778 000007fe`f8791da1 GDI32!NtGdiDdDDIWaitForVerticalBlankEvent+0×a
00000000`0287f780 000007fe`f89e1b6e dxgi!CDXGIOutput::WaitForVBlank+0×51
00000000`0287f7c0 000007fe`f89e1ae9 dwmcore!CD3DDeviceLevel1::WaitForVBlank+0×1f9
00000000`0287f810 000007fe`f89e1a9d dwmcore!CHwDisplayRenderTarget::WaitForVBlank+0×39
00000000`0287f850 000007fe`f89e1a4c dwmcore!CDesktopRenderTarget::WaitForVBlank+0×40
00000000`0287f880 000007fe`f89d3513 dwmcore!CSlaveHWndRenderTarget::WaitForVBlank+0×2c
00000000`0287f8c0 000007fe`f89d3584 dwmcore!CRenderTargetManager::WaitForVBlank+0×7d
00000000`0287f900 000007fe`f89d2661 dwmcore!CPartitionVerticalBlankScheduler::WaitForVBlank+0×7c
00000000`0287f950 000007fe`f8a1f0f4 dwmcore!CPartitionVerticalBlankScheduler::Run+0×e5
00000000`0287f9b0 00000000`7719652d dwmcore!CPartitionThread::ThreadMain+0×1c
00000000`0287f9e0 00000000`772cc521 kernel32!BaseThreadInitThunk+0×d
00000000`0287fa10 00000000`00000000 ntdll!RtlUserThreadStart+0×1d


THREAD ffffa800451d720  Cid 1418.17fc  Teb: 000007fffffdc000 Win32Thread: 0000000000000000 RUNNING on processor 2
Not impersonating
DeviceMap                   fffff8a001ce6b90
Owning Process              ffffa800442ab30    Image:          ApplicationE.exe
Attached Process            N/A           Image:         N/A
Wait Start TickCount        22295         Ticks: 0
Context Switch Count        27960
UserTime                    00:01:25.332
KernelTime                  00:00:00.015
*** ERROR: Module load completed but symbols could not be loaded for ApplicationE.exe
Win32 Start Address ApplicationE (0×000000013f0f1578)
Stack Init fffff8800723cc70 Current fffff8800723c960
Base fffff8800723d000 Limit fffff88007237000 Call 0
Priority 8 BasePriority 8 UnusualBoost 0 ForegroundBoost 0 IoPriority 2 PagePriority 5
Child-SP          RetAddr           Call Site
00000000`0021f9e0 00000000`00000000 ApplicationE+0×6cd3
```

www.ingramcontent.com/pod-product-compliance
Lightning Source LLC
Chambersburg PA
CBRC091939210326
41598CB00012B/863